LEARN, TEACH, CHALLENGE

Indigenous Studies Series

The Indigenous Studies Series builds on the successes of the past and is inspired by recent critical conversations about Indigenous epistemological frameworks. Recognizing the need to encourage burgeoning scholarship, the series welcomes manuscripts drawing upon Indigenous intellectual traditions and philosophies, particularly in discussions situated within the Humanities.

Series Editor:
Dr. Deanna Reder (Métis), Associate Professor,
First Nations Studies and English, Simon Fraser University

Advisory Board:
Dr. Jo-ann Archibald (Sto:lo), Professor, Associate Dean,
Indigenous Education, University of British Columbia

Dr. Kristina Fagan Bidwell (NunatuKavut), Associate Professor,
English, University of Saskatchewan

Dr. Daniel Heath Justice (Cherokee), Professor,
English, Canada Research Chair in Indigenous Literature
and Expressive Culture, University of British Columbia

Dr. Eldon Yellowhorn (Piikani), Associate Professor,
Archaeology, Director of First Nations Studies,
Simon Fraser University

LEARN, TEACH, CHALLENGE

Approaching Indigenous Literatures

Deanna Reder and Linda M. Morra, editors

WILFRID LAURIER UNIVERSITY PRESS

Wilfrid Laurier University Press acknowledges the support of the Canada Council for the Arts for our publishing program. We acknowledge the financial support of the Government of Canada through the Canada Book Fund for our publishing activities. This work was supported by the Research Support Fund.

 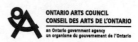

Library and Archives Canada Cataloguing in Publication

Learn, teach, challenge : approaching indigenous literatures / Deanna Reder and Linda M. Morra, editors.

(Indigenous studies series)
Includes bibliographical references and index.
Issued in print and electronic formats.
ISBN 978-1-77112-185-9 (paperback).—ISBN 978-1-77112-186-6 (pdf).—ISBN 978-1-77112-187-3 (epub)

1. Canadian literature (English)—Native authors—History and criticism. 2. Canadian literature (English)—Native authors—Study and teaching. I. Morra, Linda M., editor II. Reder, Deanna, 1963–, editor III. Series: Indigenous studies series

PS8089.5.I6L42 2016   C810.9'897   C2016-900267-5
                                                  C2016-900268-3

Front-cover image by Sonny Assu, *There Is Hope, If We Rise*, 2013.
Cover design by Sonny Assu and text design by Janette Thompson (Jansom).

This book is printed on FSC® certified paper and is certified Ecologo. It contains post-consumer fibre, is processed chlorine free, and is manufactured using biogas energy.

Printed in Canada

Every reasonable effort has been made to acquire permission for copyright material used in this text, and to acknowledge all such indebtedness accurately. Any errors and omissions called to the publisher's attention will be corrected in future printings.

Dedicated to and in loving memory
of Jo-Ann Episkenew,

teacher, mentor, friend

CONTENTS

V • CLASSROOM CONSIDERATIONS

ACKNOWLEDGEMENTS

We are immensely grateful to all those who attended "How Shall We Teach These?," the workshop staged at Simon Fraser University in February 2014, and who provided us with invaluable feedback that contributed to the shape and content of this anthology: Caitlin Barter, Tracy Bear, Lesley Belleau, Kristina Fagan Bidwell, Blake Bilmer, Miriam Brown-Spiers, Tenille Campbell, Warren Cariou, Adar Charlton, Francesca Courtade, Lindsey Cornum, Michelle Coupal, Jonathan Dewar, Renate Eigenbrod, Jo-Ann Episkenew, Jeff Fedoruk, Margery Fee, Marc André Fortin, David Gaertner, Emily Gingera, Allison Hargreaves, Sarah Henzi, Sarah Hickey, Gabrielle Hill, Roberta Holden, Dallas Hunt, Natalie Knight, Curran Jacobs, Brendan McCormack, Daniel Morley Johnson, Daniel Heath Justice, Michele Lacombe, Janey Lew, Hartmut Lutz, Keavy Martin, Tara Masaki, Sophie McCall, Sam McKegney, Ashley Morford, Laura Moss, Alex Muir, Dory Nason, Lisa Quinn, Deena Rymhs, Angela Semple, June Scudeler, Szu Shen, Isabelle St. Amand, Mike Taylor, Chris Teuton, Renae Watchman, Saylesh Wesley, Greg Younging, Lisa Taylor, and Angela Van Essen.

In addition, we would like to thank the members of the SFU MATE class, who, in ENGL 844, reviewed this anthology and made many productive suggestions. Thanks to Marina Brewer, Beth Carson Fehr, Dylan Gant, Katie Keller, Allison Kilgannon, Laura MacPherson, Matthew Metford, Cathleen Peters, Rebecca Taylor, Jennifer Thompson Whitcher, and Maria Zappone. Thanks also to past MATE students who inspired this work, most particularly Shirley Burdon, Ann Marie McGrath, Karine Guezalova, and Deborah Stellingwerff.

At Bishop's University, we would like to thank the members of the ENG 358: Approaches to Indigenous Literatures class, which tested the early version of this volume: Dylan Beland, Sean Gallagher, David Guignion, Shannon Jackson, Sarah Legge, Aislinn May, Tess Metcalfe, Matthew M. Nutbrown, Ashley Shinder, and Katherine Warriner.

We would also like to acknowledge the publishers who attended the event: Lisa Quinn of Wilfrid Laurier UP; Greg Younging of Theytus Books; and Kevin Williams of Talon Books. We thank Simon Fraser University for allowing us to host the Workshop in February 2014. We acknowledge the support of our respective university affiliations, Simon Fraser University and Bishop's University. Specifically, we would like to thank SFU's Vice President

Academic and Provost, Jonathan Driver, and SFU's Dean of the Faculty of Arts and Social Sciences, John Craig, for their support and encouragement. We would like to thank the SFU's Department of First Nations Studies, specifically Chair Eldon Yellowhorn and Department Manager Lorraine Yam, for providing an immense amount of administrative support. Thanks to the Department of English for funding the Graduate Student Mentorship breakfast. Thanks also to Bishop's University's Senate Research Council Travel Grant, Senate Research Council Publications Grant, and Experiential Learning Internship Grant, which provided funding so that we could hire Curran Jacobs to complete preliminary work on the manuscript and to allow two Bishop's students to participate in this groundbreaking event. Special thanks to the University of Manitoba's Dr. Renate Eigenbrod, whose memory continues to inspire us. Also thanks to the Centre for Creative Writing and Oral Culture, specifically the amazing work of Canada Research Chair Dr. Warren Cariou. Many thanks to the University of British Columbia's Canada Research Chair Dr. Daniel Heath Justice and the Department of First Nations and Indigenous Studies. Thanks also to the amazing team from Full Circle Performance, which annually puts on the Talking Stick Festival—specifically Margo Kane and Tanja Dixon-Warren. We would also like to express our gratitude to visual artist Sonny Assu for allowing us to use his image for our cover.

And thank you in particular to the SFU community, including Brett Romans, Maureen Curtin, Bev Neufeld, Costa Dedegikas, Andrea Creamer, Am Johal and the Vancity Office for Community Engagement, William Lindsey and the Office for Aboriginal Peoples, Dr. Sophie McCall and her two classes of graduate students in the Department of English, including the MATE program, and students Ashley Morford, Natalie Knight, Blake Bilmer, and Karen Johnson.

We are grateful to the Social Sciences and Humanities Research Council of Canada for the Connections Grant that allowed us to stage the Workshop in February 2014 and to cover the cost of the permissions related to the anthology; such funding is crucial to seeing these endeavours come to fruition. Special thanks to the team at Wilfrid Laurier University Press, including copy editor Edwin Janzen, as well as to Dr. June Scudeler and Melanie Tutino for their careful editorial attention.

Linda Morra would also like to express her love for her friends and family and thank them for all their support, especially her parents. Deanna Reder would like to thank her sons Mischa, Eli, and Sam, and in particular her partner, Eric Davis, for their unwavering support.

Introduction:
Learn, Teach, Challenge

Deanna Reder:

I distinctly remember the moment, in summer 2013, when Linda and I were talking on the phone about balancing our respective research projects with the particular demands of teaching Indigenous literatures in the university; it was then that we decided to work together to produce this anthology. At the time, we were discussing the fact that teaching Indigenous literatures so often involves having to complete the administrative work required to create such a course before we can even begin offering it to our students. Often, this administrative work grows beyond what one might imagine. For example, because there was no such course related to Indigenous literatures at Bishop's University, Linda ended up not only creating her course but also joining forces with other colleagues from History, Sociology, and Education to create an Indigenous Studies minor. Even then, Linda remarked, mentioning what those of us in the field of Indigenous Studies already know, to introduce Indigenous literary theory to her students, she had to create the course pack from scratch. There are no companion textbooks available, she observed, for the upper undergraduate and graduate student classrooms; these textbooks were crucial for students who have often and only been trained by Western models. Then, I responded, we should work with your course outline as a basis and create one. We would then figure out a way to consult with our colleagues in this field, to help us shape an anthology they will find useful.

Linda Morra:

Deanna initiated the next logical step: to apply for a SSHRC Connections Grant with the intention of bringing our colleagues together for the purpose of consultation about creating such a textbook. She suggested that it assume the form of a workshop over the course of a couple of days, and that it be held at Simon Fraser University in Vancouver. Over that summer and well into the fall, we worked together on the SSHRC grant application—and several others—to allow us to invite as many participants as we could think of to the workshop, which was eventually held in February 2014. In advance of the workshop, we developed a preliminary table of contents for the book, which was divided into five sections; then we assigned each section to a specific group of people comprised of both Indigenous and settler scholars, and established critics and graduate students. We asked members of each group to evaluate the merits of each article in their section, but also to comment more broadly on the structure of the table of contents in general and to let us know what topic or article might also be included. Had we missed any significant contribution? What else might we add? Could the range of the topics covered be even broader? Was the organization and framework of the book useful? Their feedback was invaluable.

Deanna Reder:

Although we originally titled this workshop and proposed anthology "How Shall We Teach These?" to mirror the question posed in the title of Helen Hoy's collection of essays, *How Should I Read These?* (U of Toronto P, 2001), our colleagues pressed us to go back further in time, to think of the work of Nehiowe-Métis-Anishinaabekwe scholar Janice Acoose, published in 1995. *Iskwewak-Kah'Ki Yaw Ni Wahkomakanak: Neither Indian Princesses nor Easy Squaws* insists that we recognize that English literary studies, specifically the field of Canadian literature, is an ideological instrument designed to oppress Indigenous peoples. Studying the work of Indigenous knowledge keepers— Aboriginal writers included—is the corrective. Inspired by her work, we have placed an updated introduction to her book as the first essay, with Hoy's work thereafter.

Another example of crucial feedback that helped us reshape the anthology pertained to our description of Indigenous literary nationalism. Initially, we credited Creek scholar Craig Womack's *Red on Red* with introducing the pivotal idea that specific tribal epistemologies and stories could be used to interpret stories from that nation. Our colleagues reminded us of the preceding work of Okanagan intellectual Jeannette Armstrong and Anishinaabe writer Kimberly Blaeser, in the 1993 collection *Looking at the Words of Our People*, where they proposed similar points. We placed them at the beginning of section three, before Womack.

It was not simply that our colleagues re-oriented the anthology in examples such as these; they also improved it by insisting that certain topics needed further elaboration. While we looked for articles to open up discussions about violence against Indigenous women or Indigenous queer theory, we also invited participants to include their own original work. All of the essays in the final section are therefore new publications by scholars who are likely to expand them into monographs, which will further shift the field.

Linda Morra:

Our hope is that the consultations and discussions with our colleagues will have produced an anthology that offers a solid starting place for the study of Indigenous literatures, and that will showcase the development and range of methods, conversations, and debates in the field. Above all else, we hope to prompt further discussion about the broad range of issues undergirding the study of Indigenous texts. We do not see this volume as an end point, there-fore, but rather as the beginning of many other collaborations. Although we have consulted area specialists, we have kept in mind literary scholars new to this field who might be teaching this subject for the first time. Each section provides an introduction to the essays that follow, situates them in the field, and flags key points; and each section culminates in a response that extends the conversation.

Deanna Reder:

In fact, our support for those of you who are new to this area comes with a shared understanding of the difficulties ahead. At first glance, it might appear that this textbook offers you no road map to help you deal with a hostile student who dismisses the value of the work you teach; the uncomfortable colleague who is challenged by the call to change the curriculum; or the disappointment both individuals might express about your position, whether Indigenous or non-Indigenous, depending on what they consider a scholar in this field ought to look or live like. There is, of course, no easy answer except to follow the prin-ciples as outlined in our table of contents: identify and value your position, which grants you a distinct perspective, even as it demands that you consider your intentions as you complete this work; imagine beyond the images and myths that saturate the field, so that, in the words of Niigaanwewidam Sinclair, you might "recognize the full humanity of Indigenous peoples" (301); and deliberate the various Indigenous literary approaches, not only intellectually, but, as Leanne Simpson suggests, also emotionally, physically, and spiritually (296). Although typically literary scholars have little training in holistic forms of inquiry, writings by Indigenous authors and stories encoded in ceremony might inspire you to search for wisdom and to value humility as you take on the responsibilities involved in making meaning; to integrate contemporary concerns into your analysis and pedagogy throughout the process, because there is no literature today that is as relevant to general society as that by Indigenous authors; and, finally, to emulate the creativity in the classrooms of our colleagues, who collaborate with each other and with writers to create curriculum on topics seldom taught.

Deanna Reder and Linda Morra:

The title of this anthology was inspired by visual artist Sonny Assu's print, titled *Learn, Teach, Challenge the Stereotypes.* We shortened it to *Learn, Teach, Challenge.* Certainly, teaching this literature and the corresponding theory enjoins us to challenge stereotypes, prejudice, and institutional inertia. But, of greatest importance, teaching in this field is a profound challenge to us. We hope this volume supports you in this difficult work.

A Note about Terminology

Some minor changes have been made to articles reprinted in this volume to reflect contemporary socio-political forms of expression or to conform to Press standards on Canadian spelling.

I

POSITION

1

Introduction: Position

Deanna Reder

At the beginning of every term I follow local Coast Salish customs and introduce myself to my students by acknowledging the four First Nations on whose
territories my school, Simon Fraser University, is built. Following the expected
formula, I acknowledge that I am a guest in the territory, not to suggest that
I was ever invited here, but rather a turn of phrase to recognize that even
though I have lived in British Columbia's lower mainland for most of my adult
life, this does not give me the same relationship to this land as those whose
Nations have been here since time immemorial. I identify myself as a Métis
woman with family from all around the Prairies, whose Cree-speaking side
of the family comes from northern Saskatchewan, from La Ronge, and historically from such communities as Green Lake, Sled Lake, and Isle la Crosse.
This inclusion of my communities of origin follows local traditions that value
genealogies, but is also an act of solidarity with Indigenous students, to affirm
that their ancestry is relevant in a university context not typically sensitive to
Indigenous concerns.

I also begin by positioning myself, just as other Indigenous scholars regularly do, to emphasize that all knowledge is generated from particular positions, that there is no unbiased, neutral position possible. Such is the value
of neutrality in everyday society that this is a point my students often struggle
with, even as we work to uncover the assumptions and opinions embedded in
so-called "unbiased" newspaper reports, textbooks, documentaries, legal judgments. It takes them some time to realize that I am not arguing that there is a
conspiracy of hidden agendas (although hidden agendas do exist), but that all
knowledge is positioned.

While in standard literary analysis discussion of one's position is rarely identified and discussed, it is, I suggest, a necessity in Indigenous Studies, a corrective for the fixation on Aboriginal identity that is already examined keenly, regularly discussed, legislated, regulated, questioned, dismissed, debated, and defended,[1] typically in response to questions from a member of the public or from a querying public institution. Notably, questions about identity are always focused on the Aboriginal person and whether his or her identity claims are valid legally, culturally, or genetically. (Are you an Aboriginal person if you do not register for a Status card or Métis membership? If you live an urban lifestyle? If you have mixed Aboriginal/non-Aboriginal ancestry? Etc.) The focus on the Aboriginal as object of study assumes it to be what Denise Ferreira da Silva calls an "affectable other"[2] against which the Western subject defines itself. The act of identifying one's position undermines the object/subject dichotomy and makes visible the lines of relationship that affect one's perspective.

Assumed in this declaration of position is the notion that there is more of a benefit to recognizing our relations to one another than striking a so-called "unbiased" pose. As such, I feel compelled to reveal my relationship to the following authors. Such is the size of the field of Indigenous literary studies in Canada that I can say I have met all of the contributors in this section, respect all of them, and have worked with two—the late Renate Eigenbrod and Sam McKegney—in the establishment in 2013 of the Indigenous Literary Studies Association (ILSA);[3] I count both as friends. I owe both an intellectual and an emotional debt to all the scholars in this section; the tangible work that they have done and continue to do, to bring Indigenous literatures and perspectives into the university is so removed from any experience I previously had in the classroom that my first contact with this work brought tears to my eyes.

1. Janice Acoose

While currently there is a significant body of critical work on Indigenous writing in Canada, this is a recent phenomenon. It was only in the late 1980s that scholarship on the image of the "Indian" in Can Lit emerged (King, Calver, and Hoy; Goldie, *Fear and Temptation*) and the early 1990s that articles on Indigenous writing were published (New, *Native Writers and Canadian Writing*; Armstrong, *Looking at the Words of Our People*; Hoy, "'Nothing but the Truth'"). A monograph on Indigenous literatures in Canada was not produced until 1995: Saulteaux-Métis author Janice Acoose's *Iskwewak—Kah' Ki Yaw Ni Wahkomakanak: Neither Indian Princesses nor Easy Squaws*.[4] It is a remarkable mixture of standard literary analysis and what I call "autobiography as theoretical practice." Acoose's insistence that her position—who she is, who her relatives are, and where her family comes from—is relevant, although typically invisible to Settler Canada, is evident in the very title of her book. Non-Cree speakers have little way of knowing that the main title is not the rejection of stereotype as articulated in the subtitle, *Neither Indian Princesses nor Easy Squaws*. Instead, the main title is a proclamation of her connection to her kinswomen: *Iskwewak—Kah' Ki Yaw Ni Wahkomakanak* ("I am related to all Iskwewak . . . I am related to all womankind").[5] In choosing this title, Acoose privileges Cree speakers, an audience rarely addressed in works of literary study.

Notably, Acoose mounts her critique as a master's student, outside of the typical supports that senior scholars depend upon, before much of the vocabulary critiquing settler colonialism had been coined. A decade before Daniel Coleman argues, in *White Civility* (2006), that the literary project of English Canada naturalizes whiteness—conflated with a British model of civility—as the norm for English Canadian cultural identity, Acoose expounds on her own critique of whiteness, decrying "canadian literature as an ideological instrument" that promotes the values of white european christian canadian patriarchy.[6]

Integral to her argument is her recounting of her own personal narrative.[7] Acoose foregrounds her academic analysis with the description of herself and her family, complete with government-issued scrip records from a maternal ancestor and her own certificate of birth as a "live Indian," which confirms her as a Status Indian in Canada, and subsequently condemns her to residential school. The power of these documents is reinforced by other discourses, like public school textbooks, that render invisible the histories of Indigenous people, particularly women, and the prevalence in daily society of the damaging and humiliating Indian princess and easy squaw stereotypes that she unquestioningly internalizes. But when she reads a course description of a Canadian literature class—presumably sometime in the 1980s—that describes its focus on the transformation of Canada "from no man's land to everyman's land" (30), Acoose instantly recognizes her professor's and "the institution's casual dismissal of [her] Nehiowe-Metis and Anishinaabe ancestors (both female and male) who had cared for and nurtured the land since time immemorial" (30). It is her family connections to the stories of the land, stories unacknowledged by dominant society, that provoke her to write.

It is not surprising, then, that in her monograph, once Acoose critiques the classics of Canadian literature that foster derogatory and damaging stereotypes of Indigenous women, she offers as an alternative an autobiography by a Métis woman. While Acoose celebrates the culturally sensitive and positive depictions in *Halfbreed* (1973), by Maria Campbell, she credits the book—as many do—as the inspiration for a new generation of Indigenous writers to value their positions and perspectives and to consider their writing as acts of resistance and re-empowerment (Iskwewak 109).[8]

2. Helen Hoy

It was not until 2001 that the first full-length monograph exclusively focused on Indigenous literatures was released. Helen Hoy, originally a Canadianist, was an established scholar at the University of Guelph, who, from about the 1980s, used her academic influence to open up this field. Her study of writing by Native women in Canada has a title that poses the question: *How Should I Read These?* Central to Hoy's inquiry is her position as a non-Native scholar studying Native literature, a position she identifies as "fraught and suspect" in the context of an academy that is impervious to Native presences and paradigms (48). At a time when almost all literary scholars in Canada were non-Aboriginal, Hoy and like-minded colleagues had to represent Indigenous presence, often in the absence of actual Indigenous people. While it could be argued that such scholarship opened up the university for a future wave of Indigenous students, Hoy, schooled in discussions in anti-racist and feminist theoretical circles, is hesitant to make such claims. Instead, she cites Sherene Razack to decry the "'race to innocence,' the attempt, by emphasizing one's positions of subordination and not of privilege (as a woman, say), to disclaim responsibility for subordinating others. . . . [S]uch a denial obscures the necessity, as part of ending one's own marginalization, to end all systems of oppression" (50).

In this way, Hoy provides a model of self-reflexive, multi-vocal, theoretically infused analysis that is ethically determined to consider one's position and is marked by the anxieties of this field. She cautions her readers to "resist universalizing gestures [celebrations of common humanity, for example] that ignore difference and absorb disparate historical and material realities into dominant paradigms" (41), tactics that typically do little to help dismantle "the oppressive hierarchies and the unequal distribution of power" (50). Hoy's focus on position is a strategy to make privilege, and by extension power imbalances, visible as a first step in opposing oppression.

3. Emma LaRocque

In contrast to Hoy's deliberation on the complexities of the position of the cultural outsider, Emma LaRocque gives her perspective as one of the few (and first) Aboriginal professors who taught Indigenous literatures in Canada through the seventies, eighties, and nineties. In her 2002 essay, "Teaching Aboriginal Literature: The Discourse of Margins and the Mainstreams,"[9]

LaRocque, confident in her cultural location as a Cree-speaking Métis scholar, quotes from *Indigena* (1992) to assert that "To be an Aboriginal person, to identify with an Indigenous heritage in these late colonial times, requires a life of reflection, critique, persistence and struggle" (56). She discusses her experiences in the classroom, where struggles are exacerbated by assumptions by students and general society about Indigenous literature as necessarily angry, tragic, ethnographic, infantile, or artless. These distracting stereotypes and LaRocque's work to dismantle them play out in the identities of her students, from those unwilling to give up "'the National Dream' version of the Canadian self-image" (59) to those Aboriginal students who "feel an affinity with various Native characters," many of whom struggle with confusion or deep shame, which then "leads them to new levels of awareness about their experiences" (60).

For LaRocque, anti-colonial critique is essential in the study of literature as long as it includes the appreciation of the "aesthetic possibilities" of literature (61). But what needs to define the field, she insists, is "Indigenously engaged epistemology and pedagogy" (58). LaRocque readily admits the pitfalls of defining—and delimiting—Aboriginal experience, and, by extension, literature, even as she asserts that, "there is an Aboriginal experience unique to the Canadian context" (67). But LaRocque rejects accusations that the belief in the existence of difference necessitates that she is essentialist or nativist: "It is about theory and praxis. Aboriginality as an identity is more than an amorphous grouping of persons with varied experiences who happen to have some 'Indian'"; "it is," she emphasizes, "about epistemology" (64).[10]

4. Renate Eigenbrod

Renate Eigenbrod would undoubtably agree with LaRocque on the value of epistemology. While Eigenbrod appreciates that the concept of positionality is valued by postmodern, postcolonial, and feminist theorists, she credits Indigenous theory for her use of her own story. In the introduction to her monograph, *Travelling Knowledges* (2005), she states: "it was not Western but Aboriginal thought that made me rethink notions of truth, objectivity, and scholarship . . ." (4). In the preface to her monograph cited in this volume, Eigenbrod immediately recognizes Indigenous epistemes that value personal storytelling and so addresses her readership directly, in order to destabilize the position of the distanced critic (74).

While Eigenbrod readily identifies her position as a German-Canadian scholar, she unsettles the assumption that she studies this literature because of a perceived German fascination with Indians. Instead, she shares her story as a newcomer to Canada in 1982 who was hired to teach a class of Cree students in rural Alberta. (Eigenbrod taught as a contract worker for over twenty years until she secured a tenure-track position at the University of Manitoba in 2003.) Conversations with these students so shaped her that she credits them with putting her "on the right path in a pursuit of knowledge that changed [her] life" (5). This story, which emphasizes the value of context and constant reconsideration of one's power, illustrates Eigenbrod's reading practice. When she states that she "reads from an immigrant perspective, but in a migrant fashion" (75), she wants to convey the value of a destabilized position that is constantly reevaluated as one moves through time and space. Eigenbrod's conception of position is as one in motion, influenced by the roots one has put down and the routes one has been on and will still travel.

5. Sam McKegney

The publication in 2008 of Sam McKegney's essay "Studies for Ethical Engagement: An Open Letter Concerning Non-Native Scholars of Native Literatures," in the US journal *Studies in American Indian Literature*, marked a generational shift in the discussion of positionality. McKegney confirms in his final footnote what is obvious from his first sentence, that he is intentionally provocative in a desire to stir up debate.

McKegney does not explicitly discuss his own position, other than as a non-Native scholar. He is less interested in acknowledging the limits of the non-Native critic's understanding as he is in committing to gaining critical, experiential, and cultural knowledge and engaging respectfully and responsibly with Indigenous communities and individuals. For McKegney, non-Indigenous critics ought not to direct undue attention away from Indigenous artistic agency by making the criticism too much about themselves, their experiences, and their inadequacies. Even as he, in his opening paragraph, accepts the need for intense self-reflexivity, he is not comfortable with this practice, admitting later on in the essay that what he calls "the 'Focus Inward' has always seemed to me slightly masturbatory" (82). He questions the need for the sensitive qualified statements that mark the standard work of the field, particularly the common habit to admit one's lack of cultural knowledge, what McKegney considers to be a gesture to evade accountability.

McKegney points to the tremendous anxiety among non-Native scholars to avoid doing damage to Indigenous texts, an impulse that he asserts can be ironically disabling, having the unintended effect of "obfuscating Indigenous voices and stagnating the critical field" (81). He argues that worry about misunderstanding or re-colonizing Indigenous texts only serves to convince timid critics to retreat from debate and become intensely self-reflexive, resulting in non-Native critics who take up only the work of other non-Native critics so as to avoid "exploitative critical discourse" (82), or to present—and here he mentions Hoy and Eigenbrod in particular—"only tentative, qualified, and provisional critical statements" (83). Instead, McKegney suggests more assertive claims: "Critical interventions, even when they are flawed, can forward others' thinking by inciting reactions in which new avenues of investigation and new methods of inquiry might be developed. If an interpretation is flawed, then why is it so, and how can another critic in dialogue remedy the errors?" (84).

While McKegney's words are intentionally brash, using the metaphor of the boxing ring to encourage discussion, he displays the confidence of a new generation of scholars who are working in a recognizable field.[11] But what is not evident is that had he written this article even five years before, in 2003, he would have largely only been able to address non-Native critics, since the majority of Indigenous critics in Canada present in 2008—Jo-Ann Episkenew, Warren Cariou, Daniel Heath Justice, Rick Monture, Niigaanwewidam Sinclair—either were not yet working or still early in the completion of their doctoral work. The increased participation by Indigenous scholars has lessened the anxieties typical of the previous generation of non-Native scholars. Menominee poet Chrystos makes the point in the title of one of her poems in *Not Vanishing* (1988): "Maybe we shouldn't meet if there are no third world women here"; add to this Hoy's quote of Trinh T. Minh-ha and the concern about being tokenized as Third World women: "'It is as if everywhere we go, we become Someone's private zoo'" (qtd. in Hoy, 40). While it is clear that by 2008 the field of Indigenous literary studies is no longer in the awkward stage of having only a few Indigenous scholars, this is not to say that there are enough; but there are enough that Indigenous participation no longer has to be a central point for discussion.

In the last century, scholars like Hoy and Eigenbrod completed the necessary work to establish a field, from creating curriculum to giving conference papers, all the while forging relationships with Indigenous students and communities. As Hoy states, "the inclusion of Native work in syllabi and curricula does not necessarily make the academy more hospitable either to Native students and faculty or to Native ways of seeing" (48). Given the lack of Indigenous presence on university faculties, they accrued expertise, power, and a public profile as they completed this work—somewhat uncomfortably, as Eigenbrod discusses when Indigenous students came to her to learn about their literatures (77). It is not surprising that even in their scholarship they stepped carefully and reflectively, never knowing when they were about to meet with a crying Indigenous graduate student or to step into a boxing ring, not only metaphorically in the way that McKegney employs it. Eigenbrod describes a class visit by Anishinaabe writer George Kenny, who discussed racism only to be challenged with a verbal and near physical attack by an offended student (Eigenbrod, *Travelling* 12).

6. Rob Appleford

In 2009, in "A Response to Sam McKegney's 'Strategies for Ethical Engagement,'" also published in *Studies in American Indian Literatures*, Rob Appleford enthusiastically steps into the ring with the assertion that, "My gloves are on, and I hear the bell!" (89). Appleford directs attention away from any malaise in the field to the battle he identifies at hand: "a squaring off of opponents determined to hold fast to an interpretive turf and thus establish this turf as a recognized higher ground" (90). Appleford identifies two opponents: on the one side are literary nationalists like Craig S. Womack who argue that Indigenous literatures are examples of specific tribal intellectual traditions; on the other are cosmopolitanists like Gerald Vizenor who believe that Indigenous literature invariably includes the mark of colonization and the influence of dominant cultures. The battle between literary nationalists versus cosmopolitanists, Appleford argues, is "fundamentally the struggle to marshal the imagination of the Indigenous writer . . . in the service of an immanent, recognizable, and *knowable* teleological project of ethical/ethnic self fashioning" (91); in other words, the author and text comprise the boxing ring, and the fight is over who gets to decide what it means to be Indigenous. By extension, the fight is also about what community the author is responsible to. Subsequent scholarship, regardless of which side you are on, will argue that the author is committed to his or her community, to whatever community they designate. The implication is that scholarly debates are just turf wars that ignore the author and the text, and in fact collapse the two, so that authors must represent a particular community in both the political and the textual sense. Appleford suggests this is a set-up, "shoehorning authors into political models of agency or resistance with which they may in fact have little interest or sympathy" (92).

Appleford's appeal to respect the author and text is laudable. What is missing from his recounting is an additional battle, as described in the 2004 article by Devon Mihesuah (Choctaw/Chickasaw), the editor of *American Indian Quarterly*. Mihesuah lambastes literary critics for taking over Indigenous Studies when she began her editorship in 1998, and charges these critics (or, as she calls us, "lit critters") for refusing to be uncomfortable, to be responsible for improving the lives of Native American people, or to be accountable to communities (99). To what extent then, is the battle not simply between nationalists and cosmopolitanists, but also against literary study? In what ways is the invocation of community a strategy for literary critics to persuade others about the relevance of our field to those who clearly do not believe it is that important? That such an attack on literary criticism could take place in one of the most eminent journals of Native Studies in North America illustrates widespread belief in the irrelevance of literary study. While no one would say that Mihesuah's words are measured, they do have some commerce with recent generations of literary critics who understand their scholarship to be a contribution to the fight against global warming, the fight for Indigenous Rights, and the support of Idle No More, reorienting the field in such a way to value activism.

7. Margaret Kovach

To the extent that those who study literature in contemporary contexts are extolled to conduct research relevant to communities, the final contribution to this section is not from a literary scholar, partly because the work she does has no equivalent in our field at the present time. In "Situating Self, Culture and Purpose in Indigenous Inquiry," a chapter in Cree scholar Margaret Kovach's monograph, *Indigenous Methodologies* (2009), she proposes that it is not enough for researchers to declare their position; they must also reflect on how grounded they are in Indigenous cultures and be able to articulate the purpose of their research. While participating in ceremonies and cultural traditions in one's research community (such as consulting elders or visiting sacred sites) is not easily done in literary studies, it is possible to see how such activities could illuminate certain texts. (How might attending a sweat or an Idle No More demonstration, for example, help us better understand Lesley Belleau's 2014 novel, *Sweat*?) But Kovach's other requirement, that scholars identify the purpose of their work is nearly unheard of in literary studies. At no point in any of our training are we ever asked to articulate why we are drawn—on a personal level—to do the work we do. A large value for Kovach, particularly given the sort of qualitative research that she conducts, is that "research should be collectively relevant. . . . Purposeful research was inseparable from the value in giving back, that what we do has to assist" (100). Kovach's assertion that we identify why we conduct the work that we do is a huge challenge to our field that is only now resonating in our own discussions.

Conclusion

In early 2014, Renate asked me to help her with that year's Aboriginal Roundtable held at Congress that May. Originally started by Renate, with

Kristina Fagan, in 2000 in Edmonton, where I first met them, the Roundtable has been hosted annually by the Canadian Association of Commonwealth Literatures and Language Studies (CACLALS). But with the establishment of ILSA, we suspected that many would stop attending this Roundtable in favour of the new association, and we wanted to give those involved a chance to discuss the upcoming changes. Tragically, Renate passed away suddenly in early May, and when we all assembled for the Roundtable, instead of talking about our groups' concerns, we talked about the model Renate had provided as a scholar, as a friend (for me, as a mother), and as a human being. It was there that Sam presented, on behalf of the association's founding committee, the tenets upon which ILSA is founded, and challenged us, much in the way Kovach does, to think about the implications if we take seriously our call for our work to be relevant to Indigenous people. I clearly remember him saying that if taken to its farthest implication, these tenets would involve completely changing how we train students, conduct our research, and choose research topics. Embedded in his presentation, a harbinger of the future, is the way that position and self-reflection continue as fundamental methodologies in Indigenous literary studies.

Notes

1. Aboriginal identity is legislated and regulated through Canada's Indian Act, the Constitution of Canada, Métis registration, and at the band membership level. It is also discussed regularly in Canadian society in such common comments as "Are you a real/full-blood Indian/Métis?" and "She looks (or doesn't look) First Nations," and in the public slogan associated with the membership committee at Kahnawake: "Marry out—get out." The impact of this regulation is also felt by the third generation of children since Bill C-31 in 1985, who, should their grandparents and parents not have kept track of the changed rules to status and married only those with Status cards, one day discover that they have lost legal Indian status and are effectively disinherited from their rights and privileges, such as the right to live on home reserves.

2. Andrea Smith cites the work of Denise Ferreira da Silva who argues in *Toward a Global Idea of Race* that "the post-Enlightenment version of the subject as self-determined exists by situating itself against 'affectable others' who are subject to natural conditions as well as to the self-determined power of the western subject" (Smith 42). See Smith's 2010 article in *GLQ: A Journal of Gay and Lesbian Studies*, titled "Queer Theory and Native Studies: the Heteronormativity of Settler Colonialism."

3. The inaugural meeting of the Indigenous Literary Studies Association was organized in October 2013 in Vancouver by Cherokee author and UBC Canada Research Chair Daniel Heath Justice. Justice worked with Sam McKegney (Queen's U) to bring together Renate Eigenbrod (U of Manitoba), Keavy Martin (U of Alberta), Métis scholar Jo-Ann Episkenew (U of Regina), NunatuKavut scholar Kristina

Bidwell (U of Saskachewan), Anishinaabe scholar Armand Garnet Ruffo (Queen's U), Haudenosaunee scholar Rick Monture (McMaster U), and Métis scholar Deanna Reder (Simon Fraser U) to write ILSA's founding purpose, context, and values. Its first governing board was elected in 2014, with Métis scholar Warren Cariou (U of Manitoba) acting as president and McKegney as vice-president.

4. In addition to the titles listed, there are also three anthologies of Indigenous literary history that deserve mention; all are collected by Penny Petrone between 1983 and 1990.

5. kinanâskomitin to Gregory Scofield for his help translating this into English.

6. Acoose refuses to capitalize these terms.

7. Acoose makes several changes to her 1995 version. For example, while in the original she never uses the word "genocidal," in the 2016 version she uses it four times. Also, she changes the name of her first chapter from "Reclaiming Being" to "Re-membering Being to Signifying Female Relations," evoking a more collective sense of identity. Still, her identification documents, her family pictures, and her personal narrative remain as integral features of her analysis.

8. Thanks to Janice Acoose and her publishers at Women's Press, who are working on a re-release of a revised and updated version of this classic and generously shared this chapter with us when we asked for permission to reprint this work.

9. LaRocque's essay is a part of *Creating Community: A Roundtable on Canadian Aboriginal Literatures*, edited by Renate Eigenbrod and Jo-Ann Episkenew and co-published by two small publishing houses, Bear Paw Press and Theytus Books; while it had limited circulation at the time, and uneven production values, the volume represents the growing influence of its editors. They assembled it following the first Aboriginal Roundtable—organized by Eigenbrod and NunatuKavut scholar Kristina Fagan (now Bidwell)—held during the Canadian Association for Commonwealth Literatures and Language Studies (CACLALS) in Edmonton in 2000. The Roundtable attracted most of the established and emerging scholars in the field over the years.

10. LaRocque does not discuss the possibility that her remarks might be taken as a call for authenticity because it does not concern her. She is not looking to police identity, but neither does she want to dispute its existence, since, she insists, "Aboriginal identity and Aboriginal Rights are inextricably related" (221).

11. The field in this instance is enlarged, as he is addressing both Canadian and American audiences—although necessarily since there is still no literary journal on Indigenous literatures that is based in Canada.

2

Iskwewak Kah' Ki Yaw Ni Wahkomakanak: Re-membering Being to Signifying Female Relations

Janice Acoose

I dream for our people to stop dying, to stop feeling so alienated and so marginalized. I dream for our collective and individual well being. . . . We need liberation not only from the colonial legacy of the proverbial white man, we need liberation from our own untruths.

—Emma LaRocque, *Contemporary Challenges*

Throughout my life I have been visited by powerful Spirits. During one visit, the Spirits of two old Koochums (grandmothers) came to me in a dream and beckoned me home. I responded to their Spiritual counsel by returning to my Nehiowe-Metis and Anishinaabe homelands. When at last my feet touched the earth from which I came, I felt the Spirits of Kah' Ki Yaw Ni Wahkomakanak (all my relations) welcome me home.

Following the directives from the Spiritual Koochums, I attempted, first, to re-member myself to maternal relations at my childhood Marival homeland, a "half-breed" colony set up in 1944 Saskatchewan during the "first socialist government in North America."[1] Whereas I remembered my childhood homeland as characterized by majestic rolling hills, luscious green trees, crystal-clear lakes, and bustling community life, now there was only tall dried grass, moved occasionally by wind and lonely animals. Undeterred by this stark reality, I searched a long time for my childhood home. Eventually, I found its decaying foundation buried in the earth, and as I tried to excavate memories, my fingers lovingly traced the concrete remains. Smells of the fecund earth re-membered me to important signifying maternal Nehiowe-Metis relations long gone to the realm of Spirits.

Hours later, on my second journey, I attempted to re-member myself to paternal relations on the nearby Sakimay "Indian" reserve. As soon as I arrived, relatives told me about the yearly Raindance, hosted by an old friend of my deceased father, Fred Acoose. Eager to participate, I respectfully adhered to Anishinaabe ceremonial protocol by seeking out the host and offering cloth and tobacco. He welcomed me immediately and encouraged me to take part in the celebration, subsequently instructing me to abstain from both food and water for the duration of the ceremony. Without the distraction of physical want, and with only my Spirit to guide me, over those few days I began to understand clearly the importance of re-membering Being to both maternal and paternal ancestors, and to empowering Spiritually other Indigenous families, communities, and nations. But I also came to the painful realization that, as a Nehiowe-Metis-Anishinaabekwe I was heavily indoctrinated in white euro-canadian-christian patriarchy. So, I asked the host to ceremonially re-member my Being to the Anishinaabe cultural body and relations by renaming me. To help prepare me Spiritually for the challenging journey ahead, he asked Elder Bill Standingready (from a neighbouring reserve) to rename me. As I arose re-membered to my cultural bodies as Miswonigeesikokwe, I felt strongly connected to the Great-Spirited Mother-Creator Aki (earth) and Kah' Ki Yaw Ni Wahkomakanak, but I wanted desperately for all my relations to become Spiritually and intellectually awakened. As University of Manitoba professor Dr. Emma LaRocque so eloquently writes, I "dream for our liberation in our land . . . for our people to stop dying, to stop feeling so alienated and so marginalized. I dream for our collective and individual well-being."[2] Re-membered in ceremony as Miswonigeesikokwe, however, I felt empowered to begin my journey as a Redsky woman of the Bird Clan people from Sakimay First Nation.

My ongoing journey toward liberation and empowerment has been a painful struggle that often left me feeling angry, resentful, frustrated, and confused. At numerous times throughout my journey, I felt angry and resentful because of deliberate colonial, racist, and sexist strategies used to dis-member my Being from Nehiowe-Metis and Anishinaabe cultural bodies. I also felt frustrated and confused throughout my life journey because white-eurocanadian-christian patriarchy was like a threatening spectre overshadowing community and family. Consequently, my own community and family were often rendered powerless against such strategic and institutionalized racism, sexism, and colonization, as my numerous contacts with white-eurocanadian-christian patriarchy illustrates ahead.

FORM 1

DOMINION OF CANADA

REGISTRATION OF A LIVE BIRTH OF AN INDIAN
(Within the meaning of the "Indian Act" of Canada)

901610 / 54

For use of Provincial Office only

Note.—In case of more than one child at a birth, a separate Registration must be made for each, and the number of each, in order of birth, stated.

Province Saskatchewan

Agency in which birth took place

1. PLACE OF BIRTH:

If on a Reserve (Give name and location)

or If in a Rural Municipality R.M. of ELCAPO No. 154 (Give name or number) 000-05

or If in a City, Town or Village Broadview Street House No. (Give name)

and If in a hospital or institution St. Michael's Hospital 26-16-5-W (Give name instead of street and number)

2. PRINT FULL NAME OF CHILD

Surname or last name: A C O O S E

All Given or Christian Names: MARY JANICE

3. Sex of child	4. Single, twin, triplet, or other	5. Are parents married to each other?	6. Date of birth		
Female	Single	Yes (Answer yes or no)	September (Month by name)	14 (Day)	19 54 (Year)

7. PRINT FULL NAME OF FATHER ACOOSE (Surname or last name) FREDRICK (Given or Christian names)

8. Band or tribe to which father belongs SAKIMAY

9. Residence of father SAKIMAY RESERVE, GRENFELL, SASK. (If on a reserve, give name and location) 000-05

10. Age last birthday 31 years 11. Birthplace of father SASKATCHEWAN (Province or country)

OCCUPATION 12. (a) Trade, profession or kind of work as teamster, trapper, canner, etc. Farmer

(b) Kind of industry or business as lumbering, fur trading, fish canning, etc. General

13. PRINT FULL MAIDEN NAME OF MOTHER BEAUDIN (Surname or last name) HARRIET (Given or Christian names)

14. Band or tribe to which mother belongs SAKIMAY 000-05

15. Residence of mother SAKIMAY RESERVE, GRENFELL (If on a Reserve, give name and location)

16. Age last birthday 27 years 17. Birthplace of mother SASKATCHEWAN (Province or country)

OCCUPATION 18. (a) Trade, profession or kind of work as trapper, canner, etc. AT HOME

(b) Kind of industry or business as fur trading, fish canning, etc. (If unemployed, answer "At Home")

19. Children of this mother at the time of and including this birth:

(a) How many children of this mother are now living? 5

(b) How many children were born alive but are now dead? 0

(c) How many children were born dead? 0

20. Was this a premature birth? 0 If premature, length of pregnancy in weeks

21. Name of doctor, nurse or other person in attendance at birth A. H. Campbell M.D.

22. Marginal notations: (Office use only)

23. I certify the foregoing to be true and correct to the best of my knowledge and belief.

Given under my hand at BROADVIEW this 20 day of SEPTEMBER 19 54

Signature of informant Mrs. Harriet Acoose

Status of informant if other than parent

Address Grenfell Post BROADVIEW, SASK.

24. I hereby certify that the above return was made to me at

on the day of 19

Indian Agency No. Indian Agent

A copy of my birth certificate (notice: "Live Birth of an Indian"!).

My first contact with white-eurocanadian-christian patriarchy was at birth in 1954 Saskatchewan. After nine nourishing and loving months inside my Nehiowe-Metis mother's womb, I was delivered into a cold and sterile white-eurocanadian-patriarchal catholic hospital in Broadview. There, Grey (catholic) Nuns immediately imposed christian and patriarchal authority by stealing my mother's right to name me. And, just like my three older sisters, I was named Mary, becoming the fourth nominally indistinguishable female child in my immediate family to be named after the virginal mother of christ.

My second contact with white-eurocanadian-christian patriarchy was a few days after my birth on September 14, 1954. At that time, my birth was recorded on forms for the patriarchal bureaucracy as the "Registration of a live birth of an Indian," a legal process that registered me as an "Indian" and a genocidal process that dis-membered my Being from signifying Nehiowe-Metis-Anishinaabe cultural bodies and relations. And, while some people assume that status as a "registered treaty Indian" provides me with so-called life-long privileges like "free education" and "tax exemptions," I want to make two things very clear. First, the words "free education" and "tax exemption," not unlike the words "easy squaw" and "Indian princess," belong to a body of language used to justify racist beliefs about "Indians." Second, while I am a direct beneficiary of Treaty 4 signed at Fort Qu'Appelle Saskatchewan in 1876, the treaty (which some claim irrelevant to contemporary Canada) also directly benefits all Canadian residents who enjoy a level of wealth and legal protection created by their immigrant ancestors. Moreover, those same opportunities and protections are now extended to new immigrants, whose settlement in Canada has created an interesting multiethnic facade. It appears to be a politically con-stituted multiethnic nation, but at its centre, the country is still controlled and manipulated by white-eurocanadian-christian patriarchy. In regards to treat-ies, however, both old and new immigrants benefit. While some may quarrel with treaty rights being extended to the ever-growing Indigenous population, it's important to remember that treaties are binding and foundational legal documents, regardless of the changing social conditions. For clarity, I ask read-ers to consider Canadian mortgage agreements that borrowers enter into with lending institutions. When borrowers enter into mortgage agreements, they cannot arbitrarily change the terms and conditions. Moreover, homeowners cannot decide to stop paying their mortgage because they feel it irrelevant, unfair, or unjust. Unlike the lending and borrowing activity at the heart of this simple analogy, the process that imposed a treaty Indian legal status on me is rooted in a genocidal strategy for removing "Indians" from the land and dis-membering Being from signifying relations and cultural bodies. Thus, my second contact with white-eurocanadian-christian patriarchy dis-membered me from signifying maternal relations and usurped my right to legally identify as both Nehiowe-Metis and Anishinaabe.

The imposed legal identity as "Indian," like the historically imposed patronymic naming enforced in the late 1800s, was a colonial strategy to dis-member my Being from Nehiowe-Metis and Anishinaabe cultural bodies: the goal of such genocidal strategies was to disconnect "Indians" like myself from important signifying female relations. Prior to the imposition of colonial rule and white-euro-canadian-christian patriarchy, my Anishinaabe ancestors had their own personal names, which signified both clan and biological relations. In my paternal family, the name Acoose (or Ekos/Flying Bird) was my great-grandfather's personal and only name. Known for his running prowess, Ekos was so named because traditional Bonaise Doodaem (Bird Clan) Knowledge Keepers acknowledged his flying bird-like abilities as a runner. The son of Qu'wich Acoose was noted too as a powerful caller of Spirits like his father. When he was christianized, Ekos was given the name Samuel Acoose, and all his descendants thereafter became Acoose. In other words, the change in naming to the patronymic "Acoose" irrevocably disconnected our Beings from Anishinaabe Bonaise Doodaem relational systems that encouraged environmentally respectful ways of living and governance with all of Creation. Thus, under such a patriarchal system, I would subsequently be dis-membered from both important and signifying Anishinaabe Doodaem and Nehiowe-Metis female relations. There is still more evidence that shows how my people were disconnected from important signifying relations. In my paternal Sakimay First Nation home community, for example, there are very few people who re-member themselves to Bonaise Doodaem, much less acknowledge it as important to Being. Also, in old colonial documents, in the spaces where our mothers' or fathers' names are to be inserted, the words "Indian," "half-breed," and sometimes "Indian squaw" appear. See, for example, my Down Koochum's application for "Half-Breed Scrip" below. Despite such genocidal attempts to dis-member me from signifying female relations, I was fortunate to have lived my life knowing my Down Koochum. Without that living connection to her, I could not re-member my Being (or any of my descendants) to the Nehiowe-Metis cultural body. As an Indigenous child, enriched Spiritually, intellectually, and physically with both Nehiowe-Metis and Anishinaabe relations, the legal categorization as "Indian," imposed patronymic naming practices, and efforts to dis-member my Being from Great-Spirited female relations, however, traumatically altered my life.

My third contact with white-eurocanadian-christian patriarchy was a couple of months after my birth, when I was baptized in the catholic church. Baptized as a child of the male-god-he, I was brought into the catholic church as Mary Janice Georgiana Darlene Acoose, daughter of Mr. and Mrs. Fred

Form A.

Reserved *J.A. McKenna*
James Walker

Disallowed

This Indian, married to a Halfbreed, lives away from the Reserve, but draws treaty. Is other annuity to be commuted?

J.A. McKenna

12/7/

NORTH-WEST HALFBREED CLAIMS COMMISSION.
1900.

Before JAMES ANDREW JOSEPH McKENNA, of the City of Ottawa, in the Province of Ontario, Esquire, and

JAMES WALKER, of the City of Calgary, in the North-West Territories, Esquire, COMMISSIONERS,

duly appointed and sitting as a Royal Commission at *Fort Du Appelle* in the North-West Territories, to investigate claims of Halfbreeds who were born in the Territories between the 15th July, 1870, and the 31st December, 1885, personally came and appeared *Philomine Pelletier*

_____ Claimant, who being duly sworn, deposes as follows :—

Question 1.   What is your name?
Answer   1. *Philomine Pelletier*

Question 2.   Where do you reside?
Answer   *Crooked Lake n.w.t*

Question 3.   Where were you born?
Answer   *On the North Saskatchewan River*

Question 4.   When were you born?
Answer   *Twenty nine Years ago*

Question 5.   What is your father's name?
Answer   *O Pa-cha-pis* *(Indian)*

Question 6.   What was the name of your mother before her marriage?
Answer   *Saulteaux* *(Indian)*

Question 7.   Is your father a Halfbreed or an Indian?
Answer   *Indian*

Question 8.   Is your mother a Halfbreed or an Indian?
Answer   *Indian*

Question 9.   Have you ever received land or scrip in Manitoba or the North-West Territories in commutation of your Halfbreed rights?
Answer   *No*

A copy of my Down Koochum's "Half-Breed Scrip" application.

Acoose, "Indians" from the Sakimay Reserve. Over the course of my life, I would understand the catholic church as one of the most powerful ideological colonial institutions operating on Indigenous peoples. In my communities, the catholic church wielded its ideological power through joyless, black-robed priests and nuns who closely scrutinized all activities within the Marival Half-Breed Colony and the Sakimay Indian Reserve.

My fourth contact with white-eurocanadian-christian patriarchy was in 1959 Saskatchewan. I was five years old when I was imprisoned behind the drab and dreary walls at the Cowessess "Indian" Residential School. The effects of my four-year imprisonment (1959–1963) and the Spiritual, psychological, physical, and sexual abuse that accompanied it, as well as the strategic programmed terrorism disguised as education and christianization, *live* in me, as a diagnosed psychological condition: post-traumatic stress disorder (PTSD). In my family, like in many other "Indian" families, legally sanctioned imprisonment and programmed terrorism began in the late 1800s with my great-grandparents, and as our legacy as "Indians" was carried on into my grandparents' lives, passed on to my father and his siblings, and then to me and my siblings. Anishinaabe scholar Lawrence Gross astutely describes such collective trauma as post-apocalyptic stress disorder (PASD), when PTSD lives in entire cultures over many generations.[3]

The day my mother delivered my siblings and me to the Cowessess "Indian" Residential School still haunts my memories. I'm haunted by memories of black-robed priests and nuns who terrorized me into submission. I have haunting memories of my mother being pushed out the door with a stern warning from the nuns not to get emotional about saying goodbye. I'm haunted, too, by echoes of my own screams, crying out for my mother and clinging tightly to my sister as the nun read through all the rules, which I seldom remembered and was consequently punished for disobeying. One of the rules, we quickly learned, was that boys and girls were to be completely segregated. Thus, my four-year imprisonment in the Cowessess "Indian" Residential School haunts me still, because I have painful memories of seeing my brother Fred, caged like an animal behind a barbed-wire fence I passed on my way to class. I'm haunted by memories of that first day of school, too, because I can still feel being ripped away from my sisters, herded down a long, dark hall, pushed into a room to have my hair shorn, powdered with DDT insecticide (supposedly because all "Indians" were infected with lice), and then showered with severely hot water.

Once stripped of remembrances of home, I was given a number, a school uniform, and an assigned bed in the "small girls' dormitory." Over the years, programmed terrorism effectively encouraged me to respond to the number rather than my name. The school uniform, too, stripped me of any individual identity. The army-like bunk to which I was assigned at least provided me with some small comfort, since it was positioned close to my older sister, Mary-Madeline. As part of the nighttime rituals, the nuns ordered me to always sleep facing right, with hands folded in a praying position under my head. Although it was monotonous and sometimes torturous, the daily routine helped me to survive from one day to the next. Each day I awoke very early, recited prayers, showered, dressed, ate meals (prefaced by prayers), attended catechism and school (prefaced by more prayers), and took part in rigidly programmed physical exercises. Bedtime was welcome after excruciatingly painful periods of time endured on our knees in prayer circles. And, although I cried myself to sleep at night, crying became part of the rituals that helped me to survive. Some nights I cried myself to sleep because I longed to be at home with my

This was taken the day my sister Mary Carol and I went to the "Indian" Residential School. Brother Clem is between us. Photo credit: Harriet Acoose.

family. Other times I cried at night because I remembered daily physical pun-ishments: sometimes my mouth and face were slapped; sometimes my knuck-les were pounded with a wooden block; and sometimes my mouth was taped shut for long periods of time. Too many times I was physically punished and psychologically terrorized for speaking out of turn, asking too many questions, or showing "disrespect" for their god by asking for proof of "his" existence. The

The Cowessess "Indian" Residential School I attended from 1959 to 1963.

nuns' consistent nighttime threats of eternal damnation, as well as haunting visits from satan himself and desperate Spirits from purgatory, intensified my fears. Even now, as a chronic insomniac, a part of me still struggles to overcome such psychological terrorism. Other times I cried in terror when I heard footsteps creeping up the fire escape to our little girls' dormitory. Those nights I jumped into my sister Mary-Madeline's bed and clung to her fiercely for protection as I listened to little girls' tortured whimpers, muffled screams, and desperate cries for help. I remember trying to tell anyone who would listen about those night visits to our dorm, the cruel punishments, and the deadly threats, but my voice was silenced by family fears, community pressure, and church power. As the beneficiary of four generations of programmed terrorism inflicted through the residential school, I began to doubt what I believed, felt, and saw. Those feelings were reinforced throughout my life by comments like "Surely the residential schools accomplished some good; didn't you learn to read and write?" which I now reason only masked the speaker's years of pent-up discomfort and collective guilt.

Programmed terrorism through the "Indian" residential school began when I was a five-year-old child in the formative developmental years of my life. It continued on through the years until I was nine, by then effectively programmed through terrorism to reject my cultures, languages, history, and ancestors. How was I to comprehend at five years old that forcing me to speak English rather than my own languages was part of a terrorist program that would alter my psyche and identity? How was I to comprehend the effects of programmed terrorism upon three previous familial generations forced to reject Spirituality, history, stories, and languages? Or how those seemingly innocent stories about Dick, Jane, Spot, and Puff from our Grade 1 and 2 readers served an ideological system much different than my own? I'm sure it confused me when I could not see reflections of my own wonderfully alive home life, especially since I did not have a language to name and link such literary tools to a terrorist program for "killing the Indian." How was I to understand that representations of quietly reserved, pleasantly passive, and submissive ladies in those early books were part of a body of stereotypes employed to foster white-supremacist cultural attitudes? How was I to understand, too, those seemingly simple "spot the difference" exercises from phonics workbooks as part of an "othering" process that placed me outside the ideal fostered in textbooks? I certainly did not understand the location of my "self" as marginalized, nor how such marginalization would make me feel ashamed and dis-membered from signifying relations. I'm sure it confused me even more to not find representations in schoolbooks of those Great-Spirited female relations who signified cultural Being. My homes (both the "Indian" reserve and the "half-breed" colony) were constantly enriched with female relations who thought nothing of making room for another hungry person at our already overcrowded supper table, or casually throwing blankets on the floor for visitors to sleep. Thinking back over the years, I realize now that representations of Great-Spirited Indigenous female relations rarely appeared in the pages of history books, even though they actively participated in the early development of this country. Even today, such Great-Spirited female relations are missing from many of the bodies of Indigenous literatures in books written in English! Without such cultural referents in books written in English, my fourth contact with white-eurocanadian-christian patriarchy in 1959 Saskatchewan significantly altered my cultural Being.

Throughout my life, my cultures (which were too often misrepresented as racially "Indian"), gender, Spiritual practices, and economic status set me apart from mainstream society, whose ideological power fostered exclusiveness. I felt set apart from mainstream society during my high school years between 1969 and 1973 at Miller Comprehensive High School in Regina, Saskatchewan. While most Canadians look back on their high school experience as a time for maturing development, my time at Miller Comprehensive High School was poisoned by institutional racism and sexism, ever-present in mainstream student and teacher attitudes, pedagogical strategies, and textual ideology. At that time, I did not have the political consciousness or strength of Spirit to challenge contemporaneous pedagogy or the school's dominating racism and sexism, and I therefore internalized inferiority and shame. And, not unlike so many other Indigenous women who suffer psychological, economic, Spiritual, political, and physical traumas associated with colonialism, sexism, and racism, I shamefully turned away from my history and cultures, believing that I was an easy squaw and "Indian" whore who deserved to be repeatedly violated and raped by white priests, teachers, psychologists, and other men.

Many frustrating and challenging years later, I was Spiritually reborn and politically awakened. I was reborn and awakened in part by politically astute, culturally tenacious, and Spiritually strong Indigenous activists throughout the Americas, whose collective voices empowered me to challenge the prevailing white-eurocanadian-christian patriarchy's institution of higher learning. I remember vividly that first day in 1986 when I walked through the front doors of the University of Saskatchewan's Place Riel as a politically awakened and Spiritually reborn Indigenous woman. Still aware of the effects of programmed terrorism, I felt haunted by white-christian-canadian patriarchy and shadowed by ignorant, uncivilized, savage, barbaric, heathen, dirty, pagan, drunk, no-good "Indian," and easy squaw stereotypes as I made my way to classes.

And, even though I felt politically empowered, once inside the classroom I realized that pedagogical strategies, required textbooks, and some of the professors still served a white-eurocanadian-christian patriarchy. Indeed, there were plenty of professors at the University of Saskatchewan in various disciplines who implicitly and explicitly reinforced notions of white cultural supremacy, albeit perhaps unconsciously, ignorantly, or naively.

When I contemplate the way that professors implicitly and explicitly reinforced notions of white cultural supremacy, I'm reminded of two incidents that happened at the University of Saskatchewan with two sessional instructors. The first incident occurred on day one of a fur trade history class. As the instructor reviewed his selected readings, he spoke of "Indian" women and fur traders. And, without even a bit of consideration, he characterized the "Indian" women as sexually promiscuous. When I asked him to reconsider his comment, given the obvious interpretive white-christian-male bias, he made great attempts to silence me. First, he said very matter-of-factly, "No, I don't have to consider what you call bias." Second, he did not encourage further discussion. Third, he moved very quickly onto another topic. So, rather than sit through a whole term enduring racism and sexism, I dropped the class. The second incident involved a sessional instructor hired to teach a western Canadian literature class. Upon signing up for the class, I was absolutely astounded to find that he had excluded a significant body of work by Indigenous authors. So, I asked him why he neglected to include such a significant body of work. For what I perceived to be a confrontation, I prepared myself emotionally, Spiritually, and physically, like a fierce Okichita (Anishinaabe woman warrior). Ready for battle, I asked him why he did not include Indigenous writers on his list of required reading. In contrast to my warrior-woman posturing, he answered me in a typically confident white-male academic voice, "There are none that are quite good enough." Not easily dissuaded, I confronted him, too, about the words "from no man's land to everyman's land," a phrase used in the "course description" section of his syllabus. I tried to explain that I felt very angry and frustrated at the description of the prairies as "no man's land," and I told him that I was frustrated and angry at his and the institution's casual dismissal of my Nehiowe-Metis and Anishinaabe ancestors (both female and male) who had cared for and nurtured the land since time immemorial. Although I left his office feeling the matter was unresolved, I made a personal commitment to complete his class. Later, I would write a term paper about the unrealistic, derogatory, and stereotypic images of Indigenous people that appeared in books selected for his western Canadian literature reading list. In fact, the ideas for my master's thesis were born from that battle with him. Years later, the same instructor told me that he had learned some things from my time in his class. And, when he recounts that time to others, he tells them that he has "been suitably Acoosed," which I'm not sure is a compliment or an insult.

My decision to study at the graduate level in the University of Saskatchewan's Department of English was part of a political strategy to challenge Canada's prevailing white-christian-canadian patriarchal ideological assumptions, too often encountered through classroom experience and the books included as "required readings." I became very zealous about challenging unrealistic, derogatory, and stereotypic images of Indigenous peoples in literature, and I was empowered by scholars like Dr. Emma LaRocque to speak out and "self-express because there was so much about our history and about our lives that … has been disregarded, infantilized, and falsified."[4] Like LaRocque, "I think I had this missionary zeal to tell about our humanity because Indian-ness was so dehumanized and Metis-ness didn't even exist."[5] And whereas most graduate students feel they have very little power, I felt empowered by Indigenous writers, activists, and Kah' Ki Yaw Ni Wahkomakanak. The Spiritual energies of all my relations, the political actions of activists, and the voices of scholars and

Me when I received my master's degree.

activists fuelled my educational journey, and so I began to develop ideas for Indigenizing the University of Saskatchewan generally, and the Department of English specifically. The only Indigenous woman in a program that, at least to my perception, appeared unwelcoming and resistant to pedagogic change, I sometimes felt like an avian ancestor removed from the sky world, unprotected, alone, and isolated. On numerous occasions when I challenged a selected literature's unrealistic, derogatory, and stereotypic images, I certainly felt the authoritative strength and power of white-eurocanadian-christian patriarchy.

Eventually, I realized that doing the kind of work I set out to do for my master's thesis required a lot of support. My strongest support and encouragement came from Dr. Ron Marken and Dr. Susan Gingell, two compassionate and committed activist-educators. Their support, along with the Spiritual energies of Kah' Ki Yaw Ni Wahkomakanak and many traditional Knowledge Keepers, family, friends, and professional associates, fuelled my energies to challenge the ideological basis of the Canadian education system generally, and its literary canon specifically. During the first few minutes of my master's thesis defence, I spoke about my insecurities and explained that I felt somewhat powerless as an Indigenous woman struggling against hundreds of years of whiteeurocanadian-christian patriarchy. Such feelings were intensified when one of the members of my graduate committee described my work/ideas/words as "very abrasive and disturbing" to him as a whitechristian male. And, while at first his comments unsettled me, eventually I felt a renewed commitment to intelligently sensitize those gathered at my defence. I spoke at length about the Spiritual, emotional, and physical pain and frustration I endured over the years studying in the English department. Some time later, however, I felt victorious as the first Nehiowe-Metis-Anishinaabekwe to graduate with a master's degree (and now a Ph.D.) from that department. I also felt victorious because my studies and developing critical skills helped me to begin the process of re-membering Being to Manitoukwe and Kah' Ki Yaw Ni Wahkomakanak.

Essentially, in my thesis, "Iskwewak: Kah' Ki Yaw Ni Wahkomakanak," out of which the first edition of this book grew, I argue that Canadian literature is an ideological instrument. As an ideological instrument, Canadian literature promotes the cultures, philosophies, values, religion, politics, economics, and social organization of white, european, christian, canadian patriarchy, while at the same time fostering cultural attitudes about Indigenous peoples based on unrealistic, derogatory, and stereotypic images. My own experience in mainstream university literature classes taught me a number of critical lessons that I carry with me into the classroom where I now teach. It taught me, first of all, that literature and books are powerful political tools. Because literature and books are powerful and political, I encourage students to read critically and with an awareness of their own cultural position. I realized, however, that most university students are not critical readers, thinkers, and writers on the subject of "Indians," "Eskimos," or "half-breeds." Consequently, many come to "know" Indigenous peoples only through highly selective images perpetuated through a similarly highly selective literature, which ultimately maintains the white-euro-christian-canadian status quo.

Experience in mainstream university literature classes also taught me valuable lessons about the relationship between language and power. Through my studies, I came to the conclusion that the English language is first and foremost the language of colonizers, although some contemporary scholars argue that it is also now an Indigenous language. In "Theorizing American Indian Experience," Craig Womack writes, "I do not think it a certainty that the English language is the colonizer's language. Once it landed in the New World, English picked up a lot of tribal influences from Indians, from Africans in the Caribbean, and so on. Literally there are thousands of Indian words in English. Maybe Indians colonized English instead of the other way around."[6] I agree with Womack that the English language has, like all languages, evolved to reflect social, economic, and political changes. What hasn't changed is that English continues to serve the interests of those in power: consider, for example, the influence of English internationally. In my interactions over the years with legal, educational, or communication institutions, I observed that white-eurocanadian-patriarchal interests are protected and served through English. Consider how English still upholds white-eurocanadian-christian power, as in its most important signifying male god, "he." In recent years, I have become enthused by feminist scholars' significant challenges to patriarchal language and power, particularly those Indigenous women scholars who dare to attach the word *feminist* to their scholarly work and identity.

As I am a politically awakened and widely read Nehiowe-Metis-Anishinaabekwe feminist, I can no longer ignore the effects of colonization, racism, and sexism. As I stated previously, my awakening began when I was newly re-membered to my own cultural bodies. I was also awakened politically by Indigenous activists throughout the Americas who inspired me to speak, act, and write. Thus, when I began my career as an educator, my first political act was to subvert white-eurocanadian-christian patriarchy in the selections for my required reading list for predominantly Indigenous first-year English students. Because I wanted students to make connections to the texts, to interact with them, I felt they needed to see realistic representations of themselves. So, instead of requiring them to read so-called canonical authorities like Chaucer, Milton, Jonson, Donne, Pope, Shakespeare, Wordsworth, Swift, Dickens, Whitman, Melville, Faulkner, or Hemingway, to provide them with an historical and cross-cultural reading experience I rely on Indigenous Knowledge Keepers. Thus, I encourage my students to read Kahgegagahbowh (Anishinaabe), Pauline Johnson (Mohawk), Joe Dion (Cree), Maria Campbell (Metis), Louise Halfe (Cree), Marie Annharte Baker (Anishinaabe), Beth Cuthand (Cree), Jeannette Armstrong (Okanagan), Tomson Highway (Cree), Lenore Keeshig-Tobias (Anishinaabe), Drew Hayden Taylor (Anishinaabe), Winona LaDuke (Anishinaabe), Louise Erdrich (Anishinaabe), Marilyn

Sisters Sandy and Jackie on Mom's knee, and, from left to right in the back, sister Carol, niece Shawna, me, and sister Vicky.

Dumont (Metis), Richard Wagamese (Anishinaabe), Paul Seesequasis (Metis-Cree), Robert Warrior (Osage), Craig Womack (Oklahoma Creek–Cherokee), Jace Weaver (Cherokee), and Gregory Scofield (Metis). Finding reflections of their own lives in the selected readings empowers students when they see how Indigenous knowledge is evolving, intelligent, and contributing to the world community. Using Indigenous-authored texts, I also show students how contemporary Indigenous writers use contemporary literary forms to re-member and recreate Indigenous cultures and relations while simultaneously remaining connected to essential Spiritual values and traditions.

Notes

Our thanks to the publishers at Women's Press who gave us permission to include this revised and updated edition of Acoose's original 1995 work, originally titled "Reclaiming Myself."

1. Laurie Barron, "The CCF and the Development of Metis Colonies in Southern Saskatchewan during the Premiership of T. C. Douglas, 1944–1961," *Canadian Journal of Native Studies* 10, no. 2 (1990): 243–70.
2. Emma LaRocque, interview in *Contemporary Challenges: Conversations with Contemporary Canadian Native Writers* (Saskatoon: Fifth House Publishers, 1991), 202.
3. Lawrence Gross, "*Bimaadiziwin*, or the 'Good Life,' as a Unifying Concept of Anishinaabe Religion," *American Indian Culture and Research Journal* 26, no. 1 (2002): 23.
4. LaRocque, *Contemporary Challenges*, 181.
5. LaRocque, *Contemporary Challenges*, 181.
6. Craig Womack, Daniel Heath Justice, and Chris Tueton, eds., *Reasoning Together: The Native Critics Collection* (Norman: University of Oklahoma Press, 2008), 404.

3

"Introduction" from
How Should I Read These?
Native Women Writers in Canada

Helen Hoy

The over-riding fear is that cultural, ethnic, and racial differences will be continually commodified and offered up as new dishes to enhance the white palate—that the Other will be eaten, consumed, and forgotten.

—bell hooks, *Black Looks: Race and Representation*

In "Queen of the North," a short story by Haisla-Heiltsuk writer Eden Robinson, Adelaine, a disaffected Haisla teenager, has to contend with the familiarities of a white powwow spectator hungry for sexual and cultural stimulation. Eyeing her bare legs and arms, subjecting her to a sequence of increasingly personal questions, Arnold slaps down one twenty-dollar bill after another to enforce his desire for bannock, after the booth where Adelaine is volunteering has closed down:

> I handed him the plate and bowed. I expected him to leave then but he bowed back and said, "Thank you."
> "No," I said. "Thank you. The money's going to a good cause. It'll—"
> "How should I eat these?" he interrupted me.
> With your mouth, asshole. (*Traplines* 208)

Misreading Adelaine's sardonic bow as a traditional formality (and interrupting her attempt to communicate about the Helping Hands Society), Arnold extends his cultural "sensitivity" to the protocol for eating fry bread.

Although Adelaine's polite spoken response—"Put some syrup on them"—restores to the realm of the familiar the fry bread that Arnold posits as foreign, her immediate silent riposte is more eloquent. "With your mouth, asshole" identifies and even more forcefully repudiates Arnold's act of cultural Othering. Adelaine dismisses his effort to make a basic foodstuff esoteric, to place it beyond the pale (so to speak) of recognizable human activity. Simultaneously the scene identifies and repudiates a predilection by members of the dominant group for *cultural* novelty. Decontextualized, commodifiable tokens of difference take the place of shared involvement in processes of social and political change (here fundraising for the Helping Hands Society) and the more pertinent, political cross-cultural communication that this might entail.[1]

Arnold wants to know how to eat fry bread, in proper Indian fashion. He apparently wants to consume Adelaine as well, to fill some undefined need that will show itself more longingly later, when he asks her to let down her hair:

> ". . . Put some syrup on them, or jam, or honey. Anything you want."
> "Anything?" he said, staring deep into my eyes.
> Oh, barf. "Whatever." (208)

What he does not want is to replace this one-sided acquisition and ingestion with a reciprocal exchange that might challenge racial (and sexual) difference as a source of Othering.[2]

A message of racial inferiority is now more likely to be coded in the language of culture than biology. (Razack 19)

"What do you do for poison oak?" a student once asked in a large auditorium where Mabel was being interviewed as a native healer. "Calamine lotion," Mabel answered. (Sarris 17)

The episode, discussed above, from Robinson's short-story collection *Traplines* explores creatively a subject that is increasingly a concern of literary-critical theory. Postcolonial theory—perhaps more properly termed "decolonial theory"—has challenged the reduction of minoritized peoples to the function of "self-consolidating Other" for the dominant culture (Spivak, "Three Women's Texts and a Critique of Imperialism" 273). It has interrogated their restriction, from a hegemonic perspective, to bounded cultures narrower and more visible than the culture allotted to the majority. At a conference for the Association of Canadian College and University Teachers of English in Montreal in 1995, Plains Cree–Métis scholar Emma LaRocque condemned the propensity of non-Natives to employ notions of tradition and cultural difference to explain everything Indian, from birch biting to biography. As an instance of this fascination with cultural difference, she gave the examples of the chaplain who asked, "How do you people die?" To this, she suggested, in a sentiment that anticipates Adelaine's, the obvious answer was, "We stop breathing" (LaRocque, "The Place of Native Writing in Canadian Intellectual Categories").

> "How do *you people* die?"
> "We stop breathing, asshole."

Although potentially part of a radical politics, respect for social specificity and challenges to ethnocentrism can produce, ironically, "a kind of difference that doesn't make a difference of any kind" (Hall, "What Is This 'Black' in Black Popular Culture?" 23). Or, worse, they can introduce new forms of domination. As Eden Robinson illustrates, ostentatious cultural deference ("How should I eat these?") can coexist unabashedly with a superior sense of entitlement to the cultural productions of a people and even to the people themselves. Sherene Razack warns that "the cultural differences approach reinforces an important epistemological cornerstone of imperialism: the colonized possess a series of knowable characteristics and can be studied, known, and managed accordingly by the colonizers whose own complicity remains masked" (10). Like the power relations it reflects, difference functions asymmetrically.[3]

For Native writers, the "knowable characteristics" expected to inform their writing have changed somewhat in recent days but still exert disturbing force. Cree-Métis poet Marilyn Dumont describes the pressure on contemporary Native writers: "If you are old, you are supposed to write legends, that is, stories that were passed down to you from your elders. If you are young, you are expected to relate stories about foster homes, street life and loss of culture and if you are in the middle, you are supposed to write about alcoholism or residential school. And somehow throughout this you are to infuse everything you write with symbols of the native worldview, that is: the circle, mother earth, the number four or the trickster figure."

What if you are an urban Indian, like herself, she asks ("Popular Images of Nativeness" 47). Even in the absence of specific expectations or stereotypes, the marked status of minority groups, by contrast with the unmarked status of the normative group, ties identity and authority, for the Native writer, to one overriding signifier.[4]

Whenever she addresses an audience, Muscogee (Creek) poet Joy Harjo observes that she is asked more about Native culture than about writing ("In Love and War and Music" 58). Lee Maracle, Salish-Métis writer and activist, similarly protests that her Indigenousness, her location quite specifically as "*Native* writer," not as "writer" or "woman," is the restrictive grounds of her authority for white readers or white feminists (*Sojourner's Truth and Other Stories* 60; *I Am Woman* 20–21).[5] Emma LaRocque echoes Maracle's concern, pointing out that ghettoizing of disparate writings under the category "Native" limits public access to relevant material: "For example, an analysis of the Canadian school system by a Native author is rarely placed under 'education' or 'sociology' or 'social issues'" ("Preface" xviii). Harjo seems to experience the identification as inappropriately broad—requiring her to illuminate entire peoples rather than her area of expertise, her own writing; Maracle and LaRocque as inappropriately narrow—requiring them to restrict their insights only to their own race. All three, however, object to being perceived primarily, and disproportionately, in terms of their race. Referring specifically to the tokenizing of "Third World women" on panels, at meetings, and in special issues of journals, Trinh T. Minh-ha comments, "It is as if everywhere we go, we become Someone's private zoo" (*Woman, Native, Other* 82).

≈

Where do you begin telling someone their world is not the only one? (Maracle, *Ravensong* 72)

The act of enforcing racelessness in literary discourse is itself a racial act. (Morrison 46)

≈

I hesitated, none the less, to open this book with the *Traplines* episode because the discussion might be read as arguing pluralistically for a common humanity leading to a shared perspective and understanding. "Why can't we all just get along?"—with its potential obliviousness to the inequitable access to resources and authority that engenders division—is emphatically not my argument. (Of course, as an aspiration, "Why can't we all get along?" has very different political implications coming from a Black man brutalized by white Los Angeles police officers and witnessing the interracial violence of disadvantaged groups turning against each other than from a person like me, privileged by race and class.) While resisting being turned into "otherness machine[s]" (Suleri,

Meatless Days 105), writers and theorists of colour have been equally adamant in resisting universalizing gestures that ignore difference and absorb disparate historical and material realities into dominant paradigms. "Because you sleep / does not mean you see into my dreams," writes Spokane–Coeur d'Alene poet and novelist Sherman Alexie, in his poem "Introduction to Native American Literature" (*Old Shirts and New Skins* 4).

—

> Understanding Indians is not an esoteric art. . . . Anyone and everyone who knows an Indian or who is *interested*, immediately and thoroughly understands them.
>
> You can verify this great truth at your next party. Mention Indians and you will find a person who saw some in a gas station in Utah, or who attended the Gallup ceremonial celebration, or whose Uncle Jim hired one to cut logs in Oregon or whose church had a missionary come to speak last Sunday on the plight of the Indians and the mission of the church. (Vine Deloria, Jr., *Custer Died for Your Sins* 5)

> Necessarily, we must dismiss those tendencies that encourage the consoling play of recognitions. (Foucault, "Nietzsche" 153)

—

Race and gender (among other identity classifications) may well be inventions, constructed categories that signal the deviation of marked races and gender(s) from the norm, but their effects are tangible, producing distinctive racialized and gendered subject positions. The appropriation-of-voice debate in Canada—which flourished in the late 1980s and early 1990s, with Native people challenging non-Native creative writers particularly to stop "stealing our stories"—invoked this question of difference. Although it pivoted also on questions of Native copyright, racist structures of publication and reception, and arrogation of profits, the challenge insisted on perspectives and knowledges located in the particularities of Native histories, cultural and political experiences, and storytelling traditions. "There are a lot of non-Indian people out there speaking on our behalf or pretending to speak on our behalf and I resent that very much," says Okanagan writer and teacher Jeannette Armstrong. "I don't feel that any non-Indian person could represent our point of view adequately" ("Writing from a Native Woman's Perspective" 56). The focus of the appropriation-of-voice debate has been on the non-Native creative writer who employs a first-person Native perspective or retells stories from the oral tradition. (Lee Maracle, in fact, argues that the incursion should properly be called "appropriation of story" on the grounds that voice cannot be commandeered ["Coming Out of the House" 83].) In either case, the writer is seen as both displacing the Native author and subject and presuming—and, in the process, producing—knowledge of realities at some remove from his or her own.

A broader argument is also underway in antiracist and feminist theoretical circles over the "epistemic privilege" of the socially marginalized, the superior knowledge of their own situation (and, by some accounts, that of the oppressors) available to group insiders. (For differing conclusions on such knowledge claims, see, for example, Uma Narayan, "Working across Differences," and Bat-Ami Bar On.)[6] The epistemological status of such claims is under dispute, especially in a poststructuralist framework skeptical about transcendent truths and about reality as an unmediated source of verification. Still, members of marginalized groups are pressing to be recognized as socially differentiated subjects whose understandings are distinctive, not simply interchangeable with those of other groups or instantly accessible to outsiders. Addressing non-Native feminist educators and students, Osennontion (Marilyn Kane, Mohawk) is determined to convey the message "that *we are absolutely different!*", stressing the necessity for readers to "twist their minds a little bit (or a lot) to try to get into the same frame of mind as us" (7). In the context of white cultural rapacity, one of Sherman Alexie's fictional characters in *Indian Killer*, John Smith (himself an instance of the theft of Native children for white adopting), in conversation with an Indian wannabe, mounts a grimly ironic defence of at least a minimal entitlement:

> "What is it?" Wilson asked. "What do you want from me?"
> "Please," John whispered. "Let me, let us have our own pain." (411)

In Canada, and North America more generally, the First Nations face a particular, historically grounded insistence by descendants of European settlers on obliterating difference and claiming connection. Margery Fee points out that a Euro-Canadian desire to naturalize the seizure of Native land and a Romantic hunger for "community, nature, and a personal sense of the numinous" (represented, in the white imagination, by Native people) have prompted "an identification and a usurpation" in relation to Indigenous people ("Romantic Nationalism" 25, 15).[7] (To Fee's two motives, I would add the urgent white-Canadian self-image of non-racist tolerance—often cited in contradistinction to US-American iniquity—with First Nations as the critical Canadian test case.)[8] Fee focuses her discussion of this spurious "white 'literary land claim'" on the creation of Native characters in literature and on suspect literary representation of a "totem transfer" from Native to newcomer, legitimizing the newcomer's claim to place and nostalgic reconnection ("Romantic Nationalism" 17, 21). But similar needs can drive the *reader* or critic of literature from cultures and histories other than her own. Too-easy identification by the non-Native reader, ignorance of historical or cultural allusion, obliviousness to the presence or properties of Native genres, and the application of irrelevant aesthetic standards are all means of domesticating difference, assimilating Native narratives into the mainstream. Along the way, they are a means of neutralizing the oppositional potential of that difference.

On a larger scale, the very attentiveness of postcolonial theory to the diversity of world cultures and decolonizing struggles can ironically produce, in Ann duCille's words, a colonizing "master narrative that contains all difference ("Postcolonialism and Afrocentricity" 33). The various stories become a single story, retold by sympathetic Western critics. Similarly, the postmodern crisis of meaning, destabilizing of the subject, and hermeneutics of suspicion (with their own local history and function) risk being universalized, as Kumkum Sangari cautions, to quite other texts and culture. "[A] Eurocentric perspective . . . is brought to bear upon 'Third World' cultural products," Sangari argues; "a 'specialized' skepticism is carried everywhere as cultural paraphernalia and epistemological apparatus, as a way of seeing; and the postmodern problematic becomes the frame through which the cultural products of the rest of the world are seen" (183). My own parenthetical qualification two paragraphs above—"especially in a poststructuralist framework skeptical about transcendent truths"—is an instance of this automatic application of postmodern interpretive assumptions. The difference that is ostensibly the focus of investigation, this expression of political agency, vanishes in the face of Elizabeth Spelman's "boomerang perception": "I look at you and come right back to myself" (*Inessential Woman* 12).

In the summer of 1996, my partner—Cherokee-Greek novelist Thomas King—and I were interviewed by CBC Television for an ambitious cross-country documentary or meditation on the nature of Canada. "Sense of Country," hosted by Rex Murphy and broadcast on 3 and 4 September 1996, was visually spectacular (facets of a Newfoundland lighthouse reflector blazing kaleidoscopically)—and socially and politically conservative. The search was for a singular, overarching Canadian identity; the visuals, however stunning, were predominantly rural and romantic; the tone was uplifting. To the best of my recollection, the only people of colour interviewed, apart from Tom, were an Asian-Canadian couple (possibly), members of an Ontario Black women's gospel choir,[9] and members of the Blood tribe in Alberta.

At one point in the interview, trying to challenge ideas of a fixed, given content for Canadianness, of a Canadian character, I proposed that Canada be thought of as a conversation. Shortly thereafter, the interview shifted away from me temporarily, and I began self-consciously rehearsing what I had already said and worrying at the interview questions. Tom was elaborating one of his observations about Canada when he turned unexpectedly to me: "You know. What's the word I'm looking for . . . ?"

With the camera whirring and everyone's attention refocused in my direction, I had to disrupt his argument by confessing sheepishly, "I'm sorry, I wasn't listening."

The irony of that juxtaposition didn't make the final cut for the television program, but it might well have provided a salutary corrective to some of its rosier narratives of the nation.

> "Canada is a conversation."
> "I'm sorry, I wasn't listening."

Or perhaps, transposed to the context of national rather than individual communications: "I'm sorry, but thanks to my spot in the social hierarchies, I don't need to listen."

―

> Can you ever have a valid completion of a work by an audience that is a stranger to the traditions that underpin the work? (Philip 32)

―

The question "How should I eat these?" or in the case of Native literature, "How should I read these?" can involve, then, for the outsider reader, unfortunate occasions either for absolute, irreducible distance or for presumptuous familiarity. And, of course, reifying difference and erasing it are far from mutually exclusive approaches. Himani Bannerji points this out when she describes white bourgeois feminists as failing to "position themselves with regard to non-white women—whom they rendered invisible by both ascribing difference *and* by practically and theoretically neglecting that very difference" (21; emphasis added). These simultaneous wrongs are what Pat Parker has in mind in her poem "For the White Person Who Wants to Know How to Be My Friend": "the first thing you do is to forget that I'm Black. / second, you must never forget that I'm Black" (68).

Difference from whose point of view is, of course, the question. I have framed this introduction to *How Should I Read These? Native Women's Writing in Canada* with a discussion of the dangers of fixating on or ignoring difference, because those are factors in my own responses, as a white woman, to the texts I will be discussing here. Though not, I suspect, entirely absent from consideration, difference would presumably play a much more minor role in the responses of a Blood woman analyzing Beverly Hungry Wolf's *Ways of My Grandmothers* or an Okanagan woman reading Jeannette Armstrong's *Slash*. But my intention is not so much to explicate the texts here, to provide normative readings, or to imagine how a cultural insider might read them. Instead, this book sets out to explore the problematics of reading and teaching a variety of prose works by Native women writers in Canada from one particular perspective, my own, that of a specific cultural outsider. As the title suggests, the book proffers a question, or series of questions, rather than an answer. I am less interested in resolving the question of the title than in rehearsing some of its attendant challenges and discoveries. And I am interested in locating those challenges and discoveries in the particularities of my reading and teaching experience, as potentially symptomatic of readings from similar subject locations.

Recently, Tom phoned me long distance from California. Partway through our conversation, the phone line made several weird, clicking noises and its tone became distinctly more hollow sounding.

"Hello!?"

"Hello-o!" I could hear him, but he apparently could not hear me. He could hear me, but I apparently could not hear him.

"Hello? Can you hear me?"

"Hello? Are you still there?"

"Hello? Can you hear me?"

"I'm here. Hello!?"

Eventually we managed to re-establish conversation with each other. The connection had never been broken. Each of us had heard every word of our two blank monologues.

―――

[W]hat does it mean when primarily white men and women are producing the discourse around Otherness? (hooks, *Yearning* 53)

"We read all this American Indian literature, the folklore and everything, and I don't know what I'm reading. I don't know anything about the Indians. I was hoping to know something after today. Like where to start."

"You just said it," Anita said. "You don't know anything. That's where to start ..."

The woman wrung her hands. "But then how can we know about Indians of the film? I wanted to learn something."

... "Listen," Anita said looking back to the woman, "do you know who you are? Why are you interested? Ask yourself that." (Sarris 74)

––––

At the launch of Cree poet Louise Halfe's *Bear Bones and Feathers* in Toronto in 1994, I found myself in animated conversation with a Native woman from British Columbia, both of us buoyed up by the reading and the celebratory atmosphere. The conversation eventually turned to what I was working on. When I mentioned this book, her face instantly became studiously neutral. Guarded. As mine would, too, if a white woman announced a similar project.

––––

White writers . . . must understand how their privilege *as white people*, writing *about* another culture, rather than *out of* it virtually guarantees that their work will, in a racist society, be received more readily than the work of writers coming from that very culture. (Philip 284)

––––

Most of the writers discussed in this book have indicated, either in interviews or in the texts themselves, that their primary audience is Native, an exception being Eden Robinson, for her first publication at least. (*The Book of Jessica*, being a collaborative endeavour, may have a slightly different audience than Maria Campbell's other writing.) In *I Am Woman*, Lee Maracle begins by declaring that she does not intend to write for a European in Canada, that intimate conversation with her own people is overdue.[10] Within that very paragraph, though, the third-person pronouns applied to a white readership begin to slide into direct address ("you just don't concern me now"). This slipperiness Maracle tackles directly later in the book: "It sickens my spirit to have to address your madness, but you stand in front of my people, and to speak to each other, we must first rid ourselves of you" (11, 111).

In the past decade, in particular, the establishment of Native-run presses such as Theytus Books (Penticton), Seventh Generation Books (Toronto), and Pemmican Publications (Winnipeg);[11] Native theatre companies such as Native Earth Performing Arts (Toronto),[12] De-ba-jeh-mu-jig (Wikwemikong), and the Centre for Indigenous Theatre (Toronto); Native-run journals and magazines such as *Akwesasne Notes*, *Gatherings*, *Sweetgrass*, and *Aboriginal Voices*; the Committee to Re-Establish the Trickster (Toronto); Canadian

Native Arts Foundation (Toronto); and the En'owkin International School of Writing (Penticton)[13] have all reflected the desire of First Nations people in Canada to control the contexts in which they speak with each other. In the area of literary analysis, recent publications such as *Looking at the Words of Our People: First Nations Analysis of Literature*, edited by Jeannette Armstrong, *Iskwewak—Kah' Ki Yaw Ni Wahkomakanak: Neither Indian Princesses Nor Easy Squaws*, by Janice Acoose/Misko-Kìsikàwihkwè, and *(Ad)dressing Our Words: IndigeCrit: Aboriginal Perspectives on Aboriginal Literatures*, edited by Armand Garnet Ruffo (Anishinaabe), insist on Native perspectives regarding their literature and their representation.

At the same time, Native writing, editing, publishing, performing, reviewing, teaching, and reading necessarily take place, at least partially, in contexts shaped and controlled by the discursive and institutional power of the dominant white culture in Canada. Editorial boards, granting agencies, publishing companies, awards committees, reviewers, audiences and purchasers, university and school curricula, and scholarly theorizing and analysis (of which this book is one instance) assess merit, distribute resources, enact policies of inclusion and exclusion, and produce meanings based on norms extrinsic to, even inimical to Native values and interests. Such effects are neither accidental nor simply idiosyncratic. Himani Bannerji stresses the necessity of recognizing that "a whole social organization is needed to create each unique experience, and what constitutes someone's power is precisely another's powerlessness" (74).

So what's a white girl like me doing in a place like this?

My metaphor of Canada as a conversation, for CBC's television documentary, like most figurations of Canada that have gone before—part of a wrongheaded quest for a national mythos—missed the mark. Quite apart from ignoring the problematics of language, both for conversation and for Canada's national narratives, the metaphor of conversation ignores issues of power and access. Whose conversation? Whose favourite topics predominate? Who keeps being interrupted? Whose contributions are heard only when paraphrased by someone else? Who is too strident, beside the point, political, incomprehensible? Who is even permitted to be in the room? Who is bringing the coffee? (And to go back to the question of language, is the conversation in one language? Whose? If not, is simultaneous translation possible, and is it power-neutral?) Does conversation have any effect, and who implements which conclusions? And, finally, for whom is conversation itself a luxury? I had fallen into what Chandra Mohanty dubs the "discourse of civility" (201), a pluralist celebration of diversity that reduces structural inequities to personal relationships.[14]

> The problem, so tendentiously constructed as "Why can't whites teach *about* racism?" after all should be phrased as "Why aren't non-white people teaching at all in the university about racism or anything else?" (Bannerji 116)

> Too often, it seems, the point is to promote the *appearance* of difference within intellectual discourse, a "celebration" that fails to ask who is sponsoring the party and who is extending the invitations. (hooks, *Yearning* 54)

The current academic fashionableness of issues of race, what Susan Friedman (playing on Barbara Christian's "race for theory") has called "the race for race" (4), has changed little in terms of the racial composition of university faculties and administration. Ann duCille has noted the historical amnesia around the contributions of Black women scholars and the professional profit derived in the academy by men and white women, but not Black women, from the upsurge of interest in Black women writers. "[B]lack culture is more easily intellectualized (and colonized)," she concludes, "when transferred from the danger of lived black experience to the safety of white metaphor, when you can have that 'signifying black difference' without the difference of significant blackness" ("The Occult of True Black Womanhood" 600). Her observation applies equally to the First Nations presence in the Canadian academy, where Native people are more welcomed as objects of study than as subjects of study.

The number of Native faculty in literature departments in Canada can be counted on one hand. Janice Acoose (Nehiowè-Métis-Ninahkawè) recounts her undergraduate experience of a course in western Canadian literature at the University of Saskatchewan that described the transformation of the prairies from "no man's land to everyman's land" and that included no First Nations writers (30). Patricia Monture-Angus (Kanien'kehá:ka or Mohawk), inquiring about a similar course, was informed that there was no First Nations literary work good enough for a Canadian literature course ("Native America and the Literary Tradition" 21). Despite the appearance of entire courses on Native literature, ethnocentric courses like the ones confronting Acoose and Monture-Angus continue to exist. But the inclusion of Native work in syllabi and curricula does not necessarily make the academy more hospitable either to Native students and faculty or to Native ways of seeing.

In her own academic work, Emma LaRocque has discovered that her first-hand knowledge of Native life, which at second hand would constitute field work and evidence, is in her own voice devalued as subjective and hence suspect ("The Colonization of a Native Woman Scholar" 12–13). I have observed, and doubtless contributed to, the frustration of First Nations graduate students whose isolation is compounded by the poor fit between prevailing paradigms of literary studies—meaning as endlessly deferred, identities as provisional and strategic, even the invitation to self-disclosure and self-reflexivity—and their own ways of knowing.[15] ("Poor fit" is somewhat euphemistic; in the hierarchies of graduate school, one can readily speculate which epistemology is expected to yield.) As Carole Leclair reports of her graduate experience, "I was a long distance away from expecting respect and being able to communicate naturally about my Métis values. Eventually, I learned to speak like a middle-class educated academic, but my writing, my thought processes, still reflect the deep ambivalence that living in two (often incompatible) cultural frameworks can produce" (124). I know of one Métis graduate student in literature, finally able to meet another at a national conference, who asked urgently for reassurance that in time she wouldn't cry every day. A more seasoned student shrewdly envisioned her own wary relationship to those Euro-American academic theories potentially useful to her own work as a kind of raiding expedition, during which she stole some good horses and made her escape.

She wants to be the only guest allowed
in the longhouse, and then to refuse the honour
or not to be allowed
because no guest is allowed.
She wants to obliterate herself
loudly. (Spears, "On Cultural Expropriation," *Poems Selected and New*
89–90)[16]

it will not save you
or talk you down from the ledge
of a personal building (Alexie, "Introduction to Native American Literature,"
Old Shirts and New Skins 3)

Given the imperviousness of the academy to Native presences and paradigms, then, the position of the non-Native scholar studying Native literature—my position—becomes a fraught and suspect one. The position is replete with opportunities for romanticizing, cultural ignorance, colonization—and, ironically, simultaneous professional advancement. Although discussions in white feminist, anthropological, and literary academic spheres have become more self-reflexive and self-examining over the past two decades, that development can produce more sophisticated and insidious versions of the same old offences.

Susan Friedman has examined the scripts about race and ethnicity, "narratives of denial, accusation, and confession" and of "relational positionality" (the alternative she endorses) that have recently circulated among white feminists and feminists of colour (7). One form of denial Sherene Razack and Mary Lou Fellows have named "the race to innocence": the attempt, by emphasizing one's positions of subordination and not privilege (as a woman, say), to disclaim responsibility for subordinating others. As they observe, such a denial obscures the necessity, as part of ending one's own marginalization, to end all systems of oppression (Razack 14).

Responses to the accusations of racism by women of colour, responses going beyond denial, can take many forms. As an instance of Friedman's third narrative, of confession, Ann duCille alludes sardonically to "I-once-was-blind-but-now-I-see" exposés, by white feminist critics, of our former racism/sexism vis-à-vis texts by women of colour ("The Occult of True Black Womanhood" 160). Elizabeth Spelman elucidates the limitations of such enactments of guilt: "guilt is not an emotion that makes us attend well to the situation of those whose treatment at our hands we feel guilty about. We're too anxious trying to keep our moral slate clean" (*Fruits of Sorrow* 109). Indeed, as Maria Lugones elaborates, white theorists have seemed to focus on the wrong problem, worrying more intensely about how race- and class-specific generalizations about "all women" might damage feminist theory than about how such distorted conclusions might harm women of colour or working-class women ("On the Logic of Pluralist Feminism" 41). In largely white feminist classrooms, too, I have seen the determination to "get it right," as a form of personal enlightenment about racism, take precedence over the determination to take action against oppressive hierarchies and the unequal distribution of power.

The "retreat response" is one alternative to stances either of unexamined authority or static self-recrimination. Deciding not to attempt to speak beyond one's own experience, Linda Alcoff argues, can be a self-indulgent evasion of political effort *or* a principled effort at non-imperialist engagement (although, in the latter case, with seriously restricted scope) ("The Problem of Speaking for Others" 17). A related stance is the "embarrassed privilege" accorded the "postcolonial Woman," an ostentatious deference which awards iconic, metaphoric status to the woman of colour as the representative of "the good" (Suleri, "Woman Skin Deep" 758) and simultaneously avoids engagement with particularities of her argument. Sky Lee discusses such a moment at the 1988 Vancouver "Telling It" Conference, in which no one challenged a woman of colour on her apparently homophobic remarks, for fear of demonstrating cultural insensitivity (183–84). In the classroom, Chandra Mohanty suggests, this can produce "a comfortable set of oppositions: people of color as the central voices and the bearers of all knowledge in class, and white people as 'observers,' with no responsibility to contribute and/or with nothing valuable to contribute" (194).

What this simple divide misses, Mohanty suggests, is the necessary acknowledgement of "co-implication," awareness of asymmetrical but mutually constitutive histories, relationships, and responsibilities (194). Friedman's advocacy of "scripts of relational positionality" seems to build on Mohanty's idea of co-implication. Such scripts dismiss the absolutes of the white/other binary, conceptualize identities as multiply, fluidly, and relationally defined, and recognize that power can flow in more than one direction within multiple systems of domination and stratification. So, a stance of relational positionality allows for coalition work attentive to the complexities of "shifting positions of privilege and exclusion" (Friedman 40). Denial, accusation, confession, and retreat are not the only alternatives. In practical terms Uma Narayan, noting that one can be at once insider and outsider in relation to different groups and that analogizing from one position to the other may increase one's conscientiousness, proposes "methodological humility" and "methodological caution" as strategies for the outsider. Methodological—or epistemological—humility and caution recognize presumed limitations to the outsider's understanding and the importance of not undermining the insider's perspective, in the process of communication and learning across difference (Narayan, 38).

> The objective here is not to have complete knowledge of the text or the self as reader, not to obtain or tell the complete story of one or the other or both, but to establish and report as clearly as possible that dialogue where the particular reader or groups of readers inform and are informed by the texts. (Sarris 131)

From a position of race privilege, I feel responsibility to combat structures of power and entitlement. Teaching or writing about texts by Native writers, from my position of privilege, may not do that politically efficacious work; my academic activity is seriously implicated in the very systems of stratification and dominance it critiques.[17] What *How Should I Read These?* does undertake is to keep to the forefront the assumptions, needs, and ignorance that I bring to my readings, the culture-specific positioning from which I engage with the writing. The book makes questions of location—the issues of difference and power rehearsed in this introduction—ongoing subjects of investigation, in interplay with the literary texts themselves.

Self-reflexivity and self-questioning can certainly be forms of luxury and self-indulgence. Those of us with power can afford to dispense with some of its more obvious trappings. My hope, though, is that, by making explicit various sources of my responses, I render the readings more clearly local, partial, and accountable, relinquishing the authority that clings to detached pronouncements. *How Should I Read These?* locates in my own history inside and outside the classroom both the challenges and the new perspectives that the writings by these First Nations women can produce. What I incorporate into the textual analysis are pedagogical and personal *moments*, not a comprehensive narrative. I suspect that these moments, from classroom discussions and my own story, though not representative (no culture is monolithic, and I am multiply located), may be symptomatic, clues to Euro-Canadian cultural tendencies that bear on the reception of First Nations literatures. Though a narrative of my reception might seem to risk displacing the Native text and the Native author, readings (however detached or unattributed) are always just that, readings, meetings between text and reader. As Greg Sarris (Miwok-Pomo) says about his knowledge of Mabel, a Pomo woman who helped raise him, "I cannot construct Mabel's world independent of my own experience of it.... What I can do is reconstruct my relationship to her world, at least to the extent I understand it at this time" (30).

Notes

This Introduction was first published in Helen Hoy, *How Should I Read These? Native Women Writers in Canada* (U of Toronto P, 2001).

1. Philip Deloria (Lakota), in his historical analysis of the white US-American fascination with "playing Indian," points out how knowing or reading about Indians replaces more engaged social and political interaction: "As a result, the ways in which white Americans have used Indianness in creative self-shaping have continued to be pried apart from questions about inequality, the uneven workings of power, and the social settings in which Indians and non-Indians might actually meet" (189–90).

2. The interaction in this scene is more complicated than I may have suggested. Arnold is the only person in the story to inquire about Adelaine's pallor, the result of her recent and traumatic abortion. His final request, to which Adelaine accedes, to see her hair loose, is made blushingly, with disquieted awareness (finally) that his need oversteps what he is entitled to ask. Adelaine's use of a phony name and her dismissal of Arnold, as he continues to talk—"'Goodbye, Arnold,' I said, picking up

the money and starting toward the cashiers" (E. Robinson, *Traplines* 209)—with its implicit restoration of their exchange to a financial transaction, however, confirm the impertinence of his overtures.

3. For a parody of white Othering, see Beverly Slapin's *The Basic Skills Caucasian Americans Workbook*, dedicated to "all boys and girls who love white people and animals." Its "Note from the Publisher" mordantly illustrates the power of indirection and denial to construct a people and culture as past, singular (both odd and monolithic), and inconsequential: "Our purpose for publishing *The Basic Skills Caucasian Americans Workbook* is to provide young readers with accurate accounts of the lives of the Caucasian American people, who, long ago, roamed our land. Caucasians are as much a part of American life as they were one hundred years ago. Even in times past, Caucasians were not all the same. Not all of them lived in condos or drove Volvos. They were not all Yuppies. Some were hostile, but many were friendly" (n.p).

4. Mollie Travis discusses this problem in relation to Black writers: "When readers fault African American writers for attempting to transcend race . . . we display what Nadine Gordimer calls 'the essential gesture' of criticism, which mandates that a writer living in a politically conflicted country write about the conflict, that a female writer represent the female experience, and that the culturally marginalized author write about the experience of marginality. In essentialist mandate, white male writers from politically stable Western countries—thought of as being unmarked by gender or race—are the only ones free to construct ahistorical, apolitical, and unrepresentational narratives. This essential gesture . . . reveals the white critic as a manufacturer of otherness, a curator of difference, to valorize and preserve his/her own autonomous essence—a sign of the institutional necessity of race in reading and a sign that we need to read more closely this criticism which passes for cultural work" (195).

5. During his 1997 reading tour in France, Cherokee-Greek author Thomas King, in the face of persistent Othering, took to turning the tables on his interlocutors, asking them to explain the French practice of supplying *pink* toilet paper in public facilities. Foregrounding French people's own enculturated existence, the question also presumably pokes fun at reductive approaches to culture as a superficial curiosity rather than, in Chandra Mohanty's words, a "terrain of struggle" (196). "How should I eat these?" "Why is your toilet paper pink?"

6. See also the discussion in *Signs* 22.2 (Winter 1997) among Susan Hekman, Nancy Hartsock, Patricia Hill Collins, Sandra Harding, and Dorothy Smith on the knowledge claims of feminist standpoint epistemology.

7. See also Terry Goldie's term "indigenization" to describe the "impossible necessity," for white settlers, of becoming Indigenous, sought through literary representations of Native peoples (*Fear and Temptation* 13).

8. Philomena Essed rightly observes that "the idea of tolerance is inherently problematic when applied to hierarchical group relations" and demonstrates, in her study of everyday racism experienced by Black women in California and Surinamese women in the Netherlands, "[t]he compatibility of cultural assimilationist practices and cultural pluralistic discourse" (viii, 17).

9. Dionne Brand has spoken of how, when North American media represent Blacks at all, the reassuring image chosen is often that of the gospel choir ("Jazz Ritual and Resistance").

10. This demarcation of Maracle's audience is somewhat qualified by her addition, "and those who are not offended by our private truth" (*I Am Woman* 11).

11. Smaller Native presses such as Moonprint (Winnipeg) and Rez (Kwantlen First Nation, Langley, BC), Native-focused presses, such as Fifth House (Saskatoon), and presses run by women of colour, such as Williams-Wallace (Stratford, ON), and Sister Vision (Toronto), have also contributed to this change.

12. The Weesageechak Begins to Dance Festival, providing workshops for new Native playwrights and choreographers, is a separate undertaking of Native Earth.

13. The Saskatchewan Indian Federated College (University of Saskatchewan) might be another example, along with the First Nations House of Learning (University of British Columbia), First Nations House (University of Toronto), and so on, but their location within dominant-culture institutions makes their contribution somewhat different.

14. Rather than as a genteel conversation, I could have imagined Canada as a clamour of stipulations, protests, voices in the wilderness, decrees, whispers, contracts, backroom chats, chants, judicial reports, gossip, private phone lines, party lines (in both senses), shrieks, red tape, royal commissions, songs, and multilateral agreements. Intrinsic to that formulation, though, would have to be an understanding both of the quite disparate authority of the various discourses and of the systemic interrelations—economic, legal, and so on—of the forums in which they had weight. In any case, either formulation gives undue precedence to discourses over economic, political, and social organization.

15. Willie Ermine (Cree) explores features of an "Aboriginal Epistemology," including a holistic sense of immanence connecting all of existence, to be known by inwardness and developed through community: "Ancestral explorers of the inner space encoded their findings in community praxis as a way of synthesizing knowledge derived from introspection" (104).

16. I am unclear about the political valence of Spears' poem, in terms of the issue of appropriation. Certainly it mocks the righteousness of its presumably white protagonist: "she is tender to the slightest slight / in conference papers people raced to finish." At the same time there is poignancy and rich suggestiveness, along with mockery, in the ambiguity of the final enjambment: "She does not want to hurt any more, not to hurt / any more." There, the object of hurt seems doubled, with the protagonist's capacity to cause hurt represented simultaneously as the cause of her own hurt. As an exposé of her excesses and personal investments and neo-exoticizing in the name of cultural sensitivity—"She stands at the contaminated boundary / she has raised"—does the poem ultimately extend or discredit challenges around cultural appropriation (89–90)?

17. In this regard, it is important for majority critics like myself to develop other areas of intellectual focus, so as not to become invested in the field and unprepared to "move over" for those Native scholars who choose this as their specialty.

4

Teaching Aboriginal Literature: The Discourse of Margins and Mainstreams

Emma LaRocque

Ashcroft, Griffiths, and Tiffin (1989) have argued that the study of history and English and the growth of Empire . . . proceeded from a single ideological climate and that the development of the one is intrinsically bound up with the development of the other, both at the level of simple utility (as propaganda for instance) and at the unconscious level, where it leads to the naturalizing of constructed values (e.g., "savagery," "native," "primitive," as their antithesis and as the object of a reforming zeal) (7).

Thus, a "privileging norm was enthroned at the heart of the formation of English studies as a template for the denial of the value of the 'peripheral,' the 'marginal,' the 'uncanonized'" (3). The standardization of "privileging norms" in Canadian historiography and literature has entailed, among other things, extreme devaluation and marginalization of Aboriginal cultures and peoples. Needless to say, Native literatures, both oral and written, have remained, until very recently, completely outside of Canadian literary and academic canons.

I well remember a debate I had with the Dean of Arts about the value of keeping two courses on Aboriginal literatures in our roster of courses in Native Studies. It was sometime in the early 1980s; the Department of Native Studies was not a decade into its existence, and I was even newer and definitely inexperienced in the politics of university teaching and canons. Because student enrolment in both the literature courses was low, the Dean took an economical approach and bluntly informed me that both courses were to be cancelled and taken off our calendar of course offerings. Besides student enrolment, it was clear that the Dean did not believe there was sufficient Native literary material to justify teaching Native literatures. Although I had just begun teaching the courses, I was instinctively horrified by the suggestion, and in the full splendour of my own inexperience, argued passionately for those courses. To this day, I am sure it was my naïveté and vision (and perhaps the Dean's respect for an honest exchange) that won me a compromise. The Dean cancelled the American Native lit course but I could keep the Canadian equivalent as long as the enrolment increased. I argued then that it was just a matter of time before Native literature would grow and demand pedagogical and critical attention. As it has turned out, and not surprising to those who knew the Native experience and studies, I could not have been more right in my prediction.

Today it is with pride and pleasure that I am able to state that Native literature has virtually exploded onto the Canadian intellectual, if not literary, arena, and is one of the most exciting new fields of study for those specializing in Canadian Native literature. The dramatic growth both in Native writing and critical study of it has resulted in many changes for those of us producing and/or teaching Aboriginal literature(s). This essay is not a detailed history of Native writing[1] but rather a reflective overview of pedagogical, epistemological, and canonical issues arising from two decades of teaching Canadian Native literature from the margins of Native Studies in a large mid-Canadian, middle-class mainstream university.

Location in the Empire

"To be an Aboriginal person, to identify with an Indigenous heritage in these late colonial times, requires a life of reflection, critique, persistence and struggle" (McMaster and Martin 11). I begin by briefly locating myself and thus situating the Indigenous and de/colonial basis of my pedagogy. In a number of significant respects, I have unorthodox beginnings in university teaching. At home I grew up Cree with Wehsehkehcha; in schools my senses and intellect were overrun with Settlers and Savages and neither knew anything about Wehsehkehcha, rendering me an "alien" in my own home/land. Alienation and poverty do have social consequences; in Alberta in 1971 the average grade level for Status Indian and Métis children was grade four. Statistically speaking, Native children were not expected to make it to high school, let alone to university. Quite an interesting combination of factors enabled me to pursue education in an era of devastating marginalization and bleak social conditions for my community and family. It was the resourcefulness and support of my parents, along with their engaging Cree-Métis cultural literacy, that instilled in me a love of knowledge and a spirit of determination and independence. By the mid-1970s I had worked my way to a graduate degree in Peace Studies. I then had come to the University of Manitoba on a Graduate Fellowship to work on an M.A. in (Canadian) History, which I completed in 1980.

One day while walking on campus at the University of Manitoba (and still a graduate in History), I was approached by a Métis man who introduced himself as the Head of the recently established Department of Native Studies, a department I had not known existed. He asked me to teach the summer Intro (to Native Studies) course.

In addition to my academic qualifications, I was a writer with a Cree language background, and perhaps because of that I was assigned to teach (among other courses) the two Native literature courses that the Native Studies department offered.[2] I took to teaching, particularly Canadian Native Literature, with enthusiasm and not a little creativity. Teaching Native literature in the late 1970s and even into the mid-1980s presented certain challenges. For one thing, I was finding it difficult to fill a half term course with contemporary Canadian Native fiction. To compensate for this lack in those years, I focused on three areas: oral literatures, literature *about* Native people, and non-fiction Native writing. Although the non-fiction writing (including poetry) consisted of a wide variety of styles re/mapping place, facts of biography, ethnographic explanations, legends, curriculum guides, historical and sociological expositions, response to governmental policies or proposals, and so forth, it was often lumped as social protest writing. Native writing, whether social commentary or poetry, was not appreciated as postcolonial (Ashcroft et al.) or resistance literature (Harlow), and much of it was dismissed as parochial or undermined as angry and bitter (Petrone, "Indian Literature" 383–88). As a result, there was minimal, if any, critical literary treatment of any form of Native writing; instead, reviewers concentrated on "anger," personal tragedy, or ethnography. Native Literature courses in most mainstream English departments were not generally available, and only one other Native Studies department (University of Lethbridge) was offering courses on Native American writing. Even my colleagues in our department assumed Native literature consisted mostly of "folktales" and "children's literature." These are, of course, honourable subjects but the assumptions revealed ignorance about the scope of study available in Native literatures.

In various respects, we all needed to learn how to read Native material. For example, while I understood the colonial experience addressed by most Native writers, I did not presume to understand without study the specific cultures from which each writer expressed him/herself. Being Cree does not make me some "natural" expert on all things Cree, let alone on non-Cree Aboriginal cultures. Certainly, students required a basis of knowledge from which to better comprehend and appreciate Native writers and writing. Consistent with the systemic devaluation of Aboriginal cultures in society, schools, and textbooks,[3] such basis of knowledge had not been made available to students in most Canadian-controlled educational institutions, whether in elementary or post-secondary levels, whether in residential, reserve, or public schools.

In fact, because of the educational system's abysmal failure in providing basic and balanced treatment of Aboriginal peoples in all areas significant to any peoples' history and cultural achievements, students have suffered from deeply entrenched conditioning to "see" "Indians" through "stereotypic eyes" (Pakes 1–31). Cultural differences notwithstanding, both Native and non-Native students continue to arrive in universities with a disturbing combination of absence of basic knowledge and misinformation about Aboriginal peoples and issues. This is a significant shared experience by students which informs their approaches to the study of Native peoples.

It soon became clear to me that I was teaching in no ordinary "cross-cultural" circumstances. Not only were there many cultures[4] represented in my classes, there were educational, socio-economic, and racial chasms, as well as deeply divergent political experiences. Both the differences and the similarities derived from the common school ground of western bias posed (and continue to pose) unique pedagogical challenges.[5] And there were no role models to pave the way for me. In the 1970s and much of the '80s, Native Studies was largely treated as a cultural sensitivity, remedial program, not as a serious scholarly field. Critical intellectual work was often misunderstood or dismissed as "biased,"[6] and the barely emerging handful of Native scholars had not yet developed methodological tools or languages by which to articulate what we, in praxis, were modelling, namely, Indigeneity and postcoloniality.

De-colonizing Scholarship in the Empire

In retrospect, it occurs to me that I, per force, developed in content and approach a contrapuntal anti-colonial Indigenously-engaged epistemology and pedagogy. But it was not until the 1990s that I began to articulate this as *resistance scholarship*, a critical scholarship not only based on Aboriginality but one borne out of colonial experience.[7] Such scholarship confronts knowledge which has been privileged in a dominating society and includes the critical use of "voice" and "engaged research" as well as the exploration of the social purpose of knowledge.[8] Knowledge cannot be devoid of human values. Brazilian educator Paulo Freire (*Pedagogy of the Oppressed*), for example, argued for the humanization vocation of pedagogy, a vocation that requires a conscientious criticism. Such purposeful pedagogy challenges us to use languages and styles in classrooms and publications which seeks both to demystify and to revisit western assumptions of objectivity in research and modes of distancing in teaching. Decolonizing scholarship takes to task western appearances of impartiality hidden in designatory vocabulary and methodologies which among other things, objectifies and others the peoples being portrayed or studied, usually Indigenous peoples.[9]

My interdisciplinary work on Native resistance response to "textual strat-egies of domination" (Duchemin 63) in historical and literary writing has shaped how I have taught, and in many respects continue to teach my Canadian Native Lit course. As has my Indigenous-informed knowledge. I find that this unique multidisciplinary approach and ethos offers students the possibility of a much greater appreciation of both original and contemporary Native expressions.

I should reiterate here that even though students today are generally more open and better informed, not all students are willing or able to engage with issues beyond sanctioned histories, texts, or forums. Although this is to be expected, given the school system's failure to provide critical skills, it is none-theless demanding. Teaching about the "dominant western narrative" to those who assume its hegemonic properties as well as to those who have been "oth-ered" by it—all in one classroom—invites reflection on what was/is really the subtext of colonial discourse that exists in any given Native Studies class. It adds a "racial" and political dimension to our classrooms which administration may not understand and which mainstream scholars, as a rule, do not have to deal with.[10] While many students appreciate the new perspectives, others resist re-viewing the "the National Dream" version of the Canadian self-image. Students obviously feel more comfortable with cultural portraiture, which they associate with and often expect from Native Studies than with the critical work required in the revisiting of Canadian historical and cultural records. But studies on Native peoples in universities are not cultural workshops, and how-ever "positive"[11] we want to be, Canada is centrally a colonial project and good scholarship dictates that we not teach with one eye closed. Ethnography and cultural sensitivity are of course important but not without critical awareness.

For example, Indigenous cultures have been infantilized through the linguistically literal translations of legends and myths as well as through the civ/sav interpretations. In order to demonstrate some of the problems with literal translations, I often find myself paraphrasing into modern English Wehsehkehcha stories my Nokom and Ama related to me in Cree. And of course, I make every effort to properly contextualize Native oral literatures by providing historical and cultural readings, discussions, and data. But "cultural studies" alone does not address the master narrative of "the Indian" as sav-age and/or primitive. To help students appreciate the political environment in which scholarship develops, I encourage them to discover some of the early anthropological forays into Native communities and to explore how anthropol-ogists gathered and interpreted cultural information.[12]

Appreciating oral literatures is also an effective means to appreciating contemporary written Native poetry. For the generation of Native poets who grew up with their mother languages, poetry reflects the transition from oral to written literatures. This, in part, may explain why so many Native writers have taken to poetry, often in conjunction with other genres. Of course, there are as many complex reasons for choosing the medium of poetry as there are poets, but poetry does seem to best facilitate the linguistic and thematic expression of many Aboriginal writers. There is in Aboriginal poetry both a Romantic and Resistance tradition.[13] Rita Joe, Chief Dan George, and Duke Redbird are among the earlier poets who drew on the more Romantic (both invented and reality-based) presentations of Native cultures and at the same time, protested colonial interference in their cultural and personal lives. It is also through poetry that Native individuals can express both personal and social outrage. Outrage in poetry (or poetic prose such as Arthur Shilling's *The Ojibway Dream* or Maria Campbell's *Road Allowance People*) is often exquisite. What more heart and metaphor can we find in any poetry than in the late Sarain Stump's "There Is My People Sleeping"?

> I was mixing stars and sand
> In front of him
> But he couldn't understand
> . . . And I had been killed a thousand times
> Right at his feet
> But he hadn't understood.

The quality of much Native poetry should dispel any doubts critics may have about the aesthetic value of Resistance Literature.

To help students discover the raison d'être of Native "protest writing," I still include a section on literature *about* Native peoples. I assign students to review archival sources as well as white Canadian fiction and poetry selected from various eras. For example, *Wacousta* is explored not only as a Canadian gothic novel but also as an illustration of hate literature.[14] The historio-literary interrogation helps students to better understand the imperial connection between English history and literature and why Native writers have been resisting their subordination in Canadian scholarship and society.

It also helps them better understand Native authors or characters who struggle with confusion or deep shame about their Indianness, for example, Agnes (Kane), Slash (Armstrong), Garnet (Wagamese), or the Raintree sisters (Culleton). It has been my observation that white students are often surprised by the extent of this shame. But once they learn about the dehumanizing role and power of stereotypes in the media and texts, they gain an appreciation of the Native's struggles with internalization, especially to the Savage portrayal. And many Native students feel an affinity with various Native characters which then leads them to new levels of awareness about their experiences.

I hasten to add, though, that while Native fiction (or non-fiction) serves a socio-political function in pedagogy and society, we must tend equally to its aesthetic value. Native literature is as much about art and nuance as it is about colonial discourse. That Native writing can best be understood as Resistance literature does not mean that it is singularly political or that it lacks either complexity or grace. Nor does it mean that we have to subscribe to the Noble Savage construct or nativist moral righteousness in order to create a sense of beauty. The Aboriginal landscape is full of aesthetic possibilities—be it in our cultures, faces, or resistance. Those of us who teach and/or write do so because our intellects are inspired by the creative re/construction of words and our spirits are nurtured by imagination. It is unfortunate that so many literary critics have focused on ethnography or politics and have overlooked the art of reinvention. Literary criticism needs to come back to the artistic essences of imagined words and worlds. "We are born into a world of light," writes Richard Wagamese, but "it's not the memories themselves we seek to reclaim, but rather the opportunity to surround ourselves with the quality of light that lives there" (*Quality of Light* 3).

One of the reasons I like and teach literature is because it may be one of the most effective ways to shed light on Native humanity. Perhaps it is through literature we can best illuminate Native individuality, psychology as well as fluidity, and we can do this without compromising Native cultural diversity or the colonial experience. Were critics (and audiences) adequately educated they would have long ago recognized the multidimensionality of Native works and personalities. Appreciating, highlighting, and demanding excellence as well as what is unique in contemporary Native writing should certainly become central to Native literary criticism.

Of course, this begs the question of what constitutes Native literary criticism and the role of culture in Aboriginal Literatures. Many issues intersect here, and I cannot, to my satisfaction, treat them in this essay.[15] But I will approach the issue of criticism and culture through the back door, if you will, by now turning away from art and irresistibly to the matter of mainstream English departments opening up positions in Aboriginal Literatures. It appears that all the postcolonial theorizing about western canonical hegemony and with it the relatively recent addition of "cultural studies" in English departments has led to certain allowances for "cultural differences" both in the study and hiring of non-Western peoples. While we can perhaps celebrate such efforts, certain problems are emerging in the treatment of Aboriginal scholars and studies.

I have greeted these new openings with some ambivalence, and raise a number of questions. On a more personal level, I am happy to see greater professional and job possibilities for scholars specializing in this field. The importance of the Aboriginal contribution to literature cannot be overemphasized, and I have long cautioned against the ghettoization of Native Studies, literatures, or scholars. But the question arises as to what extent and in what manner these openings should be serving Aboriginal interests, be they students, scholars, or culture(s).

In my view the new openings in English departments are not necessarily meant to facilitate Aboriginal scholars (in Aboriginal literatures), knowledge, or experience, but rather, to facilitate their new graduates specializing in these fields. For the most part, it has been scholars (the majority remain non-Native) in English departments who have had the luxury of advancing their studies in Aboriginal literatures. Such scholars are, of course, looking for positions in universities, most likely in English departments, and this fact puts into perspective the reason(s) why mainstream departments are assimilating Indigenous literatures. But is "specializing"[16] in Native literature within standard graduate programs in English sufficient criteria for teaching this literature? I am of course suggesting that it is not.

Legitimating Aboriginal Epistemology in the Empire

Aboriginal literatures represent languages, mythologies, worldviews, and experiences which require pedagogical and critical knowledge *beyond* standard western academic literary treatments. That is, those of us teaching Aboriginal Literatures have an extraordinary mandate to *know* both Aboriginal and western epistemologies and should, accordingly, have more than just western-based graduate training in English. This being so, English departments are challenged to consider extraordinary qualifications in hiring of scholars in Aboriginal literatures.

Whether English departments assume this extraordinary mandate depends, in part, on what exactly English departments mean by "Aboriginal literatures" and/or to what extent they wish to facilitate genuine cross-cultural exchange and learning. Part of the question being posed here is this: should Aboriginal literatures be fitted into the English discipline, or should English departments change to accommodate the *real* cultural differences combined with Native colonial experience suggested in Indigenous literatures? English departments will have to clarify these points in their advertisements. If English departments simply wish to offer courses on Aboriginal writing, usually fiction, with standard English literary treatments (i.e., plot, characterization, theme, and so forth), then they should specify that all is required is Western-specific pedagogy. If, however, they mean to enhance the cross-cultural, postcolonial, and Indigenous-based understanding of Aboriginal literatures, then they should consider those who do not fit the standard pattern of a candidate in English, but who are informed by several disciplines, cross-cultural experience, and epistemological and political understanding of Native/White relations which informs contemporary Native writing.

By opening up positions in Aboriginal Literatures, English departments are opening up the Pandora's box of "cultural differences." By inviting "cultural differences," at least ostensibly, then the other part to the qualification question must centrally be about Aboriginality (whether in defining a body of literature, or in assessing a candidate). What criteria will they draw on here? While much has been written about what may constitute "Native literature," little has been determined as to how Aboriginality is assessed in criticism or in hiring. For example, are having a biological (however remote) and/or ceremonial (however recent) but not epistemological (land- and language-based) connection to Aboriginality sufficient criteria for hiring "Aboriginal staff?"[17] What and whose culture might be prioritized?

The commodification of Aboriginal culture (Kulchyski 605–20) is a topic which requires much greater exploration and critique than I can give it here. Needless to say, the subject acts as political currency is both unwieldy and highly charged. The fact is both the colonizer and the colonized have been profoundly informed by centuries of oppositional politics and colonial misrepresentation. Politically and intellectually, confusion reigns in a continuing attempt to uncover (or hire) the "authentic Indian." The result has been a colourful invention of oversimplified cultural typologies and social contradictions.

But it does remain for us to try to assess the role of identity and culture in the study of Native literature. As our repeated attempts indicate, this is no easy task, for it is difficult to unravel what is real or what is important. We are confronted with the task of treating Aboriginal cultures, which respects their integrity, and at the same time taking into account colonial forces. You will note that I use the phrase "real cultural differences" throughout this essay. It is my attempt to address misrepresentation and at the same time say that there is a basis to Aboriginality, both in cultural content as well as experience. It is true that colonization has complicated and compromised Aboriginal identity, but it is equally true that there is extant a remarkable cultural ground from which and through which many of us approach our scholarship. Not all of us grew up confused or alienated from our homes, languages, or lands. Dislocated characters such as Agnes, Slash, and Garnet do find their way back to their cultural and epistemic home/lands. In other words, there is an Aboriginal ground to Aboriginal literature. The foundational bases to Aboriginal worldview refer to the modes of acquiring and arranging knowledge within the context of original languages, relationships, and cultural strategies. This ground, though, is layered and "unsedimented," for there is here a complex imbrication of cultural continuity and discontinuity. The "broadening" of Aboriginal epistemology must be treated with all the interspacial nuances and contemporaneity that this implies and demands (LaRocque, "From the Land to the Classroom").

Recently, in the context of my arguing for such a ground to Aboriginality in the teaching of Aboriginal literatures, I was taken aback by a white colleague's challenge: "But is there a Native experience?" I believe I retorted something like: "What Aboriginal literature is there if Aboriginal identity and experience is erased?" Concerns about how we define or delimit Native experience (thus literature), which may be the basis to my colleague's challenge, are well taken but what I was trying to articulate was and is more than just about "experience," as such. It is about theory and praxis. Aboriginality as an identity is more than about an amorphous grouping of persons with varied experiences who happen to have some "Indian," it is about epistemology. To what extent modern deconstructionists can comprehend this is another debate, for many may conjecture *a priori* that this place of difference is essentialist or nativist.

As is often the case under colonial existence, there are time warps and contradictions. Even as a growing number of scholars are finally taking an inclusive or "cross-cultural" approach, Native peoples are in various phases of decolonizing. For many academics, cross-cultural means their "academic right" to use Native material in the advancement of (their) research and theory without that translating into bringing Aboriginal praxis in their pedagogy. Here cross-cultural is a one-way street. Some academics even take the direction of imposing a notion of racial sameness (not to be confused as equality), some to the extent of appropriating Native identities themselves. Let's shake hands (in a culturally appropriate clasp, of course) and say we're all the same (with varied experiences, of course).

To Native peoples, cross-cultural means having "inherent right" to practise and protect their Aboriginality. Decolonization demands having to define and protect more closely their identities (languages, literatures, among other things) and what is left of their lands and resources. Aboriginal identity and Aboriginal rights are inextricably related. But even as Native peoples are attempting to shore up their colonially beleaguered identities, they are pressured to be "inclusive" or even "transcultural." Irony seems to be a singular feature of colonialism. Using only western standards for intellectual western purposes, albeit postcolonial, is hardly a balanced equation to a truly cross-cultural exchange! In the universalized name of "literature" the Native experience is again levelled. But those of us not so alienated from our *ground* especially represent what the literati is fond of talking and writing about, namely, the *real* cultural differences.

Although there is way too much ethnographication (allow me to coin this) in literary criticism on Native works, and although there is too much emphasis on our (oft stereotyped) differences generally, I am becoming increasingly concerned that mainstream literary treatments of Aboriginal writers and writing is losing sight of the *real* cultural differences that yet exist between Native and White Canadians.[18] For me this is an odd place to be. I am of course aware of the increasing complexities concerning Aboriginal identities. Change and adaptability inherent in Aboriginal worldviews and practices have long been central tenets of my research and writing. And certainly, I do not believe that Aboriginal cultures should in any way be pre-historicized (coin) or typologized. However, the recent postcolonial emphasis on "hybridity" (which is not to be confused with Métis Nation cultures), "crossing boundaries," or "liminality" can serve to eclipse Aboriginal cultural knowledges, experiences (both national and individual) and what may be called the colonial experience.

I appreciate that we all want to be "fluid," and I appreciate that none of us want to be labelled as exclusionary, and I certainly appreciate the wide-ranging experiences of Native (and non-Native) peoples, but fluidity should not mean erasing of Native identities or the Native colonial experience. Whether we like it or not, at this time in Canadian life we are all deeply colonized, white and Native alike,[19] and no amount of disassembling "the Native experience" to accommodate globalized postcolonial theories can undo this homegrown colonial burden.

Literary treatments carry political implications; whitewashing our Aboriginality means dispossessing our Aboriginal rights. For example, the reading of "métis" in English literary treatments tends to obscure both our Aboriginality and our unique Red River Cree-Métis roots.[20] Such obscuration carries serious implications concerning Métis land rights and Métis identity. Broadening "métis" to include anyone who claims to be so (without the specific cultural and historical identity markers) merely on the basis of some biological connection (however remote or recent) confuses readings and discussions on Aboriginally based Métis cultures and identities.[21] Take the Raintree sisters in Culleton's *In Search of April Raintree*. Most critics have assumed the sisters are Métis. But are they? They may be "métis" or "halfbreed," that is, they may have part Indian and part White ancestry, but they quite clearly do not have Red River Cree-Métis cultural identity. Anyone looking for such cultural markers will not find them in this novel, not even toward the end where April begins to accept her Indianness (which is not the same as Métisness). One will not be able to discern Aboriginally based knowledge systems here, yet my Cree-Métis community of Red River roots practised (in many respects continues to practise) Cree-Métis epistemology. I have found it troublesome that non-Métis critics use Culleton's portrayal (and experience) as valid for herself and her identity search, but the novel should not be used as a history book or cultural lesson on the Red River Cree-Métis. There is no question that the Raintree sisters experience racism and misogyny to the extreme, but I cannot say they represent my culture.

I do not think I am being a Métis "nationalist"[22] here; I am pointing out a cultural and historical point of difference significant to Métis identity (and good scholarship). Further, that I relate much more closely to Ruby Slipperjack's Owl (*Honour the Sun*) or to Jeannette Armstrong's Penny (*Whispering in Shadows*) than I do to the Raintree sisters is not just about literary preference. As a Cree-Métis of Red River roots, I grew up with an Indigenous worldview and experience that comes only from the land and the language.[23] Both Owl and Penny exude the ethos born out of the motherlands and languages. Yet, I have faced an odd sort of discrimination (denial of my Aboriginal rights and denial of the view that "métis" does not mean "Métis") because of the confusion around the portrayal and universalization of the term "métis."

Native identities, knowledge systems, and the colonial experience(s) are complex, mutable, uncongealed yet well-defined. It is true that some 100 different Indigenous cultures representing 10 unrelated linguistic families, or about 50 different languages, greeted Europeans (not all at once of course) at the site of first encounter(s), and, given all the historical and demographic changes experienced and yet the cultural continuity exhibited by Native peoples since this time, it may seem foolhardy to speak of a Native experience in the singular. Anthropology and History point to "a kaleidoscope" of diversities among Native peoples, but also some fundamental similarities, especially in the use of resources and spirituality (Frideres 22). There appears to be among Indigenous peoples a fairly remarkable shared understanding of life as a cosmo/ecological whole, enabling the human being to experience life past the sensory confines. We cannot build a canon of Aboriginal literature or criticism without appreciating what this means in terms of mythology, literature, and cultural strategies. As anthropologist Ridington has discovered, land-based orally-literate peoples "code their information about their world differently from those of us whose discourse is conditioned by written documents" (275). For those of us who grew up in oral cultures, it is this "code of information" we seek to impress upon and within modern scholarship.[24]

Besides cultural commonalities, Native people's sustained and multi-faceted resistance to colonization has also bonded them and provided them with "similarities." Colonial time has collapsed some fundamental differences in areas such as resources, economies, technologies, education, kinship, governance, language, religions, among others. The *Indian Act* has determined legal identity and locality, defining margins and centres even within the Native community. This is not to mention societal prejudices, industrial encroachment, and urbanization. In other words, we can speak of the "Native experience" from a number of cultural, historical, and colonial bases. This, though, does not imply or hold that Native peoples' experience is unidimensional. But it is there. Any panoramic study and Indigeneity-based reading[25] of Aboriginal writing and writers makes this abundantly apparent.

There is an Aboriginal experience unique to the Canadian context.[26] This point comes back to (and tentatively answers) the issue and significance of qualifications and Aboriginality in the hiring of faculty for positions in Native literatures. Those who have an interdisciplinary academic training and/or who code their information Aboriginally are particularly well positioned to teach both oral and written Native Canadian literatures. This kind of interdisciplinarity is more than about latching onto postcolonialism (Slemon), it is about putting into practice Aboriginal knowledge and knowledge systems, the origins of which predate and in some ways now co-exist with, as well as subversely-exist, to colonialism. I am not at all promoting nativism or essentialism. At issue is the legitimation of Aboriginal discourse. Having an Aboriginal, land-based, linguistic and cultural upbringing which provides a particular worldview does make a difference in teaching, research, writing, and criticism. As does the on-going de/colonization.

I am not suggesting that non-Aboriginal scholars cannot treat Aboriginal literatures. Insight and understanding cannot be confined to ethnic origins. Many non-Aboriginal scholars, especially those who are attuned to the Aboriginal worldviews[27] and postcolonial experience, have served to advance Aboriginal histories, cultures, and contemporary peoples. However, scholars in Aboriginal literatures need to bring to their teaching and research an Aboriginal epistemological ethos *in addition to* their western academic training and credentials. I hasten to add, I am not suggesting that a candidate for a university position should have fewer academic qualifications (even as western hegemonic standards are under review); rather I am referring to those who have *more* than the academic qualifications. Indigenous literatures bears on an area of discourse and study which cannot be dealt with effectively only by standard western models or by an undisciplinary approach.

Standardization must come under review, for "knowledge" cannot mean only or same as "western" under cross-cultural mandates. Nor can English departments assume to meet their cross-cultural mandates simply by re-routing Aboriginal scholars, writers, and writing within the Empire's old dominant narrative or the newly sanctioned theoretical models, for these canons by themselves are insufficient in the appreciation of Aboriginal cultural productions and experience. This implies that English departments, consistent with their ads, should be particularly interested in those who do model, not just theorize, *real* cultural differences. Candidates with extra-ordinary qualifications would best serve, I would think, both the cultural and postcolonial mandates in the study of Aboriginal writers and writing. And of course, in the final analysis universities must hire on the basis of research and creative achievements, publication record, community service, and years of teaching experience. For English departments such a dossier should, of course, be in the area of Native literatures but not confined to it. I must emphasize that a cross-cultural and interdisciplinary scholarship gained in fields such as Native Studies can only enhance the study of Aboriginal Literatures. For these and other reasons I believe that university resources for the development of Aboriginal Literatures should go primarily to the community of Native Studies. This is not to suggest that other departments cannot study Aboriginal Literatures but it is to declare that Native Studies should remain in the intellectual and cultural foundation to the study of Native literatures.[28] At the very least, Native Studies should be consulted and cross-referenced prior to developing literature courses extraneous to Native Studies.

Ironically, in the area of Native literatures, Native Studies departments have not kept up with the dramatic changes. Today there are young (as well as experienced) Aboriginal scholars looking for positions in Aboriginal Literatures. For those looking to Native Studies, it is the sad fact that the handful of Native Studies programs or departments across Canada have not developed in this area and so will not be able to absorb such graduates. Most Native Studies programs have gone in the direction of the social sciences rather than the humanities. Most courses revolve around anthropology, history, law, linguistics (not to be confused with contemporary Native literature), governance, socio-economic issues, and more recently "Traditional Ecological Knowledge," which is an amalgam of environmental and cultural (associated as "traditional") studies. Even my own department teaches only one half-term course on Canadian Native literature! Yet, it is my position that the study of Aboriginal literatures (and languages) ought to be among the core courses for any Native Studies program.

Pushing Paradigms

In the final analysis, our studies of Aboriginal literatures can only be advanced by the production of more Aboriginal works. Even though today a half-term of Native Lit cannot begin to touch on the literary material now available, we can never have enough Native plays, prose, and poetry. And of course, our studies are enhanced by Aboriginal literary criticism. Non-Native teachers and critics should no longer dip into Native material just for ethnographic or personal information in the advancement of their theories. They now must deal with our theories and philosophical praxis as well. How else is cross-culturalism practised, and how else shall we truly "dethrone" the Empire?

The Aboriginal bases for contemporary scholarship and criticism are in the process of development. As we seek to develop a "critical centre" (Blaeser, "Native Literature") we are also academics who must aspire for that "critical and relatively independent spirit of analysis and judgment" which Edward Said argues, "ought to be the intellectual's contribution" (*Representations of the Intellectual* 86). In my concern for intellectual freedom and fluidity in this task, I have assiduously avoided being a mere conduit of community or political voices. Critical Aboriginal scholars present complexities in that we are "pushing margins," crossing boundaries and cultures, disciplines and genres, and we do not fit the standard patterns of both western and nativist pressures. But just because we are on the cutting edge of cultures and boundaries does not mean we are abandoning our Native-specific heritage with its substantial and particular worldview(s) and knowledge base(s). And we are bringing "the other half" of Canada into light. As I have written elsewhere, we are creating a space from which to enter the mandates of western thought and format without having to internalize its coloniality or to defy our personal and cultural selves. And just because we are not abandoning our heritage does not mean we are in a quagmire of confessional subjectivity. On my part, I have strived toward a personal and intellectual liberation which, among other things, has entailed both "living" and theorizing decolonization, a "decolonization" that would ultimately be free of rigid paradigms, ideological or cultural formulas and fads, or the jargon that often comes with each of these respective methodological tools or theories. As a professor I have encouraged all my students to engage in critical thinking, reading, and writing. To that end I facilitate students to study and approach Native history, identities, literatures or any modes of cultural productions and representations from a variety of genres, eras, cultural, theoretical, and critical perspectives. I do of course emphasize "the Native experience" as is mandated by Native Studies.

Much has changed in the ideological climate within the Empire since my youthful encounter with my Dean about the value of teaching Aboriginal literatures in universities, but much work remains to be done to facilitate even greater comprehension of pedagogical and canonical issues and challenges specific to the teaching of Aboriginal histories and literatures, cultural achievements, and epistemologies.

Favourite Poem

There Is My People Sleeping
by Sarain Stump

And there is my people sleeping
Since a long time
But aren't just dreams
The old cars without engine
Parking in front of the house
Or angry words ordering peace of mind
Or steals from you for your good
And doesn't wanna remember what he owes you
Sometimes I'd like to fall asleep too,
Close my eyes on everything
But I can't
I can't

Notes

This essay was first published in Renate Eigenbrod and Jo-Ann Episkenew, eds., *Creating Community: A Roundtable on Canadian Aboriginal Literatures* (Penticton, BC: Theytus Books, 2002).

1. For a detailed chronological history of Native writing, see Petrone, *Native Literature of Canada*, 1990.
2. At the time, the English department at the University of Manitoba offered no Native literature courses; I believe they offered one course for a brief time sometime in the late 1990s. As far I know, they did not consult our department about the course.
3. Most Native writers and/or scholars have located school textbooks as significant sources in their dehumanization and alienation. For an absorbing view of the euro-centricity of textbooks, see Blaut's *The Colonizer's Model of the World*.
4. I believe cultural differences among Aboriginal students, not to mention, between Aboriginal and non-Aboriginal, are quite profound but exquisitely and increasingly more subtle. I have noticed, for example, many northern Native students express confusion and alienation from powwow or elder ceremonies which have become popularized on campuses. These practices reflect the Plains Indian tradition, if not caricature (Pakes).
5. For further comment on the many levels of political discourse that goes on in Native Studies classrooms, see my article "From the Land to the Classroom: Broadening Aboriginal Epistemology."
6. My generation of Native university instructors have had to deal with intellectual suspicion, classicism, patriarchy, and standardized evaluation systems derived from this "unconscious" climate. Though much has improved over the last two decades, much remains to be "foregrounded" about the colonial discourse or "bias" in the academic system.

7. I first described my work as "resistance scholarship" in "The Colonization of a Native Woman Scholar."

8. Feminist and decolonization criticism have advanced the concept and use of voice in scholarship. I introduced my use of voice in the context of literature in my "Preface" (1990). I have since developed the theoretical grounds for voice, engaged research, and resistance scholarship in my dissertation *Native Writers Resisting Colonizing Practices in Canadian Historiography and Literature* (1999).

9. See Duchemin's brilliant exposition of Alexander Mackenzie's imperial constructions of Indians cloaked as impartial science. Mackenzie typically indulges in "mind numbing" ethnography, all the while skilfully employing an "almost scientific" vocabulary, which, "While appearing to be neutral . . . is in fact highly evaluative and judgemental" in language and imagery ("A 'Parcel of Whelps,'" 61).

10. Other minority peoples, perhaps especially for women of colour with critical approaches, are also confronted with similar situations in universities. See, for example, Mukherjee, *Oppositional Aesthetics*.

11. There is afoot a positivist movement in our midst which views treatment of colonization as "too negative" and basically consigns "native studies" to cultural programs, particularly spirituality, ceremonial practice, or craft replications.

12. How Native narratives, or, for that matter, other cultural information, were collected and interpreted should accompany any study of Aboriginal oral literatures. Notice, too, how Basil Johnston adds an Indigenous dimension and texture to oral literatures in his "One Generation from Extinction."

13. I treat these co-existing themes in my dissertation (1999).

14. Richardson employed not just the civ/sav master narrative (the effects of which are often diluted by the blanched term "eurocentrism") but racist slander, often comparing "Indians" to "cunning" or vicious animals or reptiles. Such virulent anti-Native text qualifies as hate literature. Hate literature is associated with neo-Nazism, but it in fact forms a consubstantial part of colonial records. For more on Richardson and hate literature, see my dissertation.

15. In my dissertation (1999), I devote several chapters to the fascinating, if confusing, intersection of issues on cultural difference and criticism in light of the overwhelming history of misrepresentation.

16. What constitutes specialization: a Ph.D. thesis? A Native-authored book? A Native-themed work?

17. Apparently self-conscious on these matters, many universities now turn to the "Native community" for input on culture and hiring. But care should be taken that Aboriginal (or any other) scholars not be evaluated as if they are cultural ambassadors elected to office. Not only are candidates being subjected to many disparate communities or "cultures" but also to ideological control and non-university review (LaRocque, "From the Land to the Classroom").

18. I am not contradicting myself here about too much ethnographication, on one hand, and my concern about erasing of *real* cultural differences, on the other. Negotiating around and through these mercurial Siamese twins is convoluted. The discussion, which I pursue at some length in my dissertation (1999), is centrally about misrepresentation.

19. In substantially different ways, of course! Needless to say, colonization benefits one at the expense of the other.

20. As I show in "Native Identity and the Métis: *Otehpayimsuak* Peoples" (2001), Métis identity is complex but it is grounded in Aboriginality and is well-defined by Métis Nation peoples.

21. Margery Fee, in "Deploying Identity in the Face of Racism," treats Métis (métis?) identity cautiously.

22. Janice Acoose has so faithfully used my works, and so I find it puzzling that she refers to me in a broad stroke as a "Métis nationalist" ("The Problem of 'Searching' for April Raintree," 229), especially since I have hardly published any works specifically on the Métis. My theoretical decolonizing positioning on "voice" should not be confused with nationalism.

23. In response to so much misinformation about the Métis, especially the recent emphasis on "hybridity," I feel compelled to repeat this bit of ethnographic detail in a number of works. The repeating of information also has to do with the addressing of different audiences that comes with the interdisciplinary work now spanning more than two decades.

24. Basil Johnston's creative and ethnographic work especially comes to mind, but as I have already explained, every Native author and intellectual of my generation has tried to teach our audiences an Aboriginal "way of seeing and naming our worlds" ("One Generation from Extinction" xx).

25. As Armstrong's collection *Looking at the Words of Our People* shows, reading Native works through the eyes of Native critics does make a difference. Native writers and scholars have long been "looking at" Native words, it is just that it has not been recognized as (Aboriginal) criticism under western literary standards.

26. At the risk of "going against the grain" in the recent emphasis on "Native North America" (i.e., in the Hulan anthology), I argue for the foregrounding of *Canadian* Native literature because there are a number of significant cultural and national differences between Canadian and American Native intellectuals (LaRocque 1999).

27. For a lovely read and excellent modelling on Indigeneity-based literary treatment, see Renate Eigenbrod's "Reading Indigeneity from a Migrant Perspective: Ruby Slipperjack's Novel *Silent Words*—'log book' or Bildungsroman?" (2000).

28. Works in "traditional ecological knowledge" have established the theoretical grounds for the "science" of Indigenous methods in the "coding," recovering, and interpreting of data (Colorado, Ridington, Simpson, Smith). This field has much to teach those engaged in Aboriginal literature(s), not only in the validation of Aboriginal knowledge system(s) but also about respecting Aboriginal cultural/intellectual property rights.

5

"Preface" from
Travelling Knowledges: Positioning the Im/Migrant Reader of Aboriginal Literatures in Canada

Renate Eigenbrod

Preface

Coming to Theory

[The] image of work—whether the work of everyday life or the work of intellectuals—as travel (transformation) . . . allows us to see the complexity of intellectual alliances and disputes: sometimes people travel with you, or near you, or against you; sometimes they help you, or distract you, or interrupt you, or redirect you; sometimes we take a wrong turn, or a detour, or a dead-end; sometimes we are "hijacked" (Hall, 1988) by another position and sometimes we are the "hijackers."

—Lawrence Grossberg, "Wandering Audiences, Nomadic Critics" 377

Our model for academic freedom should . . . be the migrant or traveller. . . .

—Edward Said, *Reflections on Exile and Other Essays* 403

I remember being on the train. . . . And I am looking at the school until I could see it no more. And then I am sitting there and crying.

And a few minutes later, I am sitting there giggling. I am free, I am free, I am thinking to myself. Oh my god! Free! Nobody is going to tell me what

to do again, when to blow my nose, when to go to the bathroom, when to
pray, when to do to bed, or whatever. We couldn't even yawn. We couldn't
even cough.

—Rita Joe, qtd. in "Talking at the Kitchen Table" 278

In this book, you will follow the different paths I took in order to come to an
understanding of Canadian Aboriginal literatures.[1] I started with a phrase from
the title of an article by Sto:lo writer Lee Maracle, "Oratory: Coming to Theory"
(1990). From the point of view of orally communicated knowledge, she argues
in favour of the contextualized story, or "oratory," instead of decontextualized
theorizing. Aligning myself with her reasoning, I introduce my own work in
the personal storytelling mode, this way "speaking" to you, the reader, not just
through the persuasiveness of my intellectual arguments but also through my
lived experience. Or, "hijacking" literary critic Brill de Ramirez's "conversive"
approach, I place my scholarship within "the oral engagement" (6) of assisting
you to become a participatory listener/reader of literary texts rather than to
remain a distanced critic.

Also, in a further movement away from or beyond the written text, I begin
with a visual image: *Migration, The Great Flood*, by Anishinaabe (Ojibway)
artist Norval Morrisseau (Morrisseau). At a time when Thunder Bay, the city
where most of this book was written, was not Thunder Bay but consisted of
two towns, Fort Arthur and Fort William (amalgamated in 1970), Morrisseau
went for two years to the Indian Residential School in Fort William, and later
to the tuberculosis sanitarium in the same place. Of those years in his life he
writes: "Lets leave it void—too much Involved" (Morrisseau xv).[2] The agonies
in his life contrast sharply with the fact that, in addition to the late Bill Reid,
Morrisseau is one of the most well-known Native artists in Canada. His biography presents, therefore, one of the many paradoxes and ironies I try to come
to terms with in writing this study about Aboriginal literatures as a white,
middle-class academic.[3] There are several other reasons why I chose his paint-
ing as an introduction. For one, it visualizes one of the themes of this study,
migration; also, it crosses cultural boundaries as it depicts a story known to
many cultures, the great flood, but from a distinctly Aboriginal perspective;
thirdly, this particular kind of Native imagery, also known as the Woodland
School of Art, is often stereotypically equated with the generic definition of
"Canadian Native Art." Hence, Morrisseau's visual image suitably prefaces discussion about a positionality that hinges on personal connections with the
topic, but also emphasizes the challenges and pitfalls of cross-cultural interpretations from the vantage point of an outsider who may assume familiarity
too easily and tends to overlook differentiations.

As my book's title suggests, I read Canadian Indigenous literatures from an immigrant perspective, but in a migrant fashion. The immigrant label denotes my outsider position in relation to the Indigenous text; the migrant signification alludes to what Rosi Braidotti calls the "nomadic consciousness" (*Nomadic Subjects* 12) of any critic reading for border-crossing movements and migrations. The negotiation of both, the immigrant and the migrant perspective, acknowledging yet also crossing boundaries, constitutes the interpretive method of this study, analogous to Dasenbrock's search for a "hermeneutics of difference . . . that can understand texts *different from us* and understand them *to be different from us*" ("Do We Write the Text We Read?" 248; emphasis added). Regarding my racial identification as "white," I would argue with German scholar Hartmut Lutz that although the term *race* is "highly questionable and loaded," it "continues to be pertinent . . . for as long as racism and racist violence continues to exist" (as they do in Canada and in Germany) ("'Is the Canadian Canon Colorblind?'" 52).[4] I question Brill de Ramirez's praise of scholarship as a "tool for changing reality" (13) as long as most of the scholars are white, middle-class academics whose freedom to move in any possible way differs distinctly from Aboriginal peoples' experiences of multiple boundaries. The quotation above by Mi'kmaq poet Rita Joe expresses the relief that she felt when, finally, she was able to leave the residential school. As a third epigraph to this preface, her words, implying how she suffered from her lack of freedom to move, suggest the problematic of the rhetorical framing of theory as travel. The quotation serves a similar purpose as Carole Boyce Davies's introductory sequence of "migration horror stories" in her book on theorizing migrations of the subject (*Black Women, Writing and Identity*). However, Rita Joe's words are not just a "reality check," but, more fundamentally, a reminder of the limitations of Western theorizing. According to Cree scholar Willie Ermine, in "Aboriginal Epistemology," "[e]xperience is knowledge" (10). In residential schools, which many Native children were forced to attend,[5] students were not allowed to form their own "intellectual alliances"; education was not about choices but about conforming to rules set by an oppressive institution.[6] These schools, along with the ghettoized reserve system, the confining definitions of the Indian Act, and the racist preconceptions of Aboriginal people in the media of mainstream society, are just some examples of restrictions of physical, economic, political, intellectual, cultural, and artistic mobility through colonization.

Included in my theoretical migrations from my position of privilege are the shifting alignments as suggested by Grossberg in the first epigraph, in particular my "shuttle" movements between Native and non-Native writers and critics, emulating Krupat's ethnocriticism.[7] In tune with James Clifford's prologue to his work *Routes*, a title I can no longer read without simultaneously hearing its British and Canadian homophone, I do not provide a map but "contours of a specific intellectual and institutional landscape, a terrain I have tried to evoke by juxtaposing texts addressed to different occasions and by not unifying the form and style of my writing" (11). Clifford's assertion that scholarly genres "are relational, negotiated, and in process" (12) illuminates, in the context of my own work, my attempt at a participatory, "oral" and non-coercive study, but also corresponds with my analysis of literatures that are evolving in reaction to, and as a reflection of, rapidly changing socio-economic and political conditions and cultural changes.

The "simple" style of writing in some Indigenous texts is misleading and may effect simplistic interpretations. For example, the novel by Métis author Beatrice Culleton-Mosionier, *In Search of April Raintree* (1983), is often read reductively as either juvenile fiction or as a commentary on social problems, but not as a carefully crafted literary work. Although the interdisciplinary nature of many texts by Indigenous writers lends itself to other than literary approaches, if critical interpretations disregard the complex layering of a work, they simplify not only a style of writing but also a way of thinking. As Helen Hoy explains in her analysis of Culleton-Mosionier's work, this autobiographical novel does not simply tell "nothing but the truth" about certain Native experiences, but is constructed as a multi-layered text (*How Should I Read These?*).[8] One of my objectives is to demonstrate the complexities of Native literature—complexities one would expect from any other literature. I use migration as a central metaphor to emphasize movement and process in my readings, resistance to closure and definitiveness; however, as Meaghan Morris points out in her critical analysis of nomadic theory, "colonization may be precisely a mode of movement (as occupation) that transgresses limits and borders" ("At Henry's Park Motel" 43). Readings of Indigenous literatures within the authoritative discourse of a scholarly publication could easily become another "conquest," in Todorov's meaning of the term. Despite "the impossibility of establishing a grand synthesis in which different view points are reconciled" ("Worlding Geography" 20), as Trevor Barnes says, a migrating approach of continuosly shifting positions—or even Brill de Ramirez's "conversive" approach of the listener/reader—does not guarantee a non-colonialist reading of texts. Barnes explains with reference to Donna Haraway: "'The Western eye has fundamentally been a wandering eye, a travelling lens,' and its movements have often been instruments of coercion and oppression" (21). Therefore, as much as I am aware of the complexities of the texts under scrutiny, so do I problematize my subjectivity, the situatedness of my knowledge, and the context of my subject position in order to underscore partiality and de-emphasize assumptions about the expert: "We all write and speak from a particular place and time, from a history and a culture which is specific,"

Stuart Hall says. "What we say is always 'in context,' positioned" ("Cultural Identity and Diaspora" 222).

With Jewish scholar Arnold Krupat, I recognize that rather "than my origins explaining my ends, my ends, it seems have forced me to consider my origins" (*The Turn to the Native* 127). Part of the position from which I read Native literature is "locatable" in "the 'contrapuntal' awareness" or the "double vision" (*Framing Marginality* 38), in Sneja Gunew's words, of my hyphenated immigrant position as German-Canadian. Although I will refer to my German background throughout this study, it is the hyphen in my identification that is of at least as much importance because I was writing in the context of living in Canada and teaching Aboriginal literatures to Native students in Northwest Ontario. Therefore, I introduce my contextualized methodology with an autobiographical speech/essay that traces sites of my coming to an understanding about my topic (including my connections with Germany). I have kept the oral character of this piece, which was originally composed for a lecture on Canadian Native literature at a German university. When I was invited to give this lecture, I felt uncomfortable with my expected "expert" position, and therefore chose to situate myself in space and time, outlining "an itinerary rather than a bounded site—a series of encounters and translations" (*Routes* 11), as Clifford says, in my trajectory of "coming to theory."

Notes

This Preface was originally published in Renate Eigenbrod, *Travelling Knowledges: Positioning the Im/Migrant Reader of Aboriginal Literatures in Canada* (U of Manitoba P, 2005).

1. In this study I will use the qualifiers "First Nations," "Native," "Indigenous," and "Aboriginal" interchangeably, as they are all in use. A preference for one name falsely standardizes a varied and always changing praxis of naming, by the peoples themselves and by the government and society at large. "Aboriginal" is more often used than "First Nations," as this name includes the Métis. The more appropriate adjective in naming the peoples and their literatures would be a nation- or culture-specific identification like Anishinaabe, and whenever applicable this will be used. The word "Anishinaabe" has several spellings, and I have chosen to use this spelling for consistency. Although some Native people refer to themselves as "Indians," for different reasons, I, as a non-Native person, will not use this term because of its colonialist and racist connotations.
2. The original does not have an apostrophe for "Let's" and does capitalize "Involved."
3. Therefore, although I am differently positioned in relation to my topic than Stan Dragland in relation to Duncan Campbell Scott, I align myself with his ambivalent attitude toward objectivity for similar reasons. In his introduction to *Floating Voice*, he writes: "I haven't tried for objectivity at every point, feeling that the stresses of a study like this ought not to be concealed, feeling that I can trust the reader to weather the turbulence" (*The Floating Voice* 12).

4. I agree with Thomas Parkhill (*Weaving Ourselves into the Land*) that "'Whiteman', 'White', 'White Man', as well as their substitutes, 'non-Indian', and 'non-Native' are, in most usages, stereotypical foils for images of the 'Indian'" (5). When I use these terms, I follow the reasoning of the literature I am discussing. Given the key words in the title for this study, I often use the qualifier "migrant" and "immigrant" but also Euro-Canadian or Euro-American.

5. In her autobiography *Song of Rita Joe: Autobiography of a Mi'kmaq Poet*, Rita Joe explains how she came to enrol herself at Subenacadie Indian Residential School—a rarely told story.

6. The importance of routine and mechanically regulated days is emphasized in Basil Johnston's autobiographical narrative about residential school experiences titled *Indian School Days*. The longlasting effects of these aspects of life at the schools are analyzed by Greg Sarris in *Keeping Slug Woman Alive: A Holistic Approach to American Indian Texts*.

7. Arnold Krupat (in *Ethnocriticism*) uses the image of the shuttle when he distinguishes his ethnocritical movements "between Western paradigms and the as-yet-to-be-named paradigms of the Rest" (113) from James Clifford's "perpetual shuttling back and forth between the privileged Western narrative paradigms of tragedy and comedy" (*Routes* 112). Although I agree with Krupat's distincton, I subscribe neither to the marginalization of non-Western paradigms as "the Rest" (even if capitalized) nor to the desire to name them.

8. Her chapter on *In Search of April Raintree* is titled "'Nothing but the Truth': Beatrice Culleton's *In Search of April Raintree*."

6

Strategies for Ethical Engagement: An Open Letter Concerning Non-Native Scholars of Native Literatures

Sam McKegney

Reacting to violence perpetrated against Indigenous texts by decades of literary criticism dominated by non-Native academics wielding analytical strategies developed outside Native communities, much recent criticism of Indigenous literatures has been intensely self-reflexive about the position of the critic, whether non-Native or otherwise. Declaration of ties to particular Indigenous communities or, perhaps more crucially, confession of lack of community ties and non-Native status have become near obligatory elements of contemporary Indigenous literary criticism, and rightly so given the general desire of such criticism to intervene in and destabilize unequal power relations and the basic truth that non-Native members of the academy tend to enjoy positions of privilege, authority, and power. The current critical climate thus encourages a healthy skepticism about claims made by non-Native critics while suggesting (at times implicitly, at others explicitly) the intellectual and political value of attending to Indigenous voices within the critical arena.[1] Helen Hoy, herself non-Native, worries adroitly about "unfortunate occasions either for absolute, irreducible distance or for presumptuous familiarity" (11), which emerge for the outsider critic by virtue of cultural naïveté. Lack of cultural immersion leaves many non-Native critics unaware of the symbolic archives, historical and cultural backdrops, generic categories, and even languages relied upon by specific Native authors, all of which conspire to render interpretations by such critics suspect, if not dangerous. Hoy elaborates that "too-easy identification by the non-Native reader, ignorance of historical or cultural allusion, obliviousness to the presence or properties of Native genres, and the application of irrelevant aesthetic standards are all means of domesticating difference, assimilating Native narratives into the mainstream" (9).

Although I agree with insistence on self-reflexivity and acknowledgement of limited cultural understandings, I would argue that lack of cultural initiation and knowledge is actually a secondary reason for privileging the work of Native critics (as well as a bit of a generalization). Knowledge can be attained. Neither unproblematically, of course, nor completely, and certainly not with the depth of a lifetime of experiential learning through simple academic study, but those non-Native critics willing to put in the time and effort in terms of research, dialogue, social interaction, and community involvement can approach valid cultural understandings. (In fact, to my mind, it is our responsibility to do so if we desire our work to be relevant.) Furthermore, given colonial intervention, not all Native individuals have inherited full understandings of their tribal cultures and histories, let alone those of other Native nations. In the aftermath of attempted genocide, requisite cultural knowledge can be taken as a given by neither Natives nor non-Natives.[2]

The primary reason for privileging the work of Indigenous scholars is rather what Craig S. Womack calls the "intrinsic and extrinsic relationship" between Native communities and Native writing (11) and what Jace Weaver calls the "dialogic" nature of Native texts, which "both reflect and shape Native identity and community" (41). Native literature grows out of Native communities and in turn affects Native communities. In analyzing, contextualizing, grappling with, and elucidating Native texts, literary criticism seeks to intervene in this reciprocal process (most often to serve as catalyst). To borrow from Julie Cruikshank, criticism of Native literature generally seeks to participate in the social lives of stories.

Stories influence the extratextual world, not straightforwardly and not transparently, but stories and critical discourses about stories do influence people's lives. And in the field of Native studies, the stories under analysis, quite frankly, affect certain lives far more profoundly than others. As much as intellectual empathy and ethical commitment can pervade the work of a scholar with neither biological nor immediate social connection to Indigenous communities, the consequences of that individual's work cannot be experienced personally with the same intensity as one whose day-to-day lived experience is being Indigenous. Although I endeavour to be as sensitive and respectful as I am able, as a non-Native critic I simply do not stand to inherit the adverse social impact my critical work might engender, and this, it seems to me, impacts the way my work functions and is something about which I must remain critically conscious.

Such critical consciousness, while absolutely necessary for ethically appropriate critical and political interactions with Indigenous literatures, has produced tremendous anxiety among non-Native scholars working in the field over the past several years, leading to a series of critical reactions to which I wish to respond in this methodological discussion. I have become increasingly concerned recently that the dominant strategies adopted by non-Native critics to avoid doing damage to Indigenous texts have had unintended inverse (and adverse) effects of obfuscating Indigenous voices and stagnating the critical field. My goal in these brief remarks is to explain what I see as the ironically disabling impact of some critical postures characterized by careful, self-reflexive distance undertaken by non-Native critics and then suggest a possible alternative direction for future critical interventions. The following are the most popular among what I will refer to as strategies of ethical disengagement by non-Native scholars.

Strategies of Ethical Disengagement

Retreat into Silence

Faced with the conundrum of either misunderstanding (and therefore misrepresenting) indigeneity or recolonizing the Indigenous literary artist by "submit[ting] him or her to a dominative discourse" (Krupat 30), many non-Native former critics of Native literature have simply moved on to other areas of study. A popular site of migration has been white representations of indigeneity, which can be critiqued in terms of racism, colonial myths, and semiotic imprisonment without the fear of appropriating Native voice. This strategy has two benefits: it protects the Indigenous text against assault by the culturally uninitiated, and it opens up the field for Indigenous scholars.[3] However, this alternative of focusing even more attention on the cultural creations of the dominant society seems at the same time perplexingly contrary to the goals of respecting Native voices and forwarding the social and political objectives embedded in texts; it again takes focus away, willingly failing to heed the creative voices of those adversely affected by the legacy of colonial oppression.

Focus Inward

Intense self-reflexivity is far from uncommon in the age of postmodern literary analysis, but contemporary analyses of Native literary productions by non-Natives at times take this to a new level in which the actions of the critic become the primary site of inquiry rather than a cautionary apparatus designed to render the primary analysis more fertile. Given the dangers of appropriation and misrepresentation, the analytical process itself presents a safe site where the critic can be confident she or he is not committing violence against Native voice because the voice under scrutiny becomes her or his own. An example of this in process—although one that needs to be contextualized as an analysis of collaborative autobiography—would be Kathleen Sands' focus in *Telling a Good One* on a "narrative-ethnography methodology, in which the reader is made privy to the [non-Native] collector's self-conscious participation [in the autobiographical project] and doubly self-conscious hindsight" (50). In an effort to avoid corrupting the voice of Theodore Rios, the Native subject of the autobiography, Sands makes her own involvement in the collaborative process as much the focus of her inquiry as Rios' words.

While to a certain extent necessary, the "Focus Inward" has always seemed to me slightly masturbatory. The idea that the best way to ensure that Native voice is not stifled or misunderstood is to study another voice altogether is counterintuitive. It is kind of like the backhanded paternalism of saying, "you might get hurt in the ring, so please stay on the sidelines while I shadow box myself." In the effort to protect the oppressed, one disregards her or his decision-making authority. Yes, scholars need to be aware of their own limitations, and yes, they must be self-reflexive, but no, they do not need to make themselves the stars of their studies, especially to the ongoing neglect of Indigenous voices.

Deal in the Purviews of Non-Natives

Although only one among many, Arnold Krupat presents the foremost example of this type of reaction. Krupat's attachment to a social-scientific approach to Native literature is undoubtedly informed by awareness of his outsider status; however, his defence against producing an exploitative critical discourse is to retreat from Native narratives themselves and deal in the domains of other non-Native scholars—anthropologists, sociologists, historians, literary theorists, philosophers—which is why his 1992 book *Ethnocriticism* is, by its author's own admission, "very little concerned with specifically literary texts" (31). It deduces textual meaning predominantly through analyses of material production and cultural collision, thereby implying a deterministic relationship that obscures the possibility of enduring Indigenous agency. It suggests that the work of Native authors is determined by forces outside themselves, be they cultural, economic, or political.

To play with my earlier analogy a bit, "Dealing in the Purviews of Non-Natives" is somewhat like saying, "you may get hurt on the field, so please stay on the sidelines and watch the rest of us play." The non-Native critic examines the work of other non-Native scholars, critics, and theorists in order to explain away the textual product without having to engage much at all with the ideas of the text. "Unwilling to speak for the Indian," writes Krupat, "and unable to speak as an Indian . . . the danger I run as an ethnocritic is the danger of leaving the Indian silent entirely in my discourse" (30). Krupat identifies a mighty risk, one that seems far more threatening to Indigenous empowerment than the alternative of engaging Native literature directly, despite the possibility of misinterpretation. Non-Native critics must indeed be ever conscious of the limitations of their experiential knowledge, but this awareness cannot lead them to ignore Native voices without compromising the critical and political validity of their work. Although contextual information from a variety of sources is clearly crucial to knowledgeable engagements with any literature, such information must never replace the literary analysis, particularly among literatures that have been heretofore marginalized. The priority in Native literary studies, it seems to me, must be Native voices as evidenced by the writing of the Native author. This is not a dogmatic claim about what constitutes Native identity but rather an obvious conclusion about what it is the job of the literary critic to do. The function of literary criticism, in the Indigenous context as elsewhere, is to engage in the understanding and elucidation of specific literary texts, not to bury those texts beneath mountains of anthropological and historical data.

Present Only Tentative, Qualified, and Provisional Critical Statements

From the all-too-frequent "Please let me know if I'm saying this wrong, because I don't speak Anishinaabe" prefaces at Native studies conferences, to the two-paragraph qualifications at the beginning or end of articles tracing the author's complex subject position and her or his capacity to make only a particular type of reticent truth claim regarding these distant literatures, many non-Native critics flirt with this technique. Renate Eigenbrod, for example, is careful to "problematize [her] subjectivity, the situatedness of [her] knowledge, and the *context* of [her] subject position in order to underscore partiality and de-emphasize assumptions about the expert" (xv). Hoy similarly strives in her work to "keep to the forefront the assumptions, needs, and ignorance that [she] bring[s] to [her] readings, the culture-specific positioning from which [she] engage[s] with the writing." By "making explicit various sources of [her] responses," Hoy endeavours to "render the readings more clearly local, partial, and accountable, relinquishing the authority that clings to detached pronouncements" (18). Both Hoy and Eigenbrod take action against the power imbalance between Indigenous community and non-Native academy by forsaking access to positions of "authority" and calling into question the validity of their own readings.

Politically, this is astute, admirable, and ethical, but it does lead to questions about the point of reading work that professes to be inadequate throughout.[4] Also, when taken to an extreme, this process can potentially lead to critical license. By qualifying their statements with admissions of lack of cultural knowledge, critics can consider themselves freed from attempting to gain that knowledge, which inevitably will lead to weaker criticism. The wise person may well recognize that she or he knows nothing, but the wiser person takes this as incentive to learn.

Furthermore, remaining cognizant of limitations must not prevent the outsider critic from saying anything of note, from making the interpretive claims that are the earmarks of engaged scholarship. Critical interventions, even when they are flawed, can forward others' thinking by inciting reactions in which new avenues of investigation and new methods of inquiry might be developed. If an interpretation is flawed, then why is it so, and how can another critic in dialogue remedy the errors? According to Womack, critics of Native literatures need to "interrogate each other's work as much as celebrate it. . . . The backslapping that has characterized our discipline has not gotten us very far" (Weaver, Womack, and Warrior 169). Warrior agrees, arguing in *Tribal Secrets* that "the tendency to find in the work of other American Indian writers something worthy . . . of unmitigated praise . . . stands in the way of sincere disagreement and engagement" (xviii). Although non-Native critics can never and should never claim "big A" Authority in their discussion of Native texts, the need for endless qualification is mitigated by the dialogic nature of critical discourse. All claims unleashed upon the critical arena are offered up for debate, and those that are inept or, worse, communally damaging need to be countered with astute, powerful, and ethical responses. I apologize for any weaknesses that might emerge in my own analysis, but I do not apologize for analyzing. And I expect and desire other critics (especially those with connections to the communities for whom the issues embedded in the texts I analyze are lived concerns) to engage with some of the things I have said and to disagree with them where necessary. This is how the critical field will grow; this is how I will get better as a critic and hopefully produce more empowering and communally generative work in the future.

Strategies for Ethical Engagement

In short, I reject the reigning strategies for ethical disengagement in order to seek out strategies for ethical engagement. To respect the creative work of

Native writers, the intellectual work of Native critics, and the activist work of Native community members, one must engage—listen, learn, dialogue, and debate. The critical posture I endeavour to occupy as a non-Native critic of Native literatures, therefore, is that of the ally. Weaver states:

> We need simpatico and knowledgeable Amer-European critical allies. . . .
> We want non-Natives to read, engage, and study Native literature. The sur-
> vival of Native authors, if not Native people in general, depends on it. But
> we do not need modern literary colonizers. We only ask that non-Natives
> who study and write about Native peoples do so with respect and a sense
> of responsibility to Native community. (Weaver, Womack, and Warrior 11)

An ally, in my understanding, is one who acknowledges the limits of her or his knowledge, but neither cowers beneath those limits nor uses them as a crutch. An ally recognizes the responsibility to gain knowledge about the cultures and communities whose artistic creations she or he analyzes before entering the critical fray and offering public interpretations. An ally privileges the work of Native scholars, writers, and community members—not as a political gesture, but as a sincere attempt to produce the most effective criticism—yet she or he does not accept their work uncritically; she or he recognizes that healthy skepticism and critical debate are signs of engagement and respect, not dismissal. Further, an ally appreciates that multilayered and ultimately valid understandings of cultures, communities, and histories can never emerge solely from book research and that the ongoing vitality of Indigenous communities must serve to augment and correct what Jana Sequoya calls "the alienated forms of archive material" (458). Most importantly, the non-Native ally acts out of a sense of responsibility to Indigenous communities in general and most pointedly to those whose creative work is under analysis. Cherokee author, academic, and activist Daniel Heath Justice argues that "to be a thoughtful participant in the decolonization of Indigenous peoples is to necessarily enter into an ethical relationship that requires respect, attentiveness, intellectual rigour, and no small amount of moral courage" (9). Allied critical endeavours, it seems to me, aspire to such participation.[5]

This piece consists of a revised excerpt from the author's book *Magic Weapons: Aboriginal Writers Remaking Community after Residential School*, published by University of Manitoba Press in 2007.

Notes

This essay was first published in *SAIL: Studies in American Indian Literatures* 20, no. 4 (2008): 56–67.

1. In two of the most significant critical interventions of the last decade or so, *Tribal Secrets* (1995) and *Red on Red* (1999), Osage critic Robert Warrior and Muskogee Creek critic Craig S. Womack argue respectively (in distinct but interpenetrating ways) for analytical strategies in Native literary studies that emerge from Native people and Native communities. Warrior "explores the extent to which, after more than two centuries of impressive literary and critical production, critical interpretation of [Native] writings can proceed primarily from Indian sources" (xvi), and Womack explores the extent to which "Native literature, and the criticism that surrounds it," can be engaged through the lens of "tribally specific concerns" (1). Both critics focus on the work of other Native writers, critics, community members, and activists, not solely in response to the domination of "the 'mental means of production' in regards to analyzing Indian cultures . . . by non-Indians" (Womack 5), but also as a reasoned argumentative position regarding what generates the most effective interpretations of the literature. Reacting to "an unfortunate prejudice among scholars against American Indian critical, as opposed to fictional, poetic, oral, or autobiographical, writings," Warrior calls for "bibliograph[ies] dominated by . . . the criticism of American Indian writers" and critical discourse in which "native writers [are] taken seriously as critics as well as producers of literature and culture" (xv–xvi). Womack similarly seeks out "Native perspectives" by "prioritizing Native voices" within his work and by "allowing Indian people to speak for themselves" (4).

   The need for what Cherokee critic Jace Weaver calls a "Native American literary criticism"—as opposed to "criticism of Native American literature"—that resides "in the hands of Native critics to define and articulate, from the resources [they] choose" (Weaver, Womack, and Warrior 17) is paramount. Since the initial challenges of Womack, Warrior, and Weaver in the 1990s, the critical movement of Indigenous literary nationalism has endeavoured to address this need while building ethically responsible critical methodologies that remain committed to the endurance and well-being of Native communities and individuals. Among the most significant products of this movement is the recent collaborative collection *Reasoning Together: The Native Critics Collective*.

2. As Métis author Kim Anderson writes, "Native experience" is complicated, "because, unfortunately, part of our experience as Native peoples includes being relocated, dispossessed of our ways of life, adopted into white families, and so on" (27).

3. All scholars of Native literatures need to facilitate the development of new Native scholars through involvement in graduate courses, symposia, conferences, edited collections, and journal special issues, thereby contributing to conditions of possibility for the inevitable and necessary predominance of the critical field by Natives. To clarify, this does not mean a power-laden dynamic in which non-Native paternalist scholars "give Natives a chance" by editing their work, organizing their conferences, and teaching their grad courses. By contrast, it is a recognition that all of us, Native and non-Native, need to be involved in expanding the field and growing

the discipline so that there are multiple sites for engagement by the next generation of Native scholars who increasingly will guide the study of Native literatures in the years to come. However, we need to continue to respect and examine Indigenous creative work as a frontline to Native empowerment and agency. If we indeed desire to expand the field—something desperately needed, particularly in Canada, where I study—scholars need to welcome new insights, new critical strategies, and new critical minds (particularly those emerging from Native communities), while not ceasing to engage with Native artistic creation. The two need not be mutually exclusive.

4. I consider this to be far more of a difficulty in Hoy's work, which, to be fair, did come earlier and provide a necessary intervention in the field, than in Eigenbrod's. While Hoy's discussions in *How Should I Read These?* (2001)—note the interrogative nature of the title—often deconstruct themselves or stop short of forwarding solid critical claims by virtue of the author's reticence, Eigenbrod's *Travelling Knowledges* (2005) still posits well-researched interpretations while maintaining a high level of self-reflexivity. *Travelling Knowledges* thus provides more substance to the critical reader. Also, although I would level the following critique at the work of neither Eigenbrod nor Hoy, both of whom I respect a great deal and have learned from extensively, I do worry that qualifications like those mentioned above might, at times, be disingenuous, presented as protocol rather than sincere reservation. I am concerned that many non-Native critics believe their work to be valid, intelligent, and effective— after all, why else would they try to publish it?—and yet feel compelled to pay lip service to their unworthiness in order to appease the current critical climate.

5. I have prepared this essay to be intentionally provocative, and I desire it to stir up some discussion. Please feel free to contact me with comments, arguments, disagreements, thoughts: sam.mckegney@queensu.ca.

7

A Response to Sam McKegney's "Strategies for Ethical Engagement: An Open Letter Concerning Non-Native Scholars of Native Literatures"

Robert Appleford

You fight me, you fight the Mission![1]

—Common Anishinaabe/Ojibwa battle cry in Thunder Bay, Ontario

First off, I would like to thank both the editors of *SAIL* and literary critic Sam McKegney for asking questions about ethical engagement with Aboriginal literature that are both profoundly and historically vital. That said, my response to Sam's diagnosis of the malaise currently afflicting non-Aboriginal critics of this literature is an attempt to consider the "cure" Sam offers (albeit provisionally) for this malaise in relation to the symptoms he diagnoses. But I will put aside my medical metaphors for now and take up the more exciting—and apt, I think—"sporting" metaphorical register that Sam uses. My gloves are on, and I hear the bell!

In both his articulate identification of what prevents non-Aboriginal critics from engaging robustly and ethically with Aboriginal literary texts and his suggestion as to why these critics might migrate to other texts, Sam contrasts the internally or externally directed non-Aboriginal critics with Aboriginal critics who advocate a communally responsible literary criticism. While the current trends in Aboriginal literary/cultural studies are not the focus of Sam's discussion, I do think it is important to spell out certain premises that are currently being buttressed or challenged by Aboriginal critics in order to give context to my own concerns as a non-Aboriginal critic. I will borrow and adapt Sam's sporting analogy here and push it, if that is okay. When one considers the current state of the field of North American Indigenous literary criticism, many colourful euphemisms spring to mind. Dance marathon, king-of-the-mountain push-fest, arm wrestling. Knife fight. But one would be hard-pressed to apply a descriptor that did not carry with it a sense of combat, a squaring off of opponents determined to hold fast to an interpretative turf and thus establish this turf as a recognized higher ground. The two camps currently in melee in the United States (as many readers of *SAIL* will know, of course) have been called the "nationalist," "tribalist," "nativist," or "separatist" critics on one side and the "cosmopolitanist" or "hybridist" critics on the other. This conflict, while still evolving and fought on several fronts at once, can be summarized broadly as the struggle to establish Indigenous literature's relation to what both camps have variously (and differently) described as the "real world." For critics like the late Paula Gunn Allen, Elizabeth Cook-Lynn, Jace Weaver, Robert Warrior, Craig S. Womack, and Daniel Heath Justice, literary criticism of Native American writers must first and foremost concern itself, as Womack has succinctly put it, "with the ethics of the relationship between a text and the community it claims to represent" (*Red on Red* 149). By emphasizing the authored text as a record of lived Indigenous experience, however imaginative and idiosyncratic, these critics assert the necessity of reading these texts as responses to and reflections of particular tribal histories and struggles for political and intellectual sovereignty (for example, Creek sovereignty in the case of Womack, or Cherokee sovereignty in the case of Justice). The critics I have mentioned can and do disagree with each other about how tribal-centred reading practices can and should be developed and critiqued. But these critics share a commitment to expose and counter what they see to be the Euroamerican three-pronged strategy of co-opting these texts as part of the metropolitan canon, effacing the ethical imperative of these texts as communal documents of struggle, and diluting this ethical imperative as a generally postcolonial or pan-tribal call for justice that is nonlocatable and therefore enervating as a resistance strategy.

In the other scrum, ready to scrap, are the so-called cosmopolitan or hybridist critics. These critics include non-Native scholars such as Arnold Krupat and Elvira Pulitano and Indigenous scholars such as Gerald Vizenor and the late critic Louis Owens. Like their opponents, they make up a highly diverse and multivocal group, but they do take a particularly concerted aim at the separatist impulse that underwrites the nationalist critic's call to ethics. All four critics see the premise that literary activity can be framed as uniquely and independently Indigenous as, at worst, an exercise in bad faith or, at best, wilful ignorance. They argue that to deny the interdependence of Indigenous and colonial history, a shared trajectory, is to deny the reality of intercultural exchange and to fetishize a highly romantic reification of Indigenous stereotype that has always served as a necessary angel of colonialism. Like the nationalist critics, the cosmopolitan critics claim to be led by the literature they are interpreting, but they emphasize the hybrid nature of texts and of the identities that these texts articulate. For these critics, Indigenous identity formation, as it can be understood to be reflected in literary texts, necessarily involves the experience of hybridity as an unavoidably contemporary way of knowing the "real world" of influence and experience, a globalized marketplace of stories and their ethical legacies.

While many critics of both sides of the question have made some attempt to ameliorate the conflict between the two warring interpretative camps, the polarization of opinion has continued apace.[2] The point of preambling my discussion of what defines ethical literary criticism of Aboriginal texts with this backdrop of conflict is not simply to enjoy a courtside seat, to marvel or offer a *tsk* at the height of invective hurled—high moral grounding! and higher dudgeon! Rather, I would suggest that the struggle to establish an ethical reading practice for Indigenous North American literature, either as tribal or hybrid texts, is fundamentally the struggle to marshal the imagination of the Indigenous writer (as it is invested in the texts she or he writes) in the service of an immanent, recognizable, and *knowable* teleological project of ethical/ethnic self-fashioning.

But now, let's get back to Sam's argument. I want to bring forward Craig S. Womack's pithy statement about "the ethics of the relationship between a text and the community it claims to represent" (*Red on Red* 149), since I would think Sam would agree with Womack on the importance of this relationship. The problem I have here is with the fuzzy definition of "community" as a self-evident construction in this statement. What is the "community" for an Aboriginal writer? For the "tribalist" team, the community is necessarily signalled by the Aboriginal language/culture/biological inheritance of the writer. For example, Thomas King's community is Cherokee, in this definition. For the "cosmopolitan" team, it is equally clear that the writer's community is unstably hybrid, both local and global in its strategic deployment of identity as a political trope. For this team, Thomas King's community is variously Blackfeet/Blackfoot (since these are the communities he most often writes about in his fiction), Canadian Aboriginal (since King addresses Indigenous issues apart from Blackfoot or Cherokee ones in his critical writing), and international (since his main readership is not tied to specific communities in Canada). What does bother me in this melee is the common drive to draft the Aboriginal writer in the service of particular (and increasingly divisive) projects of political agency. Whether the project is the creation of the intellectually sovereign tribal citizen or of the interculturally fluid cosmopolitan hybrid, the literary text is supplied as evidence of the author's commitment to making identity accessible to, and useful for, the "right" reader. If the non-Aboriginal critic rejects the "parochial" nationalist interpretative strategy in favour of the more "worldly" cosmopolitan strategy, one exchanges one kind of "certainty" for another.[3]

What I see as the end result of this division is that younger scholars who are now seeking to explore critical methodologies for understanding Indigenous literature are caught in the epistemic trap that the call to ethics in the field has already set, a trap the postcolonial critic Gayatri Chakravorty Spivak identified (early on), where, "two senses of representation are being run together: representation as 'speaking for,' as in politics, and representation as 're-presentation,' as in art and philosophy" (275). These conflated senses of representation elide the discontinuity between them, where aesthetic versions of identity are misrecognized as both politically transparent and concretely metonymic "vox populi" of the "people" under representation.

Thus, several non-Aboriginal graduate students I have worked with in the last few years have evoked the term "community" in an almost talismanic fashion to justify their political readings of Aboriginal authors without offering justification for the material connection between aesthetic representation in fiction and the political representation the author is assumed to be advocating in aesthetic terms. "Community," in these cases, becomes less a way into flexible and responsible critical analysis than a justification for presumptively shoehorning authors into political models of agency or resistance with which they may in fact have little interest or sympathy. In this context, I do disagree with Sam that the problem in our field stems from non-Aboriginal critical disengagement from Aboriginal communitarian values.[4] Rather, it is what Spivak tags (again, early on) as the reintroduction of the undivided subject—the writer-as-community—into the discourse of power in the name, as she significantly points out, of desire (247). And I would also suspect that, in addition to the reasons Sam identifies quite rightly, another of the reasons why non-Aboriginal scholars might move away from studying literature is that the problematizing of representation as re-presentation that is so much a part of postcolonial and cultural studies criticism seems to have less purchase in a field where Aboriginal literary texts are seen primarily as "a front line to Native empowerment and agency," as Sam asserts (65).

To shift things a little, there is another community here, of course: the community of authors. As a critic of Aboriginal literature, I have spent more time in this community, since many of its members are writers that I consider my friends. My experience in their company has taught me that many contemporary Aboriginal writers are engaged with aesthetic issues that often lead them to "follow the story" beyond or against *either* category of ethical/ethnic communal "voice" championed by the two battling critical camps. And to be even more blunt—my apologies for the simplification here—what I have heard from these writers, in various places and contexts, is that they want to be paid well. They want to be read widely. And they want to be taken seriously as artists, not conditionally, but categorically. Sam argues through his call that non-Aboriginal critics should consider themselves allies of Indigenous communities and promote the work of "Native writers, critics . . . and activists" in their textual analyses (64). I would ask: are these three communities (writers, critics, and activists) necessarily coextensive, and are their goals necessarily the same? And can one ally oneself (in terms of critical engagement) to a notion of community that elides the instability of identification that makes these communities exciting and contumacious in the first place? So, I welcome and support Sam's exhortation to non-Aboriginal critics to commit to Aboriginal literary criticism passionately and ethically. But, to reformulate (with apologies to Sam) Sam's sporting refrain in his essay, does the call to ethics for the non-Aboriginal critic have to become, "Don't shadow box. Don't box each other. Box the text. But remember that the text is the community. And the community is watching you"? I am not convinced that this is a more attractive invitation to strap on the gloves.

Notes

This essay was first published in *SAIL: Studies in American Indian Literatures* 21, no. 3 (2009): 58–64.

1. Epigraph. "The Mission" refers to the Mission of the Immaculate Conception (1849), later a reserve in the Fort William Anishinaabe First Nation territory.
2. See especially Craig S. Womack, Daniel Heath Justice, and Chris Teuton's *Reasoning Together: The Native Critics Collective* for nationalist re-formulations of intellectual sovereignty.

    Lots of invective to go around here. The nationalist perspective has been called (with an unavoidably patronizing implication) a rhetorical rather than logical argument (Krupat, *Red Matters* 8), "naïve at best" (Owens 52), and even "fascistic" (Carson 24). Predictably, the cosmopolitan approach to criticism has been damningly linked by nationalist critics to "Whiteness" (Justice 212) and exploitative careerism (Weaver, "Splitting" 12), and cosmopolitanists' rejection of tribal-centred criticism as being naive has been characterized as "misguided," "pernicious to Indigenous agency" (Weaver, "Splitting" 19), and an "exercise intrinsically linked to the intellectual, political, and economic colonization of the Americas" (Justice 213).
3. The general gist of the cosmopolitan argument is that nationalist critics have artificially "shor[ed] up the borders of Native American discourse" (Carson 11) and deposited the contemporary Aboriginal writer within these borders, and that a

hybrid interpretive practice celebrates the uncontainable freedom of ingress and egress that the contemporary Aboriginal writer already enjoys as an ethnic border crosser and postcolonial subversive. However, I would argue that the hybridity model of discourse is in some ways equally instrumental in its expectation that the writer will make the globalized world a more legible, and if "we" are lucky, more liveable place. Gerald Vizenor's charge that "the *indian* must sacrifice the uncertainties of individual experience" in favour of a simulation to be read as having "real presence" (39) can be read equally as an indictment of the celebratory mode of much cosmopolitan criticism, where, as Paul Rabinow defines "critical cosmopolitanism," one is "suspicious of sovereign powers, universal truths, overly relativized preciousness, local authenticity, moralisms high and low" (258).

4. For an extended discussion of "communitarian" or "communitism," see Jace Weaver's *That the People Might Live.*

8

Situating Self, Culture, and Purpose in Indigenous Inquiry

Margaret Kovach

I have returned home from the Federation of Saskatchewan Indian Nations' annual powwow. As the Elder gave a prayer and the carriers raised the pipe, I stood watching the grand entry. Then the dancers enter the stadium in regalia, viscerally knowing their role in maintaining culture. I thought about my research journey, why I located as a Nêhíyaw and Saulteaux researcher. Deep down, I wanted my research journey to help uphold culture, for it certainly gave occasion to come home, and this in itself made it purposeful. From my current vantage point, I am thankful for this opportunity, yet there were days during the research when my gratitude was tempered. Indigenous inquiry is holistically demanding, and knowing purpose in what can be emotionally challenging work matters when spirits are low.

Experience and research told me that Indigenous inquiry involves specific multi-layered preparations particular to each researcher. Preparatory work means clarifying the inquiry purpose, which invariably gets to motivations. Preparation assumes self-awareness and an ability to situate self within the research. It requires attention to culture in an active, grounded way. There is no formula (nor could there be) for this preparation. Nor do the details of this work need to be explicitly retold, for they are not preparations amenable to academic evaluation. Yet, they are often referenced by Indigenous researchers, and consistently appear in tribal methodologies (P. Steinhauer, "Thoughts on an Indigenous Research Methodology"; Bastien, *Blackfoot Ways of Knowing— Indigenous Science*; Struthers, "Conducting Sacred Research"). It is these preparations that count should an Elder ask: "Why did you do *that* research, and why did you do it in *that* way?" Focusing on self-location, purpose, and cultural grounding, this chapter offers insights into the prepatory aspect of Indigenous inquiries. Integrated into this chapter, Indigenous scholar Cam Willett shares his thoughts on purpose within Indigenous research.

Locating Ourselves

Within Indigenous research, self-location means cultural identification, and it manifests itself in various ways. Indigenous researchers will situate themselves as being of an Indigenous group, be it tribal, urban, or otherwise. They will share their experience with culture, and/or they will identify the Indigenous epistemology (or epistemologies) of their research. Often, they will culturally locate in all three ways. To resist pan-Indianism, identifying the specific tribal epistemology (e.g., Plains Cree) is a necessity. For many Indigenous people, this act is intuitive, launched immediately through the protocol of introductions. It shows respect to the ancestors and allows community to locate us. Situating self implies clarifying one's perspective on the world (Meyer, *Ho'oulu: Our Time of Becoming*; Hampton, "Memory Comes before Knowledge"). This is about being congruent with a knowledge system that tells us that we can only interpret the world from the place of our experience.

Self-locating in research is common among many qualitative approaches, though the extent that it is integrated varies. Within feminist methodologies, researchers are encouraged to locate themselves, to share personal aspects of their own experience with research participants. This is a means of building "reciprocity, rapport and trust between researcher and researched" (Liamputtong 13). Anti-oppressive inquiries integrate self-location to identify and then mitigate power differentials in research. Anti-oppressive researcher Susan Strega proposes that within the "system of domination and subordination," where the perspectives of the marginalized are not fully appreciated, those of us who have this experience need to share it, voice it, and give it space (*Research as Resistance* 224). For if we do not, who will? From this perspective, self-locating is a powerful tool for increasing awareness of power differentials in society and for taking action to further social justice.

Postmodern approaches use self-location to illustrate multiple truths. Through autoethnographies and autobiographical narrative inquiries, researchers reveal how the intuitive and experiential work constructs knowledge. In this research, what is "central in autobiographical narratives is 'I,' our accounts of the world, which are constructions, made up of language and meanings, and our own histories" (Kimpson 75). This form of reflexivity allows the researcher-self to participate as co-constructor of knowledge in specific and defined ways.

Regarding the social constructivist tradition, such as phenomenology, Max Van Manen makes this comment: "How can we pursue the question of what constitutes (phenomenological) knowledge in such a way that out of addressing this question may come an example of what the question in questioning seeks to clarify?" (46). Manen's point underscores the epistemic purpose of self-location, revealing the beliefs that shape our lives and what we take as "truth" and knowledge. It is not only the questions we ask and how we go about asking them, but who we are in the asking. Van Manen goes on to clarify his point by saying that "the question of knowledge always refers us back to our world, to who we are. . . . [I]t is what stands iconically behind the words, the speaking and the language" (46). This stands in strong alignment with holistic epistemologies that emphasize self-knowledge, though always in relation to other.

Specifically within Indigenous inquiry, Absolon and Willett ("Putting Ourselves Forward" 97–126) tell us that location is important. They remind us that self-location anchors knowledge within experiences, and these experiences greatly influence interpretations. Sharing stories and finding commonalities assists in making sense of a particular phenomenon, though it is never possible (nor wise) to generalize another's experience. "Location ensures that individual realities are not misrepresented as generalizable collectives. Our ancestors gave us membership into nations and traditions; location both remembers and 're-members' us to those things" (123). Self-locating affirms perspectives about the objectivity/subjectivity conundrum in research. Cree scholar Winona Stevenson tells us that Cree Elders will most often preface statements by stating, "I believe it to be true" (*Decolonizing Tribal Histories* 19). These words espouse relational validity, qualify knowledge as personal reflection from one's own life experience, and recognize other truths. Tribal epistemologies are a way of knowing that does not debate the subjectivity factor in knowledge production—subjectivity is a given. To embrace Indigenous methodologies is to accept subjective knowledge. This is difficult for sectors of the Western research community to accept, and it is where much of the contention about Indigenous research arises.

In addition to epistemological locating of oneself within Indigenous inquiry, critically reflective self-location gives opportunity to examine our research purpose and motive. It creates a mutuality with those who share their stories with us. Critically reflective self-location is a strategy to keep us aware of the power dynamic flowing back and forth between researcher and participant. It prompts awareness of the extractive tendency of research.

As a reflexivity method of research, situating the self authorizes expression of the relevant narrative from personal experiences, those reminiscences of life rooted in our earliest experience that shape our understanding of the world. Indigenous scholars, in my study, affirmed the necessity of reflexivity in research. Laara Fitznor shares why situating self matters: "I was raised in northern Manitoba not on the reserve . . . I was Cree with Scottish and German ancestry. For me, it's always important to acknowledge those, that part of who I am." Keeping one's location front and centre is a way that individuals can consciously assist from where their strength comes, and ensure that their integrity will not become compromised by the trials of academic research. Kathy Absolon advises that if you "went and found out what it was like and if you feel that you can't be yourself, you can't be who you are, then you can leave." In my research, writing my personal story was necessary. I was raised outside the culture, yet I was researching Indigenous methodologies. I could not proceed with this research without stating that I write from a specific place. Doing this work shows respect to culture, community, the research audience, and to myself. Being truthful does not culturally disenfranchise. Michael Hart points out that the diversity of personal stories does not preclude collective belonging: "The journey you and I would take wouldn't necessarily be the same, but they are all part of being Cree." Inclusiveness is a Cree value. Within Cree culture there is a myriad of life experiences among Cree peoples. Locating oneself honours the personal among the collective.

The methods of integrating self-location within Indigenous inquiry are many, and their manifestations different among researchers. Graham Smith situates himself as Maori through a prologue to his research. Through prologue, personal story offers authenticity, and is recognized as integral to knowledge constructions. The prologue is where the writing can shape-shift from an "objective account" to a holistic narrative, revealing how the self influences research choices and interpretations.

As a method for reflexivity during my research, I kept a reflective journal. This went beyond conventional field notes to a chronicling of my struggles, dreams, fears, hopes and reflections. This excerpt is from my research journal:

> I am taking Cree, it is my first class today. Walking in the First Nations University there are Indians everywhere with shiny hair flying as both instructors and students race down the hall to class. The instructor is Cree, Plains Cree, he was raised with the language, says he has been teaching here forever. This class is full of young students, not just Indigenous but of a variety of colours and cultural offerings. Though I am comforted as the Instructor reads off the class list—Tootoosis, Cyr—these are names I know. These are the Crees. The Instructor asks who is Cree, we put up our hands. He asks why we do not know our language. He points to me. I say adopted. He nods.

My reflective journal is a mix of research observations, reading analysis, field notes, annotations of family dinners, ceremony, vibrant dreams, road trip reflections, my on and off relationship with French friends, and so forth. It was that process of consistently self-locating that assisted me in saying, "I believe this to be true."

Reflexivity was intensive within my journey. This may not be true for all Indigenous researchers. There is flexibility, though it does need to be evident in some manner to show contextualized knowing. It supposes self-knowledge. A Cree *kokum* shares a memory of her personal history and the fascination, which the fabled attractions of modern life—such as lipstick or mail order catalogues—held for her (Ahenakew and Wolfart 24). Such insights not only tell others of oneself, they tell self.

Purpose

Not long ago, I attended a workshop led by a non-Indigenous scholar who was presenting research on the socioeconomic conditions of Indigenous people. I felt that the research was fascinating and was curious as to the researcher's motivation. During the time allotted for questions, I asked him about his purpose for doing this research. What compelled him? To my mind, it was a fairly straightforward question about the motivations that provoked his study, yet he seemed a bit unsure of what I was asking. Afterward, I thought perhaps I was not clear about what I meant by purpose or maybe this just was not a common question. I was perplexed because by this time I had spent considerable energy focusing on Indigenous research approaches, and many Indigenous scholars were consistently saying that knowing one's own purpose and motivation for research was fundamental. This seemed consistent with Western research approaches, and yet my question seemed somehow out of place to that workshop leader. However, I knew instinctively that purpose—Indigenous-style—and research curiosity were deeply linked.

Research questions anchor and direct research. There is much attention to the formulation of research questions within academic research, for they can be difficult to craft. The research question ought to be specific enough to render focused findings and at the same time allow for discovery. The research question can emerge from a personal curiosity or be tailored to a specific need as identified by the public or private sector. It can be developed solely by an individual researcher, a research team, or in collaboration with a community or a stakeholder (such as a research advisory committee). Regardless of the origin of the research question, it ought to respond to a need. Furthermore, the researcher should be able to show that there is a gap in the knowledge that the proposed research can assist in filling. Often, in research textbooks, the section on developing research questions is situated by the purpose statement.

In academic research design, there is an expectation that the researcher will identify through a purpose statement the reason behind conducting the research. Here the research indicates that the researcher's curiosity and the purpose statement help clarify the research question and plan. Within Indigenous methodologies, crafting a research question remains a necessity, though it may surface more organically. However, the purpose statement is more elasticized, asking for greater commentary on personal motivation.

In his paper entitled "Memory Comes before Knowledge: Research May Improve if Researchers Remember the Motives" (1995), Eber Hampton describes the relationship between memory and research. He advises researchers to go back in time to unfold the sacred medicine bundle that holds memories and consider how memory shapes personal truth. This matters because researchers need to know their personal motives for undertaking their research, and they are usually found in story. Indigenous research frameworks ask for clarity of both the academic and personal purpose, and it is the purpose statement within Indigenous research that asks: What is your purpose for this research? How is your motivation found in your story? Why and how does this research give back to community?

In Plains Cree knowledge, value is placed on experiential knowledge. Inherent within this perspective is the value of personal responsibility in maintaining good relationships. One maintains good research relationships by identifying one's purpose and motivations behind the actions. It is about being honest. Among the scholars I interviewed, there was a consistent belief that research should be collectively relevant. In their own research, the personal meaning was bound with community relevancy. Purposeful research was inseparable from the value in giving back, that what we do has to assist. Kathy Absolon expresses a decolonizing purpose of her research found in community relations: "One of our core missions in decolonizing in our life is to figure out who are we, and in order to do that you are not going to find that out in a university, in the absence of your peers and your culture." In picking her research topic, Jeannine Carriere struggled to find a topic. After considering several options, then reconsidering, she found her research purpose (and subsequent question) in exploring the lives of Indigenous adoptees. A friend helped Jeannine focus her inquiry into the experience of Aboriginal adoptees, saying to her, "That is who you are, that is your story and that is what you should be contributing." Michael Hart articulates the connection between purpose and contemporary research. He says, "I am doing this because we can't all live in teepees forever . . . our realities have changed, and they are going to continue to change." These scholars demonstrate the strong connections between self, community, memory, reciprocity, and research. Deciding upon a research direction after having examined one's purpose makes its utility transparent and the research strong from day one.

Cultural Grounding

What does cultural grounding mean within an Indigenous research framework? For Indigenous research, cultural grounding is best defined within the context of a person's life and relationship with culture. As with non-Indigenous researchers, its significance may depend upon their life context and how they engage with culture. This commentary defines cultural grounding as the way that culture nourishes the researcher's spirit during the inquiry, and how it nourishes the research itself. There are levels of cultural involvement within research. Some customs are shared openly, others privately. This needs to be respected. Given this caveat, Indigenous research frameworks reference cultural grounding specifically or generally, and permeate the research in a manner consistent with the researcher's relationship with his or her culture.

Blackfoot scholar Betty Bastien (*Blackfoot Ways of Knowing—Indigenous Science*) provides an example of cultural grounding in her research. Her study is an inquiry into the infusion of Niitsitapi (Blackfoot) ways of knowing into Bachelor of Social Work curricula for the Niitsitapi community. It was couched within a pre-existing relationship with community and utilized methodology congruent with a Blackfoot worldview. She has a *"Kaahasinnon*—Grandfather for the Sacred Horn Society" (88) guide her research. The site of gaining knowledge from the grandmothers and grandfathers was a convocation that integrated cultural protocols, gift offerings, food, ceremony, and prayer. This cultural guidance assisted her in determining the parameters around sharing Niitsitapi knowledges in the research. "The guidance and advice shared by the grandparents about common knowledge of the *Niitsitapi* I share here is meant to be shared with the uninitiated" (95). By involving Elders, Bastien was offering cultural grounding for the research itself.

Researchers incorporate ceremonial practices to show respect and give protection to the knowledge shared. A Cree protocol is to offer tobacco to teachers. Showing respect is a consistent value among most tribal groups; the ritual for doing so is not. Thus, it becomes necessary to locate a specific tribal ontology. Cultural grounding of the research may involve ceremony, though the form of ceremony will depend upon the tribal epistemology. These are significant considerations.

Encompassing culture is part of the notion of researcher-in-relation. Betty Bastien's personal preparations for research involved visiting sacred sites and participating in ceremony. Laara Fitznor spoke of the personal sustenance that she gained from culture. There was a time during her doctoral research when she was at a loss as to how to proceed—her computer crashed with all her research on it. "I smudged my papers, I smudged my computer and I said, 'you know Creator I need help, help to get me onto the next stage.' All of a sudden I had this burst of energy and I just wrote." She called upon spirit to see her through. My own experience led me home. I had received dream knowledge that helped me to understand that my research necessitated a return. In Saskatchewan, I was able to connect culturally in a way unavailable to me in British Columbia. That said, grounding is not solely found in our ancestral territory. It can also be found in the larger Indigenous community. Returning to British Columbia, I participated in a Coast Salish ceremony on the morning of my doctoral defence. I left knowing that the ancestors stood with me.

The choices are many; there is no dogma. For this is about spirit and connecting with the ancestors. The extent to which the researcher chooses to share these efforts may be great or minimal. It does not matter that it is shared with all as there need be no thick descriptions here. What matters is that there is room within Indigenous research to acknowledge the meaningful role of cultures within our inquiries.

A Conversation with Cam Willett

Cam Willett reflects upon how personal history informs purpose by sharing the motivations behind his decision to enter into doctoral studies and research. Cam Willett is Cree from Little Pine First Nation in Saskatchewan. He received his doctoral degree from the Ontario Institute for Studies in Education, University of Toronto, and has been a post-secondary educator for many years. I offered Cam tobacco for his teachings and started by asking Cam some general questions about his background. First I asked Cam why he went back for a doctoral degree. This is his response:

Maggie: Cam, what precipitated you going back to get your doctorate?

Cam: Is it about community for me? I guess, but it seems more personal. I was thinking about that as you were talking and remembering. I think about my elementary education and my secondary education, which were fine until Grade 12. I dropped out of school because of a lot of life pressures. I was working full-time and had an hour-and-a-half bus ride to school and back. One day, these three teachers ambushed me in the hallway—going from one to the next to the next—saying things about me, "You sleep in my class, you're really lazy." I stood up and said, "Well, fine, I quit," or whatever, walked down the hallway. The vice-principal was walking down the hallway, and I say to him, "I quit right now." He said, "Well, you should think about it." And I said, "No." I got on the phone and I called my dad. He came and drove an hour to the school, and we sat down with the vice-principal. He said I should think about this and that, but I couldn't be convinced. That was it for me. I went to Saskatoon and started delivering pizza and worked for a while, then went back to school.

I think the reason I am talking about this is because at that time I was thinking to myself, "Gee, am I really capable of graduating from Grade 12? Can I do this?" I was really questioning my intellectual ability and whatever. I used to think, "Yeah, I could," because I remembered my experiences from before where I did pretty well at school. I did great and my confidence was restored, and so I went into university. It was just sort of the logical thing. What else was I going to do?

So why did I start my Ph.D. program? Because it's related to all that. I was coming out of my master's program and the opportunity was there. I knew it wouldn't always be there, and I felt I should just do it. At this point, I was starting to wonder what the heck I am doing this for. How will this benefit my community? How does this benefit me, even? I think my major reason for continuing is to finish what I have started. You don't want to just bail. I know I can do this and that's my motivation. As a young person, thinking back about my experience in high school, a lot of that was pure racism. Today, I know that, and at the time I was trying to figure it out. Has it made me happier to know that racism is so powerful in this province, in this country today? I don't know. I find now that I can't read the newspaper. I just sort of skim through it. My mind deconstructs everything very quickly and it's frustrating. I deconstruct everything, my mind is less—I wouldn't say it's totally decolonized—but it's certainly a lot less colonized than it was. I don't know. What does that do? I guess there is a benefit in teaching for the students that are there. It's not just me instructing them to teach the same old colonial curriculum. I don't want my students to go off into Black Lake and teach colonial curriculum. That's not what I am teaching them, I want them to be critical.

When I was taking a course in a master's program, I was talking to my professor during a break, and we were talking about how far I would go in my program. Would I become a faculty member or would I get a Ph.D.? Of course, when you are a student you have the privilege of being radical.

You can go into a classroom and say, "I defy school. I think we should tear down all the universities because it's all bullshit." But then he pointed out to me, "well, you know, if you don't get the Ph.D., will people ever listen to you? Will Western-minded people ever value what you have to say?" That's the thing. It's these two worlds that we are living in. The one world you are honoured with the eagle feather and the other world you are honoured with the doctoral degree. Maybe that's one of the big reasons why I wanted to finish the Ph.D. I guess finishing is partly for validation, though it's not really that important to me. But if that's what it takes for people to listen to you, well then . . .

You know, we were saying something about feeling alone and that was a pivotal point in my research. The first year you're learning all this Western stuff, reading all these books that don't have anything Aboriginal, and you're the only Aboriginal person in these classes with no Aboriginal faulty. You start to feel really alone. I think when you do any ceremony, you do reach some of these portals, and you do realize that you're not alone. People are always talking about the language disappearing, cultures disappearing. I think that's a load of bull, because if you put your tobacco down and you go to ceremonies, I believe that all transcends time and space. You can't be lost or killed because all you have to is sweat and ask, and the songs will come back to you. That's the power of them. Our knowledge and legacy can never be erased. We are very strong and that makes my proud. The legacy of our people is this land.

Cam alerted me to several significant qualities of Indigenous research during our conversation. He affirmed Hampton's advice that knowing purpose is wise in any endeavour, and that we find purpose within our personal narrative. When Cam spoke of his high school experience, I was taken back to memories of elementary school and how the residue from it left me questioning my abilities. What were my motivations for returning to school? Would I have pursued doctoral studies if I did not feel that I had something left to prove to the educational system? And when does that stop? The conversation got me thinking.

We talked about story, purpose, self, and the relevance of being holistically true to one's worldview. Was it okay to apply a worldview (e.g., feminist, Indigenous) to our research but not practise it in our lives? It was not really a question about the merits of purity or applying an impossible orthodoxy to one's life. Rather, Cam's point was that epistemology ought to be congruent with life choices in general, not just in research. I was reminded of the holism inherent in Indigenous epistemologies and thought of how we teach research methodology classes in Western universities. We assume that people can select methodologies solely in relation to a research curiosity without a reflection of the self. No wonder it can be a "head trip."

Cam spoke about the traditional knowledges that value dreams, the ancestors, and the timelessness of ceremonies, and I know that regardless of whether they were identified in our methodologies, they were guiding our search for knowledge. I left the conversation with Cam, knowing that Indigenous research frameworks require a purpose statement about one's own self-location and worldview, and that this meant honouring the *kôkums* and *mosôms* by remembering them. Right off the bat, this was no small order. Knowing why we are carrying out research—our motive—has the potential to take us to places that involve both the head and heart. We need to know our own research story to be accountable to self and community.

Note

This essay was first published as "Creating Indigenous Research Frameworks," in *Indigenous Methodologies: Characteristics, Conversations, and Contexts*, ed. Margaret Kovach (U of Toronto P, 2010).

9

"The lake is the people and life that come to it": Location as Critical Practice

Allison Hargreaves

Located at the north end of Kelowna's downtown, Knox Mountain is crisscrossed with hiking paths that converge at various lookout points, and again at the top. It's a popular destination for trail runners, mountain bikers, and casual hikers alike—and, on this summer evening, a colleague and I join the legions of after-work walkers all looking to complement a brisk bit of cardio with the reward of stunning Okanagan Valley vistas. At the top, we lean wearily on a guardrail (we've hiked one of the more athletic routes) and take in the view. The city of Kelowna is spread at our feet and Lake Okanagan stretches in either direction. Several of Kelowna's landmark buildings, beachfronts, and orchards can easily be seen from this vantage point. We're high enough now, too, to see the whole of the Tolko Industries' hulking lumber mill at the lake's edge below us, and how the highway cuts through the city and arches over the William Bennett bridge before descending into Westbank First Nation on the opposite shore. It's the lake itself, however, that draws my eye today. Standing here, waiting to catch my breath, I recall Secwepemc-Syilx writer Gerry William's words from *The Woman in the Trees*: "The lake stretches some eighty miles, north to south. It bends in the middle, like someone kicked it in the stomach, folding it over. . . . The lake is the people and life that come to it. The Syilx knew the lake when it stretched for one hundred and twenty miles north to south, and when its shores lay three hundred feet above where it now resides" (69). To see the valley and lake in this way is to glimpse something before and beyond "the cities that now dot the landscape" (69): this is the traditional and unceded territory of the Syilx, the Okanagan Nation. It is a territory of about

69,000 square kilometres in BC's southern interior, extending as far north as the Rocky Mountains and as far south as Wilbur, Washington. The Syilx have been here for thousands of years; I have lived and worked here for five. "So where are you from, anyway?" my colleague and hiking companion asks. As she turns from the lake to face me, a few different answers come to mind.

I grew up in a small town just south of Edmonton, Alberta, in Treaty 6 territory. My parents' families are mostly of working-class English and Irish background, and have lived in Western Canada for only a couple of generations. The stories of my recent ancestors' arrivals in Canada are, from what I understand, shaped by hardship and poverty—although my own upbringing was firmly middle-class. My childhood town of Beaumont, historically a French farming community known by its hilltop St. Vital Parish Church, was settled following the arrival of Catholic missionaries, the Half-Breed Scrip Commission, and Treaty 6 negotiators to the Fort Edmonton area, Cree territory, in the late nineteenth century. And, although these particular arrivals resulted in the expropriation of Cree land and in subsequent waves of displacement so recent that my hometown itself wouldn't celebrate its centennial until I was a teenager, they were arrivals and dislocations I grasped, nonetheless, only in vague, romanticized isolation from their actual colonial purpose. Meanwhile, the story of my town's settlement was but one of many social practices by which I came to know myself as unquestioningly entitled to the land I lived on as well as the resources it provided. I didn't think of myself as a treaty person with inherited responsibilities. I didn't have a *relational* way of understanding my community's public memory of place. I knew these things only by their seeming absence, as a kind of unnamed negative space contouring every daily assertion of belonging that I learned to make. These would be among my earliest lessons in the politics of location, but I wouldn't understand that until much later—and with the benefit of many other teachings. As it happens, many of these teachings would come to me through literature.

It was as a reader that I first understood my perspective as socially and historically constituted. Literature unfolded other worlds for me, worlds both like and unlike my own, which I eagerly inhabited at first solely for the sake of having somewhere else to *go*. But while reading started as a kind of refuge from a sometimes difficult home life, it soon became much more: through literature I glimpsed the situated and contingent nature of my own knowledge and experience. Perspective, it seemed, was a product of where one stood—and this meant that my own life could be known and lived differently. Imaginatively inhabiting other places and perspectives thus became a daily exercise in hope, but with this came a new and unsettling realization: if my own story could be different, so, too, could my previously unquestioned narratives of belonging and place. "Stories take place," Creek-Cherokee critic Craig Womack reminds us (*Art as* 44), and through literature I saw that there could be *other stories* attached to the places I knew. Seeking these stories out, and locating myself in relation to them over time, I gradually began to understand the place-based responsibilities I inherit as a guest in the territories where I live. Anishinaabe scholar Leanne Simpson theorizes these responsibilities in terms of Indigenous diplomatic traditions, wherein all individuals are politically accountable to their ancestors as well as the "Peoples whose homelands [they are] visiting" ("Politics" 5). As a non-Indigenous teacher and critic of Indigenous litera-tures, I now think of myself as a perpetual visitor—both to the literatures I teach, and to the homelands in which I teach them. One way I try to fulfill my responsibilities as a visitor is by observing the Indigenous methodological precept of "locating the self": for example, I begin each course I teach with an acknowledgement of where I'm from and what my purpose is, how I moved from Treaty 6 to Syilx territory, and how literature informed that journey.

The essays collected in this section consider the difficult question of "loca-tion," and how location informs literary critical practice where Indigenous-authored texts are concerned. Fundamental to these considerations are issues of place and position—and of the methods by which we make knowledge about that relationship. Many of the essays show how these methods have emerged from the literature itself. On the topic of teaching Indigenous literature in the 1970s and 1980s, for instance, Cree-Métis critic Emma LaRocque recalls that "the barely emerging handful of Native scholars had not yet developed meth-odological tools or languages by which to articulate what we, in praxis, were modelling" (58)—namely, that there is "an Aboriginal ground to Aboriginal liter-ature" (63). LaRocque advocates locating these literatures in their "cultural and epistemic home/lands" (63), and in this way understands the critic as carrying political responsibilities when he or she enters into this literary-critical terrain. These responsibilities entail grounding one's critical practice in the territories and communities that have lived stakes in the material under discussion. To foreground such concerns as important to Indigenous literary-critical practice isn't meant to "shoehorn" individual authors into "political models of agency or resistance for which they may in fact have little interest or sympathy," as Rob Appleford (92) suggests in his response to Sam McKegney's "Strategies for Ethical Engagement." Rather, it's to ask—as all of these critics have—what the responsibilities of the critic ought to be, and to take methodological cues from the literature itself in offering a response to this question.

Different responsibilities are involved for Indigenous and non-Indigenous critics. Several of the essays explore the politics of literary criticism in the context of colonialism, where analyses by "cultural outsiders" (Hoy 45) have sometimes imposed either "absolute, irreducible distance or . . . presumptuous familiarity" (44). Part of a broader history of "violence perpetrated against Indigenous texts by decades of literary criticism dominated by non-Native critics" (McKegney 79), these seemingly opposing tendencies toward either detachment or familiarity have long characterized political and intellectual debates on the question of locating the self. Troublingly, both critical stances play host to a range of colonial pitfalls. Self-conscious refrains of guilt, retreat, or disengagement may *look like* a departure from hegemonic modes of Eurocentric criticism, but in fact seek—through the fantasy of irreducible distance—a release from the "extraordinary mandate to *know*" and engage with Indigenous critical protocols (LaRocque 62). Meanwhile, confidence in one's rightful adoption of these protocols may be just as damaging—"obliterating difference and claiming connection" in order to legitimize one's position in the field (Hoy 42). Too often, appropriative rehearsals take the place of more genuine engagements involved in working for social transformation from where one stands.

In a growing body of work that has increasingly foregrounded questions of position and location in Indigenous research methods, critics are now being asked to understand "location" not only as a gesture by which we acknowledge social position relative to our research—but, rather, as a relational process grounded in Indigenous ontologies. As Kathy Absolon and Cam Willett remind us, "location is more than simply saying you are of Cree or Anishinaabe or British ancestry; from Toronto or Alberta or Canada; location is about relationship to land, language, spiritual, cosmological, political, economical, environmental, and social elements in one's life" (98). It is, Margaret Kovach says, a way of "clarifying [your] perspective on the world" by telling the story of who you are, and how you came to do the work that you do (96). From my perspective as a non-Indigenous critic, location is about trying to understand myself as a guest with a specific relation to treaty history, to historic relations of diplomacy, and to conceptions of territory and nation that precede my ancestors' arrival here. Location is the critic's practice of "narrat[ing] specific landscapes wherever he or she might 'land'" (Womack, *Art as* 44).

II

IMAGINING BEYOND IMAGES AND MYTHS

10

Introduction:
Imagining beyond
Images and Myths

Linda M. Morra

As the title of this section suggests, imagining beyond images and myths has been a preoccupation of both Indigenous literary writing and criticism for more than a century. In "Popular Images of Nativeness," for example, Cree-Métis poet Marilyn Dumont examines the ideological straightjackets by which the Indigenous had been held in the past, sometimes being identified as "*too Indian*" or "*not Indian enough*" (48). Misrepresentation, she astutely observes, is a form of domination. Elsewhere, in her poem "Circle the Wagons," she demonstrates how the process of colonization may be reinvoked when images are not subjected to careful critique: pandering to expectation will generate stereotypes, she notes, but addressing them directly also risks their reinscription.

1. E. Pauline Johnson

Critiquing those stereotypes, however, has been a necessary project in Indigenous studies. One of the first to take on this task was turn-of-the-twentieth-century Kanien'kehá:ka poet and performer E. Pauline Johnson (1861–1913). In her own literary endeavours, she would have encountered a socio-political environment in Canada that was highly charged by imperial attitudes and assumptions about what it meant to be an Indigenous person—and, more challenging yet, what it meant to be an Indigenous woman. Born to a Kanien'kehá:ka father and British mother on the Six Nations Reserve near Brantford, Ontario, she carefully negotiated her stage presence and public identity to protest against ideas of nationhood then being promulgated. That form of protest came in various forms, most tangibly in the essay she wrote and published in 1892 titled "A Strong Race Opinion: On the Indian Girl in Modern Fiction." Perhaps the earliest critical piece in Indigenous Studies, the essay examines depictions of Indigenous women in literature of the period, and, as such, is significant for revealing both the ideological underpinnings of such images and the material differences in the lives of Indigenous women in the period.

More specifically, Johnson makes several key points in this essay related to how Indigenous women had been affected by such literary depictions that had no real basis in specific knowledges about Indigenous ceremonies and customs. She argues that this lack of cultural specificity detracts from Indigenous women and limits them as essentialized subjects, as it also undermines the very nation under question. She observes that, conversely, there were a number of practices or characteristics that North American writers attributed to Indigenous women—that they were prone to committing suicide, that they were invariably daughters of Chiefs—which had no real basis in their respective cultures. Finally, she took issue with how Indigenous female characters often served to facilitate the romance of a white male hero and his white female companion, thus endorsing notions of "correct" partnerships and, more largely, a national community from which Indigenous women were simultaneously excluded. Johnson sees such writing as furthering the real indignities suffered by Indigenous nations and calls upon writers to be more just toward, and more knowledgeable about, Indigenous nations and specifically Indigenous women in their literary efforts.

2. Drew Hayden Taylor

That Drew Hayden Taylor would still be writing about such indignities over a century later suggests the tenacity of the ideas that Johnson was critiquing. As Taylor observes in "Indian Love Call," Western stories have specifically had repercussions for and skewed perceptions about Indigenous sexuality. Therein, he humorously explores how stereotypes about male and female Indigenous sexuality continue to be generated by Western literature. If, as he argues, "literature is the DNA that tells the truth about the culture that bore it" (129), then Western literature reveals its own preoccupations with Manifest Destiny, even as it is also characterized by fears about sexual contamination and violation by an Indigenous presence. The simultaneous fascination with and yet complete misapprehension about Indigenous sexuality is observable in the "uncountable number of Western/historical romance novels that populate mainstream bookstores, drugstores, airports and used-book emporiums" (134). But the images that circulate within these novels are far removed from the realities of Indigenous life and are clearly written for white patrons; indeed, he notes, they are a sharp contrast from the "massive upheaval, the perpetuation of a centuries-long genocide" (115). In such stories, the Indigenous male protagonist is cast in dimensions more familiar to a Western audience: he is thus often characterized as a "half-breed" whose appearance bears resemblance to white subjects. The female character is depicted as vying for freedom from an unhappy or abusive marriage—an irony, Drew notes, when in fact more Native women have married white husbands rather than the other way around. Such stories, he concludes, do not do justice to Indigenous realities, but rather impede proper cross-cultural understanding and reinscribe the colonization process.

3. Daniel Francis

Settler scholar Daniel Francis first published *The Imaginary Indian* in 1992, exactly one hundred years after Johnson's book and a few years before Taylor's. His work was integral to identifying the disparity between images in circulation in popular discourse about Indigenous peoples, that is, between the "Imaginary Indian" and Indigenous persons themselves. His book explores the various manifestations of the "Imaginary Indian" as mediated by White desire, and then overturns these fantasies, which have been manufactured by popular Canadian culture since at least 1850. Such fantasies served to strengthen a dominant White ideological agenda by which "Europeans also projected all the misgivings they had about the shortcomings of their own civilization" (144). The "Other" against which non-Indigenous people defined themselves, the Imaginary Indian was vital to the process of self-identification for Euro-Canadians and thus impeded any real understanding of Indigenous nations. These images were manufactured through historical cultural figures, such as Grey Owl and Buffalo Long Lance, the circulation of media images, and reconfiguration of historical events; from the Noble Savage to the Indian Princess, these images ultimately facilitated non-Indigenous interests.

Central to this process was the construction of the Canadian Pacific Railway (CPR) between 1881 and 1885, after which time Euro-Canadians began to commodify the "Indian image," specifically as postcards of Plain Indians. "Indian culture," in the form of shows, landmarks, and other cultural artifacts, became a means by which to attract tourists, even as Indigenous persons were simultaneously urged to assimilate into a dominant Western culture. On the one hand, such commodification supported non-Indigenous assumptions and stereotypes about Indigenous persons. The CPR thus appropriated images of "Indians" ostensibly to "honour" Natives, but ultimately as a means of wielding control. On the other hand, Euro-Canadian socio-political culture also indulged in an apparent nostalgia for Indigenous nations that it actively sought to repress and eradicate through both policy and cultural activity.

4. Gerald Vizenor

Considered a cosmopolitanist in the field of Indigenous studies by critics such as Rob Appleford, Gerald Vizenor (Anishinaabe) is recognized for playing a fundamental role in Indigenous literary inquiry, especially for the means by which he critiqued broadly (rather than as part of one nation state) the prevailing images of "Indianness." Vizenor's *Manifest Manners* (1994), a brief selection of which is included in this anthology, appeared two years after Francis' *The Imaginary Indian*. Like Francis, he is concerned with how Indigenous stories and voices are appropriated by non-Indigenous writers. This book is especially important in that it furnishes several key terms that have since become crucial to the field of Indigenous literary inquiry. The title itself gestures toward the colonial implications and legacies of Manifest Destiny that negatively impacted Indigenous nations. If Manifest Destiny meant that American peoples were preordained to take over the West and were identified as such by their own special set of virtues, Indigenous nations were clearly excluded from this belief. The legacies of Manifest Destiny include a set of assumptions, or what Vizenor calls "manifest manners" (156), that generated "narratives of dominance" by which an imperial presence attempted to govern Indigenous peoples and which embodied that presence's racism, supremacy, and hegemony. He spends the first section of *Manifest Manners*, therefore, identifying the various "simulations" of "Indians"—inventions of a dominant society—that have worked to undo any meaningful understanding of the specific nature of its nations, and by which Indigenous peoples have repeatedly been challenged (155). He argues that nostalgia and "the melancholia of dominance" become, for example, "common sources of simulations in manifest manners" where the "real" has been altered and supplanted by stereotypical assumptions.

    Manifest Manners also offers several other key ideas and terms to restore Indigenous agency—ideas that more contemporary critics continue to call upon in the field of Indigenous Studies. He coins the term "postindian"—that is, the Indigenous person who creates stories that are informed by "a new sense of survivance" (157). He deploys "survivance," an elision of "survival" and "resistance," as the active process by which Indigenous nations must respond to forms of dominance. "Simulators of manifest manners" are thus positioned against those who are "warriors of postindian survivance," that is, those who generate "postindian simulations" that are integral to the process of survivance.

He sees the primary tasks of the postindian warriors as writing new stories, countering manifest manners, and opposing "simulations of dominance" (157). Finally, he espouses "Trickster Hermeneutics," an Indigenous understanding of trickster stories, as central to survivance. Vizenor thus does crucial work in asserting the strategic uses of postindian narratives and in reimagining the field of Indigenous critical inquiry.

5. James Youngblood Henderson

James Youngblood Henderson (Chickasaw) does essential work in his essay "Postcolonial Ghost Dancing," wherein he tracks how such a process of colonization has been enacted globally, and the forms of dissemination that have entrenched such ideological systems. A law professor invested in restoring Indigenous cultures, institutions, and rights through the process of litigation, Henderson argues that the process of colonization is the result of Eurocentrism, or what he refers to as the "cognitive legacy of colonization" (170). That legacy offers a "differentiated consciousness" that assumes different guises in order to justify its exploitation of Indigenous peoples and informs the socio-political institutional frameworks that continue to oppress Indigenous peoples. This consciousness also works on the assumption that Aboriginal heritage is inferior, so Henderson argues for the need of critiquing the assumptions that situate these values as "universal." One such assumption is that there is a world with a single centre from which "civilizing" ideas and information emanate; this form of "epistemological diffusionism" generates a dualism that characterizes Europe as progressive and inventive, and peripheral cultures as "ahistorical, stagnant, and unchanging," and in need of "civilizing." In fact, Henderson notes, classic diffusionism posits that that emptiness characterizes the non-European world and justifies the subsequent displacement of Indigenous peoples by adopting a language that is regarded as neutral, objective, and impartial. That language, however, is also key to the racist strategies that are then exercised to maintain colonial power over Indigenous peoples. Calling upon Albert Memmi, he suggests the following practices are enacted: "Stressing real or imaginary differences between the racist and the victim; assigning values to these differences, to the advantage of the racist and the detriment of the victim; trying to make these values absolutes by generalizing from them and claiming that they are final; using these values to justify any present or possible aggression or privileges" (178). Eurocentric systems of knowledge and law, he argues, generated a grammar by which Indigenous peoples were positioned as outside civilized discourse and frameworks of understanding. That grammar assigns negative values to Indigenous differences and does so through ideology rather than through knowledge or empirical evidence. Such ideology informed the two prominent images about the Indigenous in circulation: that they were either "wild, promiscuous, propertyless, and lawless," or that they were noble and "lived with natural law without government, husbandry, and much else" (181). In making these assumptions and the corresponding values absolute, a dominant group renders a victim an object or thing that is easily expelled from human community. Should these assumptions be challenged, colonial dominators alter their logic in order to remain coherent and secure their domination. This tendency to shift and adopt different guises is how Henderson comes to conclude that colonialism is the "anti-trickster" or the "imitator of the Imitator, its twin" (184).

6. Margery Fee

It is settler scholar Margery Fee, however, who tracks the evolution of literary Indigenous studies in the latter half of the twentieth-century, and offers a detailed analysis of how certain discourses that have evolved around the trickster figure have both facilitated and impeded the process of Indigenous empowerment. The Committee to Re-establish the Trickster (CRET) established in 1986, was a means of securing greater attention for the work of Indigenous artists and opening up the space and field for such artists. Subsequent public debates and conversations in the 1990s addressed such issues as those related to the appropriation of voice, such that mainstream writers were characterized as exploiting minority communities, from which the former took their material. In particular, writer Neil Bissoondath publicly endorsed an April 1992 Writers Guild of Canada news release asserting that restricted literary freedom was tantamount to censorship; Lenore Keeshig-Tobias countered such attitudes by publishing "Stop Stealing Native Stories" in the *Globe and Mail*. Therein, she argued that writing fiction was a way of not "getting it right"—of bypassing the ethical responsibility of acquiring knowledge and learning about Indigenous people. A non-consultative process involved in the circulation of Indigenous images meant that, even as Indigenous persons were using figures such as the trickster to locate autonomy and self-expression, non-Indigenous persons were using such stories and images without public permission. Whereas non-Indigenous writers were arguing for the right to "liberal imagination" to justify such acts—what Fee refers to as a form of "democratic racism"—Indigenous persons were insisting upon their right to express their own cultures and to vocalize their own sets of concerns and interests, especially in light of, for example, the explosive White Paper of 1969. A non-Indigenous cry for freedom, Fee observes, was thus, in fact, "an attempt to stifle dissent" or to bypass the fact that such appropriation is another means by which "to cover up the theft of the land" (197). Critics who examine English-Canadian representations of Indigenous persons thus often conclude that these representations "are stereotypical and almost always serve the purposes of the mainstream rather than revealing or attempting to change misconceptions about Indigenous persons" (*Troubling Tricksters* 66).

The trickster, as it was being popularized in the period by non-Indigenous writers, was not only used to obscure the process of colonization, but was also over-determined in the process. Instead, Fee argues, to define this period of the trick-ster is "to consider the trickster not as an icon ... but as part of a historical process of rearranging social relations, a true transformation" (*Troubling Tricksters* 71). Conversely, that figure was used by Indigenous writers to facilitate self-empowerment, and explains why they responded to the appropriation debate so vocally: at the moment that they turned to this figure in the process of locat-ing cultural autonomy, non-Indigenous writers also did so, which was seen as yet another means by which to undermine this process.

7. Jo-Ann Episkenew

It is, however, the power of Indigenous storytelling, Jo-Ann Episkenew argues in "Myth, Policy, and Health," that challenges these master narratives and the "colonial myths" of the new Canadian nation-state, "which valorizes the set-tlers but which sometimes misrepresents and more often excludes Indigenous peoples" (202). The provision of a counter-story that responds to these myths is a necessary form of resistance and of healing—and not only the provision, but also the circulation and apprehension of these stories. Even as anthropol-ogists collected Indigenous creation myths, they did not properly examine or understand them; indeed, many of these stories were largely excluded from anthropological studies. As Episkenew observes, this is also the result of the stories' orality, which was not perceived as "literacy" from the point of view of European privilege; renewing oral storytelling and analyzing the latter's importance will act as a significant counterbalance to the erasure engendered by anthropological studies.

She then critiques the notion of "historical progress," yet another means of protecting white privilege and disempowering Indigenous communities. "Progress" locates Indigenous forms of culture in a purportedly unrecoverable past, and allows for a historical revisionism that elides governmental respons-ibility in relation to the colonizing process and the "psychological terrorism" (205) inflicted on Indigenous communities. Episkenew advances the import-ance of stories in challenging assumptions of progress; as one example, she cites Chief Phil Fontaine's 1990 disclosure of sexual abuse at a residential school.[1] His story effectively drew together and empowered Indigenous communities, as it also countered the colonial myth that posited the "benevolence" of Canadian government's policies and practices. Her essay significantly concludes this section by reminding us that stories, especially personal ones, are essential to healing and to countering colonial narratives.

Note

1. Phil Fontaine, "Interview with Barbara Frum," *The Journal* (CBC), 30 October 1990.

11

A Strong Race Opinion:
On the Indian Girl in Modern Fiction

E. Pauline Johnson

Every race in the world enjoys its own peculiar characteristics, but it scarcely follows that every individual of a nation must possess these prescribed singularities, or otherwise forfeit in the eyes of the world their nationality. Individual personality is one of the most charming things to be met with, either in a flesh and blood existence, or upon the pages of fiction, and it matters little to what race an author's heroine belongs, if he makes her character distinct, unique and natural.

The American book heroine of today is vari-coloured as to personality and action. The author does not consider it necessary to the development of her character, and the plot of the story to insist upon her having American-coloured eyes, an American carriage, an American voice, American motives, and an American mode of dying; he allows her to evolve an individuality ungoverned by nationalisms—but the outcome of impulse and nature and a general womanishness.

Not so the Indian girl in modern fiction, the author permits her character no such spontaneity, she must not be one of womankind at large, neither must she have an originality, a singularity that is not definitely "Indian." I quote "Indian" as there seems to be an impression amongst authors that such a thing as tribal distinction does not exist among the North American aborigines.

Tribal Distinctions

The term "Indian" signifies about as much as the term "European," but I cannot recall ever having read a story where the heroine was described as "a European." The Indian girl we meet in cold type, however, is rarely distressed by having to belong to any tribe, or to reflect any tribal characteristics. She is merely a wholesome sort of mixture of any band existing between the Mic Macs of Gaspé and the Kwaw-Kewlths of British Columbia, yet strange to say, that notwithstanding the numerous tribes, with their aggregate numbers reaching more than 122,000 souls in Canada alone, our Canadian authors can cull from this huge revenue of character, but one Indian girl, and stranger still that this lonely little heroine never had a prototype in breathing flesh-and-blood existence!

It is a deplorable fact, but there is only one of her. The story-writer who can create a new kind of Indian girl, or better still portray a "real live" Indian girl who will do something in Canadian literature that has never been done, but once. The general author gives the reader the impression that he has concocted the plot, created his characters, arranged his action, and at the last moment has been seized with the idea that the regulation Indian maiden will make a very harmonious background whereon to paint his pen picture, that he, never having met this interesting individual, stretches forth his hand to his library shelves, grasps in the first Canadian novelist he sees, reads up his subject, and duplicates it in his own work.

After a half dozen writers have done this, the reader might as well leave the tale unread as far as the interest touches upon the Indian character, for an unvarying experience tells him that this convenient personage will repeat herself with monotonous accuracy. He knows what she did and how she died in other romances by other romancers, and she will do and die likewise in his (she always does die, and one feels relieved that is it so, for she is too unhealthy and too unnatural to live).

The Inevitable "Winona"

The rendition of herself and her doings gains no variety in the pens of manifold authors, and the last thing that they will ever think of will be to study "The Indian Girl" from life, for the being we read of is the offspring of the writer's imagination and never existed outside the book covers that her name decorates. Yes, there is only one of her, and her name is "Winona." Once or twice she has borne another appellation, but it always has a "Winona" sound about it. Even Charles Mair, in that masterpiece of Canadian-Indian romances, *Tecumseh*, could not resist "Winona." We meet her as a Shawnee, as a Sioux, as a Huron, and then, her tribe unnamed, in the vicinity of Brockville.

She is never dignified by being permitted to own a surname, although, extraordinary to note, her father is always a chief, and had he ever existed, would doubtless have been as conservative as his contemporaries about the usual significance that his people attach to family name and lineage.

In addition to this most glaring error this surnameless creation is possessed with a suicidal mania. Her unhappy, self-sacrificing life becomes such a burden to both herself and the author that this is the only means by which they can extricate themselves from a lamentable tangle, though, as a matter of fact suicide is an evil positively unknown among Indians. To-day there may be rare instances where a man crazed by liquor might destroy his own life, but in the periods from whence "Winona's" character is sketched self-destruction was unheard of. This seems to be fallacy which the best American writers have fallen prey to. Even Helen Hunt Jackson, in her powerful and beautiful romance of *Ramona*, has weakened her work deplorably by having no less than three Indians suicide while maddened by their national wrongs and personal grief.

To Be Crossed in Love, Her Lot

The hardest fortune that the Indian girl of fiction meets with is the inevitable doom that shadows her love affairs. She is always desperately in love with the young white hero, who in turn is grateful to her for services rendered the garrison in general and himself in particular during red days of war. In short, she is so much wrapped up in him that she is treacherous to her own people, tells falsehoods to her father and the other chiefs of her tribe, and otherwise makes herself detestable and dishonourable. Of course, this white hero never marries her! Will some critic who understands human nature, and particularly the nature of authors, please tell the reading public why marriage with the Indian girl is so despised in books and so general in real life? Will this good far-seeing critic also tell us why the book-made Indian makes all the love advances to the white gentleman, though the real wild Indian girl (by the way, we are never given any stories of educated girls, though there are many such throughout Canada) is the most retiring, reticent, non-committal being in existence!

Captain Richardson, in that inimitable novel, *Wacousta*, scarcely goes as far in this particular as his followers. To be sure he has his Indian heroine madly in love with young de Haldimar, a passion which it goes without saying he does not reciprocate, but which he plays upon to the extent of making her a traitor to Pontiac inasmuch as she betrays the secret of one of the cleverest intrigues of war known in the history of America, namely, the scheme to capture Fort Detroit through the means of an exhibition game of lacrosse. In addition to this de Haldimar makes a cat's paw of the girl, using her as a means of communication between his fiancée and himself, and so the excellent author permits his Indian girl to get herself despised by her own nation and disliked by the reader. Unnecessary to state, that as usual the gallant white marries his fair lady, whom the poor little red girl has assisted him to recover.

Then comes another era in Canadian-Indian fiction, wherein C. Mercer Adam and A. Ethelwyn Wetherald have given us the semi-historic novel *An Algonquin Maiden*. The former's masterly touch can be recognized on every page he has written; but the outcome of the combined pens is the same old story. We find "Wanda" violently in love with Edward MacLeod, she makes all the overtures, conducts herself disgracefully, assists him to a reunion with his fair-skinned love, Helene; then betakes herself to a boat, rows out into the lake in a thunderstorm, chants her own death-song, and is drowned.

Notwithstanding all this, the authors have given us something exceedingly unique and novel as regards their red heroine. They have sketched us a wild Indian girl who kisses. They, however, forgot to tell us where she learned this pleasant fashion of emotional expression; though two such prominent authors who have given so much time to the study of Indian customs and character, must certainly have noticed the entire ignorance of kissing that is universal among the Aborigines. A wild Indian never kisses; mothers never kiss their children even, nor lovers their sweethearts, husbands their wives. It is something absolutely unknown, unpractised.

But "Wanda" was one of the few book Indian girls who had an individuality and was not hampered with being obliged to continually be national first and natural afterwards. No, she was not national; she did things and said things about as un-Indian-like as Bret Harte's "M'liss": in fact, her action generally resembles "M'liss" more than anything else; for "Wanda's" character has the peculiarity of being created more by the dramatis personae in the play than by the authors themselves. For example: Helene speaks of her as a "low, untutored savage," and Rose is guilty of remarking that she is "a coarse, ignorant woman, whom you cannot admire, who it would be impossible for you to respect"; and these comments are both sadly truthful, one cannot love or admire a heroine that grubs in the mud like a turtle, climbs trees like a raccoon, and tears and soils her gowns like a madwoman.

Then the young hero describes her upon two occasions as a "beautiful little brute." Poor little Wanda! not only is she non-descript and ill-starred, but as usual the authors take away her love, her life, and last and most terrible of all, her reputation; for they permit a crowd of men-friends of the hero to call her a "squaw," and neither hero nor authors deny that she is a "squaw." It is almost too sad when so much prejudice exists against the Indians, that any one should write an Indian heroine with such glaring accusations against her virtue, and no contradictory statements either from writer, hero, or circumstance. "Wanda" had without a doubt the saddest, unsunniest, unequal life ever given to Canadian readers.

Jessie M. Freeland has written a pretty tale published in *The Week*; it is called "Winona's Tryst," but Oh! grim fatality, here again our Indian girl duplicates her former self. "Winona" is the unhappy victim of violent love for Hugh Gordon, which he does not appreciate or return. She assists him, serves him, saves him in the usual "dumb animal" style of book Indians. She manages by self-abnegation, danger, and many heartaches to restore him to the arms of Rose McTavish, who of course he has loved and longed for all through the story. Then "Winona" secures the time-honoured canoe, paddles out into the lake, and drowns herself.

But Miss Freeland closes this pathetic little story with one of the simplest, truest, strongest paragraphs that a Canadian pen has ever written, it is the salvation of the otherwise threadbare development of plot. Hugh Gordon speaks, "I solemnly pledge myself in memory of Winona to do something to help her unfortunate nation. The rightful owners of the soil, dispossessed and driven back inch by inch over their native prairies by their French and English conquerors; and he kept his word."

Charles Mair has enriched Canadian Indian literature perhaps more than any of our authors, in his magnificent drama, *Tecumseh*. The character of the grand old chief himself is most powerfully and accurately drawn. Mair has not fallen into the unattractive fashion of making his Indians "assent with a grunt"—or look with "eyes of dog-like fidelity" or to appear "very grave, very dignified, and not very immaculately clean." Mair avoids the usual commonplaces used in describing Indians by those who have never met or mixed with them. His drama bears upon every page evidence of long study and life with the people whom he has written of so carefully, so truthfully.

As for his heroine, what portrayal of Indian character has ever been more faithful than that of "Iena." Oh! happy inspiration vouchsafed to the author of *Tecumseh* he has invented a novelty in fiction—a white man who deserves, wins, and reciprocates the Indian maiden's love—who says, as she dies on his bosom, while the bullet meant for him stills and tears her heart:

Silent for ever! Oh, my girl! my girl!
Those rich eyes melt; those lips are sun-warm still—
They look like life, yet have no semblant voice.
Millions of creatures throng and multitudes
Of heartless beings flaunt upon the earth:
There's room enough for them; but thou, dull Fate—
Thou cold and partial tender of life's field,
That pluck'st the flower, and leav'st the weed to thrive—
Thou had'st not room for her! Oh, I must seek
A way out of the rack—I need not live,
. . . but she is dead—
And love is left upon the earth to starve.

My object's gone, and I am but a shell,
A husk, and empty case, or anything
That may be kicked about the world.

After perusing this refreshing white Indian drama the reader has but one regret, that Mair did not let "Iena" live. She is the one "book" Indian girl that has Indian life, Indian character, Indian beauty, but the inevitable doom of death could not be stayed even by Mair's sensitive Indian-loving pen. No, the Indian girl must die, and with the exception of "Iena," her heart's blood must stain every page of fiction whereon she appears. One learns to love Lefroy, the poet painter; he never abuses by coarse language and derisive epithets his little Indian love, "Iena" accepts delicately and sweetly his overtures, Lefroy prizes nobly and honourably her devotion. Oh! Lefroy, where is your fellowman in fiction? "Iena," where is your prototype? Alas, for the other pale-faced lovers, they are indifferent, almost brutal creations, and as for the red skin girls that love them, they are all fawn-eyed, unnatural, unmaidenly idiots and both are merely imaginary make-shifts to help out romances, that would be immeasurably improved by their absence.

A Chance for Canadian Writers

Perhaps, sometimes an Indian romance may be written by someone who will be clever enough to portray national character without ever having come in contact with it. Such things have been done, for are we not told that Tom Moore had never set foot in Persia before he wrote Lalla Rookh? and those who best know what they affirm declare that remarkable poem as a faithful and accurate delineation of Oriental scenery, life, and character. But such things are rare, half of our authors who write up Indian stuff have never been on an Indian reserve in their lives, have never met a "real live" Redman, have never even read Parkman, Schoolcraft, or Catlin; what wonder that their conception of a people that they are ignorant of, save by heresay [sic], is dwarfed, erroneous, and delusive.

And here follows the thought—do authors who write Indian romances love the nation they endeavour successfully or unsuccessfully to describe? Do they, like Tecumseh, say "And I, who love your nation, which is just, when deeds deserve it," or is the Indian introduced into literature but to lend a dash of vivid colouring to an otherwise tame and sombre picture of colonial life[?]: it looks suspiciously like the latter reason, or why should the Indian always get beaten in the battles of romances, or the Indian girl get inevitably the cold shoulder in the wars of love?

Surely the Redman has lost enough, has suffered enough without additional losses and sorrows being heaped upon him in romance. There are many combats he has won in history from the extinction of the Jesuit Fathers at Lake Simcoe to Cut Knife Creek. There are many girls who have placed dainty red feet figuratively upon the white man's neck from the days of Pocahontas to those of little "Bright Eyes," who captured all Washington a few seasons ago. Let us not only hear, but read something of the North American Indian "besting" some one at least once in a decade, and above all things let the Indian girl of fiction develop from the "doglike," "fawnlike," "deer-footed," "fire-eyed," "crouching," "submissive" book heroine into something of the quiet, sweet womanly woman she is, if wild, or the everyday, natural, laughing girl she is, if cultivated and educated; let her be natural, even if the author is not competent to give her tribal characteristics.

Note

This essay, originally published in 1892, was previously reprinted in Carole Gerson and Veronica Strong-Boag, eds., *Collected Poems and Selected Prose* (U of Toronto P, 2002).

12

Indian Love Call

Drew Hayden Taylor

A shameless girl approached me with affrontery,
offering to keep me company, for which I thanked
her, sending her away with gentle remonstrances,
and I passed the night with some savages.

—Samuel de Champlain (qtd. in Jaimez n.p.)

The dominant culture's skewed perception of Native sexuality dates back many centuries, perhaps to the very point of contact. And the results were usually unpleasant. In the early 1500s, Hernándo Cortés had an Aztec interpreter and mistress named Malinche who, according to history, was instrumental in the downfall of Aztec civilization. Ever since, Mexicans have smeared her for her traitorous acts by giving her the unpleasant nickname "La Chingada," which loosely translates as "the Fucked One." The term is still a common insult in Mexico today. It was not an auspicious beginning.

In her essay "Sexuality and the Invasion of America: 1492–1806," Vicki Jaimez says that, "For Europeans, sexual allurement manifested itself in the forms of sex as reward (officially incurred or not) for service to country, sexual interaction as politics or sport, and fascination with Native displays of European taboos. In addition, they were led by a desire for sex for the sake of pleasure, as a form of comfort in a land far from home" (n.p.).

Western literature teems with such representations, which say a lot more than their authors intended; literature is the DNA that tells the truth about the culture that bore it. Many, for instance, have argued that Caliban in Shakespeare's *The Tempest* is a Eurocentric fantasy of Indigenous lust and depravity, the man who put the *id* in idiopathy. Ariel, another Indigenous resident of the island, was a spirit and thus physically and motivationally out of reach (but still fully controlled by Prospero), but Caliban was an Indigenous creature of flesh and blood and not a very nice person with not very nice interests:

> PROSPERO: Thou most lying slave,
>> Whom stripes may move, not kindness! I have used thee,
>> Filth as thou art, with human care, and lodged thee
>> In mine own cell, till thou didst seek to violate
>> The honour of my child.
> CALIBAN: O ho, o ho! would't had been done!
>> Thou didst prevent me; I had peopled else
>> This isle with Calibans.
> MIRANDA: Abhorred slave! . . . (1.2.346ff.)

Even more revealing, Caliban was the son of the island's resident witch (a symbol of the Indigenous culture's spiritual leader?), whom Prospero supplanted upon his arrival, forcing Caliban to serve as his slave. Manifest Destiny delivered in iambic pentameter.

In the succeeding centuries, many books told tales of sexual relations between Natives and non-Natives, and, as can be expected, the courtship was difficult. My personal favourite is Injun Joe in Mark Twain's *The Adventures of Tom Sawyer*. This half-breed speaks fondly of many depravities, from grave robbing to theft to one particular form of pleasure. Speaking to a fellow outlaw, he confides what he has in mind for a local white woman: "When you want to get revenge on a woman you don't kill her—bosh! You go for her looks. You slit her nostrils—you notch her ears like a sow's!" (185).

John Seeyle, a Twain academic, writes,

> Having been horse-whipped by her late husband, Joe plans on tying the widow to her bed and mutilating her, an episode linked by Dixon Wecter to an incident in which an actual rape (not by an Indian) may have been threatened—a theme hardly suited, as Wecter notes, to a children's book. Yet, to an adult reader, the image of a woman tied to a bed is hardly subliminal, and the episode has its literary counterparts in [*Last of the*] *Mohicans*, where the evil Huron named Magua seeks revenge against Colonel Munro, who has had him horsewhipped for drunkenness, by kidnapping Munro's daughter Cora and attempting to force her into marrying him, a "cruel fate" with a clearly sexual dimension. But Injun Joe is much more than a social menace: he is evil personified, doing bad things because he likes to. (xxii)

And, of course, he ends up starving to death trapped in a cave, outwitted by a precocious young white boy. Karmic retribution.

Over the intervening years, little has changed. There might be fewer face mutilations and less overt racism, but manifestations of Aboriginal sexuality in literature still have less fact and more fiction than they ever have. The Internet and other new media have merely opened up the possibilities for further exploitation and misinformation. The medium isn't the message anymore. It's the problem.

In the vast majority of non-Native literature, Aboriginal characters, just as they never have a sense of humour, are rarely ever viewed as sexual beings. And if they are, their sexuality is not healthy. What we did and how we did it is dark (no pun intended), foreboding, and forbidden. Kidnappings, rape and other assorted defilements are the order of the day on this particular pop culture menu. Tender love stories involving Native people are scarcer than priests at a residential school reunion. We never even had a Romeo and Juliet story. Granted, it's a tragic, dysfunctional tale (about families, ending in multiple suicides), but we'd even accept that. Over the years, there have been many rumours and legends about the true relationship between Tonto and the Lone Ranger, but that's about all we've got (and that's a whole different essay).

Speaking of cowboys and Indians, in John Ford's classic movie *The Searchers*, John Wayne spends five years looking for his niece, played by Natalie Wood, who has been kidnapped by Comanches. When he finally finds her, rather than letting her live peaceably and amicably with her Native husband and his people, he intends to shoot her to save her from such a dishonourable existence. Sort of an early American honour killing. Instead, he finds redemption by destroying the village, scalping the chief, and returning the girl to her white family.

Earlier in the movie, Wayne, as Ethan Edwards, is watching a white woman and her two daughters who have been recently rescued from Indian captivity. In the screenplay they are described as "mad," "frightened," "wild-eyed," and as making "animal noises." They are bordering on insanity.

COWBOY: It's hard to believe they're white.
ETHAN: They ain't white. Not anymore. They're Comanch.

In an essay on Ford, Joan Dagle says this scene "clearly conveys not only the absolute opposition between Indian and white settler, but also the underlying fear and threat of sexual violation and attendant madness" ("Linear Patterns and Ethnic Encounters" n.p.).

From now on, I will remember to be nicer to the white women I date.

It has only been within the last fifty years, since the era of political correctness began, that the concept of exploring Native sexuality has become possible, if not downright interesting and, in some cases, quite fashionable. In the age of the New Western, it's hard not to bring two films and their contemporary views of Native sexuality into the conversation: *Soldier Blue* (1970) and *Dances with Wolves* (1990).

In *Soldier Blue* (with a theme song by Buffy Sainte-Marie, so you know it's authentic), Peter Strauss plays a cavalry officer who "rescues" Candice Bergen, who has been kidnapped by Native people years before. The other soldiers, less in touch with their feminine side, openly gossip about how many bucks she's been with. But Bergen's character is portrayed as being much more savvy and logical than her rescuers; in the new era, turnabout is fair trade. And the cavalry officer is no longer seen as the rescuing hero—he is now less honourable than his traditional enemy. If the cavalry comes riding over the hill to rescue you from the Indians, hide and seek refuge with the Indians.

This concept is pushed even further in *Dances with Wolves*, often to a ridiculous extent. The white woman is the only person in the Indian village in desperate need of a comb, and the soldiers sent to civilize the American Plains are a ragtag bunch of mercenaries, bullies, and buffoons. For a change, the European conquerors are not portrayed in the best of light. There is no one except Kevin Costner—who at first seems so ill-equipped, both materially and mentally, to survive in this rugged landscape—to be the conscience of his people.

But perhaps the most telling part of the film was the tame sex scene in the teepee. Costner wakes up and sees Graham Greene and Tantoo Cardinal going at it. And lo and behold, Tantoo is on top. For years afterwards, I would hear women, sociologists, film students and a host of other people with too much time on their hands commenting on and approving of the fact that they had shown the woman on top. "What a progressive statement," they would say. "It showed how respected the woman was in traditional Native culture"—and various other similar opinions.

Ironically, in porn terminology that position is called "cowgirl," not "Indian girl." I sometimes think that, as a stand against Manifest Destiny, as a statement objecting to cultural genocide and Christian indoctrination, to further limit the encroachment of the dominant society's thunderous existence and virus-like contamination, First Nations people around the world should ban the "missionary position," in light of the bad historical baggage it carries. Or rechristen it the "Aboriginal position."

How times have changed. And how they haven't.

In 1983 the fledgling medium of video games crossed a new frontier when the company Mystique marketed a new game it had developed for its Atari 2600 series. It was called *Custer's Revenge*. The marketing copy went as follows:

> History was never quite like this. In a "creative interpretation" of the Battle of Little Big Horn, a rowdy and naked General Custer must make his way through a hail of continual arrows to a Native American princess tied to a pole. If Custer can survive the obstacles in his way, he then gets an opportunity to have "sexual intercourse" for big points. Whether his needs have been sated, or brought down by enemy fire, Custer will return again and again to what he wants. ("Swedish Erotica" n.p.)

Class question: How many things are wrong with that sales pitch? And if you answer that traditionally, Native Americans never had a hierarchy of royalty, so the term "princess" is inaccurate . . . well, then maybe somewhere out there is a cultural sensitivity course with your name on it. And did I say "the era of political correctness" earlier? I take that back.

I remember seeing a news report about the launch of this game and the public outcry, especially from women's groups and Native organizations, that predictably followed. It told me two things: computer games are designed by adolescent boys and their adolescent imaginations, and the battle continues. I also seem to remember a spokesperson for the company defending the game by claiming, "It's obvious the woman [tied to the pole] is enjoying it." How long would it be till Atari came out with a game like those ones where you kill zombies with guns, only with Dudley George and the OPP?

At the other end of the political spectrum, I came across an interesting ad on the Net one day, on a site called *Aphrodite Recommends: Female Sexuality*. It seems there is a substance being marketed out there called, simply, Native Woman. Evidently it's some sort of First Nations aphrodisiac:

> Throughout Europe this mushroom was known as *elixirium ad longum vitam*, the elixir of long life. Before the Western World discovered this treasure, the Haida First Peoples of the Queen Charlotte Islands, in what is now British Columbia, understood its primal purpose: connecting a woman to her deepest sexual identity.

I must confess that I have never been to the Queen Charlotte Islands, more commonly known in Native circles as Haida Gwaii, but now I am certainly looking forward to my first trip. This type of advertising reminds me of those ads for a pain ointment product called Lakota, publicly endorsed by Floyd "Red Crow" Westerman but created and owned by a Western Canadian Métis. They promote the concept that Native people have secret ways that only now, after most of our land has been taken away, our language destroyed, our culture and belief systems obliterated, are we willing to share. The time has come to show you white people how to have a good time and not feel sore afterwards.

But perhaps nowhere has the image of the sexual Aboriginal been so appropriated, so conjured, so manipulated but embraced, than in the uncountable number of Western/historical romance novels that populate mainstream bookstores, drugstores, airports, and used-book emporiums. Romance fiction is an incredibly lucrative genre, estimated to make up more than 50 per cent of paperback fiction sales. According to Lee Masterson, author of *Write, Create and Promote a Best Seller*, historical romance is one of the most successful of the eight sub-genres of romance fiction, the others being contemporary romance, fantasy romance, futuristic romance, paranormal romance, regency romance, romantic suspense, and time-travel romance.

Come on, admit it—you've picked one up. With a big muscular Indian on the cover, sweeping some poor (or lucky, depending on your perspective) white woman off her feet. You've read the back and maybe even bought one or two:

> She was a runaway wife, with a hefty reward posted for her return. And he was the best darn tracker in the territory. For the half-breed bounty hunter, it was an easy choice. His had been a hard life, with little to show for it except his horse, his Colt and his scars. The pampered brown-eyed beauty would go back to her rich husband in San Francisco, and he would be ten thousand dollars richer.
>
> But somewhere along the trail out of the Black Hills, sometime during the long star-studded prairie nights, everything changed. Now he would give his life to protect her, to hold her forever in his embrace. Now the moonlight poetry of their loving reflected in the fiery vision of the Sun Dance: She must be his. . . . (Baker n.p.)

This is the literature of the middle-class Caucasian housewife and, to be fair, your average working-class woman, who dreams of romance and escape. In the arms of an Indian. And not just any Indian. An über-Indian.

It is on the covers of these stylish and carefully crafted homages to interracial love that the image of the studly male Indian reaches its pinnacle. More often than not, he's got a solid square chin, an aquiline nose, a chiselled brow and long, flowing raven-black hair that can tell you the direction of the prairie breeze better than any windsock. So what if these traits are noticeably lacking from most Native men of that era? The broad noses seen in photos of Sitting Bull and Geronimo, both strikingly handsome men, are not celebrated on the covers of *Song of a Warrior* or *Wild Thunder*. And the Aboriginal bodies seen in these fantasies could only come from hours in a personal gym, not to mention some careful calorie counting (it's a known fact that muskrats have a higher fat content than buffalo).

Here lies an interesting contradiction. Objectively, the men on the covers all look like white men with good tans in dim lighting. Yet the reason these books are devoured so rabidly by a faithful audience is that the readers want more than just a love story—they want one encased in exoticism, one involving a distant but still embraceable culture and environment, far removed from their own existence. It is this sense of foreignness or otherworldliness that makes these stories so enticing. Kind of like going out for Korean or Ethiopian food: it's tasty, interesting and different, but chances are that you, the consumer, will never visit the land that created the meal that you are eating. Experiencing it at the local strip mall is about as close as you're gonna get.

Part of the attraction might also be our innate desire to root for the underdog. The time period in which these books take place was arguably the last flowering of Native culture in its pure form. All the world knows what came next: the Dispossessed Indian, the Tragic Indian, the Forgotten Indian. This is a way of remembering them when they were strong, proud, and free. I have yet to come across a historical romance that takes place on a reserve during the Depression. It's like telling stories about a close relative who had a stroke. More often than not, the stories will be about when he was healthy and did interesting things, not about the way he is now, bedridden and slobbering.

It's also an opportunity to experience forbidden love, a culturally unallowable tryst. Only recently—and again, this is arguable—have Native/non-Native relationships been considered non-scandalous and acceptable. But a wild Indian, savage and proud with long flowing locks and a huge powerful horse between his legs (no metaphor intended)—now that's something to get hot and bothered about, especially if you live in the suburbs, have two kids (one with the flu), drive a Honda minivan, and are married to an accountant who never puts the toilet seat down.

Truth be told, I know very few, if any, Native women who read these books. The relationships in the stories are not forbidden or exotic for them. They know the reality and the pain that came from the real nineteenth-century interrelations. It was not a particularly romantic time for First Nations. It was a time of massive upheaval, the perpetuation of a centuries-long cultural genocide. So I think it's safe to say—and I could be wrong, but I would hazard a guess—that the *vast* majority of patrons of this literary genre are white.

So, again, the men are Native but look remarkably white. This limits the dimensions of the unknown, providing a touchstone that is more familiar and acceptable. See the contradiction? And if the men are not fully Native, then they are half-breeds and therefore closer to white society. What could be more romantic than the outsider, someone torn between two cultures? In a random sampling of ten historical romances, five of the male protagonists were half-breeds. Injun Joe was not among them.

And their names . . . Lone Eagle, Swift Buck, Bear, Jesse Yellow Thunder, Chase the Wind a.k.a. The White Wolf, Strong Wolf, Wolf Shadow, Jared Redwolf (the Wolf family seems to have a real thing for kidnapped women). Traditional Native names were not always that flattering or masculine; history books will tell you of the exploits of real Indians with names like Roman Nose, Hairy Bear, Gall, Big Foot, Dull Knife, Stumbling Bear and Lame Deer. But what does reality have to do with fantasy?

The generic story usually consists of the central character, a Native or half-breed guy, who kidnaps a white woman or is hired to find a white woman kidnapped by Natives because he "knows their ways." After a chase and some adventures, he makes her fall in love with him. There are limitless variations to this template, but essentially it's the Stockholm Syndrome with a happy ending. Of course as the story progresses, there are some bridges to be built between the two cultures. Once those are constructed, the heavy panting and teepee shaking begins. Coincidently, that's how I got my prom date.

Occasionally, the white woman was also raised by Indians. For a variety of reasons she went back to her people, only to return years later in search of something. In Rhonda Thompson's *Walk into the Flame*, the female protagonist was raised by Apaches after being abandoned by her father. At the age of seventeen she returns to "civilization"; five years later, she's back. Same principle with *Wolf Shadow* by Madeline Baker, the story of Theresa Bryant, renamed Winter Rain, except that Winter Rain still lives among her adopted people. She was raised by the Lakota, and her birth parents hire Chance McCloud, "half Lakota and half white," to find her.

Also note that the women almost always have blue eyes—this seems to be a prerequisite for being kidnapped by Indians. Their hair is usually blond or red, with the occasional foray into "dark as a raven's wing." And they range in age from seventeen to no older than twenty-three or twenty-four. That seems to be their "best before" date.

A unique code of ethics also comes into play. The women are almost always young and virgins, and if they have had sex, it's usually within a marriage to an impotent or abusive man, frequently white, from whom they are struggling to escape. The Native men, by contrast, have been quite sexually active in prior years. When push finally comes to shove (again, no pun intended), they provide a more holistic, respectful, and tender form of love and sex for these women. The coupling is almost always Indian man–white woman, very seldom the other way around—ironic, because in the real world (whatever that might be), more Native women ended up with white husbands than vice versa. Champlain put it best when he said, "Our sons shall marry your daughters and henceforth we shall be one people."

These books obviously tap into a rich world of fantasy. There never seem to be any bugs. No one's hair ever needs washing, or even combing. Nobody ever has to go to the washroom. Their clothes never stink. And everyone has a full set of teeth. For that time period, these characteristics are truly fantasy.

As a Native person, how do I feel about these books? Am I insulted? No. Do I think their portrayal of Native people is dangerous? No, no more dangerous than their portrayal of all those tall, lithe, lovely, slender, curvy women that read them with their amber/grey/green/blue eyes. Does it do our culture justice? Of course not. Does it do us any harm? If anybody believes this is reality, they are more a danger to themselves than to us.

However, I prefer to think about the genre's positive influences. For the most part these books make us out to be caring, sensitive, and interesting partners, far superior to all those abusive or non-existent husbands. Not to mention fabulous lovers.

It seems our secret is out.

Their love has to be written in the stars. And their passion . . . mercy is it hot!! They give new meaning to what happens in a sweat lodge. I would sure love to be Jared Redwolf's woman.

—Benway, a fan of the book *Redwolf's Woman*

Note

This essay was originally published in Drew Hayden Taylor, *Me Sexy: An Exploration of Native Sex and Sexuality* (Douglas and McIntyre, 2008).

13

"Introduction" and "Marketing the Imaginary Indian" from *The Imaginary Indian: The Image of the Indian in Canadian Culture*

Daniel Francis

Introduction

> the Indians are not composed
> of romantic stories about them

—John Newlove, *The Pride*

I

Some years ago a friend and I decided to pay a visit to Head-Smashed-In Buffalo Jump. Located where the prairie meets the foothills in southwestern Alberta, Head-Smashed-In is a high cliff over which Native people stampeded the great herds of buffalo hundreds of years ago. Archaeologists believe that people used this place as a slaughterhouse for almost 6,000 years. The United Nations has declared it a World Heritage Site, one of the most culturally significant places in the world.

We drove south from Calgary on a sunny Thanksgiving Day. On our left the flat plain ran away to the horizon under a wide, blue sky; on our right the land folded into rolling hills all the way to the Rocky Mountains, faintly visible in the distance. There were few signposts along the way and we had begun to fear that we had missed the turnoff when at last we spotted the sign and left the highway on a meandering strip of asphalt heading west toward the mountains.

Just about the time we once again thought we must be lost, we arrived at a gravel parking lot, seemingly in the middle of nowhere. We were there.

The site at first seemed unimpressive. The visitors' centre, actually a mini-museum, is a concrete building several stories high embedded in the face of the cliff. It appears to have been built to make as little impact on the landscape as possible. Entering at the front door, we climbed up through a series of levels and emerged at the top of the cliff, at the edge of the buffalo jump, right where the stampeding animals would have run into empty space and begun the long, bellowing fall onto the rocks below.

The anthropologist George MacDonald has written that the three holiest places in Canada are a row of stone statues at Eskimo Point in the Northwest Territories, Bill Reid's large cedar carving, "The Raven and the First Men," at Vancouver's Museum of Anthropology, and the abandoned Haida village of Ninstints on Anthony Island. Well, I thought, as I looked out from the clifftop across a vast sweep of undulating prairie, lightening and darkening as billowing clouds obscured the sun and set it free again, add a fourth; if by *holy* you mean a place where the warm wind seems to be the earth breathing, a place where personal identity dissolves temporarily, where you can feel the connectedness of lives back through time to be a reality, and not just an opinion.

Back inside the museum, looking at the various items depicting the history of the buffalo and the people who hunted them, my attention shifted from the display cases to the people who were tending them. I became aware that the facility was staffed entirely by Indians (Peigan, as it turned out, from a nearby reserve). But I found myself thinking that they didn't look like Indians to me, the Indians I knew from my school books and from the movies, the Indians, in fact, who were depicted inside the museum displays I was looking at. That is where most of us are used to seeing Indians, from the other side of a sheet of glass. But at Head-Smashed-In, they were running the place. They stood around in jeans and dresses and plaid skirts—not feather headdresses and leather moccasins—talking and laughing. If curious visitors like myself asked them something, they answered thoroughly but not pedantically: as if this was something they knew, not something they had studied.

After a long afternoon learning about the buffalo, I left Head-Smashed-In dimly aware that I had changed my mind about something. It had been an encounter not just with an important place in the history of the continent, but also with an idea, my own idea about what an Indian was. If I thought I had known before, I didn't think I knew anymore. And perhaps that is where this book began. How had I come to believe in an Imaginary Indian?

II

In 1899, the poet Charles Mair travelled into the far Northwest as a secretary to the Half-Breed Scrip Commission, appointed by the government in Ottawa to carry out negotiations related to Treaty Number Eight with the Native people of northern Alberta. Negotiations began on the shore of Lesser Slave Lake, before a large tent with a spacious marquee beneath which the members of the official party arranged themselves. The Native people, Beaver and Métis, sat on the ground in the sun, or stood in small knots. As the speeches droned on through the long June afternoon, Mair observed the people as they listened to what the government emissaries had to say. "Instead of paint and feathers, the scalp-lock, the breech-clout, and the buffalo robe," he wrote:

> there presented itself a body of respectable-looking men, as well dressed and evidently quite as independent in their feelings as any like number of average pioneers in the East. . . . One was prepared, in this wild region of forest, to behold some savage type of men; indeed, I craved to renew the vanished scenes of old. But, alas! one beheld, instead, men with well-washed unpainted faces, and combed and common hair; men in suits of ordinary "store-clothes," and some even with "boiled" if not laundered shirts. One felt disappointed, almost defrauded. It was not what was expected, what we believed we had a right to expect, after so much waggoning and tracking and drenching and river turmoil and trouble. (*Through the Mackenzie Basin* 54)

Unlike most Canadians of his time, Charles Mair possessed extensive know-ledge of the country's Native people, living as he had for so many years as a merchant trader in the future province of Saskatchewan. He knew well that the contemporary Indian no longer galloped across the plains in breechcloth and feather headdress. However, Mair did expect to discover in the more isolated regions of the north a Native population closer to his image of the picturesque Red Man. His disappointment was profound when instead he found "a group of commonplace men smoking briar-roots."

III

Two very similar experiences, almost a century apart. Charles Mair, myself, and how many other White people, having to relearn the same lesson: Indians, as we think we know them, do not exist. In fact, there may well be no such thing as an Indian.

Indirectly, we all know this to be true; it is one of the lessons we learn as school children. When Christopher Columbus arrived in America five hundred years ago he thought he had reached the East Indies so he called the people he met Indians. But really they were Arawaks, and they had as much in common with the Iroquois of the northern woodlands as the Iroquois had in common with the Blackfoot of the western Plains or the Haida of the Pacific Coast. In other words, when Columbus arrived in America there were a large number of different and distinct Indigenous cultures, but there were no Indians.

The Indian is the invention of the European.

Robert Berkhofer Jr. introduced me to this unsettling idea in his book, *The White Man's Indian.* "Since the original inhabitants of the Western Hemisphere neither called themselves by a single term nor understood themselves as a collectivity," Berkhofer began, "the idea and image of the Indian must be a White conception. Native Americans were and are real, but the *Indian* was a White invention . . ." (3).

The Indian began as a White man's mistake, and became a White man's fantasy. Through the prism of white hope, fears, and prejudices, Indigenous Americans would be seen to have lost contact with reality and to have become "Indians"; that is, anything non-Natives wanted them to be.

IV

This book attempts to describe the image of the Indian, the Imaginary Indian, in Canada since the middle of the nineteenth century. During this time, what did Canadians think an Indian was? What did children learn about them in school? What was government policy toward them? What Indian did painters paint and writers write about? I want to make it perfectly clear that while Indians are the subject of this book, Native people are not. This is a book about the images of Native people that White Canadians manufactured, believed in, feared, despised, admired, taught their children. It is a book about White—and not Native—cultural history.

Many of the images of Indians held by Whites were derogatory, and many were not. Many contained accurate representations of Native people; many did not. The "truth" of the image is not really what concerns me. I am not setting out to expose fraudulent images by comparing them to a "real Indian." It is, after all, the argument of this book that there is no such thing as a real Indian. When non-Native accounts of Indians are at variance with the known facts I will say so, but my main intention is not to argue with the stereotypes, but to think about them. The last thing I want to do is to replace an outdated Imaginary Indian with my very own, equally misguided, version. My concern is rather to understand where the Imaginary Indian came from, how Indian imagery has affected public policy in Canada and how it has shaped, and continues to shape, the myths non-Natives tell themselves about being Canadians.

Every generation claims a clearer grasp of reality than its predecessors. Our forebears held ludicrous ideas about certain things, we say confidently, but we do not. For instance, we claim to see Indians today much more clearly for what they are. I hope that my book will undermine such confidence. Much public discourse about Native people still deals in stereotypes. Our views of what constitutes an Indian today are as much bound up with myth, prejudice and ideology as earlier versions were. If the Indian really is imaginary, it could hardly be otherwise.

Take, for example, the controversial 1991 decision by Chief Justice Allan McEachern of the Supreme Court of British Columbia relating to the Gitksan-Wet'suwet'en land claims case. Much of what Judge McEachern wrote about Native culture in that decision could as easily have been written by another judge one hundred, two hundred, three hundred years ago. In dismissing the Natives' claim, he wrote: "The plaintiffs' ancestors had not written language, no horses or wheeled vehicles, slavery and starvation was not uncommon, wars with neighbouring peoples were common, and there is no doubt, to quote Hobbs [sic], that aboriginal life in the territory was, at best 'nasty, brutish, and short'" (13).

It is unclear whether Judge McEachern was aware when he borrowed this well-worn phrase that Thomas Hobbes actually coined it in 1651 to describe "the savage people of America" as he believed them to be. And many Europeans agreed with him. Because Native North Americans were so different, had so few of the "badges of civilization" as Judge McEachern calls them, it was seriously debated whether they could properly be called human beings at all. I would have thought, however, that in the three hundred and forty years separating Thomas Hobbes and Judge McEachern, our understanding of aboriginal culture might be seen to have improved. But obviously not.

Of course, non-Natives have held much more favourable opinions about Indians over the years. The Noble Savage, for instance, is a venerable image, first used by the English dramatist John Dryden in his 1670 play, *The Conquest of Granada*, to refer to the innate goodness of man in a perceived "state of nature":

I am as free as nature first made man,
Ere the base laws of servitude began,
When wild in the woods the noble savage ran.

For an example closer to home, we need to look no further than the aforementioned Charles Mair, who wrote in his long poem, *Tecumseh*:

... There lived a soul more wild than barbarous;
A tameless soul—the sunburnt savage free—
Free, and untainted by the greed of gain:
Great Nature's man content with Nature's good.

Savage, when used by Dryden and Mair, means innocent, virtuous, peace-loving, free of guile and vanity that came from living in contemporary society. I don't think I have to argue the fact that many non-Natives continue to believe that Indians have an innate nobility of character which somehow derives from their long connection with the American continent and their innocence of industrial society.

Ignoble or noble? From the first encounter, Europeans viewed aboriginal Americans through a screen of their own prejudices and preconceptions. Given the wide gulf separating the cultures, Europeans have tended to imagine the Indian rather than to know Native people, thereby to project onto Native people all the fears and hopes they have for the New World. If America was a Garden of Eden, then Indians must be seen as blessed innocents. If America was an alien place, then Indians must be seen to be frightful and bloodthirsty. Europeans also projected onto Native peoples all the misgivings they had about the shortcomings of their own civilization: the Imaginary Indian became a stick with which they beat their own society. The Indian became the standard of virtue and manliness against which Europeans measured themselves, and often found themselves wanting. In other words, non-Natives in North America have long defined themselves in relation to the Other in the form of the Indian.

As time passed, colonist and Native had more to do with one another. But Euro-Canadians continued to perceive Indians in terms of their own changing values, and so the image of the Indian changed over time. Close contact revealed differences between the idealized vision of the noble savage and the reality of Native culture. As White settlement spread, conflict increased. As long as Natives remained valuable allies in the wars the colonial powers waged against each other, the image of the Indian remained reasonably positive. By the middle of the nineteenth century, however, these wars were over and whites no longer needed Native military allies. Natives had become marginal to the new issues which preoccupied Canadian colonists: how to wrest a living from the country, how to create durable political institutions, how to transform a set of isolated colonies into a unified nation.

At this point Whites set themselves the task of inventing a new identity for themselves as Canadians. The image of the Other, the Indian, was integral to this process of self-identification. The Other came to stand for everything the Euro-Canadian was not. The content of the Other is the subject of this book.

V

A word about terminology. There is much debate these days about the correct term for Indigenous Americans. Some do not object to being called Indians; others do. Alternative terms include Aboriginals, Natives, Amerindians, First Nations peoples, and probably others I have not heard. . . . I use the word Indian when I am referring to the image of Native people held by non-Natives, and I use the terms Natives, Native people, or Aboriginals when I am referring to the actual people. What to call non-Natives is equally puzzling. White is the convenient opposite of Indians, but it has obvious limitations. So, in this age of multiculturalism, does Euro-Canadian, an awkward term anyway. I hope readers will forgive me for using all three. It is part of the legacy of the Imaginary Indian that we lack a vocabulary with which to speak about these issues clearly.

Marketing the Imaginary Indian

I

In 1929, when Buffalo Child Long Lance was living in New York, the B. F. Goodrich Company introduced a new type of canvas running shoe. The "Chief Long Lance Shoe" was modelled on an Indian moccasin and endorsed by Long Lance in an extensive advertising campaign. "In our primitive life, nothing was more important than our feet," Long Lance is quoted as saying in one magazine advertisement. "I wonder if the white race would not be sturdier if they took better care of their feet in childhood—by wearing shoes that allow free exercise of the foot and leg muscles." As part of the publicity for the new sneakers, Goodrich published a booklet, *How to Talk in Indian Sign Language*, featuring photographs of bare-chested Long Lance, in breechcloth and headband, manipulating his hands (Smith, *Long Lance* 180–81).

B. F. Goodrich wished to associate its shoes with speed, strength, and durability. There was no better way to do this than to associate them with the Indian, known for his ability to run like the wind for hours at a time. Of course, shoes were not the first products to be marketed with the help of the Indian image. The association of Indians and products was a venerable one, going back at least to the travelling medicine shows of the late eighteenth century, in which potions and elixirs were peddled on the strength of their connection with Indian healing practices. The first decades of the twentieth century saw the appearance of dozens and dozens of products which tried to find favour with consumers by identifying with the Indian: Pocahontas perfume, Red Indian motor oil, Iroquois beer, Squaw Brand canned vegetables—the list goes on and on. For some products, the Indian was used as an all-purpose symbol of Canada. For others the Indian image was used to associate a product with the out-of-doors, or with strength and courage, or with the simple innocence of nature.

This tradition continued in the naming of sports teams after Indian groups—the Braves, the Redskins, the Indians. It represented an attempt to link the team with the courage, ferocity, strength, and agility of the Indian. For the same reasons, audiences at sporting events occasionally utilized the Imaginary Indian. In 1916, for example, students at the University of British Columbia came up with the following chant:

> Kitsilano, Capilano, Siwash, Squaw,
> Kla-How-ya, Tillicum, Skookum, Wah
> Hiyu Mammok! Muck-a-Muck-a, Zip!
> B.C. Varsity. Rip! Rip! Rip!
> V-A-R-S-I-T-Y. Varsity.

Later the university adopted the Thunderbird as the name for its athletic teams.[1] More recently, the Atlanta Braves baseball team had an Indian mascot named Chief Noc-A-Homa who inhabited a tipi just beyond the outfield fence. When Native groups complained, the team retired the Chief, but during the 1991 World Series, Braves' fans angered Aboriginal Americans once again by using fake tomahawks and the so-called "tomahawk chop" to urge on the team.

The irony of seeking victory by invoking the totemic power of a socially oppressed people was apparently not recognized. But a grasp of irony has never been the strong suit of White society when it wishes to appropriate elements of Native culture.

Advertising relies on a simple message to make a point. It deals in stereotypes. Once it began using images of Native people, advertising created a whole new context for the Imaginary Indian. Suddenly images of the Indian were appearing on the pages of mass-circulation magazines, on billboards, on the shelves at the local supermarket. The Imaginary Indian became one of the icons of consumer society. The result was a reduction of Aboriginal cultures to a series of slogans, a set of simplistic and patronizing attitudes. Take, for example, this jingle used by General Motors to promote the Pontiac in 1927:

> Heap Big Injun,
> Pontiac a warrior brave was he,
> One day he met Miss Sleeping Fawn
> And fell in love you see,
> Now, Sleeping Fawn was up to date,
> No birch canoe will do,
> You get a car and take me for a riding when you woo,
> Pontiac, Pontiac, Heap Big Injun Brave. . . . (qtd. in Doxtator 46)

Many of the images of Indians which appeared in advertisements were intended to be positive. They reveal a widespread admiration for certain qualities which the public associated with "Indianness": bravery, physical prowess, natural virtue. Of course, these were qualities Indians were thought to have possessed in the distant past, before contact with the White Man. Advertisements did not feature Indians in suits or dresses; they did not highlight life on the reserve or on the other side of the tracks. Instead they showed the classic Indian head in feather headdress or the Indian princess in beaded doeskin. Advertising reinforced the belief that the best Indian was the historical Indian. It used the Indian as a symbol to appeal to modern consumers who admired values they associated with pre-industrial society.

II

The marketing of the Imaginary Indian reached its peak not with a product but an experience, the experience of railway travel. More than any other single aspect of White civilization, the railway transformed the world of the Indian, especially in Western Canada. It was the railway that conveyed the hundreds of thousands of new settlers into the West. It was the railway that kept these settlers supplied with everything they needed to establish the new grain economy. And it was the railway that transported the products of the new economy to market. Ironic, then, that the railway should lead the way in marketing the image of the Indian to sell its services to travellers.

The settlement of the West did not happen all at once. The Canadian Pacific Railway was completed in 1885, but the flood of immigrants into the new land did not begin for another decade. Meanwhile, the CPR had to find some way of paying for itself. Tourism was one answer. Cornelius Van Horne, the CPR's first general manager, determined to attract travellers by offering them first-class accommodation on his transcontinental trains (Hart 12ff.). Sleeping cars were fitted out with oversize berths, richly upholstered seats, mahogany and satin-wood panelling, polished brass fittings, and bathrooms in every car. Elegant dining cars offered sumptuous meals and imported wines at tables set with white linen and gleaming silver. But comfort was not enough: travellers had to be offered spectacle. And here the CPR capitalized on one of its greatest assets—the magnificent beauty of the western landscape. Company officials recognized that the West could be sold as one great tourist attraction. The Rocky Mountains especially offered travellers some of the most spectacular scenery in the world. "1001 Switzerlands Rolled in One" was how Van Horne described them.

The railway's publicity department began churning out posters, books, and pamphlets extolling the natural wonder of Canada's West. No less an authority than the governor-general, the Marquis of Lorne, was enlisted in the cause. "Nowhere can finer scenery be enjoyed from the window of a car than upon this line," Lorne enthused in an article published by the CPR as its first promotional effort (Hart 23). Some of the country's leading painters and photographers received free passes on the trains to go west and record the scenery. The CPR then used these scenes in its publicity material, or sold them along the route as postcards, viewbooks, and individual prints. . . .

Following the examples of their southern counterparts, the CPR gradually realized that the Indians were a surefire tourist attraction. "The Indians and the bears were splendid stage properties to have at a station where both the east and west bound trains . . . stop for lunch," remarked Sladen (306). It was not entirely by accident then, that in 1894, when floods washed out the track, the company sent local guide and outfitter Tom Wilson down to the Stoney reserve at Morley to invite the Indians back to Banff to entertain the marooned travellers. The Indians performed traditional dances and competed in a number of rodeo events for prices put up by the railway company. The whole affair turned out to be so popular that the CPR and local businesses decided to make Banff Indian Days an annual summer event (Hart 59). The railway sponsored a similar pageant in Desbarats, Ontario, each summer with actors in Native costume performing scenes from a version of Longfellow's popular long poem, "Hiawatha" (Monkman 129).

Travel on the CPR boomed in the years before World War I. In 1913, fifteen and a half million passengers rode the train. Encouraged by the railway's publicity machine, many of them went west to discover the much-heralded beauty of plains and mountains. Tourists were excited at the possibility of seeing wild Indians in their natural setting from the safety and convenience of a railcar. It was every bit as exotic as visiting the depths of Africa or some distant island in the Pacific.

Reality did not always measure up, however, as the British traveller Edward Roper discovered on his cross-Canada excursion in 1890. Pausing at Maple Creek, Saskatchewan, Roper observed a group of Blackfoot lingering around the railway station. "Many of them were partly civilized in dress, though ragged and dirty, and there was very little of the picturesque about them. Some few had good faces, but the ideal Red Man was not there" (Roper 118). Later, at Gleichen, Alberta, Roper was pleased to have a chance to see some less "civilized" Natives, who impressed him with their paint and feathers and decorated clothing. These were much closer to the wild Indians of his imagination and he admired their animated good looks and clean appearance. Roper enjoyed throwing coins and oranges from the back of the train to watch young Natives scramble in the dust for them (120). In BC, he was surprised to find Indians occupying prominent places in White society. "I conclude that there must be something really good in a race which can, if only here and there, produce such specimens" (244). However, he was impressed mainly by the indifference with which Canadians seemed to view the Indians. "The Canadians," he told his readers, "seemed to regard them as a race of animals which were neither benefit nor harm to anyone, mentioning that they were surely dying out, and that when they were all gone it would be a good thing" (118). Of course, the fact that the Indians were vanishing added an urgency to the tourists' quest for novelty. If they didn't see them soon, they might never see them.

III

Once the West was settled, the Indians lost some of their appeal as advertising devices. Western Canada was no longer promoted as a wild frontier. Tourists came west for the scenery and the hiking and the skiing, not to see the primitive Red Man. Still, there remained among travellers a fascination with the Indians and their exotic culture and railways continued to capitalize off it whenever they could. One such opportunity arose in the 1920s in northern British Columbia.

For several decades, collectors had been stripping coastal villages of native artifacts and selling them to museums around the world. Most highly prized were the giant totem poles which over time had come to symbolize the people of the Northwest Coast. By 1920, hardly any of the huge monuments remained in their village settings, and those that did were in a sorry state of natural decay. A large cache of about seventy poles stood in the Indian villages along the Skeena River. During World War I, the construction of the Grand Trunk Pacific Railway through the river valley of Prince Rupert placed these villages right on the mainline of a transcontinental railway. As a result, the poles became a major tourist attraction. One Montreal newspaper calculated that they were the most photographed spot in Canada after Niagara Falls.[2]

Canadian National Railways, the publicly-owned corporation that took over the Grand Trunk after the war, recognized the value of the poles and took a leading role in their preservation, along with the Indian Department, the Parks Branch, and the Victoria Memorial Museum in Ottawa. The expense of the project was justified mainly as a stimulus to tourism and therefore to the business of the CNR, though several of the officials involved were serious ethnologists who had more scientific reasons for preserving the poles. The Skeena Valley line was advertised as the railway to totem-pole land and thought was given to the creation of a major tourist resort. The initiative for the project came from the government and railway officials, not the local Gitksan people who owned the poles. The Natives were not very interested in marketing their culture for tourists, and some of their chiefs asked the government to stop meddling with the poles. Harlan Smith, an official with the museum, reported that the Gitksan asked why a government which a few years earlier had banned the erection of new poles now wanted to preserve old ones. The Natives believed that their monuments were being used to put rail fares into the pockets of the CNR and wondered why they should co-operate. When the project finished in 1930, only about one-third of the Skeena Valley poles were restored. Still, the result was a benefit to the railway, which highlighted the totems in its publicity material.

During the summer of 1926, the artists A. Y. Jackson and Edwin Holgate visited the Skeena to sketch the poles and the Native villages. Both men believed they were witnessing the remains of a culture in decline. Jackson later wrote that "the big powerful tribes . . . have dwindled to a mere shadow of their former greatness" (Jackson 111). Wanting to take advantage of public interest in the poles, and in West Coast Natives generally, the CNR installed a "Totem Pole Room" for dining and dancing in the Chateau Laurier, its hotel in Ottawa, and commissioned Holgate to design it. The finished product, which opened in 1929, featured columns done up to resemble totem poles, large murals, and Native masks and designs festooning the walls (Reid 14–15).

The marketing of the Skeena Valley poles as a tourist attraction by the CNR was part of a curious phenomenon—the appropriation of the totem pole as an unofficial symbol of British Columbia. The trend began in the 1920s, when various public bodies became alarmed at the rapid disappearance of poles from Native villages into the hands of museums and collectors, mainly outside Canada. As the number of poles dwindled, their value as works of art rose in public estimation. White British Columbians, and Canadians generally, decided that they were an important national treasure, a visible link with the country's first peoples and a part of its heritage, which had to be preserved.

In Vancouver, the Art, Historical and Scientific Association was at the forefront of this movement. Founded in 1889, the AHS created the original Vancouver Museum to hold its growing collection of historical art and artifacts, including "a representative collection of native relics and handicrafts." Later, the AHS conceived the idea of erecting a model Indian village in Stanley Park "to give to the present and succeeding generations an adequate conception of the work and socials life of aborigines before the advent of the white man." The village did not materialize, and the association began collecting totem poles instead. The congregation of poles, which now attracts the attention of so many visitors at Brockton Point in the park, originated with these early efforts of the AHS (Goodfellow, *The Totem Poles in Stanley Park*).

Since the 1920s, totem poles have appeared at a large number of public buildings, hotels, parks, and shopping plazas in British Columbia. Almost every provincial milestone has been celebrated with the raising of a pole. Immediately following World War II, the BC Electric Company, owners of public transit systems on the Lower Mainland and Vancouver Island, altered the insignia on its vehicles to feature a large, spread-winged thunderbird, familiar from the top of so many totems. A tall Haida pole welcomes people entering Canada at the Peace Arch border crossing south of Vancouver. In 1958, when BC celebrated its centennial, the province presented Queen Elizabeth with a Kwakiutl pole, which now stands in Windsor Great Park in England. In 1966, to celebrate the centennial of the union of the colonies of British Columbia and Vancouver Island, the province inaugurated the "Route of the Totems," a series of poles erected along highways and at ferry terminals from Victoria to Prince Rupert. In the mid-1980s, Duncan, a small town on Vancouver Island, declared itself the "City of Totem Poles" and commissioned a group of poles as a way of encouraging travellers to visit (Stewart, *Totem Poles*). While Native people venerate totem poles for social and historical reasons, many non-Natives apparently share a more superstitious belief that poles have the power to make people stop and spend their money.

The totem pole is just one aspect of Native culture that has been adopted by non-Native Canadians as a symbol of their own. In 1991, the federal government unveiled a huge sculpture at the entrance to the new Canadian embassy building in Washington, DC. The "Spirit of Haida G'waii" is a five-ton bronze statue depicting a canoe spilling over with Haida myth figures, carved by the renowned West Coast artist, Bill Reid, who is part Haida himself. Reid and his work are acclaimed worldwide. He ranks among the top monumental artists in Canada. However, it must be assumed that a sculpture in such a prestigious public location is intended to be not only a work of art but more than that, a symbol for Canada itself. The choice of a giant Haida canoe is an interesting attempt by the government to absorb Haida mythology into a more general mythology of relevance to all Canadians.

These attempts are ubiquitous. Recently, I opened an American magazine to discover a government advertisement encouraging tourists to visit Canada.... A bold headline ran across two pages: "Only in God's Country could you meet such interesting souls." A stunning photograph shows two figures, presumably Native people, seated on a sandy beach. They are both wearing large raven's head masks, brightly painted, with long beaks. In the background, a third figure, carrying a ceremonial drum and wrapped in what appears to be a Chilkoot blanket, emerges from the mist at the water's edge. Offshore, islands melt into a blue haze.

The text, which begins by informing readers that "our native peoples have been entertaining visitors for centuries," incorporates a version of a creation myth. Raven beats his wings and brings the world into being. "The most revered of spirits and master of ceremonies, the Raven embodies what this land is today," continues the text. "Magic. For here the supernatural abides in all that is living." The advertisement is promoting Canada, but refers specifically to British Columbia, where apparently everyone is a pantheist and the "Animal People" are "our link to another realm."

Needless to say, this is not a British Columbia I recognize, and I grew up there. Nor is it a British Columbia which any visitor should have any reasonable expectation of encountering. The Animal People do now show themselves to tourists. This British Columbia is the fabulation of an advertising copywriter with a vivid Imaginary Indian.

The Indians in the advertisement are familiar enough. They are spiritual, mysterious Indians. They are a part of the land, like the animals, in touch with the unseen forces of nature. They appeal to the widespread conviction on the part of non-Natives that Native people experience the natural world in a way that is qualitatively different from the rest of us. As well, the Indians in the advertisement belong to history. Dressed in traditional costumes and placed in a context that evokes the past, they are not Indians as they appear to us in modern life. They are thoroughly exotic and otherworldly. . . .

IV

Many aspects of Native culture have been appropriated over the years and turned into commodities to help sell products in the marketplace. These products range from running shoes to cars to the country itself. Indian heroes like Pontiac, Indian artifacts like totem poles, Indian attitudes like the stoicism of the cigar-store Indian have all been invoked. Products are linked to the Indian in the expectation that some supposedly Native virtues will rub off. Indians themselves become commodities in the marketplace. The advertising image is based on stereotypes of the Imaginary Indian already abroad in the culture. In turn, advertising reinforces the stereotype by feeding it back into the mainstream culture in a self-repeating loop.

It may seem unimportant that images of Indians have appeared in tourist brochures and on tins of canned vegetables, coins, and hood ornaments. But the phenomenon is not a trivial one. Many writers have observed that non-Natives have experienced a persistent sense of alienation in North America ever since the first Europeans arrived here. "Americans are really aliens in North America," says Vine Deloria, the American Sioux writer, "and try as they might they seem incapable of adjusting to the continent." In their search for ways to feel at home, Deloria continues, the newcomers have looked to the first inhabitants of the continent: "Indians, the original possessors of the land, seem to haunt the collective unconscious of the white man, and to the degree that one can identify the conflicting images of the Indian which stalk the white man's waking perception of the world one can outline the deeper problems of identity and alienation that trouble him" (Deloria, "American Fantasy" x). One response to this dilemma is to "go Native," to become an Indian, or at least to take on Indian identities, either directly, as Archie Belaney did when he turned into Grey Owl, or spuriously, by appropriating elements of Indianness and making them representative of mainstream society.

Since the beginning of the country, non-Native Canadians have wanted Indians to transform themselves into Whites, to assimilate to the mainstream. But there has also been a strong impulse among Whites, less consciously expressed perhaps, to transform themselves into Indians. Grey Owl simply acted out the fantasy. Each time they respond to a sales pitch which features an Indian image, each time they chant an Indian slogan from their box seats, each time they dress up in feathers for a costume party or take pride in the unveiling of yet another totem pole as a symbol of the country, non-Native Canadians are trying in a way to become Indigenous people themselves and to resolve their lingering sense of not belonging where they need to belong. By appropriating elements of Native culture, non-Natives have tried to establish a relationship with the country that pre-dates their arrival and validates their occupation of the land.

Notes

This Introduction and "Marketing the Imaginary Indian" were originally published in Daniel Francis, *The Imaginary Indian: The Image of the Indian in Canadian Culture* (Vancouver: Arsenal Pulp Press, 1992).

1. I am grateful to my friend Jim Taylor for this reference.
2. This discussion was based on Darling and Cole, 29–48.

14

Postindian Warriors

Gerald Vizenor

President Thomas Jefferson envisioned a water course to the western coast of the nation a decade before he proposed the expedition that would become the most notable literature of tribal survivance.

Meriwether Lewis and William Clark were instructed that the objective of their mission was to explore the land west of the Missouri River that "may offer the most direct & practicable water communication across the continent, for the purposes of commerce."

Lewis and Clark reported in their journal that they wanted to be *seen* by tribal people on their expedition. They were diplomatic at a distance, to be sure, and they were certain that their mission would have been threatened not by the presence of the other, but by the absence of the tribes.

Luther Standing Bear, three generations later, was on an expedition in another direction and dimension; he was one of the first tribal students to graduate from an eastern government school. He was curious and courageous in the presence of the other, and he was threatened by the absence of reverence, honour, and natural reason.

Standing Bear, Lewis, Clark, and others, created the simulations that would honour their survivance in literature. Simulations have never been uncommon in literature, as the simulations of the other are instances of the absence of the real, but these expeditions in at least two dimensions were more than the mere simulations of savagism and civilization.

The Lewis and Clark expedition was one of the first transcontinental encounters with diverse tribal cultures; the encounters were inevitable in the new nation, but the successive encroachments on the natural presence of the tribes were vicious and barbarous. The cruelties of national and colonial authorities were widespread; the grievous outcome of avarice, perverse determinism, and the destinies that would become manifest manners in the literature of dominance.

Lewis wrote in his journal on 18 July 1805, "as we were anxious now to meet with the Sosonees or snake Indians as soon as possible in order to obtain information relative to the geography [of] the country. . . ." Four days later he wrote that Sacajawea, the "Indian woman recognizes the country and assures us that this is the river on which her relations live, and that the three forks are at no great distance."

Lewis wrote on 27 July 1805, "we begin to feel considerable anxiety with rispect to the Snake Indians. if we do not find them or some other nation who have horses I fear the successfull issue of our voyage will be very doubtfull or at all events much more difficult in it's accomplishment."

Then, about two weeks later, he wrote, "I was overjoyed at the sight of this stranger and had no doubts of obtaining a friendly introduction to his nation provided I could get near enough to him to convince him of our being whitemen." The selections are from *The Journals of Lewis and Clark*, edited by Bernard DeVoto.

"Indeed, the greatest danger the Indians could pose for Lewis and Clark arose from their absence rather than their presence," wrote Larzer Ziff in *Writing in the New Nation*. "What was later to be a cliché in Western adventure fiction, the white man's seeing Indians and taking care to remain unseen by them, was reversed as they strained to see the Indians who they knew were seeing them in order to enter into dealings with them."

Lieutenant William Reynolds, in contrast to the earlier expedition of Lewis and Clark, remained *unseen* on the deck of the *Flying Fish*, a schooner in the first discovery expedition of the United States Navy. "We never saw any one for weeks, save a few Indians now and then who brought us Salmon and Deer and who were welcome enough, but as to Society, after a hard day's labour, we might as well have been in the great desert. We did long with all our hearts to see the face of some *human* creature," he wrote to his sister on 7 November 1841, after a survey of the Columbia River.

> Once in a great while we *did* manage to run up to Astoria and have a chat with the folks there, and sometimes we saw the young wives of the missionaries, pretty, rosy cheeked women, the very sight of whom gave us the heart ache. I am disgusted with all naked Indians and primitive peoples whatever, and shall be too happy . . . when I can associate again with the more intelligent and attractive portion of the human family, who carry ideas in their heads, wear clothes on their bodies and are fair to look upon.

His aversion to the tribes would represent the racialism of the nation; in turn, that aversion to the presence of the tribes would become the cause of manifest manners and the literature of dominance.

Lewis and Clark traversed the same river thirty-six years earlier and were content to be *seen* by the tribes. Clark wrote in his journal on 24 October 1805 that the

> nativs of ths village re[ce]ived me verry kindly, one of whome envited me into his house, which I found to be large and comodious, and the first wooden houses in which Indians have lived Since we left those in the vicinity of the Illinois. . . . Peter Crusat played on the *violin* and the men danced which delighted the nativs, who Shew every civility towards us. we Smoked with those people untill late at night, when every one retired to rest.

Standing Bear seemed to envision the onset of the postindian warriors of simulations; that sensation of a new tribal presence in the very ruins of the representations of invented Indians. "I always wanted to please my father in every way possible," wrote Standing Bear in *My People the Sioux*. "All his instructions to me had been along this line: 'Son, be brave and get killed.' This expression had been moulded into my brain to such an extent that I knew nothing else.

"My father had made a mistake. He should have told me, upon leaving home, to go and learn all I could of the white man's ways, and be like them." Luther had "come away from home with the intention of never returning alive unless he had done something brave."

"Now, after having had my hair cut, a new thought came into my head. I felt that I was no more Indian, but would be an imitation of a white man. And we are still imitations of white men, and the white men are imitations of the Americans."

Standing Bear was in the first class to attend the federal school at Carlisle, Pennsylvania. Later, he taught school on the reservation, witnessed the horror of the massacre at Wounded Knee, and toured with Buffalo Bill's Wild West show in Europe. This postindian warrior was active in tribal rights movements, an actor in several motion pictures, and he wrote several books about his experiences.

The postindian warriors encounter their enemies with the same courage in literature as their ancestors once evinced on horses, and they create their stories with a new sense of survivance. The warriors bear the simulations of their time and counter the manifest manners of domination.

Manifest Destiny would cause the death of millions of tribal people from massacres, diseases, and the loneliness of reservations. Entire cultures have been terminated in the course of nationalism. These histories are now the simulations of dominance, and the causes of the conditions that have become manifest manners in literature. The postindian simulations are the core of survivance, the new stories of tribal courage. The simulations of manifest manners are the continuance of the surveillance and domination of the tribes in literature. Simulations are the absence of the tribal real; the postindian conversions are in the new stories of survivance over dominance. The natural reason of the tribes anteceded by thousands of generations the invention of the Indian. The postindian ousts the inventions with humor, new stories, and the simulations of survivance.

Standing Bear, for instance, had graduated from the government school and he was working at John Wanamaker's department store in Philadelphia when he read in the newspaper that Sitting Bull, the Lakota healer, was scheduled to lecture in the city. "The paper stated that he was the Indian who killed General Custer! The chief and his people had been held prisoners of war, and now here they were to appear" in a theatre. "On the stage sat four Indian men, one of whom was Sitting Bull. There were two women and two children with them. A white man came on the stage and introduced Sitting Bull as the man who had killed General Custer," which was not true.

Sitting Bull "addressed the audience in the Sioux tongue" and then the white man, the interpreter, misconstrued his speech in translation. "My friends, white people, we Indians are on our way to Washington to see the Grandfather, or President of the United States," and more was translated as the story of the massacre of General Custer at the Little Big Horn. "He told so many lies I had to smile."

Standing Bear visited Sitting Bull at the hotel. "He wanted his children educated in the white man's way, because there was nothing left for the Indian." The interpreter was in the room, so "I did not get a chance to tell Sitting Bull how the white man had lied about him on the stage. And that was the last time I ever saw Sitting Bull alive."

The postindian warriors hover at last over the ruins of tribal representations and surmount the scriptures of manifest manners with new stories; these warriors counter the surveillance and literature of dominance with their own simulations of survivance. The postindian arises from the earlier inventions of the tribes only to contravene the absence of the real with theatrical performances; the theatre of tribal consciousness is the recreation of the real, not the absence of the real in the simulations of dominance.

Manifest manners are the simulations of dominance; the notions and misnomers that are read as the authentic and sustained as representations of Native American Indians. The postindian warriors are new indications of a narrative recreation, the simulations that overcome the manifest manners of dominance.

The once bankable simulations of the savage as an impediment to developmental civilization, the simulations that audiences would consume in Western literature and motion pictures, protracted the extermination of tribal cultures.

Michael Blake must have been cued to continue the simulations in his novel *Dances with Wolves*. "There were Pawnee, the most terrible of all the tribes," he wrote. "They saw with unsophisticated but ruthlessly efficient eyes. . . . And if it was determined that the object should cease to live, the Pawnee saw to its death with psychotic precision."

The motion picture with the same name counts on the bankable manifest manners of the audience to associate with the adventures and discoveries of an errant cavalry officer who counters the simulations of savagism in *his* stories. The tiresome tantivy of tried and true horses with no shadows, and the Western tune of manifest manners, is the most serious deliverance of civilization ever concocted in the movies or literature. The Civil War has become one of those simulations in movies that abates the loathsome memories of more recent wars, and hastens the disabused heroes to discover their honourable pluck with native warriors. *Dances with Wolves*, for instance, must have been inspired by the men who heard the cicerones of *Broken Arrow* and *Little Big Man*. Manifestly, movies have never been the representations of tribal cultures; at best, movies are the deliverance of an unsure civilization.

Simulations are the absence of the tribes; that absence was wiser in the scenes of silence, richer in costumes, and more courageous on a ride beside simulated animals. Western movies are the muse of simulations, and the absence of humor and real tribal cultures.

"The absence of Indians in Western movies, by which I mean the lack of their serious presence as individuals, is so shocking once you realize it that, even for someone acquainted with outrage, it's hard to admit," wrote Jane Tompkins in *West of Everything*. "My unbelief at the travesty of native peoples that Western films afford kept me from scrutinizing what was there. I didn't want to see. I stubbornly expected the genre to be better than it was, and when it wasn't, I dropped the subject. . . . I never cried at anything I saw in a Western, but I cried when I realized this: that after the Indians had been decimated by disease, removal, and conquest, and after they had been caricatured and degraded in Western movies, I had ignored them too."

The Western movies, of course, are not cultural visions, but the vicious encounters with the antiselves of civilization, the invented savage. Since the national encounters over the war in Vietnam, however, the Indian is a new contrivance and encounter of the antiselves in postwestern movies. The new scenes of postwestern simulations are the melancholy antiselves in the ruins of representations; the tribal others are now embraced, a romance with silence and visions. The tragic wisdom that was once denied is now a new invention in such postwestern movies as *Dances with Wolves*.

The postindian is the new simulation in the postwestern salvation of the antiselves in the movies; the landscape, overrun to be sure, has turned even richer in postwestern movies with the rescue of natural reason and romance over the ministrations of antitribal mercantilism.

Wallace Stegner has ushered the postwestern landscape into a new theatre of literary salvation and dominance; alas, he has no obvious need to be *seen* with the tribal others as survivance. "Being a Westerner is not simple," he wrote in his recent collections of essays, *Where the Bluebird Sings to the Lemonade Springs*. He observes that, "ethnic and cultural confusion exists not only in Los Angeles but in varying proportions in every western city and many towns. Much of the adaptation that is going on is adaptation to an uncertain reality or to a reality whose past and present do not match. The western culture and western character with which it is easiest to identify exist largely in the West of make-believe, where they can be kept simple."

Thomas Jefferson, James Fenimore Cooper, Francis Parkman, George Bancroft, and other masters of manifest manners in the nineteenth century, and earlier, represented tribal cultures as the other; to them "language did the capturing, binding Indian society to a future of certain extinction," wrote Larzer Ziff in *Writing in the New Nation*. "Treating living Indians as sources for a literary construction of a vanished way of life rather than as members of a vital continuing culture, such writers used words to replace rather than to represent Indian reality."

The simulations of manifest manners are treacherous and elusive in histories; how ironic that the most secure simulations are unreal sensations, and become the real without a referent to an actual tribal remembrance. Tribal realities are superseded by simulations of the unreal, and tribal wisdom is weakened by those imitations, however sincere. The pleasures of silence, natural reason, the rights of consciousness, transformations of the marvelous, and the pleasure of trickster stories are misconstrued in the simulations of dominance; manifest manners are the absence of the real in the ruins of tribal representations.

Those who "memorialized rather than perpetuated" a tribal presence and wrote "Indian history as obituary" were unconsciously collaborating "with those bent on physical extermination," argued Ziff. "The process of literary annihilation would be checked only when Indian writers began representing their own culture."

Andrew McLaughlin and Claude Van Tyne, authors of a high school history textbook published by Appleton and Company a generation after the Wounded Knee Massacre, resisted the inclusion of more than about half a page on Indians. Manifest manners and the simulations of dominance are the annihilation, not the survivance of tribal stories.

"Simulation is no longer that of a territory, a referential being or a substance," wrote Jean Baudrillard in *Simulacra and Simulations*. "It is the generation by models of a real without origin or reality: a hyperreal. The territory no longer precedes the map, nor survives it."

Americans, moreover, pursue a "more to come" consumer simulation, wrote Umberto Eco in *Travels in Hyperreality*. "This is the reason for this journey into hyperreality, in search of instances where the American imagination demands the real thing and, to attain it, must fabricate the absolute fake." Indians, in this sense, must be simulations of the "absolute fakes" in the ruins of representation, or the victims in literary annihilation.

Wallace Stegner situates the western landscape in the literature of dominance. The land and new nation were discovered with nouns and deverbatives, consumed with transitive actions, and embraced with a causal sensation of manifest manners. The land was unnamed and became a place with names "worn smooth with use," he wrote in an essay. "No place is a place until things that have happened in it are remembered in history, ballads, yarns, legends, or monuments."

Stegner would never contribute to the annihilation of tribal cultures, but his concern over names pronounces that the land was untouched and unnamed in tribal stories. His pronominal discoveries of the land are the absence of tribal remembrance. He concedes to manifest manners in the cause of literature. "Plunging into the future through a landscape that had no history, we did both the country and ourselves some harm along with some good." Natural scenes with "no histories" are the absence of natural reason in the literature of discoveries. Tribal names and stories are real histories, not discoveries.

"We have made a tradition out of mourning the passing of things we never had time really to know, just as we have made a culture out of the open road, out of the movement without place," wrote Stegner. "No place, not even a wild place, is a place until it has had that human attention that in its highest reach we call poetry." His reluctance to honour tribal stories in the blood, land, and oral literature, the names and stories of remembrance, is the course of manifest manners; the christened names of discoveries and dominance.

The shadows of tribal names and stories are the ventures of landscapes, even in the distance of translation. Tribal imagination, experience, and remembrance, are the real landscapes in the literature of this nation; discoveries and dominance are silence.

N. Scott Momaday, the poet and novelist, reached to the remembrance of his childhood at Jemez, New Mexico. "I existed in that landscape," he wrote in his memoir, *The Names*, "and then my existence was indivisible with it. I placed my shadow there in the hills, my voice in the wind that ran there, in those old mornings and afternoons, and evenings. It may be that the old people there watch for me in the streets; it may be so." That place is so with his memories.

"The language of white thought has had to create the boundaries of its existence and to determine what will not be allowed inside," wrote Aldon Lynn Nielsen in *Reading Race*. "The signifier of whiteness continues to rewrite itself as a discourse into our institutions, including our literature, and we, as racial subject, continue to read it, to recognize it, to privilege it, and to enjoy its power."

The attention to manifest manners and the romance of the land would annihilate tribal names, languages, oral stories, and natural reason. Larzer Ziff argued that literary "annihilation, in which the representation offers itself as the only aspect of the represented that is still extant, is not, of course, physical extermination." However, in "order to conquer the savage one had to outdo him in savagery," and "the wild man within was purged even as the wild man without was exterminated."

The word Indian, and most other tribal names, are simulations in literature of dominance. Chippewa, for instance, is defined as *otchipwe*, and the invented word Indian is defined as *anishinabe* in *A Dictionary of the Otchipwe Language* by Bishop Baraga. This first dictionary of the language published more than a century ago defined *anishinabe* as a man, woman, child, of the *anishinabe* tribe, but the simulated names, not the names in tribal languages, were sustained by manifest manners in literature.

Cognation and certain loan words can be traced to the earliest use in the literature of dominance. *Canoe*, for instance, was "picked up from the Indians in the West Indies by Columbus's sailors," observed H. L. Mencken in *The American Language*. "It was taken without change into Spanish where it remains as *canoa* to this day." *Maize* is another loan word that came into Spanish and then English from the West Indies. The word *Indian*, however, is a colonial enactment, not a loan word, and the dominance is sustained by the simulation that has superseded the real tribal names.

The Indian was an occidental invention that became a bankable simulation; the word has no referent in tribal languages or cultures. The postindian is the absence of the invention, and the end of representation in literature; the closure of that evasive melancholy of dominance. Manifest manners are the simulations of bourgeois decadence and melancholy.

The postindian warrior is the simulation of survivance in new stories. Indians, and other simulations, are the absence of tribal intimation; the mere mention of blunders in navigation undermines the significance of discoveries and the melancholy of dominance. The contrivances of names, however, endures in the monologues of manifest manners and literature of dominance. The postindian warriors ensnare the contrivances with their own simulations of survivance.

Russell Means, for instance, launched a new simulation of the name. There is "some confusion about the word *Indian*, a mistaken belief that it refers somehow to the country, India," he wrote in *Mother Jones*. "Columbus called the tribal people he met 'Indio,' from the Italian *in dio*, meaning 'in God.'"

The postindian warriors bear their own simulations and revisions to contend with manifest manners, the "authentic" summaries of ethnology, and the curse of racialism and modernism in the ruins of representation. The wild incursions of the warriors of survivance undermine the simulations of the unreal in the literature of dominance.

Postindian simulations arise from the silence of heard stories, or the imagination of oral literature in translation, not the absence of the real in simulated realities; the critical distinction is that postindian warriors create a new tribal presence in stories. The simulations of manifest manners are dominance, the scriptures of a civilization in paradise. The counteractions of postindian warriors are the simulations of survivance.

The postindian encounters with manifest manners and the simulations of the other are established in names and literature. This is a continuous turn in tribal narratives, the oral stories are dominated by those narratives that are translated, published, and read at unnamed distances. Stories that arise in silence are the sources of a tribal presence. The simulations of dominance and absence of the other are the concern of manifest manners. The simulations of survivance are heard and read stories that mediate and undermine the literature of dominance.

The names of the postindian warriors are new, but their encounters are consistent with the warriors who tread the manifest manners of past missions in tribal communities. The warriors of simulations, then and now, uncover the absence of the real and undermine the comparative poses of tribal traditions.

The warrior modes and postindian interpretations, in this instance, at the closure of the colonial inventions of the tribes in literature; the warriors, then and now, observe postmodern situations, theories of simulation, deconstruction, postindian encounters, silence, remembrance, and other themes of survivance that would trace the inventions of tribal cultures by missionaries and ethnologists to the truancies and cruelties of a melancholy civilization.

The postindian warriors and the missionaries of manifest manners are both responsible for simulations; even that resemblance is a simulation that ends in silence, or the presence of an original referent to tribal survivance.

The warriors of simulation are entitled to tease the absence of remembrance in the ruins of representation, and in the tribal performance of heard stories. Simulations in oral stories arise from silence not inscriptions. The causal narratives of missionaries and ethnologists are terminal simulations of dominance, not survivance.

"But the matter is more complicated, since to simulate is not simply to feign," continued Jean Baudrillard in *Simulacra and Simulations*. "Someone who feigns an illness can simply go to bed and make believe he is ill. Someone who simulates an illness produces in himself some of the symptoms." Hence, "feigning or dissimulating leaves the realty principle intact: the difference is always clear, it is only masked; whereas simulation threatens the difference between 'true' and 'false', between 'real' and 'imaginary'. Since the simulator produces 'true' symptoms, is he ill or not?"

Jamake Highwater simulated his tribal descent, to be sure, and with such assurance that others feigned their own identities in his presence. Jack Anderson, the investigative columnist, reported that Highwater "fabricated much of the background that made him famous."[1] He was more answerable as a simulation than others were to their own real crossblood identities.

How are we to understand the common attributions of tribal descent in the simulations of postindian identities? Some postindian warriors feign the sources of their crossblood identities, the masks of a real tribal presence. Others, the wannabes, posers, and the missionaries of manifest manners, would threaten the remembrance of tribal identities with their surveillance and terminal simulations; the scriptures of dominance are the absence of tribal realities not the sources of a presence. The simulations of manifest manners have never been the masks of civilization or even the historical ironies of tribal cultures.

The Indian is the simulation of the absence, an unreal name; however, the misnomer has a curious sense of legal standing. Some of the definitions are ethnological, racial, literary, and juristic sanctions. "To be considered an Indian for federal purposes, an individual must have some Indian blood," wrote Stephen Pevar in *The Rights of Indian Tribes*. "Some federal laws define an Indian as anyone of Indian descent, while other laws require one-fourth or one-half Indian blood in order to be considered as an Indian for purposes of those laws. Still other federal laws define Indian as anyone who has been accepted as a member of a 'federally recognized' Indian tribe." Clearly, the simulations of tribal names, the absence of a presence in a mere tribal misnomer, cannot be sustained by legislation or legal manoeuvres.

Postindian autobiographies, the averments of tribal descent, and the assertions of crossblood identities, are simulations in literature; that names, nicknames, and the shadows of ancestors are stories is an invitation to new theories of tribal interpretation.

The sources of natural reason and tribal consciousness are doubt and wonder, not nostalgia or liberal melancholy for the lost wilderness; comic not tragic, because melancholy is cultural boredom, and the tragic is causal, the closure of natural reason. The shimmers of imagination are reason and the simulations are survivance, not dominance; an aesthetic restoration of trickster hermeneutics, the stories of liberation and survivance without the dominance of closure. Tribal consciousness is wonder, chance, coincidence, not the revisions of a pedate paradise; even so, for curious reasons some would hear confessions and the conversions of criminals as the evidence of a new tribal awareness.

Trickster hermeneutics is the interpretation of simulations in the literature of survivance, the ironies of descent and racialism, transmutation, third gender, and themes of transformation in oral tribal stories and written narratives. Trickster stories arise in silence, not scriptures, and are the *holotropes* of imagination; the manifold turns of scenes, the brush of natural reason, characters that liberate the mind and never reach a closure in stories. Trickster stories are the postindian simulations of tribal survivance.

The trickster is reason and mediation in stories, the original translator of tribal encounters; the name is an intimation of transformation, men to women, animals to birds, and more than mere causal representation in names. Tricksters are the translation of creation; the trickster creates the tribe in stories, and pronounces the moment of remembrance as the trace of liberation. The animals laughed, the birds cried, and there were worried hearts over the everlasting humour that would liberate the human mind in trickster stories. Trickster stories are the translation of liberation, and the shimmer of imagination is the liberation of the last trickster stories.

Trickster hermeneutics is access to trickster stories, and the shimmer of tribal presence in simulations; this new course of tribal interpretation arises from the postindian turns in literature, the reach of tribal shadows, postmodern conditions of translation, the traces of deconstruction, and the theories of representation and simulation. Trickster hermeneutics is survivance, not closure, and the discernment of tragic wisdom in tribal experiences. The tribes bear the simulations of pathos and the tragic without the wisdom of chance and natural miseries of the seasons. Simulation of the tragic has been sustained by the literature of dominance. Natural reason teases the sense that nature is precarious; however, the realities of chance, fate, and tragic wisdom were denied in the literature of dominance.

"Some say that tragedy teaches us the power of chance, of the force of contingency in determining whether the virtuous thrive," wrote Amélie Oksenberg

Rorty in *Essays on Aristotle's Poetics*. "While tragedy does indeed focus on what can go wrong in the actions of the best of men, its ethical lessons are not primarily about the place of accident and fortune in the unfolding of human life." She observed that many "tragedies represent a tale with which the audience is likely to be familiar." The tragic tribal tales, in this sense, are simulations for an audience familiar with manifest manners and the literature of dominance. Decidedly, the stories that turn the tribes tragic are not their own stories.

Manifest manners are scriptural simulations, the causal narratives of racialism, the denial of tragic wisdom, and the cultural leases of objectivism; otherwise, the mere mention of the transitive other, the antiselves in the absence of remembrance, would end in silence. The postindian warriors hear stories that arise in natural silence. Listen, oral stories are the best performance of simulations, because the reference is in the performance.

Performance and human silence are strategies of survivance. Nature is a simulation without silence. The presence of human silence and death has no simulations. The absence and the presence of death are mortal performances. "Death actually discloses the imposture of reality, not only in that the absence of duration gives the lie to it, but above all because death is the great affirmer," wrote Georges Bataille in *Theory of Religion*. "But death suddenly shows that the real society was lying. Then it is not the loss of the thing, of the useful member, that is taken into consideration. What the real society has lost is not a member but rather its truth."

Native American Indians have endured the lies and wicked burdens of discoveries, the puritanical destinies of monotheism, manifest manners, and the simulated realities of dominance, with silence, traces of natural reason, trickster hermeneutics, the interpretation of tribal figurations, and the solace of heard stories.

The various translations, interpretations, and representations of the absence of tribal realities have been posed as the verities of certain cultural traditions. Moreover, the closure of heard stories in favour of scriptural simulations as authentic representations denied a common brush with the shimmer of humour, the sources of tribal visions, and tragic wisdom; tribal imagination and creation stories were obscured without remorse in national histories and the literature of dominance.

"One of the greatest paradoxes of contemporary culture is that at a time when the image reigns supreme the very notion of a creative human imagination seems under mounting threat," wrote Richard Kearney in *The Wake of Imagination*. "The imminent demise of imagination is clearly a postmodern obsession. Postmodernism undermines the modernist belief in the image as an *authentic* expression."

In other words, the postindian warriors of postmodern simulations would undermine and surmount, with imagination and the performance of new stories, the manifest manners of scriptural simulations and "authentic" representations of the tribes in the literature of dominance.

Notes

This essay was first published in Gerald Vizenor, *Manifest Manners: Postindian Wars of Survivance* (Hanover and London: Wesleyan UP, 1994).

1.   As cited in Vizenor, "Native American Identities," 125.

15

Postcolonial Ghost Dancing: Diagnosing European Colonialism

James (Sákéj) Youngblood Henderson

Many different strategies and techniques comprise colonialism. These strategies and techniques are a maladroit manifestation by colonialists of their inherited European culture and values. These colonialists saw themselves as continuing the work of the great seventeenth-century European thinkers who created the idea of an artificial society. In remote places, they constructed colonialism on their heritage of Eurocentrism, universality, and a strategy of difference. In the process, they either rejected or overlooked the Crown's vision of treaty commonwealth in international law.

An understanding of these competing components will allow Indigenous peoples to understand the nature of postcolonial self-determination, its movements, visions, and projects. The analysis that I present will be an exercise in postcolonial ghost dancing. Perhaps, for the benefit of an international audience, I should explain why I use this term.

Eurocentric writers have categorized the ghost dance as a type of messianic movement among North American Indians that expressed a desperate longing for the restoration of the past. The vision unfolded that, if followers would purify themselves, speak the truth, love one another, and participate in a special dance, then the dead would soon join the living and all would live happily together in the old way. One vision originated in the prophet dance in eastern British Columbia and Washington. The vision emphasized an imminent destruction of the world, return of the dead, and change to more righteous ways, and it may have been the ultimate source of the later movement (Spier, *The Prophet Dance of the Northwest and Its Derivatives* and *The Ghost Dance of 1870 among the Klamath of Oregon*). Among the Plains Indians, my relatives, a related vision told that a tidal wave of new earth would cover the alien whites and Indian nonbelievers and renew the land.[1] The vision instructed Wovoka to teach people a sacred dance to be performed at regular intervals. This vision came to be known as the ghost dance.

Eurocentric writings about the ghost dance misunderstood the visions. The normative visions and the dances were not part of a messianic movement but a sustained vision of how to resist colonization. It was a vision of how to release all the spirits contained in the old ceremonies and rites. The dance released these contained spirits or forces back into the deep caves of mother Earth, where they would be immune from colonizers' strategies and techniques. Their efforts were a noble sacrifice for future generations. What is more important, the dance would allow the spiritual teachings to renew the ecology and eventually the forces of the ecology would forge a traditional consciousness of the following generations. In time, through postcolonial ghost dancing, these forces would foster a new vision of Aboriginal renewal, thus restoring the traditional consciousness and order. Part of the renewal is understanding the colonizer's strategy of Eurocentrism, epistemological diffusionism, universality, and enforcement of differences.

Eurocentrism

Among colonized peoples, the cognitive legacy of colonization is labelled "Eurocentrism." Among some Indigenous peoples, Eurocentrism is known as the twin of the trickster or imitator,[2] or the "anti-trickster." Similar to the trickster who emphasizes Aboriginal thought and dramatizes human behaviour in a world of flux, the "anti-trickster" appears in many guises and is the essence of paradoxical transformation. The "anti-trickster" represents a cognitive force of artificial European thought, a differentiated consciousness, ever changing in its creativity to justify the oppression and domination of contemporary Indigenous peoples and their spiritual guardians.

In academic professorate, Eurocentrism is a dominant intellectual and educational movement that postulates the superiority of Europeans over non-Europeans. Modernists tend to think of Eurocentrism as a prejudice that can be eliminated in the same way that attempts have been made to eliminate racism, sexism, and religious bigotry. However, Eurocentrism is not a matter of attitudes in the sense of values and prejudices. It has been the dominant artificial context for the last five centuries and is an integral part of all scholarship, opinion, and law. As an institutional and imaginative context, it includes a set of assumptions and beliefs about empirical reality. Habitually educated and usually unprejudiced Europeans accept these assumptions and beliefs as true, as propositions supported by "the facts."

Historian Lise Noël has dramatically captured the consequences of this cognitive reality:

> Alienation is to the oppressed what self-righteousness is to the oppressor. Each really believes that their unequal relationship is part of the natural order of things or desired by some higher power. The dominator does not feel the need to withdraw from his tutelage. . . . The dominator will even believe, in all good faith, that he is looking out for the good of the dominated, while the latter will insist that they want an authority more enlightened than their own to determine their fate. (79)

In Canadian universities and colleges, academic curricula support Eurocentric contexts. When most professors describe the "world," they describe artificial Eurocentric contexts and ignore Aboriginal worldviews, knowledge, and thought. For most Aboriginal students, the realization of the invisibility is similar to looking into a still lake and not seeing their images. They become alien in their own eyes, unable to recognize themselves in the reflections and shadows of the world. As their grandparents and parents were stripped of their wealth and dignity, this realization strips Aboriginal students of their heritage and identity. It gives them awareness of their annihilation.

At best, Canadian universities define Aboriginal heritage, identity, and thought as inferior to Eurocentric heritage, identity, and thought. Typically, however, Eurocentric thought explicitly and implicitly confirms Aboriginal inadequacy and asserts a negative image of Aboriginal heritage and identity. Tragically, before long, Aboriginal students will succumb and inwardly endorse Eurocentric thought and help to lay the foundations of the relationship of domination that will entrench their thoughts (Noël 79–80).

A strong critique of Eurocentrism is under way in all fields of social thought (Blaut 8).[3] This critique reveals that the assumptions and beliefs that constructed the context are not universal after all. Many are imaginative local knowledge; some are false. These critiques give rise to anguished discourses about knowledge and truths. Quickly the issue of respecting diversity slips into maintaining Eurocentric unity and canons. Roberto Mangabeira Unger has called this the burden of the past in the social theory and law:

> It is commonplace that great men impose a burden upon these who come after them. When there has been remarkable achievement in politics, art, or thought, the generation that follows in its wake, and benefits from it may suffer the paralyzing sense that nothing really important remains to be done. It may feel that the most brilliant opportunities have already been explored and turned to advantage. As a result, the successors seem faced

with a dilemma: either they become mere caretakers of the monuments the great have left them, or, desirous of independence, but despairing of excellence, they drastically narrow their ambitions and set out to till, with technical proficiency, a small field. (*Law in Modern Society* 1)

Critical scholars today are aware, as most were not a few decades ago, that the empirical beliefs of history, geography, and social science that invented the context of Eurocentrism often gained acceptance in the way in which the evidence was presented. Scholarly beliefs are embedded in particular languages and cultures and are shaped by them. This helps to explain the paradox of Eurocentrism, which is resistant to change and continues to exercise a persuasive intellectual power. Its old myths continue to be believed long after the rationale for their acceptance has been forgotten or rejected (e.g., arguments grounded in the belief that the Old Testament is literal history). Newer beliefs gain acceptance without supporting evidence if they are properly Eurocentric.

James M. Blaut argues that modernists derive this resistance from their association with the most powerful social interests of the Eurocentric elites. European colonialism initiated the development of the Eurocentric context, and its wealth formulated many academic elites. Consequently, the development of a body of Eurocentric beliefs has been, and still is, of great importance in justifying and assisting Europe's colonial activities. Eurocentrism is, quite simply, the colonizer's model of the world (10).

Eurocentrism is the colonizers' model of the world in a very literal sense: it is not merely a bundle of beliefs. It has evolved, through time, into a finely sculpted model, a structured whole—in fact, an ultra-theory, a general framework for many smaller theories: historical, geographical, psychological, sociological, and philosophical. This ultra-theory is known as diffusionism (10–11).

Epistemological Diffusionism

Eurocentric diffusionism has changed through time, but its basic nineteenth-century epistemological framework has remained essentially unchanged. Blaut argues that diffusionism is based on two axioms: (1) most human communities are uninventive; and (2) a few human communities (or places or cultures) are inventive and thus remain permanent centres of cultural change or progress. On a global scale, this gives us a model of a world with a single centre—roughly, Europe—and a surrounding periphery (12).

The dualism of an inside and an outside is central to the ultra-theory (14).[4] The basic framework of diffusionism in its classical form depicts a world divided into two categories, one of which (greater Europe, "inside") is historical, inventive, and makes progress; the other (non-Europe, "outside") is ahistorical, stagnant, and unchanging and receives progressive innovations by diffusion from Europe. From this base, diffusionism asserts that the difference between the two sectors is that some intellectual or spiritual factor, something characteristic of the "European mind," the "European spirit," the "Western man," and so forth, leads to creativity, imagination, invention, innovation, rationality, and a sense of honour or ethics—in other words, "European values." The reason for non-Europe's non-progress is a lack of this intellectual or spiritual factor. This proposition asserts that non-European people are empty, or partly so, of "rationality"—that is, of ideas and proper spiritual values.

Classic diffusionism asserts an emptiness of basic cultural institutions and people in much of the non-European world. This is known as the diffusionist myth of emptiness. This idea plays a role in the physical movement of Europeans into non-European regions, displacing or eliminating the native inhabitants. The proposition of emptiness makes a series of claims, each layered upon the others:

1   A non-European region is empty or nearly empty of people (so settlement by Europeans does not displace any Native peoples).

2   The region is empty of settled population: the inhabitants are mobile, nomadic, wanderers (European settlement violates no political sovereignty since wanderers make no claim to territory).

3   The cultures of this region do not possess an understanding of private property, so the region is empty of property rights and claims (colonial occupiers can freely give land to settlers since no one owns it).

4   The final layer, applied to all the "outside," is an emptiness of intellectual creativity and spiritual values, sometimes described by Europeans as an absence of "rationality" (15).[5]

Classic diffusionism also assumes that some non-European regions were "rational" in some ways and to some degree. Thus, for instance, the Middle East during biblical times was rational. China was somewhat rational for a certain period in its history. Other regions, always including Africa, are unqualifiedly lacking in rationality.

Diffusionism asserts that the normal and natural way that the non-European world progresses—or changes for the better, modernizes, and so on—is by the diffusion (or spread) of innovative, progressive ideas from Europe, which flow into it as air flows into a vacuum. This flow may take the form of ideas or new products through which European values are spread. Europeans themselves are bearers of these new and innovative ideas.

The diffusion of civilizing ideas from Europe to non-Europe is compensation for the confiscation of material wealth by Europe from non-Europe—although nothing can fully compensate Europeans for their gift of civilization to the colonies since the possibility exists that ancient, atavistic traits will counterdiffuse back into the civilized core, in the form of evil things such as black magic.

Blaut outlined the characteristics of the dualism between the centre and the periphery; see Table 1. This is a simplified version of the diffusionist world model. The debates between diffusionists and their opponents have been going on for more than a century in anthropology, geography, history, and all fields concerned with long-term, large-scale cultural evolution (Blaut 11).[6] The anti-diffusionists (often called "evolutionists" or "independent-inventionists") level two basic charges against the diffusionists: they hold much too sour a view of human ingenuity, and they believe in spatial elitism. Yet antidiffusionists have failed to grasp the full implication of their critique. None of them denies that the world has an "inside" and an "outside." While criticizing the diffusionists for rejecting the psychic unity of humankind, the antidiffusionists nonetheless believe that Europe is the centre of cultural evolution. Therefore, they accept the idea—explicitly or implicitly—that Europeans are more inventive and more innovative than anyone else is (13). They make this assumption explicitly when they discuss the modernizing effect of European colonialism. The basic structure of their arguments is the same as that of the diffusionists.

All Eurocentric scholarship is diffusionist since it axiomatically accepts that the world has one permanent centre from which culture/changing ideas tend

Table 1: Centre and Periphery Compared

Characteristics of Eurocentric Centre	Characteristics of Periphery
Inventiveness	Imitativeness
Rationality, intellect	Irrationality, emotion, instinct
Abstract thought	Concrete thought
Theoretical reasoning	Empirical, practical reasoning
Mind	Body, matter
Discipline	Spontaneity
Adulthood	Childhood
Sanity	Insanity
Science	Sorcery
Progress	Stagnation

to originate and a vast periphery that changes as a result (mainly) of diffusion from that single centre. This ultra-theory of Eurocentric context is the intellectual tool of European colonialism. It asserts that colonialism brings civilization to non-Europe and is, in fact, the proper way in which the non-European world advances out of stagnation. Under colonialism, wealth is drawn out of the colonies and enriches the European colonizers. In Eurocentric diffusionism, Europeans see this as a normal relationship between European and Indigenous peoples. Although Eurocentric diffusionism is constructed on some unjustifiably restrictive assumptions, it nevertheless provides the context for colonial legal and political strategy.

Universalism

Eurocentric thought does not claim to be a privileged norm. This would be an argument about cultural relativism, which asserts that values are about specific cultural contexts.[7] Instead, Eurocentric thought claims to be universal and general.[8] Noël summarizes the function of universalism in colonialism: "To present himself as the ideal human type, the dominator often invoked irreducible laws sanctioned by Nature, God, or History. In his view, the power he exercised over the oppressed was not so much the result of undue reliance on force as the effect of uncontrollable imperatives, if not a Higher Will. In relation to the universal model that the oppressor seemed to represent, the dominated always appeared to be afflicted with some defect or intrinsic failing" (149).

European scholars have always held that their civilization had two sources of inspiration that forbade them to be content with developing their own society and part of the world. The first inspiration was the search for knowledge. This quest was an outgrowth of the "wonder" that Aristotle found at the beginning of all thought and of the talk in which Socrates sought to engage each person willing to listen. Every discovery was examined for its universality, and life was to be tested by questioning its universal good. This quest for truth, the universal values, and virtue informs the idea of the universal civilization and begins to explain why Europeans left their lands and went to such efforts to discover, as they thought, the whole world and to see it as a "whole" world.

The other reason that Europeans could not rest content with perfecting their own part of the world is the messianic prophecy of monotheistic religions. Europeans had a belief in, and a commitment to, a messianic dream of a millennium: a new heaven, a new Earth, and a transformed people. The Judaic vision of linear time moved toward a predetermined end. Christianity supplemented this vision with divine commands to the disciples that they had something to do, and they were to be about it.[9]

What Socrates and the prophets of the Bible shared is the notion of a universal mission that invites the attention of all humans. It is ironic that national laws of the time attempted to end the idea of this new knowledge and the transformation to a universal civilization. The executions of Socrates and Christ were both legally sanctioned and, indeed, have served to make subsequent generations suspicious of legal order and doing justice. With these deaths came questions about the limits and nature of politics and law, which led to the idea of civil public. Central to the ideal of a civil public is a search for knowledge, truth, and a just legal order.

Universality is really just another aspect of diffusionism, and claiming universality often means aspiring to domination. Universality creates cultural and cognitive imperialism, which establishes a dominant group's knowledge, experience, culture, and language as the universal norm. Dominators or colonizers reinforce their culture and values by bringing the oppressed and the colonized under their expectations and norms. Given the assumed normality of the dominators' values and identity, the dominators construct the differences of the dominated as inferior and negative (Young 58–61). Thus arises the consciousness of the immigrant-colonizer and the Aboriginal-colonized, which the colonized have to accept if they are to survive. This binary consciousness justifies the separation of Indigenous peoples from their ancient rights to the land and its resources and the transfer of wealth and productivity to the colonialists and the mother country (Memmi, *The Colonizer and the Colonized*).[10]

Often when the colonized others become aware of the colonizers' vision of them and reject it, they experience what W. E. B. Du Bois called "double consciousness": "This sense of always looking at one's self through the eyes of others, of measuring one's soul by the tape of a world that looks on in amused contempt and pity" (45). Double consciousness occurs when the colonized assert that they are human but the dominators reject this assertion and impose their standards as universal and normal. Noël writes:

> After long endorsing the logic of a discourse taught to them as the only one that was valid, the dominated began to feel doubts. At first vague and fleeting, these doubts were aroused by the oppressor's own failure to live up to his idealized model of humanity. As the oppressed became more actively aware of their own worth, their doubts grew more insistent. Gradually, the dominated ceased to see the oppressor's defense of his special interests as the inevitable tribute owed to a superior being. Divine, natural, or historical laws that espoused such narrow designs became suspect. It eventually came to mind that these laws were pure creations of a group wishing to legitimize its privileges. (149)

The colonialist or oppressor is immune from double consciousness because, as the embodiment of the universal, the dominator has the privilege of not being considered as a member of any specific group. "Unseen and often unnamed, the oppressor thus is the implicit incarnation of the supreme model, the ideal type, and the yardstick that measures the humanity of anyone who does not resemble him. Presented as the standard of perfection, his specificity appears to coincide with the main lines of the universal. The very fact that he exercises the right to examine others confirms his belief and, for a time, the beliefs of his victim in his intrinsic wholeness" (12).

Dominators are in a position to study others who pose a "problem," present "a question," or constitute a "case" (11). In searching for the answers for others, dominators believe that they not only maintain a universal discourse but also speak the language of objectivity or impartiality.

Typically, to succeed in creating this sense of objectivity, colonizers must obscure Aboriginal memory. To strip Indigenous peoples of their heritage and identity, the colonial education and legal systems induce collective amnesia that alienates Indigenous peoples from their elders, their linguistic consciousness, and their order of the world. Only the Eurocentric oppressor is the agent of progress, either by the will of God or by the law of nature. The sum of European learning is established as the universal model of civilization, to be imitated by all groups and individuals. The oppressors' imperatives monopolize history or progress. In the Eurocentric construct of three-dimensional time, whoever masters the present moulds the past (12, 16).

In Canadian thought, for example, Aboriginal nationhood, rights, and treaties are banished from mainstream history and law and replaced by the theory of two founding nations: the English and the French. These thoughts silence or circumscribe the dominated First Nations. Born out of colonialism, anthropology was marked initially by the desire to resolve the conflict raised for European colonialists. By rescuing Indigenous peoples as objects of specific academic observation, Eurocentric anthropology effectively isolated them from history (Rosaldo 30–45).

The anomalous ability of Eurocentric academics and lawyers to energize and legitimize the rhetoric of universalism in colonial society was vast and remains powerful. Such repression of Indigenous peoples by universal standards or general law was and is effective in immunizing Eurocentric assumptions and practices from examination. As Noël states, "The opinions of the theorists and functionaries of Religion, Law and Science thus had the effect of legitimizing the relationship of domination by accrediting the thesis of the dominator as the ideal model for humanity. Taking their cue from the very inferiority that they have attributed to the oppressed, theologians and ministers of religion, legislators and magistrates, researchers and scholars believe they may claim the exclusive right to determine the fate of the oppressed" (48).

Differences

In contrast to universalism was the strategy of differences. Universal humanity was a key idea, but the dominants did not apply it universally. Because colonizers consider themselves to be the ideal model for humanity and carriers of superior culture and intelligence, they believe that they can judge other people and assess their competencies. In short, colonizers believe that they have the power to interpret differences, and this belief shaped the institutional and imaginative assumptions of colonization and modernism. Using the strategy of differences, colonialists believe that they have the privilege of defining human competencies and deviances such as sin, offence, and mental illness. They also believe that they have the authority to impose their tutelage on the colonized and to remove from them the right to speak for themselves (Kennedy).[11]

Michel Foucault locates at the outset of the colonizing period a shift in the fundamental mode whereby knowledge is acquired: "The activity of the mind . . . will . . . no longer consist in *drawing things together*, in setting out on a quest for everything that might reveal some sort of kinship, attraction, or secretly shared nature within them, but, on the contrary, in *discriminating*, that is, in establishing their identities. . . . In this sense, discrimination imposes upon comparison the primary and fundamental investigation of difference" (*The Order of Things* 55). The strategy of difference is not simply abstract or analytical. It directly affects secular Eurocentric identity and order.

The strategy of racism allows the colonialists to assert Eurocentric privileges while exploiting Indigenous peoples in an inhuman way.[12] As Albert Memmi explains, "Racism is the generalized and final assigning of values to real or imaginary differences, to the accuser's benefit and at his victim's expense, in order to justify the former's own privileges or aggression" ("Attempt at a Definition" 185). Memmi goes on to identify four related racist strategies used to maintain colonial power over Indigenous peoples: stressing real or imaginary differences between the racist and the victim; assigning values to these differences, to the advantage of the racist and the detriment of the victim; trying to make these values absolutes by generalizing from them and claiming that they are final; and using these values to justify any present or possible aggression or privileges (186).

Stressing Real or Imaginary Differences

The strategy of stressing difference between European "civilization" and New World savages recurs throughout seventeenth- and eighteenth-century texts, maintaining the separation of Indigenous peoples from colonialists. Memmi affirms that "The colonizer discriminates to demonstrate the impossibility of including the colonized into the community: because he would be too biologically and culturally different, technically and politically inept, etc." (187).

By 1800, European aristocracies controlled more than one-third of the Earth's surface. With its expansive claim to exclusive rationality and its arrogant assumption of a universal and uniform knowledge of the world, the colonialists had set a fateful dimension. Colonialists have a better claim to subjugate Indigenous peoples to Eurocentric thought if they define them as "other." These definitions are always simple and reductive (Noël 109).

Difference is an extension of the noun-based linguistic structure of Eurocentric thought. With the rejection of the noun-God's commandments and the unitary, suprahistorical intelligible human essence of classical thought (109), Eurocentric thought could only perceive categories and make inferences.[13] The two methods used to do this were logical analysis and causal explanation. Each provided an interpretation of what it means to account for something both in the sense of telling what it is like, which is description, and in the sense of establishing why it had to follow from something else, which is explanation in the strict sense (Unger, *Law in Modern Society* 9).

In the transforming Eurocentric thought, nature was distinguished from European culture.[14] Colonialists use culture to bring order to nature. The sovereign subject becomes the illimitable conduit for illimitable thought and reason. Yet the subject also retains a distinct identity from nature, asserting self-sufficiency.[15]

Not only did this process create a new European identity, but it also reduced the world to European terms. People who stood outside the universal European civilization could only be absolutely different from it. They could only be an aberration or something other than what they should be. Thus, Indigenous peoples were of nature rather than of civilization and were constantly compared to the devils of Christian belief. The identities of Europeans and their colonies were achieved by describing their foundational differences from Indigenous peoples.[16] European identity was different from a wild, disordered nature and, in particular, from "untamed . . . natural man."[17] This identity is based in racism and became the strategy that underpinned Eurocentric systems of knowledge and law.

Len M. Findlay in "The Future of the Subject" reminds us that comparative grammar and linguistics comprise an imperial project of the late eighteenth and early nineteenth centuries. It created the Indo-European identity and languages to legitimize conquest and colonization:

> The move away from cultural otherness toward a common linguistic ancestry would lead to the ruthless reconstitution of difference rather than its progressive elimination. If "we" started at the same proto-linguistic place, then why have you progressed so little relative to us? If "we" belong to the same Indo-European family, then who is to head the family household and direct its economy? If you end up as the subaltern or object and I as the sovereign subject of our erstwhile common discourse, then it is certainly no "accident." (130–31)

Assigning Negative Values to Differences

Since the first encounter with different people in the medieval crusades, Europeans have sought to prove the inferiority of those who do not share their supposedly superior value system and civilization. They use the same process to describe those from whom they wish to take something. The assigning of values in a colonial context is always to the advantage of the colonialists and to the detriment of their Aboriginal victims. To Memmi, the fact that real differences might be the basis for assigning negative values is irrelevant: "The racist can base his argument on a real trait whether biological, psychological, cultural or social—such as the color of the black man's skin or the solid tradition of the Jew" ("Attempt at a Definition" 187–88).

This comfortable strategy allows the colonizers to recognize the very differences that they themselves induce. Anthropologists saw what they wanted to see, and, because they came from the universal European culture, they assumed that their view was an objective one capable of discerning the patterns of another culture.[18]

Assigning negative values to Aboriginal differences has been a persistent strategy in slavery and colonization. It is a strategy grounded in ideology rather than in empirical knowledge, and even anthropologists' impartial accounts of Aboriginal culture complied with the ideology of colonialism:

> The Lone Ethnographer depicted the colonized as members of a harmonious, internally homogeneous, unchanging culture. When so described, the culture appeared to "need" progress, or economic and moral uplifting. In addition, the "timeless traditional culture" served as a self-congratulatory

reference point against which Western civilization could measure its own progressive historical evolution. The civilizing journey was conceived more as a rise than a fall, a process more of elevation than degradation (a long, arduous journey upward, culminating "us"). (Rosaldo 30–31)

Armchair Eurocentric theorists did not have to live among Indigenous peoples to present an authoritative opinion about them. Relentlessly, the strategy of differences reinforced the obviousness of the received idea of Indigenous peoples (Noël 109). Noël points out this process of circular reasoning: "Repetition reinforces what seems obvious. Warned that the dominated have a particular character trait resulting from their 'difference,' the dominator will not be surprised to observe its frequent manifestation. Having taken note of all those who adopt the behaviour he expects of them, he will feel entitled to conclude, in all impartiality, that the entire group to which they belong do the same thing" (116–17). Thus, Eurocentric authorities developed the negative stereotype of Indigenous peoples into a comprehensive prejudice, a stigmatized identity, and negative attitudes. Racist discursive strategy, says Memmi, "always adds an interpretation of . . . differences, a prejudiced attempt to place a value on them" ("Attempt at a Definition" 188).

The "discovery" of the Americas produced two negative and seemingly contradictory views of Indigenous peoples. The first vision was that Indigenous peoples were wild, promiscuous, propertyless, and lawless. The second vision was of the noble savage who lived with natural law but without government, husbandry, and much else.[19] Together these visions created the narrative tradition of Aboriginal deficiency and unassimilability. Racism resolved any inconvenient contradictions.

The secular European worldview affixes to the idea of race three correlates, which together underlie racism: (1) differences based on race are fundamental, intractable, and unerringly indicative of superiority and inferiority; (2) these differences exclude brown people from the domain of knowing, reason, equality, and freedom (this is more than simply excluding the enslaved or colonized from the realms of liberty and universal law, as Grotius and Locke did);[20] and (3) through taking identity against their construction of "Indians," Europeans and colonialists become bound in their own being by the terms by which they oppress others (Hegel 19).

The primary ordering of things by Europeans was visual observation (Foucault, *The Order of Things* 138). Thus, Indigenous peoples were classified according to their physical appearance, usually skin colour. Outward features were massively generalized and became signs of inner characteristics and capacities. When equipped with such visual identifying marks, the classifying gaze could produce colonial order by hierarchical racial division. The second step was "to imagine . . . that a mere negation of all our [European] virtues is a sufficient description of man in his original state" (Ferguson, *An Essay on the History of Civil Society, 1767* 75). European thinkers derive a "negative state which is styled a state of nature or a state of anarchy" from a "positive" image of European civilization. Lastly, there was the insight that Indigenous peoples in the state of nature needed European values, or the civilized "sub-jection," including the determining order of "positive" law (Austin, *Lectures of Jurisprudence* 22.2–I).

By logical or causal deduction, Europeans fabricated civilization and posi-tive law. These methods prevented the imaginary subjects of the state of nature from contradicting the Eurocentric universal. In other words, universalism created and sustained the strategy of difference; European thinkers simply ignored empirical evidence that did not fit with the patterns that they were imposing on the world.

Making Values Absolute

Colonial thought asserts that all differences are final, thus confining Indigenous peoples to alienation in perpetuity. This return to universalism is a potent ideo-logical weapon. Memmi explains: "So the discriminatory process enters the stage of universalism or 'totalization.' One thing leads to another until all the victim's personality is characterized by the difference, and all of the members of his social group are targets for the accusation" ("Attempt at a Definition" 189). Moreover, "The racist ascribes to his victim a series of surprising traits, calling him incomprehensible, impenetrable, mysterious, disturbing, etc. Slowly he makes of his victim a sort of animal, a thing, or simply a symbol. As the outcome of this effort to expel him from any human community, the victim is chained once and for all to his destiny of misfortune, derision and guilt. And as a counterpart, the accuser is assured once and for all of keeping his role as rightful judge" (190). Racism, on whatever level it occurs, Memmi asserts, "always includes this collective element which is, of course, one of the best ways of totalizing the situation: there must be no loophole by which any Jew, any colonized, or any man could escape this social determination" (177). Noël affirms this insight: "There is no aspect of the oppressed's person over which the dominator does not claim some rights, at some time, or which the dominator does not feel authorized to dispose of in some way to his advantage. The method used by the dominator may be subtle or brutal, and the discourse justifying it may be open or implicit" (96).

The inviolability of that "other" against which European identity is formed was secured by elevating some kinds of knowledge and suppressing others. All

Indigenous peoples are viewed as people in the state of nature, and collectively they suffer from defects. Because of these defects, they are doomed to extinction in the face of an imported civilization. According to the dominant society, only Euro-Christian values are a remedy for their defects, and often only words on pieces of paper—called laws—can protect their existence.

Totalization began with Locke's statement that "In the beginning all the World was *America*" ("The Second Treatise of Government" 343). As a source of savage origins, the Americas remained the predominant source of the state of nature in British thought until expanding colonization displaced this state of nature. The totalization of the negative values associated with the state of nature ignored that European intervention was burdened with the deathly disordering of a situation that already had its own subtle order. The existence of an Aboriginal order different from the state of nature, however, was to the European and the colonialist "literally unthinkable" (Memmi, *The Colonizer and the Colonized* 137). Yet, by totalizing the colonial order, the colonial dominators created for themselves the curse of getting it right. Not only did the concept of colonial order work against the colonized peoples, but it also created standards that the dominators could not hope to achieve.

By basing their power on the supposed superiority of their culture and technology, the dominators denied themselves the right to fail. By creating the myth of the ideal, they condemned themselves to eternal perfection. The inability of the dominators to live up to these myths exposed them for what these myths really were: theoretical constructs sanctioned by the groups whose privilege they served. Leslie Silko magnificently captures this predicament of the dominators: "We invented white people: it was Indian witchery that made white people in the first place" (*Ceremony* 132).

Using Values to Justify Privileges

The final essential element of colonialism relied on the deficient, dehumanized victims and their cultures to explain and justify the racists' aggression and privileges (Memmi, *The Colonizer and the Colonized* 137). Memmi notes that a racist "does not punish his victim because he deserves punishment, but declares him guilty because he is already punished" (217). The inferiority or crimes of the oppressed must justify the colonial Eurocentric order. This element establishes the intimate relationship between Eurocentric repression of devalued differences and colonialism and racism. Memmi explains:

> Whatever is different or foreign can be felt as a disturbing factor, hence a source of scandal. The attempt to wipe it out follows naturally. This is a primitive, virtually animal reaction, but it certainly goes deeper than we

care to admit. . . . However that may be, the mechanism remains the same. By an accurate or failed characterization of the victim, the accuser attempts to explain and to justify his attitude and his behaviour toward him. (192)

The cultural and biological inferiority of Indigenous peoples justifies their domination by the superior British colonizer, thus justifying his privilege:

The fact remains that we have discovered a fundamental mechanism, common to all racist reactions: the injustice of an oppressor toward the oppressed, the former's permanent aggression or the aggressive act he is getting ready to commit, must be justified. And isn't privilege one of the forms of permanent aggression, inflicted on a dominated man or group by a dominating man or group? How can any excuse be found for such disorder (source of so many advantages), if not by overwhelming the victim? Underneath its masks, racism is the racist's way of giving himself absolution." (194)

In Aboriginal thought, this process creates the "anti-trickster" or the Imitator, its twin.

In the strategy of difference, evidence was irrelevant as the Eurocentric critical mind reflected the clear and rational laws of the universe.[21] Developing difference relied on logic or causal thought and not on empirical evidence. This legacy created most elements of Canadian law and policy, particularly the false description of the lawless nature of the savage and the idea that society and law emerged with agriculture. In this process, artificial government was equated with law, and law was not deemed possible in the solitary state of the savage or the savage family.

Consequences

. . . The colonists created new hierarchies and governments that believed in the absolute superiority of Europeans over the colonized, the masculine over the feminine, the adult over the child, the historical over the ahistorical, and the modern or "progressive" over the traditional or "savage." These artificial political orders reflected ways of thinking that were defined by polarities: the modern and the primitive, the secular and the nonsecular, the scientific and the unscientific, the expert and the layman, the normal and the abnormal, the developed and the underdeveloped, the vanguard and the led, the liberated and the saveable (Nandy x). Force sometimes imposed these ideas, but just as often Indigenous peoples absorbed these ideas. These privileging norms released forces within the colonized societies that altered their cultural priorities. Colonization created new worldviews that were self-legitimizing. In this brave new world, through a curious transposition, the colonial dominators called upon the colonized to justify themselves. A historical, primitive people would one day, the colonialists said, learn to see themselves as masters of nature and thus masters of their own fate and a brave new world (Nandy ix, citing Albert Camus). The psychological consequence of this strategy is currently being unfolded as the "anti-trickster" struggling with *Nanabush*, the Anishinaabe trickster.[22] Among the Aboriginal peoples of the northern Plains, the reconciliations of these knowledge systems are viewed as restorative processes; thus, these processes are organized under the term "postcolonial ghost dancing."

Notes

This essay was first published in Marie Battiste, ed., *Reclaiming Indigenous Voice and Vision* (Vancouver: UBC P, 2000), 57–76.

1. See, generally, in Eurocentric literature, J. W. Sayer, *Ghost Dancing and the Law: The Wounded Knee Trials*; D. Lynch, *Wovoka and the Ghost Dance*; J. Vander, *Shoshone Ghost Dance Religion: Poetry Songs and Great Basin Context*; A. B. Kehoe, *The Ghost Dance: Ethnohistory and Revitalization*; R. Thornton, *We Shall Live Again: The 1870 and 1890 Ghost Dance Movements as Demographic Revitalization*; D. H. Gottesman, *The Politics of Annihilation: A Psychohistorical Study of the Repression of the Ghost Dance on the Sioux Indian Reservations as an Event in the US Foreign Policy*; W. L. Weston, *The Ghost Dance: Origins of Religion*; J. Mooney, *The Ghost-Dance Religion and the Sioux Outbreak of 1890*; D. H. Miller, *Ghost Dance*; P. Bailey, *Wovoka: The Indian Messiah*.

2. Aboriginal traditions are taught through a paradoxical force in nature known as the "trickster." The Mi'kmaq refer to him as *Klooscap* or badger, the Anishinaabe call the force *Nanabush*, among the Cree the force is known as *wisakedjak* or coyote or crow, the Blackfoot Confederacy call the force *nabi*, the Lakota refer to this force as spider, and the people of the western coast refer to this force as raven. In Aboriginal thought, these sounds present the forces of transformation or changing person. Lessons are learned from trickster actions and transformations that encourage new interpretations and awakening.

3. I have relied heavily on Blaut in my analysis of Eurocentric diffusionism below.

4. There are a number of variants of this framework. The classical division was one between "civilization" and "savagery." Sometimes this dualism is treated as sharply distinct, with a definite boundary between the two areas. (This form of the model is a familiar one; it is sometimes called the Centre-Periphery Model of the World.) Alternatively, this dualism is expressed as a clear and definite centre, but outside it there is a gradual change in the degree of civilization or progressiveness or innovativeness. Another variant depicts the world as divided into zones, each representing a level of modernity or civilization or development. The classical division was one with three great bands: "civilization," "barbarism," and "savagery."

5. See also M. Weber, *The Protestant Ethic and the Spirit of Capitalism*.
6. Blaut is citing M. Harris, *The Rise of Anthropological Theory* and J. H. Steward, *Theory of Culture Change: The Methodology of Multilinear Evolution*.
7. See R. Benedict, *Patterns of Culture*. Cultural relativists sought to demonstrate that standards of morality and normalcy are culture-bound and called into question the ethnocentric assumption of European superiority. See Alison Dudes Rentelin, *International Human Rights: Universalism versus Relativism* (66).
8. Relativists claim that such universality is a cloak for the projection of culturally specific beliefs onto other cultures that possess different worldviews or "inner logic." See Rentelin (67–72).
9. There are many examples of the search for the millennium. For example, in the Hebrew Bible or Old Testament, when the Lord asked whom he should send on the spiritual journey, Isaiah replied, "Here I am: send me" (Isaiah 6:8). In the New Testament, the disciples of Christ are told to go forth and baptize all nations and to teach the things that have been commanded to them (Matthew 28:19); Christ said to Peter, "Feed my sheep" (John 21:17). Some time later, as the Acts of the Apostles narrated, those disciples who witnessed the Ascension were told immediately that they were wasting their time standing there "looking up into the sky" (John 21:17).
10. "When all is said and done the colonizer must be recognized by the colonized. The bond between the colonizer and the colonized is thus both destructive and creative. It destroys and recreates the two partners in the colonization process as colonizer and colonized: the former is disfigured into an oppressor, an uncouth, fragmented human being, a cheat solely preoccupied with his privileges, the latter into a victim of oppression, broken in his development and accepting his own degradation" (Memmi 126). Jean-Paul Sartre stated in his preface to Memmi (24–25) that, for the immigrant-colonizer, "privilege and humanity are one and the same thing; he makes himself into a man by freely exercising his rights. As for the other [Aboriginal-colonized], the absence of any rights sanctions his misery, his chronic hunger, his ignorance, in short, his subhuman status." See Sartre, "Colonialisme et néocolonialisme," in *Situation V*.
11. The differences created, however, are fallible, and contemporary thought has witnessed the demise of most of them.
12. "Everyone has felt the contempt implicit in the term 'native,' used to designate the inhabitants of a colonized country. The banker, the manufacturer, even the professor in the home country, are not natives of any country: they are not natives at all. The oppressed person, on the other hand, feels himself to be a native; each single event in his life repeats to him that the has not the right to exist" (Sartre, "Materialism and Revolution" 215).
13. See, generally, R. M. Unger, *Knowledge and Politics*.
14. L. Jordanova, in "Natural Facts: A Historical Perspective on Science and Sexuality," states that, "While it is important to realize that nature was endowed with a remarkable range of meanings during the period of the Enlightenment . . . there was also one common theme. Nature was taken to be that realm on which mankind acts, not just to intervene in or manipulate directly, but also to understand and render it intelligible. This perception of nature includes people and the societies they construct. Such an interpretation of nature led to two distinct positions: nature could be taken to be that part of the world which human beings have understood,

mastered, and made their own. Here, through the unravelling of laws of motion for example, the inner recesses of nature were revealed to the human mind. But secondly, nature was also that which has not yet been penetrated (either literally or metaphorically), the wilderness and deserts, unmediated and dangerous nature." Foucault stated a similar conclusion—the appropriated and the yet to be appropriated share in the same universal order of things (*The Order of Things* 56–57).

15. See E. Cassirer, *The Philosophy of the Enlightenment.*

16. This is a process similar to Edward Said's notion of "orientalism." Said underscored the links between power and knowledge, between imperialism and orientalism, but showed how seemingly neutral, or innocent, forms of social description both reinforced and produced ideologies that justified colonialism and the imperialist project. Under such descriptions, the Orient was a cultural entity that appeared to be both a benchmark against which to measure Western European progress and an inert terrain on which to impose colonial schemes of development. See E. Said, *Orientalism.* See also E. Said, *Culture and Imperialism.*

17. See L. Poliakov, *The Aryan Myth: A History of Racist and Nationalist Ideas in Europe.*

18. The French sociologist Emile Durkheim was evoked as the model in British ethnology (Memmi, "Attempt at a Definition" 32).

19. See J. Y. Henderson, "First Nations Legal Inheritance in Canada: The Mîkmaq Model."

20. See J. J. Rousseau, *The Social Contract and Discourses*; D. B. Davis, *The Problem of Slavery in Western Culture*; J. Locke, "The Second Treatise in Government."

21. See, generally, G. Mosse, *Toward the Final Solution: A History of European Racism.*

22. See the elegant works of John Borrows: "Constitutional Law from a First Nation Perspective: Self-Government and the Royal Proclamation"; "Frozen Rights in Canada: Constitutional Interpretation of the Trickster."

16

The Trickster Moment, Cultural Appropriation, and the Liberal Imagination

Margery Fee

Introduction

Writing about the trickster or about a specific incarnation, such as Nanabush, the Ojibwa trickster, can be dangerous. As Drew Hayden Taylor points out in "Academia Mania," literary critics tend to over-interpret. About a critic who was sure that a crow in one of his plays represented Nanabush, Taylor writes: "If he thinks a crow is Nanabush, let him. There's a whole flock of Nanabushes living around my mother's house. He'll have a field day" (87). Taylor goes on to quote Daniel David Moses about academic literary critics: "They all like to play 'Spot the Trickster'" (88). As an academic, I am fated, paradoxically, to take the trickster seriously—and Taylor has promised to humour me: "I'm not responsible for these views and criticisms; the trickster is at fault here. The trickster made me do it. Yeah, they'll buy that" (88). The trickster may have become a hermeneutic fad, but the sudden visibility of the trickster in mainstream Canada in the 1980s came from the need to open up a space for Indigenous cultural production.[1] The trickster provided a strategic rallying place for Indigenous artists across Canada to make strong political points in a way that was healing for them and their communities, while (somewhat) dampening the backlash against their revelations of continuing colonial abuse and oppression to a mainstream audience in denial. Indigenous writers closely associated with the trickster made the point that Indigenous people were tired of being stereotyped in mainstream Canadian cultural production, tired of having traditional stories used without permission or even acknowledgement of the storytellers, and tired of being excluded from national and provincial institutions that regulated access to education, grants, and cultural capital.

The Committee to Re-establish the Trickster (CRET)

According to Moses, the idea for the Committee to Re-establish the Trickster (which they abbreviated to CRET, apparently so they could call themselves "the CRETins"; cf. Sherman) came to him in late winter or early spring in 1986 in Toronto ("Trickster's Laugh" 107).[2] He and his allies in the project—Tomson Highway and Lenore Keeshig-Tobias—were at that time all extremely active in the city's literary and performing arts world, particularly with Native Earth Performing Arts (1982–). One reason for establishing this Committee was to get attention for their work and that of other Indigenous artists. Moses observed that he had "seen what we are all doing, that it is good and worthy of attention" (107). He remembered three people with "differences in cultural values, assumptions and behaviours" who were "at odds often, but laughing almost always" (107): the issue was "what can a meeting between a Cree musician and playwright (Tomson), an Ojibwa storyteller (Lenore), and a Delaware poet with Iroquoian roots [Moses] agree to agree on?" (108). He saw their "area of agreement"—the need to re-establish the trickster—as a "rather rich irony," since they were planning to use this traditional figure to combat stereotypes, which often freeze Indigenous culture in a traditional past. Moses remarks that "the Trickster as we know or rediscover him, as Coyote or Weesageechak or Nanabush, as Raven or Glooscap is as shifty and shiftless, as horny and greedy, as lucky, as funny, as human as any of us" (109–10). What they were looking for was something that could be taken seriously enough to "open up a space for a little bit of the strange but true about us" (109). The choice of the trickster could be seen, then, as the work of compromise, as what has come to be known as a branding exercise; it could even be regarded as an act of cultural (re-)appropriation or repatriation:

> What we choose to lever open that space with is a tool some anthropologist or ethnologist came up with—digging around through our stories, taking them apart, sorting those parts and slapping labels on them, one of those labels being the category "archetype," with a subheading "Trickster." It is in us to hope that if this Trickster character was strange enough to a scientist to be marked and remarked upon, then it might also be true enough to get us all beyond the scientific attention span. (109)

The scientist referred to here is most likely Paul Radin, a student of Franz Boas, who began fieldwork with the Winnebago in 1908 and published *The Trickster: A Study in American Indian Mythology* (with a commentary by Carl G. Jung) in 1956. The trickster as an abstract concept came to Canada, then, with some anthropological and some psychological baggage. The label, invented by a non-Indigenous social scientist, was appropriated because it facilitated cross-cultural work among Indigenous cultural producers with different perspectives, it focused efforts on reviving tradition, and it attracted some non-Indigenous attention long enough to subvert the stereotypes. Indeed, Highway's play, *The Rez Sisters*, which featured a trickster hero, Nanabush, was already in rehearsal when Moses had the idea for the Committee; the play's runaway success cemented the popularity of the trickster. Intense work began on cultivating Indigenous writing: the new Indigenous canon in English was under construction.[3]

Appropriation of Voice

One of the most memorable battles for the Indigenous arts community was called the appropriation of voice debate. Mainstream writers who wrote from the position of minority cultural insiders began to be seen as exploitative imposters who were using foreign subject matter without considering the cultural or political impact on the communities from which they took it. Indigenous writing entered the awareness of the mainstream audience in the 1980s as part of a larger surge of writing by visible minority and recently immigrated Canadians, a surge marked by frustration with narrow, stereotypical, and even racist definitions of who is Canadian. Just as the Canadian nationalists of earlier eras had struggled to establish provincial and national institutions that would support Canadian culture, such as the Canada Council for the Arts (1957), these new writers struggled to found new institutions and to achieve equity of access to the resources of existing ones so that they could get their vision out. The Indigenous intellectuals involved in this struggle articulated Indigenous experiences of colonization and appropriation, and used traditional Indigenous protocols about the ownership and telling of stories to mark Indigenous difference. The insistence on control over speech and writing about Indigenous issues was a political move, even though it was made in the "soft" area of culture. Indigenous people were tired of having things done to and "for" them by government bureaucrats: to insist on a place at the table after the near-disaster of the White Paper of 1969 was essential. But some felt that to deal with the state and with the wider Canadian society rather than with their own cultures was a mistake. Jeannette Armstrong's *Slash* deals with the debates about whether Indigenous people should be involved in the patriation of the Constitution Act (1982). The hero argues that getting legal recognition was unnecessary: "We don't need anybody's constitution, what we have is our own already. We hold rights to the land and to nationhood" (241). Winning money or even land in court would be a wasted effort without a living culture; what was important was that "[t]here were young people who were . . . rebuilding a world view that had to work in this century, keeping the values of the old Indian ways" (232).[4] Most of the Indigenous writers who emerged during this period were consciously working on this project, albeit from different cultural and political perspectives. As Tomson Highway made clear in his *Kiss of the Fur Queen*, music, dance, theatre, writing, and the other arts—based on traditional roots—were to be the magic weapons with which Indigenous people would make a new world. The trickster—the transformer—became central to this movement.[5]

At the Third International Writers' Conference in 1988, Lee Maracle asked Anne Cameron to "move over" to permit Indigenous writers space to speak. At issue was Cameron's extremely successful novel, *Daughters of Copper Woman* (which has sold over 200,000 copies since first published in 1981, with all royalties going to Indigenous women's projects).[6] Part of the problem was that, in the novel, Cameron told traditional stories without public permission to do so, as was customary. Cameron, in her account of this event in "The Operative Principle is Trust," writes: "I have not been censored or stifled, or denied any freedom of speech or expression; I have been asked to take a step or two to one side. Not down. To one side . . ." (69). Cameron's reaction was relatively mild. Maracle (in the same collection) noted, "I am told by a host of the [CBC program] *fifth estate* (who has yet to air the interview with Anne Cameron and myself) that Timothy Findley, among others, is categorizing my objection . . . to such abuse and appropriation of our cultural heritage and sacred ways as fascist" (186). She concludes, however, that "[w]hat is . . . important is that women of colour are entitled to author their own stories. I do not hear any outcries from any corner of the publishing community about the penchant that women's presses have for publishing books about (white) women, written by (white) women and not men" (186).

Keeshig-Tobias, founding chair of the Racial Minority Writers' Committee of the Writers' Union of Canada (TWUC), raised the issue of cultural appropriation at an AGM in 1989 and argued "that the stories and cultures of the First Nations (and, by extension, other minorities) should not be appropriated by non-Native writers" (Moore).[7] This argument was in line with the stated goal of the Committee to Re-establish the Trickster: "to consolidate and gain recognition for Native contributions to Canadian writing and to reclaim the Native *voice* in literature" (*The Magazine* 2; emphasis mine). This imperative brought a debate that had been ongoing in feminist (cf. Niedzwiecki), ethnic minority, and Indigenous literary circles into the mainstream, where it generated a great deal of heated comment that continued to the Writing Thru Race Conference in 1994 and beyond. Later commentary on this conference, which took place when Roy Miki was Chair of the Racial Minority Writers' Committee, shows that it profoundly shook mainstream notions of Canadian culture. TWUC and other cultural institutions also underwent a transformation in thinking because of this debate. . . .

The Liberal Imagination

Although TWUC was a bastion of left liberal writers, those on the Racial Minority Writers' Committee raised an array of issues that many found unpalatable or incomprehensible. The debate epitomized "the general liberal dilemma," which is "that there will always be a moment at which liberalism will illiberally turn against those whom it perceives as not (yet) liberal (enough) in order to convert them into its own image" (Pels 153). The debate tricked many mainstream writers into exposing a systemic problem of access to the public: freedom of speech is certainly worth protecting, but, as Lorne Simon put it, you should not "use the excuse of freedom of speech to hog the conversation" (47). Discourse constructs the meanings of events, and the discourse around the debate fell into the pattern that has been described as "democratic racism": "The central discourse of democratic racism is denial, the failure to acknowledge that cultural, structural, and systemic racism exists in a democratic liberal society" (Tator 3). The negative reaction of those in the mainstream media and writing community revealed the power of dominant liberal ideas about the creative process, intellectual property, and artistic quality to exclude cultural minorities who wanted to assert a collective presence in the Canadian arts scene.

The media quickly focused on a perceived threat to freedom of speech, and reduced any potential for subtlety in the debate to near-zero. Despite many attempts to turn the discussion to the issue of access to media attention, publication, and grants, it became caricatured as a shootout between racial minority writers who were depicted as would-be censors and mainstream writers who argued the claims of the minority writers were a threat to freedom of speech. Many routes through this discursive phenomenon were possible, which burgeoned as controversies erupted around the 54th Congress of PEN held in Toronto in September 1989, and continued through the release of the Report of the Racial Minority Committee to the Canada Council in January 1992 (cf. Tator for other related controversies of the time). One could point out, as does Allan Hutchinson, that "the [Canada] council is . . . in the business of allocating public funds to support the work of writers and artists. As such, it is surely appropriate for it to channel its scarce resources to those Canadians whose cultural voice has been less often heard" (A16). But this sort of statement was rare. Moses summed up the polarization of the debate this way:

> Journalists have asked me if I condone censorship, if I don't want my stories to be told, as if my only choices were to be lied about or to be ignored. I wish to exercise a third option: I can and will tell my own stories myself. You too can try to tell Native stories if you dare, but you better be prepared to go Native, to own and be owned by these stories as we are, to do them justice. ("Whose Voice" 15)

A news release from the Writers Guild of Canada[8] (22 April 1992), which represented around 950 writers, stated that "actions that in any way restrict freedom of expression are simply a form of censorship." This assertion sounds noble enough until one realizes that, for some members, the action of complaining that someone's writing contains racial stereotypes may have counted as censorship. The cry for freedom, in fact, was an attempt to stifle dissent. . . .

Mainstream writers compared the minority writers to the fascist South African government that supported apartheid. [Neil] Bissoondath commented that "[w]hat has frightened and saddened me . . . is that . . . while in South Africa you have people recognizing that apartheid is evil and unworkable, that we seem to have groups in this country who are trying to institute a certain apartheid of the mind based on culture" (*Morningside* 37). Fascism and Nazism were also used as analogies for the approach of the minority writers. Findley, for example, said that "[i]n 1922 they burned 10,000 books at the gate of a German university because those books were written in unacceptable voices" ("Letter" D7). A column by Erna Paris, headed "A Letter to the Thought Police," suggested that "as a pleasing, tidy gesture, the Canada Council may also wish to draw up blood purity charts for jurors and hopeful authors and scholars, since everyone will need to demonstrate their biological fitness before qualifying for grants" (A16; cf. Groening, 4–13, for more on the history of the debate). While positioned in the media as Nazis and white South African supporters of apartheid, however, most of those arguing against appropriation were members of visible minorities and often they were women. (It's worth noting that Bissoondath is of Indo-Trinidadian origins, Findley gay, and Paris, Jewish—and can be understood, if not necessarily forgiven, for reacting so strongly. They had more to lose than most by being categorized as "minority" writers.) The framing of the debate othered the protesters in the public eye, turning them into unreasonable bullies rather than what they were—fellow writers trying to get a legitimate point across about the failure of that wonderful liberal imagination to produce much beyond stereotypes and the failure of major institutions to treat their work equitably.

In 1990 Keeshig-Tobias wrote "Stop Stealing Native Stories," a one-page opinion piece in the *Globe and Mail* with a title that launched a thousand uncomprehending tirades. The problem for Keeshig-Tobias was that the liberal imagination could only imagine as far as its own ingrained opinions:

> Stories are much more than just the imagination, and Canadian writers might research circumstances and events, artifacts and history, but why bother if it's fiction? And whether it is fiction or non-fiction, the fact is, stories have power. With non-fiction, non-Native authors have a better chance of "getting it right," but with fiction, God help us, here we go again, these people haven't learned. . . . And so a few canoes, beads, beaver ponds and a buffalo or two are used to prop up the whore, the drunkard or the shaman. These romantic clichés and stereotypes, however, serve only to illustrate how they, the outsiders, see or want to see Native peoples. ("The Magic of Others" 176, 174)

And these people really had not learned. Pauline Johnson had said much the same thing almost a hundred years earlier in the same newspaper (*Toronto Sunday Globe*, 1892), under the title "A Strong Race Opinion: On the Indian Girl in Modern Fiction."[9] . . .

Why do many Canadian writers, for the most part, never learn? What stabilizes these stereotypes? And, more interestingly, how does the dominant ideology manage to exclude the Other without open racism? Bissoondath describes the creative process thus:

> how my stories come about is not easily explained, for the truth is that I don't find the stories, they find me. Characters emerge unbidden . . . and I follow them into their worlds, grateful for their generosity. . . . If the characters live, they will at times do and say things I dislike or with which I disagree, but this, far from detracting from their validity, lends them a greater integrity, for literary characters should be fully developed individuals with minds and lives of their own existing in the imaginative world of the writer. They must be true only to themselves and their circumstances. They owe allegiance neither to the writer nor to the social groups to which they belong. . . . To

> oblige a character to adopt a preordained stance is to kill that character; it
> is to take away his or her individuality, to remove freedom of choice. ("I'm
> Just a Writer" C1)

This passage is compelling, but it is not Bissoondath's original creation; it is part of a long-lived Western discursive formation promulgated widely in the education system of the former British Empire. Let's look at it more closely. Characters arrive in Bissoondath's head unbidden; he writes down everything that they tell him, even if he doesn't like it; and, in effect, he runs a little democracy in his head, in which everyone has freedom of speech. . . . But where are these voices coming from? Well, usually from the often-limited experiences of the writer and from the dominant discourse, which explains why Keeshig-Tobias says, "I think the most important thing for a non-Native writer to do when they write about Native issues is to have respect—respect means research and talking to the people" (as cited in Kenneth Williams).

This vehement insistence by two important writers that the voices to which they should listen are those in their heads, rather than those of the contemporary people about whom they are writing, can be traced to the German Romantic nationalist notion of the *Volksgeist*, or the spirit of the people (cf. Rotenstreich). For J. G. Herder (1744–1803) and other later European thinkers, national legitimacy is founded on the spirit of the people, but the *Volk*, in his view, is a metaphysical entity as much as a real community. The great poet was in touch with the *Volk* at the spiritual level, which served as a kind of conduit for the national voice. This model is a useful way of justifying the activity of "speaking for" others, others who are portrayed as unable to speak because they are inarticulate, illiterate, unselfconscious, and inartistic. This idea became foundational to Romanticism and is closely tied to ideas of representing the people politically as well as culturally. . . .

The ideology of the free liberal imagination separates the aesthetic from the political and the economic, in the process reducing the power of art (since art that makes political points can be dismissed as "propaganda" and art that makes money can be dismissed as pandering to vulgar tastes). Once that is done, then elite evaluation decides what is and is not aesthetically "good." Those who resisted the idea that juries should contain appropriate numbers of minority artists argued that ethnic background was irrelevant, because the juries made their judgments on literary quality alone. Those with cultural capital provided by upbringing and education in the dominant class, when they reinscribe the status quo, appear not to be "political" at all. Further, as Pierre Bourdieu points out, dominant artists and intellectuals "have always practiced that form of radical chic which consists in rehabilitating socially inferior cultures or the minor genres of legitimate culture" (84). Finally, cultural appropriation in settler colonies is driven by a need to cover up the theft of the land. Usually, non-Indigenous immigrants to Canada do not want to learn about Indigenous people: they want to *be* Indigenous, to belong here without question, not to have to deal with the most problematic form of appropriation, that of the land (Fee 24; cf. Coleman). Despite mainstream Canadians' resistance to facing the fact that much of their power and privilege is based on this founding act of theft, land claims are still in the courts because Indigenous land claims have merit, although they are constantly being denied or obscured by a combination of cultural appropriation and the refusal to listen to Indigenous voices.

Morningside

Keeshig-Tobias was given space on the influential CBC radio show *Morningside*, along with the host, Peter Gzowski; Joyce Zemans, head of the Canada Council; authors Neil Bissoondath, Heather Robertson, and Rudy Wiebe; Michael Bliss, a historian; and Patricia Smart, a literature professor. Keeshig-Tobias said, "I don't think that things like cultural appropriation can be legislated and I'd be loath to do that. I think what has to happen is a real awareness, a waking up of *privileged*, to date *privileged* artists" (*Morningside* 35). After a long discussion in which Bissoondath reviewed his ideas, she finally declared, "your imagination comes right up to my nose, and if you try to get inside my head then I have the right to push back" (46); she described fiction about the cultural Other as "trying to crawl inside someone's consciousness before they have even vacated their physical bodies" (48). At that moment, she turned around Bissoondath's metaphor of characters freely entering his mind unbidden: she described it as a kind of violent intrusion, even a kind of vampirism. This is the Indigenous experience of the "wannabee," someone who wants to be a conduit for exotic knowledge, someone who wants to be Indigenous magically—or to channel Indigeneity—without any of the pain or learning. This explains one of Keeshig-Tobias's article titles, "The Magic of Others." Over and over again, Indigenous writers pointed out that what they needed was political solidarity and support, not to be spoken for but to be heard; however, their words were repeatedly seen as exclusionary along racial lines. In 1990, Keeshig-Tobias wrote that, "as Ms. [Maria] Campbell said on CBC Radio's *Morningside*, 'If you want to write our stories, then be prepared to live with us'. And not just for a few months. . . . Be there with the Lubicon, the Innu. Be there with the Teme-Augama Anishnabai on the Red Squirrel Road. The Saugeen Ojibway. If you want these stories, fight for them. I dare you" ("Stop Stealing" A7).

Minority writers rarely make the move of speaking for others in favour of trying to get stories about their own misunderstood and stereotyped cultures into the public eye. Heather Robertson walked directly into this difference when she said, "What I think would be much more creative and interesting is if Lenore had a whack at writing as Heather Robertson, in my voice, as a white, middle-aged woman. I think that would be fascinating"; Keeshig-Tobias responded, "I don't" (*Morningside* 42). And why would it be fascinating for Keeshig-Tobias to do what practically everything in the environment off the reserves presses her to do—that is, to assimilate? Notice, however, that Robertson assumes it is more creative to write about someone from a culture other than one's own. Members of minority groups who write about their own situation are seen as inherently unoriginal and over-political in this liberal model of creativity, and thus their writing is judged as qualitatively inferior. And, as Sneja Gunew has discussed, those minority writers who cannot be read as simply "representing" their own presumed homogeneous cultures are seen as stepping out of line in their violation of the expectation of the dominant culture of a realist narrative of Otherness (57–60).

Keeshig-Tobias sees appropriative writers as imposing just one more form of social control: "for how many more decades are we going to have Indian agents and missionaries speaking for Native people? . . . and how many times are we going to become the mission of some white-Canadian writers?" (*Morningside* 41). She notes that there is a void in which Indigenous stories might have been expected to exist, and points out that writers don't think to ask about "why the void exists in the first place and I'll tell you why it exists. It exists because this country, this place called Canada, outlawed native cultures. *Outlawed* the ceremonies. *Outlawed* the dances. *Outlawed* the clothes. *Outlawed* the languages. And with that the stories. That's why those voices are not there" (*Morningside* 41).

She also raised the issue of protocol around Indigenous stories: "You know, in our culture, people own stories. Individuals own stories. Families own stories. Tribes own stories. Nations own stories. And there is a protocol if you want to tell those stories: you go to the storyteller. And if you don't and you start telling those stories, then you are stealing" (*Morningside*, 42). Michael Bliss argued that "she is trying to create a property right in the stories and a property right in cultures in which you would sue people for doing that and, would you . . ."; she interrupted to assert, "Well, it happens all the time. Isn't that what copyright is all about?" (*Morningside* 42). Her attempt to discuss the idea of an Indigenous copyright did not get her anywhere. But the year after she failed to convince Bliss, and possibly others on this panel of eminent Canadians, the

UN passed a declaration "that the intellectual property of Indigenous peoples is theirs to own and control" (Nason 252; cf. Brown).

Things were changing, however slowly. Certainly, the trickster was over-determined in this process. . . . The willingness of Keeshig-Tobias and many others to face hostile questions, reiterate their points, hold meetings, run magazines, publish press releases, talk to reporters, and write poems, articles, plays, and novels created an alternative to the assumption that there was only one way to be Canadian—one defined by the mainstream—and that they and other minorities would have to assimilate to it or forever remain Other. The founders of the Committee to Re-establish the Trickster and those who supported them can look back on the transformation they worked at with pride—although they might just say that the trickster made them do it.

Notes

This essay was first published in Deanna Reder and Linda Morra, eds., *Troubling Tricksters: Revisioning Critical Conversations* (Waterloo, ON: Wilfrid Laurier UP, 2010), 1–18.

I would like to thank Deanna Reder for inviting me to contribute, and the Writers' Union of Canada, Renate Eigenbrod, Daniel David Moses, and especially Lenore Keeshig-Tobias for helping me with access to materials and information related to the appropriation debate, including *The Magazine to Re-establish the Trickster*. SSHRC provided a grant that allowed me and Sneja Gunew to interview several of the writers closely connected to the debate. Susan Crean, President of TWUC during much of the debate, helpfully commented on a version of part of this essay that I gave as a paper in 1993 as "Free Speech or Prison House: The Debate about Cultural Appropriation in Canada," at the conference "Post-Colonialism: Audiences and Constituencies" in Edmonton. Lally Grauer told me about the Taylor reference, which starts the essay.

1. Perhaps the critics are to be forgiven, because, for a while, everyone who was anyone wrote at least one trickster story, play, or poem. Here is a sampling: Beth Brant published a lesbian Coyote story in *Mohawk Trail* (1985); King's trickster story, "One Good Story, That One," appeared in 1988, and "The One about Coyote Going West" in 1989; Jeannette Armstrong contributed an ecologically focused Coyote story to King's *All My Relations* (1990); Lee Maracle used Raven as a muse in "Native Myths: Trickster Alive and Crowing" (1990), in *Ravensong* (1993), and elsewhere; Moses produced a play, *Coyote City*, in 1990; Keeshig-Tobias wrote a long poem, "Running on the West Wind," published in 1992; and Marie Annharte Baker's *Coyote Columbus Café* (1994), illustrated by Rebecca Belmore, featured a coyotrix with coyotisma.
2. The founding of the Committee to Re-establish the Trickster is not originary, but provides a useful moment to anchor the discussion. See Allan Ryan for a more comprehensive trickster reading list.
3. To be represented in a canon is not the same thing as having equitable access to cultural capital, that is, to an education that leads to social, political, or economic

power (cf. Guillory). New writing was showcased in *The Magazine to Re-establish the Trickster* (1988–89), edited by Keeshig-Tobias. As well, Alootook Ipellie edited *Kivioq: Inuit Fiction Magazine*, associated with the Baffin Writers' Project (1990) and named after an Inuit trickster figure, while *Gatherings* was founded in 1990 at the En'owkin Centre in Penticton, BC. In 1991, Moses, with Terry Goldie, compiled *An Anthology of Canadian Native Literature in English*, which became the first university teaching anthology.

4.   In 1986, Armstrong became Director of the En'owkin Centre with a closely related mandate: it is "an Indigenous cultural, educational, ecological, and creative arts organization . . . taking a lead role in the development and implementation of Indigenous knowledge systems, both at the community and international levels" (En'owkin Centre).

5.   The House of Anansi, founded in 1967 by Dennis Lee and Dave Godfrey to construct and speak to a Canadian nationalist audience, is named after a West African trickster, but this borrowed trickster had none of the traditional cultural or ethnic links of the Indigenous ones. Non-settler writers turned to traditional mythic creatures as characters and inspiration, too. For example, Hiromi Goto's use of the tengu in *Chorus of Mushrooms* (1994) and the kappa in *The Kappa Child* (2001), and Larissa Lai's fox in *When Fox Is a Thousand* (1995), assert a connection to ancestral culture in the face of an assimilating white settler Canadianness. Ironically, this singular Canadianness was in part constructed in publications from the House of Anansi, such as Northrop Frye's *The Bush Garden: Essays on the Canadian Imagination* (1971) and Margaret Atwood's *Survival: A Thematic Guide to Canadian Literature* (1972).

6.   See Christine St. Peter's two articles, "'Woman's Truth' and the Native Tradition: Anne Cameron's *Daughters of Copper Woman*" (*Feminist Studies* 15:3, 1989), and "Feminist Afterwords: Revisiting *Copper Woman*" (in *Undisciplined Women: Tradition and Culture in Canada*, 1997); see also Jonathan Dewar's "From *Copper Woman* to Grey Owl to the alterNative Warrior: Exploring Voice and the Need to Connect" (in *(Ad)dressing Our Words: Aboriginal Perspectives on Aboriginal Literatures*, 2001).

7.   Keeshig-Tobias was the only non-white member of the first ad hoc committee to discuss issues of racism in publishing by the TWUC, formed in 1988 (Godfrey). She was the first chair of the Racial Minority Writers' Committee, founded in 1990. See Fee's "Who Can Write as Other" for discussion of the similar debate in New Zealand/Aotearoa around Keri Hulme's *The Bone People*.

8.   Note that the Writers Guild of Canada is not the Writers' Union of Canada, which is always referred to here as TWUC.

9.   Gerson and Strong-Boag, editors of Johnson's work, suggest that this somewhat sensational title might have been supplied by the newspaper (323), and, of course, this might also have been the case with the Keeshig-Tobias piece.

17

Myth, Policy, and Health

Jo-Ann Episkenew

Myth, Policy, and Health

In my second year as an undergraduate student, I had an epiphany.[1] I realized that all knowledge worth knowing—or, more specifically, knowledge that my university considered worth teaching—was created by the Greeks, appropriated by the Romans, disseminated throughout western Europe, and through colonialism eventually made its way to the rest of the people of the world, who apparently were sitting on their thumbs waiting for enlightenment. This was the subtext of the curriculum in all classes with the exception of Indigenous Studies. Given that my experience does not differ substantially from that of students at other universities in the West, I consider myself lucky to have attended a university that offered Indigenous Studies.

What an assault! As a Métis woman, I knew that Indigenous communities had created a body of knowledge that enabled our ancestors to survive for millennia before the Johnny-come-lately new nation-state of Canada established itself on top of Indigenous peoples' lands. Because I was painfully aware of the injuries that colonialism and racism had inflicted on Indigenous communities, I was hell-bent to discover where these arrogant attitudes originated and establish who was to blame. (Although I was not young, I was still naive at the time.) The best way, I thought, to accomplish this monumental task was to study stories.

Several years later, having learned that racism and oppression had been a part of the world for much longer than I could research, I was forced to abandon my quest. I did, however, begin to learn something that I believe is more important and certainly more productive than finding out who is to blame. I began to understand the healing power of stories in general and of Indigenous literature in particular.

Not only does Indigenous literature respond to and critique the policies of the Government of Canada; it also functions as "medicine" to help cure the colonial contagion by healing the communities that these policies have injured. It accomplishes this by challenging the "master narrative," that is, a summary of the stories that embody the settlers' "socially shared understanding" (Nelson, *Damaged Identities* 6). This master narrative is, in fact, the myth of the new Canadian nation-state, which valorizes the settlers but which sometimes misrepresents and more often excludes Indigenous peoples. Indigenous literature acknowledges and validates Indigenous peoples' experiences by filling in the gaps and correcting the falsehoods in this master narrative. Indeed, Indigenous literature comprises a "counterstory" that resists the "oppressive identity [that the settler myth has assigned Indigenous people] and attempts to replace it with one that commands respect" (6).

Myth as Menace

For many years, anthropologists traversed the Americas collecting Indigenous creation myths. Their goal was to understand better the diverse peoples indigenous to the new land. Believing that Indigenous cultures, and indeed Indigenous peoples, were well on their way to extinction, anthropologists sought to preserve these stories for posterity, often mourning the loss of such noble peoples. It is not surprising that anthropologists would look to creation myths to gain a better understanding of Indigenous peoples. To understand any people, one must necessarily understand their creation story, which "recounts how the world was formed, how things came to be, for contained within creation stories are relationships that help to define the nature of the universe and how cultures understand the world in which they exist" (King, *The Truth about Stories* 10). It is ironic that, although anthropologists continue to be fascinated with Indigenous peoples' stories, they rarely examine the myths that their own people hold dear, especially those myths that tell the story of the establishment of the new nation-states that occupy North America and dominate the world. Do these stories lack the cachet of Indigenous peoples' stories, or could there be a more complex reason for their absence in anthropological studies?

In his 2003 Massey lecture, Thomas King tells his audience that "stories are wondrous things," but then adds the caveat "they are dangerous" (9). Indigenous people would certainly agree. The myth of the colonization of the Americas is truly a dangerous story, which continues to have disastrous effects on the health and well-being of Indigenous people. For millennia, attitudes of superiority were based on nation or class or religion. Only with the rise of imperialism and the establishment of European colonies in Africa, Asia, Australia, and America was the concept of "racial" identity added to the list of markers of superiority. The colonial myth is a story of imagined White superiority.

The White settler population looked at the evidence at hand—the superiority of their technology, the might of their military, their ever-increasing numbers, and the truth of their god—and judged themselves the superior race. As a consequence of this belief in the myth of White superiority, the dominant White colonial society began to confer upon its own, almost automatically, a set of privileges that they had not earned. It was not until the second half of the twentieth century that scholars revealed that the logical thought process proving White superiority had been based on a faulty premise:

> The environmental historians Alfred Crosby and William McNeill showed in the 1970s that the New World's true conquerors were germs: mass killers such as smallpox, bubonic plague, influenza, and measles. These arrived for the first time with the Europeans (who had resistance to them) and acted like biological weapons, killing the rulers and half the population of Mexico and Peru in the first wave. . . . Despite their guns and horses, the Spaniards did not achieve any major conquests on the mainland until *after* a smallpox pandemic swept through. The Maya, Aztecs, Incas, and Floridians all repelled the first efforts to invade them. (Wright, *A Short History of Progress* 112)

Although the evidence proves that the White invaders would have found it difficult, if not impossible, to overcome the Indigenous armies without their invisible biological allies first eliminating more than half of the population, the popular myths of the North American nation-states remain unchanged. The myth of White superiority has become entrenched in the psyche of the North American settler population and has resulted in their consistently positioning their darker-skinned neighbours on the bottom of the social strata. It is clear, then, that myths continue to wield enormous power, even "in a predominantly scientific, capitalistic, Judeo-Christian world governed by physical laws, economic imperatives, and spiritual precepts" (King, *The Truth about Stories* 12).

Literacy—the ability to read and write—has become another marker of superiority. Indigenous peoples were literate in their ability to "read" the land, a skill upon which the colonizers depended in their early days on this continent. Indigenous people were not, however, literate in the way that Europeans privilege.[2] Indigenous cultures were oral ones until well into the twentieth century, exhibiting great diversity but still sharing certain characteristics as oral cultures. Indigenous peoples understood that language has the power to change the course of events in both the material and the spiritual worlds. Furthermore, because Indigenous societies shared and transmitted their collective truths by way of oral narratives, Indigenous peoples placed high value on memory and honesty. Women or men were only as true as their words. Passed down through the generations, oral narratives explained the history of the peoples, reinforced cultural practices and norms, and articulated the peoples' relationship with the world. And, oral narratives were adaptable because they could be revised to meet the changing needs of their societies and, therefore, could evolve as their context changed (Gold 104). Thus, stories were central to the functioning of Indigenous societies.

What happens, then, to people of oral cultures if invaders wrest control of the education of their children? And, what happens if the invaders remain and take control of the land and of every aspect of the people's lives, systematically de-educating the children so that they lose their ability to communicate in their native languages and, therefore, lose access to those foundational narratives of their people? What happens if these invading powers supplant the myths of the people with new myths in which the people are either maligned or ignored? By way of public policy and bureaucratic action, the colonial regime that is the legacy of British and, to a lesser extent, French imperialism, executed these very actions against the people of the Indigenous nations of Canada.

Bringing "Progress" to the Natives

Both the colonizers and Indigenous peoples witnessed the settlers' numbers increasing while the Indigenous population waned, and both groups understood that an increase in population meant an increase in military might. They also observed that technological advances gave the settlers more sophisticated weaponry than that of the Indigenous peoples. European settlers believed that it was their right to take control of Indigenous peoples' land. However, if the imperial powers were to seize control of Indigenous lands they must first disempower the Indigenous population. As Joseph Gold writes, disempowerment began with disease, moved forward with increased immigration and settlement, and culminated in the creation of the Dominion of Canada in 1867. Not coincidentally, Canadian government officials began to develop policies to control the proliferation of Indigenous languages and stories shortly after the establishment of the Dominion. These policies made it "possible to falsify history in order to undermine group and individual identity and so in a sense invalidate the life experience of those [they wished] to disempower" (Gold 32). That is not to say that colonizers falsified history in a concerted and self-conscious manner. Rather, the colonizers believed so fervently in the veracity of their own mythology that they did not consider that there might be another perspective on history. Furthermore, the colonizers believed so zealously in their superiority to their fellow human beings that they considered it their responsibility to eradicate pagan superstition and replace it with "truth."

Believing that Indigenous epistemologies were merely pagan superstition, the colonizers sought to eradicate those epistemologies by imposing "modern" education and Christian evangelism. Their goal was to eliminate Indigenous cultures and bring modernity and progress to Indigenous peoples. This was what Rudyard Kipling termed the "White man's burden" (Kipling, "The White Man's Burden"). However, as Ronald Wright contends, the word "progress" is a loaded term: "Our practical faith in progress has ramified and hardened into an ideology—a secular religion which, like the religions that progress has challenged, is blind to certain flaws in its credentials. Progress, therefore, has become 'myth' in the anthropological sense. By this I do not mean a belief that is flimsy or untrue. Successful myths are powerful and often partly true" (4). What the settlers could not foresee were the consequences of the myth of progress, especially the social and environmental consequences. Today, the very ideas that formed the foundation of the myth of White superiority now threaten the survival of humanity. Nevertheless, most settlers still choose to believe in the myth of the establishment of the Canadian nation-state because it buttresses their feelings of superiority and confers upon them privileges that have become normalized.[3] It also rationalizes the settlers' seizure and occupation of Indigenous lands.

Despite a growing body of evidence to the contrary, the Canadian myth does not acknowledge that the nation was founded on a practice of psychological terrorism and theft. "When government policies and practices that systematically discriminate are juxtaposed with the Canadian state's formal commitment to democratic equality, hypocrisy is revealed," argues Dara Culhane. "In these ways, Aboriginal peoples strike repeated blows to the heart of Canada's liberal self-image and international personality" (49). Still, the Canadian myth persists, ignoring or negating all evidence that calls its veracity into question and continuing to proclaim Canada a liberal, inclusive, and multicultural nation founded on peaceful negotiation. Stephanie McKenzie contends that "contemporary attempts to justify this nation's beginnings are often arrested in the traumatic recall of the holocaust that happened here" (iii). Indeed, few settlers are willing to admit that there is "a darker aspect of Canadian history, one rarely highlighted in a country that fancies itself an angel in an imperfect world. . . . The Canadian self-image is that we have bland history that is exemplified by the perception that the American West was violent and colourful, while in Canada it was peaceful and bland" (Krauss). Culhane argues that "it is within this space between the ideal and the real that ideologies of justification are constructed in law, government, imagination, and popular culture. This is the space wherein lies are legitimized and truths silenced. In the histories of colonial laws we can see both the mendacity and the crudeness of the original lie of European supremacy" (49).

This distorted collective vision mollifies the guilt that settlers experience when faced with evidence that their prosperity is built on the suffering of others. Ward Churchill observes that

> holding Indians in a state of perpetual subordination/destitution is a pre-requisite to maintaining the relatively lavish level of comfort enjoyed by the settlers and collectively announced as their own entitlement. The implications of this cause/effect relationship are ready-made to instil a sense of guilt among beneficiaries, especially those so prideful of their self-proclaimed "humanitarian enlightenment" as the settlers. Since guilty feelings are at best an uncomfortable sensation, the implications—or the nature of the relationship itself—must be denied. (14)

Legal scholar Brian Slattery adds that belief in the myth has permeated the Canadian judicial system: "All national myths involve a certain amount of distortion . . . but some at least have the virtue of broad historical accuracy, roughly depicting the major forces at work. The myth that underlies much legal thinking about the history of Canada lacks that redeeming feature" (qtd. in Culhane 45). Thus, to assuage settler guilt and to maintain settler control of the land, Indigenous stories still reside in the margins of history and literature.

The Genesis of "White Privilege"

Admitting that their prosperity and privilege is built on Indigenous peoples' suffering would injure the collective self-esteem of the majority White settler population. In Canada, this is unacceptable. One of the unearned privileges that White-skinned people enjoy is that of denying any evidence that calls into question their right to a guilt-free existence.

Following the awakening of social consciousness in the 1960s and 1970s and supported by subsequent human rights legislation, racism in its overt forms has become a cultural faux pas among White people who consider themselves educated and enlightened. That is not to say that blatant racism does not exist in Canada. It does, and to remedy blatant racism, "cultural awareness training" proliferates. The basic premise of cultural awareness training is that if White people could only learn to understand Indigenous peoples' strange and exotic ways, they would come to appreciate us and put an end to their racist behaviours. However, cultural awareness training does not acknowledge the more subtle forms of racism—the racism of structures and systems—that are founded on and support "White privilege."[4]

Most White people do not recognize and acknowledge the benefits that accompany their skin colour. Feminist scholar Peggy McIntosh explains how she came to understand the privileges that she enjoys as a White woman: "Thinking through unacknowledged male privilege as a phenomenon, I realized that, since hierarchies in our society are interlocking, there is most likely a phenomenon of white privilege that was similarly denied and protected. As a white person, I realized I had been taught about racism as something that puts others at a disadvantage, but had been taught not to see one of its corollary aspects, white privilege, which puts me at an advantage" ("White Privilege" n.p.). McIntosh argues that "White privilege" is a more useful term than "racism" for discussing the distinctions between the Indigenous and White populations. White privilege and its foundational myth of White supremacy continue to have a profound effect on Indigenous peoples' health, both individually and collectively.

Since White privilege is a socio-cultural health determinant for the Indigenous population, its foundational myths must be debunked if Indigenous people are to improve the state of their health. Okanagan writer and activist Jeannette Armstrong asserts that "lies need clarification, truth needs to be stated, and resistance to oppression needs to be stated, without furthering division and participation in the same racist measures" ("The Disempowerment of First North American Native Peoples and Empowerment through Their Writing" 245). Without truth, there can be no reconciliation; without truth, there can be no healing; and without a shared narrative of our collective reality (past and present), there is no truth.

You Call It Policy—We Call It Tyranny!

Canada's "Indian" policies constitute a form of "psychological terrorism" which has had a profound effect on the health of its Indigenous victims. Many Indigenous people have turned the violence inherent in these policies inward, where it has become "toxic and effective self-loathing, culturally and individually" (Neu and Therrien 4). That the policy-makers fought to eradicate Indigenous knowledges and beliefs by eliminating Indigenous languages and stories suggests that they understood their power.

The health problems that Indigenous people experience today began with the occupation of their lands. At that time, Indigenous people suffered what Eduardo Duran and Bonnie Duran have termed a "soul wound," arguing that the "core of Native American awareness was the place where the soul wound occurred":

> The core essence is the fabric of the soul and it is from this essence that mythology, dreams, and culture emerge. Once the core from which the soul emerges is wounded, then all the emerging mythology and dreams of

a people reflect the wound. The manifestations of such a wound are then embodied by the tremendous suffering that people have undergone since the collective soul wound was inflicted half a millennium ago. Some of these diseases and problems that Native Americans suffer today are a direct result of the soul wound. (45)

This soul wounding has become the legacy of colonialism for the generations of Indigenous people who face the continual pressure to acculturate into settler society—the same society that created the genocidal policies and practices that continue to affect them today.

The "Indian" policies of the settler government have taken many forms, yet all have been promoted as a means of helping Indigenous people. In his 10 March 1925 radio address, Cayuga Chief Deskaheh expressed his contempt for the policies of the settler governments of Canada and the United States: "Over in Ottawa they call that policy 'Indian Advancement.' Over in Washington they call it 'Assimilation.' We, who would be the helpless victims, say it is a tyranny" (Petrone, *First People, First Voices* 152). Regardless of what the bureaucrats label their policies—assimilation, acculturation, advancement—their goal has been to make Indigenous cultures disappear. One cannot overemphasize the damage that these policies have had on the mental, physical, emotional, spiritual, and social health of Indigenous people.

Postcolonial Traumatic Stress Response and Other Health Concerns

"Acculturation stress," write Duran and Duran, "is a continuing factor in the perpetuation of anxiety, depression, and other symptomatology that is associated with PTSD [post-traumatic stress disorder]" (32). What Duran and Duran label "other symptomatology" includes violence, rarely against the settlers but rather against oneself, one's family, or one's community, and addiction as a form of self-medicating to temporarily ease the despair of personal and political powerlessness. Addiction and violence are not the only consequences of postcolonial trauma, however. In her address to researchers at the Community-Based Research and Aboriginal Women's Health and Healing Colloquium, Métis writer, playwright, and community activist Maria Campbell argued that Indigenous women suffer from chronic low-level depression that is a result of living with colonial policies and historical trauma. James Pennebaker adds that physical harm typically accompanies the psychological stress of discrimination: "The dangers of being discriminated against go far beyond psychological stress, higher than average rates of heart disease and other health problems.

Infant mortality, alcohol and drug problems, and even death due to suicide and murder are much higher than average" (176). Duran and Duran list a host of scholarly articles that hypothesize why Indigenous people suffer disproportionate rates of alcoholism. The list includes "poverty, poor housing, relative ill-health, academic failures, cultural conflict with majority society, and racism" (95). They also note that it is significant that "these articles usually do not make mention that these problems are the direct result of the policies of the . . . government toward Native American people" (95).[5]

Today, multiple generations of Indigenous people live with intergenerational post-traumatic stress disorder, which is the direct result of multiple generations of colonial policies all focused on dealing with the "Indian problem." Gerald Vizenor notes that when historical trauma is not publicly acknowledged and honoured in story, subsequent generations inherit and display the effects of that trauma: "Wounded Knee has had post-traumatic effects on several generations [of Indigenous people] because the stories of the survivors were seldom honoured in the literature and histories of dominance" ("Native American Indian Literatures"). Terry Mitchell and Dawn Maracle argue that the term PTSD is not suitable for describing the Indigenous peoples' response to historical trauma and suggest another term, "post-traumatic stress response" (PTSR) (14–25). They explain that the term PTSD "individualizes social problems and pathologizes traumatized people"; whereas PTSR as a "diagnostic profile provides a useful tool in confirming the long-term impact of colonization, which may increase access to appropriate healing resources" (17). Kuna/ Rappahannock playwright Monique Mojica highlights colonialism as the root cause of present-day trauma by using the terms "postcolonial traumatic stress disorder" or "ethno stress" ("Postcolonial Traumatic Stress Syndrome"). Perhaps the most accurate term to describe Indigenous people's response to long-term historical trauma would be "postcolonial traumatic stress response."

Revelations That Rock the Nation

Prompted by the public outcry that followed the Winnipeg police shooting death of Indigenous political leader J. J. Harper in 1988, the Government of Manitoba established the province's Aboriginal Justice Inquiry: "for two years, a panel criss-crossed the province, hearing heartbreaking stories from aboriginal people struggling to fit into the justice system. When it was over, the panel had heard from more than 1,000 people, amassing 27,000 pages of transcripts" (Sawatsky). The inquiry panel made public its report in 1991, just one year after the armed standoff at Oka between the Mohawks of Kanesatake and the Canadian Armed Forces, and once again brought Indigenous issues to the public eye. Then, in 1992, the Grand Chief of the Assembly of First Nations, Phil Fontaine, made public another shocking revelation—that he had been sexually abused as a young child while attending a residential school. "Indian" residential schools had been created by a Government of Canada policy and were operated by churches, ostensibly to "civilize the Indians" to enable them to function in a modern society.[6] Although his was not the first revelation of abuse at residential schools—the first legal suit had been filed in the courts in 1990—Fontaine's disclosure was headline news because of his stature as a public figure (Canada, "Key Events," Indian Residential Schools Resolution Canada). By breaking the code of silence, it seemed as if Grand Chief Fontaine had implicitly granted other former students permission to make public the narratives of their own experiences. A torrent of similar revelations followed Fontaine's.

Although the story of Indigenous people suffering abuse at the hands of colonial officials well into the twentieth century might have been news to mainstream Canadians, it was certainly not news to Indigenous people, who were well aware that abuse took place in far more settings than the justice system and the residential schools. Helping their people heal from the effects of historical trauma has been a priority for Indigenous governments and organizations for decades. Nevertheless, when these narratives made their way into the mainstream media, they rocked the nation and forever altered the national discourse by and about Indigenous peoples.

Even more importantly, these stories challenged the mythology of the Canadian nation-state, thereby embarrassing the settlers and their government. Because the collective esteem of the settlers was threatened, the settler government began to take action to address the concerns that Indigenous people were expressing in their stories, concerns that focused on healing individuals, families, and communities traumatized by colonial policies and practices. It was only when stories of abuse became public and the rest of the country became aware of experiences that were all too familiar to the Indigenous people that the term "healing" became central to any discourse relating to the Indigenous peoples of this country.

"Healing" does not imply that Indigenous people are sick, however. Ward Churchill argues that "to be sick is one thing, wounded another; the latter requires healing, the former a cure" (56). Colonialism is sick; under its auspices and supported by its mythology, the colonizers have inflicted heinous wounds on the Indigenous population that they set out to civilize. Although Indigenous people understand their need to heal from colonial trauma, most settlers deny that their society is built on a sick foundation and, therefore, deny that it requires a cure. White people are typically horrified to learn about the damage that their governments have caused Indigenous people. McIntosh explains that White people have been "taught to think of their lives as morally neutral, normative, and average, and also ideal, so that when we work to benefit others, this is seen as work that will allow 'them' to be more like 'us'" ("White Privilege").

Not surprisingly, few Indigenous people are able to trust today's politicians and their bureaucrats, who purport to be willing and able to help Indigenous people deal with the trauma that their predecessors and their policies have caused. Instead, Indigenous people look to their own communities to find resources with which to heal traumatized spirits. Over the last three decades, Indigenous people have witnessed the healing power of stories as they have begun to reassert their individual and collective narratives.

Linguistic Subversion and Its Applications

Indigenous peoples have believed in the healing power of language and stories since time immemorial, and today's Indigenous writers continue to apply this belief to the creation of literature and theatre in English. Although most writers would prefer to tell their stories in their Indigenous languages, many do not speak those languages. Forced upon them by the policies of the colonial regime, English has become the lingua franca for the many diverse Indigenous peoples of this land, diverse peoples who share similar experiences under colonialism and who desire to heal from those experiences. Although English is not always their language of choice, today's writers use it to create literary work that aspires to accomplish many of the same aims as the oral stories did: to explain the history of the people, to buttress cultural practices and norms, and to articulate their relationship with the world (Gold 104). Armstrong explains that, "although severe and sometimes irreparable damage has been wrought, healing can take place through cultural affirmations" (244).

Writing in English is simultaneously a political act and an act of healing that provides the foundation for the process of decolonization. Jace Weaver uses the term "communitism" to describe Indigenous literature in English, a term that he creates by combining the words "community" and "activism":

> [Indigenous] Literature is communitist to the extent that it has a proactive commitment to Native community, including what I term the "wider community" of Creation itself. In communities that have too often been fractured and rendered dysfunctional by the effects of more than 500 years of colonialism, to promote communitist values means to participate in the healing of the grief and sense of exile felt by Native communities and the pained individuals in them. (*That the People Might Live* xii)

In other words, Indigenous literature is intrinsically communal in that it seeks to heal the dislocation caused by the breaches in psychosocial integration inherent in the process of colonialism. The goal of communitism is to heal Indigenous communities by reconnecting Indigenous individuals to the larger whole.

Gloria Bird and Joy Harjo draw out attention to the subversive nature of the practice of writing in English to recover Indigenous communities. They term this subversive practice "reinventing the enemy's language":

> "Reinventing" in the colonizer's tongue and turning those images around to mirror an image of the colonized to the colonizers as a process of decoloniz-ation indicates that something is happening, something is emerging and coming into focus that will politicize as well as transform literary expres-sion. . . . It is at this site where "reinventing" can occur to undo some of the damage that colonization has wrought. (22, 24)

Clearly, there is an irony in this.[7] The language and literary traditions that the colonial educational systems forced on Indigenous peoples caused enormous damage to individuals and communities. Yet, the very language and literary traditions forced upon us are the tools of contemporary Indigenous literature in English. Contemporary Indigenous writers manipulate the English language and its literary traditions to narrate Indigenous experiences under colonialism in an effort to heal themselves and their audiences from the colonial trauma.

Although the English language cannot communicate accurately the practi-ces and norms of Indigenous cultures, it does provide Indigenous writers with some advantages regarding the distribution of their literary works. It is ironic that since the colonizers began to classify the many diverse peoples indigenous to this land using generic terms, such as "Indian," "Aboriginal," "Native," and "Indigenous," we have come to acquire more commonalities than we had in the past. We share a history of similar experiences as a result of colonial policies, and our communities suffer from similar wounds. With the exception of some Indigenous people living in Quebec, almost all speak English, even those who are still able to speak their Indigenous language. Thus, by writing in English, contemporary Indigenous writers are able to reach a large and diverse audi-ence, which Louis Owens has termed "a heteroglot gathering" that includes not only "tribal relations" but also "Indian readers from the same or other tribal cultures who may not be familiar with the traditional elements essential to the work but who may recognize the coercive power of language to 'bring into being'; and non-Indian readers who approach the novel with a completely alien set of assumptions and values" (*Other Destinies* 14). Because Indigenous writ-ers are cognizant of their diverse audience, they have embedded a multiplicity of implied readers within the text of their narratives, so that each category of implied reader will understand the narrative somewhat differently, depending on their societal positionality.

Notes

This essay was first published as the Introduction to Jo-Ann Episkenew, *Taking Back our Spirits: Indigenous Literature, Public Policy, and Healing* (U of Manitoba P, 2009).

1. Apologies to my colleagues, who have listened to me tell this story ad nauseam.
2. Thanks to Dr. Linda Goulet of the Department of Indian Education at the First Nations University of Canada, who, over kitchen-table scholarly discussions, explained to me the concept of land-based literacy that enables Indigenous people to "read" the land.
3. See Stephanie M. McKenzie, "Canada's Day of Atonement: The Contemporary Native Literary Renaissance, the Native Cultural Renaissance and Postcentenary Canadian Mythology."
4. Clark defines "White privilege" as "*a social relation*" that confers White-skinned people with unearned advantages over darker-skinned people, for example:
    1. *a.* A right, advantage, or immunity granted to or enjoyed by white persons beyond the common advantage of all others; an exemption in many particular cases from certain burdens or liabilities.
    b. A special advantage or benefit of white persons; with reference to divine dispensations, natural advantages, gifts of fortune, genetic endowments, social relations, etc.
    2. A privileged position; the possession of an advantage white persons enjoy over non-white persons.
    3. *a.* The special right or immunity attaching to white persons as a social relation; prerogative.
    b. Display of white privilege, a social expression of a white person or persons demanding to be treated as a member or members of the socially privileged class.
    4. To invest white persons with a privilege or privileges; to grant to white persons *a.* a particular right or immunity; to benefit or favour specially white persons; to invest white persons with special honourable distinctions.
    b. To avail oneself of a privilege owing to one as a white person.
    5. To authorize or license of white person or persons what is forbidden or wrong for non-whites; to justify, excuse.
    6. To give to white persons special freedom or immunity *from* some liability or burden to which non-white persons are subject; to exempt. ("Defining 'White Privilege'")
5. Duran and Duran refer specifically to the US government; however, there is no doubt that their words apply equally to the policies of the Government of Canada.
6. The Catholic and Anglican churches operated the majority of the residential schools with the United and Presbyterian churches operating the remainder.
7. This irony has not escaped Indigenous writers. See Armand Ruffo, "Why Native Literature?" in *Native North America: Critical and Cultural Perspectives*.

18

Imagining beyond Images and Myths

Renae Watchman

My maternal grandmother was originally from Shiprock, New Mexico: home of the Shiprock Chieftains. She was usually in the stands, cheering fanatically when the Lady Chiefs basketball team played on home court at the Chieftain Pit, which holds up to four thousand people. Evidence of her fanaticism and Diné Pride are captured in a few scenes of the 2001 documentary *Rocks with Wings*, by Rick Derby, as the camera pans horizontally across the crowd of Lady Chiefs fans, and at times focuses on the image of the *indian*[1] chief, which is visible on the basketball court. This image is not one that accurately represents Diné leaders of the past or of the present. Ninety-eight percent of the student body consists of Diné students. Given that this basketball court is located on the Navajo Nation, it is not in the collective consciousness to interrogate critically the myth of the image of a headdress-donning cartoon *indian* that is being recycled in my home community. Instead, national and international attention has been focused on the fierce controversy surrounding the Washington National Football League team.

On 25 September 2014, *The Daily Show with Jon Stewart* aired a segment that featured Amanda Blackhorse (Diné), Tara Houska (Anishinaabe from Ontario), and select members of The 1491s, as well as four Washington fans who claimed to have been "defamed and mocked." It is critical to note that the Washington NFL team recently had its trademark and patent cancelled in a court decision (June 2014), due in large part to the leadership of Blackhorse as the lead plaintiff. As a result, several news and media outlets refuse to publish the "r-word," and *South Park* devoted an entire episode on 24 September 2014 to "honouring" Washington owner Daniel Snyder and "his people" in an ingenious parody (in support of dropping the NFL team name). The attention afforded to the mascot issue is not new. In *Recovering the Sacred*, Winona LaDuke states that, "in the new millennium, it is time for the settler to end the process of naming that which he has no right to own, and for us collectively to reclaim our humanity" (140). Throughout the last century, several mascots were retired, yet some remain across Turtle Island. A detailed and balanced scan of the mascot controversy is well beyond the scope of this commentary, yet the heart of the controversy asks us whether or not we can imagine beyond imagery and myth when evoking the North American Indigenous collective in the public domain. To ignore the naming of sports team mascots on the backs of Indigenous peoples actively contributes to epistemicide.

The essays included in this section, "Imagining Beyond Images and Myths," treat numerous fictions of Indigeneity as seen in the written domain of Indigenous literatures; taken in their totality, the critical essays offer counter-narratives of resistance to literary hegemony defined and upheld through a patriarchal, heterosexual, Euro-collective imaginary. Non-Indigenous Canadian authors are the target, for example, of E. Pauline Johnson's "A Strong Race Opinion," written in 1892, because Johnson grew tired of the recurring stock character, the "book Indian girl," who was always a Chief's daughter, usually named Winona, and burdened with "suicidal mania" (179). She pleaded with her contemporaries to imagine something they could not. I am not convinced that things have changed much in the twenty-first century.

When it comes to mythmaking and forming a collective image of *indians*, there are unsurprising consistencies thanks to visual media: "movies have never been the representation of tribal cultures; at best, movies are the deliverance of an unsure civilization" (Vizenor 6). Indigenous literary criticism that looks at imagining images ought to acknowledge film and film criticism. *Seeing Red— Hollywood's Pixeled Skins* (2013), edited by LeAnne Howe, Harvey Markowitz, and Denise K. Cummings, provides a humorous yet critical account of film history and the depiction (the imagined images and myths) of American Indians in film. Silent pictures, early talkies, contemporary independents, documentaries, and feature-length films are critical pedagogical tools to bring real (as opposed to imagined images and myths) *indians* to our tech-savvy, media-saturated students of the twenty-first century. As another means of considering such mythmaking, I suggest that we consider the recently published winner of British Columbia's National Award for Canadian Nonfiction, *The Inconvenient Indian: A Curious Account of Native People in North America* (2012), by Thomas King, who offers a contemporary Indigenous rendering of story as history, history as story.

Indigenous stories as knowledge have been marketed as myth by mainstream North Americans, but the opposite holds true for Indigenous elders, authors, artists, scholars, and learners. Privileging Indigenous literatures over immigrant literatures (that is, anything not produced in Indigenous North America) will restore all that has been systemically fractured in contemporary education practices. While I also see the medicinal and cultural value of Indigenous stories and *ndn*-humor, I advocate for the teaching of Indigenous "meaning making" or rhetorics, such as stories found on button blankets, to wampum belts, to ledger art. Malea Powell's 2002 essay "Rhetorics of Survivance: How American Indians Use Writing" is an informative supplementary piece that would complement the Indigenous literary curriculum.

Approaching Indigenous literatures in the twenty-first century requires the recognition of, and teaching of, oratory—the body of knowledge that predates written literary production, which, as Lee Maracle argues in "Oratory on Oratory," "has ensured continuous growth and transformation." To grow and transform is to imagine beyond the static and fetishized representations of North American Indigenous peoples. Maracle adds that, "[s]eeing the self and society through story" (55) is a learning opportunity for critical reflection and goes hand-in-hand with "Imagining Beyond Images and Myths." To imagine requires an active exercising of creating, thinking, and forming to *re*-present, resist, reclaim, renew, and reframe.

While teaching Indigenous literatures in the twenty-first century necessitates re-Indigenizing the classroom and the curriculum, we can't ignore the epistemicide that pervades our attempts through seemingly harmless acts, such as downplaying the mascot controversy. While *indian* mascots on reservation schools like that of the Shiprock Chieftains will likely not see any immediate change, the mascot controversy has reached a level that is garnishing international attention. In Canada, however, the Edmonton Eskimos are not on the national radar as an issue worth public discussion. Awareness and education of how Indigenous peoples have been depicted and continue to be caricatured is critical. Imagining beyond images and myths includes challenging: literary protagonists and antagonists, advertising and marketing campaigns, activist discourse, theoretical analysis, celluloid *indians*, and sports mascots. They have actively contributed to epistemicide by ignoring the critical role that Indigenous literatures play, thus erasing Indigeneity, teachings, and knowledges.

Note

1. I use the Vizenorian notion of *indian* (from *Fugitive Poses*) throughout this commentary. "Native names and identities are inscrutable constructions; the ironic suit of discoveries, histories, memories, and many clusters of stories. Native identities and the sense of self are the tricky traces of solace and heard stories; the tease of creations, an innermost brush with natural reason, precarious visions, and unbounded narcissism. The *indians* are the simulations, the derivative nouns and adjectives of dominance, and not the same set as natives, the *indigene*, or an indigenous native, in the sense of a native presence on the continent. . . . The *indians* are that uncertain thing of discoveries, and the absence of natives, some*thing* otherwise in the simulations of the other culture. Natives are elusive creations; the *indigene*, that real sense of presence, memories, and coincidence is borne in native stories . . . native stories must tease out of the truisms of culture exclusions and the trumperies of simulations" (Vizenor, *Fugitive Poses* 69–70).

III

DELIBERATING INDIGENOUS LITERARY APPROACHES

19

Introduction:
Deliberating Indigenous
Literary Approaches

Natalie Knight

1. Jeannette Armstrong

Jeannette Armstrong's edited collection, *Looking at the Words of Our People: First Nations Analysis of Literature*, is the first anthology of Indigenous critics writing on Indigenous authors in Canada. It was published as recently as 1993, and not only did this volume open up space for critics to engage on cultural and political terms with Indigenous literatures, it also anticipated debates in the field of Indigenous literary criticism in the years that followed.

Armstrong's "Editor's Note" in that volume might appear brief and modest, but it is far from it. In an admirable economy of words, Armstrong intervenes in the dominant trends of 1990s literary criticism about Indigenous writers by suggesting three key positions. First, "that First Nations literature will be defined by First Nations writers, readers, academics, and critics" (229). Second, that First Nations literature has to be read in terms of the *specific* cultural context that has produced it, including nation-centred, urban, and pan-tribal contexts. And third, that First Nations literature is deeply significant to the "deconstruction-construction of colonialism and the reconstruction of a new order of culturalism and relationships beyond colonial thought and practise" (230). In other words, Armstrong claims that literature has a central role in the process of unlearning colonized ways of being and in rebuilding Indigenous cultural practices, social forms, and ways of living among our many overlapping communities. In these three interventions, Armstrong centrally locates Indigenous writers, critics, and students in the process of meaning-making about past and future. She suggests that Indigenous knowledges are integral to understanding Indigenous stories and poetry. And she places cultural work in the realm of political and social transformation, anticipating the cultural resurgence that is taking place in the first and second decades of the twenty-first century.

Following Armstrong's lead, the next six essays in this section approach crucial questions that continue to charge Indigenous literary criticism. These questions include: What is the relationship of Indigenous literature to Indigenous politics? What is the relationship between an ethics of reading and writing and a politics of engaging with community? How do we, as Indigenous or non-Indigenous scholars, "'present ourselves' to our communities as whole persons" (Womack, *Red on Red* 20) within the economic, political, social, and spiritual realities of contemporary settler colonialism? How is our art and criticism accountable, and to whom? And what are some methodologies that do justice to living relationships, history, *and* the future?

These questions may not be posed directly in these essays, but it is helpful to reflect on how each essay responds to them. In turn, consider how each author's positions and reflections differ, complement, and challenge one another. The conversations that are formed in this section of *Learn, Teach, Challenge: Approaching Indigenous Literatures*, and between these essays and those of the other sections, are at once current and historical debates sparked by a long history of Indigenous resistance and resilience, extending back to before the first written Indigenous stories in English. This political resistance and cultural and social resilience form the ground upon which Indigenous literatures stand. The following critical approaches by Kimberly Blaeser, Craig S. Womack, Lisa Brooks, Niigaanwewidam James Sinclair, and Leanne Simpson participate in Jeannette Armstrong's "deconstruction-construction of colonialism and the reconstruction of a new order" (230) that recovers and re-imagines stories and our interpretations of them for our Indigenous present and future.

2. Kimberly Blaeser

In "Native Literature: Seeking a Critical Center," from the collection *Looking at the Words of Our People*, Anishinaabe critic Kimberly Blaeser calls for tribal-centred criticism that arises from within Indigenous literatures and knowledges. Blaeser begins by explaining the risks of colonizing Native literature by "applying" rather than "employing" European or postcolonial theory in literary criticism. She reflects critically on her own work and that of other critics of Indigenous literature, and points to her own uses of European philosophers like Mikhail Bakhtin, the Russian critic and theorist of the "dialogic";

Jacques Lacan, a theorist of psychoanalysis; and Jacques Derrida, a central contributor to postmodern theory. These Western theories "have been helpful," Blaeser writes, but the way they have been used has tended to instrumentalize Indigenous literature and to judge the quality of the writing by how well it demonstrates a given theory (233).

Against this dominant method of doing literary criticism, Blaeser asks for criticism to rise up out of the literature it seeks to understand. She points to the "intertextuality" of Indigenous literature, by which texts speak back and forth to each other by making references and forming communities of writers and words across time, place, and nation. This awareness between texts forms a conversation that literary criticism can seek to articulate and explore more clearly. In addition, Blaeser points to the in-between, mixed "border existence" of Indigenous literature and suggests that the conversations between texts also extend to lived communities, families, heritage, and stories (234). Indigenous literature is often situated between languages, English and one or more Indigenous languages; between urban and rural spaces; between oral and written knowledges; between Indigenous aesthetics and the preferences and aesthetics of non-Indigenous communities of all kinds. In other words, Blaeser's call for a tribal-centred criticism is far from an essentialist form of criticism that would seek "real" and "pure" Indigenous knowledges.

At the same time however, theorizing Indigenous literatures as literatures of borders brings Blaeser to seek a critical centre. While the wide range of Indigenous experiences expressed in literature are, in her words, bi- or multicultural, they can, and perhaps must, be engaged with ethically, by centring nation-specific ways of knowing *before* Western modes of theory. As examples of creating theory from Indigenous literature and knowledge, she cites Gerald Vizenor's idea of "trickster discourse" (which Niigaanwewidam James Sinclair's essay in this section takes up closely), Louis Owens' "mixed destinies" and "mixed-blood metaphors," and Keith Basso's "code-switching." These concepts are methods of "recogniz[ing] both the differences between Native and non-Native perspectives and the complexity of the literary voice that arises from the convergence of these different perspectives" (235).

3. Craig S. Womack

Like "Seeking a Critical Center," Craig Womack's introduction to the book *Red on Red: Native American Literary Nationalism*, published in 1999, positions itself as another strong methodological alternative to postmodern interpretations of Indigenous literature. Like Armstrong and Blaeser, Womack centres Indigenous knowledge and stories as the first stories in North America by reminding us that, "[w]ithout Native American literature, there is no American canon" (244). Yet, he also writes, "the current state of Native literature is, at least partially, a colonized one" (245). To undo the academic colonization of Indigenous literature, Womack emphasizes the relationships between literature and community and suggests that Indigenous literatures should be read and written about from within cultural- and community-specific knowledges. He advocates for *literary nationalism*, a way to build nationhood and participate in resurgence through literary criticism. As a Muskogee Creek and Cherokee scholar, Womack works to establish a Creek national literature that pluralizes Creek experience and expression, while also practising ethical engagement with Creek ways of knowing and understanding the world. This ethical engagement is less about "authentic" Creek experience and more about contributing to a Creek body of knowledge. Authenticity, as Womack writes, is "often discussed in Native communities especially given the historical reality that outsiders have so often been the ones interpreting things Indian" (243). Although it is true that insider and outsider status are debated in non-Indigenous communities as well, the political realities of settler colonialism in North America challenge these dynamics for Natives in very different ways.

Womack's argument is, then, not to reduce or isolate authenticity but to populate the range of voices that have Native experiences, and to do so in *specific* tribal and Indigenous national ways. Womack also acknowledges "the construction of such an identity" as, to varying degrees, being just that—a construction—since the legacy of colonialism has worked through violent dispossession, isolation, and fragmentation (243). Debates about "authentic Indianness" can work against Native nationalisms by focusing on status, purity, and lineage rather than sovereignty and self-determination. Sovereignty, or the ability of a community to govern itself without interference by other communities, is one way of expressing the ethical and political calls of Indigenous literary nationalism. Likewise, self-determination, or the ability of a community to choose its relationships with other communities and form partnerships or allegiances, can be expressed through literary criticism by the choice of Indigenous critics to develop nation-specific methods, as well as employ non-Indigenous theories and methods when it seems right.

Part of the challenging work of asserting self-determination is to insist on the particularities of difference of each Indigenous nation. Womack writes that creating pan-tribal alliances is a useful tactic, too, but one that never outweighs the repopulation of Indigenous imaginations with culturally specific histories, practices, and future visions. One way that nations can develop literary methods that are culturally specific is to foreground land in the practice of Native criticism and creative writing. Womack calls for "a kind of 'Red Stick' criticism," referring to a group of revolutionary Creek writers, teachers, and leaders in the early nineteenth century who did not just refuse and resist colonialism, but also applied "tradition in radical new ways with attention given to analysis, criticism, and political reflection" (248). This is perhaps one of the most compelling parts of Womack's perspective, one that also informs his criticisms of colonized academia and the necessity of remaking both traditional and new practices without referring to Western academic standards at every turn. So it is fitting that Womack's essay ends with a playful shift in tone that reflects Creek story, place, and worldview.

4. Elvira Pulitano

What follows is an except from the work of Elivira Pulitano, whose controversial 2003 book *Toward a Native American Critical Theory* critiqued Indigenous nationalisms generally and Womack specifically. On the one hand, Pulitano was one of the first critics to give book-length attention to the subject—typically a high note in an emerging field—and on the other hand, the monograph was criticized, in the words of Lisa Brooks that follow Pulitano's, as presenting a "ravaging simplification of Native critical perspectives" (275).

5. Lisa Brooks

Reflecting a shared mode with Blaeser and Womack, Abenaki scholar Lisa Brooks begins her essay "At the Gathering Place" with historical and personal positioning. From the 2005 collection *American Indian Literary Nationalism*, edited by Jace Weaver, Craig Womack, and Robert Warrior, "Afterword: At the Gathering Place" details the "fish-in" on the Abenaki Nation of Missisquoi, which sparked a debate over Aboriginal title and land claims for more than a decade. In addition, Brooks also grounds her perspective in her maternal Polish family's intimate connections with the Holocaust, so her own understanding of liberatory nationalism is situated within both Abenaki and Polish experiences of repression and genocide. For Brooks, liberation "gathers families together," which is "perhaps, the essence of a Native nationalist literature" (272).

A revealing point in Brooks' essay is how Indigenous criticism can encourage dialogue and open space for different views and voices in ways that some forms of Western criticism may be less equipped to do. Although Brooks notes the importance of drawing from Western and postcolonial theories to help gain perspective on Indigenous experiences, she writes that ultimately she had to return to "the gathering place" to make meaning. Returning to places of knowledge and experience outside of the academy and beyond the reach of narrow critical perspectives is foundational work for the Indigenous literary scholar. This is both an ethical and an epistemological act, and it is at this intersection of ethics and epistemology that Indigenous literary criticism, and Indigenous nationhood more broadly, makes one (of many) crucial methodological distinction.

Brooks wonders why Indigenous nationalism might be controversial at all, and asks, "Is it the very persistence of Indigenous nationalism in the age of globalization that remains a disturbing reminder of what many wish to regard as the colonial past?" (280). Although nationalism as a concept also troubles her (her intergenerational and embodied knowledge of the violence of Nazi nationalism lends insight here), "Afterword: At the Gathering Place" calls for the importance of revealing and strengthening Indigenous ties to land. This is where she also questions celebrations of hybridity for their risk of overriding the political and social necessities of regaining relationships to land for Indigenous communities. She compels literary scholars to focus their work on community and conversation in order to facilitate the emergence of new voices.

6. Leanne Simpson

Anishinaabe writer Leanne Simpson's piece "Gdi-nweninaa: Our Sound, Our Voice," from her book *Dancing on Our Turtle's Back: Stories of Nishnaabeg Re-creation, Resurgence and a New Emergence* (2011), extends much of the work of the previous writers and essays in a decolonized, emergent, Nishnaabeg context. Simpson writes her perspective from Michi Saagiig Nishnaabeg territory as a member of gdigaa bzhiw doodem (Bobcat Clan). This essay introduces four concepts that Simpson has put into practice in daily life, as well as in intellectual pursuits and community responsibilities. These concepts are part of, in my understanding of it, a larger methodology that Simpson calls, in English, "learning through the language," which can "deepen our understanding of decolonization, assimilation, resistance, and resurgence from within Nishnaabeg perspectives" (289).

The first of these concepts is "Biskaabiiyang," which is like a process of decolonizing, or "returning to ourselves," as Wendy Makoons Geniusz has it in her book, *Our Knowledge Is Not Primitive*. Simpson writes that Biskaabiiyang, as both an individual and collective process, counters the assimilating and ongoing colonizing processes called "Zhaaganashiiyaadizi." She states that, "we are still enmeshed in the insidious nature of colonialism and neo-colonialism, and this means that I need to keep Biskaabiiyang present in my mind when I am making my way through the world" (290).

The next concept Simpson introduces is "Aanjigone," which expresses the need to take care and to exercise caution when making judgments, passing criticism, and deciding to change. Aanjigone supports individuals and groups to consider all the effects of a decision, from the most local to the more distant, and to consider ways of "offering criticism" of work or an idea that creates something new rather than setting out to undercut someone's words or actions that have already taken place. Remembering Blaeser's suggestion, in "Native Literature: Seeking a Critical Center," that Indigenous literary criticism does not need to empty out a text and display its guts and flaws, Simpson's retelling of the Nishnaabeg concept of "Aanjigone" might speak toward Blaeser's desire for "emerging critical language[s that] need not or should not have to base [their] existence or integrity on an oppositional relationship" (Armstrong 235).

Alongside the considered use of criticism and pursuit of change, Simpson's third concept is "Naakgonige," which suggests careful deliberation when making decisions. She writes that the concept of Naakgonige is a "culturally embedded process that require[s] individuals, clans, and communities to carefully deliberate, not just in an intellectual sense, but using their emotional, physical, and spiritual beings as well" (296). In the context of ethical literary criticism, this sense of collective deliberation on more than merely an intellectual level extends the potential responsibilities of our criticism in much greater ways; such deliberation may also be related to the tenets of ethical criticism suggested at the end of Sinclair's essay.

Finally, Simpson introduces "Debwewin," an expression that means "the sound of the heart" or truth, such that it is relative and true to each person differently. To explain and show how Debwewin is a unique sense of truth to each person and yet also constitutive of the social rules and expectations of community, she reflects on gender norms in her Nishnaabeg community, and the contradictions between the stringent roles of Western heteropatriarchy, how it has shaped her actions and views of the world, and how these gender norms differ greatly from her local understanding. The essay closes with a personal reflection that shows how "the personal is always embedded intrinsically into our thought ways and theories; and it is always broadly interpreted within the nest of the collective" (291).

Remarkable in "Gdi-nweninaa: Our Sound, Our Voice" is the language learning and Nishnaabeg living that form the basis for Simpson's perspective; throughout her retelling of coming to know these four concepts, Simpson meets and speaks with Elders who guide her understanding of Nishnaabeg epistemologies, ethics, and practices. This essay is a strong example of a criticism of resurgence—or in Simpson's words, emergence—that cultural revitalization makes possible. It also shows how quickly the field of Indigenous criticism has shifted and how much it has opened and grown since Jeannette Armstrong's groundbreaking *Looking at the Words of Our People*.

7. Niigaanwewidam James Sinclair

The final essay in this section is an excerpt from Anishinaabe scholar Niigaanwewidam James Sinclair's 2010 essay "Trickster Reflections: Part I"; Sinclair embraces the trickster, recalling Gerald Vizenor's "trickster discourse" mentioned in Kimberly Blaeser's essay. Sinclair roots his perspective and social and literary practices in the potential for trickster narratives to demonstrate "the dynamism of Anishinaabeg existence" (23). In the shorter version included in this volume, Sinclair concludes with a series of propositions for ethical Indigenous literary criticism that emerge from and speak to living, complex Indigenous communities. These propositions suggest self-reflexive and responsible ways of seeing past and future.

Like all writers included in this section, Sinclair takes up the responsibility and challenge to embed critical thought in community- and language-centred ways of knowing. From Jeannette Armstrong and Kimberly Blaeser's calls to begin this work, to Craig Womack's Creek criticism, Lisa Brooks' place-based reflections "at the gathering place," and Simpson's reliance on Anishinaabe understandings of the world, all of the essays here take up the work of cultural resurgence, suggesting different routes toward repopulating Indigenous literatures and languages. These literary approaches attest to the vital role of cultural practice to sustain and build nations through action, conversation, story, language, and ethical literary criticism.

20

"Editor's Note" from
Looking at the Words of Our People:
First Nations Analysis of Literature

Jeannette C. Armstrong

In the past two years I have been invited to address conferences convened by English departments, participate on panels about Native literature in Native Studies programs, and attend forums on postcolonialist literature and women's studies. I accepted such invitations with a certain amount of trepidation. My concern arose from my need in such circumstances to clearly express the fact that I am not an authority on First Nations literature, that I depend upon Native critical thought, and draw on it in order to contribute in a valuable way to such a dialogue.

It was with this concern that I addressed a panel called "Reading First Nations" at a Conference on Postcolonial and Commonwealth Literatures hosted by Queen's University in 1992. My concern was with reading First Nations Literature and its subsequent pedagogy. In that presentation I suggested that the questioning which forms the critical pedagogical voice might belong to the internal questioning that is first a reading and a sense-making of the culture from within which it arises.

I suggest that First Nations cultures, in their various contemporary forms, whether an urban-modern, pan-Indian experience, or clearly tribal-specific (traditional or contemporary), whether it is Eastern, Arctic, Plains, Southwest or West Coastal in region, have sensibilities which shape the voices coming forward into written English Literature.

In that sense, I suggest that First Nations Literature will be defined by First Nations writers, readers, academics, and critics, and perhaps only by writers and critics from within those varieties of First Nations contemporary practice and past practice of culture and the knowledge of it.

I suggest that in reading First Nations Literature the questioning must first be an acknowledgement and recognition that the voices are culture-specific voices and that there are experts within those cultures who are essential to be drawn from and drawn out in order to incorporate into the reinterpretation through pedagogy, the context of English literature coming from Native Americans.

I suggest that the pedagogical insistence of such practice is integral to the process. In doing so I suggest that First Nations literature, as a facet of cultural practice, contains symbolic significance and relevance that is an integral part of the deconstruction-construction of colonialism and the reconstruction of a new order of culturalism and relationship beyond colonial thought and practice.

It was with these concerns in mind that I decided to edit a collection of Native academic voices on First Nations Literature and include views on the relevance of First Nations literary analysis itself. This collection is an example of the diversity of voice and opinion from various regions and various cultural experiences. This collection includes essays which will be helpful in identifying contemporary issues related to literature, as well as very useful coverage of the first Native American gathering of writers in Oklahoma in 1992. I felt that gathering a collection of Native academic voices on First Nations literatures is one way I can insist on listening to First Nations analysis and the best way to contribute to the dialogue on English literature and First Nations voice within literature itself.

Jeannette Armstrong
November 1993

Note

This Editor's Note was first published in Jeannette C. Armstrong, ed., *Looking at the Words of Our People: First Nations Analysis of Literature* (Penticton, BC: Theytus, 1993).

21

Native Literature:
Seeking a Critical Centre

Kimberly M. Blaeser

Uncle Luther, a character in Louis Owens' *The Sharpest Sight*, offers some advice Indian intellectuals should take to heart. In Owens' novel, the old man gives his own reading of Herman Melville's *Moby Dick* and identifies the central failing of Melville's protagonist, claiming that the "storyteller in the book forgot his own story" (91). The antidote to this failing involves a balance: "You see, man's got to know the stories of his people, and then he's got to make his own story too" (91). But the stakes get higher and the tasks more difficult for Native Americans and mixed-bloods; not only must we "know the stories of our people" and "make our own story," but, as Luther says, "We got to be aware of the stories we already know" (91). We must know the stories of other people—stories from the American and world canons—especially the stories told about Indian people and we must be aware of the way our own stories are being changed: "re-expressed" or "re-interpreted" to become a part of their story or their canon because, as Luther warns, stories have political power: "They're always making up stories, and that's how they make the world the way they want it" (91). As I see it, the lesson for Indian intellectuals involves contemporary criticism and literary interpretation, because literary theory and analysis, even "canonization," can become a way of changing or remaking Native American stories.

This essay extends Luther's (or Owens') warning and challenge to contemporary scholars: it is a call, and, as its title suggests, a search for a way to approach Native Literature from an Indigenous cultural context, a way to form and enact a tribal-centred criticism. It seeks a critical voice and method which moves from the culturally centred text outward toward the frontier of "border" studies, rather than an external critical voice and method which seeks to penetrate, appropriate, colonize, or conquer the cultural centre, and thereby change the stories or remake the literary meaning.

Recognizing that the literatures of Native Americans have a unique voice and that voice has not always been adequately or accurately explored in the criticism that has been written about the literature, I have begun in the last few years to be attentive to other ways of talking about the literature of the First Peoples. Particularly, I have been alert for methods and voices that seem to arise out of the literature itself (this as opposed to critical approaches applied from an already established critical language or attempts to make the literature fit already established genres and categories of meaning). So far, I have uncovered only fitful attempts to fashion this interpretive method or give voice to this new critical language. This essay explores the most promising of these endeavours, searches for their points of convergence, and offers some comments on the inherent critical dynamics of Native American literature.

Theorizing American Indian Literature

In her discussion "Rethinking Modernism" Nancy Hartsock writes of "those of us who have been marginalized by the transcendental voice of universalizing theory" (204). Anyone familiar with the history of Native literatures in the Americas knows well the particulars—translation, re-interpretations, appropriation, romanticizing, museumization, consumerization, and marginalization—generalized in Hartsock's statement. Elements of the Native oral tradition, for example, have been dismissed as primitive, rediscovered and translated into "literary" forms, used as models for contemporary literary and cultural movements, altered and incorporated into mainstream works of literature, and almost theorized into their predicted "vanishment."

Indeed, both traditional and contemporary Native works have often been framed in and read from a western literary perspective. Hertha Wong, in *Sending My Heart Back across the Years*, and Arnold Krupat, in *For Those Who Come After*, both talk about and call into question the western theorizing of American Indian autobiography and offer alternative understandings of the form as used by Native peoples. William Bevis, in "Native American Novels: Homing In," and Louis Owens, in *Other Destinies*, perform similar service for the Native American novel. All four critics recognize in both method and intention a difference from canonical works of the Western literary tradition. Owens' study, for example, recognizes in Native stories "other destinies" and "other plots" (1992a 1). Krupat says of Native texts: "What they teach frequently runs counter to the teaching of Western tradition, and . . . the ways in which they delight is different from the ways in which the Western tradition has given pleasure" (Krupat, *The Voice in the Margin* 54). Quite naturally then, any "transcendental voice of universalizing theory" could not accurately interpret or represent the "other" voice or method of American Indian literature. The insistence on reading Native literature by way of Western literary theory clearly violates its integrity and performs a new act of colonization and conquest.

Hartsock says we should neither "ignore" the knowledge/power relations inherent in literary theory and canon formation nor merely "resist" them; we must "transform" them (204). Owens, in his discussion of the Native American writer's struggle with language and articulation, the conflicts between written and oral, English and Native languages, also calls for a kind of transformation of the existing system. Speaking specifically of N. Scott Momaday, but seeing his case as like that of "his fellow Indian writers," Owens writes: "The task before him was not simply to learn the lost language of his tribe but rather to appropriate, to tear free of its restricting authority, another language—English—and to make it accessible to an Indian discourse" (*Other Destinies* 13). His comments here on creative works have implications for the language and articulation of literary criticism as well. What Owens in his own critical work and many other Native American and non-Native scholars have attempted is to "tear free of its restricting authority" the existing critical language and "make that language accessible to an Indian discourse." Scholars like Owens, Gerald Vizenor, James Ruppert, Gretchen Ronnow, Arnold Krupat, Elaine Jahner, and myself have employed, for example, postmodern theory, the critical language of the likes of Mikhail Bakhtin, Jacques Lacan, and Jacques Derrida, in the reading of Native American texts.[1] We have made use of the intersections of Native works with postcolonial and semiotic theory, and with any number of other established critical discourses.

While I believe these theories, like Bakhtin's distinction between monologue and dialogue and between linear and pictorial writing styles, have been helpful, they still have the same modus operandi when it comes to Native American literature. The literature is approached with an already established theory, and the implication is that the worth of literature is essentially validated by its demonstrated adherence to a respected literary mode, dynamic, or style. Although the best scholars in Native studies have not applied the theories in this colonizing fashion but have employed them, the implied movement is still that of colonization: authority emanating from the mainstream critical centre to the marginalized Native texts. Issues of Orientalism and enforced literacy apply again when another language and culture, this time a critical language and the Euro-American literary tradition, take prominence, and are used to explain, replace, or block an Indigenous critical language and literary tradition.[2]

This distinction between applying already established theory to Native writing versus working from within Native literature or tradition to discover appropriate tools, or to form an appropriate language of critical discourse, implicates my own work to date just as it implicates the work of most other scholars of Native literature. I am not suggesting our critical attempts have all been for naught. However, I am hopeful that future efforts will proceed with greater awareness of the precarious situation that Native American literary criticism is heir to.

In fact, the situation is still more complicated than these comments have so far indicated because the literary works themselves are always at least bi-cultural: though they may come from an oral-based culture, they are written. Though their writer may speak a tribal language, they are usually most wholly in the language of English. And though they proceed at least partly from an Indian culture, they are most often presented in the established literary and aesthetic forms of the dominant culture (or in those forms acceptable to the publishing industry). The writers themselves have generally experienced both tribal and mainstream American culture and many are in physical fact mixed-bloods. Beyond this, the works themselves generally proceed from an awareness of the "frontier" or border existence where cultures meet. The criticism, too, even if written by Native Americans, is also (and for many of the same reasons) at least bi-cultural. Perhaps to adequately open up the multicultural texts of Native American literature, it must be.

Having briefly sketched the complexities of this critical intersection, I still do not rescind my call for an "organic" Native critical language. If we need a dual vision to adequately appreciate the richness of Indian literature, the Native half of that vision has still been conspicuously absent. Krupat has also articulated a call for new literary criticism, most recently in *Ethnocriticism: Ethnography, History and Literature*, and in his introduction to *New Voices in Native American Literary Criticism*. He claims [in the latter], for example:

> In recent years some academic researchers have wanted very much to take seriously, even, indeed, to base their research upon not only Native experience but Native constructions of the category of knowledge. Still, as I have said, the question remains: How to do so? It is an urgent question. (xix)

Contextual Experiments

Perhaps the most frequently employed mode for articulating what Krupat calls "Native constructions of the category of knowledge" has been oppositional. Lines have been drawn, for example, between cyclical and linear, biological and anthropological, communal and individual. In his 1985 introduction to *New and Old Voices of Wah'kon-tah: Contemporary Native American Poetry*, Vine Deloria Jr. distinguishes Native poetic expression with just such oppositional rhetoric: "Indian poetry may not say the things that poetry says because it does not emerge from the centuries of formal western thought. . . . It is hardly chronological and its sequences relate to the integrity of the circle, not the directional determination of the line. It encompasses, it does not point" (ix). Although this and many of the oppositional distinctions may have been necessary early on to underscore the difference, the distinct voice of Indian literature, and although they do contribute to an understanding of the Native literary character, they actually proceed from and reinforce an understanding of the dominant position of the Euro-American literary aesthetic, constructing their own identity as they do by its relationship to that master template.

Again taking up the ideas of circularity, Gordon Henry more recently coined the term "sacred concentricity" to describe both the form and the intension of much Native writing.[3] However, he framed his theory without invoking or writing itself against either the secular or the enshrined linear aesthetic. He simply set out to explain the movement and form he observed in novels like *Ceremony*, *Love Medicine*, and *House Made of Dawn*, whose story he felt created a sacred centre (which might be place, person, event, etc.) from which emanated ripples of power and connection (and might involve healing, return, forgiveness, etc.). The aesthetic form and movement described in Henry's language has, of course, been noted in various ways and in various degrees by other scholars: the seasonal cycles of *Ceremony* have been noted, the cyclical structure of *House Made of Dawn* explored. Owens writes of the "centripetal" orientation of *Ceremony* and of the "web" it creates. Paula Gunn Allen writes of "the sacred hoop" or "medicine wheel" as the informing figure behind much Native writing (56). The emerging critical language expressing these central aesthetic characteristics of Native literature need not or should not have to base its existence or integrity on an oppositional relationship.

Several of the intriguing experiments in Native critical discourse recognize both the differences between Native and non-Native perspectives and the complexity of the literary voice that arises from the convergence of these different perspectives. They take as their mode of operation dialogue or mediation between these two critical and cultural centres. Gerald Vizenor's "trickster discourse," Keith Basso's "code-switching" and bicultural "linguistic play," Arnold Krupat's "ethnocritiques" or "ethnocriticism," and Louis Owens' "mixed-blood metaphors" all proceed from an awareness of the border quality of Native speech, writing, and criticism. Although each scholar theorizes and enacts their theory in varying ways, they all seek to enrich the understanding of

Native literature by drawing their interpretation from the same multicultural experience, which informed the creation of the text. They attempt to explore the wavering and delicate balance in the frontier text between tradition and innovation, to untangle the braided cultural contexts, to acknowledge what James Ruppert calls the "meditational discourse," which "strives to bring the oral into the written, the Native American vision into contemporary writing, spirit into modern identity, community into society, and myth into modern imagination" (210). In Vizenor and in Basso's theories, much of this mediation is accomplished with playfulness and humour and self-conscious satire. Beneath or within the humour, cultural contexts and conflicts are bounced off one another. Understanding here is always in motion.

The Predicament of Theory

However, as Jana Sequoya points out, even the theoretical position of mediation carries with it the possibility for a new form of dominance. The full representation of difference involves multiple sites of literary and cultural knowledge. However, in the creation of this multicultural dialogue, this new national story, Native stories may again be changed or taken out of context. "In the oral tradition," Owens has claimed, "context and text are one thing" (*Other Destinies* 13); but it is the separation of the two that Sequoya foresees in "their expropriation for the literary market by the cultural mediator" (467). She writes of the different ways of "having" stories and claims that removing sacred oral stories from their actual culture context to place them within a literary context destroys their social role (460, 468). If this is true, to what degree might all critical endeavours be said to destroy the most immediate social or aesthetic value of those works it seeks to interpret? Alexander Nehamas speaks of the "cruelty of the commentator" and claims that the "elevation" of cultural story to the level of "literature" destroys its moral function.[4] Vizenor warns against the "dead voices" of "wordies" who situate the story in the "eye and not the ear" (7). Krupat, too, discusses the quandaries of criticism particularly as it applies to oral tradition and notes that "Indian people . . . have no need to produce a body of knowledge *about* it [oral performative literature] that is separate and apart *from* it" (*Ethnocriticism* 187).

Although the task of contemporary Native theorists seems fraught with difficulty, in the last comment by Krupat we find what may be a direction to take and we find the circularity of this discussion for his comment inadvertently brings us back to the idea of criticism as existing within and arising from the literature itself. Traditional Native literature has always entailed both performance and commentary, with, in Dennis Tedlock's language, the "conveyer" functioning as the "interpreted" as well. We get, says Tedlock, "the criticism at the same time and from the same person" (47–48). In a similar fashion, contemporary texts contain the critical contexts needed for their own interpretation, and, because of the intertextuality of Native American literature, the critical commentary and contexts necessary for the interpretation of works by other Native writers.

If we return to Owens' *The Sharpest Sight*, for example, we find the story centres partly on identity and Cole McCurtain's search for an Indian identity. Cole is told by Hoey McCurtain, "You are what you think you are," which throws Owens' text immediately into dialogue with N. Scott Momaday's "The Man Made of Words," especially his oft-quoted statement, "We are what we imagine. Our very existence consists in our imagination of ourselves. Our best destiny is to imagine, at least, completely, who and what, and *that* we are. The greatest tragedy that can befall us is to go unimagined" (*Indian Voices* 55). Owens' Cole disputes Hoey (and Momaday) scoffing, "As if . . . you could really choose what you are going to be instead of just being what it was you had to be" (15). These statements fall early in Owens' novel. The remaining story and the various characters' searches for identity will be read in the broader context Owens has implied. And Momaday is but one of many authors whose ideas or literary works are invoked by Owens in *The Sharpest Sight*. His text comes equipped with many of its own tools of literary interpretation.

Indeed, the dialogues enacted in and between Native texts offer scholars not only rich opportunities for interpretation, but much of the language and organizing principles necessary for the construction of a critical centre. Vizenor, for example, offers us the idea of "shadow writing" and "mythic metaphors." Erdrich offers the possibility of kinship as a formal structuring principal, and the visual images of "buried roots" and "a globe of frail seeds" (215). Momaday gives us the metaphor of the ritual "runners after evil" (*House Made of Dawn* 91–92), Owens the metaphor of an "underground river" (*The Sharpest Sight* 260), and Janet Campbell Hale (see *Bloodlines: Odyssey of a Native Daughter*) and D'Arcy McNickle (see *The Surrounded*) offer metaphors of confinement. Our sources also provide intertextual metaphors and critical terms as the texts in their richness quote and comment on one another, and as the authors frame their own works in the context of the writings of other Native authors. Maurice Kenny, for example, titles a collection of tribal poetry "Wounds Beneath the Flesh," taking the phrase from Geary Hobson's "Barbara's Land Revisited—August 1978," and Paula Gunn Allen takes the title for one section of *The Sacred Hoop* from Vizenor's critical commentary on "word warriors." Add to this literary self-consciousness and intertextuality, the multiple connections with oral tradition and the theorizing within the literary works themselves. Add, for example, Silko's intermingling of the traditional and contemporary story, Diane Glancy's and Linda Hogan's comments on the political powers of language and literacy, and Vizenor's theories on the trickster.[5]

The critical language of Mikhail Bakhtin and Walter J. Ong may profitably be applied to Native American literature, but as Owens' Uncle Luther reminds us, we must first "know the stories of our peoples" and then "make our own story too." And, he warns, we must "be aware of the way they change the stories we already know" for only with that awareness can we protect the integrity of the Native American story. One way to safeguard that integrity is by asserting a critical voice that comes from within that tribal story itself.

Notes

This essay was first published in Jeannette C. Armstrong, ed., *Looking at the Words of our People: First Nations Analysis of Literature* (Penticton, BC: Theytus, 1993).

1. See, for example, *Narrative Chance: Postmodern Discourse on Native American Indian Literatures*, ed. Gerald Vizenor (Albuquerque: U of New Mexico P, 1989).
2. I discuss literacy and Orientalism in "Learning 'the Language the Presidents Speak': Images and Issues of Literacy in American Indian Literature," *World Literature Today* 66, no. 2 (1992): 230–35.
3. From conversations with Henry about his notion of "sacred concentricity" and from his verbalization of it at a lecture at the University of Wisconsin–Milwaukee in 1992.
4. Discussed by Nehamas in a lecture, "What Should We Expect from Reading? (These Are Only Aesthetic Values)," given at the University of Wisconsin–Milwaukee, 1993.
5. For a more complete discussion of Glancy, Hogan, and many of these authors under discussion, see Kimberly Blaeser's 1992 article, "'Learning the Language the Presidents Speak.'"

22

Introduction.
American Indian
Literary Self-Determination

Craig S. Womack

My purpose in writing *Red on Red* is to contribute, probably in a small way, toward opening up a dialogue among Creek people, specifically, and Native people, more generally, regarding what constitutes meaningful literary efforts. My attempts toward such a conversation, I hope, are more suggestive than prescriptive, more a working-out of beginnings rather than endings, more gauged toward encouraging tribal people to talk about literature rather than dictating the terms of such a dialogue. My greatest wish is that tribes, and tribal members, will have an increasingly important role in evaluating tribal literatures. It goes without saying that I cannot speak for Creek people or anyone else; however, I do have the responsibility as a Creek-Cherokee critic to try to include Creek perspectives in my approaches to Native literature, especially given the wealth of Creek wisdom on the subject. This book arises out of the conviction that Native literature, and the criticism that surrounds it, needs to see more attention devoted to tribally specific concerns.

This study, unfortunately, does not include all Creek writers and artists. A number of people, such as Vincent Mendoza, Eddie Chuculate, Susanna Factor, Helen Chalakee Burgess, and others, deserve to be included. Jim Pepper's horn probably belongs in here somewhere. Creek author Thomas E. Moore, writing under the *nom de plume* William Harjo, continued his version of the Fus Fixico tradition in the 1930s for Oklahoma City and Tulsa newspapers in a regular Sunday feature entitled "Sour Sofke." Stephanie Berryhill's wonderful series on original Creek allottees, in which she records the language of elders in all its beauty without trying to shape it into "proper" English, is superlative work that has been appearing as a regular instalment in the *Muskogee Nation News*. Durango Mendoza's short story "Summer Water and Shirley" is a beautiful evocation of a Creek worldview that could be discussed in these pages.[1]

Earlier writers offer further possibilities for study: Charles Gibson, a journalist and contemporary of Alexander Posey, wrote comic caricatures in Red English,[2] and G. W. Grayson recounted his Civil War experience in a very interesting autobiography (*A Creek Warrior for the Confederacy: The Autobiography of Chief G. W. Grayson*). In the final analysis, limited by the demands of time and the strictures of publication in terms of length requirements, I made the trade-off between writing a "perfect" book and a book that actually appears in print.

Just as there are a number of realities that constitute Indian identity— rez, urban, full-blood, mixed-blood, language speakers, nonspeakers, gay, straight, and many other possibilities—there are also a number of legitimate approaches to analyzing Native literary production. Some of these, I will argue in this book, are more effective than others; nonetheless, *Red on Red* is merely a point on this spectrum, not the spectrum itself. I do not believe in a critical approach that preempts or cancels out all those that came before it. In fact, I will try to point out the ways in which tribal authors are influenced by those writers in their own tribes who preceded them. Although we are in dire need of examination of new ways to engage in the discipline rather than unquestioned acceptance of what we have inherited under the rubric of Native Studies, we have nevertheless been passed down an important intellectual tradition built not only on the last thirty years or so, in terms of the rise of Native Studies programs in universities, but on past generations of Native writers and thinkers.

Indian people have authored a lot of books, a history that reaches back to the 1770s in terms of writing in English, and hundreds of years before contact in terms of Mayan and Aztec pictoglyphic alphabets in which were written the vast libraries of Mesoamerica. As rich as oral tradition is, we also have a vast, and vastly understudied, written tradition. *Red on Red* assumes that attention to this Native-authored written tradition should prove valuable toward formulating literary theory. We have a large group of authors available for study, including Samson Occom, David Cusick, William Apess, George Copway, Elias Boudinot, John Rollins Ridge, Peter Dooyentate Clark, Elias Johnson, Sarah Winnemucca, William Warren, Alice Callahan, Simon Pokagon, and E. Pauline Johnson, as a mere sampling of Native people writing before the turn of the century. This does not even include those writing for periodicals and newspapers, or the early-twentieth-century writers who are often overlooked, as well. These are some of our ancestral voices, the pioneers, those who came before us whose writings paved the way for what Native authors can do today. Nineteenth-century Indian resistance did not merely take the form of plains Warriors on horseback; Indian people authored books that often argued for Indian rights and criticized land theft. In addition to publishing books, many of these authors engaged in other rhetorical acts, such as national speaking tours lobbying for Native rights. Their life stories, as well as their literary ideas, provide a useful study of the evolution of Native thought that has led up to contemporary notions of sovereignty and literature. Not nearly enough of this intellectual history has been brought to bear on a study of contemporary Native writings. Most approaches to the "Native American Literary Renaissance" have proceeded as if the Indian discovered the novel, the short story, and the poem only yesterday.

Because of these factors, I do not bother much in this book with the skepticism of postmodernism in relation to history. It is way too premature for Native scholars to deconstruct history when we haven't yet constructed it. We need, for example, to recover the nineteenth century, especially in terms of understanding what Native writers were up to during that time and how their struggles have evolved toward what Indian writers can say in print today, as well as the foundational principles they provide for an Indigenous criticism. Abenaki poet Cheryl Savageau, in a personal correspondence that she gave me permission to publish, said this:

> I never even encountered the word "essentialist" before coming to grad school, and then it was thrown at me like a dirty word, mostly because I wrote something about Native writers and the land in a paper.
>
> . . . The same professor who labeled me "essentialist," said there was no truth, no history, just lots of people's viewpoints. I argued that some things actually did happen. That some versions of history are not just a point of view, but actual distortions and lies.
>
> It is just now, when we are starting to tell our stories, that suddenly there is no truth. It's a big cop out as far as I'm concerned, a real political move by the mainstream to protect itself from the stories that Native people, African Americans, gay and lesbian folks . . . are telling. If everybody's story is all of a sudden equally true, then there is no guilt, no accountability, no need to change anything, no need for reparations, no arguments for sovereign nation status, and their positions of power are maintained.
>
> . . . As I write this [statement about intellectuals who seem smart and have garnered a lot of power] I can hear my grandmother saying, "but smart and good aren't the same things." Such an essentialist, huh?

So, at least until we get our stories told, especially in terms of establishing a body of Native criticism in relation to nineteenth-century writings, postmodernism may have some limitations in regard to its applicability to Native scholarship. Encouragingly, things have started to change, and we see more and more Native scholars examining the nineteenth century and tracing developments in this century, as well, which lead up to the great outpouring of Indian literature we have seen recently. Osage writer Robert Warrior, I think, has provided us with incredibly important models in these regards, especially the way he traces out the intellectual underpinnings of the Indian movement through several decades this century in his work *Like a Hurricane: The Indian Movement from Alcatraz to Wounded Knee*. His work will influence many of us in the years to come.

I would like to think, then, that I have not written *Red on Red* in a rejectionist mode but that, to the contrary, I seek to examine these histories to search for those ideas, articulated by Indian people, that best serve a contemporary critical framework. More specifically, in terms of a Creek national literature, the process has been based on the assumption that it is valuable to look toward Creek authors and their works to understand Creek writing. My argument is not that this is the *only* way to understand Creek writing, but an important one given that literatures bear some kind of relationship to communities, both writing communities and the community of the primary culture, from which they originate.

In arguing, then, that one viable approach is to examine Creek authors to understand Creek texts, or, more generally, Native authors to understand Native textual production, this study assumes that there *is* such a thing as a Native perspective and that seeking it out is a worthwhile endeavour. I do not subscribe, in other words, to the notion that a Native perspective is, at best, problematic, if not impossible. I feel that Native perspectives have to do with allowing Indian people to speak for themselves, that is to say, with prioritizing Native voices. Those voices may vary in quality, but they rise out of a historical reality wherein Native people have been excluded from discourse concerning their own cultures, and Indian people must be, ultimately will be, heard. Native viewpoints are important because, to quote Métis scholar and activist Howard Adams, the state, rather than Indians, controls "the mental means of production" (*A Tortured People* 38). Adams goes on to say:

> Aboriginal consciousness cannot be a facade; it is an intrinsic or inner essence that lies somewhere between instinct and intuition, and it evolves from the humanness and spirituality of our collective, Aboriginal community. Without an Indigenous consciousness, Indians, Métis, and Inuit

peoples' only claim to Aboriginality is race and heritage. That is not enough to achieve true liberation. To accomplish self-determination, we need more than racial pride. We must have Aboriginal nationalism, an understanding of the state's capitalist ideology and its oppression, and, ultimately, a counter-consciousness. (45)

The idea of a Native consciousness interests me. The critics of Native literary nationalism have faulted Native specialists with a fundamental naïveté, claiming we argue that Native perspectives are pure, authoritative, uncontaminated by European influences. This misses the point. Native viewpoints are necessary because the "mental means of production" in regard to analyzing Indian cultures have been owned, almost exclusively, by non-Indians. Radical Native viewpoints, voices of difference rather than commonality, are called for to disrupt the powers of the literary status quo as well as the powers of the state— there is a link between thought and activism, surely. Such disruption does not come about by merely emphasizing that all things Native are, in reality, filtered through contact with Europe, that there is no "uncorrupted" Indian reality in this postcontact world we live in. This is an assimilationist ideology, a retreat into sameness and blending in.

To be sure, there is no one pure or authoritative act that constitutes Native literary criticism. We can only take such a notion so far, though. The postmodernists might laugh at claims of prioritizing insider status, questioning the very nature of what constitutes an insider and pointing out that no pure Creek, or Native, viewpoint exists, that Native and non-Native are constantly deconstructing each other. In terms of a reality check, however, we might remind ourselves that authenticity and insider and outsider status are, in fact, often discussed in Native communities, especially given the historical reality that outsiders have so often been the ones interpreting things Indian. Further, it seems foolhardy to me to abandon a search for the affirmation of a national literary identity simply to fall in line with the latest literary trend. The construction of such an identity reaffirms the real truth about our place in history—we are not mere victims but active agents in history, innovators of new ways, of Indian ways, of thinking and being and speaking and authoring in this world created by colonial contact.

Whatever we might say about the inherent problems concerning what constitutes an Indian viewpoint, we can still reasonably assert that such a viewpoint exists and has been silenced throughout US history to the degree that it finally needs to be heard. Whatever one might argue about postmodern representation, there is the legal reality of tribal sovereignty, recognized by the US Constitution and defined over the last 160 years by the Supreme Court, that affects the everyday lives of individuals and tribal nations, and, therefore, has something to do with tribal literatures as well.

Take as an example earlier writers: let's say the novelists, autobiographers, and poets of the nineteenth century; as another group, the writers, such as Charles Eastman, Carlos Montezuma, and Gertrude Bonnin, associated with the Society of American Indians (SAI) in the early part of this century; then, finally, the Native novelists of the 1920s and 1930s. In many cases, these earlier writers were uncertain or hesitant about whether a Native voice, a Native viewpoint, the narration of tribal life, or even a Native future was possible. In a short time, Native writing has come a long way toward legitimizing tribal experience as an appropriate subject for writing and, most importantly, toward assuming tribal life will continue in the future. The uncertainty of this earlier epoch seems a little like a first cousin to the ambiguity of the later postmodern criticism with its tendency to decentre everything, including the legitimacy of a Native perspective. This kind of criticism hearkens back to the earlier days of questioning whether a Native voice was even possible. No matter how slick the literary strategy that gets us there, this seems the wrong political move to me.

To take this one step further, the primary purpose of this study is not to argue for canonical inclusion or opening up Native literature to a broader audience. Efforts toward that end may be necessary for forming broader alliances, and others have taken up these issues in other books. This study takes a different tack. I say that tribal literatures are not some branch waiting to be grafted onto the main trunk. Tribal literatures are the *tree*, the oldest literatures in the Americas, the most American of American literatures. We *are* the canon. Native people have been on this continent at least thirty thousand years, and the stories tell us we have been here even longer than that, that we were set down by the Creator on this continent, that we originated here. For much of this time period, we have had literatures. Without Native American literature, *there is no American canon*. We should not allow ourselves, through the definitions we choose and the language we use, ever to assume we are outside the canon; we should not play along and confess to being a second-rate literature. Let Americanists struggle for *their* place in the canon. (Understand this is not an argument for inclusion—I am saying with all the bias I can muster that *our* American canon, the Native literary canon of the Americas, predates *their* American canon. I see them as two separate canons.)

Some Native American writers have made inclusionary arguments, claiming that they do not wish to be considered "just an Indian writer." My problem is with the word "just," and my question is, why not? When we use this kind of language, admitting lesser roles for ourselves, to what degree are we internalizing dominant culture racism? What's wrong with being an Indian writer? Why is that a diminished role among writers? Who made up these rules? Why should we want to adhere to them? Does a description of Faulkner as a Southern writer make him any less an important figure? Should his Nobel Prize be taken back because he was "just a Southern writer"? Just what is there to write about that is more important than Native authors testifying to surviving genocide and advocating sovereignty and survival? Here, I am endorsing Flannery O'Connor's well-known argument that the deeper an author delves into her own home country, the more universal and powerful her writing becomes.

The current state of Native literature is, at least partially, a colonized one. This colonization can be seen in many forms, but I'll mention a few examples from the academic end, since that is an arena I operate in frequently. One is the way Native literary specialists must present their work at Modern Language Association conferences (not a bad thing in and of itself); but as of yet, MLA has few, if any, ties to Indian communities. The degree to which such participation is voluntary for Native lit scholars is somewhat questionable, since he or she must go to MLA for job interviews and to present papers, or to other conferences equally removed from Indian communities, to remain credible in his or her department and to get tenure if the scholar works, or ever wants to work, in an English department. Of course, MLA has begun to open up spaces for building a body of interest in important, underdeveloped areas of Native literary inquiry, such as panels on nineteenth-century Native authors, so again, the institution, as monolithic as it is, is not to be totally discredited.

Another example of the colonized state of Native literature might be the way in which teaching jobs in the field are often advertised as "ethnic literature" slots, or housed in "ethnic literature" departments, calling for academics who have broad comparative backgrounds rather than training in tribally specific cultures. Often, the candidate soon discovers, even jobs advertised as Native lit positions are really minority lit jobs. Having experience with a specific tribe often discredits the applicants for these positions. Departments often look for someone to do multicultural literature rather than Native Studies; teach an Amy Tan novel now and then, throw in a little Ralph Ellison, a Native author once in a while, and string it all together with the same damn Bakhtin quotes we've all heard a million times, reducing literary studies to little more than an English department version of the melting pot. Everybody loses—this is demeaning and destructive to Asian American Studies, African American Studies, Native American Studies, and other minority literatures, a system that makes it difficult to hire those with close ties to the subject matter they teach. Fortunately, this is not always the case—a number of English departments, and even some of the ethnic literature departments, have hired people for very solid Native lit jobs where the candidate teaches only Native literature and develops a core program of Indian literature courses within the department—but enough of the multicultural recruiting exists to cause concern.

Another example of colonialism related to teaching and hiring might be the number of search committees for slots in Native literature with no Native people on the committee. As difficult as that is to justify from an Indian viewpoint, I know I have sat in many a job interview facing that very situation, answering questions posed by people who did not even know what to ask. Or what about this—Native studies programs with few or sometimes even no Native faculty? What would we say about African American Studies or Chicano Studies programs that were run without African Americans or Chicanos? The appropriation of Native issues by non-Natives is still acceptable in Native studies in ways that have long been unacceptable in regard to other minorities. Native scholars have faced variants of these stories in a thousand different ways, so there is no use in belabouring the point here, other than to say that surely we need to work toward creating a better space for Native literary studies than what we have inherited. Perhaps we need some retrospection at this point—a time of self-scrutiny as to where Native literature has been, where it is going, and to what degree Indian people should control how it gets there.

Although her comments reference written histories, perhaps Anna Lee Walters's cogent remarks apply here, as well:

> Scholars or authorities from academia, from outside tribal societies, do not necessarily know tribal people best. There is an inherent right of tribal people to interpret events and time in their worlds according to their own aesthetics and values, as a component of American history, even when this interpretation is different from that of mainstream history. (*Talking Indian* 86)

I might add, *especially* when the interpretation is different from that of the mainstream.

Finally, as Native writers, our own resistance to forming a substantive body of critical discussion surrounding our own literature and our willingness to turn the task over to outsiders, to "those who write criticism," or "those who do theory," may indicate the degree to which we have internalized colonization. We have gone too long thinking that storytellers cannot also talk about stories, that fiction writers and poets do one thing and critics and academics quite another. When I am back home (that is, in Indian communities in Oklahoma), I am always amazed when I encounter individuals who are encyclopedic in their knowledge of their own tribe—they sort of put me in a state of awe. Though often having no formal connection to the academy, they have read every book on their tribe; they can recall family tribal histories with a breadth that is astounding; they have an amazing sense of place and culture. I often wonder why *these* people are not doing literary criticism and writing book reviews. Of course, I know some of the reasons why they are not; nonetheless, I lament this loss and wish some of these folks, the real Indian experts, could have a more prominent place in the development of our literary approaches.

I was reminded of these things at Tahlequah recently, at a Native writers' festival, after I heard what seemed like the umpteenth-million poem (read by writers whining about being mixed-bloods) about nice, kindly Indian grand-mothers, and was having difficulty recognizing any of the Indian women I have known in these highly tamed, docile old ladies. Surely, there are other areas of discourse we can give our attention to while paying the appropriate kind of respect to ancestral voices. My point is this: I was dismayed at just how little formal discussion there was among Indian writers concerning who controls Indian literature, what is the purpose of Indian literature, what constitutes Native literatures of excellence, how such criteria should be determined, what set of ethical issues surrounds being a Native writer, and what role should tribes play in the whole process. What happens, it seems to me, is that when we abandon such a discussion, we give away all our power to a group of outsiders who then determine our aesthetics *for* us, and this happens without even a fight!

A more subtle form of the colonization of Native literature may occur as an aftereffect of a phenomenon that has been overall very positive. Literary critics have attached a great deal of relevance to the "Native American literary renaissance," the great outpouring of texts authored by Native writers over the last thirty years, noting, among other things, that Native people have taken up the pen to speak rather than be spoken for. To quote Vine Deloria's polemic title, *We Talk, You Listen*, Native literature is ahead of the game compared to other areas of Native Studies, in that one can teach courses on Native lit, and now even on Native literary criticism, assigning as texts, books authored exclusively by Native people. This is much harder to do in history or anthropology or other areas of inquiry (though not impossible, and it seems to me that the minimal requirement for a Native Studies course should be that every classroom text is written by a Native author; otherwise, how can we possibly lay claim to presenting Native perspectives?).

To continue in regard to the "renaissance" and this great outpouring of Native-authored texts, one overwhelming theme of the authors writing Native creative literature is that the cultures of which they are writing have not vanished. These works seek creative and evocative ways to argue that Native cultures continue to survive and evolve. Perhaps, however, some further questions need to be asked about this renaissance, given that so much ground has been gained in the areas of fiction, especially in the forms of short stories, novels,

and poetry. In addition to the many positive aspects of this burgeoning literature, does the frontier for fiction serve partially to deny Native peoples a place
in the nonfictional world, in the arena where sovereignty, religious freedom,
treaty rights, land claims, language retention, tribal education, and many other
elements of culture continue to affect the daily destinies of tribes? Why haven't
Native-written histories or political analyses, for example, experienced a renaissance of the same magnitude?[3] Does the fictional work of the "renaissance"
effectively present these Native social realities?

Overall, it seems to me, Native-written fictional stories about reconnection to Native culture enjoy a much wider popular appeal than non-fiction
written by Indians concerning their tribe's land claims or politics. In terms of
fiction itself, take as an example the glaring difference between the attention
given to Leslie Silko's *Ceremony*, a novel about a warrior's reintegration into
Laguna society, and the same author's *Almanac of the Dead*, a novel that posits
that Indigenous peoples throughout the Americas will take back their land.
America loves Indian culture; America is much less enthusiastic about Indian
land title.

Does the Native American literary renaissance, in addition to its many
positive qualities, also play, in troubling ways, into the vanishing notion by
allowing Native people to be fictional but not real? In this study, I will con-
centrate on the idea that Native literary aesthetics must be politicized and
that autonomy, self-determination, and sovereignty serve as useful literary concepts. Further, I wish to suggest that literature has something to add
to the arena of Native political struggle. The attempt, then, will be to break
down oppositions between the world of literature and the very real struggles
of American Indian communities, arguing for both an intrinsic and extrinsic
relationship between the two. I will seek a literary criticism that emphasizes
Native resistance movements against colonialism, confronts racism, discusses
sovereignty and Native nationalism, seeks connections between literature and
liberation struggles, and, finally, roots literature in land and culture. This criticism emphasizes unique Native worldviews and political realities, searches for
differences as often as similarities, and attempts to find Native literature's place
in Indian country, rather than Native literature's place in the canon.

What is called for, perhaps, is a kind of "Red Stick" literary criticism. I am
referring to the group of traditionalist Creeks in 1813 to 1814, who, seeing
their land invaded from all sides, with demands for land cessions increasing
all the time, had to come up with radically different ways of dealing with a
threat that hitherto had not existed. What they had to develop was a vision
that was not simply reactionary, but the application of tradition in radical new
ways with attention given to analysis, criticism, and political reflection. This

anticolonial movement, fuelled by religion and myth, was both influenced by Shawnee ally Tecumseh's apocalyptic teachings and rooted in the Creek square grounds. In Joel Martin's book on the Red Sticks, entitled *Sacred Revolt*, the author says, "Not only did they react and rebel against colonialism—they also innovated on tradition and initiated new ways of life within the world created by contact" (179).

There is a difference here that is vital. In looking at Creek literature, I want to emphasize "innovat[ion] on tradition" and "initiat[ion of] new ways of life" rather than "the world created by contact." European contact is a given; toward the purpose of contributing something toward Native studies, however, I am more interested in what can be innovated and initiated by Native people in analyzing their own cultures, rather than deconstructing Native viewpoints and arguing for their European underpinnings or even concentrating on white atrocities and Indian victims. When cultural contact between Native Americans and Europeans has occurred throughout history, I am assuming that it is just as likely that things European are Indianized rather than the anthropological assumption that things Indian are always swallowed up by European culture. I reject, in other words, the supremacist notion that assimilation can only go in one direction, that white culture always overpowers Indian culture, that white is inherently more powerful than red, that Indian resistance has never occurred in such a fashion that things European have been radically subverted by Indians.

In terms of Native literature, I relate this to a more radical "Red Stick" approach—the assumption that Indian viewpoints cohere, that Indian resistance can be successful, that Native critical centres are possible, that working from within the nation, rather than looking toward the outside, is a legitimate way of examining literature, that subverting the literary status quo rather than being subverted *by* it constitutes a meaningful alternative.

I am not claiming that such a task is a particularly easy one, especially given that we have had five hundred years of being whipped into believing we have no intellectual history of our own making that might provide such frameworks for analysis, and we have critics who would still have us believe this to be the case—that the ones we do have are not "pure enough" to be taken seriously as Indian, that Europe is as much the centre of these writings as Native cultures.

If we take the Spanish book burnings of the Mayan codices in the 1540s as an example, we might describe this act of cultural genocide as one culture finding itself threatened by the profundity of the Other's literacy. These were illiteracy campaigns, sponsored by the group claiming to be the most literate. Symbolically and literally, this campaign still continues; how many Native writers have commented on their long struggle simply to believe in the legitimacy of tribal voices in racist America, where they have been taught that such voices are not possible? In dominant culture, the term "Indian intellectual" is an oxymoron. Yet we have produced written intellectual texts for centuries, not to mention Indigenous-based intellectual knowledge, so much a part of the oral tradition.

And in contemporary literary criticism, it is still a struggle simply to legitimate Native approaches to Native texts, to say that it is OK for Indians to do it their own way. Indian critics, like any others, should be subject to critique, but sometimes the critique has approached the absurd when they have been accused of being atheoretical for wanting to examine their own cultures or for using their own authors as sources for building literary ideas, or when their ideas about looking at Native intellectual history have been characterized as a belief in the pristine quality of all things Indian. Rather than taking more time to present counterarguments against the ridiculous, I hope this study provides a positive example of why looking toward primary Native cultures, authors, and histories can enrich Native literature. If we Native critics share the fault of being "theoryless," my contention would be that this comes from not looking *enough* at our home cultures, not from looking *too much* at them. Naturally, this process does not call for abandoning literary theory, and if one examines the work of most Native critics, one will find that few of us have anyway.

Even postcolonial approaches, with so much emphasis on how the settler culture views the other, largely miss an incredibly important point: how do Indians view Indians? Literature departments have done little to answer this question, and this area of history we must dig up ourselves. Let me give a concrete example of Indian literary history not being uncovered by postcolonial or other approaches. In its thirty-year history, the Institute of American Indian Arts (IAIA) at Santa Fe, New Mexico, has turned out a tremendous number of Native artists, more than three hundred. The way art was taught at IAIA, especially from the mid-1960s to the early 1970s, and the movements that have come out this school (such as Native abstractionism) have had a tremendous influence on Native poetry, and, to a lesser extent, Native fiction. Yet none of this literary history has been uncovered by those practicing conventional Native literary criticism. This is a missed opportunity, and our understanding of contemporary Native literature suffers as a result.

Native literature, and Native literary criticism, written by Native authors, is part of sovereignty: Indian people exercising the right to present images of themselves and to discuss those images; and tribes recognizing their own extant literatures, writing new ones, and asserting the right to explicate them constitute a move toward nationhood. While this literary aspect of sovereignty is not the same thing as the political start of Native nations, the two are, nonetheless, interdependent. A key component of nationhood is a people's idea of themselves, their imaginings of who they are. The ongoing expression of a tribal voice, through imagination, language, and literature, contributes to keeping sovereignty alive in the citizens of a nation and gives sovereignty a meaning that is defined within the tribe rather than by external sources.

The point that Elizabeth Cook-Lynn makes so well is that there *already* exists a Native literary critical school:

> The second worry for the nativist is the question of whether or not opening up the American literary canon to include Native literary traditions and contemporary works will have much relevance, given its own set of unique aims—the interest in establishing the myths and metaphors of sovereign nationalism; the places, the mythological beings, the genre structures and plots of the oral traditions; the wars and war leaders, the treaties and accords with other nations as the so-called gold standard against which everything can be judged. These are the elements of nationalism which have always fueled the literary canon of tribal peoples and their literary lives. In my own tribal literary traditions, there is a fairly long list of Dakota/Lakota writers and storytellers as well as a huge body of ritual and ceremony against which everything may be compared. Reference to the body of nationalistic myths, legends, metaphors, symbols, historical persons and events, writers and their writings must form the basis of the critical discourse that functions in the name of the people; the presence of the Indian nation as cultural force a matter of principle. (*Why I Can't Read Wallace Stegner and Other Essays* 84–85)

Tribal authors have the right, as well as the responsibility, to explore these national literary tendencies in order to pass on the traditions of their respective tribal nations to the next generation. If Indian writers write only about tribes other than their own, and if critics fail to look at Native philosophies and philosophers in developing their criticism, what happens to the next generation in their own communities back home? What have we left for them? Perhaps it is time to really dig in, to entrench ourselves with what we have inherited from our home cultures.

Standing Rock Lakota scholar Kelly Morgan makes an impassioned plea for national literatures. She argues that imaginative literature—fiction and poetry—is a more accurate gauge of cultural realities than the ethnographic, anthropological, and historical record; that, in fact, given the absence of Lakota women at all in non-Indian accounts (except for women as docile drudges), the imaginative writings of Lakota women are vital. Literature, Morgan posits, contributes to Lakota cultural survival because it extends knowledge of cultural practices to future generations.[4] In comparison to rigid non-Indian "scientific" depictions, literature is unfixed, ever growing and evolving, and influenced by "the diversity of Lakota people themselves." As an example, Morgan states that traditional Lakota oral stories, even in their written forms, can teach Lakotas valuable kinship roles that have been a part of Lakota world-views for centuries. She goes on to say that these texts have the potential to aid in the cultural survival of the people, especially for young people who have suffered a loss of self-esteem from racism and stereotypical dominant culture depictions of Indians. One way this loss of identity occurs is when Native children have replaced what they have learned at home with external definitions of Indianness from fixed anthropological, ethnographic, and historical texts, or portrayals from popular culture. Morgan believes that the primary audience for Lakota texts are Lakota people themselves, and she sees the written word as a vehicle for carrying forward oral stories. This kind of nation building, I believe, is vital to the authorship and critical response of the future.

To legitimize a space for national critical studies and Native intellectual history, scholars of Native literature need to break down the oppositional thinking that separates orality and literacy wherein the oral constitutes authentic culture and the written contaminated culture. The aforementioned Mayan codices, written in Mayan pictoglyphic symbols before contact, and in Mayan in the Latin alphabet afterward, are a fascinating study in these regards because recent scholarship has shown that these books were used as a *complement* of oral tradition rather than a *replacement*.[5] The books were recited and even read in precontact schools to educate the young in the oral tradition.

The idea, then, of books as a valid means of passing on vital cultural information is an ancient one, consistent with the oral tradition itself, in the case of the Mayans. This example opens up a space for Native intellectual discussion, in the form of textual production, in contact, not competition, with the oral tradition. Surely, in today's literate society, this represents one hope for Native people in terms of passing on culture. In these regards, the Mayan codices are also interesting in terms of their national literary character; the texts taught Mayans what it meant to be Mayan—their history, their cosmogony, the evolution of their political system, and so on.

Another aspect of Native literatures that needs to be discussed in terms of their national character is their mimetic function, the link between literature and social realities that is a natural part of the oral tradition. Many authors have discussed the pragmatic nature of literatures in oral traditions, where a song, poem, or chant is used toward utilitarian ends such as fostering successful hunting relationships, warding off evil, germinating crops, curing illnesses, going through the day with respectful thoughts and actions, and so on. In a classroom essay, Kirk Zebolksky, one of my Native literature students at the University of Nebraska at Omaha, made an interesting comment on the way

Native literatures continue to link themselves with Native politics, a contemporary form of this unique mimesis:

> Implicit in this description of the U.S. as "stolen" is the presumption that parts or all of it should be returned. Thus Louis and other Native authors have an important role in dialogue about Native land rights. Perhaps they have the most important role in terms of getting across the point that Indigenous land rights have been grossly violated. American Indian writers are assuming a unique role—being the primary and most articulate voices in calling for major political changes and property transfers in the country which is the world's only superpower and the most militarily powerful nation in history.[6]

Native artistry is not pure aesthetics, or art for art's sake: as often as not, Indian writers are trying to *invoke* as much as *evoke*. The idea behind ceremonial chant is that language, spoken in the appropriate ritual contexts, will actually cause a change in the physical universe. This element exists in contemporary Native writing and must be continuously explored in building up a national body of literature and criticism—language as invocation that will upset the balance of power, even to the point, as Zebolsky argues, where stories will be preeminent factors in land redress. . . .

Notes

This essay was first published in Craig S. Womack, *Red on Red: Native American Literary Separatism* (Minneapolis: U of Minnesota P, 1999).

1. Durango Mendoza's short story "Summer Water and Shirley" is analyzed in the original dissertation version of this book, as is the work of Thomas E. Moore (William Harjo) and Susanna Factor. "Summer Water and Shirley" is anthologized in Natachee Scott Momaday's book *American Indian Authors*. Thomas Moore's work *Sour Sofke* was published in Muskogee, Oklahoma, by Hoffman Printing Company and can sometimes be found in places like the Creek National Council House Museum in Okmulgee. Vincent Mendoza has an interesting autobiography about growing up Mexican American and Creek entitled *Son of Two Bloods*. Eddie Chuculate is a budding Creek creative writer published in various anthologies. Susanna Factor has written bilingual children's books used in schools in the Creek Nation. Helen Chalakee Burgess is a Creek writer, essayist, and journalist who has worked for the Creek Nation. Jim Pepper was an outstanding jazz saxophonist interested in syntheses of tribal music and jazz.
2. See Daniel F. Littlefield for many of Gibson's letters, as well as other early Creek writers who appeared in print in *Native American Writing in the Southeast: An Anthology, 1875–1935* (Jackson: UP of Mississippi, 1995).

3. The genesis of this idea began for me in a conversation with historian Tony Hall, who was commenting on the way in which Native issues in Canada are so much more prominent in public discourse than they are in the United States. Hall observed that perhaps Indians are allowed to exist only as fiction in the States.

4. I am indebted to Morgan for allowing me to read and cite her Ph.D. dissertation-in-progress (University of Oklahoma) on the subject of Lakota women writers. Morgan has since successfully defended her dissertation and earned the Ph.D. in the spring semester, 1997.

5. See, for example, Leon Portilla's essay "Have We Really Translated the Meso-American Word?", in *On the Translation of Native American Literatures*, ed. Brian Swann (Washington: Smithsonian Institution P, 1992).

6. Kirk H. Zebolsky wrote a student paper for a Native American literature class at the University of Nebraska at Omaha. The title of the paper is "Recent Works of Louis, Harjo and Silko: Emphasizing Land Rights, Subsuming Native Culture."

23

"Introduction" from
Towards a Native American Critical Theory

Elvira Pulitano

One of the assumptions most frequently made about critical theory is that it is the elite language of the social and culturally privileged. Attacks against such a monolithic, hegemonic form of discourse—whether it is called *pure theory*, or *academic jargon*, or simply *incomprehensible language*—have characterized most critical and cultural debates in the past few decades. It is said that *to do theory* means to be working in an Olympian realm, a realm safely located within the confines of an imperialistic West, and thus to ignore the historical realities that invest the rest of humanity. Yet is undeniable that something called *critical theory* has had a tremendous impact in shaping literary and cultural studies over the past twenty years—to the extent that the foundations of theory itself (in its monolithic, Eurocentric mode) are now being tested.

To begin a discussion about something called *Native American critical theory* means to run into seemingly innumerable problems, the first of which concerns the argument itself. Is there such a thing as a Native American critical theory? If so, how should we define it? As a non-Native critic, am I entitled to define it? Does my "speaking about" necessarily mean "speaking for"? Would my attempt be a further heavy-handed appropriation of the Other, since, for more than two millennia, theory has been, as many would argue, the product of Western thinking? These are some of the questions that I intend to pose in the present study, with the hope of beginning a discussion that, far from being definitive or conclusive, might in the end generate further arguments for debate.

In *The Voice in the Margin*, Arnold Krupat claims that "what chiefly marks the Americanist critic from the Native Americanist critic today is the relation of each to that thing called theory" (5). Drawing from Paul de Man's argument concerning the suspicious attitude toward poststructuralist, Derridean, and deconstructivist theories in the past few decades, Krupat laments that, in Native American studies, there has been and continues to be a "resistance to theory tout court" (6). According to Krupat, this resistance results from the general assumption that theory is aligned with the first terms of those binary sets (abstract/concrete, West/East, theory/praxis, etc.) so common within poststructuralist practice, and, ironically, so often discredited by poststructuralist and Derridean theories themselves. In *For Those Who Come After*, Krupat posits that "those who do study Native American literatures have thus far tended to avoid critical theory as if it were indeed the French disease, a foreign corruption hostile or irrelevant to their local efforts" (xxviii–xxix). Such "resistance to theory" (*Voice in the Margin* 6), Krupat argues, inevitably continues to perpetuate an us/them universe, keeping apart two worlds and two worldviews that could and should talk to one another. As a non-Native critic working in the specific field of Native American studies, Krupat's ongoing project is to eliminate this separatist attitude, by approaching Native American literature, not as an "other" literature, but as a corpus of works that parallel (in their difference) the literary production of Euramerican culture. Krupat's significant lamentation, however, merits consideration.

Despite the fact that many contemporary authors—Native as well as non-Native—have theorized about issues related to Native American culture and literature in particular, to date no monograph-length theoretical account exists that might indicate the development of a Native American critical theory, nor can we talk about a school or circle that has grown up around such a critical endeavour. Even Krupat's own attempt to forge an "ethnocritical" discourse, one originating from "a frontier condition of liminality" and embracing a dialogic approach toward Native American literature, remains substantially a tentative project. As Krupat puts it, "What might be called an 'indigenous' criticism for Indian literature remains to be worked out" (*Ethnocriticism* 44).

Although Krupat's reasoning bears some truth, I will argue, nevertheless, that, in the past few years, rather than simply relying on literary theories borrowed entirely from the West, a number of Native American writers have developed discursive strategies concerning Native American culture and literature, strategies that suggest a theory of reading generated largely, although by no means exclusively, from Native American cultural and intellectual traditions. Paula Gunn Allen, Craig Womack, Robert Warrior, Greg Sarris, Louis Owens, and Gerald Vizenor have produced, from rather different critical positions

and cultural backgrounds, a corpus of works that could represent the beginning of a Native American critical theory, a complex, hybridized project that,
while deeply embedded within narratives of Native American oral tradition
and Native epistemology, inevitably conducts dialogues with the larger critical
discourse of contemporary theory and significantly disputes the scholarly
assumptions of a resistance to theory within Native American studies. Aware
that the accepted modes of academic discourse cannot sufficiently explicate
the arguments of Native American literature written in English, a literature
in which a traditional oral rhetoric is still very much apparent, the above-
mentioned authors argue for a literary criticism that brings to light Native
ways of articulating the world and that uses Indigenous rhetorics along with
the instruments of Western literary analysis. A close analysis of their work will
give me the opportunity to discuss the different approaches taken toward this
complex enterprise and to illustrate how persuasive these different authors'
theories are, relative both to one another and to the larger field of critical and
cultural studies. Since no substantial study has been done on any of the works
that I have selected, I want to engage them as closely possible in my analysis
in order both to establish their major premises, arguments, and interrelations
and—equally important—to subject them to as rigorous a scrutiny as I can.

As with any discourse involving Native American problematics, the present
one cannot escape the overarching question of Indian identity, an identity that
is, as Louis Owens points out in *Other Destinies*, a "treasured invention." "The
Indian," he writes, "in today's world consciousness is a product of literature,
history, and art, and a product that, as an invention, often bears little resemblance to actual, living Native American people" (4). Indeed, the question of
how to define a Native American critical theory, as well as how the authors
under analysis in this study define it, is primarily determined by such a conception of identity, an identity that, as I will argue, has a rather different meaning for some of these critics than it has for others.[1] Within the specific field
of American literature itself, discussions and arguments have been produced
from so many disparate sites and for so many disparate purposes that to conceive of a single consistent theoretical methodology characterizing such literature is often counterproductive. Similarly, to envision a monolithic discourse
that authenticates an ideal form of Native American theory is quite reductive,
since the needs and contexts that such a discourse would conflate are far too
different. While my project does not intend to be prescriptive, it does, however,
acknowledge some basic premises, premises heavily determined by the nature
of the texts under analysis.

First of all, in using the term *Native American theory*—as opposed,
for instance, to *Native American criticism*—I incorporate in my study the

recognition that there is no nontheoretical criticism. Theoretical assumptions and implications lurk behind the most practical forms of criticism, even the most text-oriented interpretations and evaluations. As Terry Eagleton points out, "Any body of theory concerned with human meaning, value, language, feeling, and experience will inevitably engage with broader, deeper beliefs about the nature of human individuals and societies, problems of power and sexuality, interpretations of past history, versions of the present, and hopes for the future" (170). Despite the resurgence of anti-intellectualism within leftist thinking in the past few years, the same orientation that has incited the most vigorous attacks against poststructuralist, deconstructivist, and postcolonial critical discourses, I argue that there is a point at which theory and praxis meet and that the intellectual armchair remains a crucial sphere of influence, a place from which it is possible to agitate through and to propose, as Michel Foucault does, "an insurrection of knowledges that are opposed . . . to the effects of the centralizing powers that are linked to the institution" (*Power/Knowledge* 84).

A second and most important recognition is that no critical theory produced from the so-called margin escapes the question of functioning within a "dominant" discourse, not even a Native American theory. Writing about the relation between Native American literature and Western literary theory, Owens claims that

> we do not have the luxury of simply opting out, because whether or not we are heard by Said, Sollors, or others, we already function within the dominant discourse. To think otherwise is naïve at best, for the choice was made for us generations ago. Half a millennium of European attempts to both eliminate and reimagine the Indian has resulted in a hybridized, multicultural reality clearly recognized in fiction as long ago as the 1920s and '30s by such Native American writers as Mourning Dove, McNickle, and Matthews. . . . The very act of appropriating the colonizer's discourse and making it one's own is obviously collaborative and conjunctural. (*Mixedblood Messages* 52)

Along with Owens, Krupat points out the "conjunction of cultural practices" characterizing the Euramerican and the Native American production. He writes that, "from 1492 on, neither Euramerican intellectuals nor Native American intellectuals could operate autonomously or uniquely, in a manner fully independent of one another, for all the differences in power relations" (*The Turn to the Native* 18).

Within the contemporary scenario of the various "post" isms (postmodernism, poststructuralism, and postcolonialism), where and how would a Native American critical theory fit? Would it be just be a new form of colonial enterprise with these authors picking up the master's tools in order to demonstrate that they can function at the same level of the dominant centre, and, as Owens puts it, "to prove that we [i.e., Native Americans] are tool-using creatures just like him and therefore worthy of intellectual recognition" (*Mixedblood Messages* 53)? Or would it rather be a separatist form of discourse, one that argues for a "Nativist" approach but that inevitably runs the risk of remaining trapped in essentialist positions by merely reversing Western binary structures? Or might it rather be an attempt to mediate between differing discourses and epistemologies? Writing in *Black Literature and Literary Theory* about the validity of applying Western methodologies to black literature, Henry Louis Gates Jr. anticipates the dilemma now facing contemporary Native American authors. "Do we have to 'invent' validly 'black' critical theory and methodologies" in order to explicate the "signifying black difference?" Gates asks. "How 'original' is the use of contemporary theory to read black texts?" (3, 9). By claiming that, in this critical methodology, originality relies more on the process by which the methodology is applied, Gates posits that "the challenge of [this] endeavor is to bring together, in a new fused form, the concepts of critical theory and the idiom of the Afro-American and African literary traditions" (9–10). To those who fear a risk of parroting the paradigms of the academic centre, Gates replies by saying that "one 'repeats,' as it were, in order to produce *difference*" (10).

In the specific case of Native American studies, where and how is a "signifying" Native difference produced? Does the development of a Native American critical theory necessitate the creation of new critical languages, or does it rather imply a problematic but unavoidable participation in a Western discourse? In *Manifest Manners,* Gerald Vizenor writes: "The English language has been the linear tongue of colonial discoveries, racial cruelties, invented names, the simulation of tribal cultures, manifest manners, and the unheard literature of dominance in tribal communities; at the same time, this mother tongue of paracolonialism has been a language of invincible imagination and liberation for many tribal people in the postindian world" (105). According to Vizenor, the "same coercive language of federal boarding schools" has now become a language of creative "resistance" and "survivance" among distinguished Native American authors in the cities (106). By challenging the logic of English in its basic structure and subverting the acceptable literary forms, Vizenor, as well as the other theorists discussed in this study, finds a place on the written page by attempting to incorporate patterns and strategies from the oral tradition—what he calls, with a twist on Derrida, "the traces of oral stories" (*Fugitive Poses* 62). If the connection between critical theory and oral tradition might at first appear to be untenable, in the context of my study I argue that it becomes the most subversive and creative way in which to forge a Native voice within the major critical discourse, or, to put in Gates' terms, to produce a "signifying [Native] difference" by repeating. Notwithstanding ideological and methodological differences as far as defining the parameters of a Native American critical theory, and notwithstanding the heterogeneity of discourses produced by the authors under analysis in this study, crucial to all of them is the idea of incorporating the vitality of the oral into the written text while bringing Native epistemology to the attention of First World ideology. Such a basic assumption is what makes them part of a dialogue on Native American critical theory to begin with, and, more significantly, perhaps, what makes their work worthy of being explored.

Within such a specific common view, Allen, Warrior, Womack, Sarris, Owens, and Vizenor articulate a unique discursive mode that adequately addresses the complexity of Native American literary texts, including the richly textured and layered worlds of the oral tradition out of which these texts originate, while significantly reflecting their borderland position as mixed-blood authors working at the juncture of different discourses and worldviews. While heavily and inevitably drawing from Western hermeneutical discourse (even when their main intent is to promote a rigidly tribal-centred approach), the above-mentioned authors emphasize a reading of theory that reveals unique characteristics by allowing the Native oral tradition to speak for itself about its nature and various functions, providing the tools, concepts, and languages necessary to a discussion of Native American literature, and adding to the rhetorical systems of Western critical theory. By bringing the liberating and extraordinary vitality of the spoken word onto the written page, these authors suggest in their own ways how the oral tradition can inscribe its own theories of its nature, function within the elaborate hermeneutical systems of the Western tradition, and, ultimately, demystify the curious notion that theory is the exclusive province of Western thought. Instead of taking a resisting stance toward theory, as many scholars have argued should be done, the above-mentioned authors are now "resisting theory" from within, forging identity out of rupture and inevitably remapping the boundaries of theory itself.

My decision to select Allen, Womack, Warrior, Sarris, Owens, and Vizenor from among the many Native American authors who have written critical works about Native issues—as well as to exclude non-Native critics (e.g., Krupat, Alan Velie, Elaine Jahner, and James Ruppert) who have consistently applied Western methodologies to interpret Native American literary texts—reflects the primary goal of this study: an attempt to define a Native American critical theory in which the discursive modes are largely generated from within a Native epistemology, while, of course, also subsuming the forms and methods of Western discourse.[2]

Specifically, the authors selected rely heavily on Native American cultural and intellectual traditions in the attempt to create discursive strategies that might explicate the richly layered texts of Native American literary works. Acknowledging the vitality of the oral narratives, Allen, Womack, Sarris, Owens, and Vizenor in particular incorporate into their written texts strategies and patterns from the oral tradition, in an attempt to re-create/reimagine the dialogic quality of the oral exchange.[3] Both in form and in content, their works have, within a specific point of commonality, begun to define the characteristics that make Native American theory different, to a certain extent, from Eurocentric discourse. At the same time, by demonstrating the crucial ways in which this theory is, of course, in dialogue with, relies on, and subsumes Western discursive modes, they produce substantially multi-generic, dialogic, and richly hybridized works, texts that shuttle back and forth between worlds and worldviews and "mediate" strategies that challenge Western ways of doing theory.

Although a dialogic or crosscultural approach appears as the most natural and effective way to discuss the highly hybridized nature of Native American theory—an approach that, it should be pointed out, not even all the authors selected in the present study seem to agree on—I am also aware of the significant objections that such a position might raise. Within the current debates over cultural identity and political positioning in postcolonial studies, an emphasis on hybridity and plural identity has generated significant criticism by scholars such as Robert Young and Benita Parry, who see in such a tendency a perpetuation of the old notion of humanism.[4] Within the specific context of cultures, they argue, the term *hybridity* is, much like its opposite reality, *authenticity*, unintelligible without a notion of cultural purity. Such a hybridized perspective, they posit, tends to homogenize the centre more or less implicitly and make it monolithic in ways that simply do not do justice to the variegated (peripheral) realities. On the other hand, in the so-called border zones of cultures, such as Africa, the Caribbean, and the Indian Ocean, the term *hybridity* is conceived as a site of powerful creative resistance to the dominant conceptual paradigms. According to Françoise Lionnet, the message proclaimed by contemporary art and literature from Africa and the Caribbean involves a "move [that] forces individuals to stand in relation to the past and the present at the same time, to look for creative means of incorporating useful 'Western' tools, techniques, or strategies into their own cosmology or weltanschauung" ("Logiques Métisses" 325). By appropriating the term *transculturation* as it was earlier used by the Cuban poet Nancy Morejon, with the prefix *trans-* suggesting the "act of traversing, of going through existing cultural territories" (326), Lionnet insists on a "métissage of forms" and identities that is the result of crosscultural encounters.[5] In such a case, she argues, *transculturation* becomes, unlike *acculturation* and *assimilation*, the terms usually associated with hybridity, "a process whereby all elements involved in the interaction would be changed by that encounter" (323). On a more radical level, Chris Bongie envisions, in his historical and theoretical study of the "Creolization" process, the Creole identity as something incessantly produced out of the global crossings of cultures as well as out of identitarian ways (63).[6] Careful to avoid the essentializing trap of opposing the notion of Creolization to the colonial legacy, something that Lionnet herself, according to Bongie, does not do, he insists on the double identity of the Creolization process, a shifting middle ground between a rooted and a relational identity (65).[7] On a discursive level, these advocates of Creolization celebrate the mutual contamination of styles while pointing out how the former colonized culture has, by borrowing from the metropolitan culture, succeeded in the process to subvert and indigenize it.

In the context of my study, I see the hybridized or crosscultural perspective of the Native American discursive modes paralleling more closely the ideological intentions of the Caribbean critics' notion of identity rather than engulfing the assimilationist and pluralist tendencies of its opponents. Those familiar with something called *Native American literature* are fully aware that such literature is, in the end, the product of conjunctural cultural practices, the Euramerican and Native American, and that, whatever our geographical, cultural, or ideological position, we cannot dismiss such a crucial premise in our interpretative acts. Written primarily in English by authors possessing a consistently high level of education, these works are already heteroglot by nature— even as they rely heavily on elements from Native epistemologies, specifically the reality of myth and ceremony as embodied in traditional oral literatures. Novels such as Silko's *Ceremony*, Momaday's *House Made of Dawn*, Welch's *Winter in the Blood*, Carr's *Eye Killers*, Owens' *The Sharpest Sight*, and Vizenor's *Bearheart*, to mention but a few, brilliantly convey this richly hybridized dialogue—or "meditational" strategy—connecting two different worlds and worldviews. The same could be said for the poetry of Luci Tapahonso, Simon Ortiz, and Joy Harjo—and, in fact, for all the literary genres that have contributed in the past few years to the development of Native American literature. Within this context, charges of assimilationism against a theory that relies on the same hybridized strategies and discursive modes utilized by the texts that it sets out to interpret seem, in the long run, an ironic contradiction. How could a Native American theory aim at a "pure" form of (Native) discourse, untouched by the strategies of Western tradition, when Native American literature itself a product of a crosscultural encounter, what Thomas King labels "interfusional literature, blending the oral and the written" (xii)? How could Native American theorists aim at developing a separatist form of discourse when they are heavily and inevitably implicated in the discourse of the metropolitan centre? As I will point out in my discussion, while such separatist sentiments appear legitimate to fervent representatives of nationalist approaches, they become all the more dangerous as they continue to ossify Native American literary production, as well as Native identity, into a sort of museum culture.

Equally important for my study is the relation that a Native American critical theory bears to current postcolonial discursive modes. Krupat argues, for example, that, in the current climate of literary studies, "it is tempting to think of contemporary Native American literatures as the postcolonial literature of the world" (*The Turn to the Native* 30). Certainly, he suggests, as the product of the "contact zones," a product originating in response to or in dialogue with the metropolitan representation, the ideological perspective of the literature produced by Native American authors bears interesting parallels with the ideological perspectives of other postcolonial literatures and postcolonial theory. On the other hand, recognizing that there are many forms of postcolonialism, and that there is nothing at all "post" about some of these forms, some critics (even within the postcolonial field itself) argue that we must draw distinctions; such critics accuse postcolonialism of being another totalizing method that fails to account for differences, in this case the culturally and historically variegated forms of both colonization and anti-colonial struggle. . . .

As critics have pointed out, America never became postcolonial, and what is usually considered Native American literature still operates in an ongoing process of colonialism. To further illustrate this point, we should mention the forceful critique of postcolonial theory conducted by the historian Amy Kaplan, who argues, "The history of American imperialism strains the definition of the postcolonial, which implies a temporal development . . . that relies heavily on the spatial coordinates of European empires, in their formal acquisition of territories and the subsequent history of decolonization and national independence" (17). Obviously, Kaplan suggests, such a "Eurocentric notion of postcoloniality" (17) does not apply to the history of American imperialism, both at home and abroad, where the United States predominates in a power relation often called *neocolonial*. Even Krupat claims, after a first, enthusiastic impulse to align Native American literature among the "postcolonial literatures of the world," that "there is not yet a 'post' to the colonial status of the Native Americans" (*The Turn to the Native* 30). However, while admitting that Native American literature is produced in an ongoing condition of colonialism, and that cultural, historical, and ideological differences are crucial in a postcolonial approach to Native American literary production, Krupat convincingly argues that both Native American and postcolonial writers (and theorists) are involved in an intensely subversive ideological project. Drawing from Talal Asad, Krupat uses the term *anti-imperial translation* to conceptualize the tension and differences between Native American fiction and the imperial centre (*The Turn to the Native* 32).

Such ideological parallels might explain why more and more critics, including Native scholars, have in the past few years turned to the rhetorical strategies of postcolonial theory to elucidate Native American literary narratives. Carleton Smith, for example, explores the cultural and literary borderlands between Native American, postcolonial, and postmodern theories of cultural representation in order to explicate Frederick Jackson Turner's famous frontier thesis in terms of the repressed Other. More specifically, Smith adopts Bhabha's notion of a "third space" as an interpretive lens through which to read Louise Erdrich's *Turtle Mountain* series of novels. In *Mixedblood Messages* . . . Owens finds Mary Louise Pratt's terms *contact zone* and *auto-ethnographic text* particularly useful in the context of Native American literature. More extensively, in his "As If an Indian Were Really an Indian," Owens compares the situation of the "migrant, diasporic Native American writer" to the liminal condition of the postcolonial critic (people such as Gayatri Spivak, Homi Bhabha, Trinh T. Minh-ha, and Edward Said, among others) while pointing out how, even within this increasingly anticolonial theoretical site of resistance, the erasure of Native American voices constitutes the norm (209–10). Owens posits that a reader must turn, almost with surprise, from Said's extraordinary denigration of Native Americans in *Culture and Imperialism* and Bhabha's silencing of the Indigenous inhabitants of the Americas in his panoply of minority voices in *The Location of Culture* to Trinh's critical narratives, in order to find mention of Leslie Marmon Silko's storytelling and Vizenor's trickster, as if the works produced by Native Americans are less marginal and less anticolonial than those produced by African American, Asian American, or Chicano writers.[8]

Elaborating on Owens' and Krupat's formulations, the present discussion will indicate ways in which Native American theory and postcolonial strategies speak to one another despite ideological, historical, and geopolitical differences. Against those who insist on cultural specificity, arguing that the colonization of India, Cuba, or Algeria is not the same as the colonization of the Indians, Cubans, and Algerians, I argue that cultural specificity does not exclude some very real cultural commonalities, and that, by overemphasizing (cultural) difference for its own sake, we run the risk of exoticizing the cultures in question. Using Spivak's notion of "catachresis," I will illustrate how Native American theorists both use and go beyond the discursive strategies of postcolonialism by testing its ideas primarily against Native American problematics and predicaments.[9] While the works of Spivak, Bhabha, Trinh, Said, and

Fanon, among others, will provide me with a critical vocabulary with which to interrogate the texts of Native American theorists, at the same time, and perhaps more significantly, these same texts will provide me with examples of discursive modes that in most cases challenge the parameters of Eurocentric theory itself. The trickster trope of Vizneor's hermeneutics, as well as the overall patterns from the oral tradition to which almost all the authors I set out to discuss subscribe, provides discursive strategies that speak, actually "perform," the same (anticolonial) lexicon of postcolonialism. In addition, more subversively and provocatively than the often cerebral, Eurocentric grid of postcolonial texts, such strategies succeed in bringing together differing epistemologies and discursive modes. In the words of Homi Bhabha, Native American theorists are, indeed, accomplishing acts of "(cross)cultural translation" (*The Location of Culture* 228), bringing to the attention of the dominant culture other discursive tropes while destabilizing the margin-centre opposition so dear to traditional Western hermeneutics.

Notes

This essay was first published in Elvira Pulitano, *Toward a Native American Critical Theory* (Lincoln: U of Nebraska P, 2003).

1. The contemporary debate over tribal identity, integrity, and authenticity also accounts for my semantic choices. In this study, I most often use the term *Native American* as opposed to, e.g., *aboriginal* or *indigenous*, mainly because it is accepted and commonly used by the writers whose work is the subject of this study. For the sake of convenience, I occasionally retain the familiar *Indian*, even though I am perfectly aware of the heavily colonial overtones invested in it. As Gerald Vizenor forcefully points out, the term *Indian* has been used since Columbus to create manifold representations of Indians. Yet the *Indian* never existed in reality: "The word Indian . . . is a colonial enactment . . . [a] simulation that has superseded the real tribal names" (*Manifest Manners* 11).

2. Within this context, Native writers and critics such as Jace Weaver have also been excluded from my discussion. *That the People May Live*, Weaver's critical analysis of Native American literature in the last two hundred years, an analysis substantiated by his interesting concept of "communitism," adds very little to a discourse on Native American critical theory that is attempting to generate rhetorical strategies of its own. Similarly, a work such as Owens' *Other Destinies* clearly responds, in its Bakhtinian approach to Native American fiction, to a purpose other than which my study intends to pursue.

3. While contributing to a discourse on Native American theory and criticism in many important ways, showing how attention to Native intellectual figures such as John Joseph Matthews and Vine Deloria Jr. might benefit a Native American critical discourse, Warrior's critical strategy follows a more traditional Western rhetorical pattern.

4. While Parry's and Young's critiques are mainly directed against Said's idea of the *human*—which he exposes to the Western representation of the Orient, but which, ironically, Parry and Young argue, is itself derived from the Western humanist tradition—those critiques acquire conceptual force in the context of a conception of hybridization intended as a synthesizing, dialectical, and progressive teleology. See Parry 30; and Young 131–32. On the notion of *the hybrid*, see also Bhabha, *The Location of Culture*, 102–22.

5. The concept *transculturation* was, as Lionnet points out, first advanced by Fernando Ortiz, for whom the term meant the assimilation of Afro-Cuban culture into Hispanic culture. Unlike Ortiz's, Morejon's view of transculturation is, according to Lionnet, a "more dialectical phenomenon," and better responds to Lionnet's notion of *métissage*. See "'Logiques Métisses'" 341.

6. Drawing from Edouard Glissant (one of the most influential theorists of the Creolization process), Bongie posits that all essentialist glorifications of unitary origins—what Glissant refers to as "the univocal pretensions of the indentitary"—run contrary to the hybridized arguments that have gained such prominence of late in postcolonial theory (Bongie 53). Yet, Bongie argues, in order to avoid the hierarchical thinking often underlying the notion of Creolization, it is necessary to acknowledge the paradoxical coexistence of two different logics. He writes: "What this statement suggests is that the connection between fixed and relational identities is not (simply) a matter of either/or but (also) of both/and" (66).

7. Elaborating on Glissant's formulations, Bongie reads the critic's phrase *identitérelation* in an equivocating manner, suggesting that the hyphen does not so much separate as join both elements interstitially, "the old world of a necessary circumscribed local identity, and the new world of an increasingly chaotic and globalized cross-cultural relation" (70).

8. Other critics have addressed the homogenizing tendency of postcolonial theory. For a more detailed discussion, see Chapter 3.

9. As Owens points out, Said's reference to Native American writing as "that sad panorama produced by genocide and cultural amnesia which is beginning to be known as Native American literature" makes a statement about the kind of imperialist terminology often adopted by postcolonial theorists ("As If an Indian" 210).

24

Afterword:
At the Gathering Place

Lisa Brooks

There was a time, in the early 1990s, when anyone who wanted to write to me, whether family, friend, or bill collector, had to address their correspondence to the Sovereign Abenaki Nation of Missisquoi, which had a zip code that matched that of Swanton, Vermont, but was (and has always been), in many ways, an entirely different space.[1] I have been thinking lately about the meaning of such an act. We know the power of words. N. Scott Momaday reminds us in his landmark essay that "we are all" people "made of words" ("The Man Made of Words" 162). Craig S. Womack, in *Red on Red*, notes that "as often as not Indian writers are trying to *invoke* as much as *evoke*." For our words, he writes, have the potential to "actually cause a change in the universe" (17). In the Abenaki language, it is quite clear that the written word has the power to create and solidify changes in the landscape.[2] I have been thinking about what it meant for so many people to write those words on a daily basis. Words that enacted recognition of our nation, all over the state of Vermont, all over New England, all over the world.

It seems a strange request for me to write this Afterword in a volume on Native literary nationalism. According to the papers manufactured by the state and nation-state that purport to have jurisdiction over Abenaki people (Vermont and the United States), the existence of such a nation is tenuous. We do not have a reservation; we do not have a casino; we are not, as of this date, a "federally recognized tribe." When Abenaki people rose up in the 1980s to assert their continuing right to fish in the Missisquoi River, a place where families such as mine have stories that suggest that fishing is as essential to physical and cultural survival as drinking water, a court battle ensued that would last for the better part of a decade. The case began with an organized "fish-in" and rested on the doctrine of Aboriginal title. Although often abrogated by treaty, removal, or federal recognition, Aboriginal title represents the sovereignty that is inherent in an Indigenous people's relationship to land.[3] According to US law, Aboriginal title exists a priori; it can be extinguished by treaty or federal proclamation, but its existence does not rely on recognition by the United States or its colonial predecessors. The doctrine recognizes the jurisdictional right of an Indigenous nation in the land they have inhabited and utilized over an extremely long course of time. What made the Missisquoi case so significant was the idea that Aboriginal title continues to exist (if a Native nation continues to enact it), *regardless* of whether a nation-state (in this case, the United States) had formally recognized it as such.

During the fish-in trials, the judge at the district court level gave the case a thorough hearing and deliberated carefully, concluding that the Abenaki Nation of Missisquoi and its interdependent relationship to land continued to exist long into the twentieth century *despite* colonial encroachment. The court concluded that "the State [had] failed to prove . . . that the Missisquoi abandoned or ceded their Missisquoi homeland or that their Aboriginal rights were extinguished by either an express act or an act clearly and unambiguously implying any sovereign's intent to extinguish those rights. Accordingly, the Missisquoi's Aboriginal right to fish in their Missisquoi homeland continues to exist today" (*State of Vermont v. Harold St. Francis, et al.*). This was a huge victory for the nation. It represented recognition without relinquishment. It meant families could continue to fish without interference. It solidified, in writing, a relationship that had long existed in the daily practice and stories of Abenaki families. Powerful words, indeed.

The events that occurred in the aftermath of this decision could make for an electrifying novel or political thriller. I will give you an abbreviated version. During some of those years, I was working in the tribal office. As a repatriate and an idealistic undergraduate, I felt myself a part of a transformation in the political landscape. The tribal office, housed in an old railroad depot nearby the Missisquoi River, was a chaotic but energized place. Much of our energy went to working this case. In the meantime, tribal members faced harassment from local police, fear and opposition from local landowners and sports fishing outfits, as well as the struggle with the daily battle of poverty, lack of basic health care, increasing encroachment of development, growing reports of diseased and mercury-laden fish, internal conflict, and despair. It seemed that everything rested on this one case. Consider what it means to understand yourselves internally as a Native nation while those governmental mechanisms that directly affect your lives literally do not see that you exist.

There are advantages, if you can manage to survive. But if your resources are being directly threatened by increased development and pollution, and you have no legal recourse as a political body, the future can seem bleak indeed. In the wake of the fish-in decision, it seemed that this disempowered community might actually be able to regain control.

As the fish-in case developed, a couple of words began to circulate that threatened to cause a change in the universe: "land claim." This phrase made its way into the newspapers, into gossip networks, into law journal articles, and university lectures. Title insurance companies began to add clauses that protected them against land claims by the Abenaki Nation of Missisquoi. It was those two phrases together that caused all the trouble. A lot of power resides in words. Through a series of rhetorical manoeuvres, the Vermont attorney general was able to seek an appeal of the lower court decision. At the level of the Vermont Supreme Court, we saw the meticulous work of the district court judge undone. In the absence of a legal doctrine that would support colonial occupation as eradication of Aboriginal title, the Court invented a concept that haunts me to this day. I remember the day the decision came in to the tribal office. I remember seeing those little words typed on paper: the judges on the Vermont Supreme Court decided that Abenaki Aboriginal title had been "extinguished . . . by the increasing weight of history" (*Vermont v. Eliot*).

Although the court did not dispute that the "tribe" continued to exist, the judges asserted that their rights to their homeland did not. How one could separate out the "tribe" from its land, particularly when subsistence was still essential to existence, was incomprehensible to me. Imagine that . . . nations could be extinguished by . . . history. It's no wonder that for those few Abenaki people who have access to academia, the bulk of us have chosen to pursue an understanding of words, and to almost obsessively comprehend the work, and the "weight," of history.

―――

To turn for a moment to the other side of my family, it has been helpful to me, in trying to understand the weight of history and the complex character of nationalism, to draw on the stories from my mother's family as well.[4] My mother was born a "displaced person" in a Nazi labour camp, the sixth child in a Polish family that had been given the choice, in 1939, either to go with the Germans to their work camps in the east or wait for the Russians, who would arrive shortly to ship them to their work camps in Siberia. This forced submission to the will of neighbouring imperial nations had a long history. For a period of some 125 years (until the end of World War I), the nation of Poland was not allowed to exist. The political map of the landscape was divided up among Russia, Austria, and Prussia. I have heard that it was illegal, in some areas, even to speak the word "Poland." However, in the stories and minds of Polish families, in the music and in the attachment to land, Poland carried on. If asked, my mother will always identify herself as Polish, but she has never been to her homeland. When my mother's family came to the United States in 1950, it was not to pursue some idealized version of the American Dream; they simply had no other place to go. The Soviet Union controlled their country, and they could not return. The United States was the only country that would take a family of nine "displaced persons," and then only because their relocation was sponsored by a Catholic mission. When my grandmother died and was revived by paramedics at her house in Connecticut in 1995, she yelled at her surprised saviours. She told us that, when they woke her up, she had been on the hill she had grown up on as a girl in rural Koszarawa, surrounded by flowers. She had returned home, and they had taken her away, again.

Like my Polish ancestors, my Abenaki relations have also defined nation-hood differently from the imperial and colonial powers that have sought to eradicate the existence of the Native nation and its inextricable relationship to land. In the Abenaki language, as Joe Bruchac points out in his book, *Roots of Survival*, the word for "tribe" is *Negewet kamigwezo*, or "those of one family." The word for "nation," however, is *Mizi Negewet kamigwezoi*, meaning "families gathered together" (30). Thus the activity of nation-building, in the Abenaki sense, is not a means of boundary-making but rather a process of gathering from within. To echo Jace Weaver's term, it is a process of "upbuilding" ("Splitting the Earth" 6). Historically, Abenakis are famous for cycles of gathering and dispersal within particular territories, travelling to up-country havens either to get where the hunting is good, or to avoid being hunted themselves, and then returning to central village places, to fish, to plant, and to gather.[5] When calamity hits, families may disperse, but they never "disappear." Always, they end up gathering together when the storms clear.

During the 1990s, we were involved in an intense gathering time. As families within Missisquoi solidified around the fishing case, other families arrived from all over New England carrying stories, songs, papers, and photographs. We gathered together, exchanging words, trading stories, slowly rebuilding trust. In contemplating the power of words, I've been thinking about what it meant for my father to call me every week at the tribal office and hear about the "upbuilding" project in which I was engaged, what it meant for him to come to tribal gatherings at the old fish hatchery on the shore of Lake Champlain, back to the place, at the village centre, where his own grandfather had been born, how he took me upstream to the places along the Missisquoi River where he fished as a boy, the places where they gathered berries, the delight with which he recalled the stories of huge extended family gatherings. I've been thinking about what it meant when I asked my grandfather to recall the stories of maple sugaring, rum running, and rabbit tracks that linked us with other Abenaki families along the river of his birth, what it meant for my sister to visit Missisquoi as a teenage girl, to recognize this place in a way I never would have imagined, to come to know her name. What it has meant for me, in this lifetime, to connect my family with others whose stories we share, to gather with others who understand the literature of my family, who recognize our name.

However, I have also been thinking about the dispersal that occurred after the "weight of history" decision came down. Anyone who wanted to understand internalized oppression could have come to Missisquoi, to the tribal office in 1992–93, to witness that phenomenon in action. I don't know that lawmakers fully understand the impacts of their own decisions, but that year the "weight of history" felt like lead on our shoulders. When we raised the seemingly insurmountable sum that an appeal to the US Supreme Court required, and that Court simply decided it wasn't prepared to hear the case, we were left with no legal recourse. Many other options were discussed, explored, and pursued, but ultimately, the conflict and infighting that arose with that defeat, with those words of nullification (to echo William Apess), created a dispersal.[6] It is only now, over a decade later, that it feels to me as if families are beginning to come together again. Yet, I've noticed that the decision that was handed down a decade ago did not change the perception of the families from Missisquoi. In fact, if anything, that long, drawn-out legal battle only solidified the relationship between families and the land to which we belong. And what the stories that outlast the papers say is that as long as families continue to gather in place, the nation will exist. However, as Greg Sarris observes in *Keeping Slug Woman Alive*, this gathering process is never idealistic or easy:

> Families bickering. Families arguing amongst themselves, drawing lines, maintaining old boundaries. Who is in. Who is not. Gossip. Jealousy. Drinking. Love. The ties that bind. The very human need to belong, to be worthy and valued. Families. Who is Indian. Who is not. Families bound by history and blood. This is the stuff, the fabric of my Indian community. (117)

As my father's family gathered recently around the sudden and violent death of a beloved and central woman in our extensive network of relations, I was reminded once more of how very fragile our loves and lives are, how tenuous our connections to each other in this world. The words I heard like a refrain in my own mind over the course of those days were from Simon Ortiz: "We must take great care with each other" (as quoted in Weaver, *That the People Might Live* 4).[7] After all, family gatherings can be painful, tumultuous events. When we most need diplomacy and condolence, they can foster divisiveness and anger. I am painfully aware that our eyes and ears are not yet cleared from the violence that our families have endured. But I was grateful for and proud of my family in those days as we told the stories that would make meaning from my cousin's death. We confronted the anger and violence, the madness that was the hidden fabric beneath her carefully woven life. We reminded each other of all the things she said and did that made us laugh. We told stories that envisioned better, more hilarious versions of ourselves. A huge gap in the web of our family required the mending that only stories can do; those strands reinforce the relations between us, remind us of our shared history, let loose the laughter the gives us the reassurance that we can, as a family, endure. This, perhaps, is the essence of a Native nationalist literature, a literature that gathers families together. We turn to the stories for sustenance and meaning; they enable our survival, not just as individuals, but, in the words of Samson Occom, "as one family," as a "whole" (Samson Occom Papers, Folder 16).[8] As Simon Ortiz writes in his seminal essay, "Towards a National Indian Literature," "Because of the insistence to keep telling and creating stories, Indian life continues, and it is this resistance against loss that has made that life possible." As Ortiz seems to suggest, the process of "story-making" and the process of nation gathering may be one and the same (II).

$$=$$

As my family came together for my cousin's passing, I found that the deepest and most painful of stories, as well as the most hilarious strands we wove, seemed to emerge as we gathered around my cousin's table in the evening, with scraps of food and paper, old photographs, flowers scattered haphazardly (perhaps blasphemously) across the space she had kept so neatly clean and organized. Of course, this was no surprise to the women in my family, among whom it is a well-known secret that the kitchen is where all the stories are made. When my sister-in-law revealed to me some time ago that she felt a little out of the loop when we went to the big extended family gatherings, I told her, "Just go help out in the kitchen." Sure enough, she returned from a gathering for which I was absent to tell me, "You're right. Everything happens in the kitchen." Once she made her way to the village centre, and got in on the conversation, she felt included in the gathering. And my aunties later said to me, "You know, it was so nice that Amy came into the kitchen this year. . . ." Tellingly, it was my cousin's unusual absence from the kitchen at the last family gathering that was the biggest signal to us that there might be something wrong. As Joy Harjo writes, reflecting a reality I now know too well: "The world begins at a kitchen table. No matter what, / we must eat to live" (*The Woman Who Fell from the Sky* 68). The women in my family would surely recognize themselves in her poetic lines:

> *Our dreams drink coffee with us as they put their arms*
> *around our children. They laugh with us at our poor*
> *falling-down selves and as we put ourselves back*
> *together once again at the table. . . .*
>
> *Perhaps the world will end at the kitchen table,*
> *While we are laughing and crying,*
> *Eating of the last sweet bite.* (69)

I remember well the experience of sitting at Chief Homer St. Francis' kitchen table at the village centre during those turbulent years at Missisquoi. There was always lots of food (whether it was Patsy St. Francis' homemade rabbit stew or "breakfast for dinner") and lots of conversation to go around. You never knew who you might meet there, could be a fisherman who you didn't recognize at all, but who turned out to be one of the guys who instigated the fish-in for which you were fighting every day. Could be a leader from another nation who came to consult or commiserate. Could be a relation, could be an enemy, could be a hungry stranger off the street. Everyone, it seemed, was welcome at Homer's table; everyone would be fed, but that didn't mean you were safe from confrontation. Many a fight broke out at the table, many a man was challenged. I remember hearing that the heads of families gathered there in the seventies and eighties to discuss their rights as Indian people. I remember the first night I sat at that table, and I stayed so late talking, I was invited to stay over, take up an extra bed, but I declined the offer. For some reason, I wanted to walk back to the tribal office, walk by the river, even though it was around 3 or 4 a.m. There was something about the quiet of the night on the river. I stopped by the bridge, peered over the edge, listened. All around me, it was dark, silent, except for the ebb and flow of the water below. It was like I could hear the weight of history running past, travelling downstream.

Many years later, when I was still trying to figure out that history, still attempting to understand the forces that seemed to tear the gathering apart, I found myself at a lot of kitchen tables, all over Indian Country. At the same time, there were gatherings of Native writers erupting in universities and conference centres, and I found myself drawn into those conversations.[9] It was interesting to me, when I later entered graduate school, that while literary critics in English departments were battling each other in the so-called "theory wars," Native writers and literary scholars were gathering together, engaging in "upbuilding," discussing the interrelatedness of their work and its implication for and in their home communities. I saw creative minds from Alaska to Mexico discussing what it meant to be a Native writer, the responsibilities and potential conflicts with home communities, the joy at reading each others' works in print, and the exhilaration of hearing those words come to life. The exchanges at those gatherings were nothing short of a feast.

When I first read Craig Womack's *Red on Red*, I recognized his voice from those gatherings, and I admired deeply the bravery of his project. To me, he was daring to bring the conversation at the kitchen table to print. At the time I was engaged in graduate study at Cornell. I remember feeling that being in a university was something akin to being in the belly of the beast, but it also offered a haven, a place away from the village where I could take the time to think. I remember being energized by a meeting in the Green Dragon Café with Robert Warrior just prior to reading Womack's work, discussing my ideas for writing a "creative" dissertation that would revolve around the voluminous writings from the Native Northeast that had been repressed by the nineteenth-century American literature of vanishing. I remember him telling me that he thought many people beyond my own region would be interested in coming to know the Native Northeast, that people would want to know what it was like to be Samson Occom sitting in the study of his house on Mohegan Hill, what it meant to be a writer, teacher, and leader in the midst of the Mohegan nation. I remember being grateful for his encouraging words, but I also remember doubting whether anyone would let me do this, particularly under the auspices of a department of English literature. And then I remember how reading *Red on Red* suddenly made my own project seems more possible, more achievable, more acceptable in what I perceived to be a somewhat hostile academic environment. Womack's writing enabled my own articulation, helped me to "find my talk," to echo Jace Weaver's citation of Rita Joe's poem. In short, his work gave me hope.

To turn to the subject of Womack's essay herein, I should note that my reaction to reading Elvira Pulitano's book was entirely the opposite: not only was her work discouraging, but it seemed to me that she and I had read entirely different books. I remember immediately driving over to (Abenaki poet) Cheryl Savageau's house, sitting down at her kitchen table, and before she could even make me a cup of tea, launching into what her husband Bill recognizes as a quintessential Abenaki woman's rant on what I regarded as Pulitano's ravaging simplification of Native critical perspectives (note the plural). I believe Womack does a fine job of fully articulating the problems of that text, so I won't belabour the point. In short, Pulitano's work diminishes my belief in the prospect of real dialogue, makes me *less* hopeful that our voices will be heard, and fearful that the complexity and depth of what many of us are writing about will be simplified, translated, and tossed back to us in a form that says much less than what we had intended. To me, this kind of critical activity seems too close a kin to the ethnographic translation of Indian "myths," reminding me of the way those old stories got translated, simplified, slaughtered, stripped of context and meaning, to be reshaped into a recognizable artifact. It may be appealing to facilely characterize and dismiss work such as Womack's (or Warrior's, for that matter) as "nativist" or "essentialist," but to do so would be to misrepresent, or, at the very least, misread the work. I would hope that sophisticated literary scholars would take care to do what I suggest to all of my students who are reading historical and literary criticism: strive to comprehend what the author is trying to communicate or argue first, before deciding what you wish to agree with or critique. I would hope that they would seek to fully understand the author's framework before applying their own critical lens to any work. One of the great privileges and downfalls of contemporary intellectual life is that we all have too much to read, and therefore we sometimes hastily categorize a work in terms that are already familiar. I want to caution against this impulse, for my fellow critics as well as myself, because, if we follow it too quickly, we might miss out on the most original and provocative of the burgeoning ideas in our fields.

I suspect that critics like Pulitano, who admit to few interactions with Indian students, scholars, or their friends and families, have little conception of the pressure that is on Native scholars to conform to the models for which she advocates. I was lucky. Unlike Womack and other folks in the generation that preceded me, I was trained in a Ph.D. program where I could take a graduate course in Native American literature every semester, with students and professors, both Native and non-Native, who had spent a lot of time at the kitchen table. I had courses in Native history and linguistics and participated in Cornell's first graduate seminar in American Indian studies, which formed the core of a newly developed graduate minor. I was interested, too, in exploring postcolonial, feminist, and other cultural theories that might help me to unpack and understand the internal dynamics that had thrown my nation into turmoil, the colonial politics that allowed for a state to erase us with a phrase as enigmatic as "the weight of history," and the stories that would allow for restoration. I did a great deal of gathering in those years. Many of my professors insisted that the theories they taught would provide the best route for my thinking, and I was told over and over again that my work needed to be comparative and had to engage with critical theory, so that my scholarship would be "marketable." But, to paraphrase Scott Momaday (quoting William Gass), I wasn't writing for myself (and my potential career), because that would have been "self-serving"; I wasn't writing for my audience (here, I suppose, literary critics and the departments that might or might not offer me a job), because that would be "pandering." I was writing "for the thing that was trying to be born" (Isernhagen 35). Like Robert Warrior (in his discussion of Said), I learned from and drew on what I learned in those classes in literary and cultural theory. But those theories were not enough. Ultimately, I had to return to the gathering place in order to find the theories and methodologies that allowed me to answer the questions with which I was most concerned. I found those answers in Native space, in the networks of Native writers in the Northeast, in the complexity of language and oral literature, and in conversation with the network of relations, writers, and intellectuals that is alive and flourishing today. Without them, without those kitchen-table conversations both inside and outside of class, this thing called "The Common Pot" would not have been born. Perhaps those models for which Pulitano advocates seem quite radical and liberatory in relation to the mainstream, or to the history of European and American philosophical thought. That, I'm sure, is true. However, if we limit ourselves to the culture of academia, or to that of literary criticism, those methodologies for which she advocates seem to me fairly conventional, even hegemonic, to use the lingua franca of our discipline. To strike out on our own self-determined paths, developing methodologies that seek to interpret and read literature of our own choosing based on models drawn from our own, often collective, knowledge and experience, that seems pretty liberating to me. I think I can say that all six of Pulitano's chosen subjects have done just that, and I would honour them all for that achievement. Thankfully, I find myself able to do this without creating a hierarchy of difference, or a "great chain of being," as Craig S. Womack suggests herein, a methodology, I should note, which has fairly ancient roots itself.

Returning fondly to my graduate school memories, I want to contrast Pulitano's organizing framework with that of Jace Weaver's in his introduction to *That the People Might Live*. I remember sitting in that first graduate seminar in American Indian studies discussing the book with my colleagues. I told them that one of the reasons I liked Weaver's work was because he seemed to bring the conversation among critics and writers in Native American literary studies to the page. I could see the way he was drawing lines between them, setting voices up in dialogue with each other, creating a space for interaction, and even, perhaps, synthesis. Over the years, I've found Weaver's introduction particularly useful for teaching students who are new to the field, giving them the opportunity to pick up on the conversations in the landscape of Native literature and providing a foundation from which to begin addressing the critical and historical problems with which, as Robert Warrior points out herein, all of us who enter the field are faced. In contrast, Pulitano's framework fails to create a space where multiple voices can be heard. Instead, she assumes the role of ventriloquist and puppeteer. Rather than placing the work of Native literary critics in dialogue, in relation to each other, in a network of critique and exchange, she divides these critics into individual slots, and then puts them in a hierarchical order, performing, to my mind, a recolonization, an allotment and redistribution, a process of ordering and containment. The worst part is that I have my doubts as to whether Pulitano is aware of the implications of her own methodological framework. If she had brought her work to the kitchen table, however, she certainly would have become aware of those implications, and quite early on. She might have found herself sitting there alone until she made some really good stew that drew everyone back to the table. I hope that, given her level of intelligence, she would have come to understand far more before she decided to commit this work to print. You see, I am advocating that she should have come to the kitchen table not for our sake, but her own.

To turn from theoretical grounds to more pragmatic ones, I want to speak to the usefulness of literary nationalist approaches in teaching. I now find myself back in New England, living close to my family and teaching Native American literature and history to a mix of Native and non-Native students who constantly keep me on my intellectual toes.[10] I cannot express how valuable it is to have tribally specific readings of Native texts in the classroom. I can give my students an incredibly rich, complex, and detailed understanding of the political, cultural, historical, and literary landscape of the Northeast, but when it comes to other regions, I am particularly grateful for the guidance of scholars such as Craig Womack and Daniel Heath Justice, who are immersed in those areas. Although I am not Creek or Cherokee, I teach Creek and Cherokee literatures, and the work of these scholars has enabled me to teach them in a way that is much more complex, profound, and knowledgeable than before their books existed. Maybe other gatherers are more skilled, but I could not possibly develop a full knowledge of all of the regions about which I teach, even if I had a lifetime's worth of travelling and the trust and opportunity to learn from the best plant folks around. I find the accusations of isolationism and exclusiveness to be particularly ironic given that one of the most encouraging aspects of this field is the generosity of its practitioners in their willingness to gather and distribute for us all.

This past fall, I taught a course called "Native American Literature: Narrations of Nationhood," a seminar that was built around the idea that the imagination of nations is a continuing communal process, in which narration, including writing and literature, plays a strong role. It was organized regionally and relied on tribally specific readings and criticism. As a newly conceptualized course, it was an experiment in which the whole class was engaged. During the course of the class, I noticed that the Native students in particular were especially pleased to see their and others' tribally specific traditions explained eloquently and with complexity in texts like *Red on Red* (which, you all know, is not always the case with academic texts about Indians). So many of my questions from Native students reflected their own interests in finding out how things are done in different nations, and what the histories and cultural traditions have been in different regions, as well as their desire to increase their knowledge and engage in analysis of their own regional and tribal histories and traditions. They were equally interested in thinking about how other Native intellectuals have grappled with the problems and questions with which they are faced and did not hesitate to challenge those with whom they disagreed. While I certainly deal with issues of representation, most Native students already know way too much about how they have been represented, stereotyped, and utilized by American literature and history. In fact, this is something that I always have to teach with a strong sense of irony and humour, because on so many levels, the figure of "the Indian" is just tired. In my experience, non-Native students, too, are often intellectually paralyzed by the endless circular gymnastics of representation, but find themselves empowered as writers and scholars when they can rely on the political, historical, and cultural traditions of specific nations to guide their readings and their writings. They can put writers from particular regions and nations in conversation, in conflict, use them to illuminate each other. With the aid of tribally specific teaching and criticism, students can, with great skill and complexity, unpack the many layers of a poem like Harjo's "The Flood" or "A Map to the Next World" with an understanding of the many overlapping worlds that exist simultaneously in the space of the poem, speaking to Creek, Navajo, Iroquois, and urban Indian contexts that intersect with and illuminate each other, without needing to rely on a simplifying framework that suggests that the characters, speakers, or authors of the poem are "caught between" anything. All of the students in this course seemed to prefer grappling with the complexity of the texts on their own terms, rather than moving to explain them only through the frameworks they have gained from studying cultural theory.[11] What is most interesting to me is the way the students in the class turned that lens around, as they took frameworks drawn from treaty literature, oral traditions, and contemporary criticism and began to apply them to other literatures, histories, and contemporary issues, treating Native American writers as sophisticated intellectuals who have something to say to the world at large, as well as to their tribally specific communities.

I remain befuddled as to why literary nationalism represents such a controversial approach for literary studies. To compare with another field, it has long been accepted practice for scholars to focus on particular regions or nations when doing Native American history.[12] Furthermore, we have long had fields designated to British, French, and German literature, so why would writing a book on Creek or Cherokee literature, particularly given the extensive literary output of these nations, be so controversial? And who better than someone who is from that nation to write about its national literature? Why would suggesting that these literatures might be able to stand on their own as literary traditions be a move that suggests alienating or excluding someone? I am Abenaki, and I do not feel excluded by such work (and I'm a fairly sensitive person). Nowhere does Craig S. Womack say that only Creeks can write about Creek literature, or that only Natives can write about Native literature. If some critics *feel* excluded, or sense that exclusion is *implied*, perhaps it would be a useful exercise to engage in the kind of personalized critical exploration exemplified by Greg Sarris in *Keeping Slug Woman Alive*, where he explores the feelings and senses he experiences in reaction to statements made by Pomo grandmothers like Mabel McKay and Violet Chappell. (I am not being facetious, here; I truly think this would be worthwhile.) Just as I admire Womack's boldness in bringing the kitchen table to academia, I admire Sarris' brave honesty in revealing and discussing his own position at the kitchen table, his willingness to expose his inability to peel potatoes, his lack of knowledge, and his attempts at gathering. However, I would never want Womack to write Sarris' book, or vice versa. I would never suggest that either is the "more subversive" way to do Native scholarship. I am thankful for the presence of both of these models in the world. But, to return to my own befuddlement, I want to ask, why is it so offensive to suggest that a Creek might have more insight into Creek literature than a non-Creek, or that contemporary Creek concerns might be relevant to Creek literature and literary scholarship, particularly given the invisibility and displacement of such literatures and concerns from the mainstream? Is it not a worthy goal to attempt, as Warrior suggests, to "be methodologically self-conscious in attending to perspectives that ha[ve] been ignored, debased, discounted, and marginalized" ("Native Critics in the World" 195)? Is it the tone of Womack's book that gets under people's skins? Again, to me, that tone is recognizable, because it comes directly from the kitchen table. In my family, if you are getting teased, you know you are part of the group. Or is it the insistence that the group, the family, the notion of nationhood still exists? Is it the refusal to be the subject of the scholar and the State? Is it the very persistence of Indigenous nationalism in the age of globalization that remains a disturbing reminder of what many wish to regard as the colonial past?

I want to turn now to the notion of hybridity, and to a concept that I believe may be much more useful for conceptualizing the ongoing activity of transformation within Native space, including those changes that have taken place in relation to colonization. One of the central problems with the way hybridity theory has been applied to Native texts is that it does not seem to account for the relationship between community and land. Rather, culture and identity seem to rest within the individual "subject," who seems oddly out of place, displaced, caught between two assumed worlds or perspectives so intertwined that they no longer exist independently of each other. Okay, fine, but where does relationship to land figure into all of this? Is this a way basically to say that we are all native to this land because European and Native American cultures are so intertwined as to melt together into a single multicultural mass? Have assimilation and the extinguishment of Aboriginal title been accomplished? Should we just drop our tribal delusions and go home? That is . . . if home could then ever be found.

When I was a visiting instructor at Colorado College, I was very grateful that my apartment was located nearby a pond that had a resident heron, as well as a family of beavers. I admit that I only liked it because it reminded me of home, made me feel less out of place in that wide expanse of a western city. I took my students there on the last day of class so they would understand what I was talking about when I emphasized the notion of adaptation.[13] Those beavers who moved into the tin man-made pond made that place their own. Like the beavers back home who reclaim a marshy field once occupied by their ancestors by recognizing beaver space, those western victims of recollection and termination, logging and development, were able to recognize a beaver pond, whether they came from up in the mountains or a nearby urban haven. Pretty good deal, too, considering how little dam-building would be involved. Visitors to the park usually wouldn't see that family there, because they didn't expect to see beavers in their landscape, and that family, they kept to themselves. They would usually only come out when no one else was around. Even their lodge was carefully disguised to become a part of the small brushy island that afforded some cover. My students didn't see them at first, either, and then they couldn't figure out how those beavers, assumed vanished, had gotten there in the first place. "They must have been relocated from elsewhere," one said. Another responded, "But why would they want beavers here? They will probably block the drains and eat up the vegetation." "And why would they stay?" another wondered. That's when we turned to the reading for the day, Leslie Silko's *Gardens in the Dunes*, to the pages at the end of the novel that describe young Indigo's garden, a lovely working mix of indigenous plants, and transplants she's gathered in her travels, where "bright ribbons of purple, red, yellow, and black gladiolus flowers" are "woven crisscross over the terrace gardens, through amaranth, pole beans, and sunflowers" (474). This place in the desert dunes of the Arizona/California border is a location that Silko purposefully does not name, evoking all of those Native places and histories that were not marked by reservation boundaries or American catalogues, that remained *recognizable* only to those families who had always gathered there.

The novel begins with a portrait of the child Indigo among her Sand Lizard family in the dunes, learning to tend plants under her grandmother's tutelage. Although the family must disperse when the forces of colonization enter their Native space, its members separated and displaced, Indigo and her sister find their way back to the gathering place and begin to build a new family from within. Drawing on the knowledge she has gained during her travels across two continents, Indigo finds new uses for "the old gardens," cultivating the seemingly ornamental gladiolus as companions to the indigenous plants, and as the irises transform in relationship to the landscape and to Indigo's tending, the extended family finds the new plants useful for trade as well as food. Their friends, the twin sisters, use the flowers' unusual beauty to repair relations with the churchgoers in the city, a move that protects them in their place, and Indigo offers the twins a stew made with "tasty" gladiolus sounds when they come to visit (476). In the changing landscape, "those flowers turned out to be quite valuable after all." Silko's vision of adaptation and regeneration within the landscape is encapsulated in one of the novel's final passages:

> When the girls returned to the old gardens the winter before, Grandma Fleet's dugout house was in good condition but terrible things had been done at the spring. . . . Strangers had come to the old gardens; at the spring, for no reason, they slaughtered the big old rattlesnake who lived there; then they chopped down the small apricot trees above Grandma Fleet's grave.
>
> That day they returned, the twins helped Sister Salt and Indigo gather up hundreds of delicate rib bones to give old Grandfather Snake a proper burial next to Grandma Fleet. They all wept as they picked up his bones, but Indigo wept harder when she looked at the dried remains of the little apricot trees hacked to death with the snake.

Today Indigo and Linnaeus ran ahead of the others with the parrot flying ahead of her. At the top of the sandy slope she stopped and knelt in the sand by the stumps of the apricot trees, and growing out of the base of one stump were leafy green shoots. Who knew such a thing was possible last winter when they cried their eyes sore over the trees? (476)

Silko's imagery—of springs, of snakes, of leafy green shoots—speaks of the regenerative capability of this particular landscape, which is nothing more, or less, than the combined activity of all of its inhabitants, including humans, who can tend it like a garden or conquer it like an enemy, who have interdependent relationships with the plants and other living beings that grow up from within the place, regardless of whether they acknowledge those relationships or not. All of these beings adapt and change within the landscape, thereby transforming the "garden" itself. This is an ongoing activity in which we have always been engaged, and in which we will engage as long as we are part of this earth. As I've learned myself, from watching those closest to me regenerate and die, the hope for transformation and adaptation, for survival within the land, lies within the regenerative ability of the land itself. And it is stories that make meaning of those changes, allow experience to be translated into expression. It is literature that gives life to the words, solidifies them in the landscape, allows them to be gathered and carried on.

Over the last few decades, we have seen a remarkable change in the landscape here in northern New England, a recovery that has paralleled the regathering of families in this place. I look out now on a forest that hosts nearly every animal and plant indigenous to this land, with many additions that are well adapted to its changing form. There are enduring threats to its continuance, to be sure, but who could have envisioned, a hundred years ago, that the forests would return to claim the towns and fields? That the beavers would return to re-create the marshes and ponds? That coyotes would come from the west, mate with wolves on their journey, and begin to be transformed by the landscape themselves, so that even my young nieces, when reading an old story, call out the name of the eastern coyote when they see a picture of wolf? Who could have predicted, at the moment of nadir, that Abenaki families would gather together in old village places to reproclaim their place as a nation? There will be stories told about this remarkable time, I am sure, for many generations to come. And to be truthful, there have always been stories about this time; it's just that those stories have been kept quietly, tended carefully, so that one day, they would be able to feed the whole. The process of recognition belongs to them.[14]

I'll admit that talk of nationalism makes me wary. For me, like many, it calls to mind the setting of boundaries, both physical and cultural, and defending those boundaries with force. It calls to mind the sounds and images of patriotism and jingoism that have been destructive and detrimental to both sides of my family. It recalls the potential for violence. As a typical big sister, as the daughter of a war survivor, and now, as an auntie, such proclamations cause me unease. However, I have a different kind of nationalism in mind, which I hope lies in concert with the calls of those within: a nationalism that is not based on the theoretical and physical models of the nation-state; a nationalism that is not based on notions of nativism or binary oppositions between insider and outsider, self and other; a nationalism that does not root itself in an idealization of any pre-Contact past, but rather relies on the multifaceted, lived experience of families who gather in particular places; a nationalism that may be unlike any of those with which most literary critics and cultural theorists are familiar. As envisioned herein, American Indian literary nationalism is a dynamic model that posits the existence of a field of Native American literature and supports (but does not advocate exclusively for) scholarship that draws on theoretical and epistemological models that arise from Indigenous languages and literatures, as well as the many, varied, complex, and changing modes in which Native nations have operated on the ground, in particular places, over a wide expanse of time.[15]

Like the gathering and dispersal of families, the gathering and dispersal of knowledge must be "processual," as both Robert Warrior and Jace Weaver suggest, and adaptive. As Warrior adds herein, we cannot merely focus on the "gathering of information" but "on creating frameworks in which to understand the broad ways in which knowledge has operated ideologically and politically in bringing the Native world to the state in which it currently exists" ("Native Critics in the World" 198–99). Gathering is a process in which we are engaged, an activity that sustains us and our families. Yet, like the gathering plants, intellectual and artistic gathering relies on carefully considered knowledge of the landscape and our impacts on it. Gathering without knowledge could get you and yours sick, could purge you. Gathering without foresight can destroy the roots of the very plants on which we rely for nurturance and healing. Gathering also requires distribution. One does not gather merely for oneself. Even my niece, who is only six, knows this. She is excited to share her knowledge of plants with her older cousins, but is cautionary with them, telling them how and why the plant should be taken, and what should be given back. American Indian Literary Nationalism is a model that does not view knowledge as something to be gathered within a vessel and preserved, or as a process of steady accumulation, of ever-growing accuracy or progress. Rather this gathering relies on a process of exchange, which will constantly shape and change the state of the field. It requires careful tending and nurturing. It requires a continual give and take. Sometimes it will require us to gather together; sometimes we will only want to go out in small groups, to avoid damaging the plants or scaring away our fellow inhabitants; sometimes we will have to disperse, go our own ways, with the knowledge that we will always return. I want to see what kind of "national" space we might build, if the tools, methods, and materials are not "determined for us," in Jace Weaver's words, but rather we are allowed the intellectual freedom to determine this process for ourselves.

To those who might think that I am excluding them from this process, I urge you not to jump to such conclusions. I ask you to listen for a few minutes more. To those who would dismiss this volume because it appears to advocate for an exclusionary model, or one that is isolationist or provincial, I ask you to consider carefully, "the weight of history." As Robert Warrior demonstrates herein, "Everyone . . . who takes up the task of researching and writing about the Indigenous world comes into an arena of inquiry already left in ruins by generations of bad faith." Undoing this legacy is a burden we all share. What happens when we consider "literary nationalism" or "intellectual sovereignty," as I believe the writers have herein, not only in relation to the ideals of literary cosmopolitanism or humanistic inclusiveness, but in relation to assimilation and its coercive, often violent, history? Can we take a moment to consider the actual experiences of Native nations in relation to this American ideal? What happens when we consider the rhetoric of deconstruction in light of the policy of Termination or the extant legal doctrine of extinguishment? Until Native literatures and histories, and in particular, Native voices, are part of the curriculum, until they rise to the surface of common knowledge, I believe we may have many misunderstandings of the intent and purpose of Native American literary criticism, as with the example of Pulitano's work critiqued herein. Despite all the rhetorical claims of "hybridity," it does sometimes seem as if we are speaking from different worlds, and it is Native critics who are so often called on to play the role of translator, who are asked to travel from the village centre to the academic council and explain themselves. In writing the books that we have, and in writing this volume that you are reading now, I believe that we are inviting everyone to make their way to the kitchen table, to come to the gathering place. I am not saying that you (or we) will always be welcome there, given the weight of history, or that it will be an easy journey, but I can promise that there will be some food and good conversation waiting for those who come willing to listen, and to reciprocate, in turn.

Notes

This essay was first published in Jace Weaver, Craig S. Womack, and Robert A. Warrior, eds., *American Indian Literary Nationalism* (Albuquerque: U of New Mexico P, 2006).

1. Missisquoi is an Abenaki village on the northeast shore of *Bitabagw*, or Lake Champlain, that has been continually occupied by Abenaki families for over twelve thousand years. During the seventeenth and eighteenth centuries, it also served as a refuge for many Algonquian families escaping colonial wars, and was the main site from which the famous war leader, Grey Lock, launched his reclamation raids on Massachusetts settlements. On paper, the "Abenaki Nation at Missisquoi" leased a large swath of land on the Missisquoi River to James Robertson in 1765, which was supposed to expire after one hundred years. In the wake of the violence of the French and Indian wars, the American Revolution, and the colonial settlement of the Green Mountain Boys and their cohort, Abenakis went underground but remained steadfastly in their old territories. The subsistence and family-centred communal lifestyle of Abenaki families continued to exist, despite the development of the state of Vermont and the Union to which it belonged, long into the twentieth century, when the combined effects of the Vermont Eugenics program of the 1920s and '30s (which resulted in the sterilization and institutionalization of countless Abenaki people), the establishment of the Missisquoi Wildlife Refuge in the 1940s, the subsequent increase in surveillance by Fish and Wildlife officials, and rising development in the region forced the leadership to seek alternatives outside of the community. At the same time, tremendous political changes in Indian Country, from the fish-ins on the Northwest coast, to Wounded Knee II, to increasing political activity amongst neighbouring nations to the east and south, provided an opening for Abenaki voices to address the outside world. For additional information, see, for instance, Colin G. Calloway, *The Western Abenakis of Vermont, 1600–1800: War, Migration, and the Survival of an Indian People*; William A. Haviland and Marjory W. Power, *The Original Vermonters: Native Inhabitants, Past and Present*; Frederick Matthew Wiseman, *The Voice of the Dawn: An Autohistory of the Abenaki Nation*.

2. I have written about the words a*wikhigan* and *awikhigawôgan* in my dissertation, *The Common Pot: Indigenous Writing and the Reconstruction of Native Space in the Northeast*. While *awikhigan* represents writing that has become manifest, words or images that have taken shape, solidified (a book, a map, a letter), *awikhigawôgan* is the activity of writing, drawing, or mapping something in which we are engaged.

3. Aboriginal title "arises from a tribe's occupation of a definable, ancestral home-land before the onset of European colonization ... the validity of aboriginal title is not dependent on treaty, statute, or other formal government recognition ... the phrase 'aboriginal title' or 'Indian title' describes the ownership interest retained by Native Americans in lands which European nations appropriated," *State of Vermont v. Raleigh Elliot, et al.* (1992).

4. This story represents only one example of how, as Womack points out herein, the concept of a monolithic Europe is just as problematic as that of a monolithic Native America.

5. See, for example, Bruchac, *Roots of Survival*; Colin G. Calloway, *The Western Abenakis of Vermont, 1600–1800*; Gordon M. Day, *The Identity of the Saint Francis Indians*; William A. Haviland and Marjory W. Power, *The Original Vermonters*; and Frederick Matthew Wiseman, *The Voice of the Dawn*.

6. See William Apess, *Indian Nullification of the Unconstitutional Laws of Massachusetts Relative to the Mashpee Tribe; or The Pretended Riot Explained*, in *On Our Own Ground: The Complete Writings of William Apess, a Pequot*.

7. I first encountered this line in Jace Weaver's *That the People Might Live: Native American Literatures and Native American Community*.

8. See also Lisa Brooks, *The Common Pot*, Chapter 2.

9. I should relate that one gathering truly led to another. It was two writers from my own nation, Joe Bruchac and Cheryl Savageau, who were responsible for drawing me into these larger circles of Native writers. I think it is entirely likely that without them, I would probably still be holed up in a cabin in New Hampshire, covered under pages of writing that nearly no one was reading but myself.

10. I agree with Craig S. Womack that teaching about the nonexistence of the Indian in a class full of Native students would be a good way to find yourself sitting alone at the kitchen table. Again, let me remind you of the very real impact of legal decisions that seek to eradicate the existence of Indian nations, not to speak of the physical dispossessions and acts of violence that wage this battle on human bodies.

11. That Native American literatures "deserve to be judged by their own criteria, in their own terms" is one of the key arguments, of course, of Womack's *Red on Red* (242–43).

12. The well-known and well-respected historian Colin Calloway began his career with a history of my nation, the manuscript of which I remember passing around during those old days at Missisquoi in a yellow three-ring binder. I remember reading it with great interest when I was working on my own undergraduate thesis in a trailer in St. Albans, Vermont; his scholarship was welcome in the community, and its impact on my own sense of nationhood was significant. I distinctly remember coming to work one day to find him sitting on the couch in the tribal office, chatting with the chief, the tribal judge, and the tribal historian. To me, the quality of his work reflects not only his own immense intelligence and aptitude for research, but his willingness to sit at the kitchen table, his engagement with Native individuals and communities over the long course of his career. My argument is not that scholars of Native American history and literature *must* engage with Native people, but rather, that, as scholars, *our* work is enriched when we do. This is true, as Jace Weaver points out, for both Native and non-Native scholars alike.

13. I purposefully want to juxtapose the linguistic roots of these two terms for your contemplation. Note these definitions from *Webster's*:

> *adaptation*, n. 1. the act of adapting or the state of being adapted. 2. something produced by adapting: an adaptation of a play for television. 3.a. any beneficial alteration in an organism resulting from natural selection by which the organism survives and multiplies in an environment. b. a form or structure modified to fit a changed environment. c. the ability of a species to survive in a particular ecological niche, esp. because of alterations of form or behavior brought about through natural selection. 4. the decrease in response of sensory receptor organs, as those of vision or touch, to changed, constantly applied

environmental conditions. 5. the regulating by the pupil of the quantity of light entering the eye. 6. a slow, usu. unconscious modification of individual or collective behavior in adjusting to cultural surroundings. [1600–1610]

adapt, v.t. 1. to make suitable to requirements or conditions; adjust or modify fittingly. 2. to adjust oneself to different conditions, environments, etc. [1605–1615; Latin *adaptare*, to fit, adjust]

hybrid, n. 1. the offspring of two animals or plants of different breeds, varieties, or species, esp. as produced through human manipulation for specific genetic characteristics. 2. a person produced by the interaction or crossbreeding of two unlike cultures, traditions, etc. 3. anything derived from unlike sources, or composed of disparate or incongruous elements; composite. 4. a word composed of elements originally drawn from different languages, as *television*, whose components come from Greek and Latin. adj. 5. bred from two distinct races, breeds, varieties, or species. 6. composite; formed or composed of heterogeneous elements. [1595–1605; Latin *hybrida*, a crossbred animal] Note that the word "hybrid" assumes the existence of two pure, authentic, and disparate originals prior to the new being that is formed, whereas the notion of adaptation relies on a dynamic model for conceptualizing relational identity and cultural survival. *Random House Webster's College Dictionary* (New York: Random House, 1997), 15, 638.

14. The concept of adaptation that I have been foregrounding here has been prominent within Native American literary studies for some time. All of the authors herein highlight the adaptability of Native communities in their scholarship. Jace Weaver notes that "Native cultures have always been highly adaptive, and they continue to evolve constantly." He rightly observes, "Native interest in incorporating elements from other cultures long predated the European encounter. Vast trading networks carried goods throughout North America, and trade argots were developed to facilitate commerce—all before any had seen a white man. Natives showed themselves adept at adopting and adapting anything that seemed to be useful or to have power" ("Splitting the Earth: First Utterances and Plural Separatism" 29).

This process of adaptation and adoption did not begin, but rather continued, when Europeans entered Native space. In "Towards a National Indian Literature," Ortiz writes of the way in which the incorporation of Catholic saints' days into ceremonial life at Acqumah "speak[s] of the creative ability of Indian people to gather in many forms of the socio-political colonizing force which beset them and then make these forms meaningful in their own terms." He notes that, because in every case where European culture was cast upon Indian people of this nation, there was similar creative response and development, it can be observed that this was the primary element of a nationalistic impulse to make use of foreign ritual, ideas, and material in their own—Indian—terms. Today's writing by Indian authors is a continuation of that elemental impulse (8).

In speaking of the revitalization of Native culture during the latter half I of the twentieth century, Robert Warrior writes in *Tribal Secrets*,

The return to tradition . . . cannot in Deloria's analysis be an unchanging and unchangeable set of activities, but must be a part of the life of a community as it struggles to exercise its sovereignty. . . . To understand what the "real meaning" of traditional revitalization is, then, American Indians must realize that the power of those traditions is not in their formal superiority but in their *adaptability* to new challenges. (93–94; my emphasis)

Finally, Craig S. Womack argues in *Red on Red*,

I wish to posit an alternative definition of traditionalism as anything that is useful to Indian people in retaining their values and worldviews, no matter how much it deviates from what people did one or two hundred years ago. The nostalgic anthropological view, by contrast, creates a self-fulfilling prophecy. Only cultures that are able to adapt to change remain living cultures; otherwise they become no longer relevant and are abandoned. Yet anthropology often prioritizes the "pristine." Anthrospeak claims that things must be recorded because they are soon to die out, yet the anthropological definition of culture denies cultures the very thing that will allow them to survive: the possibility of changing and evolving with the times [and the place within which they operate]. Literature . . . allows for this kind of creative change. (42)

15. Let me join with my fellow contributors in reiterating that this is not to say that Native American literature is not in dialogue with, influenced by, and influential on American or Canadian literature, but rather to insist that its complexity and specificity, its diversity within and its divergence from without warrants its recognition as a full body of literature, and demands interpretation and critique, in Craig S. Womack's words, "in its own terms" (*Red on Red* 242).

25

Gdi-nweninaa:
Our Sound, Our Voice

Leanne Simpson

Indigenous languages carry rich meanings, theory, and philosophies within their structures. Our languages house our teachings and bring the practice of those teachings to life in our daily existence. The process of speaking Nishnaabemowin, then, inherently communicates certain values and philosophies that are important to Nishnaabeg being. Breaking down words into the "little words" they are composed of often reveals a deeper conceptual—yet widely held—meaning. This part of the language and language learning holds a wealth of knowledge and inspiration in terms of Aanji Maajitaawin. That is because this "learning through the language" provides those who are not fluent with a window through which to experience the complexities and depth of our culture. The purpose of this chapter is to use this approach to deepen our understandings of decolonization, assimilation, resistance, and resurgence from within Nishnaabeg perspectives.

Biskaabiiyang

Biskaabiiyang is a verb that means "to look back."[1] The Seventh Generation Institute, located in the northwestern part of Anishinabek territory, has been working with several Elders to develop an Anishinabek process for their M.A. program in Indigenous thought. They call the first part of their process Biskaabiiyang. In this context, it means "returning to ourselves," a process by which Anishinabek researchers and scholars can evaluate how they have been impacted by colonialism in all realms of being (Geniusz, *Our Knowledge Is Not Primitive* 9). Conceptually, they are using Biskaabiiyang in the same way

Indigenous scholars have been using the term "decolonizing"—to pick up the things we were forced to leave behind, whether they are songs, dances, values, or philosophies, and bring them into existence in the future. Wendy Makoons Geniusz, an Anishinaabe scholar from Wisconsin, uses this approach in her Ph.D. dissertation research and explains:

> Biskaabiiyang research is a process through which Anishinaabe research-ers evaluate how they personally have been affected by colonization, rid themselves of the emotional and psychological baggage they carry from this process, and then return to their ancestral traditions. . . . When using Biskaabiiyang methodologies, an individual must recognize and deal with this negative kind of thinking before conducting research. This is the only way to conduct new research that will be beneficial to the continuation of anishinaabe-gikendaasowin (knowledge, information, and the synthesis of personal teachings) and anishinaabeg-izhitwaawin (anishinaabe culture, teachings, customs, history).
>
> The foundations of Biskaabiiyang approaches to research are derived from the principles *of* anishnaabe-inaadiwiwin (anishinaabe psychology and way of being). These principles are gaa-izhi-zhawendaagoziyang: that which was giving to us in a loving way (by the spirits). They have developed over gen-erations and have resulted in a wealth of aadizookaan (traditional legends, ceremonies); dibaajimowin (teachings, ordinary stories, personal stories, histories); and anishinaabe-izhitwaawin (anishnaabe culture, teachings, customs, history). Through Biskaabiiyang methodology, this research goes back to the principles of anishinaabe-inaadiziwin in order to decolonize or reclaim anishinaabe-gikendaasowin. (*Our Knowledge Is Not Primitive* 9–10)

The power of Biskaabiiyang as a process is that once engaged in this process, it becomes obvious and necessary to think of Biskaabiiyang not just in relation to research, but also in relation to how we live our lives as Nishnaabeg people. In our current occupied state, it becomes important to carry the essence of Biskaabiiyang with me through my daily life; it is not something that I can do at the beginning of a project and then forget. We are still enmeshed in the insidi-ous nature of colonialism and neo-colonialism, and this means that I need to keep Biskaabiiyang present in my mind when I am making my way through the world. Biskaabiiyang is a process by which we can figure out how to live as Nishnaabeg in the contemporary world and use our gaa-izhi-zhawendaagozi-yang to build a Nishnaabeg renaissance.

Biskaabiiyang has to be an ongoing individual process. However, we can-not effectively engage in Biskaabiiyang in an isolated fashion. As communities of people, we need to support each other in this process and work together to stitch our cultures and lifeways back together. In this way, Biskaabiiyang is both an individual and collective process that we must continually replicate. This is why the larger critical Indigenous intellectual community is important. The contestation of imperial domination becomes our collective and individual starting point, and the lens through which to view our own liberation. As demonstrated in the coming chapters, the personal is always embedded intrinsically into our thought ways and theories; and it is always broadly interpreted within the nest of the collective.

Within Nishnaabeg theoretical foundations, Biskaabiiyang does not literally mean returning to the past, but rather re-creating the cultural and political flourishment of the past to support the well-being of our contemporary citizens. It means reclaiming the fluidity around our traditions, not the rigidity of colonialism; it means encouraging the self-determination of individuals within our national and community-based contexts; and it means re-creating an artistic and intellectual renaissance within a larger political and cultural resurgence. When I asked my Michi Saagiig Nishnaabeg Elder Gdigaa Migizi about Biskaabiiyang, the term immediately resonated with him when English terms such as "resistance" and "resurgence" did not. He explained Biskaabiiyang in terms of a "new emergence,"[2] noting that he lives his own interpretations of the teachings he received from his Elders, just as my generation has the responsibility of finding meaning in the teachings our Elders share with us.

I first encountered the concept of Biskaabiiyang in Wendy Makoons Geniusz's *Our Knowledge Is Not Primitive: Decolonizing Botanical Anishinaabe Teachings*. The concept resonated with me; but because she is from the northwest part of our territory and I do not know her personally, I took the concept first to my language teacher and then to my Elder. I did this because I have learned that unless concepts have local meaning, it is difficult for them to have local resonance. I also thought that, as a Michi Saagiig Nishnaabeg person, I could· only really learn to understand this concept from within the web of relationships of my existence. While Biskaabiiyang might be an important and powerful cultural way to ground decolonization and resurgence work in other places, it was only going to be useful to me if it had meaning within my current relationships. Both my language teacher and my Elder immediately recognized the word and identified with the concept, which is not always the case when I bring them writing and words from Nishnaabeg writers. Biskaabiiyang then became a very useful and important Nishnaabeg way of grounding resurgence or decolonization as a "new emergence," because it carries wide meaning and has resonance throughout our territory. To me, Biskaabiiyang means not just an evisceration of colonial thinking within individuals before a research project begins; it is a constant continual evaluation of colonialism within both individuals and communities. It also encompasses a visioning process where we create new and just realities in which our ways of being can flourish. Nonetheless, it is not just a visioning process. We must act to create those spaces—be they cognitive or spatial, temporal or spiritual—even if those spaces only exist for fragments of time.

While Biskaabiiyang encompasses the process for decolonizing, the term Zhaaganashiiyaadizi encompasses the process and description of living as a colonized or assimilated person (159–96).[3] Zhaaganashiiyaadizi occurs when a person tries to live his or her life as a non-Native at the expense of being Nishnaabeg. In other words, they become assimilated. Zhaaganashiiyaadizi is a process by which choices are made to the detriment of being Nishnaabeg. The key is "at the expense of being Nishnaabeg," so one may adopt the ways of the non-Natives only to the extent that it does not negatively influence the core of one's being. I would caution against a racialized understanding of this term. My understanding of this word is indicative of the processes or the continual decisions that one might chose to make—decisions and choices which, in this case, supplant all of the beautiful and diverse ways of living as a contemporary Nishnaabeg. To me this means that we do not need to "go back" to "hunting with bows and arrows," but we do need to practise ways of being and living in the world that are profoundly Nishnaabeg. It also means that there is a diversity of ways of being within a Nishnaabeg value system that encompasses being Nishnaabeg. For me, that means that there isn't a single way of being Nishnaabeg. Rather, there is a set of processes, values, and philosophies embedded in our language and culture that one needs to embrace in order to live as Nishnaabeg. When viewed through a cultural lens, Biskaabiiyang is far from promoting an essential Nishnaabeg identity; instead, it promotes a diversity of political and cultural viewpoints within the Nishnaabeg worldview. There are many good ways to be Nishnaabeg, but those ways are constructed and exist within our knowledge and our language.

However, to be able to appreciate that fluidity and diversity, one needs an in-depth knowledge of culture, language, philosophies, and anishinaabegikendaasowin.

When we speak broadly about Indigenous resistance, we are essentially speaking about processes we engage in to prevent Zhaaganashiiyaadizi (our people becoming colonized or assimilated). To me, that means we need to act against political processes that undermine our traditional forms of governance, our political cultures, our intellectual traditions, the occupation and destruction of our lands, violence against our children and women, and a host of many other issues. We must learn Nishnaabeg Gikendaasowin and Nishnaabemowin.

While Biskaabiiyang is a useful context to begin to explore what liberation and resurgence looks like within Indigenous thought, it is just the beginning. For Nishnaabeg people, our political and social cultures were profoundly non-hierarchical, non-authoritarian, and non-coercive.[4] Our culture placed a profound importance on individuals figuring out their own path, or their own theoretical understanding of their life and their life's work based on individual interpretation of our philosophies, teachings, stories, and values. In combination with their own interpretation of the name or names they held within their society, clan responsibilities, and personal gifts or attributes, individuals were afforded a high level of autonomy within the community for exploring and expressing their responsibilities. This is sometimes framed as an "ethic of non-interference"[5] on the part of other community members. It is also coupled or twinned with individual responsibilities of figuring out one's place in the cosmos and how to contribute to the collective while respecting oneself and one's inner being.

Aanjigone

In exploring this "ethic of non-interference" with Elder Gdigaa Migizi, the Nishnaabeg concept of Aanjigone emerged. Aanjigone is the idea that one needs to be very, very careful with making judgments and with the act of criticism. Aanjigone is a concept that promotes the framing of Nishnaabeg values and ethics in the positive. It means that if we criticize something, our spiritual being may take on the very things we are criticizing. It promotes non-interference by bringing forth the idea that, if someone else does wrong, the "implicate order"[6] will come back on that person and correct the imbalance in some other way. Take an example from Gdigaa Migizi: if we "destroy the land to build a monster cottage on the side of a lake, we can expect this to come back on us in a negative way."[7] There is then no need to criticize or be angry with the perpetrators, because they will pay the price for their destructive action, one way or another, and this will be mediated by the spiritual world. Our responsibility is to live our lives according to the teachings and values that were given to us with great love by Gzhwe Mnidoo.[8] But where does Aanjigone leave us in terms of building resurgence and protecting our lands? And what does Aanjigone mean in terms of the interrogation of colonialism? Of academic critique?

Aanjigone ensures that if change or transformation occurs, it promotes Nishnaabeg ways of being and prevents Zhaaganashiiyaadizi. It also ensures that the interrogation or critique of decisions—or the consideration of all the possible consequences of a particular decision—is focused on the concept or decision rather than an individual. In a sense, critique is an internal process and the outcome is an individual action rather than an attack on another. Indeed, when an Elder is displeased with an action of one of his or her students, the Elder does not criticize that action, but is silent. Often at a later point, the Elder will use a story or an activity to convey a particular teaching in an indirect manner.

Very early on in my academic career as a Ph.D. student, a non-Aboriginal academic began attacking my work and the work of my colleagues, writing that we had invented Indigenous Knowledge to propel our own careers, and that no such intellectual capabilities exist within Indigenous Peoples. The paper was immediately accepted for publication. My immediate reaction was to write a scathing academic critique of this particular paper. I consulted Anishinaabeg Elder Robin Greene-ba and asked for his thoughts. I particularly wanted to know if it was ethical for me as a Nishnaabekwe to intellectually attack the paper and critique this scholarship. There was no doubt in my mind that this was the correct thing to do as an academic. Robin answered my question by telling me a story. What I understood from his story was that the better way to proceed was to write a paper about what I thought Indigenous Knowledge was, about why it is important, and about how to promote it in a good way. He made sure I understood that I had a responsibility to do something. But he told me that particular story so I understood that what was truly important was *how* I took on that responsibility.

To me, this means that we must not spend all of our time interrogating and criticizing. We need to spend an enormous amount of energy recovering and rebuilding at this point. Critique and revelation cannot in and of themselves create the kinds of magnificent change our people are looking for. We can only bring about that change by engaging in Biskaabiiyang. To me it means we need to be careful with our criticism. We should not blindly follow the academy's love affair with criticism, ripping apart other Indigenous academics' work—with whom we probably have more in common than virtually any other academics in the world. Instead, we should highlight the positive within each other's work, and save our criticism for the forces that continually try to rip us apart. As Nishnaabeg legal scholar John Borrows writes, "[what Treuer views as authentic and inauthentic voices in Native American writing] I view [as] different styles and methods of writing within Anishinabek genres and traditions. Recognizing diversity within Anishinabek expression allows for variations between authors, including the use of mixed metaphors, misplaced dialects, fragmentary memories, and fluid identities" (*Drawing Out Law* 233).

Aanjigone, as I understand it, means to focus within. Although I believe that part of Biskaabiiyang requires criticism and critical thinking, I think Aanjigone propels me toward the idea of focusing the majority of my energy on Nishnaabeg flourishment. Focusing within, I believe Nishnaabeg philosophies are telling me to live my life using Biskaabiiyang and Aanjigone to the best of my gifts and abilities. My interpretation of Aanjigone does not exclude taking action against the colonizer to protect our lands, our knowledge, or our lives. Rather, it encourages us to think carefully and strategically about our responses rather than blindly reacting out of anger.

Naakgonige

The third concept I want to discuss by way of introduction into Nishnaabeg resurgence is Naakgonige. Naakgonige is a culturally embedded concept that means to carefully deliberate and decide when faced with any kind of change or decision. It warns against changing for the sake of change, and reminds Nishnaabeg that our Elders and our Ancestors did things a certain way for a reason. For instance, Nishnaabeg did not (and do not) tell traditional Aandisokaanan stories in the spring, summer, and fall. When I asked Gdigaa Migizi why, he explained that the spirits were farther away from the earth in winter, and less likely to be offended. But he also said that it was his understanding that "something had happened," or an Elder "saw something," that caused them to conduct themselves in a way to avoid danger. He explained that we need to trust our Ancestors on certain things. When I asked him how he felt about contemporary storytellers and writers ignoring the tradition of only telling certain stories in the winter, he avoided passing judgment. He told me that he has no idea what they might have done beforehand to ensure that it was a good thing to do. Perhaps they had prayed and asked the spirits for guidance, and that led them to make the decision. He only knew that he would not tell certain stories unless there was snow on the ground. In a similar way, Edna Manitowabi explained to me that we do not tell Animal stories or Nanabush stories in the spring, summer, and fall, because these beings are awake and active during this time and they could be around when we are speaking about them. While she was speaking, I thought about how my children react when I tell stories about them while they are present. They are often embarrassed, even if the stories are delightful in nature. In fact, most adults would feel the same. It makes complete sense that Nishnaabeg would offer the same level of respect to animals and spiritual entities.[9] It also ensures that we take our time with the winter stories and allow ourselves plenty of time to think about them. Similarly, Nishnaabemowin language expert Shirley Williams explained to me that the word Aandisokaanan also means that one is calling the spirits you are talking about,[10] something that should be done according to protocol and tradition. Naakgonige encourages one to deliberate and consider the impacts of decisions on all aspects of life and our relationships—the land, the clans, children, and the future. In a sense, it protected our people from engaging in

Zhaaganashiiyaadizi because the process of Naakgonige meant that change, even on a personal level, was a long and deliberate process.

Naakgonige encourages Nishnaabeg people to make decisions slowly and carefully. Other words in Nishnaabemowin have meanings that are related to Naakgonige, warning to be careful or mindful. However, Naakgonige has a larger conceptual meaning. Another related word is Naanaagede'enmowin, the art of thinking to come to a decision. This is similar to Naakgonige in that it asks a person to sit and reflect on the weighing or measurement of a problem in order to figure out what needs to be done. It is a sorting of one's thoughts so that a decision can be made, a plan to help out the caring part of the individual to listen and care for the heart and do the right thing. The heart must help or guide the mind to come to a good decision.[11]

To me, both the concepts of Naakgonige and Naanaagede'enmowin exemplify resistance. First, because they protect against Zhaaganashiiyaadizi. Second, they are culturally embedded processes that require individuals, clans, and communities to carefully deliberate, not just in an intellectual sense, but using their emotional, physical, and spiritual beings as well. For instance, if a language speaker were to engage in Naakgonige and Naanaagede'enmowin to decide whether or not to speak Nishnaabemowin to their children, they would have to consider the impact of that act on the child's ability to perform their cultural responsibilities to their family, clan, community, and nation. They would have to consider how that choice would impact the values of the child and their relationship to their territory. They would have to assess how that child would interact with Elders and the spiritual aspects of Nishnaabeg culture. They would have to consider the impact on that child's identity, and their ability to comprehend what it is to be Nishnaabeg. The speaker would have to consider not only that child, but also the subsequent generations of the family; and they would have to allow their heart, or their emotional intellect, to guide that decision. By engaging Naakgonige and Naanaagede'enmowin, far fewer people might choose to speak only English to their children; or at the very least, more people may try to mitigate some of the negative impacts that loss of language might have on their family. Rather than blindly accepting the colonizers' truths or acting out of fear, Naakgonige and Naanaagede'enmowin demand presence of mind and heart, engagement, thorough analysis, and a critical evaluation of the long-term impacts of decision making in terms of promoting mino bimaadiziwin and preventing Zhaaganashiiyaadizi—which, in my mind, is what resistance is all about.

I have thought a lot about how my Ancestors lived in the world. And over the past two decades, the values that have always stood out to me or that have been demonstrated to me, particularly through Elders, has been one of profound gentleness and profound kindness. In an interview with the Office of Specific Claims and Research in 1976, Nishnaabeg Elder Peter O'Chiese relayed that one of the first things given to the Nishnaabeg by Gzhwe Mnidoo was to be kind and have a gentle heart.[12] This idea permeates our culture and is expressed through countless words, stories and teachings. The word "Nengaajdoodimoowin—the art of being gentle or of doing something gentle to someone,"[13] is one expression of this idea. Gentleness was seen as strength because gentle people are highly sensitive to potential threats against mino bimaadiziwin. They are highly in tune with peace, the proper use of power, and heart knowledge. It is that heart knowledge I would like to consider next.

Debwewin

Nishnaabeg Elder Jim Dumont explained the origins of the word debwewin to a group of students and community members at Trent University's Annual Elders Conference in 2010. The word is normally translated as truth, and Dumont explained to us that he had difficulty breaking it down into its components, until an Elder told him to place the letter "o" in front of it. When one does that, the first component of the word is "ode" which means heart. The component "we" means "the sound of." So (o)debwewin is "the sound of the heart"; or, more specifically, in my own case, it is the sound of my heart. This means my truth will be different from someone else's.[14] This idea has also been described by Murray Sinclair as a plurality of truth ("Aboriginal Peoples and Euro-Canadians" 19). Elder Peter O'Chiese explained that each of the seven original clans has their own truth; and, when you put those together, a new or eighth truth emerges (*Final Report of the Royal Commission on Aboriginal Peoples*, vol. 3, ch. 2). These understandings are philosophically similar to Basil Johnston's explanation:

> Our word for truth or correctness or any of its synonyms is *w'dae'b'wae*, meaning "he or she is telling the truth, is right, is correct, is accurate." From its composition—the prefix *dae*, which means "as far as, inasmuch as, according to," and the root *wae*, a contraction of *wae-wae*, referring to sound—emerges the second meaning, which gives the sense of a person casting his or her knowledge as far as he or she can. By implication, the person whom is said to be *dae'b'wae* is acknowledged to be telling what he or she knows only insofar as he or she has perceived what he or she is reporting, and only according to his or her command of the language. In other words, the speaker is exercising the highest degree of accuracy possible given what he or she knows. In the third sense, the term conveys the philosophic notion that there is no such thing as absolute truth. (*Anishinaubae Thesaurus* x)

These explanations are consistent with John Borrows' explanation of diversity in terms of Nishnaabeg thought. Borrows explains that difference exists within Nishnaabeg thought. Rather than positioning this difference as "tension," or in an oppositional framing, diversity and difference are seen as necessary parts of the larger whole. The views expressed in this book are my own interpretations as a Nishnaabekwe from the gdigaa bzhiw doodem (Bobcat Clan) of the Michi Saagiig Nishnaabeg territory, as a mother, as an intellectual, and a language learner. For me, gender plays an important role in my own perspective, but my understandings of gender are not fully shared by other members of my nation. I have been taught that, in the past, gender was conceptualized differently than as the binary between male and female expressed in colonial society (Ladner 35–61). For Nishnaabeg people there was fluidity around gender in terms of roles and responsibilities. Often one's name, clan affiliation, ability, and individual self-determination positioned one in society more than gender, or perhaps in addition to gender. While I am not comfortable being confined to an essentialized version of Native womanhood defined by child birth (LaRocque, "Métis and Feminist" 63), I am also someone who has been profoundly transformed through giving birth, nursing, and mothering. I will not apologize for fully participating in those ceremonies and honouring the teachings given to me through those ceremonies.

Andrea Smith reminds us that a critical interrogation of heteropatriarchy must be at the core of nation building, sovereignty, and social change (*Native Americans and the Christian Right* 255–72). I would argue that this requires a decolonization of our conceptualization of gender as a starting point. Nishnaabeg thought compels us to place the sovereignty of Indigenous women at the core of our movement; but it also compels us to critically evaluate how we are contributing to raising our boys as agents of patriarchy, instead of as agents of Biskaabiiyang.

In my own life, I recently used Biskaabiiyang, Naakgonige, Aanjigone, and Debwewin to decide whether or not I would wear a long skirt to a sunrise ceremony that took place in my territory. This is an issue full of tension in my territory, and I am guessing perhaps in other Nishnaabeg territories as well. In the reclamation of this ceremony, women are generally asked to wear long skirts as a way of showing respect to both our traditions and the conductor as acknowledging our innate power as women and life givers. I have always felt conflicted about this issue. At times, I have worn my skirt to demonstrate respect to the Elders and knowledge of those teachings. When I was pregnant and nursing my children, I wanted to be in the skirt to honour those processes. But I have never believed that my value as a woman was tied to my ability to reproduce; and there have been many times when the idea I was *required* to wear a skirt frustrated and angered me. So a few months ago, when I decided to go to the sunrise ceremony, I decided to listen to the part of me that was profoundly irritated with the required attire.

I first spoke to one of my Grandmother Elders. She explained the teaching, but also said that no one should be forced to wear something or do something they are uncomfortable doing. I put semaa (tobacco) down. I prayed. Then I thought about why I felt so irritated about the skirt in the first place. I thought about how in colonial society, the skirt carries meaning that maintains the rigid boundaries in a two-gendered system. My understanding of gender within my own culture is one that was much more fluid. I thought of my Ancestors and how they might feel watching me at the ceremony in pants. I thought of a photo that hangs in my parents' house of my great-great-Grandmother, on her trapline in pants. I thought of the some of Nishnaabekwe my own age—how we roll our eyes at the skirt rule—and I tried to think of a more ethical response. I thought of how my being would appear to the spirits if I wore the skirt but resented it. I thought of Gzhwe Mnidoo, the one that loves me in total acceptance and understanding, in warmth, in protection. I thought that Gzhwe Mnidoo cared about who I was, not what I was wearing. I thought about the coming generations. I thought about my four-year-old daughter Minowewebeneshiihn, and then I made my decision.

Gdi-nweninaa

Listening to the sound of our voice means that we need to listen with our full bodies—our hearts, our minds, and our physicality. It requires a full presence of being. It requires an understanding of the culturally embedded concepts and teachings that bring meaning to our practices and illuminate our lifeways. In regenerating our languages, an enormous task in and of itself, we must also ask our Elders and fluent speakers to teach us through the language, using specific words as windows into a deeper, layered understanding. We must listen and take with us those sounds that hold the greatest meaning in our own lives and in our resurgence.

Notes

This essay was first published in Leanne Simpson, *Dancing on Our Turtle's Back: Stories of Nishnaabeg Re-Creation, Resurgence, and a New Emergence* (Winnipeg: Arbeiter Ring, 2011).

I would like to acknowledge that the title of this chapter came from a language book of the same name written by Shirley Ida Williams, *Gdi-nweninaa: Our Sound, Our Voice* (Peterborough, ON: Neganigwane, 2002). In this chapter, I explore four interrelated

Nishnaabeg concepts that provide a window through which people who do not speak Nishnaabemowin (and I am a language learner, not yet a speaker) can begin to understand how concepts of decolonization, resistance, resurgence, and truth are expressed within Nishnaabeg existence. While these concepts were not chosen randomly, they are not the only windows into these ideas within the language; there are many, many others.

1. Explained to me by my language tutor Vera Bell, Peterborough, ON, 19 June 2010.
2. Doug Williams, Waawshkigaamagki (Curve Lake First Nation), 15 July 2010.
3. This term was also familiar to Doug Williams, Waawshkigaamagki (Curve Lake First Nation), 15 July 2010.
4. I've read about this in Kiera Ladner, "Women and Blackfoot Nationalism," 35–61; and it has been demonstrated to me through example by several Elders, including Doug Williams, Waawshkigaamagki (Curve Lake First Nation), and Robin Greene-ba (Iskatewizaagegan).
5. As described by Rupert Ross, *Dancing with a Ghost: Exploring Indian Reality*, 11–38.
6. I am borrowing the term "implicate order" to refer to the spiritual world, from James Sákéj Youngblood Henderson, *First Nations Jurisprudence and Aboriginal Rights*, 144–53.
7. Doug Williams, Waawshkigaamagki (Curve Lake First Nation), 15 July 2010. Shirley Williams corrected my spelling of this word, 12 September 2010.
8. I am using the verb *Gzhwe* rather than *Gchi* or *Kichi* because, according to Doug Williams, *Gzhwe* represents awe, warmth, love, total acceptance, protection, and understanding, rather than an authoritarian Creator imbued with fear and punishment. Doug Williams explained this to me in Waawshkigaamagki (Curve Lake First Nation), 15 July 2010. Shirley Williams had the same understanding of the word in Peterborough, ON, 12 September 2010.
9. Edna Manitowabi, Stoney Lake, ON, 13 December 2010.
10. Shirley Williams, Peterborough, ON, 13 September 2010.
11. Explained to me by Shirley Williams, Peterborough, ON, 19 September 2010.
12. Also see Jim Dumont's "Anishinaabe Izhichigaywin," in *Sacred Water: Water for Life*, 13–57.
13. Shirley Williams, Peterborough, ON, 15 September 2010
14. Jim Dumont, Presentation, Elders Conference, Trent University, Peterborough, ON, 20 February 2010.

26

Responsible and Ethical Criticisms of Indigenous Literatures

Niigaanwewldam James Sinclair

To teach Indigenous literature with a belief in the full humanity of Indigenous people is to inevitably engage in an act of political resistance.

—Daniel Heath Justice, *Renewing the Fire:*
Notes Toward the Liberation of English Studies (52)

If Thomas King is right, and "the truth about stories is that's all we are," as Justice points out, "then the work of the literary scholar has profound ethical implications. Our vocation is the telling, preservation, interpretation, and creation of stories. Stories are what we *do*, as much as what we are" (*Our Fire Survives the Storm* 206; original emphasis).

This is why, I assert, scholars theorizing Indigenous literatures must continue to formulate responsible critical tenets for our field, and reflect on ethics. Of course, this is a process that began well before me, but it is my intention to encourage more of it here by suggesting some possible trajectories scholars might want to keep in mind in their works while studying Native stories. Importantly, these are meant as starting points, not end points, and I profess to be no expert— only an interested party among many. As evident by the multiple voices that follow, this trail has already started. I hope many of us walk it together.

Responsible and ethical criticisms of Indigenous literatures recognize the full humanity of Indigenous peoples.

As Justice identifies in the epigraph to this essay, criticism has for too long been invested in dehumanizing Indigenous peoples while furthering a project of colonialism in the Americas. To invest in a criticism that explores the full humanity (which includes tribal-specificity) of Indigenous peoples is to invest in a truly revolutionary act. Most of all, engaging this wide-ranging complexity is part of upending colonial discourses and meaningfully participating in the interests of Indigenous knowledge systems. Speaking of the politics of Indigenous erotica, arguably one of the greatest literary threats to colonialist hegemony and Indigenous erasures, Kateri Akiwenzie-Damm remarks that after five hundred years of mainstream misrepresentation, bastardization, and ignorance, "We need to see images of ourselves as healthy, whole people. People who love each other and who love ourselves. People who fall in love and out of love, who have lovers, who make love, who have sex. We need to create a healthy legacy for our peoples" (148). Human beings (and their stories) come with interests and ties that are political, social, sexual, material, and more. These must be included in studies of Native literatures.

Responsible and ethical criticisms of Indigenous literatures situate stories in specific times, places, and contexts.

Native peoples, like all human beings, tell stories that reflect specific experiences, influences, and interests. These are always contextual and often promote a method of continuance somehow related to the interconnected nature of our communities, our families, and the world around us. Criticism should take this up. As Womack writes, "We need to prioritize dates, events—in short, history. Not just distant history but recent events. Instead of making universal, overarching assumptions about Indians, the compassionate critic should delve into historical particulars. We need an improvement over the kind of literary work that has been so very popular in relation to Native literature in which people avoid historical research and base their criticism exclusively on tropes and symbols" (*American Indian Literary Nationalism* 171). In Abenaki critic Lisa Brooks' new study, *The Common Pot: The Recovery of Native Space in the Northeast*, she brilliantly shows how Native literatures of this region have deep historical ties to land, as well. This attention brings criticism closer to First Nations peoples and their current situations, interests, and struggles. Justice points out that this is also a directive from Native writers and their literatures, too, as

> one thing is certain from the work of most Indian writers: being Cherokee, Creek, Choctaw-Cherokee, or Anishinaabe, or any of the self-designations of the Indigenous peoples of this hemisphere, includes a fundamental affirmation of the Indian nationhood of a specific community that expresses a tribal-specific identity that's rooted somewhere in a tribal-specific language, sacred history, ceremonial cycle, and geography. Why else would we cite tribal

affiliation? Why would we acknowledge kin, ancestors, and spirits if not to acknowledge their specificity? Why would so many use their Indigenous language to name particular spirit beings, or give geographic details of a particularly meaningful place, if not to locate them in a specific linguistic, geographic, and sometimes historical relationship? (*Our Fire Survives the Storm* 214)

Scholars such as Bonita Lawrence (in her important book *"Real" Indians and Others: Mixed-Blood Urban Native Peoples and Indigenous Nationhood*) show that pan-tribal literatures can certainly be considered in specificities as well.

Responsible and ethical criticisms of Indigenous literatures respectfully consider Indigenous-centred literary approaches as fruitful possibilities.

Indigenous storytellers are, in countless ways, politically invested in the sustenance and continuance of the relationships and communities in which they reside. As stated, this is usually embodied in some aspect of Indigenous community, but not always. Stories are the lifeblood between storyteller, community, and universe—how they relate, how they interact, how they change as a result. This interconnectivity is a fruitful space that is as full of perspectives, creativity, and growth as it is full of controversy, polemics, and politics. Speaking of this literary tradition, Armand Ruffo points out in his essay, "Why Native Literature?" that "it is said that one cannot be a Native writer and not be political; it comes with the territory" (670). As Ruffo argues, it is these claims for Native aesthetics and perspectives where "the literature itself tells us what it is" and "theories of criticism, ways of approaching the literature" emerge (667). While these might not be the sole interest of a Native storyteller, they are almost always a strong one.

Responsible and ethical criticisms of Indigenous literatures legitimate a long-standing and wide-ranging Indigenous intellectualism and recognize this intellectual history.

Tomson Highway remarks that

Native people have a literary tradition that goes back thousands of years before 1492. Mainstream audiences in Canada don't know that we have a mythology that is every bit as potent as mythologies anywhere else—not least of all Christian mythology—and that it is applicable to the specific landscape and the relationship of a specific people to that landscape. . . . Our literature, our literary tradition, our history, our language, our culture is first rate. (qtd. in Preston 140)

It is also in the best interests of theorists, if they are *sincerely* interested in accurately developing meaningful approaches to North American cultures, canons, and critical legacies, to investigate Indigenous intellectual traditions, for they are the most expansive, wide-ranging, and influential knowledge processes in this area of the world. I agree with Womack when he writes: "Tribal literatures are the *tree*, the oldest literatures in the Americas, the most American of American literatures. We *are* the canon. Native peoples have been on this continent at least thirty thousand years, and the stories tell us we have been here even longer than that, that we were set down by the Creator on this continent, that we originated here. For much of this time period, we have had literatures. Without Native American literature, *there is no American canon*" (*Red on Red* 6–7; original emphasis). We need all critics to engage critically with these (hi)stories—embodied in the works and words of Native writers, thinkers, and community members—and simultaneously contribute to the intellectual processes of which they are a part. As critic Sam McKegney writes, this means that "one must engage—listen, learn, dialogue, debate," and allow oneself to be informed by Indigenous thinkers but remain critically and honestly engaged, without apology (44). And, as Osage critic Robert Warrior points out in his seminal book *Tribal Secrets: Recovering American Indian Intellectual Traditions*, this also includes the crucial recognition that Indigenous peoples have continuing critical and intellectual histories worthy of examination on their terms (xvi–xvii).

This body of work, of course, is underpinned by its own theories, approaches, and knowledge bases, none of which have ended, as well. Critics engaging in these literatures must take this into consideration, particularly when investing so heavily in criticisms formulated outside of Indigenous contexts, histories, and experiences. And, without really needing to be said, responsible literary criticisms of Native literatures listen, employ, and make Native intellectual voices a central tenet.

In terms of poststructuralism and postcolonialism, King reminds scholars in his important essay "Godzilla vs. Post-Colonial" that these lenses are useful, but that

> the term ["post"] itself assumes that the starting point for the discussion is the advent of Europeans in North America. At the same time, the term organizes the literature progressively suggesting that there is both progress and improvement. No less distressing, it also assumes that the struggle between guardian and ward is the catalyst for contemporary Native literature, providing those of us who write with method and topic. And, worst of all, the idea of post-colonial writing effectively cuts us off from our traditions, traditions that were in place before colonialism ever became a question,

traditions which have come down to us through our cultures in spite of colonization, and it supposes that contemporary Native writing is largely a construct of oppression. (*World Literature Written in English* 11–12)

Simply, Native writers write about more than resistances to colonialism. To use Womack's metaphor, European invasion of our territories is a branch on the tree, albeit a heavy one, but ultimately only a branch. Criticism should take up all struggles of our intellectual traditions that embody the entire spectrum of Native existences.

Responsible and ethical criticisms of Indigenous literatures are responsible to an audience that *includes* real-life, modern Indigenous peoples in it.

I assert that no research or literary criticism is objective, and should be (at least) interested in methods of Indigenous continuance. Métis critic Jo-Ann Episkenew reminds us, "When analyzing literary works, most scholars are very conscious that ideology is embedded in the text; what they often forget is the ideology that they bring to their reading" ("Socially Responsible Criticism" 54). In the ideological, imagined, and intended audience of a body of criticism on Native literatures, if there are intentionally mutated, mutilated, and/or fantastically deformed representations of Native peoples (or worse, completely erased), necessary questions should be posed as to the critic's politics, what their purpose is in using this information, and what their work's implications are. As NunatuKavut scholar Kristina Fagan (now Bidwell) points out in "'What About You?' Approaching the Study of 'Native Literature,'" "critics need to be honest about their fundamental critical assumptions. What is our guiding theory? How are we defining our terms and categories? What do we believe is the purpose of 'Native Literature?'" (247).

Responsible and ethical criticisms of Indigenous literatures do not assume that Native cultural expressions are "ending," nor do they adopt a "deficit" model of change, especially if reality says otherwise.

Cultural adaptability, innovation, and growth have always been a tenet of Indigenous cultures. How could they have maintained themselves for millennia otherwise? Tribal and pan-tribal communities, cultures, and nations have always changed with influence, and on some degree by their own terms. Characterizing Native cultures as inherently weak, passive, and lacking in the face of Western advancement, particularly considering the history on this continent regarding that gesture, is to deny countless evident and multivalent resistances, and ultimately to participate in an imperialist justification for their erasure. Native nations, one must remember, have not disappeared, and are very much dynamic, complex, and alive today. Speaking of literary approaches invested in describing Native cultures as incapable of reconciling change, deficient, and disappearing as a result of cultural influences from the West, Weaver reminds us that "Native interest in incorporating elements from other cultures long predated European encounter. Vast trading networks carried goods throughout North America, and trade argots were developed to facilitate commerce—all before any had seen a white man. Natives showed themselves adept at adopting and adapting anything that seemed to be useful or to have power. Yet each new item, tool, or technology was used to strengthen, not weaken, their people" (*American Indian Literary Nationalism* 29). Instead of seeing Native cultures, peoples, and literatures as the problem, we need to see that, for the most parts, the issues have been in critical lenses themselves. If past, problematic theories continue to be revisited, this must be considered.

Responsible and ethical criticisms of Indigenous literatures dream of (and point to) important new possibilities for literary criticisms of Indigenous writing, as well as leave space for the reader to dream of (and point to) possibilities too.

Indigenous signification has a long and storied history on this continent. No Native community, I would argue, has ever been "illiterate," but has used forms of writing in multitudes of ways. Equally, we have told stories in complex and diverse ways. For instance, the use of Roman orthography should not be the start or end point, nor the be-all and end-all of Indigenous literacy, intellectualism, or stories. Also, although I recognize how important historically constituted studies of orality in Native literatures have been, these have also proven to be reductivist and limiting in scope, particularly in relation to Indigenous signification systems continuing today (such as books, drums, tattoos, sand teachings, wampum, tagging, and footprints).

Grounded political and historical approaches, as I have tried to suggest in this essay, are one way to examine this history. Speaking in his 1981 essay "Towards a National Indian Literature: Cultural Authenticity in Nationalism," Simon Ortiz identifies, quite rightly, that it is "the oral tradition" which has sustained and manifested Indigenous communities, histories, and stories, and "given rise to the surge of literature created by contemporary Indian authors" (10). However,

It is not the oral tradition as transmitted from ages past alone which is the inspiration and source for contemporary Indian literature. It is also because of the acknowledgement by Indian writers of a responsibility to advocate for their people's self-government, sovereignty, and control of land and natural resources. And it is to look at racism, political and economic oppression, sexism, supremacism, and the needless and wasteful exploitation of land and people, especially in the U.S., that Indian literature is developing a character of nationalism, which indeed it should have. It is this character which will prove to be the heart and fibre and story of an America which has heretofore too often feared its deepest and most honest emotions of love and compassion. It is this story, wealthy in being without an illusion of dominant power and capitalistic abundance, that is the most authentic. (12)

Ortiz's approach is only one route. Literary approaches considering Indigenous technological and environmental innovation, semiotics, and theology are some directions scholars may want to invest in and use to uncover Indigenous narrative theories (and some have).

Responsible and ethical criticisms of Indigenous literatures promote dialogic exchanges that include all interested parties, Indigenous or otherwise.

Even the staunchest Indigenous sovereigntist agrees: we are all interconnected. Indigenous peoples, allies, and other interested parties must all be at the table, bringing their honest concerns, beliefs, and interpretations of Indigenous literatures for a true dialogue to happen, continue, and grow. These must be initially without judgment, recognizing that all positions, disagreeable or not, have historically situated contexts. Although we will undoubtedly make mistakes and be quick to judge (including me), we should invite everyone to the literary feast (even if they might not come). Everyone, though, must bring some food so that everyone will benefit. And, with respect, everyone should try each other's food, even if we don't love it.

Responsible and ethical criticisms of Indigenous literatures provoke, evoke, and invoke change, growth, and beauty that are understandable by many, even if devised by few.

Speaking of Indigenous theorizing, Lee Maracle writes in "Oratory: Coming to Theory" that "[t]here is a story in every line of theory. The difference between us and European (predominantely white male) scholars is that we admit this, and present theory through story. We differ in the presentation of theory, not in our capacity to theorize" (236). Ultimately, she claims,

> No brilliance exists outside of the ability of human beings to grasp the brilliance and move with it. Thus we say what we think. No thought is understood outside of humanity's interaction. So we present thought through story, human beings doing something, real characters working out the process of thought and being.
>
> For Native people, the ridiculousness of European academic notions of theoretical presentation lies in the inherent hierarchy retained by academics, politicians, lawmakers, and law keepers. Power resides with the theorists as long as they use a language no one understands. In order to gain the right to theorize, one must attend institutions for many years, learn this other language, and unlearn our feeling for the human condition. Bizarre.
>
> If it cannot be shown, it cannot be understood. Theory is useless outside human application. (238–39)

Simply, we all have a responsibility to listen respectfully to, learn from, and engage with Indigenous peoples and communities with whom we live, from whom we draw, and with whom we share this world. As many have documented, Indigenous storytellers make their worlds through words, sentences, stories. As literary critics of these literatures, we have an exciting opportunity to participate in this process. By maintaining responsible, real-life connections with Indigenous peoples and their stories, we hold the potential to invoke positive change, inspire, and perhaps even contribute to the process of more creations. We can also add to an everlasting process of Indigenous continuance. By being mindful of our past legacies—some brutal, some beautiful—we can define trajectories including real, living Indigenous peoples as a central part of the world. And maybe, just maybe, we can devise some responsible approaches, have a few conversations, and have a few visions of our own.

Note

This chapter was excerpted from Niigaanwewidam James Sinclair, "Trickster Reflections: Part II," in *Troubling Tricksters: Revisioning Critical Conversations*, ed. Deanna Reder and Linda M. Morra (Waterloo, ON: Wilfrid Laurier UP, 2010).

27

Many Communities
and the Full Humanity of
Indigenous People:
A Dialogue

Kristina Fagan Bidwell
and Sam McKegney[1]

Kristina Fagan Bidwell: You know, when we look at this section of the anthology, it's called "Deliberating Indigenous Literary Approaches," but don't you think that it really revolves around the emergence of Indigenous Literary Nationalism?

Sam McKegney: Looking back, it's really quite striking how much Jeannette Armstrong, who starts the section, predicted what was basically going to unfold in the two decades that follow. She was calling for a literary criticism that builds from Indigenous worldviews and reaches to the experts within the cultures themselves.

KFB: But even back in 1993, Armstrong didn't want to focus only on the tribally specific nation but on what she called "First Nation cultures in their various contemporary forms" (229), including the pan-tribal and the urban. A common critique of nationalism is that it is too restrictive, too limiting in terms of how it defines Indigenous identity, but a few years after Armstrong we see Womack arguing for opening up tribal-specific subject matter as much as we can, and then Brooks saying that we need to look at Native nations as complex, changing, evolving things. So we see these nationalist critics pushing to keep the boundaries of the nation quite flexible. Do you think we need a new term, one that doesn't have the restrictive connotations of nation?

SM: Well, one possibility might be the band, which Robert Innes explores in his book, *Elder Brother and the Law of the People*.[2] He describes his own band, the Cowessess First Nation, as an inclusive multicultural and intercultural collective that is still understood by its members as a political unit. The band model actually bears some similarities to confederacy frameworks that are prominent where I live in Haudenosaunee territory.

KFB: Those are great examples. They point toward ways to think about Indigenous identity as complex and multiple and yet still traditional. Others would be the work of Lisa Brooks and Tol Foster, who focus on a specific region and the ways that different groups of people within that region relate to that place and to each other.[3] In a similar vein, we have Daniel Justice arguing for a much more inclusive and expansive version of Indigenous identity that is built around kinship rather than the ever-diminishing measures of blood or of cultural purity. Because you can always become kin, everyone is potential kin. All of these move us away from the damaging idea that if Indigenous people belong to multiple communities or claim multiple identities they are going to lose something, that they are inevitably going to become diluted or hybrid.

SM: But from some politicized critical perspectives, that is exactly what is perceived to be at stake. There is a sense, a fear, that such unraveling might occur if particular identities aren't defined rigorously and protected. That's why the language of nation retains such currency.

KFB: I think that part of that fear is based in the limits of language, and in the discourse that we use when we talk about Indigenous identity. We don't have a full language or theory yet—though we're moving toward it in some of the examples we've talked about—for articulating how people can have multiple identities or multiple communities without becoming less of any one thing, without becoming less Indigenous, for instance. It's like we assume that each identity is separate. So, our language is based in fragmentation and dilution: saying that we're half something and half something else. Or we talk about intersecting identities, which again implies that you have two separate identities that occasionally cross paths. We need better language.

SM: Do you worry that claiming such multiplicity might imply hierarchy rather than mutuality? And if claiming connection to community in one way, does identifying in a different way inevitably threaten the political validity of the original connection?

KFB: It could be framed that way—that different collective identities push against one another. But I think that it's richer to think of multiple identities as informing one another, or as mutually constituting each other. One example is Maria Campbell's *Halfbreed*. When Campbell was writing it in the seventies, she was part of an urban activist community and sometimes her language is a very politicized, activist discourse. At other times, she's writing in a way that has been shaped by her Elders, what Gail McKay's essay in *Indigenous Poetics in Canada* calls "Elders' discourse" (351). So we could say that these two different discourses conflict with each other in the text, but I think it's more interesting and more real to think about how they inform and shape one another. How did the fact that Campbell was a young activist change how she thought about and articulated the words of her Elders, and how did the words of her Elders shape how she articulated the political language of the seventies? It's a way of thinking that views Maria Campbell as a whole person with multiple identities that expand one another, rather than detract from or impoverish one another. Too much language constructs Indigenous people as fragmented and as a person of mixed ancestry myself, I resist that construction. That's not how I experience my life. I don't see myself as pieces of different things. I'm one person with multiple connections that enrich my life. Theorist Michael Hames-Garcia uses the metaphor of a photograph (4). All photos are actually made up of only three primary colours, but we can see those colours only in relation to one another. If we try to look at them separately, we're missing the whole picture, so to speak.

SM: Well put. Our relationships with various communities inform our identities in dynamic, not just delimiting, ways. Your point makes me think of what Jo-Ann Episkenew, in *Taking Back Our Spirits*, calls the "complete and coherent personal myth" (15), where all the aspects of one's personal and collective experience are brought together imaginatively to forge a full and healthy sense of self. However, I've got to admit that I've always been a bit anxious about valorizing the coherent personal myth, at least partially, because I believe the personal myths of settler Canadians are often very coherent and in very damaging ways. So coherence isn't, to my way of thinking, inherently positive. Also, I would argue that it's important to find a vocabulary that registers conflict and contradiction—and not as a deficit. We're always, all of us, conflicted in certain ways. I may believe wholeheartedly in certain things that don't gel with other things I believe in wholeheartedly, and that's just part of being human. As Lee Maracle says, "We cannot *not* be ourselves" (*Masculindians* 37).

KFB: Perhaps coherence is not the right word, but it's crucial that we recognize that internal contradiction does not necessarily lead to personal fragmentation. We have the ability to cope with contradiction and to live in contradiction.

SM: The term that I would lean toward is integrity, because all of those elements can be understood as integral to one's identity, even if some are in conflict with one another. They don't have to be coherent, but they are interconnected and mutually generative.

KFB: I like that term. It reminds me of Niigaanwewidam Sinclair's argument in his essay that ethical criticism of Indigenous literatures needs to "recognize the full humanity of Indigenous peoples" (301). To me, full humanity evokes both integrity and contradiction. We all belong to multiple communities: urban communities, social media communities, activist communities, scholarly communities, artistic communities, queer communities, workplace communities, sporting communities. . . . We need to be able to talk of these as not being isolated from one another, and as all contributing to Indigenous identity.

SM: There's a tendency in criticism to imagine communities as stable and discrete.[4] The question for critics often becomes: what is the community of most value to a particular piece of literature? And then the critical process involves zeroing in on that community while letting other (potentially relevant) communities recede into the background. Even when an individual is understood to have ties to multiple communities, those ties can generally only be talked about in succession—one after the other. This makes them appear temporally or spatially distinct. An individual might be part of a tribal-specific community on her reserve and also a multicultural activist community in the city, yet we'll tend to focus on the tribal-specific community while she's in ceremony and the activist community while she's at a rally; but in reality those communities are both always already at play in her actions and self-understanding—they're integral. So that's what you seem to be talking about: a critical methodology agile enough to grasp multiplicity *and* simultaneity.

KFB: Yes, while still recognizing connection to community as a crucial Indigenous value. And literature is often much better at sustaining the messy multiplicity of communities than is criticism. Perhaps that's why we're seeing a turn in recent criticism toward the aesthetic. It's what Kimberly Blaeser described back in 1993 as being "alert for critical methods and voices that seem to arise out of the literature itself" (232). But we see it in work like the new anthology *Indigenous Poetics in Canada* and Mark Rifkin's recent work on the erotic.[5] Rifkin, in particular, seems to be trying to move beyond limited visions of what counts as a community, and to do it he's looking at sensation and affect—the classical domains of literary art.

SM: Yeah, Rifkin's argument is pretty compelling: the affective experiences of belonging to communities and territories tend to be categorized by the state as either unintelligible or private, and therefore treated as politically irrelevant. Yet because these sensual, emotive experiences speak to Indigenous modes of persistence that transcend the legal language of the state, they offer an incredible arsenal for imagining other possibilities. They offer creative and political potential through the emotions, which brings us back to literature. After all, literature doesn't just depict or speak to communities, it creates them. As Gerald Vizenor might say, through literature, "we touch ourselves into being with words" (Coltelli 158).

KFB: Returning to the idea that our language may not yet be quite right, when we incorporate the realms that Rifkin is talking about, then we're pushing the idea of "nation" or "sovereignty" way beyond the logic of the nation state.

SM: Our conversation today has come full circle because, of course, the language of nationhood among literary nationalists was initially informed by the need to speak back to the attempted erasure of Indigenous communities as self-determining entities. "Nation" was a tactical manoeuvre designed to assert prior occupation and nation-to-nation relations with the settler states of Canada and the United States. But it was a tactical move that has at times obscured the experiential realities of Indigenous persistence that critics like Rifkin are now trying to acknowledge and illuminate.

KFB: And we need to remember that we are literary critics and not political scientists. In the end, if we look to the art, we get something richer, larger, and more complex than what's legible under the law or in political rhetoric. That's what is exciting about our field—it pushes our understandings and our imaginings beyond the narrow confines of the legal/political sphere, which is where Indigenous issues are so often seen as belonging. Perhaps that's the value of what we do.

SM: We honour the full humanity of Indigenous individuals and their many communities by engaging sincerely with Indigenous literary art.

Notes

1. In an effort to foreground the complex, interpersonal relationships that animate our discussion of Indigenous literary criticism in this chapter, we decided to retain the substance of our conversation as a dialogue rather than massage it into a collaborative argument that feigns a singular critical voice. Noting that our reflections here are informed not only by our unique backgrounds, experiences, and relationships, but also by our ongoing engagements with each other's ideas, those of the authors of chapters in this section of the book, and those of the focus group with which we discussed these entries back in early 2014 in Vancouver, we have opted to foreground perspectival interaction in our piece's form. That being said, we condensed our initial recorded conversation considerably and have edited it in places. The authors would like to thank Adar Charlton for her assistance with transcription, editing, and general critical conversations.

2. Robert Innes, *Elder Brother and the Law of the People: Contemporary Kinship and Cowessess First Nation* (Winnipeg: University of Manitoba Press, 2013).

3. Please see Lisa Brooks, *The Common Pot: The Recovery of Native Space in the Northeast* (University of Minnesota Press, 2008), and Tol Foster, "Of One Blood: An Argument for Relations and Regionality in Native American Literary Studies," in *Reasoning Together: The Native Critics Collective*, Acoose et al., ed. Craig Womack, Daniel Heath Justice, and Christopher B. Teuton (Norman: U of Oklahoma P, 2008): 265–302.

4. This is for both political and practical reasons—political, because it helps us affirm the persistence of Indigenous communities as sovereign entities, and practical, because focusing on a single community makes things clearer and less messy.

5. Please see Mark Rifkin, *The Erotics of Sovereignty: Queer Native Writing in the Era of Self-Determination* (Winnipeg: University of Minnesota Press, 2012), and the introduction to Mark Rifkin, ed., *When Did Indians Become Straight? Kinship, the History of Sexuality, and Native Sovereignty* (New York: Oxford University Press, 2011).

IV

CONTEMPORARY CONCERNS

28

Introduction:
Contemporary Concerns

Daniel Morley Johnson

If the contemporary period of Indigenous studies in Canada—and Indigenous literary studies in particular—were to be defined by dominant themes, these would arguably be: (1) the resurgence of Indigenous nationhood and national-ism (and again, specifically, literary nationalism), (2) the emergence of settler-colonialism as the leading theory for analyzing ongoing histories of colonialism, (3) discourses of reconciliation, set in motion most visibly by Canada's Truth and Reconciliation Commission (TRC), (4) the interrelated study of Indigenous genders and sexualities, and (5) activism and scholarship about the well over one thousand recorded murdered and missing Indigenous women (MMIW) in Canada since 1980.

The emergence of Indigenous literary nationalism—influenced by the work of Simon J. Ortiz (Acoma Pueblo), Kimberly Blaeser (Anishinaabe), Daniel Heath Justice (Cherokee), Craig Womack (Muskogee/Cherokee), Robert Warrior (Osage), Jace Weaver (Cherokee), Jeannette Armstrong (Okanagan), and Janice Acoose (Cree/Saulteaux), to name but a few—marked an import-ant turn toward studying Indigenous literatures from both a tribally specific and explicitly political standpoint. At the same time, scholars have increasingly employed theories of settler-colonialism, often using Patrick Wolfe's scholar-ship, to analyze the structural particularities of colonial domination. Wolfe writes: "Settler colonization is at base a winner-take-all project whose domin-ant feature is . . . replacement. The logic of this project, a sustained institutional tendency to eliminate the Indigenous population, informs a range of histor-ical practices that might otherwise appear distinct—invasion is a structure not an event" (163). For Wolfe, settler-colonialism involves the replacement of

Indigenous people with settlers. This process is sustained and institutional, and it is an ongoing structure of domination, not a series of distinct events.

1. Deena Rymhs

Reconciliation is integral to combatting this structure of domination. "What happens to guilt—and specifically, the owning of guilt—in the process [of reconciliation]?" asks Deena Rymhs in her essay, "Appropriating Guilt: Reconciliation in an Indigenous Canadian Context." Published after the beginning of Canada's era of apology and reconciliation—which is focused specifically on the Indian Residential Schools (IRS) system to the exclusion of other oppressive policies and practices—Rymhs' essay links official inquiries in Canada (such as the Marshall Inquiry and the Royal Commission on Aboriginal Peoples) to Indigenous literatures. She surveys writing about the Canadian IRS system by authors like Tomson Highway (Cree), Basil Johnston (Anishinaabe), Maria Campbell (Métis), Rita Joe (Mi'kmaq), and Joseph Boyden (who is of Anishinaabe ancestry). One theme Rymhs discusses is guilt—though without substantial discussion of its corollary, blame—and asks two important questions: "Can guilt be turned into tangible political action?" and "How much does the process of reconciliation help those who have been unjustly treated?" For Rymhs, a concern is that guilt can be "swept into colonial history," attributed to past policies and governments or faceless institutions and "at times bypassing the attribution of responsibility altogether." For scholars like Roland Chrisjohn (Onyota'a:ka), naming the perpetrators and placing blame is indeed useful and necessary in terms of moving toward restitution and restoration. Sometimes it is particularly useful to ascribe guilt. Hence the importance of naming and blaming, as well as recognizing that individuals put policies into practice and are complicit with institutions when injustice takes place. As well, we must acknowledge the ways that our contemporary realities are built on the foundations of colonial oppression (which is, of course, ongoing). We are certainly not blameless in the present.

Attempts at reconciliation through official inquiries run the risk of continuing to "displace the wronged party" (the perpetrators forgive themselves, and their ancestors, while little substantial change has occurred for the survivors). Rymhs correctly illustrates how official inquiries (like Marshall and RCAP) fail to adequately critique or question the legitimacy of the system; instead, they produce "a false sense of material change" (333). Inquiries can create the illusion that injustices are aberrations, rather than glaring examples of a violent, oppressive colonial structure, resulting in a false consciousness that substantial change has occurred, when actually the underlying power structures have been reinforced.[1] As a result, according to Rymhs, "reconciliation's successes have been more illusory than real" (337). One indicator of this would be the ongoing disproportionate representation of Indigenous peoples in the prison system, which Rymhs correctly links to residential schools: "In its forced relocation and confinement of Indigenous children, the residential school was historically a precursor to the prison system in Canada, used to control and contain Aboriginal subjects for colonial as well as penal purposes" (331). Rymhs references autobiographical works by Anthony Apakark Thrasher (Inuvialuit) and Leonard Peltier (Chippewa/Lakota), both of whom were incarcerated in boarding schools as children and in prisons as adults.

2. Amber Dean

In her contribution to this anthology, "Moving Beyond 'Stock Narratives' of Murdered or Missing Indigenous Women," Amber Dean illustrates how these oppressive legacies have directly affected Indigenous women. In particular, she examines sustained and structural colonial domination in her analysis of Sarah de Vries' poetry and life writing. Both de Vries (who was last seen in downtown Vancouver in 1998) and Dean turn stock narratives into complex stories about racial and ethnic self-identification and of systemic racism in the child welfare system. They link these to human struggles for justice, sovereignty, and what scholar Andrea Smith has called "bodily integrity."[2] In quoting de Vries' poetry, and by pointing out that "the indictment de Vries makes is not of a generalized or anonymous 'society': it is directed to a 'you,'" Dean reminds us all of our complicity in settler-colonialism and our responsibility as witnesses. Reading de Vries' lines, "Just another day / Just another death / Just one more thing you so easily forget," it is difficult not to link the hundreds of missing and murdered Indigenous women (and men) with the residential school system, the racist Canadian criminal justice and prison systems, child welfare displacements, Indigenous "homelessness," and so on. It would seem that de Vries clearly assigns blame for the injustices faced by Indigenous and other people of colour in what is now called Canada, and does so with an appropriate sense of indignation.

In his recent book on the TRC, *Truth and Indignation* (2013), Ronald Niezen writes that indignation is "a close emotional correlate of injustice. And, in the context of the truth commission, it is all-pervasive" (16). For Niezen, indignation is "set in motion by simultaneous feelings of love, loyalty, and compassion. Indignation builds energy through personal or personalized relationships that are close to the source of error or harm at its origin." We feel indignation at injustice the closer we are to it. Perhaps it is indignation—rather than reconciliation—that should emerge from our relationships in an era marked by the government of Canada's apology for the IRS system (June 2008), the IRS Settlement Agreement (2007), the TRC (established in 2008), and then prime minister Stephen Harper's concurrent denial of Canadian colonialism and its pervasive termination agenda.[3] Indignation points a finger, it places blame. Reconciliation is so often passive, and the emotion it gestures toward is guilt.

3. Daniel Heath Justice

In "'Go Away, Water': Kinship Criticism and the Decolonization Imperative," Daniel Heath Justice weaves together a compelling piece about creating an ethical Native literary criticism, acknowledging the complexities of Indigenous identities, communities, and concerns, and the importance of kinship to Indigenous nationhood and nation-building. He writes: "Stories expand or narrow our imaginative possibilities—physical freedom won't matter if we can't imagine ourselves free as well" (353). A way to counter cognitive imperialism is through literature, through storytelling; Indigenous literatures attest to community continuance despite settler rhetorics of removal.

Like other literary nationalists, Justice emphasizes community continuity over disappearance, and in particular, the continuity of Indigenous peoples (and their intellectual and literary traditions) *as Indigenous peoples*. "Continuation doesn't matter if we continue in the image of individualized Eurowesterners," writes Justice. "It is as peoples that we endure, through our obligations to kinship and balanced relationships" (362). He points to kinship as a more inclusive way to constitute Indigenous communities and nations, particularly when compared to race-based notions of citizenship. An individual's race or authenticity can be challenged or questioned by insiders and outsiders alike; race, he points out, is "a threatened constitutive commodity," always at the risk of being "washed out to the point of insignificance" (362). Kinship allows for communities to grow—for example, through adoption, marriage, or treaty—while race or blood quantum can be thinned, thus shrinking the community (Section 6 of Canada's *Indian Act* would be one example of diminishing citizenship by racial legislation). Justice offers a critique of race-based claims to absolute Indigenous authenticity in his readings of Delphine Red Shirt (Oglala Lakota) and Elizabeth Cook-Lynn (Crow Creek Lakota). He suggests we might formulate an ethical literary criticism based on the integrative elements of kinship and the attendant callout to be responsible relations: "Such kinship isn't a static thing; it's dynamic, ever in motion. It requires attentiveness; kinship is best thought of as a verb rather than a noun, because kinship, in most Indigenous contexts, is something that's *done* more than something that simply *is*" (352).

4. Jeff Corntassel, Chaw-win-is, and T'lakwadzi

Kinship and Indigenous literatures are linked to the "cultural and political resurgence of Indigenous nations" in the essay "Indigenous Storytelling, Truth-telling, and Community Approaches to Reconciliation," by Jeff Corntassel (Cherokee), Chaw-win-is (Nuu-chah-nulth), and T'lakwadzi (Kwakwaka'wakw). These authors refer to the *haa-huu-pah* of Nuu-chah-nulth peoples as "teaching stories or sacred living histories" connecting the people to their homelands, and these stories are part of the core teachings that people pass on to future generations. Corntassel et al. amplify community voices with a focus on action-oriented movement toward decolonization: "Processes of restorying and truth-telling are not effective without some larger community-centred, decolonizing actions behind them" (374). For these authors, decolonization rooted in *haa-huu-pah* is presented as an alternative to "the state's vision for reconciliation, which seeks to legitimize the status quo rather than to rectify injustice for Indigenous communities" (374). Aside from financial compensation, the IRS settlement agreement and TRC offer little to nothing by way of restitution to Indigenous peoples, communities, and nations. However, the authors found that by "emphasizing the cultural and spiritual dimensions of survivors' experiences [their] research could serve as an alternative to the political/legal constraints of the TRC process" (375). As Corntassel and his colleagues point out, the TRC has done little to "reunify and regenerate families and communities dispersed and dislocated by the trauma of these schools." In fact, today the child welfare system continues to dismantle Indigenous families on a scale that rivals the residential school system at its height.

With an emphasis on resurgence, this essay offers an analysis of the IRS settlement agreement and TRC that prefigures the Idle No More/Indigenous Nationhood Movement in its rejection of the status quo and the vision of reconciliation offered by the perpetrators. Survivors are given a take-it-or-leave-it, limited-time-only chance at reconciliation and financial compensation (which is offered to individuals who are able to prove the abuse they survived). There is perhaps no better example of a decolonized approach to the IRS legacy than the authors' description of the demolition of the former residential school building on the territory of the Tseshaht First Nation. The demolition, conducted by the community along with ceremony and a community feast, is an example of what the authors call restorying, demonstrating the sort of transformative action that can contribute to community healing. The authors write: "Given that reconciliation is not an Indigenous concept, our overarching goal as Indigenous peoples should not be to restore an asymmetrical relationship with the state but to restory our communities toward justice" (380). Viewing the IRS system as just one aspect of the Canadian settler-colonialism that removed Indigenous peoples from their homelands, the truth-telling and restorying engaged in by the authors and survivors they interview offers an alternative to the state-sponsored model of reconciliation, which arguably aims to strengthen the settler state, not to decolonize it. These community voices urge us to reject simple reconciliation in favour of Indigenous cultural and political resurgence.

5. Kateri Akiwenzie-Damm

"Indigenous erotica is political," writes Kateri Akiwenzie-Damm (Anishinaabe) in her essay "Erotica, Indigenous Style." She argues that this is the case not only because Indigenous sexuality and erotic art exemplify the peoples' resistance to colonization and genocide—particularly the damaging influence of missionaries—but also because simply existing, having sex, and procreating was, and still is, a direct challenge to settler government attempts to solve "the Indian problem" by assimilating/legislating/exterminating Indigenous peoples out of existence. As such, the repression of Indigenous erotic life and artistic expression is symptomatic of Indigenous oppression as a whole. Fighting against stereotypes that deny the complexity of Indigenous sexual identities, Akiwenzie-Damm suggests that reclaiming Indigenous erotica is a way for Indigenous people to recognize themselves "as healthy whole people" who are more than caricatures, but who make love, have sex, and are human and sexual beings. Akiwenzie-Damm was writing, compiling, and publishing Indigenous erotica since the early 2000s, and comments, in her 2001 essay, on the re-emergence and resurgence of erotic art. She writes: "To reclaim and express our sexuality is part of the larger path to de-colonization and freedom" (400). In the years that followed, other writers and scholars have taken up this project of reclamation and decolonization.

6. Qwo-Li Driskill

"Doubleweaving Two-Spirit Critiques: Building Alliances Between Native and Queer Studies," Qwo-Li Driskill's (Cherokee) contribution to the groundbreaking "Sexuality, Nationality, Indigeneity" issue of *GLQ: A Journal of Lesbian and Gay Studies*, offers a thorough critique of the settler-colonization of Indigenous bodies, which provides a model of intersectional analysis rooted in the tradition of Cherokee basket weaving. A doubleweave is one of the oldest and most difficult traditions of Cherokee basket weaving, consisting of two baskets woven one inside the other, often resulting in two independent designs.

Driskill uses this as a metaphor for the interweaving of two fields of study, "in order to doubleweave queer and Native concerns into a specifically Indigenous creation." Driskill is successful in formulating a theory that is tribally specific and grounded in Indigenous epistemologies, which is particularly notable given the influx of scholarship in queer Indigenous studies over the past ten years (in addition to the trailblazing work of activists and scholars like Beatrice Medicine [Lakota]). Driskill provides a theory that takes into account race, sexuality, and empire as LGBTQ studies have done, but more importantly "the relationships between sexuality, gender, colonization, and decolonization" (403). One goal of this approach is to refocus gender and sexuality studies so that they are no longer marginal in discussions that, as Driskill reminds us, are taking place on Indigenous lands.

Driskill asks: "Whose land are you on, dear reader?" In a time when Indigenous Studies scholars habitually acknowledge territory at the beginning of our presentations, Driskill reminds us to take this question seriously and learn about localized Indigenous histories before and after—as well as Indigenous resistance to—settler-colonialism and occupation. Hir essay reminds us that sexual and gender oppression have always been tools of settler-colonialism and the formation of "heteronormative nationalisms." A doublewoven critique, then, does not aim for inclusion or simple equality; Driskill quotes the Menominee poet Chrystos: "This continent is morally and legally our land, since no treaty has been observed. . . . Logically, then, we remain at war in a unique way—not for a piece of the 'white pie,' but because we do not agree that there is a pie at all" (410–11). Driskill's essay may be read as the logical extension of literary nationalism; the doublewoven critique encapsulates all forms of oppression (e.g., sex, gender, ethnicity, Indigeneity, imperialism, settler-colonialism, legal, governance, removals, etc.) faced by Indigenous peoples and nations. Driskill asserts, "by doubleweaving splints from queer studies and Native studies, Two-Spirit critiques can aid in the resistance struggles of Native communities and help create theories and movements that are inclusive and responsive to Native Two-Spirit/LGBTQ people" (419).

7. Katsisorokwas Curran Jacobs

Though Indigenous nationhood, resistance, and resurgence define the texts in this section, all published after the resistance at Kanehsatà:ke and Kahnawá:ke in 1990, in her contribution Katsisorokwas Curran Jacobs (who was "born in the midst" of the above-named "Oka Crisis") states emphatically, "My people have never really been idle." In an important response to the Idle No More

(INM) movement, Jacobs points to both the historical resistance of her nation as well as the unity that INM inspired amongst diverse Indigenous nations and peoples across Turtle Island. Curran importantly points out that "obliging to [Canada's] authority shows that you agree with its policies, its corruption, its 'best interests,' and its every move" (424). Jacobs reminds us that it is the small acts—voting for any Canadian political party, participating in state-sponsored reconciliation—that mean not only supporting, but endorsing the settler-colonial Canadian state. This is not indicative of separatism; rather, Jacobs' linkage of INM and nationhood is a statement of Indigenous sovereignty and autonomy. Indigenous literary critique in an era of truth and indignation seeks more and greater autonomy, not assimilation repackaged as inclusion or reconciliation. The articles in this section emphasize that the contemporary concerns of Indigenous peoples, literatures, and literary studies are intersectional, complex, and multifaceted; their common response, however, would appear to be one that is in collaboration with Indigenous communities, rooted in kinship and alliances, and transformative of the status quo structures in settler states like Canada and the United States.

Notes

1. See Glen S. Coulthard, "Subjects of Empire: Indigenous Peoples and the 'Politics of Recognition' in Canada," *Contemporary Political Theory* 6 (2007): 438–39, 446–450.
2. See Andrea Smith, *Conquest: Sexual Violence and American Indian Genocide* (Cambridge, MA: South End P, 2005), especially chapter 1.
3. See David Ljunggren, "Every G20 Nation Wants to Be Canada, Stephen Harper Insists," *Reuters*, 26 September 2009.

29

Appropriating Guilt: Reconciliation in an Indigenous Canadian Context

Deena Rymhs

If the twentieth century was, in Elie Wiesel's words, "the age of testimony," the late twentieth and early twenty-first centuries might be called "the age of forgiveness." In the last twenty years, forgiveness and reconciliation have become part of an international discourse. South Africa's Truth and Reconciliation Commission (1995–98), Tasmania's apology to the Stolen Generation (2006), and Britain's apology to the Maori (1995) are just a few recent instances of reconciliation across different national contexts. In Canada, the Royal Commission on Aboriginal Peoples (RCAP) represented a similar gesture, as the country confronted its colonial past and awakened to the insistence of that past in the present. Two years after RCAP released its 1996 report, the Canadian government issued a "Statement of Reconciliation" to former occupants of residential schools, stating it was "deeply sorry" for the collective and personal damage of these institutions on Indigenous communities ("Statement of Reconciliation"). Shaped by global politics, these attempts at reconciliation reflect a current sensibility of revisiting national history.

More buried in these public attempts at reconciliation are questions about their ideological underpinnings and the interests they serve. In what ways does reconciliation function as a way for the nation to re-imagine and perform itself—less, that is, as a deconstruction of national master-narratives than a reconstruction of one? To what degree does the process of reconciliation satisfy wronged parties? Ten years before RCAP, the Royal Commission on the Donald Marshall Jr. Prosecution (1986–88) undertook a public inquiry into the wrongful conviction and eleven-year imprisonment of Donald Marshall (Mi'kmaq).[1] The Marshall Inquiry was not void of value: the commission and its subsequent report identified a crisis in the criminal justice system, particularly in its treatment of racial minorities. Beyond recognizing problems like cultural misunderstandings between defence counsel and clients, the foreignness of the courtroom to defendants of different cultural backgrounds, and institutional racism in policing bodies and the courts, the commission made a number of larger, structural recommendations. On a local as well as a national scale, the royal commission set the ground for constitutional reconsiderations and legal reform by sounding a call for self-government, respect for treaty rights, and the implementation of Indigenous, community-based models of justice.[2]

Yet, the Marshall Inquiry, like RCAP and other reconciliation processes globally, can also be read as part of a national narrative. Baldly criticized as "Canada's favourite substitute for action,"[3] these commissions are often seen as offering only a discursive balm for historical injustices that have profound, and potentially unsettling, political implications. Arguably, the Marshall Inquiry was motivated more by the hope of restoring public faith in the federal government (epitomized by Brian Mulroney's election promise of a public inquiry and a million-dollar compensation package for Marshall) than by a willingness for various parties to admit responsibility for the personal toll suffered by Marshall and his community. Some contend that the Royal Commission on the Donald Marshall Jr. Prosecution originated from the Nova Scotia government's desire "to find scapegoats" (Wall 20), to redirect responsibility to other parties. On one level, then, the commission elided notions of guilt and responsibility, as federal, provincial, juridical, and policing bodies looked to other places to assign blame.

In addition to questioning its efficacy, one might also ask how the reconciliation process violates the understanding of forgiveness as a reciprocal act. In determining the notion of reparation and change—indeed, in deciding what the appropriate response of the wronged party should be—how does "reconciliation" erode the wronged subject's agency? What happens to guilt—and, specifically, the owning of guilt—in the process? Is reconciliation's function strictly performative? Is it capable of producing more than an affective response from the national community? That is, if reconciliation is a largely performative process, how might otherwise genuine feelings of guilt become merely the performance of guilt? Can guilt be turned into tangible political action? Put in more practical terms: how much does the process of reconciliation help those who have been unjustly treated?

While public attempts at reconciliation signify an alternative hearing for individuals and communities to testify to injustices, they also serve as a means for a broader national community to work through its implication in the blighted parts of its history. Guilt, in effect, becomes a dissolute concept, swept into colonial history, attributed to past government policies, or directed at faceless institutions rather than being individually or personally owned. At times bypassing the attribution of responsibility altogether, the process of reconciliation overlooks the logic that asking for forgiveness does not imply the granting of it. The success always implied by the act of reconciliation dissolves the wronged subject's agency as the public, the government, and its institutions forgive themselves.

For Indigenous communities, literature has been an important forum for testifying to past and present injustices and for setting the interpretive framework of such articulations. The proliferation of residential school writing in the 1980s and 1990s provided an outlet for individuals and communities to work through the effects of these institutions. In his 1998 work *Kiss of the Fur Queen*, Tomson Highway uses the novel's heteroglossic potential to stage a mixing of Cree and non-Cree frameworks. Highway draws on Indigenous concepts like the Windigo and Trickster to represent trauma and the potential for moving beyond that trauma. Anishinaabe author Basil Johnston, in his 1988 memoir *Indian School Days*, retells this part of public history in a way that departs from an emphasis on tragedy and loss. A curiously nostalgic work, *Indian School Days* emphasizes above all else the resilience of the boys. Both writers emphasize renewal in their narratives—Highway in the resilience embodied in the Trickster, and Johnston in affirming the collective solidarity of his community of peers who, he insists, were not broken by the residential school.

Reading literature in the current tenor of reconciliation, this essay looks at how Indigenous authors explore guilt in their writing and how, in turn, recent public discussion appropriates and transforms that guilt. Within and outside of literature, Indigenous communities are repositioning themselves under sovereign political identities and conceptions of governance. This repositioning has radical implications politically as well as academically. In the latter instance, critics are proposing new ways of approaching Indigenous writing with readings that track the influence of Indigenous intellectual traditions on Indigenous writers and the place of cultural knowledge in their writing. These new methodologies prompt a renewal and self-reflexiveness in literary criticism that are not always well received by its practitioners.[4] Channelling attention to the influence of political developments like Indigenous nationalism on Indigenous authors, these emergent approaches are interested in the different critical positions and vocabularies that Indigenous writing might generate. Next to these political and intellectual developments is the public dialogue that comes out of the context of reconciliation. This public dialogue also influences the ways Indigenous authors are read and the types of narratives readers construct. The discussion that followed RCAP and the Marshall Inquiry arguably remapped Indigenous people under Euro-Canadian ideas of justice by promoting an "alternative" justice that emerged from a framework of reconciliation. Rather than overhauling existing political configurations, reconciliation (as a process rather than an outcome) more often produces an affective response from the national community. Re-enacting a narrative of "victimry," to use Gerald Vizenor's term, these affective responses in a sense appropriate guilt. This liberal guilt is not limited to discussions that come out of RCAP and the Marshall Inquiry; rather, it is part of a larger cultural sensibility that underlies academic readings of Indigenous history and literature. What results is a discursive re-enactment of past roles that overlooks the distance that Indigenous people are asserting as they redraw notions of governance, political identity, and nationhood.

This essay considers, then, the role that guilt plays in both literature and public discussions. The bifurcated focus of this examination proceeds from the recognition that literature and criticism are not written in isolation from larger public dialogues. Just as Indigenous writers engage in political discussion, so, too, are academic treatments of literature part of social contexts and familiar discourses. As this essay identifies how the discourse of guilt spills over into academic treatments of texts, it implicitly asks what ethical and intellectual responses might lie beyond guilt and the false promises of "reconciliation."

Guilt in a Colonial Context

In an Indigenous context, guilt is indelibly part of colonial history. The fraught relationship between Indigenous people and the law—writ large in the over-representation of Indigenous prisoners in provincial and federal institutions—points to that history's legacy in the present.[5] Guilt is an ideological construct, produced by a set of processes in which cultural difference becomes transposed as moral difference. The prohibition of Indigenous practices like the potlatch from 1885 to 1951 or the threatened imprisonment of parents who refused to send their children to residential school punished cultural difference while criminalizing indigeneity. Many Indigenous authors expose the ideological and cultural bias of the justice system, or, as it has been mockingly dubbed, the "Just Us" system. Justice, notes Kanien'kehá:ka law professor Patricia Monture-Angus, is a word that has no direct equivalent in some Indigenous languages (her examples are Blackfoot, Musqueam [Salish], and Kanien'kehá:ka [Mohawk]). In the Anishinaabe language, the closest equivalent is *ti-baq-nee-qwa-win*, which means "to come before a system for something that has already been done wrong" (238). Monture-Angus interprets this reference to a "system" as a reference to a Euro-American system of law. The Anishinaabe word for justice, then, is possibly a postcontact term, the product of a colonial relationship. Justice carries with it a historical "residue," to borrow Wai Chee Dimock's term, ensconced in a set of relations in which it can only prevail.

Guilt in a Legal Context

The criminalization of Indigenous ways of life appears widely in the writing of Indigenous authors from the nineteenth century to the present. In her 1973 touchstone autobiography *Halfbreed*, Maria Campbell recalls two Mounties visiting her home. Investigating allegations of her father's poaching, the officers single out the young Campbell for questioning. Caving in to their bribe of a candy bar, Campbell shows the officers where her father keeps the meat. The guilt that immediately ensues as Campbell sees her father being hauled away to prison lingers over the rest of the autobiography. In Joseph Boyden's 2005 novel *Three Day Road*, a now elderly Niska tells her nephew, Xavier, about a similar experience watching her father be taken by the North-West Mounted Police. A spiritual figure known as a windigo killer, Niska's father is arrested for murder and dies in prison. His imprisonment marks the shifting world of Niska's community. These changes are reflected not only in the incarceration of Niska's father, but, more poignantly, in the fact that other Cree tip-off the authorities. "'Unspoken law said Cree business remained Cree business and was not to be discussed with the *wemistikoshiw* [white man],'" Niska remarks. 'But rum is a sly and powerful weapon'" (46–47). Like the arrest of Campbell's father, Niska's father's imprisonment is the result of internal disloyalty and, in an uncanny similarity, individual appetite. "I sold out for an 'Oh Henry!' chocolate bar," Campbell self-reproachingly remarks (60). For both Niska and Campbell, this experience is a moment of political awakening, one that develops the antagonistic relationship between Indigenous people and the law.

The prison looms large in Indigenous literature, appearing in the writing of canonical as well as less well-known authors. Much of this writing treats incarceration as a collectively known experience, dissolving the boundary between those inside the prison and those ostensibly outside it. In addition to writing that explores the continuities between imprisoned and non-imprisoned populations, the prison narrative stands as a discrete literary genre in Indigenous literature. Works like Anthony Apakark Thrasher's *Thrasher: Skid Row Eskimo* and James Tyman's *Inside Out: Autobiography of a Native Canadian* are both written about the prison experience by authors who were incarcerated. In such works, the prison is often the site of a nascent political consciousness where the imprisoned subject begins to recognize his experiences as continuous with those of a larger cultural community. Tyman, because of his adoption into a white middle-class family, is estranged from a Métis identity for much of his early life. It is not until he goes to prison that he recognizes himself as Native. From the prison, Tyman gains a profound vantage point from which to understand and critique the social forces contributing to his criminality.

The prison autobiography as a genre extends earlier back to Louis Riel, whose largely spiritual reflections he collected in diary form while awaiting execution. In a recent context, the most immediate Indigenous political prisoner to come to mind might be Anishinaabe-Lakota activist Leonard Peltier. Peltier, who was convicted of killing two FBI officers on the Pine Ridge Reservation in 1975, pleads his individual innocence in the crimes of which he was convicted, but he also insists that innocence does not exist for Indigenous people within the justice system. Peltier has become, for many, synonymous with the continued persecution of Native peoples and the criminal justice system's failure to prosecute fairly. His *Prison Writings: My Life Is My Sun Dance* is paradigmatic of the prison memoir as a genre. In it, he emphasizes the intersections between his experiences and those of other Indigenous people: "My own personal story can't be told, even in this abbreviated version, without going back long before my own birth on September 12, 1944, back to 1890 and to 1876 and to 1868 and to 1851 and, yes, all the way back through all the other calamitous dates in the relations between red men and white" (50). Peltier's story collapses into a larger history to reveal a notion of self that is in metonymic relation to that of an entire people. Identifying the prison as a disciplining mechanism over Indigenous people, Peltier explores the racialized dimensions of guilt. Like the memoirs of other prison authors, Peltier's work functions as a necessarily "alternative hearing," allowing him to respond to the law's authority over his public and personal identity.

Guilt is also a significant consideration for authors writing about the residential school. Peltier speaks about his entry into Wahpeton Boarding School as his "first imprisonment" (78). The guilt ingrained in the children, Peltier suggests, would come to characterize their later dealings with legal institutions. In her account of Shubenacadie Residential School in Nova Scotia, Mi'kmaq author Isabelle Knockwood remarks that the very name of the school evoked associations with miscreants and criminals. "'Don't do that or you'll be sent to Shubie,' was a standard threat to children," Knockwood recalls. "The school was so strongly associated with punishment in children's minds that those who were 'sent to Shubie' as a result of their family's circumstances constantly wondered what crime they had committed" (86). Basil Johnston similarly likens the residential school to the prison when he remarks, "Our treatment implied that we were little better than felons or potential felons" (138). These authors explore guilt as a cultural construct, showing that guilt is not necessarily correlated to criminality. In its forced relocation and confinement of Indigenous children, the residential school was historically a precursor to the prison system in Canada, used to control and contain Aboriginal subjects for colonial as well as penal purposes. These narratives testify to the racial guilt instilled in the occupants and to this structure's function as a disciplining mechanism over Indigenous people.

Reconciliation and Liberal Guilt

For Indigenous authors, literature has been an important medium not only of discursive and political resistance but of historical recovery as well. The emergence of residential school narratives in the 1980s and 1990s signified an important recuperation of history. In *The Circle Game: Shadow and Substance in the Indian Residential School Experience in Canada*, Roland Chrisjohn and Sherri Young point out a dearth of historical accounts of the residential school:

> When it comes to providing details of individuals' experiences in Residential School, or drawing generalizations about the form and function of the institution, there's . . . official silence. The churches and federal/provincial governments have produced no histories, incident reports, legal opinions, psychologies, or sociologies of Indian Residential Schooling. There is uniform inattention to these particular details. (27)

A subsequent explosion of residential school accounts by those who experienced these institutions has helped redress the ellipsis that Young and Chrisjohn identify. Works like Basil Johnston's *Indian School Days* and Isabelle Knockwood's *Out of the Depths* perform a collective act of witnessing while also crossing a variety of disciplines—literature, history, and therapy. Emerging in tandem with reconciliation movements, these writings played a crucial part in adjusting public perceptions of these institutions.

While residential school and prison narratives explore guilt as a colonial construct, much of this writing enacts a movement away from this guilt. Rejecting the ideologies that culturally coded guilt, these works reveal an insistent desire to move beyond colonial constructions. Basil Johnston's *Indian School Days*, for instance, foregrounds his classmates' roguish resistance to the priests' authority. Focusing on the social bonds formed in this place, his work refuses to tell a story of trauma. In a 1990 review of this book in *Canadian Literature*, Menno Boldt notes with disappointment Johnston's glossing over the pain of this experience.

Boldt criticizes the lack of emotional development in the narrative, as well as Johnston's refraining from an explicit indictment of this institution. "[I]t seems the author has evaded or repressed the true meaning of his experience," Boldt concludes (312). Boldt's criticisms are interesting, because they unwittingly reveal the type of expectations formed by the wave of media attention to residential schools. Jamie S. Scott, on the other hand, finds Johnston's refusal to submit to these preformed judgments to be a strength of this text. Johnston's "delicate balance between justified indignation and considered appreciation for the mixed blessings the school conferred upon its students," Scott maintains, is "a refusal to play upon the guilt-ridden posture" of a liberal readership (151). Johnston, as these authors point out, avoids a scriptedness in the way he represents this experience, submitting neither to assumptions of social disintegration nor to a dominant readership's desire for a cathartic narrative.

In her reflections on her residential schooling, Rita Joe similarly insists that she and others who experienced this place must focus on the good, on the value and instruction that might be wrested from it. Her discussion of the residential school attempts to balance criticism and praise:

> I think some of the problems, or a lot of the problems that we see today are really the result of the residential schools. And that must never happen again! . . . But let me tell you about the positive part. . . . [T]he positive part was: the people that came from it, the good ones, learned a lot from there. And so many people have gone on, and they have become chiefs, counsellors, and social workers, and they went on to learn! (Lutz 257)

In her autobiography, Joe describes telling her husband that they must "forget and forgive" the wrongs that were done (48). Joe's adage to "forget and forgive" is a point with which David Newhouse, reviewing Joe's *Song of Rita Joe* takes issue. "[W]e must forgive, but we must not forget" is Newhouse's response (51). He adds that Joe's writing "will help us not forget" (51). Much of Joe's writing in *Song of Rita Joe*, as Newhouse adeptly points out, admits the damage of these institutions, yet her statement reflects a desire to move beyond guilt and, arguably, beyond the redirection of guilt to a white readership. In the individual ways they choose to reconcile their pasts, Joe and Johnston shape not only the historical narrative but a present and future narrative as well.

Even as Indigenous communities achieve a distance from this guilt and re-imagine themselves politically, the response that comes out of RCAP and the Marshall Inquiry rehearses tragic versions of history. Reconciliation has often been faulted for its failure to recognize the autonomy of the wronged parties. These failures point to a necessary recognition that reconciliation is a cultural concept that may not always respect the ideological and political differences of individuals asked to participate in its process. In 2002, the *PMLA* devoted part of an issue to the topic of forgiveness, urging reflection of forgiveness "not just as a theme in literature or history, but also as a critical framework" (Rice 278). For instance, several of the contributors to the issue point out the Christian origins of forgiveness.[6] This Christian framework often emerges in the discourse and teleology of the reconciliation process. In the first meeting of the Truth and Reconciliation Commission, Anglican Archbishop Desmond Tutu, chair of the TRC, articulated its mandate: "We will be engaging in what should be a corporate nationwide process of healing through contrition, confession, and forgiveness" (qtd. in Gallagher 303). Tutu's statements point to the Christian structure framing the proceedings of the TRC. The object of the TRC, as Tutu articulated it, was a spiritual, national cathexis. Along with its religious associations, forgiveness—or what this essay prefers to call reconciliation—might be regarded in secular terms. It can be seen as a political and ethical response, or as a therapeutic act. In an interview on forgiveness, Julia Kristeva points out that many of the problems accompanying reconciliation as it has been rebaptized in a present context are the result of this identity crisis. With its overlapping therapeutic, ethical, political, religious, legal, and historical registers, reconciliation can in fact obfuscate notions of guilt and responsibility. In the contest of these different mandates, the intra-subjective space of mourning can become swallowed up in larger political projects of nation building and the "international politics of restitution" (Weigel 322).

The Marshall Inquiry revealed an insipid desire on the parts of the provincial and federal governments to transform its institutions. Put simply, the Nova Scotia and Canadian governments were less concerned with Marshall than they were with restoring faith in legal, juridical, and legislative process and in asserting the legitimacy of these institutions' jurisdiction over Indigenous people. While the Royal Commission on the Donald Marshall Jr. Prosecution represented an alternative forum for seeking justice, its structure and outcome did not, Joy Mannette argues, question the prevailing judicial model, nor did it "consider what kind of justice system Aboriginal peoples could respect" (92). With its quasi-juridical format, the Inquiry adhered to the "juridical epistemology and bureaucratic process" of the legal system it was critiquing (65). Mannette concludes that the Royal Commission ultimately served to "allay public doubt about judicial process, state legal coherence, and administrative rationality" (65). The Inquiry, in her thinking, produced a false sense of material change:

> Having been seen to publicly and authoritatively take charge of the assignment of blame, the state process of official discourse transforms an

> ideological phenomenon (that is, eroded public confidence in judicial process) into a material event (that is, the inquiry and its report). The material event is worked up according to principles of administrative rationality and legal coherence (for example, the use of lawyers, judges, quasi-judicial format, etc.). (Mannette 71)

This materiality creates an illusion of intervention and action. Former leader of the Assembly of First Nations, Matthew Coon Come, makes a similar observation of RCAP: while RCAP'S report represents a significant, comprehensive study of the conditions of Indigenous people, Coon Come laments that it has become "buried and ignored by the government of Canada" (5).[7] Rather than challenge the framework of the criminal justice system from an epistemological and cultural level, the Royal Commission on the Donald Marshall Jr. Prosecution, Mannette argues, pointed out "that 'what went wrong' was a malfunction of an essentially reformable system. The integrity of the judicial *system* was not impugned. On the contrary, it was human fallibility, in the guise of individual incompetence, which caused the apparent systemic breakdown" (65; original emphasis). The voices of minority constituents in the Commission hearings amounted to what Mannette further identifies as a superficial sense of inclusion. While Mi'kmaq representation figured symbolically in the consultation process of the Inquiry, she argues that the "tribal voice from the margins did not fracture the ethnic hegemony which the Marshall Inquiry sought to restore" (68). According to Mannette, the Marshall Inquiry failed to question its own epistemological underpinnings. Employing a quasi-juridical process, it assumed a role not unlike the fiduciary authority of the institutions it was criticizing. These observations point to the ways in which reconciliation, paradoxically, can displace the wronged party. Heidi Grunebaum makes a similar observation in her discussion of the Truth and Reconciliation Commission:

> While rituals of confession, apology, forgiveness, and reconciliation were facilitated by TRC, encouraged by the faith communities, enacted by individuals, widely disseminated by the national and international media, and assimilated into public discourse, the teleology of such parties transformed reconciliation into a fetishized claim that both devalues and displaces the experiences of those who were wronged. (308)

In a Canadian context, reconciliation has been driven by a public wish to atone for its colonial past. The process invites an appropriation and subsequent dissolution of guilt through affective responses to history. At the present cultural moment where the media and general public are stalled in tragic narratives of Indigenous life, the question arises of what political and interpretive possibilities exist beyond guilt—beyond, that is, the colonial guilt attributed to Indigenous groups in the past and beyond the liberal guilt that defines the present moment.

While the desire for reconciliation might reflect a changing public consciousness, its process has been criticized for obscuring notions of guilt and responsibility. Some argue that in its Statement of Reconciliation regarding residential schools, the Canadian government purposefully falls short of acknowledging its guilt in the grief suffered by Aboriginal peoples. John McKiggan, a lawyer representing over five hundred former students from the Shubenacadie Residential School, makes the case that the federal government's 1998 Statement of Reconciliation "does not apologize for government actions. It recognizes the pain. It doesn't admit responsibility for that pain" (Cox, "Government Paper"). Many critics maintain that the $350 million "Healing Fund" created by the federal government for former residents of these schools is an attempt to avert lawsuits and monetary reparation. Roland Chrisjohn and Sherri Young similarly criticize the rhetoric of healing and the pathologizing of the residential school experience that emerged during the RCAP proceedings. In their view, this focus served to neutralize discussions of legal recourse and monetary redress. Curiously, South Africa's Truth and Reconciliation Commission deployed a similar metaphor of healing in its discourse and mandate. As Pierre du Toit summarizes: "The medical metaphor, according to the Archbishop, found expression in the image of old wounds that had to be dressed, instead of being allowed to 'fester.' The process of healing would entail that such wounds be opened, cleansed and then treated with 'balm'" (161). Determining not only the format in which one testifies to injustice but also appropriate responses to that grief, the healing metaphor diverts attention away from the agency of the wronged. Peter Brooks' observation that when "the psychotherapeutic model . . . leaches into the public sphere, it works some mischief" (298) augurs the tensions that arise from reconciliation's intertwining of personal and public processes.

Literary Criticism and Its Contingencies

Given the departures seen in the writing above—these authors' resistance to discourses of guilt and to the public expectations formed by the current mood of reconciliation—we might expect criticism to follow suit. However, criticism has been slower to come, perhaps because of its practitioners' closer ties to institutional structures and thus to the ideological inertia of guilt. Critics like Gerald Vizenor observe that academic discussions of Indigenous people and history often dwell on tragic narratives rather than on the ways that Indigenous people have re-imagined themselves in the present. In "Settler Fantasies, Postcolonial Guilt: The Compromised Postcolonialism of Jane Urquhart's *Away*," Cynthia Sugars queries the popularity of recent writing that explores Canada's settler-invader past. Pointing out the often nostalgic and sentimental tenor of this writing, she asks, "Does the enjoyment of such narratives place the postcolonial critic in a compromised—even guilty—position?" (105). Sugars questions the metatextual implications of the current taste for settler narratives and the role that guilt plays in the popularity of such works. Drawing on Stephen Slemon's argument that the settler subject inherits and internalizes dichotomies of "oppressor and oppressed, colonizer and colonized" (Slemon 238), Sugars concludes that "it is therefore inevitable that settler cultures are never able to fully reject the imperial legacy they inherited, since this is a constitutive element of national—even postcolonial—identity" (104). The discussion that comes out of the process of reconciliation similarly re-enacts these colonial dichotomies of oppressor-oppressed, colonizer-colonized. Rather than exceeding these old dichotomies, such responses repeat and rehearse them. In his work on the connections between nationalism and portrayals of Indigenous people, Terry Goldie points out the ways in which the Indigene becomes a repository for white settler desires. Such semiotics would prompt us to be wary of affective identifications with Indigenous history promoted by the process of reconciliation. At a moment when literary and critical engagements with Canada's colonial past risk remaining caught in "the colonialist machineries they seek to displace" (Slemon 238), the question is whether or not academic discussions can move beyond its past dichotomies, beyond this economy of guilt.

Recent scholarly developments show the emergence of new methodologies for reading Indigenous literature. These approaches look to the political developments taking place in Indigenous communities. Kristina Fagan, for instance, proposes how Indigenous nationalism might coalesce into academic treatments of Indigenous literatures. While "[i]t may surprise some to hear the claim that the study of Native literature avoids politics when so much criticism in the area deals with questions of power and colonization," Fagan points out, "[l]iterary scholars ... have tended to stay away from specific Political (with a big *P*) topics within Native literature, such as land ownership, law, and governance. They tend instead to focus on small-*p* politics—that is, on power relations—and on large-scale issues such as colonization, sexism, and so forth" (14). Indigenous nationalism has not, in Fagan's view, made its way into the study of Indigenous literature in Canada. Instead, a culturalist approach, or what Maureen Konkle calls the "culture concept," most often used by literary critics, diverts attention away from nationalist impulses, and, in doing so, avoids recognizing the political stance of many Indigenous authors. Fagan continues:

> While it is easy to understand general concepts of colonialism, it is much more difficult and time consuming to learn about the specific traditions, languages, histories, and political priorities of particular First Nations. Moreover, while it is easy for non-Natives to decry Native dispossession, it may be less easy to support Native people's specific claims to self-determination, claims that have material consequences. (15)

According to Fagan, literary criticism avoids dealing with the larger political issues that may shake at its own foundations. Fagan's questions about the extent to which Indigenous authors' reflections on political organization, governance, and intellectual colonialism are heard apply both to public response that reconciliation has produced, as well as to readings of Indigenous texts.

A performative rather than a constative process, reconciliation prompts an affective response in the national community. Casting Indigenous people in a state of victimization, yet simultaneously calling on Indigenous communities to "heal" despite continued poverty, differences in education, and a hostile criminal justice system, means that reconciliation's successes have been more illusory than real. The public dialogue that comes out of reconciliation empties historical experiences of their political valence while discursively and statically rehearsing such roles in the present. This essay's criticisms of reconciliation are not intended to take away from the value of publicly declaring responsibility, error, or fault but, rather, to question the degree to which that responsibility is felt. Can there be forgiveness if there is no remorse? What happens to guilt in the current postcolonial moment? Reconciliation risks becoming a scripted process that stages a repetition of roles, but which cannot move beyond them.

Reading in the current global moment of reconciliation requires a self-consciousness about the ways that reconciliation movements shape a national as well as historical narrative. Reconciliation might be seen as continuing to strip Indigenous people of their separate conceptions of political identity. The answer may be, as Fagan argues of literary criticism, that interpretive frameworks need to be rebuilt, and not from the old centres either. While the outpouring of testimony has opened up important inter-cultural dialogue, one of the questions that remains of these commissions is whether or not they can mobilize more than an affective response from its public audience—whether or not they can move beyond the recognition of racism by initiating substantive political reorganization and intervention. Sometimes, as Sarah Brophy, nodding to Derrida, urges, we have to be wary of "the exorcisms that seek to justify self-satisfied assumptions of power" (268) and the way that liberalism continues to hide, sometimes by attempting to exorcise, its troublesome ghosts.

Notes

This essay was first published in *English Studies in Canada* 32, no. 1 (March 2006): 105–23.

1. Before the Royal Commission Inquiry, the province had granted Donald Marshall a sum of $270,000 for wrongful imprisonment. At the time of that offering, Marshall had lawyers' fees amounting to over $100,000. In the wake of his overturned conviction and the meagre compensation he received for his wrongful imprisonment, the Union of Nova Scotia Indians, the Black United Front, opposition politicians, and concerned citizens applied pressure to the Nova Scotia government for an inquiry into Marshall's case. The province maintained that compensation was not its responsibility since Marshall was convicted under the federal Criminal Code and that, as an Indigenous person, he was the responsibility of the federal government (Wall 19). It was amid mounting public pressure and charges of the provincial government's stonewalling that the Royal Commission was formed. Police misconduct was left off the table in Marshall's 1982 appeal hearing; many parties petitioned for public discussion about the role of police in orchestrating Marshall's conviction and the reasons for his protracted prison sentence when Sydney police and RCMP had long had evidence pointing to another suspect. Hearings began in Sydney's St. Andrews Church Hall in 1987. Ninety-three days of public hearings followed, producing fourteen thousand pages of recorded testimony by over one hundred witnesses. A total of $8 million was spent on the inquiry and its subsequent report.

2. The Marshall Inquiry made eighty-eight recommendations, some of which summarily led to the restructuring of legal-juridical institutions in Mi'kmaq communities. One of the developments spawned by the Marshall Inquiry was the 1997 establishment of the Mi'kmaq Justice Institute (MJI). While primarily a Native court worker program, the MJI became an umbrella organization for other justice initiatives. Controlled by state funding, the MJI struggled to develop sustainable pilot projects and eventually ceased operation in 1999. Some of the initiatives that emerged in tandem within the MJI, however, continued after its collapse. A current driving force of community-based restorative justice for Indigenous peoples in Nova Scotia is the Mi'kmaq Legal Support Network, which operates a customary law and court worker program. While improvements in housing and educational opportunities, along with developments in self-government, have also followed from the Marshall Inquiry, the province of Nova Scotia remains decidedly conservative in its implementation of the inquiry's central recommendations. One of the key recommendations made by the commission that has not been implemented is an Indigenous criminal court. For further information on legal-judicial developments post-Marshall, see Don Clairmont and Jane McMillan, *Directions in Mi'kmaq Justice: An Evaluation of the Mi'kmaq Justice Institute and Its Aftermath.*

3. "A Forum for Native People," editorial, *Edmonton Journal*, 25 April 1991.

4. For a recent distillation of this debate, see Dean Rader's, Chris Teuton's, and James Cox's reviews of Elvira Pulitano's *Toward a Native American Critical Theory*. Privileging postcolonial theoretical notions of cultural hybridity and favouring Indigenous texts that work with Western hermeneutics and intellectual traditions, Pulitano dismisses the methodologies proposed by critics like Robert Warrior and Craig S. Womack, who work from tribal-centred traditions and who are interested in the influence of Indigenous intellectual traditions on authors.

5. In Canada, Indigenous people constitute the largest incarcerated minority in federal, provincial, and territorial correctional facilities. While they make up roughly 3 percent of the general population, they account for just over 20 percent of the prison population. This disproportion is most pronounced in the Prairie provinces and Ontario, where Indigenous prison populations run seven to ten times greater than the percentage of the provincial populations they represent. Indigenous women comprise 30 percent of the female prisoner population and in Saskatchewan and Manitoba account for roughly 85 percent of all female admissions.

6. It is worth noting that the Christian notion of forgiveness centres on a relationship between individuals and God. This framework bypasses the role of the wronged party in granting forgiveness. The assumption would be that a "good Christian" forgives those who wrong him/her without the guilty party asking for forgiveness.

7. As an example of RCAP's receding presence in the minds of politicians, Coon Come describes the backlash from former cabinet member Robert Nault, who criticized Coon Come for his "inflammatory" rhetoric about RCAP at the World Conference on Racism in Durban in September 2001. The then Minister of Indian and Northern Affairs demanded an apology from Coon Come for language that, in Coon Come's words, came "from official reports with which he should be very familiar" (7). See Isobel Findlay's "Working for Postcolonial Legal Studies: Working with Indigenous Humanities."

30

Moving beyond "Stock Narratives" of Murdered or Missing Indigenous Women: Reading the Poetry and Life Writing of Sarah de Vries

Amber Dean

By 2007, sixty-five women who lived or worked in Vancouver's Downtown Eastside neighbourhood were listed by a police task force as missing. Today, the common phrase "Vancouver's Missing Women" tends to evoke a kind of stock narrative about the lives of the women the phrase is meant to represent. Although one could never hope to specify all of what "Vancouver's Missing Women" might signify, depending on context, audience, and framing, it is often made to stand in for a set of assumptions about a shared life narrative (troubled childhood, "broken" family, abuse, children's services, adolescent rebelliousness, and then a "fall from innocence" brought about by drug experimentation, prostitution, addiction, mental illness, criminality, and so forth). These assumptions about the women's lives are both true and not true, both over-determined and vastly oversimplified (Jiwani and Young 897). This is the sort of cultural work that a short-hand phrase like "Vancouver's Missing Women" performs, conjuring a stock narrative to represent so many diverse and complex lives.

Yet politically, drawing attention to the things many of the women had in common was an important strategy for forcing police and officials to pay attention at last to the increasing numbers of women "being disappeared" from the same neighbourhood.[1] Before they were linked together, it appears police found it easy to dismiss the women's absences as a sign of their "transient lifestyles."[2] So, in spite of the risks of evoking the stock narrative, linking the missing women together through a focus on what they *did* have in common is important for challenging false assumptions (like those of former prime minister Stephen Harper) that their disappearances or deaths should be interpreted merely as individual crimes, rather than as indicative of wider social patterns of violence.[3] For example, a statement like Harper's simply cannot help us understand why a shockingly disproportionate number of the women missing from the Downtown Eastside were Indigenous.[4] The Native Women's Association of Canada (NWAC) estimated in 2010 that at least 582 Indigenous women have been murdered or remain unaccounted for across the country since the mid-twentieth century.[5] And in 2014, the RCMP reported that the number of murdered or missing Indigenous women in Canada is actually much higher still: in a review of their files dating back to 1980, they discovered 1,181 police-recorded incidents.[6] Today, the story of "Vancouver's Missing Women" must be contextualized as one aspect of a much larger national story about the murder or disappearance of women rendered more vulnerable to violence by how they are constituted as subjects, primarily through racist discourses of disposability, discourses that we can trace back to the logics of colonialism.[7] If the disappearances or murders of these women are *not* linked together, this broader social pattern is easier to dismiss.

How can we simultaneously refuse stock narratives, yet still acknowledge the commonalities that indicate the systemic nature of the violence experienced by murdered or missing Indigenous women? The poetry and life writing of Sarah de Vries, a woman who was last seen in Vancouver's Downtown Eastside on 14 April 1998, models such complexity. Adopted by the de Vries family as an infant, Sarah's biological parents were "of mixed race—black, Aboriginal and Mexican Indian as well as white" (de Vries 1). Her placement in a white, middle-class family in 1970 is consistent with the pattern of the Sixties Scoop, a determined government effort to use child welfare practices to remove Indigenous children from their birth families and place them mainly in white households under the auspices of assimilation and integration into Euro-Canadian cultures and communities.[8]

Sarah's sister Maggie de Vries notes that Sarah's adoption fits the pattern of its time: her racial and cultural background were deemed irrelevant to her placement, as was any ongoing contact with her birth family, her extended biological kin, or her racial or cultural heritage. Sarah wrote about how this affected her in a journal entry later in life:

> Man, I don't understand how the adoption agency could let a couple that are both of the opposite colour as the child become this child's legal guardians.

I understand that they were not as strict as they are today on things of race, gender and traditions. But, come on, did they honestly think that it would have absolutely no effect on my way of thinking or in the way I present my persona? I'm not accepted into the Caucasian social circle nor am I accepted in the black social circle, for I am neither white nor black.... I'm stuck in the middle and outside both. I have no people. I have no nation and I am alone.[9]

Despite her Indigenous as well as black heritage, Sarah recognized herself (and I suspect was mainly recognized by others, based on her photographs) as black, and the convergence of these identities—black, Indigenous, white—in her claim, "I have no nation and I am alone," signals something of the complex and intertwining oppressions and violence of white supremacy (and its myths of racial purity), Western imperialism, and the colonization of North America. By linking her adoption to the Sixties Scoop or discussing her as one of many murdered or missing Indigenous women, I do not intend to eclipse de Vries' identification as a black woman; as Wayde Compton reminds us, "blacks . . . so often get minimized out of existence when people comment on the demographics of Vancouver. There are none, people often say" (114). Instead, I think we can read de Vries' journal entry as drawing our attention to the complexity of the processes by which she is identified (and identifies herself) as "of" a particular racial category. In many publications aiming to draw explicit attention to murdered or missing Indigenous women, for example, de Vries' story is prominently profiled. In Amnesty International's (2004) report, *Stolen Sisters*, de Vries' birth parents are described with a somewhat different emphasis: her mother is described as "an Indigenous woman from the West Coast of Canada, who was also of European and African Canadian ancestry. Her father was an Indigenous man from Mexico" (51). De Vries' indigeneity need not eclipse her blackness, but at times it has been important to emphasize her indigeneity in order to draw connections between the violence that ended her life and the ongoing crisis of murdered or missing Indigenous women. Her life writing, by contrast, allows us to trace the imprint of all of these racial categories; her claim to have "no nation," after all, can be read as a lament for centuries of Indigenous and black struggles for sovereignty and racial justice in the wake of the usurpation and violent decimation of bodies, lands, communities, and governance structures resulting from colonialism. It seems important, then, to read against representations of de Vries that invite us to imagine that race is a matter of clear and distinct biological markers rather than a system of categorization that is constituted discursively and serves particular political purposes. Her life writing invites us to instead read with more attention to the complexity of racial categorization in her life.

De Vries' journal entry echoes the words of many trans-racial adoptees, especially many Indigenous people adopted outside of their communities (Sinclair). The singular, personal event of Sarah de Vries' adoption is swept up in the complex and multifaceted histories of colonialism and imperialism, enacted in part through black slavery in North American and through Indian residential schools, as well as through racist child welfare policies that are wielded against black and Indigenous communities with particular force. In fact, de Vries' biological father was himself adopted, suggesting again that her personal narrative is bound to wider histories of racial injustice with very long legacies indeed. In Sarah's writing, then, we can read traces of these wider histories of injustice, traces that challenge the stock narrative and draw our attention to the complex ways that these histories render some lives more vulnerable to suffering and violence than others.

Similarly, in one particular poem, de Vries addresses her readers directly by challenging an anonymous reader's indifference to the murder of another woman from Vancouver's Downtown Eastside:

Woman's body found beaten beyond recognition.
You sip your coffee
Taking a drag of your smoke
Turning the page
Taking a bite of your toast
Just another day
Just another death
Just one more thing you so easily forget
You and your soft, sheltered life
Just go on and on
For nobody special from your world is gone (in Maggie de Vries 233)[10]

De Vries' lines, "Just another day / Just another death," repeated throughout the stanzas of this poem, reflect her clear sense that her own death might pass as anonymously and unremarkably as just another day gone by. This poem testifies not only to the murder of another woman who touched de Vries' life, a woman with whom she likely had quite a bit in common, but also to a sentiment of indifference to the woman's death among some whose lives are less susceptible to such violence: "You and your soft, sheltered life / Just go on and on / For nobody special from your world is gone" (in Maggie de Vries 233). But the indictment de Vries makes is not of a generalized or anonymous "society": it is directed to a "you," and I think this mode of address is important because it challenges us as readers to take up the role of witness that de Vries herself enacts in the poem. We can read the poem as calling upon us to attend collectively to wider histories of injustice and their legacies, for it is mainly the stock narrative that allows the "you" in the poem to maintain a disinterested distance from the woman whose violent death de Vries recounts.

Other lines in the poem also challenge us as readers to look beyond the "stock narrative" as an adequate explanation for the violence the woman experiences:

> Just another day
> Just another death
> Just another Hastings Street whore
> Sentenced to death
> No judge
> No jury
> No trial
> No mercy
> The judge's gavel already fallen
> Sentence already passed

Here, de Vries draws our attention to more than just the horror of the violent death of the woman in her poem (and, inadvertently, her own), for the lines of her poem suggest that the woman's struggles to survive actually began long before the moment of her murder. These lines draw our attention back to that key issue of how we *see* the woman, not just after her death but also *in life*, and, by doing so, de Vries asks us to look past stock narratives and consider how some lives are sentenced to death not as a result of their personal histories of trouble but because of how they are *socially* abandoned, their sentence "already passed." In this way, de Vries' writing models for us a method of engaging with representations of murdered or missing Indigenous women that pushes beyond any simple stock narrative, because we can read in her work an urgent call for us to attend to the complex ways that personal histories are indelible from the wider histories of injustice and struggle in which we are all, in one way or another, implicated.

Notes

1. There are compelling reasons for referring to murdered or missing women from the Downtown Eastside as "disappeared women" and compelling reasons against doing so. Disappearance as it was practised in Argentina (and many other places in the world) often refers to the state-sponsored, systematic disappearance of people, sometimes in the interests of quelling political dissent, and as such it has characteristics that distinguish it from the violence directed at women from Vancouver's

Downtown Eastside. The United Nations, for example, defines "enforced disappearance" as "the arrest, detention, abduction or any other form of deprivation of liberty by agents of the State or by persons or groups of persons acting with the authorization, support or acquiescence of the State, followed by a refusal to acknowledge the deprivation of liberty or by concealment of the fate or whereabouts of the disappeared person, which place such a person outside the protection of the law" (*International Convention for the Protection of All Persons from Enforced Disappearance*, Article 2). The evidence that is available suggests that the state and police are not *ordering* the violent acts against women from the Downtown Eastside, for example, so this is not a state-ordered system of disappearance, and as such it seems essential to hold on to a distinction between what's happening in Vancouver and elsewhere in Canada and what happened in Argentina, for example, during the so-called "dirty war." That said, though, lengthy periods of government inaction invite one to argue that the disappearance of women from the Downtown Eastside is certainly state-*supported*, and if, as several scholars and organizations have argued, the state-sponsored system of terror known as settler colonialism is indelibly tied to the present-day, ongoing disappearance of disproportionately Indigenous women from the Downtown Eastside (and across the country), then there are good reasons to deploy the language of enforced disappearance to describe these acts of violence. For a more in-depth discussion of this issue, please see my recent book, *Remembering Vancouver's Disappeared Women: Settler Colonialism and the Difficulty of Inheritance* (U of Toronto P, 2015).

2. For more about police failures to investigate reports of missing women from Vancouver's Downtown Eastside, see the Missing Women Commission of Inquiry reports, available online at http://www.missingwomeninquiry.ca (last accessed 2 October 2014).

3. To defend his continued refusal to launch a national inquiry into the ongoing crisis of murdered or missing Indigenous women, then prime minister Stephen Harper insisted that violence against Indigenous women was not a "sociological phenomenon" and should be viewed instead "as crime." See: http://www.cbc.ca/news/canada/manitoba/harper-rebuffs-renewed-calls-for-murdered-missing-women-inquiry-1.2742845 (accessed 2 October 2014).

4. There remains some debate about how many murdered or missing women from the Downtown Eastside were Indigenous, but even conservative estimates suggest that around a third likely were, and this percentage could be as high as half. When one considers that Indigenous women make up just less than two percent of the total population of adult females in Vancouver, it becomes obvious that their numbers here among the women from the Downtown Eastside who have been murdered or remain unaccounted for are enormously out of line with their representation in the overall population of the city. See Statistics Canada's *Aboriginal Peoples Highlight Tables, 2006 Census, All Census Metropolitan Areas (CMAs) and Census Agglomerations (CAs)*, available online at http://www12.statcan.ca/english/census06/data/highlights/Aboriginal/Index.cfm?Lang=E (accessed 12 May 2008).

5. See the Native Women's Association of Canada's "Fact Sheet: Missing and Murdered Aboriginal Women and Girls," available online at: http://www.nwac.ca/wp-content/uploads/2015/05/Fact_Sheet_Missing_and_Murdered_Aboriginal_Women_and_Girls.pdf (accessed 20 March 2016). Information about

the Native Women's Association of Canada's "Sisters in Spirit" project, which conducted research from 2005 to 2010 on the disappearances or murders of Indigenous women in Canada, is available online at http://www.nwac.ca/policy-areas/violence-prevention-and-safety/sisters-in-spirit/ (accessed 10 March 2016). Adding insult to injustice, the project's federal funding was not renewed in 2010.

6. See the RCMP report, "Missing and Murdered Aboriginal Women: A National Operational Overview," available online at http://www.rcmp-grc.gc.ca/pubs/mmaw-faapd-eng.pdf (accessed 7 July 2014).

7. For an important analysis of how sexual violence has been used against Indigenous women around the globe as a tool of genocide, see Smith, *Conquest*. For a compelling essay about the connections between globalization, neoliberalism, and the intensification of discourses of disposability in relation to Indigenous women in Canada, the US, Mexico, and Guatemala, see Erno, "Political Realities." For an analysis of a discourse of disposal in public and official discussions of outdoor sex work in Vancouver, see Lowman, "Violence."

8. For more on the Sixties Scoop, which some authors argue extended into the 1970s and is both intensified and ongoing today, see Fournier and Crey, *Stolen*, Sinclair, "Identity Lost," and Dubinsky, *Babies*.

9. This excerpt from Sarah de Vries' journal is reprinted in a profile included in Amnesty International's *Stolen Sisters* (2004) report. The profile can be read online at: http://www.amnesty.ca/sites/amnesty/files/amr200032004enstolensisters.pdf (accessed 20 March 2016). Excerpt © Maggie De Vries. Reprinted with permission.

10. Sarah de Vries' poem © Maggie De Vries. Reprinted with permission.

31

"Go Away, Water!": Kinship Criticism and the Decolonization Imperative

Daniel Heath Justice

It was the unlikely alliance of the Thunders and Water Spider that brought Fire to the world. The world was wet, cold, and cheerless in those days. Taking pity on the Animals who shivered in the darkness (this was before the time of Humanity), the Thunders sent lightning to the Middle World, where it burned in a hollow log on an island. The Animals tried to get Fire, but each was unprepared for the dangers of the strange red glow: it singed Raven's feathers a glossy black, scarred Screech Owl's face, and ringed the eyes of other Owls with clinging black soot. Other Animals made the attempt, but those who did always returned to their companions in soggy defeat, their bodies charred and blackened from the strange smoke and heat.

At last, when all the larger Animals had failed, the little Water Spider made the attempt. She didn't have Raven's swiftness or Blacksnake's agility, but she had a gift that was unlike anything her friends had: she knew how to weave. For a long time she drew the silk from her body, weaving it into a stout translucent bowl, broad in the centre and tapered slightly at the top. When she was satisfied that the bowl would serve her purpose, she skittered across the waters, grabbed a hot coal of the lightning-struck wood, dropped it into her silken bowl, and carried it on her back to the others.

Water Spider could have hidden this rare and wondrous warmth from the others; she could have dropped it into the water to punish the other Animals for doubting her, for scorning this small, shy creature who was so easy to overlook and dismiss. But she honoured her kinship obligations and brought Fire to share with all the Animals in the Middle World. Fire gave warmth and light; the cold shadows now had a limit to their reach. Darkness didn't disappear when Fire came to the Animals; it still stalks at the edge of the flickering light, greedier now that it has resistance.

But our eyes ever seek the firelight through the shadows. This is the gift of the Thunders and Water Spider: we want to join others around the dancing flames, not wander alone in the dark waters of the night.

This essay is written in Fire; it's about relationships and the attentive care we give to the ongoing processes of balanced rights and responsibilities that keep kinship going in a good way. Kinship, like Fire, is about life and living; it's not about something that *is* in itself so much as something we *do*—actively, thoughtfully, respectfully.

This essay is one part of a larger project that puts kinship principles in practice. In this essay, my aims are threefold: to propose the interpretive significance of the relationship between kinship, peoplehood, and decolonization; to employ the concerns of this mutually affecting relationship as a critical lens through which to regard recent controversies in Native literary criticism; and to offer reflections on the complicated possibilities promised by work that attends to similar concerns.

This essay speaks to others in the volume; the texts (and their authors) are also engaged in a relationship and a community. Together we respond to the ideas and questions of other Native literary critics; we travel through the imaginative mindscapes of Indigenous writers; we respond to the driving call for decolonization that echoes through those mindscapes; we attend to many of the values and concerns of our families and tribal nations.

Yet we write in Fire. This book isn't the allotted boundary of the conversation. The pages are brittle and crumble to dust or ash too easily; they don't share anything on their own. We have to be the ones to feed them, to take them beyond white space and root them—and ourselves—in rich red earth and memory.

We have to give voice to Fire, even if it means our tongues will burn.

"Go Away, Water!"

In her analysis of Seminole continuity in what is now Florida, *The Tree That Bends: Discourse, Power, and the Survival of the Maskókî People*, Patricia Riles Wickman relates the following episode:

> In 1736 . . . ostensibly Christianized Natives left Spanish hegemony, both ideologically and geographically, when a viable alternative presented itself. They transferred their allegiance to the British, because the British offered

them arms and more trade goods and did not require them to commit cultural suicide in order to get those things. Baptized Natives simply struck themselves on the forehead saying, "Go away water! I am no Christian!" (204)

This event intrigues me for a couple of reasons. First, it's a (literally) striking example of Indigenous agency and self-determination, wherein outside impositions are named, defined, and challenged in a ritual repudiation of Christian baptism. Second, and no less important, is the way in which this concise ritual of verbal exorcism and physical action—and with it, the implied return of Indigenous specificity—speaks to one of the larger goals of *Reasoning Together*, where this essay first appears, namely, the turn of the critical discussions in Indigenous literatures to the centrality of Indigenous contexts, both through a direct response to those creeds and definitions that have been imposed upon Native peoples and through the affirmation of a renewed way of understanding the ethical relationship between the critic and Indigenous literatures.

In thinking of an ethical Native literary criticism, it seems to me to be quite fruitful to reflect on community and kinship—both in their broadly theoretical forms and in their context-specific manifestations—as interpretive concepts in our analyses. In this way, we can be fully attentive to the endurance of Indigenous peoples against the forces of erasure and determine, in various ways, how the survival of Indigenous peoples is strengthened by the literature we produce and the critical lenses through which we read them.

Toward that end, I want to return again to Wickman's account. Its inclusion is not provided simply as a critique of Christianity, even though I generally tend to take a rather jaded view of all monotheistic traditions, and this particular creed's militant impacts on the world. Neither is it the symbolism of water itself that is being rejected; indeed, the ritual of "going to water" was and remains one of the most significant components of the Muscogeean ceremonial calendar shared among traditional Creeks, Seminoles, Cherokees, and other southeastern nations.[1] Rather, I read the episode above as an empowered response to the forced *imposition* of any outside definition—here, the coercive, transformative ritual of Christian baptism—and the accompanying assertion of self-definition.[2]

Similarly, in applying the example to the realm of the literary, this isn't a slam against a wide range of interpretive lenses, either, for, like the example of Christianity, it's much less about which lens we choose to read through than it is about which options are available to us, and how clear or distorted our understanding may be depending on the choice we make. I'm a literary nationalist, but I've never believed that literary nationalism is the only intellectually defensible way to approach a thoughtful understanding of Indigenous literatures. On the other hand, principles of nationhood and the tribal-specific study of our own texts certainly have an important role to play in the analysis, interpretation, and dissemination of Indigenous literatures—particularly if there is any hope of making such study relevant to Native communities and the larger issues of concern to the Indigenous Americas. Such relevance can take place only in an intellectual environment wherein respect and equality are guiding principles.

Thus, to my mind, "Go away, water!" isn't a statement or ritual that's fundamentally about rejection, because rejection for its own sake is ultimately impotent and self-defeating. Rather, it's about shifting away from the terms of "cultural suicide" that Wickman notes above, and opening room for the return of those models of self-determination that speak to the survival and presence of Indigenous *peoples*, not simply the durability of individuals of Indigenous ancestry. Certainly, to open that space, we have to uproot those rank ideologies of fragmentation that have defined us and our scholarship against our will, which lay claim to our words but offer little but angst and alienation in exchange. We have to challenge the idea that the hyperindividualist creeds of industrialization and atomization are the wellsprings of intellectual sophistication. Indigenous intellectual traditions have survived not because they've conceded to fragmenting Eurowestern priorities, but because they've *challenged* those priorities. We exist today as Indigenous nations, as peoples, and the foundation of any continuity as such is our relationships to one another—in other words, our kinship with other humans and the rest of creation. Such kinship isn't a static thing; it's dynamic, ever in motion. It requires attentiveness; kinship is best thought of as a verb rather than a noun, because kinship, in most Indigenous contexts, is something that's *done* more than something that simply *is*. As such, the relationship of our literatures to our communities—and the role of that relationship in ensuring the continuity of Indigenous nations into the future—is the primary interest of this exploratory essay, and, indeed, the larger collection as a whole.

Peoplehood and the Decolonization Imperative

Literary expression—in its broadest and most inclusive definition—is a profoundly powerful exercise of the ways in which that relationship is made manifest. This is the heart of the decolonization imperative of Indigenous literatures: the storied expression of continuity that encompasses resistance while moving beyond it to an active expression of the living relationship between the People and the world. Spokane writer Gloria Bird reminds us that "writing remains more than a catharsis; at its liberating best, it is a political act. Through writing we can undo the damaging stereotypes that are continually perpetuated about Native peoples. We can rewrite our history, and we can mobilize our future" ("Breaking the Silence" 30).

The decolonization imperative in our literature both *reflects* Indigenous continuity of the past and present, and *projects* that continuity into the future. Stories—like kinship, like fire—are what we do, what we create, as much as what we are.[3] Stories expand or narrow our imaginative possibilities—physical freedom won't matter if we can't imagine ourselves free as well. To assert our self-determination, to assert our presence in the face of erasure, is to free ourselves from the ghost-making rhetorics of colonization. Stories define relationships, between nations as well as individuals, and those relationships imply presence—you can't have a mutual relationship between something and nothingness.

Indigenous nationhood is predicated on this understanding of relationship. The idea of "the nation" has fallen into disfavour over the last decade; it's no longer viewed by most scholars as an inevitable or even desirable way of constituting group identity. Yet for Indigenous peoples in North America and elsewhere, community is the constitutive measurement of selfhood. Indigenous nationhood should not, however, be conflated with the nationalism that has given birth to industrialized nation-states. Nation-state nationalism is often dependent upon the erasure of kinship bonds in favour of a code of assimilative patriotism that places, and emphasizes, the militant history of the nation above the specific geographic, genealogical, and spiritual histories of peoples.

Indigenous nationhood is more than simple political independence or the exercise of a distinctive cultural identity; it's also an understanding of a common social interdependence within the community, the tribal web of kinship rights and responsibilities that link the People, the land, and the cosmos together in an ongoing and dynamic system of mutually affecting relationships. It isn't predicated on essentialist notions of unchangeability; indeed, such notions are rooted in primitivist Eurowestern discourses that locate Indigenous peoples outside the flow and influences of time. In his contribution to *Reasoning Together*, Creek scholar Tol Foster addresses this dynamic state of being (and the presumptions of agents of nation-state nationalism) with enviable clarity. He writes:

Others who act on tribal people will certainly be considered Other, but they will not be considered "modern" against some sort of tribal premoderns. This is a construct, we should notice, of the antitribal nation-state, which wishes to posit historical breaks as a way of building up an incommensability between then and now, just as tribal stories often construct a vague rupture between now and the time when crucial myths were in play. That was then, but this is now, we hear the government judge proclaim, but for tribal people, such explanations are inadequate, and indeed dangerous. Following from Native epistemology we must add to such narratives of difference the notion of the relational. History and events are part of the story, but they are not the determinate parts. Relations are the primary axis through which we can understand ourselves and each other. (151)

Agents of change exist in relationship to one another and demonstrate by those interactions their ability both to influence others and to be self-determining; as Foster points out, the representations of Indians as absolute Others relegate us to the role of museum artifacts of ever-diminishing authenticity. The recognition of some sort of relationship between and among peoples—the ever-contextual contours of kinship—returns us to the physical realm of the participatory. At their best, these relationships extend beyond the human to encompass degrees of kinship with other peoples, from the plants and animals to the sun, moon, thunder, and other elemental forces. The central focus of Indigenous nationhood, then, is on *peoplehood* (or, to use Chickasaw scholar Amanda Cobb's term, *peopleness*), the relational system that keeps the people in balance with one another, with other peoples and realities, and with the world. Nationhood is the political extension of the social rights and responsibilities of peoplehood.

Peoplehood, too, is the abiding concern of Indigenous literatures. Jace Weaver (Cherokee) defines this emphasis as "communitism"—a synthesis of "community" and "activism" that implies an active, participatory engagement in the creation and maintenance of a people as a culturally distinctive body. Under this definition, community isn't a stable or static group of people; rather, it's an ever-adaptive state of being that requires its members to maintain it through their willingness to perform the necessary rituals—spiritual, physical, emotional, intellectual, and familial—to keep the kinship network in balance with itself and the rest of creation. The ground is always shifting, the People are always responding to change within and without, new challenges require new or revised responses. A community—with all its constituent members and social concerns, past and present—is alive, and the People are responsible for its survival through attention to their kinship rights and responsibilities and through their response to the continuity fuelled by the decolonization imperative.

Though related, the decolonization imperative is not the root of Indigenous peoplehood and self-determining sovereignty, as Amanda Cobb points out:

[A]lthough the journey of sovereignty moves from survival to continuance, taking into account the colonization experience and providing for decolonization, it is important to note that sovereignty and decolonization are not synonymous terms. Tribal sovereignty existed before colonization and does (or will depending on your point of view) exist after colonization. Sovereignty is *the going on* of life—the living. The path to survival and the path to continuance each consist of more than "step" or what I choose to call, "action," a term I use to underscore Native agency in a given moment or context. (unpublished manuscript)[4]

The decolonization imperative gives fuel to sovereignty and continuity, but without "the going on" that Cobb addresses, it runs the risk of being merely reactionary, not creative or transformative. At its best, peoplehood is shaped by relationships and lived purpose, fuelled by a desire to create something that will last beyond the pains of oppression. Indigenous writing, in this context, is both an act of love for the People and the product of that love, whether it speaks of joy and possibility or pain and alienation. "Going on" is more than endurance; it is, as Cobb demonstrates in her analysis of the work of Acoma Pueblo poet Simon Ortiz, the expression of a sovereignty of hope and possibility.

The intersections between community, continuity, and purpose, then, seem a useful relational constellation to analyze in an essay on ethical Native literary criticism. If peoplehood is a fundamental concern of our literature, then it follows that it should also be a fundamental concern of our criticism of that literature. Native critics have responsibilities to our tribal nations, but we also have responsibilities to the broader community of Native literary studies, and it's the latter that is sometimes the most vexing and difficult to navigate, as the individualist ethos of Eurowestern academe doesn't fit very smoothly with the communitistic principles of Indigenous nationhood. Yet we must find a way to travel these difficult waters if we have any hope of bringing the study of literature and the social concerns of Indigenous peoples together in a meaningful way.

Of course, broad notions like "community," "people," and "nation" are tricky to work with. We can't very well use them without immediately qualifying them: Each community is different; no community is monolithic and without dissent, or even conflicting ideas about what exactly constitutes the group; the principles underlying tribal nationhood aren't necessarily those that give rise to the nationalism of industrialized nation-states; and so on. Yet we can still talk about ideals as functional principles without erasing the specific contexts in which those principles operate; though members of a group might differ in their understandings of that community's composition, they nonetheless work to articulate the shifty, unstable, but ultimately embodied notion of purposeful collectivity.

It's this struggle between different definitions of community that interests me, and the spaces between, within, and among those definitions. For example . . . early in my studies of the Cherokee literary tradition, I realized that my initial supposition that there was a single, unitary idea of "Cherokeeness" was both naive and, ultimately, impossible, especially given the long and tangled realities of Cherokee social history. Yet I also came to realize that though there are many different ways of understanding what it is to be Cherokee—some more suited to the preservation of Cherokee nationhood, communitism, and decolonization than others—each way is still an attempt to give shape to an idea of what it is to be, think, and live Cherokee. Thus, easy assertions of a unitary definition break down, and the complicated living realities of the Cherokee people are revealed. The definitions might differ, but all the definitions still speak to the idea of Cherokeeness. The fires of Cherokee nationhood still burn: around the kitchen table, in the council house, in the churches, in the ceremonial grounds, and in the classroom.

As a literary critic studying literature in which metaphor and symbolism are so powerfully evocative, I too easily fall back upon uncritical language, assume an easy, uncomplicated certainty that so rarely exists in the messy realities of life. We can talk about words giving shape to meaning, literature as a social force that can enhance our sovereignty, poetry as rebellion, without ever really grappling with all the difficulties of those assertions. I did it with the earlier drafts of this essay, and I'm probably doing it now, too, in spite of my cautious hopes otherwise. It's the bigger concepts—the ones we so often assume to have a uniform meaning among all readers—that really get us into difficulties. What happens, for example, when a concept like sovereignty shifts from Indigenous empowerment and responsibility and is instead used as a hammer to stifle dissent within the community, especially when it comes from client chiefs and sell-out council members who feel a larger obligation to the colonialist nation-state than to the dignified survival of their own people? What happens when appeals to "tradition" are used to justify bigotry, abuse, neglect, or corruption, or when the traditions of one Indigenous community are used to dismiss the very existence of other Indigenous peoples? What do we do when Eurowestern values of individualism, antagonistic dualism, and market-driven commodification and commercialism replace older traditions of sacred kinship, communal concern, and complementarity, thus becoming the de facto constitutive traditions of the community? We can advocate the contextualized principles of political sovereignty and tradition without assuming that political independence or appeals to a context-specific tradition alone will be the cure-all for Native empowerment, or that empowerment without ethical consideration or reflection is inevitably a good thing. Those kinds of certainty are comforting in the short term—and for those who desire power over others—but they are ultimately ineffective in revealing truth, giving respectful voice to experience, or pushing us to face the big challenges facing Indigenous peoples today.

Indigenous communities are shaped by principles of kinship, and kinship itself is a delicate web of rights and responsibilities. In order to explore ethical criticism, we have to be prepared for complexity and eschew simplistic explanations that do little to illuminate the world and much to obscure it. [. . .] I engage here with texts about Indian identity more to question their significance to issues of kinship than to privilege notions of "race," which are fundamentally incompatible with Indigenous epistemologies.

Rather than simply presenting a linear list of ethical considerations for Native literary scholars, I'm interested in a more philosophical reflection on current Indigenous realities and the possibilities for a responsible relationship between the sociopolitical realities of Native America and the literary criticism that emerges from our diverse and complicated communities. In other words, I want to explore how the principles of kinship can help us be more responsible and, ultimately, more useful participants in both the imaginative and physical decolonization and empowerment of Indigenous peoples through the study of our literatures.

"To Cut Off the Remembrance of Them from the Earth"

We should never forget that the very existence of Indigenous literatures, not to mention the decolonization imperative of Indigenous peoplehood, is a rebellion against the assimilationist directive of Eurowestern imperialism. Empire is driven as much by expedience and simplification as by hunger for power or resources. Simplification is essential to the survival of imperialism, as complications breed uncertainty in the infallibility of authoritative truth claims. Empire contains within it the insistence on the erasure of the Indigenous population, through overt destruction or co-optation; indeed, the very *memory* of an unbroken Native presence is often furiously repressed by the colonizers.

Two telling examples illustrate this point. The first is the destruction of the Mayan codices by the Spanish invaders. As Craig S. Womack (Muscogee Creek-Cherokee) notes, this act can quite clearly be seen as an "act of cultural genocide [with] one culture finding itself threatened by the profundity of the Other's literacy. These were illiteracy campaigns, sponsored by the group claiming to be the most literate" (*Red on Red* 13). The destruction of the means of knowledge dissemination was crucial to the policy of colonization, as the dominating creeds of Europe could only flourish in the perceived absence of the Indigenous epistemologies. And the written codices themselves were not the only target; the Spanish also destroyed the sites of Indigenous learning (Leon-Portilla, "Introduction" xlvi).[5]

Take, too, the case of the Pequots. In his masterful introduction to the writings of William Apess (Pequot), Barry O'Connell writes: "In 1637 [the Pequots] were the objects of the first deliberately genocidal war conducted by the English in North America. . . . Some Pequots survived but were compelled to sign a treaty that declared them extinct as a people and forbade the use of their name forever" (*On Our Own Ground* xxv). Historian Michael Freeman adds: "[T]he colonial authorities forbade the use of the Pequot name in order, in Captain [John] Mason's words, 'to cut off the remembrance of them from the earth'" ("Puritans and Pequots" 289). In reflecting on the work of Apess within a larger Native intellectual genealogy, Robert Warrior (Osage) observes that "while the Pequots managed to survive the genocidal designs of the New England Puritans, their existence for the next three hundred years would be marked by social deprivation and constant threats to the status of their lands. And their reservation-based population continued to decrease" (*People and the Word* 11).

Empires can't survive by acknowledging complexity, so whatever complications they can't destroy or ignore are, if possible, commodified, co-opted, and turned back against themselves. The struggle to uproot imperialism, then, too often becomes myopic, as the colonized in many cases too often seek to find expedient, simplistic solutions to their many difficulties. The result is turning against one another in frustration, thereby destroying themselves and one another in service of the very empire they seek to dismantle. Although between one-third to three-quarters of the Pequots survived the English campaign, the symbolic erasure of the Pequot presence in the Northeast didn't stop with the English colonists. It's continued into the present age, contributing today to an enduring prejudice that presumes the inauthenticity of the Pequots and other eastern Native communities—and given unfortunate voice by high-profile Native people.

An illuminating example: in December 2002, a letter appeared in the *Hartford Courant* that caused quite a stir on various Native academic email lists. (The letter has since been republished in the *American Indian Quarterly*, and all citations here are from this publication.) In her letter, Oglala Sioux writer and scholar Delphine Red Shirt, an adjunct professor at Yale University, castigates those "newly born" Indians of Connecticut—and, by extension, the entire East—whom she does not recognize as "real" Indians. She writes, "What offends me? That on the outside (where it counts in America's racially conscious society), Indians in Connecticut do not appear Indian. In fact, the Indians in Connecticut look more like they come from European or African stock. When

I see them, whether they are Pequot, Mohegan, Paugussett, Paucatuck or Schaghticoke, I want to say, 'These are not Indians.' But I've kept quiet. I can't stay quiet any longer. These are not Indians" ("These Are Not Indians" 643).

Red Shirt goes on to assert that "[t]here are no remnants left of the Indigenous peoples that had proudly lived in Connecticut. . . . The blood is gone." She follows the line of logic used by many anti-Native forces, namely, that blood quantum and phenotypically "Indian" features are the fullest measure of cultural authenticity and that those who are lacking in these qualities are, by definition, no longer Indian—if they ever were. The success of Indian casinos in Connecticut draws Red Shirt's particular scorn, as she connects the US recognition process to "a new arena for profit making," whereby "[p]eople who had been indigent elsewhere can come here and claim lineage and book a cruise to the Caribbean islands or move into a spanking new retirement home on casino income as a tribal member" (643).

There's no intellectual engagement in this letter with the histories or contemporary realities of these communities; it's all hyperbolic Sturm und Drang. In spite of brutal cultural oppression, forced migrations of much of the population, and material suffering, the Pequots have maintained an active presence in their homelands, which Robert Warrior addresses in his recent discussion of William Apess:

> Clearly, just the continuing existence of the Pequots in the face of all they experienced is testimony to the resilience of generations of political leadership that refused to give up on the idea of the Pequots as a people. That idea, of course, required a land base, and some Pequot people held on to that land base with ferocious tenacity. In the process, those Pequots managed to carve out a place for themselves in which they managed to endure. Their descendants would be the ones who, much later, set the stage for the contemporary rebirth of the Pequots as a people. (*People and the Word* 11)

Red Shirt's rhetoric both ignores and perpetuates the racist inconsistencies and genocidal practices of US Indian policy and those of its invader predecessors on eastern tribes.[6] When she asserts that "on the outside (where it counts in America's racially conscious society), Indians in Connecticut do not appear Indian," she overtly subjugates Indian identity to the slippery perceptions of bigoted, self-interested observers who generally refuse to see even the Indians who, like her, "appear Indian." Visual recognition is a dangerous thing to put one's faith in; it's all too easy to close your eyes.

Disconnected from history or the current kinship practices of the peoples she dismisses, Red Shirt's argument draws instead on longstanding Eurowestern stereotypes about Indians, which Robert F. Berkhofer Jr. addressed over twenty years earlier:

> In spite of centuries of contact and the changed conditions of Native American lives, Whites picture the "real" Indian as the one before contact or during the early period of that contact. . . . Since Whites primarily understood the Indian as an antithesis to themselves, then civilization and Indianness as they defined them would forever be opposites. Only civilization had history and dynamics in this view, so therefore Indianness must be conceived of as ahistorical and static. If the Indian changed through the adoption of civilization as defined by Whites, then he was no longer truly Indian according to the image, because the Indian was judged by what Whites were not. Change toward what Whites were made him ipso facto less Indian. (*White Man's Indian* 28–29)

Red Shirt's recognition of Indianness requires both a tacit acceptance of the Eurowestern stereotype of the unchanging Indian and, at the same time, a tribally specific assertion that places her own cultural identity—that of an Oglala Sioux—as the absolute standard against which all other Indians are measured: "I am Indian and have had to live with all that means. I do not claim to descend from a full-blooded Indian. I am it. What I am witnessing in this casino-mad state is a corruption of my heritage. I am outraged by it. These are not Indians" (644). While the Pequots, Mohegans, Paugussetts, Paucatucks, and Schaghticokes make no claim to being Oglala Sioux, their assertion of a broader identity as "Indian" is seen by Red Shirt not merely as inaccurate but as insulting, deeming it a "corruption" of her own Oglala heritage.

It might seem a bit gratuitous or self-serving for a light-skinned, mixed-blood Cherokee to devote so much attention to a single letter, yet my interest here isn't so much to justify the Indianness of the Pequots and others who don't appear phenotypically Native. Rather, I've chosen this document to illustrate what I see as a widespread avoidance of kinship and context, both on the part of Red Shirt herself and others of like righteousness as a preemptive response to some of the more predictable (but no less vexed) responses to her arguments. Her letter exemplifies both the complexity of the sociopolitical status of American Indians today and a significant lack of sensitivity to the larger significance of kinship to Indigenous continuity. Her fierce response to the claims of eastern tribes can be seen as mere geographic and blood-quantum bigotry, but to dismiss it simply as such would be to ignore some of the very historical realities that she herself erases. Those communities from the eastern edge of the continent have a much longer history of dealing with the immediate effects of European invasion than do many of the communities in the northern US and southern Canadian prairie: for at least two hundred years, the tribal peoples Red Shirt dismisses acted as a buffer that protected many western communities from the full brunt of white expansion. The bodies that Red Shirt doesn't recognize are the living testaments to that legacy—a legacy that her people now benefit from in a country that prizes blood purity above kinship obligations.

Similarly, among most eastern Indigenous nations—indeed, among most tribal nations in this hemisphere—intermarriage was an honoured method of developing kinship bonds with other peoples, either Indigenous or invader, an act both intimately familial and overtly political—and many of us reflect that tradition in our skin and features. But as colonization spread its crimson claws across the continent, and as traditional kinship structures became increasingly weakened by Eurowestern values (patriarchy, capitalism, rampant individualism, etc.), this tradition also became a site of conflict, even among communities with previously liberal traditions of intermarriage.[7]

While examining these conceptual weaknesses in Red Shirt's argument, it's also vital to keep firmly in mind the culturally specific contexts from which they themselves emerge. The current home of the Oglala Sioux tribe—the Pine Ridge Reservation in South Dakota—has one of the most devastated ecologies and economies in the United States, as Winona LaDuke (Anishinaabe) points out: "Alcoholism, unemployment, suicide, accidental death, and homicide rates [among the Oglala Lakota of Pine Ridge] are still well above the national average. Indian Health Service statistics indicate that alcoholism death rates in the Aberdeen, South Dakota, area are seven times the national average and almost three times that of all Indian people. The suicide rate on one of the Lakota reservations is almost seven times the national average and generally is at least three times the suicide rate of all non-Indians in the state of South Dakota" (*All Our Relations* 148). Add to these grim statistics an unemployment rate of at least eighty percent, the brutal racism of their white neighbours (and a number of unsolved murders of Lakota men whose bodies have been found on the edge of the reservation), decades of conflict between the BIA-endorsed government and the grassroots Oglala leadership, loss of lands to allotment and flooding, destruction of the buffalo herds, Wounded Knee I and II, and the incursions of white ranchers into the area. For the Oglalas, and for many western Native peoples, this is the immediate reality of being Indian: "Pine Ridge is a testimony to survival. It is also a testimony to genocide. . . . The Oglalas are survivors. They are like the Yellowstone [buffalo] herd: besieged, shot down, but still alive" (148).

The sad reality is that the Oglalas are among the most brutalized Native communities in the continental United States, and still they endure. Given the immediacy of the Oglala struggle, it's not difficult to imagine that the phenomenal economic success of the Connecticut tribal casinos and their relatively recent federal recognition is a difficult pill for Red Shirt to swallow, especially when the Native people who benefit economically and politically do not share the physical or cultural characteristics that she recognizes as "Indian" and yet benefit from that designation.

If kinship and context are important to the Indigenous scholarly enterprise, we have no choice but to challenge Red Shirt's claims, especially those that view Indigenousness in solely racial terms—a product of nineteenth-century Eurowestern science—rather than the relevant Indigenous epistemologies and familial relationships. The colour coding of "race" in America may be a material reality, but it's not a natural state of affairs—it was constructed by human minds and biases, and it can be unmade in ways that are more responsive to the complicated realities of Indigenous value systems. While addressing the problematic nature of Red Shirt's claims and examining the historical contexts of Pequot assertions of nationhood, however, we also have to embed those claims in a context that recognizes the continuing racism and oppression suffered by the Oglala Lakotas.

To erase the endurance of either the Pequots or the Lakotas requires a dangerous movement away from the expansive qualitative standard of kinship toward that of race, which depends on an ever-diminishing quantitative standard. Kinship is adaptive; race, as a threatened constitutive commodity, always runs the risk of becoming washed out to the point of insignificance. Extending this discussion to both this text and to Native literature in general, we find that kinship criticism is far more responsive to the historicized contexts of Indian communities in all their complexity, whereas race-reading—rooted as it is in Eurowestern stereotypes and deficiency definitions—can only view Indians through a lens of eventual Indian erasure. If, as is the consensus of communitistic analyses, our literatures assert a consciousness of land and ancestry, of community and kinship ties, of traditions and ceremonies, of survival and presence outside of colonialist death narratives, shouldn't our criticism attempt to do the same? As Native literature is arguably centred in the continuation of the People, the aesthetic moral imperative from which Indigenous meaning, purpose, and identity are derived would be well served by a similar concern in our criticism.

Continuation doesn't matter if we continue in the image of individualized Eurowesterners—it is as *peoples* that we endure, through our obligations to kinship and balanced relationships. A solitary flame without fuel dies quickly. This is as much the case for Native writers and scholars as it is for tribal nations themselves; as Chris Teuton (Cherokee Nation) demonstrates so masterfully in his detailed genealogy of Native literary criticism, we who are contributing to this volume do so because our literary peers and ancestors gave shape and substance to these discussions (and were themselves engaged with those of non-Native scholars in the field) and because we want to contribute to the endurance of this flame beyond the short flicker of our own warmth. Our ideas and voices are now being woven into those conversations, and we add to the continuity of this small community. By participating in these acts of kinship, we keep the community and its history alive.

This isn't to say, however, that all the conversations are harmonious; if anything, the intimate relationship between our nations and our scholarship pretty well guarantees that the stakes are high. Our investment in these issues is more than an anemic intellectual exercise. We ask questions of the literature and its writers that generally aren't asked in other fields, and we place a lot of weight on the answers that emerge. At times, our kinship duties are pushed aside in our insistence on the answer we want to hear.

For example, what relationship do Native literature and criticism have to the protection of lands and treaty rights? Given that so much of this material is, at least superficially, concerned with affirming the author's Indianness, can such literature be considered ethical? Can it even be considered Indigenous? Ostensibly simple questions, but—as with most things—far more complicated than they seem. Examining these complications through a relational lens might provide us with an option beyond false either/or binaries, where the conversation and the opinions it elicits become part of the process of kinship. In this way, divisive debates are stripped of some of their corrosive qualities, and they become oriented more clearly toward continuity.

Embodied Sovereignties

Over half of American Indians and large numbers of Mexican and Canadian Natives do not live on traditional lands. In the United States and Canada, government policies of removal, land seizure, and allotment, erosion of successful Indigenous trade networks and sufficiency economies, excessive taxation, termination of government-to-government relationships with tribal nations, boarding and residential schools, disruption of families and kinship communities, forced assimilation and relocation were the primary forces of Native land dislocation in the nineteenth and twentieth centuries. These issues, connected with government definitions of Indianness that disenfranchised tens of thousands of Native peoples while simultaneously undermining Indigenous conceptions of peoplehood, have resulted in large populations of Native peoples who, while not grounded to an ancestral land base, nonetheless maintain their Native identities and struggle to reestablish their survival. Community recognition at a local level is, as a result, often difficult to establish or maintain, particularly for multiracial Native writers. When one is uprooted from ancestral lands, the next landscape under siege becomes the body and its identities.

The Indigenous body is more than flesh, blood, and bone; as both Womack and Warrior point out in their discussions of Native erotica, Native bodies are sites of both colonized conflict and passionate decolonization. Some of the earliest European iconography of the "New World" imagined the Americas as an exotic/erotic brown-skinned woman, open and yielding to the penetrating thrust of European imperialism. Invasion depended on the subjugation of Indigenous women and their frequent positions of authority as much as it depended on the erosion of affirming sexual pleasure and diversity of gender roles and identities. It's no surprise, then, that as part of a larger movement of Indigenous empowerment and decolonization, queer Native women like Joy Harjo (Muscogee), Chrystos (Menominee), and Beth Brant (Mohawk) have worked tirelessly to reclaim sexuality from centuries of myopic misogyny and homophobia.

Yet in speaking of sex and bodies, we must also attend to other dimensions of that relationship. These are the particular landscapes/bodyscapes that provoke some of the most incendiary discussions between Native intellectuals, between those who would see it fully mapped and clearly navigable, and those who desire a more amorphous and ambiguous terrain. The vexed relationships between individuals, tribal communities, and colonialist governments make easy answers or unyielding positions difficult to maintain, as unflinching attention on any one of these elements blinds the viewer to the powerful influences of the others. This is nowhere more evident than in the debates regarding the nature of sovereignty and Native cultural identities between Crow Creek Sioux scholar Elizabeth Cook-Lynn and the late mixed-blood (Choctaw-Cherokee) theorist Louis Owens. The nature of their often heated discussions regarding the place of the mixed-blood narrative in Native literature in many ways mirrors the role that blood quantum plays among Cherokees (and other early white-contact tribes) and those tribes who experienced the full impact of white colonization toward the latter half of the nineteenth century.

Cook-Lynn has long been warning Indian country of the dangers inherent in a strong focus on mixed-bloodedness rather than on sovereignty and asserting tribal land rights; she founded the *Wicazo Sa Review* in part to ensure that there was one venue for Native scholars and writers to focus their attention toward those latter aims. For Cook-Lynn, the stories we tell are, above all, moral stories, and the strongest ethical position that Native scholars and writers can take is one of dedication to the exercise of political, social, spiritual, and territorial sovereignty. As she noted in 1993,

If history is to tell us anything, it tells us that land seekers are, and always have been, the dangerous ones. And, if the study of literature tells us anything, it is that the stories hold the secrets to our lives as much as does the land. That is the dilemma in American literature and particularly in the Great Plains, and that is why the question, "Who gets to tell the stories?" is not only never far from our thoughts, it is the political question of our time. ("Who Gets to Tell the Stories" 64)

Cook-Lynn has also written about mixed-blood tribal groups and what she sees as their dangers to Indian communities—the unspoken implication being that they are no longer Indians or Indigenous themselves:

[Wallace Stegner's] description of the metis, or half-breeds, as a buffer race, which means that they are "a small, neutral race or state lying between potentially hostile ones," is, in terms of their relationship to Indians, the beginning of a deception which allows the turning away from what was really happening in Indian communities. The metis would hardly have been called neutral by any of the plains peoples and societies for whom the arranged marriage patterns of ancient times were a tool of cultural survival. Instead, the metis were and probably still are seen by native peoples as those who were *already converts* to the hostile and intruding culture simply through their marriage into it. (*Why I Can't Read Wallace Stegner and Other Essays* 35)

Similar to the rhetorical avoidances in Red Shirt's letter, Cook-Lynn's focus on mixed-bloodedness as *the problem* draws attention away from the colonial powers that turned intermarriage into a colonizing state. Bonita Lawrence (Mi'kmaq) points out in reference to urban mixed-bloods that because "it appears as if 'the problem' resides solely with mixed-bloodedness or urbanity, not with dehumanizing identity legislation[, t]he role that identity legislation has played in *creating* mixed-bloodedness (and urbanity) as problems for one's Indianness falls out of the picture" (*"Real" Indians and Others* 46). Cook-Lynn's focus on a purity/assimilation binary and conflation of multiraciality with lack of national spirit seems counterproductive to an argument on sovereignty that respects tribal specificity; it also betrays a particularly US bias that doesn't reflect the general recognition of the Métis in Canada on both social and political levels. The autobiographical writings of Maria Campbell, the poetry of Gregory Scofield, the political historiography of Howard Adams, and the work of other Métis writers and scholars have demonstrated time and again the degree to which their distinct communities have suffered under colonialism, yet without the same treaty and land-base protections of other First Nations peoples in Canada, writings that Cook-Lynn does not discuss or acknowledge.

Indeed, this larger argument overlooks what is one of the most fundamental concerns in the struggle for land and sovereignty: the *relationship* of the People to the earth. Womack's question—"Is human knowledge the only kind of knowledge there is?"—can guide us well here, as it speaks to the vital significance of the rest of creation to the lives and intellectual concerns of Indigenous peoples. While the land herself is of central concern to most Indigenous epistemologies, we don't know her outside of our relationship(s) to her (or to the other peoples who depend on her for survival). We often call her Mother; we— like the Animal-people and Tree-people—are her kindred, and ours is a relationship of reciprocity. She gives life and sustenance to us; we (ideally) give her respect, honour, and care. Beyond the earth itself are our relationships with other spirit-beings and peoples, all of which depend on attentive engagement; as Kimberly Blaeser (Anishinaabe) indicates, kinship on the microcosmic level gives evidence of the health and significance of the macrocosm: "Perhaps we rejoice at the smallest encounter of relatedness because it signals the greater" (unpublished manuscript).[8] While the language of treaties all too often erases relational understandings and replaces them with the Eurowestern language of land-as-object, the guiding purpose behind the defence of treaty rights is as much (or more) about ensuring the ongoing maintenance of the ceremonies and rituals that ensure good relationships with the rest of creation as it is the defence of limited natural resources.

When Cook-Lynn focuses on land and treaty rights to the exclusion of kinship, she leaves important questions unaddressed. Louis Owens takes up some of these questions when he responds to Cook-Lynn's assertions; in doing so, he illuminates some of the different ways in which various tribal nations have experienced the ravages of colonialism, yet he falls into something of the same avoidance of kinship concerns. Owens comes from communities deeply impacted by diaspora—the Choctaw and Cherokee removals and their subsequent social upheavals—and he approaches Native literature and issues with a significantly different perspective than does Cook-Lynn, whose people have remained generally in the same geographic location for many generations (and who themselves have long been regarded by many of their Indian neighbours such as the Omahas and Poncas as imperialists). For Owens, Native self-determination isn't simply about the physical land itself; it's also about the interior sociopsychic landscape:

> Tribal people have deep bonds with the earth, with sacred places that bear
> the bones and stories that tell them who they are, where they came from,
> and how to live in the world they see around them. But of course almost

all tribal people also have migration stories that say we came from some-place else before finding home. The very fact that tribal nations from the Southeast were so extraordinarily successful in making so-called Indian Territory a much beloved home after the horrors of Removal and before the horrors of the Civil War underscores the ability of indigenous Americans to move and in doing so to carry with them whole cultures within memory and story. (*Mixedblood Messages* 164)

Owens responds to Cook-Lynn's assumption that the most valid Indian narra-tives are those embedded in the ancestral homelands of the writer's commun-ity; such an assumption would erase any land ethic or spiritual relationship of those Indians removed from their homelands by the US government and would certainly erase the voices of nearly every Indian in what is now Oklahoma:

there are indeed countless thousands of people in the positions of a Momaday, Silko, [Thomas] King, Vizenor, and so forth: people who do not live in reservation communities and who, if they are artists, may create art about urban or rural mixedblood experience at a distance from their tribal communities. Should the stories of such people, the products of colonial America's five hundred years of cultural wars against Indigenous peoples, not be told because they do not fit the definition of what one Lakota critic thinks is tribally "real"? Are their stories not ones that "matter" or have "meaning"? Contrary to what Cook-Lynn asserts, this is a powerful liter-ature of resistance, a countervoice to the dominant discourse that would reduce Indians to artifactual commodities useful to tourist industries. (158–59)

While Owens perhaps oversimplifies Cook-Lynn's point—after all, rooted-ness in the land is a central ethic of most Indigenous worldviews—he quite accurately represents the reality of a large number of Indigenous people in this hemisphere.

Yet Owens' argument, too, suffers from a lack of engagement with kinship principles, namely, because he places individual and family stories of displace-ment at the centre of analytical concern, asserting the Indianness of "move-ment," "distance," and the "products of colonial America's five hundred years of cultural wars" without placing this "powerful literature of resistance" firmly within a conversation about the relationship of the People to one another, to their histories, their futures, and to the rest of creation. In challenging Cook-Lynn's erasure of these narratives of motion and displacement, Owens goes to the other side, representing motion as a push away from the land that features so significantly in the orature and written literatures of the People, not a back-and-forth movement of departure *and* return, separation *and* (re)integration.

Owens' voice is most resonant, his understanding most incisive, when he engages specific places, specific voices, and his relationships to them. He embeds his response to Cook-Lynn in a larger discussion of his family's complicated "blood trails" across Oklahoma, Mississippi, and California, including photographs, family stories, and reflections on the relationships between those travellers of the past and his own experiences as an inheritor of those experiences. Even then, however, the "blood trails" Owens follows here exist at a distance from this specificity of landed relationship, except as a reflection of past connection or as a more generic commentary about large-scale Indigenous values related to land and history. He writes, "If loss of parents or grandparents or tribal community is the residue of difficult history, then you recreate community beginning with the nucleus of family and extending through memory and imagination and nation" (165). Yet when a family, a community, or a nation is fully removed from the land of its origins, that land doesn't cease to shape the People's cosmos, even when they're building new relationships with a new land; their links to it change, but they rarely vanish, just as separation from a loved one inevitably changes but doesn't necessarily erase our relationship to that person. "Memory and imagination" are important, but so too are the relational rituals that bind the People to both their rights and responsibilities within the larger familial web. Besides, even migration accounts take place in a world of identifiable features—each landscape has a distinctive personality, and as the People come to understand that personality and their own relationship to it, they weave it into their understanding of themselves and the rest of creation.

The Cook-Lynn/Owens debate, then, is less about which vision of the purpose of Native literature is "right" or "wrong," but how both arguments are limited by their partial attention to the principles within which both Indigenous lands and identities are rooted. Just as Red Shirt's argument about Pequot survival attends only to her own kinship contexts and not those of the Pequots, Mohegans, Paugussetts, Paucatucks, and Schaghticokes in whose land she now lives, both Cook-Lynn and Owens place their own contextualized experiences as the sole defining lens of North American Indigenousness, to the diminishment of all.

A Sacred Trust

What, then, might be a useful approach to thinking about ethical Native literary criticism, one that (hopefully) avoids the blistering burn of fire left neglected? For me, at this time, the best approach is about relationships, about attending to the cultural, historical, political, and intellectual contexts from which Indigenous texts emerge. This engagement provides a rich range of interpretive possibility, and it sensitizes us to the multiple relationships and contexts that make such study morally meaningful. It reflects many of the complicated realities influencing our lives, not just theoretical considerations. Cherokee literary critic Sean Teuton's essay in *Reasoning Together* speaks directly to this concern when he reminds us, through the consideration of the writing of Native prisoners in Auburn Prison, that Indigenous writing is, at its heart, a political assertion of the "going on" addressed earlier by Amanda Cobb. It is, in all the best ways, a *worldly* exercise of peoplehood and continuity:

> I thus argue . . . that an ethical American Indian theory must enter the world to change and be changed by the world. To do so, I turn to our intellectual tradition of historically engaged political writing to introduce a theory of Native praxis. Then, in closing, I return to the classroom—to the writing of Indigenous prisoners—to demonstrate this theory. What drives Indian intellectuals to political action? In moments such as described above, when we are overwhelmed by the experience of Native criminalization—and, more broadly, other observations of anti-Indianism—American Indian scholars awaken politically and begin putting their ideas to work. I term that demand for justice "the callout." (165)

In [*Reasoning Together*, the members of the Native Critics Collective] are, I hope, expressing our own versions of "the callout," and doing so in a way that does honour to those whose own voices have been (and remain) silenced, marginalized, and unheard.

Teuton and others call out; it's an invitation for response. This project expresses, in its own small way, peoplehood in practice. . . . The living kinship traditions and literatures of each People—from ancient ceremonialism to Christian syncretism and pan-Native perspectives, from birch-bark scrolls and wampum belts to poems, novels, and web pages—rather than being perceived as a frozen set of principles or texts of merely ethnographic interest, are instead seen in their own enduring beauty as a strong but flexible structure that gives guidance for continuity even in the winds of change. The green cedar bends with the wind and endures; when the sapwood dies and the tree grows rigid, sometimes even the slightest wind can bring it crashing down. Dead wood burns too quickly; green wood warms longer. Trusting in the principles of kinship and their relevance to our lives today and tomorrow keeps our work flexible, because the roots are strong. We won't always agree with one another, and that, too, is a vital aspect of this work: it's important to remember that dissent is an important aspect of self-determination. Debate and discussion are time-honoured intellectual and social practices shared in the older political traditions of most Indigenous peoples in the Americas, with status conferred on eloquence, not coercion. To return to earlier reflections, by contextualizing Red Shirt's invective against the Connecticut tribes and the Cook-Lynn/Owens debate, we shift from a discursive model of conflict and silencing to one of respectful relationship. The flames might burn white-hot, but they leave rich ash behind. The seeds that survive will be strong . . . and there's room in this fertile soil for many seeds.

This essay ends in Fire.

Kinship—in all its messy complexity and diversity—gives us the best measure of interpretive possibility, as it speaks to the fact that our literatures, like our various peoples, are *alive*. The decolonization imperative gives us hopeful purpose for our "going on." Our council fires burn still. Tobacco, cedar, sweetgrass, and sage still rise up in cleansing smoke and prayer. The heat of passion connects us with others in body and spirit, driving away cold shame and isolation, just as our embodied words burn these connections onto the page, onto the heart, onto the mind. There can be no higher ethical purpose than to answer "the callout" and tend to those kin-fires; it's a sacred trust.

It's what we do for family.

Notes

This essay was first published in Craig S. Womack, Daniel Heath Justice, and Christopher B. Teuton, eds., *Reasoning Together: The Native Critics Collective* (Norman: U of Oklahoma P, 2008).

1. See, for example, Kilpatrick, *Night Has a Naked Soul*, especially 99–100; Conley, *Cherokee Medicine Man*, especially 68–70; and Lewis and Jordan, *Creek Indian Medicine Ways*, especially 48–50.
2. The fact is, most Cherokees—and a good percentage of other Indians in North America—are at least nominally Christian, and for most of these folks, there's no necessary conflict between their Christian beliefs and their identities as Native peoples. Besides, the last five-hundred-plus years have seen the gradual indigenization of Christianity among many peoples in the Americas, so, like European languages, one can no longer accurately claim the absolute alienness of these invader ways. To willingly *choose* one particular path among many, or to bring together elements of different traditions in a way that still affirms the nationhood and self-determination of the community, is a very different thing from being forced by outsiders to walk a narrow, painful path to the exclusion of others.
3. I've quoted Thomas King's comment on these concerns ad nauseum, but it's still relevant here: "The truth about stories is that that's all we are." See King, *The Truth about Stories*, 3.

4. In possession of the Native Critics Collective.

5. This anthology of extant responses of Aztecs and their descendants to the Spanish invasion is a powerful testament to the endurance of Native voices against nearly overwhelming oppression. A more recent collection, *Mesoamerican Voices* (ed. Restall, Sousa, and Terraciano), gives further context for the literary responses to this bloody era.

6. Pequot survivors resisted erasure, however, and maintained their traditions and name, even two centuries later, although their invisibility to outsiders often continued under various institutional means. O'Connell writes of many reasons why New England Natives were marginalized in later years. Many of these reasons focus heavily on the Pequots' loss of lands and economic independence, forcing migration to those places with the best available jobs: "Censuses notoriously miss such people. Those people who might be found and who might have identified themselves as 'Indian,' or by the name of a cultural group such as 'Mohegan' or 'Pequot,' could not have been registered in most federal censuses in the nineteenth century because there was no category for them. One could only be 'white,' 'colored,' or 'mulatto'" (*On Our Own Ground* lxiii).

7. Intermarriage has been embraced by many Cherokees, as well as by the majority of non-Native "Generikees" who claim Indian identity through a Cherokee great-great-grandmother (who is often a "princess"), thus leading to the proliferation of jokes in Indian country that have as their premise the diluted blood quantum of Cherokees. Intermarriage is not, however, universally embraced among Cherokees, especially among some traditionalists, who have long asserted that such practices endanger both Cherokee identity and the nation's sovereignty. See, for example, Sturm's *Blood Politics*, a fascinating study of the complications of Cherokee identity.

8. In possession of the Native Critics Collective.

32

Indigenous Storytelling, Truth-Telling, and Community Approaches to Reconciliation

Jeff Corntassel, Chaw-win-is, and T'lakwadzi

Indigenous storytelling is connected to our homelands and is crucial to the cultural and political resurgence of Indigenous nations. According to Maori scholar Linda Smith, "'The talk' about the colonial past is embedded in our political discourses, our humour, poetry, music, storytelling, and other common sense ways of passing on both a narrative of history and an attitude about history" (19). For example, when conveying community narratives of history to future generations, Nuu-chah-nulth peoples have relied on *haa-huu-pah* as teaching stories or sacred living histories that solidify ancestral and contemporary connections to place.[1] As Nuu-chah-nulth Elder Cha-chin-sun-up states, *haa-huu-pah* are "What we do when we get up every day to make the world good." *Haa-huu-pah* are not fairy tales or entertaining stories for children—they are lived values that form the basis for Indigenous governance and regeneration. The experiential knowledge and living histories of *haa-huu-pah* comprise part of the core teaching that Indigenous families transmit to future generations.

The state of Canada offers a very different version of history than those of Indigenous nations—one that glosses over the colonial legacies of removing Indigenous nations. The residential school era, which can be said to begin in 1874, is one example of the racist policies that were imposed on Indigenous people.[2] Designed to strip Indigenous people of their languages and cultures, the residential schools were administered by the government of Canada and run by four well-known denominations or churches. By the time the last residential school closed in 1996, over one hundred thousand Indigenous children had been forcibly removed from their homes.[3]

According to Paulette Regan, Euro-Canadian scholar and academic liaison to the Truth and Reconciliation Commission of Canada (TRC), settler Canadians have much to account for:

> Settler violence against Indigenous people is woven into the fabric of Canadian history in an unbroken thread from past to present that we must now unravel, unsettling our comfortable assumptions about the past. At the same time, we must work as Indigenous allies to "restory" the dominant culture version of history; that is, we must make decolonizing space for Indigenous history—counter-narratives of diplomacy, law, peacemaking practices—as told by Indigenous peoples themselves. (2)

Given the monumental task ahead to restory the settler version of history, this essay explores the structure of the Truth and Reconciliation Commission along with some of the criticisms that have emerged recently from residential school survivors regarding the shortcomings of Canada's attempts at reparations for residential school survivors in the form of Common Experience Payments (CEP). We anchor our discussion in *haa-huu-pah* as a form of truth-telling in order to demonstrate how Indigenous stories of resilience are critical to the resurgence of our communities. Moreover, *haa-huu-pah* are fundamental to teaching our families and communities who we are and how to govern ourselves on this land, intending to lead us toward action. After all, "Awareness of trust ... compels some kind of action" (Waziyatawin 11). Processes of restorying and truth-telling are not effective without some larger community-centred, decolonizing actions behind them.

Thus, *haa-huu-pah* signify a starting point for renewing Indigenous family and community responsibilities in the ongoing struggle for Indigenous justice and freedom. *Haa-huu-pah* also represent an alternative to the Canadian state's vision for reconciliation, which seeks to legitimize the status quo rather than to rectify injustice for Indigenous communities.

As Taiaiake Alfred and Jeff Corntassel point out, "[T]here is a danger in allowing colonization to be the only story of Indigenous lives. It must be recognized that colonialism is a narrative in which the Settler's power is the fundamental reference and assumption, inherently limiting Indigenous freedom and imposing a view of the world that is but an outcome or perspective on that power" (601). A restorying process for Indigenous peoples entails questioning the imposition of colonial histories on our communities. The origin of the name

Canada provides some clues regarding the scope of injustices that need to be rectified before restitution and reconciliation can actually be achieved. Alfred, a Kanien'kehá:ka (Mohawk) scholar, reminds us that the word Canada is derived from a Kanien'kehá:ka term, Kanatiens, which means "They sit in our village." A contemporary translation of this term would be "squatter." Given the origins of Canada, what can descendants of squatters or settlers offer Indigenous peoples by way of reconciliation? Where does one start in terms of reconciling Canada?

This research project on restorying Indigenous justice started shortly after Cherokee Nation scholar Jeff Corntassel participated in a 2008 TRC conference in Montreal, focusing on the TRC's potential for trust-telling and public engagement as it began its five-year mandate. Questions posed by Lyackson First Nation scholar Qwul'sih'yah'maht were especially thought-provoking: What will the TRC do with survivors' stories? And how will the resilience and power of these stories be represented in the testimony? After reflecting on the colonial legacy of boarding schools in the US and their detrimental impacts on Indigenous nations, Corntassel saw the need for intergeneration survivors in Canada to speak with each other within a community context and learn from other survivors' stories of resistance and resilience. Around this time, T'lakwadzi, a Kwakwaka'wakw student, approached Corntassel about serving as a faculty mentor on reconciliation via the University of Victoria's LE,NONET research apprentice program.[4] As T'lakwadzi and Corntassel set up a research project that entailed interviewing Indian residential school survivors, they realized that by emphasizing the cultural and spiritual dimensions of survivors' experiences this research could serve as an alternative to the political/legal constraints of the TRC process.

During the summer of 2009, T'lakwadzi conducted seven in-depth interviews with residential school survivors and encouraged each participant to focus on the community, family, and individual impacts of residential school on their lives rather than framing the discussion around Indigenous reconciliation with Canada. Nuu-chah-nulth doctoral student Chaw-win-is was asked to join this project after the interviews had been completed in order to provide some insights into Nuu-chah-nulth perspectives on survivor truth-telling and to draw on her expertise in *haa-huh-pah*. This collaboration of Indigenous scholars and survivors from different nations and generations offers unique insights into community notions of truth-telling and justice.

Overall, while the Indian Residential School Settlement Agreement and the formation of the TRC are designed to address the devastating legacies of residential schools, they run the risk of framing these questions in a narrow way that neglects to fully appreciate the ongoing impacts of residential schools on communities, families, and individuals, and the lived experiences of resilience and resurgence that need to be shared with intergenerational survivors and other Indigenous peoples. State-centred processes of reconciliation attempt to repair the damages caused by residential schools but do little to reunify and regenerate families and communities dispersed and dislocated by the trauma of these schools. As Nuu-chah-nulth Elder Barney Williams Jr. explains, "Our Nuu-chah-nulth methodologies are missing from the TRC—our ways, like many other Native peoples' ways, have sustained us for centuries and will continue to do so if we continue to use them in our families and communities."

In this [essay] we focus on Indigenous methodologies and experiential knowledge as a counter-narrative to the Canadian state's notion of reconciliation. The section that follows lays out the structure and mandate of the TRC along with theoretical and applied approaches to the concept of reconciliation. A subsequent section on restorying justice focuses on the methodology and the findings from the seven interviews conducted by T'lakwadzi. Drawing on the Quu'asa family way and storytelling methodologies, we view these interviews as living histories and truths that need to be conveyed to future generations so that movements toward decolonization and justice can be realized. Additionally, the seven interviews serve as a counter-narrative to the political/ legal testimonies of the TRC and are contemporary versions of *haa-huu-pah* as well as community-centred visions for resurgence and renewal.

The Apparatus of Official Reconciliation in Canada

Websites relating to the "Indian Residential School Settlement Agreement" epitomize some of the confusion over the notion of reconciliation in Canada. One such website has a photograph of what appears to be a Yonega or Maamaathni ("white settler" in Cherokee and "boat people that have no land and live on the ocean" in Nuu-chah-nulth) arm outstretched and cupping a small eagle feather. The caption states "The healing continues." Just what is the message being conveyed, here? Is it the dominant society either giving something back to Indigenous peoples or holding something for us? More importantly, where are the Indigenous peoples in this picture? Are they willing to receive what is being offered? And by what authority does the Government of Canada, as a colonial entity illegally occupying Indigenous homelands, make such an offer of redress?

The Truth and Reconciliation Commission of Canada was formed on 1 June 2008 to address the genocidal legacy of residential schools resulting in the forced removal of Indigenous children from their families and homelands. The TRC is the cornerstone of May 2006 Indian Residential School Agreement,[5] which was in "response to numerous class action claims involving over 120,000 individual litigants" (Morse 283) and signed by the Government of Canada, the Assembly of First Nations, regional Inuit representatives, representatives of the four churches who once administered the residential schools, and the several lawyers involved in the negotiation process. While the TRC was sidelined for over a year due to the resignations of the former chair and commissioners, three new commissioners were appointed in June 2009, and the TRC has begun to pursue its mandate once again by undertaking a truth and reconciliation process with Indigenous survivors, which will include educating the general public about residential schools and producing a comprehensive report along with recommendations based on their findings at the conclusion of the five-year mandate. This is the first TRC ever to focus exclusively on crimes committed against Indigenous children, and it has a five-year time frame in which to undertake its mission.

Despite the comprehensiveness of the Indian Residential Schools Settlement Agreement, a question that we posed at the beginning of this section still lingers: where are the Indigenous peoples in this picture? One response came in November 2008, when Indigenous Elders from the Indian Residential School Survivors Society (IRSSS) gathered in Calgary to lay out their perspectives on the TRC and issue an official statement to the government of Canada.[6] Here are three of their main points:

- Today we gathered because of our children and grandchildren. . . . You are keepers of who we are. To Canadians we say: Take responsibility for educating yourself and your children.
- The TRC has to address the need for ongoing healing. Once the stories start to flow we will have embarked on a journey across a tidal wave of pain. Care is being provided for persons preparing to offer their truth to the commission and we would ask that spiritual support be available for people after they have presented.
- The TRC needs to recognize where all survivors, families, communities, and nations are in terms of readiness for reconciliation. We must go slowly. We cannot force reconciliation.

The IRSSS statements highlight the need for a community-based impetus to move beyond the TRC mandate toward restorying at the family and community levels. Additionally, there is a call for youth and other inter-generational survivors to be involved in the process. Furthermore, spiritual support, not just monetary support, is crucial for all people involved in the process. These recommendations might be implemented in a number of ways. The 2009 community-led demolition of Peake Hall Residential School in Port Alberni, British

Columbia, offers insight into one community-centred event emphasizing the connection between truth-telling and acting to restore justice.

On 10 February 2009, the demolition of a former residential school building took place on the territory of Tseshaht First Nation. Peake Hall had originally opened its doors in 1920 and was closed by 1972. During its fifty-two-year operation, Peake Hall was regarded as one of the worst Canadian residential schools in terms of the violence it imposed on Indigenous children: its operations produced "stories whose basis still keeps survivors awake at night, in fear, shame and dread" (*ciquiuł* 1). The Tseshaht Nation hosted a ceremony for all survivors and their families (including other Indigenous communities impacted by the violence of Peake Hall) and started by holding a pre-demolition day at Peake Hall, "using traditional and cultural methods to take the power away from the school once and for all" (*ciquiuł* 2). Crowbars and sledgehammers were also provided to anyone who wanted to pry off pieces of the building for a burning. Throughout the day, two fires were kept going so that survivors could burn "pieces of the discarded siding from the building" (*ciquiuł* 8). Sage and cedar were also burned with the pieces, in order to "cleanse and allow the trapped spirits to be finally freed" (*ciquiuł* 8). Ray Guno, a sixty-four-year-old Nisga'a from Terrace, reflected on the demolition ceremony: "Ten guys I know, some of them my closest buddies, died in the '50s. Not from natural causes, but from sexual, emotional, and physical abuses. Not to have come down [to tear apart the old school] would have cheapened their lives and their experiences" (Winks). After the demolition, families came together for a community feast in Maht Mahs. With over two hundred places set, there was only standing room available. According to Tseshaht Elder, Willard Gallic, who led the ceremony, "I feel very comfortable that what was set out was accomplished. Listening to the survivors helped us to help them" (*ciquiuł* 8). This event is just one example of restorying and resurgence occurring within Indigenous communities as a way to counter the ongoing colonial legacies of residential schools. The community demolition of Peake Hall demonstrates the kind of political and spiritual or healing work that is needed in order to begin working toward restitution. Indigenous peoples acting together in this way by linking political action and cultural teachings begin to draw the focus back to community and family processes of restorying justice and history, as a means to challenge the colonial relationship with Canada.

According to the preamble for the TRC mandate, "There is an emerging and compelling desire to put the events of the past behind us so that we can work towards a stronger and healthier future. . . . The truth of our common experiences will help set our spirits free and pave the way to reconciliation" ("Mandate of the Truth and Reconciliation Commission"). The stated desire to "put events of the past behind us" and unite a deeply divided society expresses the underlying logic of most truth commissions, which view reconciliation processes in terms of a "preparedness of people to anticipate a shared future" through forgiveness, but also shared strategies for moving forward collectively to repair existing relationships (Rigby 12). However, as anthropologist Stephanie Irlbacher-Fox points out, "The result is that, by conflating specific unjust events, policies, and laws with 'history,' what is unjust becomes temporally separate from the present, unchangeable. This narrows options for restitution: we cannot change the past" (33). Such a convenient framing of the issue allows political leaders and settler populations to deal with residual guilt on their own terms, which often follows all too familiar scripts of "forgiving and forgetting," "moving on from the past," and "unifying as a country," all the while brushing aside any deeper discussions of restitution or justice. Reconciliation becomes a way for the dominant culture to reinscribe the status quo rather than to make amends for previous injustices.

According to Alfred, "The logic of reconciliation as justice is clear: without massive restitution, including land, financial transfers, and other forms of assistance to compensate for past harms and continuing injustices committed against our peoples, reconciliation would permanently enshrine colonial injustices and is itself a further injustice" (152). Any meaningful reconciliation effort must confront colonialism not only historically but as part of an ongoing process that continues to impact present generations of Indigenous youth and families. It is an uncomfortable process, but, as scholars have noted, regardless of which truth-seeking strategy is chosen, one must come to terms with "the unavoidable tensions, the lack of tidiness involved in any response to large scale evil" (Verwoerd 265). As philosopher Claudia Card states, "Sometimes it is wise to reconcile only conditionally on the offenders living up to obligations of reparation or restitution" (179).

Not only do state applications of reconciliation tend to relegate all committed injustices to the past while attempting to legitimate the status quo, but there is another underlying motive at play: certainty. As anthropologist Paul Nadasdy points out, "Without certainty of title, there is always the danger that a corporation might lose its investment as the result of a lawsuit brought against it by aboriginal people" (86). Given an overarching desire to secure a stable land base to facilitate corporate investment, the Government of Canada, as well as certain provinces, including British Columbia, have begun to use the language of reconciliation in negotiations with Indigenous peoples (for example, in the BC Treaty Process, as well as in the proposed "New Relationship" legislation) in order to establish the "certainty" of a land claim in such a way as to facilitate the extinguishment of original Indigenous title to the land.[7] When state objectives, such as certainty and legitimation, tend to override questions of justice, it becomes clear that any pursuit of reconciliation with the state must first acknowledge the asymmetrical power relationships between states and Indigenous peoples, which can so easily derail questions of justice and decolonization.

At its core, reconciliation is a Western concept with religious connotations of restoring one's relationship to God. Given that reconciliation is not an Indigenous concept, our overarching goal as Indigenous peoples should not be to restore an asymmetrical relationship with the state but to restory our communities toward justice.

There is no word for reconciliation in Nuu-chah-nulth. The Nuu-chah-nulth word *oo yoothloothl*, or "looking after" or "looking beyond," exemplifies a commitment to move forward or beyond the problem. According to Nuu-chah-nulth Elder Barney Williams Jr., when communities need to deal with challenges, the process begins with family. *Hishimyoothoothl* means "to gather our family." This means the family will meet to discuss the problem and together they will strategize how best to deal with the situation. There may be several meetings with families before they reach out to the broader Nuu-chah-nulth communities. For Nuu-chah-nulth, the next step may mean planning a larger gathering called *nuushitl* or *maathmaya*, where we call on other communities to both witness and rectify the situation. Working within the familial system is especially adhered to when dealing with children and child-rearing practices. At the closing of these feasts or gatherings, the Nuu-chah-nulth will often say the words *yoots pah nah ahts mish*, or "We will be careful as we go." This is said with love and care as relatives leave to travel back to their homes, reminding everyone of our responsibility to travel home safely and for each of us to live every day in *iisaak*, in a respectful way.

Processes of renewing community responsibilities through feasts or gatherings are not necessarily available in the TRC structure. Additionally, rather than use the state-centred language of reconciliation, our focus is on family-centred community resurgence and restorying justice. In the section that follows, we discuss some of the findings from our interviews of seven residential school survivors from Nuu-chah-nulth and Kwakwaka'wakw First Nations.

Restorying beyond the TRC Mandate

Legal scholar Teresa Godwin Phelps has outlined the ways in which truth commissions can provide justice through storytelling; among them, the restoration of dignity and "the ability to speak in one's own voice," the "correction" of false stories, the communication of the "experience of pain and suffering between people who normally cannot understand each other," and the occasioning of forms of remembering, which can heal and even "actualize a radically new kind of constitutive history for an emerging democracy" (55–56).

While Phelps' list includes some important aspects of storytelling, the emphasis is still largely on forgiveness and unifying societies in relation to the state. Furthermore, there is no reference here to the issue of Indigenous peoples and land. The TRC was designed to fit within a Western model of justice where individuals may seek compensation (usually financial) for their losses. The issue of land is treated as a separate issue from that of the residential school, ignoring the fact that the issues with which survivors from the residential school era contend are rooted in the forced removal of entire families and communities from their homelands.

Lyackson scholar Qwul'sih'yah'maht (Robina Thomas) outlines a storytelling methodology that is useful for our purposes: "Delmar Johnnie once said that it is such a shame that every time someone who went to residential school dies without telling his or her stories, our government and the churches look more innocent. Telling these stories is a form of resistance to colonization. . . . I believe that storytelling respects and honours people while simultaneously documenting their reality" (241–42, 244). As Qwul'sih'yah'maht's words indicate, restorying can facilitate both truth-telling and acts of resistance. It can also expose some blind spots in Phelps' discourse on storytelling, namely that Indigenous restorying processes cannot be disentangled from ongoing relationships to their homelands.

Elaborating on a storytelling methodology, Chaw-win-is uses a "Quu'asa family way," which is an Indigenous-centred methodology presently used within Nuu-chah-nulth communities as a way of regenerating *haa-huu-pah* through relational accountability and truth-telling. This Quu'asa family way views *haa-huu-pah* as a layer of community governance and leadership that emphasizes the renewal of Indigenous roles and responsibilities to the land and community. Using a Quu'asa family way storytelling methodology allows us to draw linkages between themes of land, family, living histories, and acts of resistance, while offering an alternative narrative to state-centred reconciliation presented by the TRC.

In the summer of 2009, T'lakwadzi (Kwakwaka'wakw) conducted interviews with seven male residential school survivors in Nuu-chah-nulth and Kwakwaka'wakw communities.[8] While there are always risks in discussing the traumatic experiences that occurred in residential schools, we tried to reduce the risk by providing free access to culturally relevant counselling options for each participant along with frequent follow-up phone calls by T'lakwadzi. T'lakwadzi's follow-ups with the participants also allowed each person to double-check the transcripts and express any reservations about wanting his stories told. All of the participants emphatically stated that they wanted their stories told and stressed in different ways and that there was no room within the current TRC process for a community perspective to be really heard.

Using a Quu'asa family way storytelling methodology, we identified four main themes that each participant addresses to varying degrees: homeland, family, restitution, and restorying. These concepts were all interrelated and offered some insights into how community-based restorying differs from state-based reconciliation efforts.

Homeland

When asked whether land should be a part of a reconciliation process, Hayawolthlit (Wally Samuel Sr.) from Ahousaht First Nation expressed concerns that the reconciliation process was ignoring the fact that most survivors were currently living outside their home territory (often in urban areas): "What would make it genuine if they were actually doing this, talking to the individuals. And not to the nations, because eighty percent of us live away from home. Especially residential school people and their families are all away from home."

James Quatell (Wei Wai Kum First Nation) went even further by pointing out that the reconciliation process purposefully excluded land from the discussion:

> **T'lakwadzi:** What about land? Do you think land will and should be part of the TRC?
>
> **James Quatell:** Not sure that anything can be done because that subject falls under the treaty aspects. It is not that I don't think it should be a part of it all, but they have gone and capped it. They have capped it under the one word—reconciliation.
>
> **T:** But do you think it should be a part of the process?
>
> **JQ:** It should be the biggest part of all because all the people were taken from their land and resources and they would have had that if they were not taken from their communities and villages. We weren't educated to do this. We weren't educated to get all these resources, the education of it was never going to be there. So how can I say that never affected it, it did!

Dan Quatell (Wei Wai Kum First Nation) also described the importance of homeland to his family and community and how these relationships have been disrupted:

T'lakwadzi: Moving on to the next question, which is about land, should land be part of the TRC?

Dan Quatell: Definitely, look at what the government is doing to our lands, look how big we are and look at how small our land is becoming. We're fighting for our land, I can remember my grandfather having two or three big houses down at the spit and now we're fighting for that land. The land where Save On is, it was and is band land. But they say we have to go to court for now, but we allowed the Old Elm school and the church to go on our land and now they are saying it is not our land.

As the above responses indicate, for Indigenous peoples, our homelands are our future and cannot be separated from our grounding in community, languages, living histories, and ceremonial lives. These interconnected relationships all form the foundation for effective resistance to contemporary colonialism.

Family

When asked about the impacts of residential schools on intergenerational survivors, Kwi-ahts-ah-pulth from Ahousaht First Nation spoke bluntly about the importance of family members in the reconciliation process:

T'lakwadzi: What about family members, first- and second-generation family members that didn't go to residential schools; just wondering how you think they can be included in the equation, or if they should be included in the equation at all?

Kwi-ahts-ah-pulth: That is a tough one because there is still effects with our siblings, with our children, with our nephews, nieces, our grandchildren—there is still effects. But I can still see possible, possibility they could be. Playing devil's advocate, thinking from the perspective of the government that would have to pay, there is no way that they would, and I understand that, I understand why. But in lieu of that maybe what the government can be doing to support the families that want to heal themselves, those of a first, second, and third generation and the generations of children and grandchildren that have gone to residential schools, that some programs should be made available for them to understand the impacts of what residential schools did to their siblings, their parents, to their aunts, uncles, and grandparents. Get a firmer understanding of what transpired and what happened, that is one way of parties possibly working together for that benefit.

T: If you had any suggestions for the process, what would they be? Or if you could frame the TRC the way you would like it to be how would that look?

K: Make it real, I would want the committee to listen to everyone's story, that every life, every person, that it is important to hear everyone's story. Not only hear their stories but find solutions; how can we help this person, how can we help the community? How can we help this family? What is the best way? This band is in so much debt and this chief has a lot of wealth. So we have adapted very well to that European concept and business concept of money. In my opinion, we need to get back to our grassroots and our traditions and cultures and the wealth of a person and the wealth of a community is family, is the culture, is the traditional teachings. It is the land, the sea, the resources—that is what we talk about when we say how "rich" a chief is! Because a chief can be very rich if he has access or practices his access to the resources in his territory. There is an abundance of it! The wealth is our culture, it is our naming ceremonies, our potlatches, our wedding ceremonies, our memorial potlatches, it is our masks, it is all the wonders of art that come from an artist who has great teachings and knowledge of practice of what mother nature has given us. To me that is more real, and we need to get back to those ways, and those kinds of teachings is the way we are going to be able to move forward as a person, as a family, as a community.

Hayawolthlit (Ahousaht First Nation) spoke of how residential school traumas were being passed down through the generations and the need to address this reality within community:

They should offer programs that include all family members. Again I'd like to see more local planned programs for families. A lot of us don't realize [what] our attitudes are, that we do it to our own kids. Stand up, straight, sit down, all those stringent rules we had, we can't go on until the dishes are washed, but this is normal.

Even since the last federally funded residential school closed in 1996, Indigenous families have continued to be under attack by government agencies, such as the Ministry of Children and Family Development. In fact, there are more Indigenous children in government care today than at the height of residential schools (Matas). Despite comprising only 4.4 percent of the overall population in British Columbia, Indigenous children make up a staggering 52 percent of children in government care (Matas). Furthermore, Indigenous children are 6.3 times more likely to be admitted into care and, once accepted into care, 12.4 times more likely to remain in care (Matas). These statistics offer a sobering view of the current state of reconciliation in Canada involving Indigenous families, who continue to struggle against the contemporary manifestations of colonialism in Canada.

Restitution

A common theme in the interviews around issues of compensation for years spent in residential school through the Common Experience Payments (CEP) was one of representation. James Quatell (Wei Wai Kum First Nation) described what he witnessed at the consultation meetings:

> Mr. Fontaine's answer to one of the elders from the Squamish Nation [who asked]: "where did you get such a ludicrous figure that you're taking this to the Supreme Court?" His answer was: "Oh no, no, no, this is not written in stone. This is just for him to take there and negotiate on your behalf." It was $10,000 for finding out you were there for the first year and $3,000 for every year after that. The retired Supreme Court judge was going in and they told us the decision would not be made until around March of the following year; however, a decision was made in November of that same year. Which was way before the said time. Guess what, it was ten and three. My question to Mr. Fontaine was because I never was consulted. I can take you to court for misrepresentation.

Another theme in the interviews was the inadequacy of the CEP amount. After all, in 1989, after investigations demonstrated that priests physically and sexually abused white minors at the Mount Cashel Orphanage in St John's, Newfoundland, between 1951 and 1960, the compensation being offered to the victims was significant (Burns). Between 1996 and 2004, $27 million was paid by the Newfoundland government and the Christian Brothers in compensation to approximately eighty-five Mount Cashel victims (*CBC News*). This is roughly $270,000 for each victim of residential school abuse, which is far more than the current CEP being offered to Indigenous survivors.

When asked if he received the CEP monies, Hayawolthlit (Ahousaht First Nation) stated: "Yes, but it did not make life any better [lots of laughter]. The sad part is we missed out on a lot of cultural aspects, we were put in a mixed environment, we couldn't speak our languages, we all had to speak English. I got some of the money but not enough [laughs again]."

Luke George (Tseshaht First Nation) elaborates on the points that the CEP money does not begin to account for cultural loss:

> Even with that money it still didn't make me feel better. [If] the government really want to reconcile with us they would make funding for language more accessible. I cannot leave my job to go and focus on learning the language because I need to make a living. Maybe take a certain time off each year so we can learn a language. Something bigger and more real than just talk, because it is just talk all the time.

Survivors also reflected on the impact that the CEP monetary payout had on the individuals, families, and communities receiving the money. Due to some deep misunderstandings regarding the extent of "historical unresolved trauma" within Indigenous communities as well as "ongoing multigenerational processes of dispossession and oppression," the CEP process runs the risk of exacerbating these unresolved personal and community traumas given that it does not address the roots of Indigenous survivor suffering (Alfred 19). While adequate restitution cannot be denied to Indigenous peoples simply because of historically unresolved trauma, it points to the need for deeper community-centred processes, such as the burning of Peake Hall, to facilitate healing and renewal among families and individuals. The following survivor testimonies regarding the impact of the CEP must be examined within a broader context of ongoing colonialism, unresolved historical trauma, and the systematic disruption of their traditional sources of strength: community, homeland, language, ceremonial life, sacred living histories, etc. In 2008, the Indian Residential Schools Survival Society (IRSSS) sent out surveys to Indigenous communities in British Columbia and found that, "An increase in alcohol use has been recorded especially in the North; an increase in depression and suicide rates in the interior region" ("Residential School Cash"). According to IRSSS worker Brenda Reynolds, "In B.C., as far as we know, there are 24 deaths that different communities attribute to the Common Experience Payment" ("Residential school cash has deadly fallout"). Overall, CEPs to Indian residential school survivors have led to suicides, substance abuse, and depression across Canada. Kwi-ahts-ah-pulth (Ahousaht First Nation) remembered his response to receiving the CEP:

> Looking back at that day I can remember pulling off to the side of the road just being a mess very mixed emotions and had a good cry and phoned my wife up and told her what was going on, there is no sense of satisfaction, there is no sense of gratification. It is a small amount of payment for what

a survivor or any survivor had to go through. We as Kuu'us, as Nuu-chah-nulth, we always say we value life, that life is precious. It makes you think is my life only worth $3,000 dollars a year; after the first year your life is worth $10,000, after the second year your life is worth $13,000, three years you're worth $16,000, and on and on and on. It's miniscule to the amount of pain and suffering that generations and generations and generations of people had to go through from . . . the late 1800s right to 1983.

Restorying

When addressing the G20 in Pittsburgh, Pennsylvania, on 25 September 2009, then Canadian prime minister Stephen Harper made the infamous statement that "we" in Canada "have no history of colonialism" (Ljunggren). Interestingly, Prime Minister Harper's statement came less than a year after he offered an apology to Indigenous peoples in Canada for the colonial policy of residential school. Such a clear contradiction only heightens the need for Indigenous restorying and resurgence. So we asked seven residential school survivors what, if given the opportunity, they would tell the government and the public about their residential school experiences. Their answers gave us some insights into the contemporary struggles for restorying Indigenous futures, as they stressed their disappointment with the resolutions offered by the state. Two respondents, Kwi-ahts-ah-pulth (Jack Little) and Heywaladzi (Campbell Mark Quatell), offered particularly insightful comments regarding engaging with the general public on the legacies of residential schools and the overall resilience of these survivors:

Kwi-ahts-ah-pulth (Jack Little): To the public I would say "listen." Listen to my story, listen to our story. This is reality, this is what happened to me, this is what happened to my siblings, this is what happened to my parents, this is what happened to my grandparents. And I would paint a scenario and let them know how we were treated. My father would get beaten to a pulp by supervisors and he still talks about it and he is almost 74 years old. I would paint the scenarios of when residential schools came. I would want them to be in my shoes if they could. I would explain my story in a skit, and ask for participation; I would appoint certain people to be students of residential schools, two people: mother and father, maybe grandparents, the government officials, and I would say I hope it is worth it, and then I would say I am the law, Kuu'us, we are the law—natives. You now have to come to our institutions, come to our reserves, you now have to learn Indian, you now have to learn our culture, you now have to learn our religion and how we do things. And guess what, you can't speak English anymore, German, Italian, French—take away their language, take away their custom, and I would paint that scenario and say now the government agent is coming to your home and taking your child away. How would you feel? . . . I am a well respected orator and I will use my skills and . . . then paint some scenarios: here is what happened to me, you are hungry and you didn't eat that day and so you stole from the kitchen. They taught us how to steal. If you got caught, heaven help you if you got caught, then you really got punished. So tell my story and give them nothing but facts, and ask them how they feel. So that is what I would do to the public at large.

To the government, that is a different story! The governments are hard to deal with. They do not listen to reason, so you really can't treat them and talk to them like the public at large—they have feelings, you can reach the people; the government is pawns, they are pawns for their constituents, all they are worried about is the issue of the day. It may be an issue today but tomorrow or next week it is not an issue. The government is a lot harder to deal with but I would let them know that I am very hurt by what happened to myself, my siblings, my family. Honestly ask them if a life is only worth this much? . . . If there were a way of compensation other than money, I think that would be an ultimate medium where you might be able to meet. Money is not going to solve it! I have heard horrendous stories of when people got their money. Money is not going to solve it. You can't buy respect, you can't buy love!

Heywaladzi (Campbell Mark Quatell): They are never going to fix what they did to me, because all money and all the tea in China is never going to make that go away. . . . I'm stuck with feeling like a nothing for the rest of my life because that was what I was told from a very early age. . . . [T]he mental and physical abuse, starvation—how were we supposed to prove all this when most of our correspondence has been blacked out and we only have our word? I asked, "what if I go way over the maximum amount of points"; they said, "you will not receive any more than the $275,000. . . ." I said, "you are not talking serious and you have no regard for my story."

Heywaladzi's observations bring our discussion full circle. Ultimately, restorying is just a first step toward remembering and revitalizing our collective and individual consciousness. As Regan points out, these restorying efforts form the basis for "decolonizing spaces" for Indigenous "counter-narratives of diplomacy, law, and peacemaking practices." It is within these decolonizing spaces that Indigenous resurgence movements take shape.

From Truth-telling to Community Mobilization

We have seen how reconciliation as framed by Canada has served to legit-imize and reinforce colonial relationships, thus maintaining the status quo. *Haa-huu-pah* and strategies for Indigenous restorying offer alternatives for resisting contemporary colonial realities and legacies of residential schools. *Haa-huu-pah* have many layers and are inextricably linked to our homelands and family responsibilities. Throughout the interviews with the seven resi-dential school survivors, there is an acknowledgement that homeland, family, restitution, and restorying are all interconnected. Given that colonialism is ongoing, the renewal of family and community responsibilities are starting points for committing to larger Indigenous movements in pursuit of justice and freedom.

The Nuu-chah-nulth Stop the Violence March (May 2006) is a current example of how haa-huu-pah can be applied to the internalized oppression we experience within communities. The march evolved from political organ-izing by the women of Tla-o-qui-aht (Tla-o-qui-aht is one of fifteen Nuu-chah-nulth nations). In 2005, a young woman from Tla-o-qui-aht participated in her coming-of-age ceremony, known as the Ayts tuu thlaa. Tragically, two weeks later this young woman was severely beaten by a man from her own community. The women of Tla-o-qui-aht were outraged and decided to hold a march to demand an end to violence. Fifteen young Nuu-chah-nulth people decided to carry their powerful message throughout all the Nuu-chah-nulth communities. After some wise council from a relative, the participants agreed that their efforts needed to be directed toward countering internalized hatred with *yaauukmiss* (love) when restoring balance in Nuu-chah-nulth communities through *haa-huu-pah*. They did this by bringing a shawl (made and donated by House of Win-Chee clothing designer Denise Williams) to each community, so they could then choose a young woman who would be "gifted" the shawl. The communities would then each host their own *Ayts tuu thlaa* ceremony. *Ayts tuu thlaa* embodies *haa-huu-pah* regarding respect for all women as the life-givers of our nations. Further, this ceremony is about a reciprocal commitment between men and women to support the overall well-being of the community. Importantly, in this ceremony Nuu-chah-nulth people do not look to Canada for solutions. In fact, Nuu-chah-nulth people view state-centred processes as further dividing communities—or trapping us in a cycle of ongoing oppression. In the march, Nuu-chah-nulth people engaged a *haa-huu-pah* that breathed hope and possibility for the future grounded in our own worldview.

Notes

This essay was first published in *English Studies in Canada* 35, no. 1 (2009): 137–59.

1. The Nuu-chah-nulth word *haa-huu-pah* is plural in its usage. Also, the *ha'houlthee* (chiefly territories) of the Nuu-chah-nulth peoples cover approximately three hundred kilometres of the Pacific Coast of Vancouver Island, from

    Brooks Peninsula in the north to Point-no-Point in the south, and includes inland regions. The fourteen Nuu-chah-nulth First Nations are divided into three regions: Southern Region: Ditidaht, Huu-ay-aht, Hupacasath, Tse-shaht, and Uchucklesaht; Central Region: Ahousaht, Hesquiaht, Tla-o-qui-aht, Toquaht, and Yuu-cluth-aht; and Northern Region: Ehattesaht, Kyuquot/Cheklesaht, Mowachat/Muchalaht, and Nuchatlaht.

2. Bradford Morse provides 1874 as the date from which "[T]he Canadian government began to play a role in the development and administration of the Indian residential school system" (280).

3. See Roland Chrisjohn and Sherri Young, with Michael Maraun, *The Circle Game* (1997). For an in-depth look at the history of Indian residential schools, as well as truth and reconciliation processes in Canada, see the two-volume series published by the Aboriginal Healing Foundation, *From Truth to Reconciliation* (2009), and *Response, Responsibility* (2008).

4. The Kwakwaka'wakw (formerly known as the Kwakiutl) are an Indigenous group of First Nations living in northern Vancouver Island, as well as the adjoining mainland and islands of British Columbia. They number approximately fifty-five hundred people.

    LE,NONET is a Sencoten (Straits Salish) word meaning "success after enduring many hardships." The LE,NONET Project (2004–09) was designed to help facilitate opportunities for students for community internships, peer mentorship, and research apprenticeships with faculty members at the University of Victoria.

5. See: 2007 Indian Residential Schools Settlement Agreement (www.iap-pei.ca/content/pdf/irssa-settlement.pdf). As part of the Indian Residential Schools Settlement Agreement, financial compensation in the form of a Common Experience Payment (CEP) is to be awarded to residential school survivors once they verify their attendance at these schools. According to the settlement agreement, the amount of the CEP is determined by the following criteria:
    (1) Ten thousand dollars ($10,000) to every Eligible CEP Recipient who resided at one or more Indian Residential Schools for one school year or part thereof; and
    (2) An additional three thousand ($3,000) to every eligible CEP Recipient who resided at one or more Indian Residential Schools for each school year or part thereof, after the first school year; and
    (3) Less the amount of any advance payment on the CEP received.

6. The IRSSS was created in 1994 as a working committee of the First Nations Summit and currently represents approximately seventy percent of all Indigenous peoples in British Columbia. See: www.irsss.ca/about.

7. See, for example, research by Carole Blackburn and Andrew Woolford on this topic.

8. While we originally planned to interview several female residential school survivors, the following seven men were the only ones available for interviews during our

timeframe: Kwi-ahts-ah-pulth (Jack Little) from Ahousaht First Nation (Nuu-chah-nulth); Hayawolthlit (Wally Samuel Sr.) from Ahousaht First Nation (Nuu-chah-nulth); Luke George from Tseshaht First Nation (Nuu-chah-nulth); Huu-ay-aht (Stephen Lucas) from Hesquiaht First Nation (Nuu-chah-nulth); James Quatell from Wei Wai Kum First Nation (Kwakwaka'wakw); Daniel Wallace Quatell from Wei Wai Kum First Nation (Kwakwaka'wakw); and Heywaladzi (Campbell Mark Quatell) from Wei Wai Kum First Nation (Kwakwaka'wakw).

The amount of time these survivors spent in residential school ranged from one to ten years. In keeping with community protocols, we provided a gift to each participant in order to honour the knowledge and time shared with us. As part of the University of Victoria's research ethics requirements, each participant signed a consent form, which stated that if he chose to withdraw from the study at any time and for any reason, his interview data would be destroyed and not used in the analysis. None of the participants chose this option.

33

Erotica, Indigenous Style

Kateri Akiwenzie-Damm

Many artists recognize that stories of the erotic have long been the source of inspiration and renewal in their communities.

—Lee-Ann Martin, "Reclaiming Desires,"
Exposed: Aesthetics of Aboriginal Erotic Art (44)

Sex in the First Person

About five years ago, I started thinking about sex. Seriously. I started thinking seriously about sex and sexuality and the utter lack of it in Indigenous writing. Or so it seemed to me. I've since realized that, of course, there was some erotic writing by Indigenous writers around—it just took some searching. A lot of searching. Too much searching. A person could reach puberty, live her entire adult life, go through menopause, and still not have stumbled across a single erotic poem or story by a First Nations writer. Or, to make it even more depressing, I realized one could live and die as an Indigenous person and not come across a single erotic poem or story by an Indigenous writer from Canada, the US, Australia, Aotearoa (a.k.a. New Zealand) . . . I know, I looked. And although I didn't quite reach menopause before I found some, in a sense I cheated—I asked Indigenous writers to send erotica to me and I started writing it myself.

What Is Indigenous Erotica?

Indigenous erotica is political. More than that, it's stimulating, inspiring, beautiful, sometimes explicit. It's written by Indigenous writers, painted by Indigenous painters, filmed by Indigenous filmmakers, photographed by

Indigenous photographers, sung by Indigenous singers. But, for better or worse, because of the societies surrounding us, it is, like everything else we do, political. When one asks, "what is Indigenous literature?" it's a political question and the answer is political regardless of one's personal politics.

Until now, it wouldn't have occurred to most people that Indigenous literature could encompass not only "protest" literature, legends, myths, transcribed oratory, various forms and styles of storytelling, creative non-fiction, biography, autobiography, poetry, drama, and fiction, but erotica as well. Somehow it was separated out from the perception of what Indigenous literature is or could be, and excluded to the point that for the most part, we didn't even think of it. Yet, we know that our teachings and our perspectives as Indigenous peoples are inclusive and holistic. We know that "First Nations languages contain numerous words, stories and jokes depicting sexuality and the erotic as an important, and frequently humorous, aspect of life, love and spirituality" (Martin, "Reclaiming Desires" 36). All the more strange, therefore, that this aspect of our creative cultural and personal expression should be so absent.

Jo-Anne Grace, a Maori friend in Aotearoa who is a weaver and student in an arts program at a Maori university, tells me that many of the old waiata and chants were beautifully "erotic" and that the erotic was so much integrated into life and arts and song that these waiata or songs were not considered at all shocking or even different, despite their explicitness. This, as I understand it, is similar to the attitudes and traditions of the Anishinaabe and other First Nations and Inuit in North America. Old-time stories included all aspects of life—sexuality was certainly not excluded. It was an accepted aspect of life.

Another friend, Haunani-Kay Trask, a Native Hawaiian poet and leader in the Hawaiian sovereignty movement, once told me that for Native Hawaiians, the world is eroticized: often food, the land, and all elements of the natural world are eroticized in Native Hawaiian song and poetry. Certainly this is evident in Haunani's poetry. In one of her poems, titled "Ulu," Haunani describes the breadfruit tree according to a traditional Hawaiian perspective in which ulu is, as she explains in a note, a male symbol and embodiment of male mana or power:

> testicles full
> with seed sweet milk
> bubbling at the tip (Trask 82)

In many Indigenous societies, like that of the Anishinaabe, the earth and all who dwell within it contain a manitou, a vibrant energy that is creative and procreative, and thus, I would argue, sexual.

So What Happened?

In my estimation, the answer is simple: colonization and genocide. When the colonizers arrived, who we are as Indigenous peoples was disrupted and controlled. No longer was it a natural result of living as we always had in our own homelands. On the one hand, we were defined and categorized by the colonizers. Set on small parcels of land called reserves, marae, and missions, we were renamed and then those names were defined and legislated so as to separate us from the colonizers and settlers. On the other, we were beset by missionaries bent on offering us "salvation" for our sinful ways, and in the view of many of them sex is a sin, unless for procreation.

Neither the colonizing governments with their missions of genocide and assimilation nor the missionaries with their sexually repressive dogma of "good" and "evil" cared to accept our attitudes to sexuality, and certainly not any open expressions of it, cultural, artistic, creative, or not! Certainly they didn't want us procreating. That wasn't the solution to "The Indian Problem"—we were supposed to vanish, to die, to assimilate into oblivion, not procreate for God's sake! Although miscegenation was not acceptable, it was tolerated because at least it fit in with the Master Plan of wiping us out. After a few generations of mixing our recessive genes with their dominant ones, we'd be as good as White, no problem. Besides, we were simple creatures who needed to be taught proper civilized behaviour. To this end, a good many of our ceremonies were banned, and of course we were taught that those "erotic" songs and stories, which were so much a part of our cultures, were unacceptable in a civilized society.

Why?

As Joy Harjo has said, "To be 'in the erotic,' so to speak, is to be alive." Yes, eroticism presents political problems, cultural difficulties, religious problems, because the dominant culture can't function with a society of alive people" ("The Spectrum of Other Languages" 108). To deny the erotic, to create an absence of erotica, is another weapon in the oppressor's genocidal arsenal. When this part of us is dead, our future survival is in jeopardy.

So What Happened?

Many of the songs were "translated" into English in a way that changed them into something more acceptable. Stories were repressed and hidden away like some dirty secret. Or they were collected and retold by people like Herbert Schwartz in *Tales from the Smokehouse* in such a way as to be more acceptable (though still titillatingly risqué and scandalous) for a non-Native audience.

As Lee-Ann Martin says, "The legacy of colonialism contributed to the collision between the worldviews of Aboriginal and Euro-Canadian communities. Eventually, many Aboriginal stories became silenced and the images invisible" (Martin 36). No longer told or written by us or for us, the stories seemingly were only acceptable within academic contexts, for the gaze and study of anthropologists and such Others. *Fascinating.*

Unfortunately, it seems we got the subtle and not-so-subtle messages about the acceptability of Indigenous sexuality. By the late 1980s and early 1990s, when I was working on an AIDS awareness campaign for First Nations communities in Canada, I realized that, in terms of sexuality, many of our communities were at least as repressive (and hypocritical?) as the colonizing cultures that surround us. Though I didn't know it at the time, this was when my own awareness of the sexual repression of Indigenous peoples really began. Imagine trying to inform vulnerable First Nations communities of the potential onset of a health disaster like AIDS and being told that in some First Nations communities, it wasn't acceptable to discuss sex in public. How do you inform people of the risks of AIDS so they can protect themselves if you can't make any reference to sex? In retrospect, as a result, we did a lousy job of it. Today AIDS is rampant in some First Nations communities, just as was predicted.

So is it political? Damn right it is.

Erotic Without Reservation

Since I became consciously aware of all of this, I have spent more than five years collecting and editing an anthology of erotica by Indigenous writers. From the outset, the intention of the project was to advance an alterNative to some of the stereotypes and misconceptions about Indigenous peoples, particularly with regard to relationships and sexuality. Like many others, I was tired of images of Indigenous men as violent, monosyllabic studs, abusers of Indigenous women, and ravishers of White women, or as noble-savage-type shamans, warriors, and chiefs. I was sickened by stereotypes of Indigenous women as promiscuous, drunken whores or sexless Mother Earth types. All of those stereotypes and images that make us less than the whole, complex, loving, sexual, spiritual beings we are.

I began to realize that there were few positive, affirming portrayals of relationships, especially romantic and sexual relationships, *between Indigenous peoples* in the arts or mass media (even by our own artists and communicators). Like Janice Acoose, who, in one of her essays in *Iskwewak—Kah' Ki Yaw Ni Wahkomakanak: Neither Indian Princess Nor Easy Squaws*, asks "how stereotypical images like the Indian princess or easy squaw affect our values, beliefs, and attitudes" (49), I began to wonder how the stereotypes, combined with the lack of realistic images, was affecting our self-image, especially in the minds of our young people, many of whom have dealt either directly or indirectly (through intergenerational impacts) with violence, abuse, cultural deprivations, and the forced imposition of foreign values.

It seems to me that the repression of erotic art is symptomatic of our oppression and signifies a deep psychological and spiritual break between a healthy and holistic tradition and an oppressed, repressed, shamed, and *imposed* sense of reality. If erotic art is "a vital aspect of the human condition—of being human" (Davis, "Forward" 7), then our very humanity is attacked and skewed when our erotic arts are repressed. Writing particularly about Native women, Acoose says,

> Stereotypic images of Indian princesses, squaw drudges, suffering helpless victims, tawny temptresses, or loose squaws falsify our realities and suggest in a subliminal way that those stereotypic images are us. As a consequence, those images foster cultural attitudes that encourage sexual, physical, verbal, or psychological violence against Indian women. (55)

Not only do these images affect us and our communities, they are absorbed by the societies around us and provide a sort of self-fulfilling justification of their genocidal actions on both political and social levels. Racism, violence, and disrespect are so much easier when the targets of it have been dehumanized.

Eroticism is uniquely human. To deny it in any culture or individual denies a basic aspect of the individual or group's humanity. "Erotic art determines the boundaries of sexuality that are permissible within historical and cultural categories of the aesthetic" (Martin 36–37). The silencing of our erotic expression says our sexuality is not "permissible," that its expression is unacceptable, that we must remain unseen and ignored, that we must accept the dehumanizing impacts of being oppressed and colonized.

I, like others, absolutely refuse! The erotic must be reclaimed, expressed, and celebrated as an aspect of our humanity. When I became conscious of the importance of being alive and whole in the erotic, I decided to put together an anthology of Indigenous erotica and to begin discussing "erotica" with other Indigenous writers.

One intent of this decision was to break down some of the barriers within our communities and within ourselves. How can we be healthy in a holistic way if we are deprived of this view of ourselves, or if we only see ourselves portrayed as damaged and unhealthy? I don't believe we can. Overcoming this requires that we rid ourselves of the poison of those stereotypes and lies. To heal, I believe that our own stories, poems, and songs that celebrate our erotic natures must be part of the antidote. As Linda Hogan says in *Listening to the Land*:

> [W]ords have a great potential for healing, in all respects. And we have
> a need to learn them, to find a way to speak first the problem, the truth,
> against destruction, then to find a way to use language to put things back
> together, to live respectfully, to praise and celebrate earth, to love. (122)

We need to see images of ourselves as healthy, whole people. People who love each other and who love ourselves. People who fall in love and out of love, who have lovers, who make love, who have sex. We need to create a healthy legacy for our peoples.

I have spoken to quite a few Indigenous writers, many in person, about erotica over the past five years. A few years ago, when I first started this, erotica was not as mainstream as it has become in the past few years. More to the point, it was not *at all* so in the Indigenous community. There was virtually no talk about erotica within the Indigenous community and very little in the Indigenous arts community. I was determined to change this, but I was a little nervous initially that I would be laughed at or shunned. I imagined whispered conversations at Native lit gatherings filled with speculations about the real reasons I was asking people to send me erotica, *nudge nudge wink wink.*

Thankfully, these small fears were unfounded. There was no laughing, well, actually there was a great deal of laughing and joking around, but none aimed *at* me. No shunning. And, to the best of my knowledge, no speculating. Like the serious artists we are, we discussed it seriously. Because it is serious. There is something seriously wrong when sexuality and erotic expression are repressed. In an individual person, it might raise a few eyebrows. Amongst a whole people, it raises a red flag. Among Indigenous peoples from various parts of the world, it raises enormously serious concerns with huge implications about our futures.

What is interesting (though not surprising) is that the underlying political aspect of Indigenous erotica was a reality that virtually every Indigenous writer and artist I spoke with seemed to recognize immediately. Although I was prepared to explain the deeper significance of my undertaking, it was unnecessary. As in so many cases, when Indigenous peoples speak with each other, there is an unspoken understanding of our situation that does not require explanation. Consequently, I did have some wonderful discussions and conversations with other Indigenous artists and writers, including Lee-Ann Martin, Jo-Anne Grace, Haunani-Kay Trask, Joy Harjo, Sherman Alexie, Richard Van Camp, Morgan Wood, Geary Hobson, Melissa Lucashenko, Armand Garnet Ruffo, Briar Grace-Smith, Beth Cuthand, Joseph Bruchac, Kenny Laughton, Susan Heavens, Gregory Scofield, and many others. Engaging in these discussions has been one of the most inspiring, gratifying, worthwhile, and fun aspects of this quest.

Defining the Ineffable

So what is Indigenous erotica? From the outset, I have resisted defining "erotica." I prefer to allow Indigenous artists and writers and the work they produce to define this on their terms and using their own perspectives, aesthetics, and cultural perspectives. This is also what I have chosen to do in my own work. To re-discover the erotic voice. To give voice to the erotic, the loving, the sexual, the repressed, the oppressed; the "dirty," outrageous intimacies of womanhood and sexuality that had only been hinted at in my earlier work. What I have been interested in is providing the opportunity, or at least the catalyst, for other writers and artists to consider the erotic and what it means for us, as writers from specific cultures and homelands with our own artistic, cultural, and literary traditions.

To me, this sort of diversity is important. By defining, limits are set and barriers created. I have chosen to let this notion of what Indigenous erotica is emerge in a more organic way. To leave it open so that we can create a canon together, for ourselves, is to allow our erotica to be free of those imposed boundaries. I call it erotica "without reservation."

What I can say, based on my work in this area, is that in a broad sense Indigenous erotica speaks about the healing nature of love, about love that celebrates us as whole people, about love that is openly sexual, sensual, emotional, and spiritual. Love, and the expression of it, is a medicine to heal the pain of oppression, hatred, lovelessness, and colonization. It is a way for Indigenous writers and other artists to freely express themselves and their ideas about love and sexuality, without being constrained by imposed moral codes or definitions. Like the artwork in *Exposed*, Indigenous erotica serves to "reject the colonial history that has hidden Aboriginal erotic images for too long . . . [and] reaffirm the important place of the erotic in human existence" (Martin 44).

Over the past few years a real breakthrough has occurred. Gregory Scofield's collection of poems *Love Medicine and One Song* was released in 1997, and contains some of the most beautiful erotic poetry I've read. Reading it for the first time affirmed to me the importance of rediscovering and celebrating the Indigenous erotic voice and provided encouragement to me in the early stages of this work. Then, throughout 1998, I spoke to Morgan Wood and Lee-Ann Martin about an exhibition of First Nations Indigenous visual art they were co-curating. This controversial and incredible exhibition, *Exposed: Aesthetics of Aboriginal Art*, opened at the MacKenzie Art Gallery in late 1999, along with an exhibition catalogue that included erotic poetry by Aboriginal writers. *Exposed* subsequently toured to the Ottawa Art Gallery, where I was able to see the exhibit and read selections of erotic literature from my own work and from the work I had been collecting from Indigenous writers internationally. During the exhibition, I was interviewed about erotica for an Aboriginal Peoples Television Network (APTN) show and performed a reading of an erotic poem for another APTN program. The *Exposed* exhibition, which includes work by Norval Morrisseau, Thirza Cuthand, Rosalie Favell, G. Ray McCallum, Robert Markle, Ahasiw Maskegon-Iskwew, Daphne Odjig, Lawrence Paul Yuxweluptun, and Patricia Deadman, has continued to tour. Finally, I hear through the moccasin telegraph that Drew Hayden Taylor is conducting research for the National Film Board on Indigenous erotica.

Beyond these more "high profile" advancements, I frequently hear from artists and writers about various erotic works they are contemplating or completing. This is perhaps the most positive step forward—that individual artists and writers are accepting and portraying the erotic in their everyday work. To me it signals an important shift. I predict that over the next few years the erotic will regain its rightful and natural place in our arts. Although it may become an increasingly "hot" topic or fad for the next while, I believe that eventually it will settle into a more normal and intrinsic aspect of Indigenous arts.

In my own work, I believe I am finally breaking through most barriers and can write freely, without obliviously dragging along the hang ups that I acquired as an Anishinaabe woman who was raised under the *Indian Act,* as a Roman Catholic, without having seen an erotic story or poem by an Indigenous writer until I was in my late twenties. I can be, and have been, undaunted in giving readings where the mention that I might read some love poetry or erotic poetry produces initial shock and surprise from the audience. No worries. I enjoy it. I enjoy writing it, reading it, presenting it, talking about it. In a way, it's like sex—once you do it, it becomes a part of who you are. Just one more aspect of life, one more element of what you do.

To be so much a part of the movement to look at erotica and, consequently, the huge and vast array of issues that surrounds it, is a gratifying and passionate pursuit. I see very clearly that this is a huge political statement. To reclaim and express our sexuality is part of the larger path to de-colonization and freedom. And so the work continues, because I believe passionately that when Indigenous people de-colonize ourselves we'll not only free our minds, we'll free our bodies, our spirits, our whole selves. We'll live without reservation.

Without reservation. *Mashkow-aendun.*

Note

This essay was first published in Armand Garnet Ruffo, ed., *(Ad)dressing Our Words: Aboriginal Perspectives on Aboriginal Literatures* (Penticton, BC: Theytus, 2001).

34

Doubleweaving Two-Spirit Critiques: Building Alliances Between Native and Queer Studies

Qwo-Li Driskill

In the beginning of the twenty-first century, Indigenous Two-Spirit/GLBTQ people are asserting uniquely Native-centred and tribally specific understandings of gender and sexuality as a way to critique colonialism, queerphobia, racism, and misogyny as part of decolonial struggles. Radical Two-Spirit cultural work in the United States and Canada during the late twentieth century cleared a path for Two-Spirit people to form our own modes of critique and creativity suited for Native-focused decolonial struggles.[1] While our traditional understandings of gender and sexuality are as diverse as our nations, Native Two-Spirit/GLBTQ people share experiences under heteropatriarchal, gender-polarized colonial regimes that attempt to control Native nations. These experiences give rise to critiques that position Native Two-Spirit/ GLBTQ genders and sexualities as oppositional to colonial powers. Necessary in this process are critiques of both the colonial nature of many GLBTQ movements in the United States and Canada, and the queer/transphobia internalized by Native nations. Two-Spirit critiques—through theory, arts, and activism—are a part of larger radical decolonial movements. Decolonization in most of the United States and Canada is a process that looks very different from decolonial and postcolonial movements in other parts of the world. By using the term *decolonization*, I am speaking of ongoing, radical resistance against colonialism that includes struggles for land redress, self-determination, healing historical trauma, cultural continuance, and reconciliation. I don't see decolonization as a process that necessarily ends in the clearly defined "post-colonial" states of South Asia, Africa, and other parts of the world. Our colonial realities in most of the United States and Canada are substantially different, as colonial governments are still here and still maintain power and control over Indigenous communities.

Linda Tuhiwai Smith points to the problem with the concept of postcolonial:

> Post-colonial discussions have . . . stirred some Indigenous resistance, not so much to the literary reimagining of culture as being centered in what were once conceived of as the colonial margins, but to the idea that colonialism is over, finished business. This is best articulated by Aborigine activist Bobbi Sykes, who asked at an academic conference on post-colonialism, "What? Post-colonialism? Have they left?" There is also, amongst Indigenous academics, the sneaking suspicion that the fashion of post-colonialism has become a strategy for reinscribing or reauthorizing the privileges of non-Indigenous academics because the field of "post-colonial" discourse has been defined in ways which can still leave out Indigenous peoples, our ways of knowing and our current concerns. (*Decolonizing Methodologies* 24)

It is impossible to generalize about the decolonial needs of each Indigenous community, but it is possible to imagine together what decolonization means and could look like, within our particular political contexts. It is this imagination that is the strongest part of our decolonial struggles. As Joy Harjo states in her poem "A Postcolonial Tale," "Our children put down their guns when we did to imagine with us. We imagined the shining link between the heart and the sun. We imagined tables of food for everyone. We imagined the songs."[2] Instead of seeing decolonization as something that has a fixed and finite goal, decolonial activism and scholarship ask us to radically reimagine our futures. For Native Two-Spirit/GLBTQ people and our allies, part of imagining our futures is through creating theories and activism that weave together Native and GLBTQ critiques that speak to our present colonial realities. Within queer studies, critiques examining the intersections of race, sexuality, and empire— what Martin F. Manalansan IV names "the new queer studies" (*Global Divas*)— have at once held promise, and then disappointed, those of us concerned with bringing Native studies and queer studies into critical conversations, or what Malea Powell calls "alliance as a practice of survivance" ("Down by the River" 38).

Our hope for these emergent critiques lies in the thought that perhaps a turn in queer studies to articulate more carefully issues of race and nation will open up conversations about ongoing decolonial struggles and the relationships between sexuality, gender, colonization, and decolonization. Our disappointment lies in the recognition of an old story within "the new queer studies": Native people, Native histories, and ongoing colonial projects happening on our lands are included only marginally, when included at all.

This disturbs me. It disturbs me because I think that the radical potential of these critiques is dissipated through all but ignoring Native people. It disturbs me because I think that this erasure colludes with, rather than disrupts, colonial projects. It disturbs me because I think that this work is brilliant scholarship that is deeply necessary, and I *want* it to do better in its relationship with Native people and Native struggles than other intellectual movements in the academy. Sadly, I think it presently falls short of my own impossible desires.

If you are reading this in the United States or Canada, whose land are you on, dear reader? What are the specific names of the Native nation(s) who have historical claim to the territory on which you currently read this article? What are their histories before European invasion? What are their historical and present acts of resistance to colonial occupation? If you are like most people in the United States and Canada, you cannot answer these questions. And this disturbs me. This essay is meant to challenge queer studies not only to pay attention to Native people and Native histories, but also to shift its critiques in order to include a consciousness about the ongoing colonial reality in which all of us living in settler-colonial states are entrenched. Further, my goal is to challenge queer studies to include an understanding of Native Two-Spirit/GLBTQ resistance movements and critiques in its imagining of the future of queer studies. Finally, this essay articulates specific Two-Spirit critiques that are simultaneously connected to and very separate from other queer critiques. Two-Spirit critiques share commonalities with queer critiques that challenge heteropatriarchal dominance and notions, gender binaries, and the policing and control of sexualized and gendered bodies. Emergent queer of colour critiques are imagining theories that place queer people of colour at the centre of discussion and arguing that "nonheteronormative racial formations represent the historic accumulations of contradictions around race, gender, sexuality, and class," a stance that Two-Spirit critiques can draw from to understand how heteropatriarchy and heteronormativity are a part of colonial projects (Ferguson, *Aberrations in Black* 17). However, Two-Spirit critiques diverge from other queer critiques because they root themselves in Native histories, politics, and decolonial struggles. Two-Spirit critiques challenge both white-dominated queer theory and queer of colur critique's near erasure of Native people and nations, and question the usefulness to Native communities of theories not rooted in tribally specific traditions and not thoroughly conscious of colonialism as an ongoing process. Two-Spirit critiques, and this essay, ask for queer studies in the United States and Canada to remember exactly on whose land it is built.

Two-Spirit Critique

The term *Two-Spirit* was chosen as an intertribal term to be used in English as a way to communicate numerous tribal traditions and social categories of gender outside dominant European binaries. Anguksuar (Richard LaFortune) explains: "The term *two-spirit* . . . originated in Northern Algonquin dialect and gained first currency at the third annual spiritual gathering of gay and lesbian Native people that took place near Winnipeg in 1990. What we who chose this designation understood is that *niizh manitoag* (two-spirits) indicates the presence of both a feminine and a masculine spirit in one person" (*Two-Spirit People* 221).

In 1993, a conference funded by the Wenner-Gren Foundation for anthropological research titled "Revisiting the 'North American Berdache' Empirically and Theoretically" was held during the American Anthropological Association meetings. During the conference, participants challenged the use of the word *berdache* as "being derogatory and inappropriate and as not reflecting gender roles, identities, and sexualities as lived by Native Americans" (10). Because of this, *Two-Spirit* has become both a term for contemporary communities and identities and an alternative to colonial terms such as *berdache*.

I am choosing the term *Two-Spirit*, rather than other terms I could use, such as *Native queer* or *Native trans people*, for several reasons. The term *Two-Spirit* is a word that is intentionally complex. It is meant to be an umbrella term for Native GLBTQ people, as well as a term for people who use words and concepts from their specific traditions to describe themselves. Like other umbrella terms—including *queer*—it risks erasing difference. But also like *queer*, it is meant to be inclusive, ambiguous, and fluid. Some Native GLBTQ folks have rejected the term *Two-Spirit*, while others have rejected terms such as *gay*, *lesbian*, *bi*, *trans*, and *queer* in favour of *Two-Spirit* or tribally specific terms. Still others move between terms depending on the specific rhetorical context.[3] The choice to use the term *Two-Spirit*, as well as the numerous tribally specific terms for those who fall outside dominant Eurocentric constructions of gender and sexuality, employs what Scott Richard Lyons calls *rhetorical sovereignty*: "The inherent right of *peoples* to determine their own communicative needs and desires in this pursuit, to decide for themselves the goals, modes, styles, and languages of public discourse" (*Rhetorical Sovereignty* 449). Further, contemporary Two-Spirit politics, arts, and movements are part of what Robert

Warrior terms *intellectual sovereignty*, "a decision—a decision we make in our minds, in our hearts, and in our bodies—to be sovereign and to find out what that means in the process" (*Tribal Secrets* 123).

Two-Spirit is a word that itself is a critique. It is a challenge not only to the field of anthropology's use of the word *berdache*, but also to the white-dominated GLBTQ community's labels and taxonomies. It claims Native traditions as precedents for understanding gender and sexuality, and asserts that Two-Spirit people are vital to our tribal communities. Further, *Two-Spirit* asserts ceremonial and spiritual communities and traditions and relationships with medicine as central in constituting various identities, marking itself as distinct from dominant constructions of GLBTQ identities. This is not an essentialist move but an assertion that Indigenous gender and sexual identities are intimately connected to land, community, and history.[4]

Two-Spirit is also useful because it recentres discussion onto gendered constructions, both from within and outside Native traditions. While important work is being done around transgender, genderqueer, and other "gender non-conforming" people and communities, *queer* too often refers to sexualized practices and identities. *Two-Spirit*, on the other hand, places gendered identities and experiences at the centre of discussion. Indeed, many of the traditions that scholars and activists such as Brian Joseph Gilley, Beatrice Medicine, Will Roscoe, Wesley Thomas, and Walter L. Williams have identified that fall under the category of Two-Spirit are not necessarily about sexuality; they are about gendered experiences and identities outside dominant European gender constructions. No understanding of sexual and gender constructions on colonized and occupied land can take place without an understanding of the ways colonial projects continually police sexual and gender lines. Two-Spirit critiques, then, are necessary to an understanding of homophobia, misogyny, and transphobia in the Americas, just as an analysis of queerphobia and sexism is necessary to understand colonial projects.

Doubleweave

To contribute to decolonial and tribally specific theories, I would like to look to Cherokee doublewoven baskets as a model for articulating the emergent potential in conversations between Native studies and queer studies. As a rhetoric scholar and a basket weaver, I am particularly interested in the rhetorical work involved in *doubleweaving*.[5] For my purposes here, I would like to conceive of the conversation between queer studies and Native studies as a doubleweaving that can result in emergent critiques both within and between these disciplines.

Doubleweave is a form of weaving in Cherokee (and other Southeastern Native) traditions that has its origins in river cane weaving. Sarah H. Hill writes: "One of the oldest and most difficult traditions in basketry is a technique called doubleweave. A doubleweave basket is actually two complete baskets, one woven inside the other, with a common rim" (*Weaving New Worlds* 44).[6] Doublewoven baskets can have two independent designs as a result of the weave, one on the outside and one on the inside. Doubling is likewise employed as a Cherokee rhetorical strategy outside basketry, in which two seemingly disparate rhetorical approaches exist concurrently.[7] Using doubleweave as a metaphor enables me to articulate a methodological approach that draws on and intersects numerous theoretical splints—what Smith calls *dissent lines* (13)—in order to doubleweave queer and Native concerns into a specifically Indigenous creation.

I draw the concept of doubleweave as a feature of Cherokee rhetorical theory and practice through Marilou Awiakta's book *Selu: Seeking the Corn-Mother's Wisdom*, which is deliberately constructed after doublewoven baskets. She explains, "As I worked with the poems, essays and stories, I saw they shared a common base. . . . From there they wove around four themes, gradually assuming a double-sided pattern—one outer, one inner—distinct, yet interconnected in a whole" (34). The Cherokee scholar and creative writer Daniel Heath Justice uses doubleweave as an interpretive device in an essay focusing on the balance created between homeland and identity in Awiakta's work. He writes, "The Cherokee philosophy of balance . . . is the basic foundation upon which Awiakta crafts her work. Intimately connected with the concept of balance is that of *respect*—one cannot exist without the other" ("Beloved Woman Returns" 74).

Native and queer studies, when conceptualized as intertwined walls of a doublewoven basket, enable us to see the numerous splints—including Native politics, postmodern scholarship, grassroots activisms, queer and trans resistance movements, queer studies, and tribally specific contexts—from which these critiques are (and can be) woven. Such a weaving, then, moves beyond a concept of intersectional politics. Though intersections do take place in doubleweaving, the weaving process also creates something else: a story much more complex and durable than its original and isolated splints, a story both unique and rooted in an ancient and enduring form. The dissent lines of Native studies and queer studies can be used as splints to weave what I am calling Two-Spirit critiques. It is from this stance that I wish to look a bit at "the new queer studies" in order to put these analyses in dialogue with Native studies and build stronger alliances between our disciplines.

Disidentifying with the New Queer Studies

In his book *Disidentifications: Queers of Color and the Performance of Politics*, José Esteban Muñoz writes: "Disidentification can be understood as a way of shuffling back and forth between reception and production. For the critic, disidentification is the hermeneutical performance of decoding mass, high, or any other cultural field from the perspective of a minority subject who is disempowered in such a representational hierarchy" (25). Muñoz's work has been instrumental in the emergence of what Roderick A. Ferguson calls "queer of color critique" (*Aberrations in Black* 3) and what Gayatri Gopinath calls "queer diasporic" critiques (*Impossible Desires* 3). Ferguson says that, "queer of color critique employs cultural forms to bear witness to the critical gender and sexual heterogeneity that comprises minority cultures. Queer of color analysis does this to shed light on the ruptural components of culture, components that expose the restrictions of universality, the exploitations of capital, and the deceptions of national culture" (24). One of the strongest aspects of these critiques is their ability to employ a multiplicity of tactics to decode nationalist (both colonizing and colonized) strategies.[8] These critiques employ both queerness and race as a tactic to disrupt white supremacist heteronormative strategies that constitute themselves through marginalizing people of colour, nonheterosexuals, and people outside rigid gender norms. Further, they seek to employ queerness as a tactic of resistance to heteronormalizing nationalist discourses.

Another important feature of these critiques is their insistence on drawing from a variety of intellectual and political genealogies, including "women of color feminism, materialist analysis, poststructuralist theory, and queer critique" (Ferguson 149). By drawing on numerous locations, queer of colour critique is able to simultaneously speak from multiple locations to numerous audiences. Such critical interventions are necessary to reimagine queer studies as a space that focuses on intersecting experiences of oppression and resistance. What queer of colour and queer diasporic theorists offer to queer studies, as well as the numerous interdisciplinary fields they are connected with, is of the utmost importance because they help us understand the very specific ways empire is built through heteropatriarchal control and how queer people of colour resist empire and heteronormative nationalisms.

However, the fact that Native people have largely been left out of these critiques points to major ruptures in queer theories. Not only are Native people and Native resistance movements rarely a subject of analysis, the specific political and historical realities of Native people seem outside queer studies' purview. This means that—at best—analyses of race, nation, diaspora, history, sexuality, and gender are deeply lacking and that—at worst—these critiques risk colluding with master narratives both inside and outside the academy that, as Powell describes, *un-see* Native people: "Material Indian 'bodies' are simply not seen so that the mutilations, rapes, and murders that characterized . . . first-wave genocide also simply are not seen" ("Blood and Scholarship" 3).

When Native people are mentioned in the new queer studies, it is usually only in passing, and often within lists of other people of colour.[9] Even while Gopinath locates her notion of "the impossible" in José Rabasa's interpretations of Zapatista resistance, the connections between Zapatista decolonial movements and similar movements in the United States and Canada remain *un-said* and *un-seen* (*Impossible Desires* 19–20). While it may be true that "through the lens of queer diaspora, various writers and visual artists such as Nice Rodriguez, Ginu Kamani, Audre Lorde, R. Zamora Linmark, Richard Fung, and Achy Obejas . . . can now be deciphered and read simultaneously into multiple queer and national genealogies," a lens of queer diaspora—as it is currently imagined and formulated—does little to elucidate the work of Native (and arguably diasporic) writers and artists such as Clint Alberta, Louis Cruz, Thirza Cuthand, Daniel Heath Justice, Deborah Miranda, or Craig Womack (27–28).

Though this may be contrary to the intent of the authors, the mere inclusion of Native people within lists of other groups of colour unwittingly contributes to the erasure of the specificity of Native claims to land and to the particular relationships Native people and Native nations have with Euro-American colonial governments. People who are Indigenous to the places now called the United States and Canada complicate notions of queer diasporic critique in important ways. While many of us are indeed diasporic, notions of diaspora must be deeply questioned and revised in order to be inclusive of our experiences.

Queer of colour critique and queer diasporic critique have rightly looked at the misogyny and queerphobia too often present in nationalist struggles and have offered queerness as a tool that deconstructs and reformulates concepts of nation. Gopinath argues: "A consideration of queerness . . . becomes a way to challenge nationalist ideologies by restoring the impure, inauthentic, nonreproductive potential of the notion of diaspora. Indeed, the urgent need to trouble and denaturalize the close relationship between nationalism and heterosexuality is precisely what makes the notion of a queer diaspora so compelling" (11). Such a critique is important for Two-Spirit people as well, but needs revision to include Native nations. The current legal place of federally recognized Native nations within the United States as "domestic dependent nations" and the many struggles for sovereignty both within and outside this legal category troubles concepts of nation and nationalism that fall under these queer critiques. For Native people in often-tenuous relationships to colonial powers, nationalist struggles and politics are a centre of resistance against colonialism. Andrea Smith offers Native feminist critiques as a way to think of nationalism and sovereignty "beyond the nation-state":

> Whereas nation-states are governed through domination and coercion, Indigenous sovereignty and nationhood are predicated on interrelatedness and responsibility. In opposition to nation-states, which are based on control over territory, these visions of Indigenous nationhood are based on care and responsibility for land that all can share. These models of sovereignty are not based on a narrow definition of nation that would entail a closely bounded community and ethnic cleansing. So, these articulations pose an alternative to theories that assume that the endpoint to a national struggle is a nation-state and that assume the givenness of the nation-state system. (Smith, "American Studies without America" 312)

Native Two-Spirit/queer people position ourselves and our identities as productive, if not central, to nationalist, decolonial agendas. Within Native politics, being part of nationalist struggles is not an assimilationist move but instead a move against the colonial powers that have attempted to dissolve or restrain Native sovereignties. As I discuss below, Two-Spirit critiques can simultaneously push queer studies to a more complex analysis of nation while also incorporating the critiques of heteropatriarchal nationalisms that queer studies offers in order to fight against heterosexism, homophobia, and rigid gender binaries in decolonial theories and activism.

Siobhan B. Somerville does include some analysis of the portrayal of Native people in literature, specifically in Pauline E. Hopkins's *Winona* and Leslie Feinberg's *Stone Butch Blues*. However, her analysis tends to look at how Indianness signifies race more generally, rather than examine how constructions of race in the United States are built on constructions of "the Indian." Somerville disclaims an analysis of race inclusive of Native people by writing:

> My analysis of "race" in this study is limited to constructions of "blackness" and "whiteness," primarily because prevailing discourses of race and racial segregation in the late-nineteenth- and early-twentieth-century American culture developed this bifurcation more pervasively than other models of racial diversity. . . . I do not specifically interrogate the cultural constructions of Asian, Jewish, or Native American bodies, for instance, but recent work by scholars such as Lisa Lowe, Sander Gilman, and others suggests that this line of inquiry deserves further research. (Somerville, *Queering the Color Line* 13)

While Somerville at least addresses the limitation of her analysis, what remains troubling is the question of whether constructions of "blackness" and "whiteness" can actually be meaningfully analyzed without an attention to constructions of "Indianness." I would argue that—in fact—they cannot, especially within the contexts of US colonialism. And while dominant discourses of race that focus on a black–white dichotomy may indeed be those that consciously prevail, this is certainly not because of a lack of discourse around Native people and politics from the late nineteenth and early twentieth centuries. US politics are rooted in the "Indian Problem," the question of exactly what to "do" with the Indigenous people already living on land that the United States wants. This is a central political debate throughout US history, and certainly central to racial politics, creating voluminous "documents and histories written *about* Native peoples by folks who had something to lose if Indians were seen as fully human" (Powell, "Dreaming Charles Eastman" 116). The "Indian problem" was (and continues to be) a central dilemma of US empire. Race cannot be understood in this country if Native people, Native nations, and Native bodies are un-seen.

Does this mean that I expect the writers I mention above—or those in the new queer studies that are not mentioned—to focus their work on Native people? Of course not. We each have our work to do, and it is perfectly understandable to me that Gopinath's work focuses on diasporic South Asian communities, that Manalansan's work focuses on diasporic Filipino gay men, or that Somerville's work focuses on black-white constructions of race. What is troubling, however, is the way that an analysis of an ongoing colonialism and a Native presence is made absent in these critiques. This un-seeing—even if unintentional—perpetuates a master narrative in which Native people are erased from an understanding of racial formations, Native histories are ignored, Native people are thought of as historical rather than contemporary, and our homelands aren't seen as occupied by colonial powers. This brings us to question whether Native people, histories, and decolonial struggles are actually part of scholarly and political consciousness and imagination. While I don't think that scholars need to change the focus of their work, I *do* expect scholars to integrate Indigenous and decolonial theories into their critiques.

Native people are not only another group of colour that "new" queer critiques should include. The experiences of Native people differ substantially from other people of colour in North America, and these differences give rise to very particular forms of resistance. Chrystos writes: "It is not a 'simple' (I use this term sarcastically) war of racism, which is the struggle of other Peoples of Color living here, although we also fight racism. This continent is morally and legally our land, since no treaty has been observed. . . . Logically, then, we remain at war in a unique way—not for a piece of the 'white pie,' but because we do not agree that there is a pie at all" (*Fire Power* 127). While I do not necessarily agree that all non-Native people of colour are fighting for inclusion in an already existing system, Chrystos brings up a major paradigm shift that must take place for solidarity work to happen with Native people: *the United States and Canada are not postcolonial.*

I am suspicious of emergent queer critiques, as valuable as they might be, because of the startling absence of Native people and the colonization of Native nations in these theories. Native people must *disidentify* with the very critiques that claim to be decolonial and counterhegemonic interventions for queer people of colour in order to make them viable for our communities. Through disidentification, other critiques emerge that centralize Native peoples, nations, identities, land bases, and survival tactics, which can be called Two-Spirit critiques. Two-Spirit critiques emerge from this disidentification to create theories in which Two-Spirit people and decolonization are centralized. These critiques not only serve to disidentify with queer of colour and queer diasporic critique; they also create more robust and effective interventions in systems of oppression from which both Native studies and queer studies can benefit. By pulling together splints from both disciplines, we can doubleweave Two-Spirit critiques that challenge and sharpen our scholarship and activism.

As part of this doubleweaving, I would like to invite an alliance between queer studies and Native studies that can interrupt the un-seeing of Native people that serves to bolster the colonial project. Powell writes:

> We cannot separate scholarship in the United States from the "American tale." We cannot separate the material exterminations of first-wave genocide in North America (beginning in 1492) from the intellectual and cultural exterminations of second-wave genocide, a process that has been ongoing since the Indian Removal Act of 1830. But we can begin, by consciously and explicitly positioning our work within this distasteful collection of narratives, to open space for the existing stories that might run counter to the imperial desires of traditional scholarship, stories that have been silenced by its hegemonic drone. ("Blood and Scholarship" 4)

Part of the colonial experience for Native people in the United States is that we are constantly disappeared through the stories that non-Native people tell, or don't tell, about us. Too often, other people of colour are as complicit in acts of un-seeing Native people as Euro-Americans. Native studies poses a challenge to queer studies, including its most recent waves of scholarship, because it problematizes many of the theories that queer of colour critique draws from.[10]

Native people often have an uneasy relationship with other struggles for social justice because the specificity of our struggles—rooted in sovereignty and a claim to land—is too often ignored. This uneasiness pertains to many of the radical theories that queer of colour critique draws from. For instance, women of colour feminisms—which Gopinath (*Impossible Desires*), Muñoz (*Disidentifications* 21–25), and Ferguson (*Aberrations in Black* 4) have all articulated as central to queer of colour critiques—certainly have an important place in the struggles of Native people. But, like postcolonial theory, they do not necessarily include Native concerns in their formations. Native feminist analyses often see patriarchy as a tool of colonization and understand our current situation as colonial, not *post*colonial. Chrystos writes, "What we experience is not patriarchy, but the process of colonization, which immigrant women have profited from right along with the greedy boys. Patriarchy is only one of many tools of colonizer mentality & is often used by women against other women" (128). Similarly, Smith addresses how patriarchal violence is used in genocidal projects launched against Native people: "The extent to which Native peoples are not seen as 'real' people in the larger colonial discourse indicates the success of sexual violence, among other racist and colonialist forces, in destroying the perceived humanity of Native peoples" (*Conquest* 12). Native feminisms, while allied with other women of colour and radical feminisms, have very clear decolonial agendas, see patriarchal violence as a tool of colonialism, and see themselves as part of struggles for sovereignty, land redress, and cultural continuance.

If queer of colour critique claims intellectual genealogies with traditions that un-see Native people, what can it offer to Two-Spirit communities? I am not saying it has nothing to offer us. On the contrary, it has immense potential for Two-Spirit scholars and activists. Queer of colour critique is an important means to disrupt discourses of empire, hold nationalist agendas accountable, and build theories and practices that understand racism, queerphobias, and gender oppressions as always entwined. Two-Spirit critiques push queer of colour critique to pay attention to the unique situations and politics of Native Two-Spirit/GLBTQ people living under US and Canadian colonialism.

Doubleweaving the Splints of Two-Spirit Critiques

I want to make clear here that I am not attempting to posit Two-Spirit critiques as new or singular. There isn't *a* Two-Spirit critique. And, while I use Two-Spirit critiques as an umbrella term, it is meant to open up possibilities for tribally specific, Two-Spirit/queer critiques rather than to create a single, pantribal critique.[11] And these critiques are already being theorized not only in scholarship but also in artistic and activist movements. While the work of Two-Spirit activists, artists, and scholars has largely been left out of queer studies, we have been present and writing and resisting in various activist, artistic, and academic communities for what is now decades (and more). What I would like to do here is tug on a few of the splints of this work, our dissent lines, to doubleweave Two-Spirit critiques into the centre of a conversation.

While these are not the only features of Two-Spirit critiques, there are several things that I think Two-Spirit critiques *do* that are important to ongoing struggles for social justice and radical scholarship. I would like to outline these practices and briefly address them.

Two-Spirit critiques see Two-Spirit people and traditions as both integral to and a challenge to nationalist and decolonial struggles.

While Two-Spirit critiques hold Native nations and peoples accountable for misogyny and homophobia, they simultaneously see Two-Spirit people and traditions as necessary—if not central—to national and decolonial struggles. Or, in Womack's words in his discussion of Southeastern Native conceptions of difference, "Rather than disrupting society, anomalies actually reify the existing social order. Anomalous beings can also be powerful; queerness has an important place" (*Red on Red* 244). Two-Spirit critiques see Two-Spirits as valuable participants in struggles for sovereignty and decolonization, even while they call into account the hetero-sexism and gender oppressions taking place in Native communities. In addition to seeing "queerness" as deconstructive of some nationalist agendas, Two-Spirit critiques see Native Two-Spirit/GLBTQ people as necessary to nationalist struggles for decolonization and sovereignty.

Two-Spirit critiques are rooted in artistic and activist work and remain accountable to overlapping communities.

Two-Spirit critiques are created and maintained through the activist and artistic resistance of Two-Spirit people. Contemporary Two-Spirit movements take place in spaces cleared by Two-Spirit activists and artists who work in numerous communities including their nations, Native urban spaces, non-Native GLBTQ communities, feminist movements, and non-Native communities of colour. Many of our most important poets have been, and are, Two-Spirit and/or GLBTQ-identified, including Beth Brant, Chrystos, and Paula Gunn Allen. Through collections such as Brant's *Gathering of Spirit* and Gay American Indians and Will Roscoe's *Living the Spirit*, Two-Spirit people have used arts as Two-Spirit critiques. Two-Spirit critiques within academic writing, then, should not only look to these artists as models but also remain accountable and accessible to Two-Spirit people outside the academy. Native studies insists on methodologies and theories that are rooted in, responsible to, and in service of Native communities. Like women of colour feminisms, Native studies positions itself as activist scholarship that centralizes the relationship between theory and practice. Unfortunately, queer and feminist theories in the academy have a history of "theorizing" themselves away from grassroots communities. Many feminists of colour have offered useful critiques of academic appropriations of radical grassroots movements. For instance, bell hooks has this to say about academic feminism:

> While academic legitimation was crucial to the advancement of feminist thought, it created a new set of difficulties. Suddenly the feminist thinking that had emerged directly from theory and practice received less attention than theory that was metalinguistic, creating exclusive jargon; it was written solely for an academic audience. . . . As a consequence of academization of feminist thought in this manner undermines feminist movement via depoliticization. Deradicalized, it is like every other academic discipline with the only difference being the focus on gender. (*Feminism Is for Everybody* 22)

A similar critique is offered by Aurora Levins Morales:

> My intellectual life and that of other organic intellectuals, many of them women of color, is fully sophisticated enough for use. But in order to have value in the marketplace, the entrepreneurs and multinational developers must find a way to process it, to refine the rich multiplicity of our lives and all we have come to understand about them into high theory by the simple act of removing it, abstracting it beyond recognition, taking out the fiber, boiling it down until the vitality is oxidized away and then marketing it as their own and selling it back to us for more than we can afford. (*Medicine Stories* 69)

Not only do Two-Spirit critiques remain accountable to both academic and nonacademic audiences, they are informed by Two-Spirit artist and activist movements. Being Two-Spirit is a tactic of resistance to white supremacist colonialism. Two-Spirit critiques see theory practised through poetry, memoir, fiction, story, song, dance, theatre, visual art, film, and other genres. Theory is not just about interpreting genres: these genres *are* theory. Warrior argues that Native poets provide a model of the practice of intellectual sovereignty and should be used as a model for Native critical studies (*Tribal Secrets* 115–22). Two-Spirit critiques remember that "the only difference between a history, a theory, a poem, an essay, is the one that we have ourselves imposed" (Powell, "Listening to Ghosts" 15).

Two-Spirit critiques engage in both intertribal and tribally specific concerns.

The growing number of Two-Spirit organizations and gatherings in the United States and Canada focus on creating Two-Spirit communities across tribal nations, using the common goal of (re)claiming Two-Spirit identities as a way to bring Native people together.[12] While intertribal, Two-Spirit critiques also insist on tribally specific approaches as a way to create intertribal alliances and coalitions. Just as there is no such thing as a generalized "Native" person, there is no such thing as a general "Two-Spirit" identity. Thus, while Two-Spirit people come together across lines of region and nation, Two-Spirit identities and tactics are "rooted in a solid national center" (Womack, *Red on Red* 223).

Kathy Reynolds and Dawn McKinley's legal battle against the Cherokee Nation of Oklahoma (CNO) to be legally married under Cherokee law, for example, was specifically a Cherokee struggle not only to validate a same-sex union under CNO law, but also—through the hearings that resulted in this attempt—to reestablish specific Cherokee cultural memory of same-sex relationships and unions and challenge the notion that community recognition of same-sex relationships is outside Cherokee cultural precedent.[13] Non-Native radical queer movements might misunderstand Two-Spirit efforts to position ourselves within nations as assimilationist, or, as what Lisa Duggan calls *homonormative*, rather than acts of intellectual and rhetorical sovereignty (*The Twilight of Equality?* 50). The stance that we are—and should be—an integral part of our communities, that our genders and sexualities are something that actually *are* "normal" within traditional worldviews, marks Native Two-Spirit/queer politics as very separate from non-Native movements. Being *a part* of our nations and communities is actually an anti-assimilation stance against colonial projects—such as boarding/residential schools and forced Christianization—that have attempted to assimilate Native people into non-Native culture and tried to eradicate Indigenous sexualities and gender systems. Two-Spirit critiques call into question, then, how radical queer politics replicate colonial taxonomies and realities even as they attempt to disrupt them.

Does this mean Two-Spirit critiques don't call into account Native nationalisms that replicate colonialism? Of course not—the legal challenge to the definitions of marriage in the CNO mentioned above did just that. But it does mean that the challenges against homophobic and heterosexist Native nationalisms are not seen as antinationalist but as part of larger nationalist and decolonial struggles.

Two-Spirit critiques are woven into Native feminisms by seeing sexism, homophobia, and transphobia as colonial tools.

While queer of colour critique draws on and expands women of colour feminisms, Native feminisms are central to Two-Spirit critiques, which see heterosexism and gender regimes as manifestations and tools of colonialism and genocide. Homophobia, transphobia, and misogyny are part of colonial projects intent on murdering, removing, and marginalizing Native bodies and nations. As Smith argues: "U.S. empire has always been reified by enforced heterosexuality and binary gender systems. By contrast, Native societies were not necessarily structured through binary gender systems. Rather, some of these societies had multiple genders and people did not fit rigidly into particular gender categories. Thus, it is not surprising that the first peoples targeted for destruction in Native communities were those who did not fit into Western gender categories" (*Conquest* 178). Such Native feminist analyses, already critiquing heteropatriarchy and colonialism, are crucial to Two-Spirit critiques. The theories of Two-Spirit and queer Native women—such as Chrystos, Brant, Janice Gould, and Miranda—establish Two-Spirit-centred feminist critiques that challenge misogyny and queerphobia (Gould, "Disobedience (in Language)" 32–44).

As mentioned earlier, the enormous presence of queer women in Native studies as central to arts and scholarship has meant that these women can't be ignored. However, they are often included without queerness being discussed. Out queer men in Native studies are only recently being published to a degree that intervenes in the field, and too often the queerness of these artists and scholars remains in barely tolerated margins. The presence of trans people in the field, as in much of academia, remains largely underrepresented. In queer studies, Native people are largely ignored unless as "subjects" of anthropological and historical research that demonstrate an idealized "queer" past that can bolster non-Native queer identities.[14] Native feminisms offer critiques and activist agendas that work for decolonization by understanding heteropatriarchy as a colonial tool.

Two-Spirit critiques are informed by and make use of other Native activisms, arts, and scholarship.

Two-Spirit critiques use the materials available to weave radical and transformational critiques. Native Two-Spirit/queer people are already participating in several Native activist, artistic, and academic movements. These movements—even if not "Two-Spirit"—are part of the splints that doubleweave Two-Spirit resistance. Within our scholarship, critical theories in Native studies help strengthen Two-Spirit critiques. American Indian literary nationalisms, for instance, can aid in developing Two-Spirit critiques that are simultaneously tribally specific and speak to intertribal concerns (Weaver, Womack, and Warrior). To offer another example, both Winona LaDuke's (*All Our Relations*; *Recovering the Sacred*) and Melissa K. Nelson's (*Original Instructions*) scholarship and activism can push Two-Spirit critiques to articulate how issues of environmental justice and traditional knowledges intersect with and inform Native Two-Spirit/queer identities and struggles.[15] Two-Spirit critiques contextualize themselves as part of decolonial work already in motion.

Two-Spirit critiques see the erotic as a tool in decolonial struggles.

Two-Spirit critiques see the erotic as a power that can aid in decolonization and healing of historical trauma. Miranda speaks to how Native women's erotic lives disrupt genocidal misogyny and holds colonial powers accountable for past and present abuses: "If Native women, who bear the scars from five hundred years of erotic murder in this country, suddenly become visible, there is hell to pay. . . . The living history of Native women's bodies reveal that the mythic foundation of the United States is not a bedrock of democracy and freedom, but a shameful nightmare of unstable and treacherous sandstone, crumbling with each true vision of a Native woman's erotic existence" ("Dildos, Hummingbirds, and Driving Her Crazy" 145).

Miranda also calls for an Indigenous-centred, healing erotic that she calls *grace*, which "has a particular context for this particular continent: the perpetual act of balanc*ing*—always working toward balance through one's actions, intent, and understanding of the world" (*The Zen of La Llorona* 4). Similarly, I have suggested that a *sovereign erotic* can be used as a Two-Spirit tactic for healing historical trauma and as a tool in decolonial struggles ("Call Me Brother" 223–34; "Stolen from Our Bodies," 50–64). Numerous Native Two-Spirit/queer writers and artists, such as Alberta (*Deep Inside Clint Star*), Brant (*Mohawk Trail* 31–35), Chrystos (*In Her I Am*), Justice ("Fear of a Changeling Moon" 87–108), and Gregory Scofield (*Love Medicine and One Song*) have likewise formulated the erotic as central to Indigenous resistance. Two-Spirit critiques pay close attention to our erotic histories and lives, the way colonization attempts to disrupt and injure Indigenous erotics, and examines how Indigenous erotics disrupt colonial power over our sexualities and bodies.

Two-Spirit critiques see Two-Spirit identities in relationship with spirituality and medicine.

This, I think, is an important difference between Two-Spirit critiques and (other) queer critiques. Two-Spirit critiques position Two-Spirit identities as part of responsible spiritual relationships with Native communities, land bases, and historical memory. LaFortune asserts that the term *Two-Spirit* "in no way . . . determine[s] genital activity. It does determine the qualities that define a person's social role and spiritual gifts" ("Postcolonial Colonial Perspective" 221).

The stance that Two-Spirit people carry very *particular* medicine—which is not to be misunderstood as more (or less) important than men's or women's particular medicines—is one rooted within Native worldviews and land bases, and separates itself from non-Native belief systems as part of larger practices of maintaining and continuing Native cultural practices. While radical white-dominated queer movements often attempt to reject religion because of institutionalized homophobia and heterosexism or—on the other hand—create spiritual movements and communities that often appropriate Native practices, Native Two-Spirit/GLBTQ people insist that we already have a place within traditional religious and spiritual life. It is this part of our identities that many Two-Spirit movements emphasize. This is not a way to desexualize our identities in order to be acceptable to non-Two-Spirit/GLBTQ people, as non-Native radical queer movements might argue. It is a way to acknowledge our specific roles in cultural continuance. Two-Spirit oppositional politics are oppositional to colonial powers and to colonial values and epistemologies, including those internalized by Native communities. However, while radical non-Native queer movements formulate queerness as oppositional and antinormative, Two-Spirit critiques locate Two-Spirit and queer Native identities as integrated into larger Indigenous worldviews and practices. Two-Spirit activism works to mend and transform the relationships Native communities have with Two-Spirit and queer people. In this way, radical Two-Spirit politics are not oppositional in the way radical queer movements are; they seek to create and maintain balanced relationships and power dynamics in our communities as part of decolonial activism.

Taking these splints of Two-Spirit critiques and doubleweaving them into a conversation with queer studies pushes queer studies in the United States and Canada toward decolonial work that is responsible to the land and lives it builds itself on. Two-Spirit critiques simultaneously challenge and strengthen work in queer studies that seeks to decentralize white, male, middle-class formulations of queerness.

David Eng, Judith Halberstam, and Muñoz have asked, "What does queer studies have to say about empire, globalization, neoliberalism, sovereignty, and terrorism? What does queer studies tell us about immigration, citizenship, prisons, welfare, mourning, and human rights?" (2). While these moves in queer studies are creating productive theories, they haven't addressed the complicated colonial realities of Native people in the United States and Canada. In an attempt to answer the questions posited above within specifically Native contexts, Two-Spirit critiques point to queer studies' responsibility to examine ongoing colonialism, genocide, survival, and resistance of Native nations and peoples. Further, they challenge queer studies to complicate notions of nationhood and diaspora by paying attention to the specific circumstances of nations indigenous to the land bases the United States and Canada are colonizing. To push the above questions farther, I would like to ask what Two-Spirit critiques can tell us about these same issues. In addition, what can Two-Spirit critiques tell us about nationhood, diaspora, colonization, and decolonization? What do they have to say about Native nationalisms, treaty rights, citizenship, and noncitizenship? What can they tell us about the boarding/residential schools, biopiracy, the Allotment Act, the Removal Act, the Relocation Act, the Reorganization Act, and the Indian Act? How can they inform our understandings of the roles of misogyny, homophobia, transphobia, and heterosexism in colonization? What do they have to say about Native language restoration, traditional knowledge, and sustainability? What do Two-Spirit critiques teach us about survival, resistance, and continuance?

Two-Spirit critiques are part of ongoing weavings to resist colonialism. "On our separate, yet communal journeys," Brant tells us, "we have learned that a hegemonic gay and lesbian movement cannot encompass our complicated history—history that involves so much loss. Nor can a hegemonic gay and lesbian movement give us tools to heal our broken Nations. But our strength as a family not only gives tools, it helps *make* tools" (*Writing as Witness* 45). Two-Spirit critiques are a *making* that asks all of our disciplines and movements to formulate analyses that pay attention to the current colonial occupation of Native lands and nations and the way Two-Spirit bodies and identities work to disrupt colonial projects.[16] By doubleweaving splints from queer studies and Native studies, Two-Spirit critiques can aid in the resistance struggles of Native communities and help create theories and movements that are inclusive and responsive to Native Two-Spirit/GLBTQ people.

Wado to my ancestors for getting me here alive. Wado to the People of the Three Fires, the Tawakoni, and the Tonkawa Nations whose lands this essay was written on. Wado to the editors, the outside reviewers, and to Lisa Tatonetti for their comments and feedback on earlier versions of this essay. Wado to all of the Native Two-Spirit and queer folks whose conversations, art, and activism deeply inform my work.

Notes

This essay was first published in *GLQ: A Journal of Lesbian and Gay Studies* 16, nos. 1–2 (2010): 69–92.

1. My discussion in this essay focuses on Native Two-Spirit/GLBTQ politics in the United States and Canada, and—because of my own geographic and political locations—mostly the former.
2. Craig S. Womack, in writing about Harjo's work, has likewise talked about the centrality of imagination in decolonial processes. He writes, "The process of decolonizing one's mind, a first step before one can gain a political consciousness and engage oneself in activism, has to begin with imagining some alternative" (*Red on Red* 230).
3. My own slippage between numerous terms in this essay is intended to move to reflect these practices.
4. This is not because Two-Spirit people are somehow more spiritual than non-Two-Spirit people, as the appropriation of the term by New Agers might suggest. Rather, spiritual and ceremonial traditions are part of a continuance of cultural memory that Two-Spirit people, like other members of Native communities, are often a part of. Beverly Little Thunder writes, "In the non-Native community of lesbians and gay people I have been told that being two-spirited means that I am a special being. It seems that they felt that my spirituality was the mystical answer to my sexuality. I do not believe this to be. My spirituality would have been with me, regardless of my sexuality" ("I Am a Lakota Womyn" 207).
5. Wado to both Angela Haas and Malea Powell to their ongoing work on material rhetorics.
6. While I understand Hill's description here, it is also a bit misleading. Doublewoven baskets are not two complete baskets with a common rim, though they might look this way. The process of doubleweaving—in brief—involves weaving the inside base and walls of the basket, then turning the same splint back down over itself to weave the outside walls and base. Doublewoven baskets are one continuous weave.
7. While there is not space to articulate this line of thought in this article, my ongoing work examines doubleweave as a Cherokee rhetorical theory, practice, and methodology.
8. Michel de Certeau distinguishes between *strategies* and *tactics* that are based in power differentials. He writes that a *strategy* is "the calculation (or manipulation) of power relationships that becomes possible as soon as a subject with will and power . . . can be isolated. . . . It is an effort to delimit one's own place in the world bewitched by the invisible powers of the Other." A *tactic*, on the other hand, "is a calculated action determined by the absence of a proper locus. . . . The space of a tactic is the space of the other" (*The Practice of Everyday Life* 35–37). This distinction is important because it pays attention to the specific ways in which those in power engage in practices to stay in power (*strategies*) and those who are oppressed employ practices that subvert those in power and resist oppression (*tactics*).
9. For instance, Muñoz, *Disidentifications*, 29; Ferguson, *Aberrations in Black*, 15, 17.
10. While this article focuses on the interventions Two-Spirit critiques can make in queer studies, Two-Spirit critiques also offer important challenges to both Native

studies and Native nations by pushing at who exactly is included within current formations and movements of Native nation building and sovereignty struggles.

11. Part of my current work, for instance, is to theorize Cherokee-centred Two-Spirit and queer critiques. Because *asegi* is a Cherokee word that means "strange" and is being translated as *queer*, I am thinking of these particular critiques as *asegi stories*. The intersections of Native and queer studies can help us imagine numerous tribally specific Two-Spirit/queer critiques.

12. For an in-depth discussion of these movements, see Brian Joseph Gilley's *Becoming Two-Spirit*.

13. For further information on the Cherokee same-sex marriage case, see N. Bruce Duthu, *American Indians and the Law*, 147–50.

14. For further analysis of this pattern, see Scott Morgensen, *Spaces Between Us: Queer Settler Colonialism and Indigenous Decolonization* (U of Minnesota P, 2010).

15. More information on LaDuke's activism can be found through the Native Harvest/White Earth Land Recovery Project: nativeharvest.com. More information on Nelson's activism can be found through the Cultural Conservancy: www.nativeland.org.

16. The use of the term *making* here to describe an intellectual and rhetorical practice is drawn from Powell's work on Material Rhetorics and personal conversations with her during and after visiting her Material Rhetorics graduate course at Michigan State University in the spring of 2008.

35

Finding Your Voice:
Cultural Resurgence and
Power in Political Movement

Katsisorokwas Curran Jacobs

My people have never really been idle; in fact, protest and political movement are at the forefront of my daily life, from the moment I present my status card to a store clerk, to the moment I disclose my ethnicity and cultural beliefs to a stranger. I do believe that my people are all born fighting the system. In the past, we have seen mobilization and solidarity among the First Nation's population in the wake of trauma and disagreement. I was born Mohawk, in the midst of Oka, yet I have no personal recollection of the events, but rather a collective one from the story of my birth and the general memories of my community. The Oka crisis remains a point of reference I continue to reflect upon; it is a point of reference for my entire community, as we move forward through the decolonization process.

Another point of reference is the Idle No More (INM) movement. The movement began as a call to arms in opposition to policies and bills presented by the Harper administration. Native people from across Canada (and eventually the US, as well) came together to oppose the proposed legislation, but the resistance carried greater weight than just opposition to legislation. Non-Aboriginal Canadians, generally confused by the specific acts and legislations affecting our lives and typically isolated from our concerns, were mobilized to join us. This movement brought us together as a whole, as co-habitants of this land called Canada, united in the opposition to the government, a political power that is the result of hundreds of years of imposed legislation and oppression and that is not representative of where we should be.

Segregation took several forms within Canada's borders. The reservation system physically segregated Aboriginal and non-Aboriginal Canadians, which is a source of contention. Conversations often surround the Native people of Canada as being "here," but without our ever really being seen. Reserves are approached as remote worlds of their own, wherein the Native people sort of exist and allegedly drain tax dollars. Often, I have heard the notion that Native people need to "get it together and stop wasting federal money." This kind of comment suggests that the "us and them" dichotomy extends well beyond physical location. Fundamental cultural differences as well as conflicting worldviews create a divide. This divide is based on racial lines—although even these blur, as many non-Native Canadians have traces of Indigenous ancestry—but also and more specifically on political lines.

A non-Native Canadian may have the utmost respect, understanding, support, and positive interaction with the First Nations; however, in their support of the Canadian government, whether conservative or liberal, they are automatically connected to that government's oppression. Deferring to its authority shows that you agree with its policies, its corruption, its "best interests," and its every move. For some, understanding this concept enabled a fundamental shift in the "us and them" dichotomy that undergirds Canadian society. Not all non-Native Canadians, however, partake in the "them" in this equation. The "them" are those in this country who continue to perpetuate the political infrastructure that is responsible for having put us (Native people) through distress, and that is continuing to create legislation in the same, undemocratic manner. The term "Settler Ally" has thus become a frequent identifier for any non-Aboriginal Canadian citizens who joined the protests and supported the movement. This distinction is important.

During the early days of the Idle No More movement, I was quick to jump on the bandwagon, because, finally in my adult life, I found an opportunity to show solidarity and voice my opinions about my identity as a young Kanien'kehá:ka woman, what it meant to claim this title, and what I believed was wrong with the proposed legislations. With the help of one of my professors, I organized a teach-in at my university with the intent of educating the mostly white undergraduate population about what was happening and how they, too, were implicated in the proposed bills. Participants in my teach-in asked me "what can I do?" or "how does this affect me?" rather than "what are you fighting for?" It became our fight: First Nations and Settler Allies.

INM was like an explosion caused by a slow leak. The founders of this movement mobilized and began sharing their perspectives to the surrounding people. In Saskatchewan, Sylvia McAdam approached her friends Nina Wilson, Jessie Gordon, and Sheela McLean, and, as a collective, they created

Idle No More. Their intentions stemmed from the ominous Bill C-45, which they believed would erode Indigenous rights and inevitably be detrimental to the environment. Through social media and the channels opened between First Nations communities across the country, the fire ignited. Around the same time, Chief Theresa Spence of the Attawapiskat First Nation began her hunger strike as a protest to address the housing crisis in her community. With Chief Spence in the news, and the four women who initiated INM continuing to spark enthusiasm from the prairies, the fire grew. Very quickly, Nations across the country were mobilizing teach-ins, protests, and, most famously, the flash mob round dances that took place in shopping centres across the country. It seemed as if people came together overnight. While the shopping centres were quiet in my college town, through social media and news reports, I watched the birth of the movement evolve. What was most inspiring about this moment brings me back to my own community. Several round dances and protests were organized in the city centre of Montreal. I even made the drive out to one of them with some of my newly found Settler Ally friends. While many people from home participated in those events, in true Kahnawáke fashion, they took matters into their own hands. Unlike the hostility of Oka's blockade, my community staged a peaceful protest and stopped traffic on the bridge for a short yet powerful moment. It was beautiful to see so many Kahnawákeró:non come together and fly their flags, play their drums, and march for their rights and beliefs. Whereas communities are often divided, this movement gave us a taste of what can be achieved if we come together and leave our differences checked at the door. It was an inspiring, eye-opening experience.

This movement was unique because it was predominantly youth-driven. Idle No More acted as a catalyst for youth like myself to step forward and be reminded that we do have a voice. Ironically, the most assimilated of us, enrolled in western institutions to pursue higher education, used our education to speak out and speak out loudly. Yet Aboriginal youth from a wide variety of experiences and backgrounds were stepping up, and, in some cases, literally walking from their communities to Ottawa to have their voices heard. For example, a small group of Great Whale Cree[1]—consisting of six youth and a forty-nine-year-old—walked a distance over one-thousand kilometres in the middle of winter to arrive in Ottawa, in order to draw attention to Aboriginal issues. The path one walked made no difference in one's approach to this movement—it was the intentions that aligned. Ultimately, Idle No More sparked what I consider a resurgence of Indigenous cultures across Turtle Island. It was and remains an example of decolonization in action.

The term decolonization is new to my vocabulary and relatively new to the discourse of Canadian and First Nations relations. Aligning our concerns and our understanding of the history of our country, and reconciling our past are all a part of the process of decolonization. This reconciliation extends far beyond public apologies, money grants, and false promises. It is a claiming of history from both sides, and understanding the changes that need to be done to move forward. On a small scale, this is what was happening during Idle No More. INM was more than a political movement; it was an opportunity for social healing. Native and Non-Native together, as I experienced it, were working on understanding and reconciling our differences.

Democracy is often linked to the ancient civilizations of Greece. Over on Turtle Island, we continuously forget who our own ancients were, and how democracy has roots there, too. Western attitudes suggest to us that the Indigenous of Canada only date as far back as contact. While we have no written documentation due to our languages and oral traditions, I can say that, at least for the Haudenosaunee (or Iroquois Confederacy), a democracy has existed for centuries. The Grand Council of the Confederacy initiated a fair, cooperative form of governance that managed to sustain us. You can only imagine the other ways in which other Nations managed to survive, up until the point of contact. This is a fundamental truth: the democracy we are asking for is different than the democracy of the western world. The ideologies of *us* and *them* will never be the same, and will never fulfill both our societies' wants and desires. But what we are looking for is greater than simply winning this battle we've begun. It's about coming to a compromise. It's about coming to an understanding and an agreement, a common ground. It's about fulfilling the promises of the Two Row Wampum, to be able to coexist with one another in peace and harmony along the river. Most importantly, however, it is about planning for our future generations. I can guarantee that if things are not changed now, then there will be no future for the generations.

My father and I have sat down and discussed the state of our people and the country we have come to live in. We talk about the importance of building and maintaining the Mohawk Nation and our cultural traditions, but even more often we discuss the importance of keeping the land safe and cared-for. These conversations, however, need to happen beyond the confines of my living room, with those who are not seeing these truths: non-Aboriginal Canadians. This was the reason for organizing a teach-in at my university. Rather than allowing them to be bystanders, merely observing through Twitter and news reports, I invited them to join the conversation and to understand their role in the equation. Furthermore, I wanted to share a little piece of our worldview and to provoke critical thought with regard to the current democratic system of power. Unlike the standard lecture model of a teacher providing facts simply meant to be absorbed, another method of teaching—a more organic kind—was my approach. Engaging in critical thought and discussion of a complex situation was the order of business, especially since they were all implicated in the issue at hand.

In the closing remarks of the teach-in that I organized, I read a piece I had written in the heat of the moment. It was a collection of my thoughts and feelings surrounding the movement; it also was the skeleton of this piece. One of the last things I said to the audience before closing was a recounting of a conversation I had with my mother. I voiced my distrust in the world; I told her that I didn't like our world enough to want to bring children into it. However, as I experienced the power of people coming together and what they can achieve, I changed my mind. I am going to bring children into this world, because I can help to change it and make it a better place. Idle No More did this for me.

Note

1. The six young men, Johnny Abraham, Stanley George Jr., Travis George, David Kawapit, Raymond Kawapit, and Geordie Rupert, were accompanied by Elder Isaac Kawapit. They are better known as the Nishiyuu Walkers.

36

From *haa-huu-pah* to the Decolonization Imperative: Responding to Contemporary Issues Through the TRC

Laura Moss

As one in a series of seven National Events, the Truth and Reconciliation Commission of Canada (TRC) came to Vancouver in the fall of 2013. The event was intended for survivors to tell their stories, and for others to learn more about the history of the Indian Residential Schools (IRS) system and the legacies of the Indian Act. The University of British Columbia's Faculty Senate "voted to suspend classes on September 18th to honour the opening of the Truth and Reconciliation Commission's BC National Event and to help develop a better awareness and understanding of the Indian Residential School system that operated in Canada from 1875–1996, and how its effects are still with us today." UBC staff and students were encouraged to attend the TRC events at the Pacific National Exhibition grounds. Further, faculty were encouraged to integrate the history of Indian Residential Schools into course curricula across the disciplines, and the university offered workshops on how to do so. The First Nations and Indigenous Studies Program also hosted a "Teach In" to discuss the problems both of the TRC itself and of trying to bring the long history of discrimination, abuse, inequitable treatment, and exploitation of Indigenous peoples in Canada into the classroom. Together, the educational initiatives leading up to the TRC Event, alongside the TRC itself, illustrate the complexity of contemporary issues for Indigenous and non-Indigenous communities in Canada. The essays in this section of the anthology probe subjects pertinent to the TRC, such as Canada's settler-invader history, ongoing forms of both colonization and decolonization, negotiating guilt, reconciliation, kinship, personhood, and the doubleweaving of Two-Spirited and Native Studies. Drawing on some of the ideas raised in these articles, in this afterword I briefly consider the benefits and limitations of bringing the TRC onto the campus, and then discuss the South African TRC as a companion case.

One recurring argument in the articles in this section concerns the need for historical and contextual specificity and the urgency of re-considering methodologies. Such a recognition of the need for reframing was also key to the institutional approach to the TRC undertaken at UBC. In one workshop in preparation for the Vancouver TRC Event, Amy Perrault (Métis), Coordinator of Aboriginal Initiatives for the UBC Centre for Teaching, Learning, and Technology, recommended that, at a basic level, all classes at UBC should always begin with a "thank you to the Musqueam people for welcoming UBC students, staff, and faculty onto their territory and into their community." It is notable that other people at the university phrase this acknowledgement more directly and publicly recognize that UBC sits on the unceded territory of the Musqueam people. With this gesture, Perrault emphasized the link between the present, the institution, people, place, and story. She focused on the value of teaching students to acknowledge the relationship between where they are and what has occurred in that place over decades and centuries. Perrault's comments echo those of Jeff Corntassel, Chaw-win-is, and T'lakwadzi on the Indigenous methodology of *haa-huu-pah* (or teaching stories) as a form of restorying place and gesture toward Daniel Justice's "decolonization imperative."

Part of the mandate of the TRC was to "promote awareness and public education"[1] and to bring the larger Canadian community into the "process of reconciliation." In recognition of these goals, UBC suspended classes and established what they branded as "Our Truth." The conjunction of the words "our" and "truth," here, deserves attention. On the one hand, the institution recognized the significance of the TRC and worked toward disseminating knowledge about some of the most damaging parts of Canadian history. The desire was, I think, to bring history into the present, to acknowledge complicity publicly, and to refuse to adhere to an us/them binary by asserting that the IRS was all of "our" truth. In voting to suspend classes, the UBC Senate tried to ensure that students and staff could not lean on an excuse of ignorance, as many have in the past, and say they didn't know about the residential schools. The university took responsibility for a social justice educational imperative and urged its constituency to engage in the valuable process of decolonizing knowledge. At its best, bringing the TRC onto campus was meant to teach awareness of history and to consider that history in the framework of decolonization and anti-colonial struggles. In *Pedagogy of the Oppressed*, educational reformer Paulo Freire argues that students need to develop critical conscious-ness (*conscientização* in Portuguese) with the ability to read the word and the world. Through public engagement with the stories of the abuse and systemic injustice of the IRS, ideally—perhaps idealistically—the TRC's mandate was to develop critical consciousness in the broad Canadian community. UBC tapped into that goal. With the TRC ongoing, the attainment of a national critical con-sciousness, as well as local recognition, is still very much up for debate.

On the other hand, however, I am concerned that by claiming the hist-ory of the IRS as "our truth," the institution co-opted the testimonies and the experiences of those who survived the residential schools. I am troubled by the potential tokenism and pathologization of victimhood and survival. I am anxious that faculty untrained in the necessary history might only have been able to give a potted version of events without a depth of understanding of hundreds of years of treaties and policies. Could they have answered student questions about how and why? Is a potentially superficial history better than no history? I worry that by historicizing the IRS, people might think systemic discrimination and colonization are things of the past. More broadly, in terms of the commission, I question when individual stories are used for communal healing at the potential expense of the individuals telling their own stories. What happens, I ask, when an individual person's stories/history/memory are presented for the greater good of civic and national reconciliation? Several UBC colleagues articulated further concerns about the TRC itself at the "Teach In" that preceded the day of suspended classes. Sunera Thobani asked four powerful questions: Who benefits from the TRC? What kind of reconciliation is possible among unequal power entities? Where is justice in the TRC? What happens to justice when the focus is on healing? In discussing the "politics of resentment" and the "apology industry," Glen Coulthard (Yellowknives Dene) wondered whether the concepts of reconciliation and forgiveness, while offer-ing important solace to some people, might just be "a Band-Aid that never actually heals the wound." Dory Nason (Anishinaabe) emphasized Native women's perspectives on reconciliation and the effects of patriarchal and col-onial laws on Indigenous women. She also argued for the need to hear the stories of life and violence that Native women tell through art, literature, and film, and she expressed concern that such stories might be subsumed under larger communal narratives. The article in this anthology by Leanne Simpson provides Nason's points with a useful background in theories of Indigenous feminism and in terms of gender, sexuality, language, violence, and healing. One of the most critical contemporary concerns today in Aboriginal and non-Aboriginal communities is the degree to which there is unstopped vio-lence against women, and that the number of missing and murdered women in

Canada continues to rise. The article by Amber Dean speaks to this important issue. Deena Rymhs' article in this section further complicates the notion of reconciliation and the appropriation of guilt. Together, these articles provide an important grounding for consideration of private and public acts of remembering, witnessing, speaking, and storytelling.

Over the past decades there have been truth commissions in Argentina, Chile, and South Africa, to name a few. I teach both Canadian and South African literatures, and I often hear the South African Truth and Reconciliation Commission (SATRC, 1995–97) referred to as a precedent for the Canadian one. This comparison should be made with caution because of deep historical differences and because of the limitations acknowledged by the SATRC. In their excellent book, *Truth and Reconciliation in South Africa: Did It Deliver?*, Audrey Chapman and Hugo van der Merwe point out that "South Africa's Truth and Reconciliation Commission quickly became the model for other countries trying to come to terms with a past characterized by pervasive ethnic conflict, severe human rights abuses, and societal violence. Our experience with the TRC, however, suggested that the accolades at the least needed to be qualified" (vii). While I leave it to South African scholars to discuss these limitations in their proper context, it is useful to note that the SATRC's final report gestures toward its own shortcomings by citing Michael Ignatieff, who claims that "All that a truth commission can achieve is to reduce the number of lies that can be circulated unchallenged in public discourse" (111). The report further cites Ignatieff as offering a warning to "outsiders [who] have been sentimental about the South African process, as they have been about Nelson Mandela, the rainbow nation and so on. Everyone likes to watch a catharsis, especially if it is someone else's. For insiders, citizens in South Africa, Truth and Reconciliation was not a spectacle; it wasn't entertainment" (15). This also holds true for Canada and the Canadian TRC.

While the problem at the core of each system is discrimination based on racism and a colonial commitment to white supremacy, the historical specificities of South Africa and Canada vary considerably. Yet some of the lessons about the possible benefits and limitations of public engagement with individual testimonies learned in South Africa are pertinent to the Canadian context.[2] Given the context of "our truth," in particular, it is useful to look at the manner in which the SATRC represents the link between storytelling and truth. The report published by the SATRC articulated the purpose of "the Commission's quest for truth" and that its attempt "to uncover the past had nothing to do with vengeance; it had to do, rather, with helping victims to become more visible and more valuable citizens through the public recognition and official acknowledgement of their experiences" (1 (5) 27). In seeking recognition and acknowledgement, the South African TRC was the first truth commission to call for testimony to be held in public so that all South Africans (and, by extension, a global audience) could witness the abuses in the nation's past. Particularly relevant here, the South African TRC highlighted the importance of narrative, storytelling, and listening in the process of reconciliation and healing. The report notes that, "in contrast with criminal prosecutions, the purpose of a truth commission is to provide a narrative of a specific period and/or regime, determine the major causes of the violence, and make recommendations of measures to undertake so as to avoid a repetition in the future" (3). Further, the report cites "the words of Ms. Thenjiwe Mtintso, former chairperson of the Commission on Gender Equality and currently Deputy Secretary General of the ANC, at the opening of the Commission's hearing on women in Johannesburg, 29 July 1997: This hearing 'is the beginning of giving the voiceless a chance to speak, giving the excluded a chance to be centred and giving the powerless an opportunity to empower themselves'" (1 (5) 27). Mtintso articulated the need for restorying as a form of deep political and personal empowerment. Still, even when one's personal story is told in a public forum, that story becomes part of the larger process of narrative collection. As Lars Burr notes, in South Africa victims' testimonies were made to adhere to TRC's protocols: "the memories of victims materialized first as narratives, and then, through a chain of translations, became *signs* of gross human rights violations under apartheid, inscribed in statement protocols, the database, investigative reports, the Commission's archives, the final reports, and ultimately, the national archives" (80; original emphasis). The worry about the individual story being subsumed by the larger national narrative has been present in Canada as well, with some survivors who have chosen to testify in private and others who make their own stories heard in public, but with concern about what might happen to both the stories and the people.

One area in which those adherents to "our truth" might learn most productively from the South African Commission would be in its recognition of multiple kinds of truth. Shortly after commencing the TRC hearings, the South African Commission recognized that a singular concept of truth was limiting to the overall mandate. To acknowledge the complexity of the testimonies, speech, storytelling, and memories being presented from a variety of people and perspectives, they introduced "four notions of truth: factual or forensic truth; personal or narrative truth; social or 'dialogue' truth, and healing and restorative truth" (1 (5) 110). The first, "forensic truth" recognized the existence of objective, reliable, and corroborated evidence on an individual level and a contextual level. It asked, "what happened to whom, where, when and how, and who was involved?" (1 (5) 110). The second, "personal truth," acknowledged individual truths or stories victims might tell in their own languages. In allowing space for storytelling, "the Commission not only helped to uncover existing facts about past abuses, but also assisted in the creation of a 'narrative truth,'" and explicitly accepted the healing potential of telling stories. At a hearing of the Commission in Port Elizabeth on 21 May 1996, Archbishop Tutu said: "This Commission is said to listen to everyone. It is therefore important that everyone should be given a chance to say his or her truth as he or she sees it" (1 (5) 111). The third, "dialogue truth" is the "social truth, the truth of experience that is established through interaction, discussion and debate," which includes the act of listening carefully and participating actively. Finally, "healing and restorative truth" is articulated as "the kind of truth that places facts and what they mean within the context of human relationships—both amongst citizens and between the state and its citizens" (1 (5) 113). According to the *Truth and Reconciliation Commission of South Africa Report*, for truth to be restorative, acknowledgement "that a person's pain is real and worthy of attention [is] central to the restoration of the dignity of victims" (1 (5) 114). These four types of truth illustrate how the South African TRC members altered their methodology to account for the narrative realities of storytelling, testimony, and witnessing. Perhaps this notion could be brought into the Canadian TRC in regard to how stories of the past and the present are considered.

In the end, I come back to the desire, articulated in several of the articles in this section, for new, distinct or alternative, specifically Indigenous methodologies for storytelling and listening. From the focus on *haa-huu-pah* to the decolonization imperative and gendered engagement, the articles in this section help us rethink ways of approaching contemporary issues.

Notes

Thank you to Tracy Bear, Daniel Morley Johnson, Deena Rymhs, and Saylesh Wesley for discussing this anthology section at the "Approaching Indigenous Literatures in the 21st Century: How Shall We Teach These?" workshop in Vancouver at the Simon Fraser University Harbour Centre, 1 March 2014. My gratitude also extends to Linda Morra and Deanna Reder for conceiving of this anthology, encouraging collaboration at the workshop, and being committed to community engagement throughout.

1. See the section titled "What is the TRC," at http://trc.ca.
2. Rosemary Jolly writes about how the South African Commission itself has been misunderstood outside of South Africa because it is often read outside the specifics of history, and because of a liberal interpretation of justice that does not accord with a process that was based on an attempt to achieve reconciliation through amnesty (amnesty was a negotiated precondition for the democratic election of 1994 to go forward). This is a key distinction. Whereas in Canada, the TRC was a court-mandated instrument for social justice, recognition, and national education,

in South Africa, the TRC was, as Jolly notes, "a tool for democracy" (697). In South Africa, victims testified (the terminology is key here—the word *victim* was used rather than *survivor*, the term more commonly employed in Canada) and perpetrators of human rights abuses also testified (seeking amnesty). Perpetrator testimony has not been part of the Canadian TRC process and survivors have not been given the opportunity to look in the eye those responsible for the IRS and its abuses as they detail their own histories.

V

CLASSROOM CONSIDERATIONS

37

Introduction:
Classroom Considerations

Deanna Reder and Linda M. Morra

In support and celebration of the Idle No More movement, Kwakwaka'wak art-ist Sonny Assu created a series of panels called *There Is Hope, If We Rise.*[1] Most of the panels share the same abstract Northwest Coast First Nations image. At the bottom of each is an imperative: Rise; Round Dance; Confront; Resist. The first line on this series of panels is "Idle No More," which becomes by the second line, "Idle Know More." Subsequent instructions have to do with edu-cation: Teach, Learn, Challenge the Stereotypes. This call by Assu to "Know More" poses several challenges to Indigenous literary critics who live within, even as they push the limits of, the field.

First, as most Indigenous literary critics have come to understand, there are longstanding challenges in the classroom. It is still not uncommon for stu-dents, from first year to graduate school, and even for university faculty and staff to have no or limited knowledge of basic facts about the histories and social contexts of Indigenous peoples in North America. It is subsequently dif-ficult to make casual references to the damaging effects of legislation like Bill C-31 when students are not even aware of the pervasive influence of the Indian Act on Indigenous identities or the complexities of band membership, treaty rights, or the regulations that govern Status.

Second, even though there has been a significant increase in the intro-duction of Indigenous texts to university curricula, it is still not unusual to have literature students at the upper undergraduate level and even the gradu-ate level who have never read a book by an Indigenous writer. Without some familiarity of even a small sampling of Indigenous works, it makes it difficult to foster critical discussion of such texts as part of vibrant literary traditions, never mind inviting comparative analyses between Canadian and American or Cree and Sto:lo literatures.

Third, it is unlikely that literature students have even a cursory understanding of subjects like Inuit literature, Indigenous protocols governing orature, or the experience of listening to a classic *wîsashkêcâhk* story. However, given the prevalence of testimony in Canada provoked by the Truth and Reconciliation Commission, there likely *is* some experience of reading or listening to traumatic narratives. Also, since media innovations have been a cornerstone of such Aboriginal artist/activist collectives, such as beat nation or the Healthy Aboriginal Network, there is likely to be some familiarity with Indigenous hip-hop, or graphic novels, or on-line films. Still, the strategies and vocabularies required to engage with specific Indigenous storytelling traditions and with the history of colonization remain limited.

And these are just some of the challenges that scholars teaching Indigenous literatures will be obliged to face. The essays that follow address some of these challenges and a range of complexities related to Indigenous pedagogy. Although they do not provide fully articulated alternatives to standard literary methods and epistemologies, they emphasize the importance of familiarity with Indigenous stories, and broach some issues that critics and students alike need to contemplate. They remind us that the questions that are raised in classroom settings need to be brought, as Lisa Brooks would suggest, to the kitchen table for proper discussion and consideration.

1. Keavy Martin

In "On the Hunting and Harvesting of Inuit Literature," Keavy Martin draws parallels between hunting for food, and readers who approach Inuit oral narratives and song-making. She suggests that, in spite of its more controversial aspects in "southern, urban spaces," and in contrast to the public outcry against the harvesting of seals, hunting is really a "complex ethical system, a set of relationships between humans and animals" (446). Just as hunters rely on animals and are invested in the well-being of wildlife populations, so readers must be accountable to the texts they read; she argues that Inuit hunting practices thus offer a model for ethical ways of "consuming and using Inuit texts." Martin ultimately posits that, rather than posing as expert readers aware of the damage the West has and could inflict on these texts—or eschewing these texts altogether and participating in what Sam McKegney has elsewhere referred to as "ethical disengagement"—readers need to approach reading and studying Inuit literature as a means of relating to Inuit communities. In so doing, readers must consider their responsibilities to that relationship.

2. Marc André Fortin

At face value, it would seem that Marc André Fortin's essay, "'Ought We to Teach These?' Ethical, Responsible and Aboriginal Cultural Protocols in the Classroom," stands in contradiction to that of Martin: he asserts that there are texts that ought not to be taught. Yet Martin discusses a corpus largely ignored in university classrooms and suggests that reading Inuit texts helps to facilitate the establishment of ethical and reciprocal relationships between readers and Inuit storytellers and communities; by contrast, Fortin critiques a modernist novel produced in the dying days of "the museum age," what Gloria Frank calls "the lunge for anthropological artefacts on the Northwest Coast [that] took place between 1875 and 1925" (165). Anthropologists from this period have become renowned for their lack of accountability to the cultures and the peoples from whom they amassed a wealth of materials, and for reducing storytellers to informants. He uses as a case study *The Downfall of Temlaham* (1928), a novel ostensibly written by famed ethnographer Marius Barbeau, but actually heavily reliant on privately owned Gitxsan stories, which, according to Gitxsan protocols around intellectual property, he had no right to tell. Barbeau's interventions demonstrate how these stories were mediated by settler authority. Fortin's essay serves as a reminder that unmediated Gitxsan stories *do exist*, but outside the control of settler authority: while it is best that Barbeau's version is not taught in classroom settings, its apparatus may still serve as a means to identify the process by which such authority was once claimed, and, simultaneously, direct readers to the existence of Indigenous oral narratives that emerge apart from a highly mediated context.

3. Warren Cariou

Métis scholar Warren Cariou's essay "Who Is the Text in This Class? Story, Archive and Pedagogy in Indigenous Contexts" also looks at oral stories. He draws on the language of Performance Studies to understand how to preserve what Diana Taylor would call a "repertoire" that, by its very nature, is temporary and impermanent, subject to the vagaries of memory. His description of a class that focused on storytelling, without recourse to print texts to verify the memories of listeners, challenged fundamental assumptions upon which literary study is based. Indeed, he notes, in spite of the discomfort engendered by such "textlessness," students began to realize that, in oral storytelling practices, there is *"only* citation" rather than perfect re-enactments of an oral story, but also that these stories are meant to be ephemeral and subsequently forgotten. Rather than providing instances of "unreliability," however, such oral narratives are developed by the relationship between storytellers and their audiences. Transformation is pivotal: as he keenly observes, "keeping and transforming is what oral stories do best" (475).

4. Michelle Coupal

Algonquin scholar Michelle Coupal's essay, "Teaching Literature as Testimony," is also about responsibility to the storyteller and story; in this case, however, she asserts that Indigenous authors can transform personal suffering into what she calls "fictional testimony" as a way to articulate unspeakable trauma. Calling upon Robert Arthur Alexie's *Porcupines and China Dolls* as her example, she showcases how students can productively approach such semi-autobiographical fiction as an alternative literary form to address "the complexities, ambivalences, and contradictions" of the legacies of trauma, and to offer an "imaginative rethinking of what public disclosure could be if fiction were a sanctioned mode of testimony" (485). Coupal suggests that, in this kind of critical process, the reader is implicated in the storyteller's "creative act of disclosure"; such disclosures invite a relationship that demands a different methodology other than standard approaches in literary analysis.

5. Sarah Henzi

Sarah Henzi's text, "'Betwixt and Between': Alternative Genres, Language, and Indigeneity," also emphasizes the inadequacies of traditional definitions of literature given the explosion and generic innovations of Indigenous artists, particularly those in the twenty-first century. As one of the handful of experts on Indigenous literatures in North America in both English and French, Henzi is particularly sensitive to the artificial borders that have separated the study of Indigenous artistic expression, whether it be through national, linguistic, or generic divides. Inviting a reconsideration of genres and borders calls attention to how fields of study have also been "territorialized," and may inspire a "cross-border genealogy of North American Indigenous Studies" (491). In other words, new spaces and new contexts are required to read, critique, and approach Indigenous stories.

6. David Gaertner

In "A Landless Territory? Augmented Reality, Land, and Indigenous Storytelling in Cyberspace," David Gaertner tackles one of the foundational assumptions about Indigenous New Media, that cyberspace is landless and therefore not relevant to Indigenous concerns. In fact, he argues, the digital can be as complicit in generating colonized spaces—and as innovational in disrupting this process and revitalizing traditional stories. He discusses innovative new art forms that use technology to reinscribe stories onto land, introduce other land-based methodologies, and prioritize Indigenous pedagogies.

These essays share a desire to extend readings of Indigenous literatures to classroom situations, and to consider how to resolve approaching such literatures when Western pedagogical strategies are not helpful. They consistently make a concerted effort to consider how to read Indigenous texts with a finely developed sense of ethics and of accountability—to the storytellers, to the cultures, and to the peoples from which they emerge, and, ultimately, to the stories themselves.

Note

1. A version of Assu's *There Is Hope, If We Rise* graces the cover of this book. For more information on the artist, see sonnyassu.com.

38

The Hunting and Harvesting of Inuit Literature

Keavy Martin

I put some words together,
I made a little song,
I took it home one evening,
Mysteriously wrapped, disguised.
Underneath my bed it went:
nobody was going to share it,
nobody was going to taste it!
I wanted it for me! me! me!
Secret, undivided! (quoted in Lowenstein 46)

This iviusiq—an embarrassing song meant to expose or correct bad behaviour—was recorded by Knud Rasmussen in Angmagssalik, Greenland, as it was sung to a man who had "been in the habit of fetching meat from his store during the night while other people in the house were asleep" (quoted in Lowenstein 46).[1] This particular composition fulfills its function—in this case, embarrassing a miserly person—while also telling its listeners something about the value and importance of songs themselves. The "little song" described here is being hidden and hoarded, restricted for personal use, rather than properly "tasted" by other members of the household. Songs, we learn, are a source of sustenance, and therefore a resource to be shared according to the community's protocols.

Although many Inuit stories and songs have much to teach about the dangers of hoarding, my interest here is in the poetic correlation of songs with food, or, more specifically, with meat. Rasmussen recorded this comparison elsewhere, too: the song shared with him at the trading post at Naujaat (Repulse Bay) by the elder Ivaluardjuk features a hunter lying on the ice, where he sings as he waits for an animal to appear. Finally, he sings: "I seek and spy / something to sing of / The caribou with the spreading antlers!" (quoted in Rasmussen 18). The hunter—the singer—is thus seeking and finding two things simultaneously: both the animal that he is hunting and the subject of his song, something to sing about—and something to eat. The processes of hunting and song-making go hand-in-hand.

In this chapter, I consider the implications of understanding songs and stories, which can also be known as "literature" or "literary texts," as nourishment, as meat, or as animals to be hunted and harvested. This comparison might be challenging for some urban readers, many of whom are uncomfortable with the idea of killing a wild animal for food or fur. After all, southern grocery stores and malls make our reliance on animal products either conveniently abstract, or, in some cases, nonexistent. Hunting is thus often understood as something to be carried out only in the case of great necessity, because people have no other choice (as, for instance, in the Arctic, which does not support agriculture). Inuit hunting and harvesting is not carried out, however, only for survival; rather, it is part of a complex ethical system, a set of relationships between humans and animals that is often at odds with southern, or at least urban, sensibilities.

I suggest that the protocols of Inuit hunting and harvesting can provide valuable guidance in the pursuit of ethical ways of "consuming" Indigenous texts. While the language of "hunting" and of "feasting upon" texts will strike many as violent, particularly in light of historic and ongoing abuses of Indigenous intellectual culture by academics, I believe that an informed perspective on hunting reveals that the metaphorical "killing and eating" of texts need not be understood as violent so much as intimately interconnected and powerfully transformative. As we witness in the 2009 short film *Tungijuq*, the relationship between Inuit and animals relies on the generous *gift* of animal bodies and is perpetuated by the observance of particular laws. Likewise, the hunting and harvesting of Indigenous texts offers readers the opportunity to enter into reciprocal relationships—and to transform their scholarly practice accordingly.

"Denying Relationship"

Keeping in mind Deanna Reder's work on the significance of writing autobiographically, and also the reluctance of Inuit elders to speak about things that they have only heard about second-hand, I would like to begin with a brief story from my own experience. When I worked as an instructor with the Pangnirtung

Summer School in Nunavut, part of my job involved taking southern students out visiting. Having been a student of the program myself, I knew the hamlet's living rooms and kitchens to be crucibles for intense contemplation, as even the process of entering them involved, for southern students, major clashes of culture.[2] In these homes, there was almost always tea and palauga (bannock) available, and, sometimes, there would be a meal in progress. Our hosts would invite us to share whatever was available, but almost inevitably, the students would politely decline. There was something about *not* accepting food ("No, thanks—I just ate!") that made them feel more at ease. When we discussed their reasons for this later, they would say that they did not want to be a bother; they did not want to inconvenience their hosts; most of all, they did not want to be a drain on limited resources. In some cases, they were unsure or even squeamish about eating what was being offered: nattiminik uujuq (seal stew), quaq (frozen fish), or the coveted delicacy that is mattaaq (raw beluga skin).[3]

While few people in Pangnirtung try overtly to correct the behaviour of qallunaat (white people, or southerners), I was grateful to a young friend who, one day, said quite directly to her southern visitors, "I find it very insulting when you don't eat with us!" She helped us to realize that refusing to eat was a way of remaining at a safe distance, without incurring obligation—it was, ultimately, a refusal to enter into a relationship with our hosts. Instead, we had to learn to take the risk of accepting, of participating, and of acquiring the responsibility to reciprocate for what had been shared with us. When a meal has been shared, after all, there is the possibility, even the requirement, of returning to that house, and maybe next time bringing along a bag of groceries or another offering—even a song.

Anthropologists have been writing for almost a century about the ways in which the exchanging of gifts creates and sustains relationships. As Marcel Mauss wrote in his classic 1925 *Essai sur le don*, "To refuse to give, or to fail to invite, is like refusing to accept—the equivalent of a declaration of war; it is a refusal of friendship and intercourse" (11).[4] The refusal of the gift is the rejection of the relationship—and this can be a dangerous act, leading to the breakdown of social relations. The Papaschase Cree scholar Dwayne Donald takes this further, pointing out in his University of Alberta lectures that, "colonization is the extended process of denying relationship." I understand this to mean that the process of colonization is characterized by and perhaps dependent on a series of refusals: the persistent refusal to acknowledge connection and also the refusal of the responsibilities that relatedness entails. These colonial denials may function on numerous different but interlocking levels, becoming blind to relationship between peoples ("Indigenous issues have nothing to do with me"), relationship of the past to the present ("get over it" or "it wasn't me who put them in residential schools"), and especially relationship with the land ("the oil-sands industry provides us with jobs and revenue"). Arguably, these denials enable the settler-colonialist and capitalist state to function, as it imagines itself to be free of responsibility to Indigenous peoples, to the land, even to future generations—and therefore free to pursue with impunity its goals of exploiting this territory for its natural resources.

Is the reluctance of southern students to share the food of an Inuit host part of this same process? Is "polite" refusal ultimately a colonizing action? To be sure, most qallunaat students visiting Pangnirtung are strongly motivated by the desire *not* to be colonizers. Yet when this priority compels us to shy away from potentially complicated and entangling encounters, we may wind up rehearsing those individualist and separatist practices that ultimately feed the colonial process by liberating its agents from responsibility to others. The solution to this conundrum would be the flip side of Donald's theorem: that *de*colonization might be understood as the extended process of acknowledging or honouring relationship. But what does that look like? And how might it be enacted within Indigenous literary studies?

Hunting Ethics

In order to unpack these questions, I turn now to a recent Inuit "text" (I use the term loosely): Igloolik Isuma Productions' 2009 short film *Tungijuq*.[5] "Tunngijuq" means "he, she, or it transforms" or "shapeshifts."[6] At the opening of this five-and-a-half-minute film, we meet actor and internationally renowned throat singer Tanya Tagaq playing a wolf in pursuit of a caribou. As the pack—rendered by computer animation—brings down their kill, we see Tagaq again, this time in the form of the dying prey. Then she lies naked on the ice, a large and bloody slab of caribou meat clutched to her breast like a newborn baby or a lover. Rolling to the floe edge and into the sea, she becomes a ringed seal swimming up to its breathing hole, where it is quickly and cleanly shot. Throughout these initial transformations, Tagaq's human body is apparent—even quite prominent—and so we see the hunted caribou not in its animal form, but as a *person*, bleeding, weakening, and dying. Here, there is no convenient dehumanization of the quarry; instead, the film seems to invite its human audience to imagine viscerally the caribou's suffering and surrender. At the end, Tagaq appears in the form of a human woman, seated with her husband next to the body of the ringed seal about to be butchered, caressing the opening in its belly and taking her first delicious bite of fresh, raw seal liver, before she looks directly into the camera with what I understand to be defiant pleasure.

Tagaq has good reason to be provocative. This film appeared in the same year that then governor general Michaëlle Jean sparked a media frenzy by taking a bite of raw seal heart at a community feast in Rankin Inlet. Canadian news services emphatically described Jean as having "gobbled" a "dripping chunk" of meat and then wiping the blood from her fingers (Potter; Panetta). Reactions from animal rights groups evoked the language of barbarism even more strongly; in the words of Dan Mathews, senior vice president of media campaigns of People for the Ethical Treatment of Animals (PETA), "It amazes us that a Canadian official would indulge [in] such blood lust. It sounds like she's trying to give Canadians an even more Neanderthal image around the world than they already have" (quoted in Potter). A media climate in which a ceremonial public figure's participation at a community feast sparks such sensationalist and racist statements is strongly in need of some correction; this is the climate in which *Tungijuq* invites its viewers to a feast at the floe edge. Had Jean been eating a piece of steak, it's unlikely that her dinner would have made headlines. Strangely, the consumption of raw organ meat from a seal is not understood as being equivalent—or as better, given that any other kind of food would have to be flown in from thousands of kilometres away, like the majority of Nunavut's vastly overpriced groceries.

The hunting of seals in Canada, whether for food or for fur, has long been a subject of controversy. In the late 1960s, the International Fund for Animal Welfare (IFAW) began using images of the commercial Atlantic seal hunt to sway public opinion against the sealing industry, which had been a major coastal economy for centuries. In the 1970s, Greenpeace joined the campaign, as did celebrities such as the French actress Brigitte Bardot, who helped to skyrocket the issue to international attention by snuggling up to white-coated harp seal pups for the cameras. These efforts resulted in the 1983 ban by the European Economic Commission on importing Canadian whitecoat seal products. Although the ban targeted only whitecoats (that is, harp seals less than twelve days old, harvested in the Atlantic commercial hunt), and therefore exempted the Inuit seal hunt (which primarily focuses on adult ringed seals), the result of the ban was the near-total collapse of the market for seal products. The impact on Inuit communities, which had only very recently been moved off the land and into permanent settlements, where they were required to adjust to a different economic model and to try to find sources of income, was nothing short of devastating: "The Government of the Northwest Territories estimated that 18 of 20 Inuit villages in the N.W.T. lost 60 per cent of total annual community income," although the statistics were worse in some places ("Anti-Sealing").[7]

Although greatly diminished, both the commercial Atlantic and the Inuit seal hunts have continued, as have the protests. With celebrities like Pamela Anderson and Paul McCartney working with PETA to sway public opinion against the hunt of such "cute" animals, Inuit have had to launch their own rhetorical campaigns. In 2006, Inuit students Tommy Akulukjuk and Corenna

Nayulia cuddled up to a baby cow to create a poster with the slogan "Save the Baby Veal; Avoid Cultural Prejudice." Current Inuit Tapiriit Kanatami president Terry Audla has tried to redirect animal-rights activists' attention to the problems of the beef, pork, and poultry industries, which typically raise and slaughter animals in close captivity, with the liberal use of hormones and antibiotics, but away from the cameras. And Inuit scholars and spokespeople like Aaju Peter have pointed out that the limited and sometimes only source of income from seal hunting allows Inuit families to go to the store to buy milk or coffee—at exorbitant prices—and also to buy the fuel and ammunition that allows them to keep hunting (Peter 7). In other words, seal hunting not only provides income and sustenance, it also maintains the hugely important cultural aspects of harvesting animals, which allow families to work together to acquire and to share healthy and delicious traditional food as a continuation of ancient practices, despite several decades of attempted assimilation.

Tanya Tagaq's erotic depiction of the hunting and eating of seal meat thus offers a wonderful twist on the tradition of busty blond bombshells cuddling up enticingly to seals on the ice. Again, the film makes no attempt to downplay or conceal the violence or gore of the hunt, but rather lingers on the sensuousness of the animals' bodies, even as they are butchered. We are invited to witness Tagaq's passionate embrace with the tuttuminik ("former caribou," or caribou meat) and to contemplate the intimate, almost vulva-shaped incision that reveals the delicious organs of the seal. For years, graphic images of hunting have been the worst enemy of hunters, as they are taken out of context and used to shock and provoke urban audiences into moral outrage and political action. The film thus takes a major risk in using this explicit imagery, particularly in combination with sexuality, that other provocateur. Given the reaction of the mainstream media to Michaëlle Jean's single bite of seal heart, how do the filmmakers imagine audiences will respond to this image? As Tagaq lifts her gaze and slowly savours her mouthful, she seems to dare her viewers to respond using the language of "savagery," "barbarism," or "bloodlust." This feast is not a process in which she is engaging unawares or even out of necessity; rather, this is a conscious, deliberate, and, perhaps most importantly, pleasurable act, one carried out without moral conflict or shame.

The reason why *Tungijuq* represents the hunt so honestly, so unashamedly, is because it has nothing to hide. *Inuit hunting is ethical.* Although its appearance has changed somewhat with the adoption of rifles, engines, and Christianity, it is still embedded within an ancient tradition of relations between humans and animals. The maintaining of this relationship is of the utmost importance to Inuit, whose survival has depended on it for thousands of years. As the Amitturmiutaq Inuit elder Ivaluardjuk said famously to Knud Rasmussen, "The greatest peril of life lies in the fact that human food consists entirely of souls. All the creatures that we have to kill and eat . . . have souls, like we have, souls that do not perish with the body, and which must therefore be propitiated lest they should revenge themselves on us for taking away their bodies" (quoted in Rasmussen 56).

George Wenzel explains that, "Inuit relate to animals not as dominators, managers, or even stewards of wildlife . . . but as co-residents who share the same conceptual ideology" (62). Instead of being poor, hapless victims of the cruelty and cunning of Man, animals are known to be silatujuq ("intelligent") and also keenly "aware of the thoughts, speech, and actions of hunters" (Wenzel 138). They therefore make the conscious, deliberate, and generous decision to share their bodies with worthy hunters; the human recipients of this generosity are then required to be generous themselves, sharing the meat with others (Wenzel 63).

Elders warn, furthermore, that should animals be treated disrespectfully— if they are made to suffer, if they are boasted about, if they are quarrelled over, or if a hunter is stingy about sharing meat—there will be repercussions. "We were told to be fearful of something bad happening to us if we abused wildlife," Mariano Aupilaarjuk explains. "We were told to take good care of our wildlife and our land" (Aupilaarjuk et al. 33). In fact, from the perspective of many Inuit elders, the actions of wildlife biologists and conservationists (in particular, tranquilizing, tagging, collaring, and helicopter monitoring) *interfere with and torment* intelligent animals, thereby endangering not only the animal but also the relationship between animals and humans. In the 2010 Isuma documentary *Qapirangajuq: Inuit Knowledge and Climate Change*, elder Rita Nashook of Iqaluit speaks powerfully to the southern policymakers who place restrictions on Inuit hunting in the name of animal protection: "I'm a protector of animals," she says, "a real animal rights activist! When animals are mistreated, I'm reminded of my late grandmother's teaching: 'Unless you're going to kill an animal, do not cause it harm.' . . . Wildlife biologists are the ones endangering wildlife! Then they suspect Inuit overharvesting as the cause. We are told, 'You must not touch protected animals.' Inuit do not endanger animals, nor do they cause needless suffering. We love our animals."[8]

This love for and even intimacy with animals is strongly apparent in *Tungijuq*. As Tagaq transforms from wolf, to caribou, to seal, and ultimately back into the form of a human woman, she seems to be saying, "I am these animals; they are me."[9] Like the old tale of Arnaqtaaqtuq ("he gets a woman/ mother"), the story of the soul of a miscarried child who is reborn in many different animal bodies before returning to a human mother again, *Tungijuq* affirms the parallel and deeply interconnected personhood of animal beings.[10] The boundaries between species, here, are flexible and fluid; rather than existing in separate spheres, these different peoples rely deeply on one another. The death of one being moves swiftly into the life of another; in this way, the film pursues a procreative theme accentuated by its persistent sexual and reproductive imagery.[11] Tagaq plunges naked into the dark waters and floats foetus-like in a cloud of blood before swimming, now in a seal-body, toward yet another incarnation. The image of the breathing-hole passageway is then echoed in the visceral opening of the seal's belly—another portal through which life passes. The blood, gore, and suffering that colour the screen are, I would argue, not markers of violence so much as emblems of birth. The renewal of life, the film reminds us, is reliant upon the bodies of others, and those bodies are always transformed in the process.

So what of those who decline to participate in this cycle of transformation and renewal by refusing the gift of animal bodies? Inuit tradition, with its respect for each person's intellectual autonomy, would calmly allow vegetarians go about their business. But as for those who interfere in Inuit life based on the assumption of inhabiting a higher moral ground? I question their morality. Humans who attempt to remain wholly non-reliant upon animals (and who urge others to do likewise) can boast of only very distant relationships with animals, and they cannot possess the same commitment to long-term and sustainable animal wellbeing that is maintained by hunters. By retreating to the safety of perceived separateness, anti-hunting activists forget not only the colonial nature but also the broader consequences of their actions, which would compel northerners to rely almost exclusively on food imported from thousands of miles away and on clothing made from synthetic, petroleum-based fibres—all while stripping hunting communities of sustainable livelihoods and thus opening the door to thoroughly *un*sustainable resource-development projects, which pose tremendous risks to animal habitat.

In *Tungijuq*, we glimpse a world in balance, as humans and animals participate knowingly in an ancient partnership. The pleasure evinced by Tagaq is the pleasure of living well and living ethically, with gratitude for the continued abundance of the animals and the assurance that they provide of Inuit cultural survival. In sharing this series of feasts with viewers worldwide, the filmmakers invite us to relate better to Inuit lands and communities—and to the animals, too. In this way, the film provides an entryway into the cycles of kinship and responsibility that have existed in the Arctic for thousands of years.

Reading Ethics

I offer this recounting of the seal hunt controversy—and by controversy, I mean the damage inflicted by misinformed and near-sighted southerners—as a kind of reciprocity for the gift of *Tungijuq*, just as I wear my sealskin clothing proudly and speak about it to whomever will listen. I hope that this speaking and sharing will, even if infinitesimally, improve the ways in which other qal-lunaat relate to Inuit communities. But I also need to say, here, that the above account of Inuit hunting, and of the relationship between humans and animals, only skims the surface of a very deep pool. While I have eaten seal many times, I have only been on a handful of seal hunts; in other words, my knowledge of this subject is primarily second-hand. While this is acceptable in an aca-demic context, in an Inuit context it means that I don't know very much at all.[12] But something that I *do* have experience with, something that I therefore feel more entitled to speak about, is the reading of literary texts. I want to come back around, then, to the idea with which I opened: that literary texts are ani-mal-like, or meat-like, and that the ethics of Inuit hunting can guide us in our reading practice.

Most readers would agree that texts are "nourishing" in some sense. They feed us emotionally, intellectually—and for literary critics, they actually do put food on our tables. Many of us likely also feel that texts have a life or spirit of their own, whether they owe that to their author/community of origin or whether it is something that they possess in their own right. As the Cherokee scholar Daniel Heath Justice reminds us, "our literatures, like our various peoples, are *alive*" (28). This attitude is reflected in most criticism of Indigenous literatures, which has had to continually confront the complicated ethics of its own relationship to the text. Settler critic Sam McKegney points out the anx-iety that these high ethical stakes can produce in non-Indigenous readers, who, in hopes of not replicating colonial aggressions in their critical practice, often retreat into what he calls "strategies for ethical disengagement" (*Magic* 39). Yet like the vegetarians or "animal rights" activists who prefer to remain at a safe distance, critical dis-engagers risk perpetuating subtler kinds of violence that result from shirking relationships, such as ignoring Indigenous literatures and the transformative potential that they contain altogether.[13] McKegney asserts instead the need for ethical *engagement* with Indigenous texts: "I apologize for any weaknesses that might emerge in my analysis," he writes, "but I don't apologize for analyzing" (Magic 44).

To be sure, we might pose some questions about what exactly analysis is, where the practice comes from, what baggage it carries, and what kind of relationship it establishes between reader and text. Etymologically, an analy-sis is an "action of loosing or releasing, [a] fact of dissolving, [a] resolution of a problem" ("analysis"); it takes apart, however reverently, what has been lovingly put together. I always recall Susan Sontag's startling image of the critic *excavating* the artwork, which, she says, cannot survive the process.[14] For writ-ers, this dissection, this dismantling, this "jotting and prodding" can feel like an imposition, or even an annexation, as the Métis poet Gregory Scofield writes in his haunting poem "The Dissertation" (8).[15] But what if we were to think of analysis as a kind of *butchering*, not in a horror-movie sense, and without the colloquial connotations of "really wrecking something," but rather in the sense portrayed by *Tungijuq*: as a reverent, celebratory, and communal (both collective and connective) activity carried out in preparation for a feast? How might this change the relationship that is established with the text, with its author, and with its place of origin?

"Butchering" and then "feasting upon" texts—these metaphors may sound a bit disturbing to some (why is our language for the eating of meat so heavy with grim connotation?). Non-Indigenous peoples, after all, have being carving up and consuming Indigenous cultures for decades, whether it is the sacred objects that linger in museums, the faux-Navajo fashion items adorning our students, or the snippets of Indigenous texts cited in the articles and books of settler academics. The Métis artist and scholar David Garneau notes:

> The colonial attitude is characterized not only by scopophilia, a drive to look, but also by an urge to penetrate, to traverse, to know, to translate, to own and exploit. The attitude assumes that everything should be accessible to those with the means and will to access them; everything is ultimately comprehensible, a potential commodity, resource, or salvage. The academic branch of the enterprise collects and analyzes the experiences and things of others; it transforms story into text and objects-in-relation into artifacts to be catalogued and stored or displayed. (23)

In order to try to separate myself from this habit of consumption, then, in order to undertake a different kind of practice, I need to come to the table not seeking to take possession and to profit, but rather to enter into and acknowledge relationship. I need to seek ways of *being in relation to* that do not lapse into assimilation or appropriation, those twin addictions of empire.

In seeking this relational state of working and of being, I am fortunate to have many examples to follow. Daniel Heath Justice has long reminded his students to think not so much about their *rights* as readers of Indigenous literature, but rather about their *responsibilities*. The larger Indigenous literary nationalist community, meanwhile, has for decades advocated for improved, informed, and invested relations between readers of Indigenous texts and the nations from which these texts originate. More recently, Sam McKegney has called for "relationships of reciprocal responsibility" between readers and Indigenous texts: "we should seek," he writes, "to honour the words of Indigenous poets by responding to cues to criticism within the poetry itself, using those cues to form rigorous albeit non-definitive understandings, and striving to extend the poetry's capacity to engender positive change" ("Writer-Reader" 47, 52). Into this already vibrant conversation, I want to bring two principles drawn from the ethical practice of Inuit hunting. These are ideas that have profoundly influenced my teaching over the past several years, and I hope that they will provide others involved in the same work with some food for thought.

Here is the first practice. The elder Emile Imaruittuq emphasizes in *Perspectives on Traditional Law* that the way that people *speak* about animals can have serious repercussions on the human–animal relationship. "There was a man who grumbled and said bad things about wildlife," he recounts. "Because of what he said, one lake was rapidly depleted of fish and today it is a very bad fishing place, even though it is a large lake which should have fish" (quoted in Aupilaarjuk et al. 39). It is not only mocking, boasting, or complaining about animals that is dangerous, however. Imaruittuq explains, "When we started dealing with land claims we had to talk a lot about wildlife. This created a lot of fear amongst the elders. They used to tell us not to quarrel about wildlife, because this was a very dangerous thing to do. . . . We should not quarrel about wildlife or it will take revenge on us" (38).

Words, we learn, have tremendous power; even the unwritten words referred to here carry intentions over great distances and can reverberate dangerously outside of our control. The *manner* of human speech, then, becomes very important in maintaining good relationships. And although most readers of Indigenous literature strive to speak respectfully about the texts with which they are engaged, they wouldn't think twice about *arguing* about them—occasionally in a combative sense and always in pursuit of persuasion. This Inuit piqujaq (customary law) has made me wonder about the pervasive academic practice of arguing, of seeking to persuade. Stepping outside of this rhetorical mode carries dangers for a scholarly reader/writer: it might carry away with it one's feeling of authority and purpose, and it might leave one's paper or presentation seeming weak and directionless. But this serves as a reminder that rhetorical traditions vary widely, and that scholars of Indigenous literatures might think more seriously about putting Indigenous rhetorical traditions into practice in their own conversations. Imaruittuq seems to remind his listeners of the importance of maintaining peaceful and respectful relations via the way that we speak to one another. How would this change the work that academics do? In my classes, I now ask my students to write at least one essay that purposefully departs from the thesis-proof format that they have jammed almost all of their ideas into since high school. While most find the exercise terrifying, the honesty, feeling, and personality that emerges in their work makes it worthwhile. While Imaruittuq notes that arguing was necessary when it came to negotiating the land claim—as it is, I think, when dealing with anti-hunting activists—I seek the courage and ability to pursue this rhetorical shift in my own writing.

The second law for hunters is just as crucial to the maintenance of good relationships with animals—and therefore, to the securing of good "harvests." This is the requirement, referenced at the beginning of this essay in "Song to a Miser," that the gift of animal bodies be not hoarded but rather shared among family and community. This profoundly anti-capitalist ethic has struck me deeply every time that I have travelled to Inuit territory, from the very first day that I was in Pangnirtung, when a person whom I had never met before gave me an entire Arctic char fresh from his net, simply because "it's for sharing." Many qallunaat working in the north, meanwhile, find this sharing, and the expectation of sharing, irritating, as they wonder why local people never seem to save (hoard) money, why they rely so heavily upon the generosity of their relatives, etc. These practices, after all, grate beautifully on cherished southern ideals of self-reliance and individualism, to which the academy is no stranger.

So, how might an ethic of sharing be put into practice in the work of literary critics? Many of us already share eagerly the "resource" of Indigenous literary texts, and teach and publish about those that have impacted us deeply, thus hopefully augmenting the flow of royalties back to the author. In my classes, I also encourage students not to hoard the nourishment that they have gained from reading, but instead to build further relationships by passing along what they have learned outside the class, whether from a blog, an anonymous leaflet left on the bus, or a particular friend/family member. At times, they have even had the opportunity to share their work—often a creative response—with the visiting author him- or herself. For the students, this raises the stakes of assignments considerably by allowing them to step outside of the usual, somewhat impoverished custom of spending their energies solely on the individualistic goal of acquiring course credit. Likewise, I am trying to implement my own responsibility to share these nourishing texts and the transformative ideas they contain, not only while accruing (profitable) publications, but also outside of the academic merit system, with my family and community. While these are mere baby steps within a crushingly neoliberal institution, they provide me with a chance to emulate the practice of community that I have so admired in Inuit territory.

It is in that spirit that I offer this essay, both to my own community of academic readers and to the northern communities with whom, through the realities of climate change, of misguided bans on seal products, and of Canada's interest in Arctic sovereignty, to name only a few vectors, we are interconnected. I write in gratitude for the gift of Indigenous texts and stories, and for the transformations that they have brought about for me. To those who are unsure about reading Indigenous literatures, as I have often been, I say: go carefully, but heed also the words of Gregory Scofield: "Astâm, pî-miciso"—"come and eat" (126).

Instead of remaining safely (rudely, dangerously) at a distance, take the risk of entering into relationship. The results are truly transformative.

Notes

1. Iglulingmiutaq elder Emile Imaruittuq (albeit speaking a different dialect of Inuktitut than that spoken in southeastern Greenland) discusses the genre of the iviusiq, which Rasmussen referred to as "songs of derision," in *Perspectives on Traditional Law* (Aupilaarjuk et al. 208).

2. As the program's founder and director Peter Kulchyski notes, the only people who knock before entering a home in Pangnirtung are the social workers or the police; others simply open the door and walk in, thereby, Kulchyski argues, engaging in an "embodied deconstruction" of the cherished Western institution of private property (267).

3. Also spelled maktaaq. I default to using Pangnirtung dialect, which often "assimilates" double consonants for Inuktitut terms.

4. Mauss's original has "l'alliance et la communion," where the translator has "friendship and intercourse": "Refuser de donner, négliger d'inviter, comme refuser de prendre, équivaut à déclarer la guerre ; c'est refuser l'alliance et la communion" (18–19).

5. This film can be viewed online at www.isuma.tv/tungijuq/tungijuq720p.

6. Although the filmmakers use the spelling "Tungjiuq" to render their Inuktitut title into Roman orthography, "Tunngijuq" is the more direct transliteration of the syllabics. I am grateful to filmmaker Félix Lajeunesse and to Lucy Tulugarjuk for clarifying the meaning of this term for me.

7. This problem continues today. In 2014, the World Trade Organization upheld the European Union's 2009 ban on importing sealing products. Although this particular embargo included an exemption for "Inuit seal-products result[ing] from hunts conducted 'traditionally,' which contribute to the 'subsistence' of Inuit" (Peter 4), it also resulted in a further dramatic drop in seal prices and the sale of *not one* of the eleven thousand available seal pelts at the 2009 fur auction in North Bay, Ontario. In other words, the exemption for Inuit hunters is not working.

8. Other elders and hunters interviewed in the film also point out that tampering or interfering with animals can endanger them. Simon Idlout (Resolute Bay) explains that helicopter noise can damage bears' sensitive hearing, while Nathaniel Kallak (Resolute Bay) says that putting radio collars on bears can prevent them from reaching their heads into seal breathing holes—and that starving collared bears have been seen by hunters.

9. Or, as Tagaq said in an interview on The National, "We're equal. We're all meat" ("Tanya Tagaq").

10. For a thorough discussion of the Arnaqtaaqtuq story, see Blaisel.

11. My thanks to Professor Christopher Trott, who first drew my attention to the reproductive imagery of the film.

12. As the late Pangnirtung elder Inuusiq Nashalik said of the qallunaat understanding of bears, they "only know them by what they read, and have never interacted with them. We know our wildlife intimately" (quoted in *Qapirangajuq*).

13. As McKegney writes, "I see the alternative of avoiding Native literary works and focusing even more attention on the cultural creations of the dominant society as contrary to the goal of respecting Native voice and forwarding the social and political objectives embedded in text; it again takes focus away, willingly failing to heed the creative voices of those who feel the impact of Canadian colonial oppression" (*Magic* 42).

14. "The modern style of interpretation excavates, and as it excavates, destroys" (Sontag 6).

15. "But then arrived the microscope / and she set to work, the academic, / prodding and jotting, / jotting and prodding. / She even annexed his speech, / the Indian words she was so drawn to" (Scofield 8).

39

"Ought We to Teach These?": Ethical, Responsible, and Aboriginal Cultural Protocols in the Classroom

Marc André Fortin

When I first began the process of producing an edition of *The Downfall of Temlaham* (1928), a text infused with oral stories from the Gitxsan people but published by distinguished anthropologist Marius Barbeau, I set forth with the traditional Western understanding of the procedures and practices of such an undertaking in relation to copyright law. I began by contacting a number of institutions and individuals to determine who owned the copyright to the novel. It was first published by Macmillan Publishers in 1928; a second edition was published by Hurtig Publishers in 1973, for which they paid $100 to lease the rights. Macmillan Publishers no longer exists as a publishing house in Canada, but their records indicate that Barbeau signed a contract for the publication of his book after receiving approval from his employers to do so. The publishing contract stipulates that copyright of the first edition belongs to Macmillan Canada, with the added acknowledgement in the introduction of the National Museum of Canada. The acknowledgement, written by Barbeau, is expressed as follows: "To the National Museum of Canada we acknowledge our debt for our knowledge of the Aboriginal sources, which we have ourselves studied at first hand, in the course of several seasons among the natives of the Skeena" (viii).

Throughout the years, the museum has changed its name a number of times, with its most recent incarnation being the Canadian Museum of History, although all of my research was undertaken while it was called the Canadian

Museum of Civilization (CMC). When I contacted the CMC to begin my research in the Marius Barbeau Fonds at their archives in Gatineau, I described the project's goal and ultimate product. I was informed that copyright for *The Downfall of Temlaham* was held by the CMC. This information was based on an erroneous understanding of Barbeau's acknowledgement, and the idea that a government employee's work remains the copyright of the government. Although it was quite easy to prove that Barbeau had been given approval to publish his work as creative fiction, beyond his role as an ethnographer and employee of the state, by pointing to the correspondence and legal documents signed by the various individuals and institutions involved, the tone and message of the CMC's attempt to claim ownership of the novel clearly signalled that the stories *inside* the novel were thought to be owned by the museum. It was at this point that I began to recognize the inherent flaw in assuming that I could publish an edition of this complex novel using traditional Western editing and publication practices.

Barbeau's novel is filled with and surrounded by contradictions. His moralistic tone as expressed in the introduction gestures toward the adverse effects of colonialism on Indigenous peoples, as it simultaneously suggests that no such Indigenous peoples continue to exist in Canada. In part, this contradiction emerges as the result of his own context: he began his employment as an assistant ethnologist with the newly created Anthropological Division of the Geological Survey of Canada, which was housed at the Victoria Memorial Museum in Ottawa, in 1911, after he attended Oxford University as a Rhodes Scholar and took courses at the Sorbonne. Although he was prolific in his writings on Indigenous cultures, and although he was able to purchase or acquire numerous cultural artifacts to display to others in institutional settings back in Ottawa, he was always faced with a cultural divide: the first that was premised on both his Oxford-educated view of the "disappearing Native," and the second on the social and cultural perspective of the Gitxsan, who attempted to maintain their own independence during a period of violent physical, psychological, and political attempts by both government agents and missionaries to re-socialize the Northwest Pacific Coast communities.

This contradiction can also be seen in the images used in the text, as well as those displayed at the famous "Exhibition of West Coast Art, Native and Modern" (1927), which Barbeau helped organize. Discussing the exhibit, Gerta Moray explains how the imaginary *terra nullius* ideology helped shape Canadian settler practices of actual erasure: "In predominantly white settler colonies and in former colonies (such as the United States), as Aboriginal peoples were subjugated and their land rights and traditional cultures eroded, they were classified as 'vanishing races.' This classification was accompanied by

the construction of romanticized images of what was seen as their spirituality and rootedness in the land" (71–72). Barbeau's novel performs this contradictory romanticization of a "vanished" Indigenous culture by using the stories
from the very culture he claims has vanished. What is thoroughly problematic
about the construction of his novel is that it signals its status as fiction, even as
it simultaneously incorporates textual methods that position it as a work of science, such as the novel's appendix, which lists nearly every version from which
Barbeau borrowed and "paraphrased" the stories that are included. By claiming
authority through his role as an anthropologist, his novel is able to represent
the vanished Indigenous subject's story both as romance and absolute "truth."
The novel thus purports to allow readers to understand better a people who no
longer exist through a highly mediated interpretation of those peoples' stories,
which can also be studied in their original telling at the museum.

Of course, Barbeau knew that the Gitxsan still existed—and indeed they
still do exist. The stories told to Barbeau by the Gitxsan, moreover, were
part of individual members' *adawx*, the personal history of the individual,
which defines his or her origins, life, territory, and relations.[1] His Eurocentric
anthropological vision of the primitive other, however, was frustrated by the
inauthentic and "tainted," colonized individuals he found while looking for the
authentic "primitive" that he imagined he would find. As he could not write
scientifically about an imaginary subject, he created one instead—an archived
Indigenous other, who once existed in time and space, and who could be
found in the interpretation and "correcting" of the stories he had recorded.
Specifically, *The Downfall of Temlaham* is built upon individual stories told to
Barbeau by different members of the community at different times throughout
his years spent in the field. These fragments were then knit together to form a
version of the "whole" story, despite the fact that, or perhaps because, they constituted the differences, contradictions, and inconsistencies of Gitxsan culture.
Rather than consider the practice of storytelling itself as a cultural element
that could lead to a better understanding of Traditional Knowledge, Barbeau's
European ethnographic understanding of Indigenous culture led him to find
the pieces of knowledge that were consistent across all stories, and to undermine and even to erase the very act of confirmation of truth by producing his
own version of other peoples' stories.

I began to realize that I could not, ethically, republish the stories that
Barbeau had collected, edited, and published as a representation of the erasure
of the Indigenous, despite the text being an excellent example of early modernist fiction in Canada: it contains illustrations by A. Y. Jackson, Edwin Holgate,
Langdon Kihn, Annie Savage, and Emily Carr. Thoreau Macdonald designed
the dust jacket, the Canadian Pacific Railway helped pay to have some of the

artists taken to the Skeena to paint their works, Vincent Massey was involved, and Barbeau himself spoke to Parliament about turning Gitxsan traditional territory into a national park, with the traditional territory of "Temlaham" turned into a tourist attraction. The entire production of the novel, and the events outside the novel, speaks to a nationalist period of modernity within Canada that was predicated on the representation of the end of Indigenous cultures in Canada. The stories were taken from the Gitxsan and placed within a nationalist, institutional interpretation of "Canada." If I were to republish the text in a new edition that contained the stories that Barbeau had published, I would be effectively participating in the colonial project of claiming ownership of the stories simply because they were re-interpreted by Barbeau and published as a novel. I chose not to do this.

A Repatriated Edition

Dara Culhane points out that "classical anthropology is undergoing a thorough re-examination by those 'subjects' who were constituted as 'objects' of study by earlier generations of ethnographers. . . . Errors in fact are being corrected" (20). Barbeau's attempt to "correct" the Traditional Knowledge of the Gitxsan, and that of others, needs to be revisited, re-corrected, and revalued in response to the narrative of absence that Barbeau imagined was the condition of the twentieth-century Indigenous subject. But what would such a correction look like?

While I had originally set out to publish a new edition of *The Downfall of Temlaham* in order to make the text accessible as a pedagogical tool that spoke to the history of representation and appropriation of Indigenous culture in Canada, I realized that in doing so I would be accepting the fact that the stories that Barbeau drew upon for his own work are not owned by anyone under Western copyright law. To produce a new edition that includes the full text of Barbeau's work would continue to situate the text as a document of historical ownership of the ethnographic tradition that allowed for the unequal sharing of Traditional Knowledge to occur in the first place. The edition of *The Downfall of Temlaham* that I now imagine involves the erasure of the elements of the text—represented by the insertion of blank pages—that are owned by the Gitxsan, whether that means communal or individual ownership of the stories therein. The repatriated edition of Barbeau's novel will give back the stories through their absence, and symbolically respond to the ideology of *terra nullius* that permitted the work to be produced as an unowned object of scientific discourse.

This edition of the text, which marks the absence of the stories that belong to the Gitxsan and which will still include the elements of the text that are solely the work of the author and his collaborators, will be, for me, a pedagogical tool that one may explore and critique as an object participating in the process of repatriation, and what that means in relation to the history of its production. The absent text is not an instance of censorship, but of (re)placing the text in dialogue with both historical and present questions of ownership, which privileges written documentation over oral stories, and ethnographic scientific studies over traditional knowledge. Patricia Dawn Mills explains how important the *adawx* is for the Gitxsan, from which we can understand its significance to this particular text:

> Title, tenure, and legitimate use of Gitxsan land and resources are determined by birth, affinity, common residence, social status, or a combination of these. Those who cannot demonstrate knowledge of its history through the recitation of the *adawaak* (oral histories) and knowledge of the *ayuk(s)* (symbols of title) cannot claim rights to it. (25)

By granting access to the stories that make up the *adawx(s)* of the individuals involved in Barbeau's novel, one participates in a dialogue that is removed from the recognized social structure of the Gitxsan, their legal practices, their models of ownership, their way of life, and their rights to property. By having access, one is able to further the position of authorship and authority, which Barbeau claimed was his natural right as a European-trained anthropologist and member of the dominant social and political group in Canada.

The stories in Barbeau's novel represent more than just anthropological evidence of a historical moment in anthropology and Canadian nation-building. They make up the laws and rights of the individuals who own those stories. Bruce Granville Miller argues that the oral stories that make up Indigenous Traditional Knowledge, particularly in relation to their use as evidence in Western settler law courts, do not become static once they are written down, and must be used cautiously: "[Oral narratives] are *still* told in communities, as the Crown is clearly aware, given the effort to disqualify oral narratives because of variation over the years and between storytellers. . . . They come in particular genres but are delivered orally with distinctive styles and in response to the occasion. . . . Thus they are not simply historical documents like any others" (171; original emphasis). The repatriated edition of *The Downfall of Temlaham* works within this model of ethical care with regard to Traditional Knowledge. It allows for a return of the oral stories to their rightful owners by marking the inability to record a "truthful" version of the stories that were shared with Barbeau (but which he did not handle appropriately). Barbeau's own act of erasure of the stories' distinctive nature, their particular ownership, and the very nature of their being spoken only at certain times and in certain places requires a further act of erasure to "correct" Barbeau's original and misguided corrections. The repatriated edition recognizes that the stories that were in the original novel are still being told today, that they have not vanished, and that they cannot be decontextualized by removing them from the land and people to which they belong.

The contemporary movement to repatriate the objects and artifacts taken from Indigenous communities during the (ongoing) colonization of Canada is a complex and difficult process for all sides. Nevertheless, such a move has proved important for the regeneration of Indigenous communities in Canada, as well as for other North American and international Indigenous communities. The problem with Barbeau's novel is that it is an appropriation of oral stories published in material form, and thus cannot simply be "returned" as a traditional object is returned. Yet the repatriated edition opens up a space for rethinking the relationship between settlers and Indigenous peoples. The goal of this edition is to use the erasure of the text, and the blank space it produces, as pedagogical tools for students and teachers to discuss issues related to colonialism, contemporary relations between the state and Indigenous communities, and the relationship between knowledge (in the Western sense) and Traditional Knowledge. Because of the importance of the novel to a particular moment in the growth of the Canadian nation state, its connections between anthropologists, industry leaders, politicians, and artists, the publication of this edition can also offer a discourse on Canadian history, nationalism, aesthetics, and modernist literary production.

The blank pages represent the very act of colonization that Barbeau himself undertook, which is to imagine a *terra nullius* in which Western settlers and science held the rights and authority to claim ownership of those lands for their own ends. Whereas Barbeau's erasure of Indigenous peoples took the form of appropriation, the repatriated edition of *The Downfall of Temlaham* erases the act of appropriation by showing that the stories that were in the original edition exist outside and beyond the control of settler authority.[2] The repatriated edition is meant to undertake the acts of resistance toward settler injustices and of decolonization of settler control over Indigenous peoples. It is meant to return the stories to those to whom they belong, and in doing so acknowledge the inherent rights of those whose stories have been stolen from them.

Notes

1. According to the strict protocols that govern this culture, only the owner of any individual *adawx* can tell his or her story. Publishing them in a narrative that deals

with the politics of colonialism thus generates complexities: what seems to be a simple retelling of historical events along the Skeena River in British Columbia in 1888 actually defines many of the ways in which industrialization, politics, nation-building, and science constructed contradictory beliefs about the ideas of progress, modernization, and civilization. The novel inadvertently maps out a multi-layered and multi-centred politics of representation that can only be understood in relating the ways in which such disparate entities such as tourism, trains, federalism, art galleries, museums, civil disobedience, universities, totem poles, masks, guns, disease, law, geography, and science come together to produce a large-scale recording of one moment in the history of Canada, and in the history of the Gitxsan, that encompasses far more than is suggested by the number of pages within its covers.

2. In the opening section of *For Indigenous Eyes Only: A Decolonization Handbook* (Santa Fe: School of American Research, 2005), Waziyatawin Angela Wilson and Michael Yellow Bird explain to their readers what they have done: "Congratulations! In opening this book you have engaged in an act of decolonization. We hope this will be one of the many steps on your journey towards liberation. As Indigenous Peoples we have an inherent right to be free in our own lands. We have an inherent right to self-determination. Though these statements represent truths and they speak of rights we once possessed, these rights have been systematically stripped from us. When others invaded our lands and stole them from underneath our bodies, when they destroyed our ways of life and injured our peoples, they prevented us from living the way we were intended to live. Reclaiming our inherent rights will require tremendous struggle. It will require learning to meaningfully resist the forces of colonialism that have so detrimentally impacted our lives. It will require the decolonization of North America" (1).

40

Who Is the Text in This Class?: Story, Archive, and Pedagogy in Indigenous Contexts

Warren Cariou

I am trying to remember the story. It's there somewhere, waiting to be unpacked, tracked down, navigated, activated. I've carried it with me all these months, a weightless invisible thing, a gift, a spirit maybe, and now I want to call it back so I can tell you about it, so I can offer an interpretation. Or, at least, so I can cite my sources.

It was about Weesakaytsak, I know that—Weesakaytsak and the herd of caribou. The season was winter, and Weesakaytsak was cold and hungry as usual, and as he wandered through the north he stumbled on a group of caribou digging down through the snow to find something to eat. And when we heard about that, I think we all assumed he was going to find some way to eat those caribou. We had met Weesakaytsak before; we knew about his legendary gluttony. But this time the old trickster had another trick up his sleeve: instead of eating those caribou, he decided to become one of them. Yes, that's how it went. Weesakaytsak turned himself into a caribou. He leaned his head down toward the ground, and gigantic antlers sprouted out of his temples, and his face stretched forward, and his nose turned dark and shiny, and his hands and feet began to harden into hooves, and his skin sprouted a thick covering of fur. Something like that. I think. He was warm for the first time in months. He dug down into the snow with his wide hooves, and he cleared the way with the pad-dle-shaped blades on the front of his heavy antlers, and he began to nibble the lichen that was growing there on the rocks. Normally, he would have scoffed at the idea of eating such "rabbit food," but now it tasted as delicious as . . . well, as caribou stew.

However, even though the food was delectable, and his stomach was empty from days of starvation, Weesakaytsak didn't spend much time eating. He had other things on his mind. You see, when those antlers grew huge out of his head, and when the fur grew around his body, and the hooves grew out the ends of his fingers, something else had grown too. The herd of caribou he had seen were all females, and he had noticed that before making his transformation. So when he became a caribou himself, he decided to turn into a male. And, as it turned out, he had chosen his timing right, too, because it was the season of the rut, and the female caribou took notice of him right away. One of them in particular started giving him that look, the look that he was hoping for. So Weesakaytsak sidled over to her and introduced himself, and, before long, one thing led to another and the two of them had a very good time indeed. After that was finished, Weesakaytsak was congratulating himself, when he glanced up and noticed that—yes, indeed, there was *another* female caribou giving him that same look. So he puffed out his furry chest and galloped over to say hello . . . and, as you might have guessed, this new relationship progressed very quickly as well, and soon he and his new friend were having about as much fun as two caribou can have.

As the sun travelled low across the horizon and disappeared beneath the distant hills, Weesakaytsak continued to get lucky. All that night, and all the next day, he continued his routine: seeing the look, galloping over, introducing himself, enjoying himself. But by the end of the second day, Weesakaytsak was a wreck. He'd had nothing to eat since his first taste of lichen, and his whole body ached, and his legs could barely hold him up. Still, when he cast his head from side to side in search of a drink of water, all he saw was another pair of caribou eyes, giving him the look yet again.

And then . . . I don't remember. I have tried at least a hundred times, but I can't recall what happens after that. How does Weesakaytsak get himself out of that sticky situation? I know somehow he finds a way, somehow he is able to turn himself back into his previous form. But I can't recall how he does it.

And, as I look back at the account I have written above, I realize that I have introduced all kinds of things into it that are not, strictly speaking, in my memory of the story at all. The paddle-shaped antlers, the rabbit food, the caribou stew. Those were me being a writer. They were things I wrote to give substance to the gauze of memory.

The fact is, when I try to look closely at the story, to remember it exactly as it was, it seems to disappear.

Maybe I should try it again, then. Here is another way of telling it, perhaps more true to the sketchiness of my memory:

Weesakaytsak hungry, cold, horny. Sees caribou. Transforms. Antlers, hooves, fur, penis. Eats, ruts. The good life. *miyo-pimâtisiw.* But females unsatisfied. He ruts and ruts. No time to eat, no energy. No sleep. Somehow he escapes, turns back to his regular form.

But, of course, that version isn't right either. It tells the events of the story, but it doesn't have any specificity or presence; it wouldn't stick in anyone's memory. There was so much more to the story, so much different. Of course one of the most important things that my two versions don't record is the presence of the man telling the story: Louis Bird, Pennishish, renowned Omushkego Cree storyteller and Elder, honorary *mosôm* to all of us in the group. Louis was our teacher in a class on Cree Stories at the University of Manitoba in August of 2010. I was listed on the course outline as the professor, but I was just as much a student as anyone in the room. My main contribution was that I would mark the essays. I also made one fateful and possibly somewhat frustrating decision about the class. We would have no textbooks. Even though Louis Bird had written two celebrated collections of Omushkego Cree stories, we were going to encounter those stories only in their oral versions as he chose to tell them to us. Even Louis himself was a little surprised when I told him there would be no textbooks, but he was very willing to go along with this experiment in oral education. He learned the same way from his own Elders, after all, or at least he had done so for part of his storytelling apprenticeship. Over the course of many years he had also made a collection of audio recordings during his sessions with the Elders of his community, and he had kept those tapes with him for most of his adult life, listening to them sometimes as he tried to commit to memory as much of the Omushkego tradition as he could find. He was incredibly successful at this, and could tell any of the hundreds of stories without a moment's hesitation. They lived in him in such a way that he had no need to refer to his own or anyone else's books on the subject.

But the students were much less comfortable with the idea that there would be no texts. They were terrified that they would forget the stories and then be unable to study or write their essays, lacking access to the so-called primary texts. For the first couple of days, a number of the students tried to write down every word that came out of Louis Bird's mouth. I have never seen such furious note taking. However, it became clear when we discussed the stories each afternoon that these "transcriber" students couldn't recall a single thing about the stories without consulting their notes. They had mistaken writing for learning. We never introduced an outright ban on note taking, but, as the course proceeded, I saw that fewer and fewer of the students were transcribing the stories.

Eventually, by the last couple of days, the pencils were idle and all of us were focused on experiencing the stories together as living, unfolding performances that we were fortunate enough to share in. We still had a great deal of trouble with our memories, and in fact much of our discussion time in the class was devoted to our collective attempts to remember what had happened in each of the stories. Essentially, we re-told the stories to one another at the same time as we talked about what they might mean. It was probably the most engaged and genuinely interactive teaching experience I have ever been involved in.

When it came time for the students to write their essays, however, the anxiety of textlessness returned with a vengeance. The students were unsure what, exactly, they were supposed to be writing about, since they didn't trust their memories of the stories. One student asked, "If we don't have textbooks, how are we supposed to cite our sources when we write our essays?" It was a better question than it initially seemed, and it is something I have thought about ever since, because it points out how different an oral story really is from a written text or even a recording. When a story resides only in memory, how *do* we "cite" it? Is it even a singular thing that can be referred to as an entity, an object that can be demarcated and therefore interpreted? Or is the interpretation always bound up in the memory of the story: do we only remember the parts that support an interpretation we have already brought to it? One might come to the conclusion, then, that the very practice of citing is simply not appropriate for oral stories. And yet one could argue on the contrary that every story is inevitably a citation of the other versions that have gone before, that there is *only* citation and not "original" in the case of oral stories.

I have to admit that at times I shared the students' fears about "losing" the stories, and I nearly reached for my pen a few times when Louis was telling them. But I did resist that temptation. And what I came to think, long after the class was over, was that maybe forgetting is part of the story. Maybe it is necessary for us to lose or misplace some aspects of the story in order to remember it as a coherent thing. I am reminded of Nietzsche's provocative statement: "Forgetting is essential to action of any kind" (62). Is this true? Is my failing and overly literate memory the problem here, or is there something important about the way in which our memories process oral stories, something that is lost or changed when we write them down or record them?

Of course we also forget the stories we have *read*, but we don't have the same anxiety about "losing" them, because they are still there in the form of external objects—books or digital files. So we think of the forgetting differently with oral stories. We worry more about loss, because the stories seem to "exist" only in our memories, and we pine for the safety net of an external receptacle that could preserve the stories independently of our own fallible selves.

When I think back on those unwritten, oral stories now, they refuse to be settled, to be reified. In some ways that's because I don't remember them properly. I only have an imperfect recollection of how they went, and what order the events in the stories happened. But I think there is more to this than simply the weakness of memory. The stories persist in my mind as a memory of an event, a community, a particular set of circumstances—including the fact that it was incredibly hot that week, and we were sweltering in the room. And there was the sound of the fan that was facing Louis as he led the discussions. And the faces of the students as they listened to him. All of that is part of my recollection of them. With a text, it is an entirely different experience. In reading, there is the "absence of the book," as Maurice Blanchot so deftly described it. The medium of the text itself disappears as we read, and we are focused on other things. Of course, with a book we can return to it again and again, so that it is absent in a sense only *while* we are experiencing it as art. With oral stories, it is the opposite: they are present to us while we are experiencing them, and then afterward they are more absent (although not totally, so long as our memory lasts). What I remember of those stories now is not particular words or phrases, but rather echoes of Louis' voice and also the events, characters, and scenes he presented. It's as if the story was composed of something other than language, as if its medium was perhaps memory itself. Or maybe the medium was our community, the sharedness of bodies in a space, a time.

And now, when I read written versions of Louis' stories, I am struck very much by the differences between them and what we encountered in the class. Of course, I knew these things to a certain degree intellectually beforehand; I knew of the many differences between orality and literacy, and between an oral story and a work of "orature." But experiencing this difference is somehow not the same as knowing it in abstract terms. When I read Louis' stories now, they are still fascinating and rich, but they don't belong to me (or rather to "us," the class, the audience) in the same way that they belonged to us then. In some crucial ways, they are the same stories—say, the one about Weesakaytsak and the Geese, which I still remember quite well. But in several important aspects the stories are different, even in terms of the events that are recounted. Some people might say this is an example of the unreliability of oral narratives, the fact that they are based upon the fallible memory of the storyteller. But I don't think it is so simple as that. I think instead that Louis was telling us these stories in a particular way because he felt that was the way we needed to hear them. He was tailoring our experience of the stories to the teachings he had been giving us in other parts of the class. He was utilizing the strengths of orality, rather than worrying about its possible weaknesses.

———

I began this piece with my story of a disappearing story, because I wanted to highlight the continuing value of oral stories *as* oral stories in the contemporary world, rather than solely as source material for archival documentation, which is so often how oral stories are treated when they are recorded or written down. Researching oral stories these days is sometimes essentially a process of recording them, turning them into objects that can be collected and preserved in an archive, whether that archive is a collection of tapes in someone's basement, or an online database, or a book. One of the important functions of an archive is that it provides a nexus of "citationality," a specific and finite location for each piece of valued information, so that many different people can access it and can point toward it, and everyone knows what "it" is. In an archive, a story becomes a specific, measurable thing in a way that it may not have been in its oral incarnation. Stories become archivable only after they are written down or recorded, turned into material objects. I think this has implications for our understandings of memory, memorialization, and ultimately community identity, pedagogy, and political action. Even as I am now involved in projects that record and, in a small way, archive versions of oral stories, I am sometimes troubled by some of the assumptions that tend to go along with this process—especially the need for certainty, the need to make the story conform to my notions of the document, the thing.

What I haven't mentioned yet is that I made some audio recordings of Louis Bird during our class, and possibly even on the day when he may or may not have told the story of Weesakaytchak and the Caribou. Those recordings are on my computer, but I haven't yet replayed them. I could do that right now, scroll back through the days and maybe even find a recording of the story itself. I could play it, "refresh" my memory, as it were. But I have resisted the temptation so far because I have a feeling that if I played the recording, then I would believe I "have" the story. I would be able to give you the "actual" words Louis used. And I'm pretty sure I would think of the story in an entirely different way than I think of it right now. I would be more comfortable with it, more sure of my responses, because I could listen again and again, and I could even transcribe sections of it. I would know what the story was, and where it was: i.e., outside of myself, in a location that could be identified and shared with others. For now, at least, I prefer not to be so sure, not to place the story so firmly into the order of things and into a network of certainty. It lives for me right now in a way that I want to ponder and cherish for a while longer. At the same time, I realize that it is already being transformed by the fact that I am writing about it.

Things I will always remember about the story, even though crucial elements of it have already long disappeared from my recollection: Louis Bird impersonating Weesakaytsak impersonating a caribou. The way he shook his antlers, pawed at the frozen earth, gazed hungrily at the tantalizing rumps of the imagined female caribou. The way he mimed utter exhaustion, his shoulders slumped, his head waving back and forth in delirium. I can call to mind his smile and his laughter, and even the singsong echo of his Cree accent, but for some reason I can't remember any of his words. I can't recall *exactly* how he described Weesakaytchak's antlers, or the rumps of the female caribou, or the sensation of Weesakaytchak transforming into one of the four-leggeds. And yet all of those beings and events are emblazoned in my memory. And so many contextual experiences are also connected to the story in my memory: Louis' extraordinary warmth and generosity toward each and every person in the class. His sly mention that my last name was almost the same as caribou. And even a little adventure we had outside of class time, when Louis accidentally left his ID and travel documents outside overnight after doing a TV interview in the yard beside his apartment. There was a rainstorm that night, and, when the janitors found the sodden package of his ID the next morning, they spread everything out in an office to dry. He laughed so hard when he saw that, his official identity transformed into wet tents of nearly indecipherable pulp. An archivist's nightmare. When he laughed at the spectacle of his "official life" spread out like laundry on a line, I saw in a new way the absurdity of paper identity and the documented self, especially for an Aboriginal person who had every reason to distrust the transformational power of documents.

I guess that's what I'm trying to understand here: transformation. Weesakaytchak changing his shape, and stories changing theirs, and the great storyteller's identity melting away in the rain. McLuhan meets the trickster. Something persists, even in the midst of the changes, I know. Weesakaytchak was still himself when he was a caribou, wasn't he? Or was he? The story is still the story when it's a document, a recording—isn't it? How can we ever be sure? I worry that, once a story becomes a document, a location in an archive, it no longer has the capacity to change, to become relevant to a new situation, a new audience. It gains a kind of longevity and cite-ability, but perhaps it loses some of its adaptability. Almost certainly, it loses the ability to disappear (which I believe *can* be an ability, as well as a threat). And yet, even despite my reservations, I have found myself working on several projects that involve recording and archiving stories. It seems I am always ambivalent when it comes to this question of the persistence of stories. I change my mind, transform my thinking. Sometimes when I'm listening to a live story, I revel in the specificity of the moment, and I try to keep that moment with me in my memory. But then I worry about what will happen to the stories when people like Louis Bird have gone on to the next world, and so I get out my recorder, my camera, my notebook. And *then* after doing that, I am reluctant to look at my notes, to listen to my recordings. This may be my own particular version of narrative insanity, but I have a feeling it is a larger phenomenon of ambivalence, of mind-changing, that many of us find ourselves in at this particular moment in the history of representation, when technologies have made it possible to capture performances in new and more "realistic" modes: high fidelity, high definition, panoramic, polyphonic. It seems a shame not to do that when we have the tools. But it is perhaps even more of a shame when we mistake the representations for the lived experience of the stories themselves.

In the last couple of years I have been fortunate to learn from another teacher almost as wise and learned as Louis Bird: the performance studies theorist Diana Taylor, whose book *The Archive and the Repertoire* is the most nuanced exploration I have found of the differences between these two versions of story. She describes it in terms of the differences "between the *archive* of supposedly enduring materials (i.e., texts, documents, buildings, bones) and the so-called ephemeral *repertoire* of embodied practice, knowledge (i.e., spoken language, dance, sports, ritual)" (18). For Taylor, the archive and the repertoire are two fundamentally different but often intersecting cultural realities, one of them more closely attached to systems, nations, and colonialism, and the other more allied with indigeneity, folk culture, and the unofficial. Despite the suggestions of that lineage, she doesn't merely disparage the archive and celebrate repertoire. She sees them instead as alternate and competing forms of cultural practice and meaning. She has also been engaged in an ongoing project of recording and archiving hundreds of performances from across the Americas, which are preserved in the Hemispheric Institute Digital Video Library. She says of this process, "A video of a performance is not a performance, though it often comes to replace the performance as a *thing* in itself" (20). Perhaps most importantly (and the scholar in me loves being able to quote from her eminently citable text just because it is so *there*, so much a *thing*), Taylor adds, "The repertoire requires presence: people participate in the production and reproduction of knowledge by 'being there,' being a part of the transmission. As opposed to the supposedly stable objects in the archive, the actions that are in the repertoire do not remain the same. The repertoire both keeps and transforms choreographies of meaning" (20).

As many scholars and even policy makers have noted, any archive is constructed "against forgetting." It also, of course, involves a particular construction of community memory, as distinguished from individual memory. But what Taylor shows us here is that repertoire, too, is enacted against forgetting. It "keeps and transforms" the meaning through embodied practices that move from one body to another, held in memory, distributed across a community, over space and time. Keeping and transforming is what oral stories do best, I think, even though we worry about their fragility. They remain themselves, in some way, even when official recognition of that identity washes away, and they remain so because they are open to new possibilities, new contexts. Perhaps their transforming *is* their keeping, even though that may seem like a loss from some perspectives.

I think maybe the oscillation between the archive and the repertoire in Taylor's work is what resonates most for me in my sense of ambivalence about stories. What her work and Louis Bird's example tell us is that an archive can be dangerous if it is the final resting place of a story. But it doesn't have to be that way. In fact, their work makes clear that in the present moment we have to find ways of preserving or encouraging the *practice* of telling our most important stories. We have to find ways of animating those stories *as repertoire*, even if (and perhaps especially if) they have been stored in archives. It is not and should not be a one-way process, from testimony to document to archive. We have to invest just as much energy and time and political commitment to making those archives back into repertoire, enabling them to maintain that sometimes troubling but also vital status as embodied memory. I think this is a crucial function of pedagogy in Indigenous contexts: teaching can, at its best, bring life to the archive and show us that the stories live in new ways for each new community of listeners.

And Louis Bird provides a model for this process as well, since after all he is archivist as well as storyteller. As I mentioned earlier, part of his training as a storyteller was to make recordings of the Elders, first on reel-to-reel tapes and later on mini-cassette tapes, which are now part of an archival collection housed at the University of Winnipeg and available online at ourvoices.ca. Many of the stories that he knows by heart now were ones that he recorded and replayed for himself over the years. But I know Louis would be the first to tell us that creating the archive was not enough. Just making the tapes and storing them under his bed would not have given them any life. What he devoted himself to doing was listening to them, learning them, asking the Elders about them. Turning the archive back into repertoire was in a sense his life's work. The recording and the collecting of the stories were only the most basic starting points. As we move toward a new era of digital archives and nearly omnipresent technologies of recording, I think we can learn a great deal from his commitment and his practice.

Works Cited

Blanchot, Maurice. "The Absence of the Book." *The Infinite Conversation.* Trans. Susan Hanson. Minneapolis: U of Minnesota P, 1993. 422–434.

Nietzsche, Friedrich. *Untimely Meditations.* Ed. Daniel Breazeale. Trans. R. J. Hollingdale. Cambridge: Cambridge UP, 1997.

Taylor, Diana. *The Archive and the Repertoire: Performing Cultural Memory in the Americas.* Chapel Hill: Duke UP, 2003.

Works Uncited

Bird, Louis. Untitled Story [in which Weesakaytsak Becomes a Caribou]. Incompletely recalled, yet living in the memories of those who heard it at the University of Manitoba, ca. August 10, 2010.

41

Teaching Indigenous Literature as Testimony: *Porcupines and China Dolls* and the Testimonial Imaginary

Michelle Coupal

Although not all Indigenous literatures in Canada fall into the category of what I call *fictional testimony*, my contention is that much of it does. Indigenous fictional testimony is literature that gives evidence to the experiences of individuals or communities, often with pedagogical, therapeutic, or activist impulses for a broad, that is, both Native and non-Native, reading public. What follows is a précis of some of the strategies I employ when I teach Indigenous literature as a form of testimony, which I anchor, for the purposes of this discussion, in Robert Arthur Alexie's *Porcupines and China Dolls* (2002). I ask students to reflect upon the following questions: can a semi-autobiographical fiction such as Alexie's offer up an alternative form of testimonial to residential school abuses, and a creative act of instruction about its legacies, as a supplement to the work of the TRC? Can fiction function as a legitimate form of testimony? I argue that, in its semi-autobiographical staging of Alexie's alcoholism and suicidal thoughts following his stay at Stringer Hall, its initial reticence consciously to articulate the sexual abuse suffered at the hostel, followed by its exaggerated and repeated public disclosures of child sexual abuse by multiple adult characters in the novel, and its ambivalent relationship to healing, Alexie's novel was written as a means for him to testify to the complexities, ambivalences, and contradictions of his experiences and their legacies in an imaginative strategy to speak the truth in ways that the fact-based, adversarial court system would not permit. To my knowledge, *Porcupines and China*

Dolls is the only public forum in which Alexie tells the story of sexual abuse at the hostel, and he does so indirectly through fiction.[1] The fictional form of the novel grants Alexie a means of articulating traumas without compromising his entitlement to privacy. The novel form also provides Alexie with a vehicle to open up a conversation with his community through story outside of more formalized practices, such as healing circles or workshops. As Alexie says, "I'm not going to get five thousand Gwich'in to listen to me tell a story, so I give them my book. Maybe they won't read it now, but they might in five or ten years. At least they'll have the *chance* to read it, and that chance will be given to others as well" (Richler 119; original emphasis). *Porcupines and China Dolls* arguably stands in as a storied proxy to conventional testimonials, and, through its circulation to both Native and non-Native readers, represents the *chance* for change.

James, who is modelled after Alexie himself, represses but ultimately cannot contain his memories of childhood sexual abuse. Repeated disclosures of sexual abuse by James' friends prompt his own disclosure, as members of the community attempt to recover by sharing their stories of trauma with each other. Unlike Western-style talk therapy, however, the "talking cure" here is public, communal, and story-based. The public disclosure at the two-day healing workshop literalizes through performance the therapeutic release of inner demons on a public stage in a magical spectacle in which the whole community takes part. This creative act of disclosure is a testimonial fantasy of what public accounts of abuse could be—that is, acts of empowerment rather than rituals of shaming. Community and individual healing is radically disrupted, however, through a critique of the closure that healing implies. For me, the novel is both testimony and therapeutic journey, as well as a critique of testimony and the promise of healing.

There are many reasons not to testify publically to childhood sexual abuse, whether testimony is through the court system or through the safer but still public forum provided by the TRC: the shame that sexually abused children feel is often carried forward into adulthood, and the difficulties associated with speaking about violations in which victims often feel complicit are compounded by the fear of being disbelieved. Public disclosures can be especially fraught for men who have been abused as children by other men, because the heteronormative imperative still at work in society can further contribute to the shame. In the novel, for example, when Jake Noland tells his girlfriend about his sexual abuse, "He hung his head to hide his shame" (97). Fiction can provide the distancing necessary to make an account of one's traumas without having to face directly a potentially incredulous, homophobic, or otherwise critical public audience.

Alexie admits that he finds it easier to tell his story from a narrative distance. In an article written for *Indian Country Today* entitled, "Robert Arthur Alexie—An Author in Waiting," Alexie writes about himself in the third person: "Robert graduated [from high school and Stringer Hall] in June 1974 and returned home to work and party and this he did with wild abandon." Nonetheless, in 1989 Alexie became Chief of the Teetl'it Gwich'in Band Council in Fort McPherson, where he lived with his common-law wife and three children: "And through it all, Robert continued drinking and was now becoming something he never planned on: an alcoholic and an abuser. He was sentenced, on two occasions, to time in jail." In the early 1990s, "after years of abuse and abusing, Robert decided to seek treatment and went to Toronto. He's not had a drink since, but the road to recovery and healing was not easy. It's a daily struggle and he relapses into his old way of thinking every now and then." When reading the article, it is easy to forget, as I did, that the author is Alexie himself. It is only in the final lines that Alexie confesses: "Robert is me, or I am Robert. And sometimes he finds it better to write in the third person." The third-person voice allows Alexie the narrative distance he seems to require to tell his story, whether he tells it in an article about himself or in his novel.

The third-person singular employed by Alexie in the article seems also to grant him the freedom to state the semi-autobiographical form of his novel clearly: "The fact that the main character is tall, dark and wears a black leather jacket should not surprise anyone. The story is semi-autobiographical and the character is not an easy person to like." When Noah Richler met Alexie, he described him as "a handsome man with dark hair, evidently not prone to smiling . . . wearing black shades, black jeans, and a black leather vest over a khaki hunting shirt" (108). *Porcupines and China Dolls* opens with the following description of James Nathan: "He stood alone beside the highway in the Blue Mountains like he'd done so many times before. His tall, dark figure looked foreboding against the dark clouds. His black leather jacket glistened like blood-soaked armour from another time. His scowl told everyone and everything to keep their fucking distance. He looked like Death ready to go on a rampage" (1). The passage is an important signifier of Alexie's masculine testimonial style, by which I mean that James is portrayed as a strong, fearsome warrior, whose public disclosure of his childhood sexual abuse will be staged in terms of warrior and battle imagery. Interestingly, while the third-person article makes the connection between Alexie and James unequivocal, with Alexie freely confessing his alcoholism and abusive behaviour, the article remains silent about whether or not Alexie suffered childhood sexual abuse at Stringer Hall.

Alexie's Testimonial Imaginary

The culmination of the therapeutic process represented by the cathartic promise of the healing workshop occurs, significantly, not at the end of the novel, as
with James Bartleman's healing circle in *As Long as the Rivers Flow* (2011), but
about two-thirds of the way through. One expects healing to occur following
the workshop and the workshop itself to be a therapeutic end point; however,
James remains suicidal to the novel's concluding pages. These deviations in
standard processes of healing are even more interesting when one considers
the fantastic elements of the public disclosure. Alexie seems to suggest that the
public disclosure of trauma is as much an act of the imagination as healing, and,
more radically, perhaps he is suggesting that testimony should be a fantasy or
can only be an act of the imagination. Alexie's staging of public testimony is at
once an extended metaphor for the therapeutic process of releasing one's inner
demons to heal and a critique of the limitations of such an endeavour. In his
discussion with Noah Richler, Alexie describes the underwhelming community response at a Gwich'in gathering when an Elder disclosed his sexual abuse.
He was the first community member to do so, and, as Alexie says, "'It was like
nothing had been said'" (108). Alexie's frustration at his community's apathy
and failure to engage with the traumas of the Elder before them is one possible
reason why Alexie stages such a grand spectacle of disclosure in the novel:

> The anger that I felt in [*Porcupines and China Dolls*] was helpful because
> it allowed me almost to *scream* what I wanted to say. . . . I remember writ-
> ing the part where the Chief gets up and discloses and the story almost
> goes into a kind of magical realism. It was a period in the community where
> everybody was going about their business as if it was *normal*—normal to
> drink, normal to buy bootlegs, normal to be sexually abused. . . . It's so dys-
> functional, it's *normal*. (Richler 113–14; original emphasis)

If *Porcupines and China Dolls* was meant to wake up his community to the
abuses suffered at residential school, Alexie's over-the-top theatrical staging
of public disclosure holds out the possibility of doing so by reinvigorating an
engagement with testimony in a way that avoids the pitfalls of public confession. Over one hundred community members arrive for the workshop looking
like "they were there for some root canal work and wished it was over so they
could get on to more important things like bingo or poker," and "few, if any,
had a genuine interest in the healing process" (181). Alexie seems to suggest,
however, that they do like to be entertained and they also enjoy a good story. By
employing oral storytelling techniques with magical realist conventions, Alexie

creates a spectacle of masculine empowerment as an antidote to the shame the characters have been feeling as they disclose their abuse to each other. I am calling the testimonial aesthetic that Alexie creates "masculinist" because of its emphasis on male power, super-human strength, and the story-line of warriors battling their inner demons rather than victims suffering through their confessions. Chief David is the first "warrior" to take the stage at the workshop. As with Bartleman's healing circle, a talking stick is used, except in Alexie, its power is literalized. The band's talking stick, which "gave them power and courage," has been ignored for years—*"Gone like so many of our traditions"*— but when Chief David picks it up, he grows ten feet tall (183). He begins by disclosing his abuse in a straightforward, testimonial style: "Thirty years ago I was sexually abused in the hostel" (184). The narrative tone that immediately follows the disclosure is not earnest or sympathetic, as one would expect, but rather funny and magical: "One hundred people did a double take. They looked around to see if others had heard. *What 'a hell did he say?* The sound of so many empty heads reverberating in the community hall woke a million, trillion gazillion demons, dreams and nightmares from their slumber. They poked their ugly little heads out of the ceiling, walls and floor to see what the fuck was going on" (184). It is hard to imagine what a fresh take on the public disclosure of childhood sexual abuse might look like, and yet that is precisely what Alexie provides, in my view, so that his readers awake from their somnolence to witness a legend-in-the-making that they will remember and talk about in the future.

Alexie's mythmaking testimonial strategy is intended to draw in audience members (and readers) to the disclosure process, and is deeply rooted in some of the hallmarks of oral storytelling: repetition, the number three, hyperbole, engagement with the audience, and, for Alexie, a tongue-in-cheek style of humour. The Chief begins each of his disclosures with, "Thirty years ago," and, after each successive disclosure, the audience shouts, "Shit!" then "Holy shit!" and finally, "Holy fuckin' shit!" (184). "Chief David then grew twenty feet and held himself like a Warrior of Old" (184). Rather than testimony being a diminishing experience, it is legitimizing. The more Chief David discloses, the taller and fiercer he becomes. Again, note the use of repetitive syntactical formations governed by the number three: "Chief David grew thirty feet tall and spoke of suicides, killings and death. He spoke of anger, rage and terror. He spoke of hurt, shame and sorrow. He spoke of demons, dreams and nightmares, He spoke of the future, hope and healing" (185). This repetitive strategy is used, as it is with oral stories, to help the audience understand and incorporate the information into their working memories. The disclosure evolves from giving an account of suffering into an extended metaphor for conquering traumas by laying them bare: "Chief David then did something very few people have ever done. He reached deep down into the very depths of his tormented and fucked-up soul, pulled out the rage, anger, hate, sorrow and sadness by their roots and threw them on the floor for the world to see. He then proceeded to choke the little fuckers like they deserved it" (185). Despite the sparks which by this point fly from the talking stick, the Chief ends his disclosure story in a realistic mode: "After a million years, he looked at his People like he'd just come from battle. . . . 'This is where it ends. . . . This is where we make the change for ourselves an' for our children'" (185). The Chief is storied as a returning warrior fomenting the rebirth of his community by way of his own process of healing.

It is in this mode of realistic testimonial discourse that Alexie reveals his always ambivalent relationship to testimony and healing. Initially, the audience responds with wonderment as they watch the Chief grow taller and taller; however, when the disclosure ends with their Chief-warrior looking tired and like a real-life human being, they respond with skepticism: *Is he tellin' the truth? Is he lyin'? Is he doin' this for sympathy? Is he nuts?"* (185). Questioning the veracity, motives, and sanity of those who publically disclose childhood sexual abuse is an all-too-common response, both by the judicial system and the general public. Questions such as those of the audience in the novel are one of the main reasons why victims of child sexual abuse do not publically confess their abuse. The potential for incredulous witnesses to straightforward testimonies may also be why Alexie chooses magic realism as his principal narrative mode to disclose sexual abuse. In this, the suggestion is that perhaps people are more likely to believe a story, even if that story is clearly fantastical.

Alexie builds up his story of public testimony to epic proportions as Chief David's disclosure is followed by Jake's, and then, finally, James' as the climax. The chapter title, "The Battle for Souls," is an early marker of the therapeutic, masculinist aesthetic at work in the scene, an aesthetic of mythic combat rather than gentle healing through cathartic talk. I do not think it is a coincidence that James' public disclosure is the climax of the scene and also the height of Alexie's employment of magic realism. Alexie not only writes an indirect testimony to abuse through the novel; his fictional engagement with public disclosure is also an act of fantasy, story, and the creation of a legend. When James discloses his abuse to the audience, which has by that point doubled in size because word of the spectacle has spread, it is a testimonial-action-thriller and blood sport. James as the hero of this epic battle opens with his typical humour and ferocity: "He grinned that friggin' Nathan grin, then let loose such a horrendous godawful battle cry of rage, hatred and vengeance that the roof of the community hall blew off and scattered to the four winds" (191). James' "demons, dreams and nightmares shivered in their rubber boots" (191), with good reason: "James Nathan started laying demons out left, right and centre. Demon arms, legs and heads were flying everywhere. One head fell into the lap of Old Pierre. He picked it up, poked out his beady little eyes and threw it on the floor" (192). Rather than their previous, distanced incredulity, the audience becomes actively involved in James's "therapy" as witnesses and co-slayers of inner demons. An italicized narrative voice periodically interjects lines seemingly aimed directly to the reader as a further solicitation to engage with James' "testimony": "*He was a fucking sight to behold! I shit you not. You really had to be there!*" (192).

James is not ashamed, nor is his veracity in question: he is a one-hundred-foot-tall warrior whom young girls dream of marrying and young boys dream of becoming (192). Alexie piles on cultural references to his warrior-hero of disclosure, James, in an excess of imagery aimed to entertain: "James Nathan was like a knight in shining armour. He was like Kevin Costner in *Dances with Wolves*. He was like Crazy Horse charging into battle. He was like Geronimo at his best" (192). Jake and Chief David join James to kill more demons as the audience starts "singing some old Indian war song": "It sounded like the Mormon Tabernacle Choir singing *The Messiah* on acid. It sounded like a million Plains Indians all singing at once" (193). While completely over-the-top and replete with *non sequiturs*, the scene attempts to capture the scale of what is happening and to show the event as the work of healing, while retaining its sense of humour and its purposeful intent to wake up the community to the legacies of residential school: "The three Warriors heard this war song and it gave them strength and courage. There was such a fucking commotion what with blood, guts, arms, legs and heads flying every which way that no one breathed or blinked an eye lest they miss a thing" (193). In the end, "James, Jake and Chief David stood above slain demons and nightmares like great big fucking Warriors of Old covered with blood, sweat, guts, tears and pride" (193).

The spectacular disclosure scene represents what public testimonies should be but rarely are—empowering for the people giving the testimony and enlivening for their witnesses. Cool air blows through the community hall following the slaying of demons: "It smelled clean. It smelled like new beginnings" (194). The audience is filled with admiration for the three disclosure-warriors. They are not shame-filled victims, but rather proud heroes literally standing tall. Furthermore, rather than being an emasculating process, the disclosure actually enhances the virility and desirability of the warriors (194–95). Alexie writes an idealized, very male fantasy of public disclosure, but then undercuts it by bringing the narrative back to the much starker reality of realistic testimony the following day: "What really happened at the community hall in Aberdeen that day? Despite all the blood and gore, it was all very simple: three men disclosed. They talked honestly about a sexual abuse that occurred thirty years ago. They spoke of oral sex and sodomy. They spoke of the shame and the pain of being alone" (197). Alexie's disclosure scene is a wonderfully magical remediation to what he goes on to show is the painful process of bearing witness to testimonies of childhood abuse.

The contrast is perhaps most striking in the courtroom scene at the preliminary trial of Tom Kinney, the man who abused Chief David, James, Jake, and many others. James sees Kinney "smirk" as he is led out of the courtroom (266). James loses his composure and threatens to kill the man. When a rookie RCMP officer suggests that he could lay charges against James should he attack Kinney, James lashes out at the officer: "Where the fuck were you when that bastard stuck his cock up my ass!" (266). There is a significant disparity between the therapeutic and magical disclosure scene and the traumatic reality of the courtroom, where James is not growing taller in the confrontation with his demons but rather must be restrained lest he slay his real demon, Tom Kinney. The graphic language of James' abuse, while typical of the horrific detail expected of victims in the courtroom, is precisely what witnesses or readers are most likely to tune out because it is too unsettling and explicit to hear and too difficult to discuss. Alexie's magical disclosure scene accomplishes the task of confession without falling into the graphic testimonial discourse revealed in the court scene.

Porcupines and China Dolls performs and debunks testimony as surely as it enacts and deconstructs healing. For all of the demon slaying dramatized at the healing workshop, the push and pull between healing and not healing is still in evidence. Although forty feet tall and having staked himself to the stage to battle his demons, Jake is empowered but not healed. Following his disclosure, he shouts his now familiar refrain: "Healin' is a journey—there is no end!" to which James responds, "Ain't 'at 'a fuckin' truth!" (188). Keavy Martin observes that, "Alexie flouts his readers' expectations regarding the preordained progress of a healing journey" ("Truth, Reconciliation, and Amnesia" 49). Indeed, the morning following the workshop, when Brenda asks James what his plans for the day are, James thinks to himself, "*Maybe blow my brains out*" (205; original emphasis). As Daniel David Moses declares in dialogue with Terry Goldie, "some people just cannot be healed. Their wounds—or at least the wounds in their community—are so deep and abiding" (Moses and Goldie ix).

The novel emphasizes that there is no straightforward path to healing and no closure. For the community members, the workshop sparks dialogue about the event and reinstates an interest in their traditions. They gather as a community and bring out their ceremonial drums, and their Elders start speaking to each other in their own language (201–03). The reclamation of traditional

Indigenous values and practices is a marker of healing, yet Alexie troubles this healing narrative: "People were calling their relatives in other parts of the territories and in other parts of Canada. In one week, Chief David, James and Jake would be known all over the NWT. In two weeks, they would be forgotten" (199). Alexie's novel is not without hope; rather, it seeks to capture the complexities of the healing process precisely as a *process*, not an end in itself. As Chief David says, "In the last few days, we've seen something happen in our community. We've seen People disclose an' we've seen the drum return if only for one night. I wish I can tell you it's going to be like this forever, but we all know it isn't. Not unless we work together to keep it" (222). For Martin, Alexie's refusal to bring closure to the work of healing becomes a sort of meta-narrative for the potential of Canadian national reconciliation discourse to assuage non-Native guilt by bringing closure and thus forgetting to the issues:

> The end points of healing, or of closure, here remain continually beyond the grasp of readers and characters alike, and denied this state of grace they are forced to continue to grapple with the challenges of the *process* of healing— or simply of continuation. Government rhetoricians and average Canadians alike have much to learn from this inconclusivity; as Alexie demonstrates, this push for closure is in many ways a longing for oblivion—for the luxury of forgetting and for the absolution of amnesia. (61)

The push for closure, which Martin deftly perceives as part of a rhetoric in the service of public amnesia, is, in the first instance, a critique of the healing promise of public testimonies to residential school traumas. *Porcupines and China Dolls* offers an imaginative rethinking of what public disclosure could be if fiction were a sanctioned mode of testimony. If "Aboriginal trauma theory" arises, as Kristina Fagan (now Bidwell) contends, from the stories Aboriginal peoples tell, then Alexie's trauma theory radically subverts Western conceptions of healing (206–07). His story and thereby his theory reclaim storytelling and the imaginative capacity to reshape experience by opening and closing sutures to wounds that can never fully heal. Yet such storytelling and imagination always have the capacity to transform—by imagining other ways of talking, by thinking of new ways to testify, and by inspiring a community of readers to think creatively about the legacies of the residential schools.

Porcupines and China Dolls is, for me, the most non-confessional confession I have ever read. As he acknowledged, Alexie prefers to write about himself in the third person. With the exception of the seemingly tacked-on ending of healing through the love of a woman, Alexie opens and closes his novel with James Nathan taking a gun from his truck on the highway over-looking the mountains, putting the gun in his mouth, and imagining the shot. On 9 June 2014, Alexie was found dead, lying by his vehicle on the Dempster Highway overlooking the mountains outside of Fort McPherson. I dedicate this article to the memory of Robert Arthur Alexie, who wrote his life and death in his own way, dreamed of healing, reimagined testimony, and, I suggest, offered up a radical rethinking of trauma and healing.

Note

1. Alexie has not publically indicated whether or not he personally suffered sexual abuse at Stringer Hall, so while the novel is "semi-autobiographical," it is not clear that Alexie was sexually abused.

42

"Betwixt and Between": Alternative Genres, Languages, and Indigeneity

Sarah Henzi

As the different essays in this anthology show, Indigenous literary production has exploded across Canada. Whereas criticism of the 1980s and 1990s saw the past predominating thematically with a clear emphasis on the socio-political, more and more authors are looking toward the future and making use of different media and modes of intervention; critics are thus privileging the aesthetic, genre experimentation, language revitalization, and intermediality. It has become clear that learning to read across and beyond boundaries—whether literary, linguistic, or national—is a necessity if one is to articulate Indigenous literary and political concerns properly. Although the colonial language has become, without a doubt, a crucial site of reappropriation, Indigenous languages have also become important sites of resistance and decolonization: such as Natasha Kanapé Fontaine's slam poetry and spoken word, which combines French and Innu; Samian's Franco-Algonquian hip hop; Tomson Highway's use of Cree in his writing and cabaret performances; and the "linguistic soundscape through aural elements of Cree" (beatnation.org) of Kevin Lee Burton, to name only a few. These new combinations of language, genre, and media raise many interesting questions: How are traditional oral stories and classic Indigenous thought—such as *Ajjiit: Dark Dreams of the Ancient Arctic* (Tinsley and Qitsualik) or *Red: A Haida Manga* (Yahgulanaas)—brought up to date within new spaces of diffusion and discussion? What are the effects created by the decision to use Indigenous languages, and how does it de-familiarize the Anglo/Franco reader? What happens in between the spaces of translation?

What kinds of interaction are possible and how do we go about understanding these processes of interaction? And, perhaps most importantly, how do these cross-genre and multilingual works subvert, break away, or expand the existing field of Indigenous literary studies and critical scholarship? Clearly, these kinds of works not only speak to contemporaneity and transdisciplinarity, they are attentive to the political, social, and cultural contexts of their source communities, be they remote or urban. For these reasons, many believe that the future of Indigenous Studies resides in a cross-cultural exchange, by means of which one is required to look at such productions from both a communal and territorial (though not necessarily in their spatial sense) perspective. Taken together, this article seeks to offer new ways of thinking about such interventions, without them being constrained by fictitious frontiers, national, generic, linguistic, or institutional.

―――

"So much history can be lost if no one tells the story—so that's what I do. I tell the stories. This is my way of fighting for social change" (Alanis Obomsawin, qtd. in Monk 80). Storytelling can take many forms. Thus far, the field of Indigenous literary scholarship has largely focused on the novel, drama, and poetry. But what of those genres that have not been given sufficient, if any, critical reception, such as science fiction, speculative fantasy, graphic novels, gothic novels, slam poetry, film script, and erotica? These are, at the very least, redefining and expanding upon what we have considered thus far as "literature." Similarly, with regard to film, attention has been given primarily to the documentary; recently, however, more and more Indigenous filmmakers are turning to fictional film, whether feature, like *Rhymes for Young Ghouls* (2013) and *Mesnak* (2011), or short, experimental and/or animation (Wapikoni Mobile Productions). Is not, for instance, Jeff Barnaby's "warrior cinema" a new vision for Indigenous media, a new "cinema of sovereignty," following in the footsteps of Alanis Obomsawin? In the words of Algonquian filmmaker Kevin Papatie, cinema is being regarded as "the new talking stick" (Bertrand 285). Thus, if anything, the emergence of and capitalization on "upset" literary and visual/virtual devices as the products of a redefined, yet liminal existence warrants a necessary change in worldview and a reflection on the direct link to a colonialist past and the undeniable connection to imperialism's contemporaneity.

The question of genre is a slippery notion in the field of Indigenous Studies: the line between literary and non-literary is at times blurred, while the mixing and upsetting of genres and devices is a common practice for many artists. It is worth noting that conventional theories of cultural studies and popular culture

do not account for the historical and political specificities of Indigenous productions. For instance, Eden Robinson's 2000 novel *Monkey Beach* not only
successfully resists and withstands the categorization of its author as "Native,"
despite its predominantly Haisla content, it does so in terms of genre categorization: by experimenting with a variety of genres, such as Canadian gothic,
resistance novel, feminist novel, coming-of-age novel, and revenge novel,
Robinson circumvents the expectations of her readership. She does so by meddling within the universal, narrative issues of human suffering and family relationships, as well as more contextualized legacies, such as residential schools,
loss of culture, and the destruction of traditional land. It is in this sense that
I contend that such works are performative interventions, rather than merely
productions, which bring the supernatural, the mythological, and often the
repressed into dialogue with the modern world. In other words, these works
mix "traditional protocols and modern storytelling," to borrow the subtitle of
Robinson's *Sasquatch at Home*, to create a liminal/virtual space for meeting
and sharing multidimensional manifestations, in which literary and film representations take place and enable a dynamic that underlines the active presence of Indigenous peoples in contemporary North America.

Moreover, the prevalence of Indigenous new media and the audio-visual
and digital worlds provides an exceptional entry point to the land and territories (whether spatial, discursive, aesthetic) to which artists may no longer have
access. *Skins*, for instance, a Kahnawake-based storytelling and video-game
workshop, was developed "to encourage First Nations youth to be producers
of media, not just consumers," and "to experiment with ways individuals and
communities might leverage digital media as a tool for preserving and advancing culture and languages" (skins.abtec.org). Similarly, and in line with Kevin
Lee Burton's 2007 film *Writing the Land*, Chris Bose and David McIntosh's
recent urban installation and collection of short stories, *Vancouver, Crawling,
Weeping, Betting*, explores Indigenous presence and sovereignty within the
city of Vancouver, which is situated on the traditional lands of Musqueam,
Squamish, and Tsleil-Waututh. Such projects literally inscribe the "memories,
reanimated wraiths and spirits" that imbibe the city into "reports and boundaries that document [the artists'] embodied experiences of Vancouver" (Bose
and McIntosh). In these two transcontinental examples, the individual is both
embodied and embedded into a visual/virtual landscape—a mediasphere—
which s/he can (re)claim and from which s/he may (re)assert sovereignty.
This technique is even more important given that, for the most part, "everyday encounters with popular culture and new media take place in landscapes
where Indigenous history is erased by markers of state authority" (Robinson,
"The Arts of Public Engagement"). Thus, what interests me here is not only

how the notion of narrative—or storytelling—is stretched/expanded to include interventions that explore the intersections between text and image, text and performance, and text and territory, but how the complexity of the process of textualizing or otherwise materializing storytelling traditions is conveyed.

Furthermore, these unconventionalities provide young Aboriginal writers from Quebec writing in French with the necessary "entry points" to enable an artistic dialogue with their Anglophone counterparts, and this, despite the linguistic boundary.[1] For instance, Innu poet and Idle No More activist Natasha Kanapé Fontaine's combination of slam, spoken work, blog entries, Facebook posts, and performances gives voice to and renders visual both her art and her political claims;[2] she roots these claims in a fierce, bilingual sense of territorial belonging—*mamawolfunderline, "slammeuse territoriale"*—that oscillates between her urban home in Montreal and Nitassinan, the ancestral homeland of the Innu, which she is only now discovering.[3] Hers is not a narrative of (dis) location; rather, it is one of inter-location, and is made manifest in the many intersections of her artistic and political interventions.

Evidently, the combination and juxtaposition of different genres, media, and languages calls for a revisiting of what is now perceived as traditional criticism of Indigenous productions. The exploratory and ephemeral character of the latter requires an investigation as to whether, for instance, nationalism, sovereignty, and locality are sufficient to address the contemporaneity of the productions and the artists themselves. Is the shocking and violent nature of Louis-Karl Picard-Sioui's unexpected performance[4] at the vernissage of his exhibition *The Indian Act Revisited* a continuum of the rhetorical violence/ revenge narrative explored by previous authors, such as Sherman Alexie (in *Flight*) or Eden Robinson (in *Monkey Beach*)?[5] Or, are they—in the words of Susan Orenstein—"a tribute to the blur that is our reality and a tribute to how the word, and the image, and the reader can lift that penumbra" (n.p.)? For, in order to be both ethically and pedagogically challenging, these two examples rely on the audience's sensuous and intellectual experience of and response to the abject, both in bearing witness to indiscriminate or retributive violence, and, ultimately, on their acceptance of, indifference, or reaction to its different representations. Thus, the staging and juxtaposition of unclear, malleable, and transitional elements, including genre, media, language, venue, and participants, is created in such a way to trigger some type of response, whether verbal, physical, or emotional.[6] They are performative interventions that permit an exploration of the continuities and discontinuities between the literary and the visual, as well as the unexpected occurrences that take place "betwixt and between."

In the preface to his *500 Years of Resistance Comic Book*, Gord Hill emphasizes the importance of bringing together "many diverse methods of communication—including newsletters, books, videos, music, posters, stickers, banners, and t-shirts—because no single one will be successful by itself" in the effort "to raise the levels of historical understanding and warrior spirit among Indigenous peoples and others" (6). If the comic book is representative, according to Ward Churchill, of "the best of both worlds"—literary and visual, accessible and informative—then it is in this sense that these contemporary works enable the transmission, as well as the restoration, of creative and cultural practices. They suggest the consideration and analysis of literary and visual productions as performances, and not only about their content. In this way, it is crucial to take up the different boundaries, categories, and cultural constructs when teaching Indigenous literatures and media, and learn to read across and beyond them, and to bring into dialogue these cross-genre, cross-border, multi-lingual works because of their specific and shared political and linguistic histories. From Kevin Lee Burton to Chris Bose to Natasha Kanapé Fontaine, how might these cross-genre "entry points" offer new perspectives on exiguity and sovereignty, given the status of "exiguous uncededness" that both provinces—BC and QC— share? How might such productions inform or be applied to the Aboriginal context in Francophone Quebec? The outcomes of such a practice not only underline how literature and media have mapped and territorialized the fields of study in which we work, but they may be the very inspiration for a cross-border genealogy of North American Indigenous Studies. This practice will not only offer new reflexive avenues for approaching questions of identity and artistic production, it will also enable new "entry points" to analyze the importance of multilingual, visual, and virtual artistic works produced by Indigenous writers and filmmakers; ultimately, it will aid in the creation of a new space to voice, create, resist, restore, and reaffirm experiences, histories, and memory, and to rectify the falsity of colonial imagery.

Notes

1. Although several recent critical works have focused on raising awareness and promoting these works, the actual literary texts remain largely unknown to Anglophone scholars. In addition, there is little—if any—artistic dialogue between the Anglophone communities, mainly Mohawk (Kanien'kehá:ka), and the Francophone ones, placing many in a position of—as coined by François Paré— "double exiguity" (the former, however, find more resources in Ontario and the

United States, since their territory straddles the intersection of international borders and provincial boundaries).

2.   See her spoken word performance at Cacouna, QC, "Les jours des feux, des tambours et des meutes" (https://www.youtube.com/watch?v=u2QJzj1sKzo); I have written more extensively about this piece in my article "Bodies, Sovereignties and Desire: Aboriginal Women's Writing of Quebec" (*Quebec Studies*, forthcoming in 2015).

3.   At the end of the text, below the poet's name, "Chemin du retour. Juillet 2013, route 20" is written. She is referring to Highway 20.

4.   Can be viewed online at http://www.cbc.ca/8thfire/2012/02/the-indian-act-revisited.html.

5.   This could be said also of the exploitative and gory character of Elle-Máijá Tailfeathers' short film *Bloodland*.

6.   Unaware of its ulterior nature, an Elder intervened and physically attacked Picard-Sioui's onstage aggressor, resulting in discord and confusion among the performers, viewers, and general public—much to, in finality, Picard-Sioui's content.

43

A Landless Territory?: Augmented Reality, Land, and Indigenous Storytelling in Cyberspace

David Gaertner

"How do we articulate cyberspace (a landless territory) within the discourse of Critical Indigenous Studies?" This is the question I begin and end my Indigenous New Media course with. As "a world that is both everywhere and nowhere" (Barlow), cyberspace throws into sharp relief questions of sovereignty, agency, identity, and territoriality, and asks particularly resonant questions about the digital "frontier" and Indigenous contestations of these storytelling spaces. For good reason, however, Critical Indigenous Studies (CIS) remains a land-based field—while cyberspace is still largely conceived as placeless. This essay looks at the intersections between cyberspace and land, and illustrates how the former can be used to articulate key issues of CIS in the classroom.

In 1996, on the very cusp of the Silicon Valley bubble, Cree/Métis film-maker and critic Loretta Todd offered a discerning Indigenous reading of cyberspace—any computerized medium, including the Internet, generating a notional communication environment—identifying it as an extension of the Western *episteme*. The term "cyberspace" was coined by William Gibson in his 1984 novel *Neuromancer*, but, as it has been taken up by authors, critics, and programmers in the subsequent thirty years, the meaning of the word has altered significantly, coming to signify "the exercise of political power" (Lehto et al. 1). For Todd, cyberspace makes manifest the dualism at the core of Western philosophy. Presumed as "a new site for the 'heart and mind' of man" (181), Todd sees cyberspace as facilitating a neo-Cartesian insistence on a presence of mind that persists beyond the body, inspiring users "to outrun the drag of the 'meat'" (181) and leave the physical environment behind: "would we [Indigenous people] have created cyberspace?" Todd asks. "I think not—not if cyberspace is a place to escape the earthly plane" (182).

While primarily a rejection of cyberspace as a space for Indigenous storytelling, Todd's article ends by gesturing toward a more hopeful future for Indigenous new media, calling for a cyberspace that connects users to the land and the body: "as cyberspace develops, perhaps it will examine augmented versus immersive technology. Perhaps it will explore narrative forms in which you do not leave your body or soul" (193). Over two decades later, Indigenous new media artists are fulfilling Todd's prospective digital future, employing new technology to "augment" reality via geographic information systems (GIS), Quick Response (QR) codes, Hypertext Markup Language (HTML), as well as video and audio to connect users to land and place through story. The Okanagan writer and scholar Jeannette Armstrong tells us that, "the land speaks. It is constantly communicating. Not to learn its language is to die" (176). Via augmented reality, Indigenous new media artists are communicating the language of the land and the presence of Indigenous people. With the proper critical apparatus in place and even a low-level understanding of technology, Indigenous cyberspace opens up productive and challenging spaces to further investigate key principles in Critical Indigenous Studies and provide students with interactive ways to engage with Indigenous knowledges and methodologies.

Augmented reality (AR), as opposed to virtual reality (VR), layers digital objects onto the material world using mobile computing devices. Whereas VR was about the subject crossing the frame into the art (thereby eliding the medium per se), AR is about "combin[ing] views of the physical world with computer generated graphics" (Bolter and Grusin 272) making land and landscape the platform from which users engage. In the classroom, AR storytelling connects students to land and Indigenous epistemology via fun, critically engaging, and easy-to-use technology that gets them out of the classroom and onto the land—a practice that Leanne Simpson and Glen Coulthard identify as the basis of Indigenous pedagogy (par. 6).

One of the most popular pieces of AR I teach in my Indigenous literature and Indigenous new media classes is a "podplay." Podplays are site-specific, interactive pieces of digital theatre that audiences download onto a smartphone and then take with them to a specific place on the land. The website podplays.ca describes them as

> downloadable plays designed specifically for your ears. Some are best listened to in a certain location or site, some ask you to be a spectator "on the move" and to listen while you walk or run a certain route, and some ask you to simply download, plug in your earphones and close your eyes.

Podplays provide an aural experience of an environment that draws on the augmentative conventions of soundwalks, creative audio guides, and personal walking tours—which museums and art galleries have been employing since the early days of the Walkman.

Vancouver is home to one of the world's premier podplay production teams, Neworld Theatre. Working with a variety of artists and production companies, Neworld has produced a series of eleven plays set in various Vancouver locations.[1] The plays are available for purchase by the public for under $6—a fraction of the cost of a novel or textbook—and the majority of them combine the production values and intellectual heft of a contemporary piece of theatre. Unlike a traditional play, however, podplay performances are available on demand, and they promote active engagement with the city. I regularly teach a Neworld production co-designed by Musqueam writer Quelemia Sparrow and the Indigenous production company Raven Spirit Dance. The piece is called *Ashes on the Water*, and it takes place in CRAB Park, a small piece of public property on the Vancouver waterfront between the docks and Main Street.

Some context in relation to the space is necessary to fully grasp Sparrow's intervention as a land-based cyberspace artist. CRAB Park and the surrounding areas have a rich Coast Salish legacy. However, this history has been at least partially erased by a multivalent settler ideology that appropriates Indigenous politics toward "reclaiming" land for non-Indigenous peoples via the logic of what Coulthard calls *urbs nullius* (176)—urban space fallaciously deemed void of Indigenous presence. CRAB stands for "Create a Real Accessible Beach," a name designated to the space in the 1980s, when settler activists occupied the beach in order to protect it from commercial development. At that time, in tandem with the east-side gentrification accompanying Expo '86 (Blomley), the space was earmarked for private development, but (primarily white) activists contested privatization, arguing it was not a city park at all, but rather a "collective property" (Blomley 58), an open-access commons accessible to the community that uses and maintains it.

As Nicholas Blomley has illustrated, the question of to whom the park "belongs" is a matter of deep contestation. CRAB Park is the legal property of the Vancouver Port Corporation (VPC), a federally operated institution that leases the land to the City of Vancouver (Blomley), which holds the space's "official" name, Portside Park. In *Sḵwx̱wú7mesh*, however, the space is known as *luk'luk'I*, or "grove of beautiful trees" (Suttles 12); while in *hən̓q̓əmin̓əm̓*, the language of the Musqueam and Tsleil-Waututh peoples, it is *q̓emq̓emeláy̓*, or "big leaf maple trees" (Blomley 122). That the park is known (and signed) as "CRAB" is indicative of how that particular narrative inscribes the space within the terms of settler colonialism.

In his research on CRAB Park, Blomley argues that the space has been protected and "reclaimed" from corporate developers. The geographer powerfully illustrates the ways in which community "unsettles the legitimacy of state ownership," mobilizing a Hegelian rhetoric of ownership that is maintained as a result of individual labour (59). Less explicitly, however, Blomley's analysis also illustrates how Indigenous culture risks appropriation by settler politics, as it is mobilized to "reclaim" space from corporate entities. For example, when protestors occupied the site during their "camp out" in 1985, one of their first acts was to construct "a white-man's totem" (Blomley 58), which Blomley suggests staked claim to the land by signifying its material use by white settler community members (59).

This problematic layer of settler history—problematic insofar as this activism is framed as anti-state and anti-capital, and therefore *in line with* Indigenous politics—contributes to the ideology of *urbs nullius* that elides the Coast Salish histories in the city, and, in typical settler colonial fashion, constructs settlers as "Native" or "proper" users of the land. At the core of the issue is a critically under-analyzed intersection between Indigenous and leftist politics. While the goals of both parties may align, the former must clearly not be held in service to the latter, for doing so risks reiterating colonial ideology from a "progressive" (or even "radical") perspective. If there is an "unsettling" to be had in CRAB Park, Indigenous history and presence in the space must be foregrounded in the critical and community discourse.

Ashes on the Water interjects into the settler colonial history of CRAB Park by layering repressed Coast Salish history onto the material colonial present and (re)interjecting Indigenous stories into land. *Ashes* tells the story of Vancouver's Great Fire—which decimated the city in 1886—and the heroics of *Sk̲w̲x̲wú7mesh* people, particularly *Sk̲w̲x̲wú7mesh* women, who rowed canoes across the Burrard Inlet to rescue settlers from the inlet's south shore. The narrative, voiced by Margo Kane, Elizabeth McLaughlin, and Quelemia Sparrow, with sound design from Noah Drew, is based on the "Women's Paddle Song," written by *Sk̲w̲x̲wú7mesh* peoples shortly after the rescue to commemorate the event.[2] The song has been passed down through the generations, eventually finding its way to Sparrow, who was approached by *Sk̲w̲x̲wú7mesh* dancer and choreographer Michelle Olson to aid in its revitalization. While Sparrow is Musqueam, she worked closely with Olson and *Sk̲w̲x̲wú7mesh* cultural advisor Bob Baker in order to respect those protocols of storytelling and best represent the song. Olson explains, "When they [her *Sk̲w̲x̲wú7mesh* relatives] went over, they gathered survivors, and when they had them in their canoes and brought them across the water, the song came out. It was to comfort the people going through the devastation of having Vancouver burn down" (qtd. in Smith, "Michelle Olson turns to her roots at Dancing on the Edge").

In remediating the "Women's Paddle Song"—that is, in retelling it via new storytelling technology—Sparrow illustrates the ways in which traditional stories can be disseminated and revitalized through cyberspace while decolonizing deeply embedded settler claims to territory. *Ashes on the Water* puts audiences on the land and in the mindset necessary to look past the deeply encoded narrative of CRAB park toward *luk'luk'I* and *q̓emq̓emel̓ay*. In doing so, Sparrow facilitates Indigenous pedagogy and methodology while interrupting the dominant, colonial narratives of space. As Coulthard puts it, "If colonization involved a violent separation of our peoples from those social relations of land, then any education aimed at decolonization must fundamentally correct that violence" (Coulthard and Simpson). *Ashes* puts people in relation to land.

AR is changing the way new media theorists conceptualize cyberspace. AR interrupts the idea that cyberspace is placeless, that it is abstracted from the mind and the body, by using the land as the platform through which users engage with stories and ideas. In work such as *Ashes on the Water*, the previously indurate line separating the material and the digital—which Loretta Todd astutely identified at the onset of the cyberspace revolution—is being disrupted, generating the space to project Indigenous presence onto deeply colonized spaces like CRAB Park, while providing for the resurgence of First People's histories and traditions. These features alone make it a vital teaching tool. Integrating AR into the classroom is an exciting way to engage students with technology while teaching the fundaments of CIS via the same land-based methodologies taught in the classroom. With AR, Indigenous cyberspace lecturers can augment their syllabi with land-based learning and literatures set on the land, and change the way their students *practise* CIS.

Notes

1. For a full list of Neworld podlays, see: http://neworldtheatre.com/portfolio-item/podplays/. To find a podplay in your city, see: http://www.podplays.ca/.
2. For more details regarding the production of *Ashes on the Water*, visit the Indigenous Performing Arts Alliance (IPAA): http://ipaa.ca/events-performances/ashes-water/.

44

Positioning Knowledges, Building Relationships, Practising Self-Reflection, Collaborating across Differences

Sophie McCall

A recent panel discussion in Vancouver entitled "Resurgence: New Directions in Indigenous Literary Studies" was organized to celebrate the publication of new books in the field. The panelists, who included the scholars and writers Niigaanwewidam James Sinclair, Neal McLeod, Daniel Heath Justice, Joanne Arnott, and Sarah Henzi, were asked the following questions: Are we witnessing a renewed momentum in Indigenous literary studies? What do you see as possible new directions? The participants responded in wide-ranging ways and explored the relationship between their research and their personal histories, the connections between land, story, and community, their commitments to movements for social change and cultural revitalization, and their engagement with groundbreaking work by contemporary Indigenous artists and writers.

In listening to the speakers, I noticed a recurrent invocation of four guiding concepts or approaches that helps me understand the work I do as a settler teacher and scholar working in this field: positionality, relationality, self-reflexivity, and collaboration. To put this another way, the speakers modelled for the audience the importance of positioning oneself in relation to knowledges; building relationships between and across the boundaries of cultures, languages, territories, disciplines, and academic fields of study; turning inward to unlearn the shaping role of one's foundational assumptions, experiences, and training; and practising collaboration as a way to further challenge the horizons of one's own necessarily partial perspectives and interpretive frameworks. Although mutually constitutive and interdependent, these concepts at the same time hold one another in tension. In what follows, I have supplied some examples of how I see these strategies of positionality, relationality, self-reflexivity, and collaboration working in the classroom and other spaces of learning (particularly here on unceded Coast Salish territories in Vancouver), demonstrating how deeply intertwined these concepts are, as well as the dynamic tensions between them.

In recent years, post-secondary institutions across Canada have begun to hire more Indigenous scholars in both English and Indigenous Studies departments, and, although this is a step in the right direction, there is an ongoing need to broaden and deepen these changes in order truly to transform these institutional spaces. Inviting Indigenous writers, artists, storytellers, scholars, and/or community workers to interact directly with my students, either by arranging visits to the classroom, or by bringing my students to readings, panel discussions, performances, or exhibitions, is integral to how I perceive my role as a teacher and researcher in this field. Adequately compensating these writers and artists is also a vital part of my responsibility. Teaching material that enables students to reflect upon the land where they live demonstrates concretely how knowledges are positioned. Sarah Henzi's and Dave Gaertner's chapters in this section invoke what's possible artistically and pedagogically when we look beyond the book to digital platforms like podplays, in which the audience must contend with how questions of land and sovereignty are embedded within the landscapes and mediascapes they move through on a daily basis. Lee Maracle's "Goodbye Snauq," a story I teach often, asks readers to think about the relationship between where one stands and how one understands. The story moves between the institutional spaces of a university classroom; the colonial spaces of Vancouver's history of land dispossession; the creation of the reserve system; the urban, toxic-industrial, and now gentrified spaces of False Creek, Vancouver; and the memory spaces of Snauq, once a place of abundance and nourishment for Squamish, Tsleil-Waututh, and Musqueam peoples for millennia. Looking at maps in which the transformation of these lands can be traced ideologically, topographically, and historically enables the students to ask questions about where we live and how we unlearn the histories we have been taught.

For many years, now, scholars and writers have challenged the notion of doing research "on" Indigenous communities, and increasingly people working in Indigenous studies prioritize a process of engaging with and tangibly giving back to communities with which they are working. But how does this expectation play out in the field of Indigenous literary studies? In February 2015, SFU Theatre students publically staged what they called "an encounter" with Marie

Clements' *The Unnatural and Accidental Women*, a play I was teaching at the time in a graduate seminar on Indigenous literatures. The play is about a serial murderer who targeted Indigenous women on Hastings Street in Vancouver's Downtown Eastside in the 1970s. The director, Steve Hill, with participation from Clements as the term's artist-in-residence, hired Métis theatre scholar Lindsay Lachance to work with the cast, a diverse group of non-Indigenous students, to facilitate discussions about identity, the politics of representation, and the process of building connections to the neighbourhood's communities. After working through her own questions about her role, Lachance focused on "the rehearsal process as a space for Indigenous involvement, cultural and spiritual exchanges, and relationship building between the actors and the reality behind the content they are working with" (Lachance). During the rehearsals, she and the cast worked with Indigenous artists, scholars, and cultural workers to learn about how to create the conditions for reciprocal exchanges of knowledges, skills, and culturally grounded practices. The challenges of staging Clements' play are significant, and not only because ongoing violence against women in this city remains an open, often unacknowledged wound. *How* to create the basis for community engagement and the crafting of affiliative politics in respectful and participatory ways is a time-consuming process of building relationships. The production itself foregrounded vital questions of representation, voice, and the transformation of public spaces by having the students read most of the play, only occasionally embodying the characters. Having the action going on behind and around the audience defamiliarized the space and encouraged the audience to remain active in processing how, and through whose mediation, we were "encountering" the script.

In the mid-1990s, at a time when the politics of representation and voice were heightened in university contexts, Helen Hoy posed a question that touched a nerve for the predominantly non-Indigenous scholars working on Indigenous literatures: "How should I read these?" Marc André Fortin's essay in this section transforms the question to: "What ought I not teach?" His well-taken point is that, on the one hand, there is no way to re-circulate the sacred Gitxsan material that anthropologist Marius Barbeau collected without permission. On the other hand, contemporary Indigenous artists and writers like Nisga'a poet Jordan Abel in *The Place of Scraps*, Métis Dene playwright Marie Clements in *The Edward Curtis Project*, Cree scholar and poet Neal McLeod in *Cree Narrative Memory*, and Garry Thomas Morse in *Discovery Passages* (a book of poems that explores his mother's Kwakwaka'wakw ancestry), are revisiting their own families' encounters with anthropologists and collectors of stories, images, and material culture. For example, while Fortin proposes to publish a version of Barbeau's 1928 novel *The Downfall of Temlaham*, with blank pages to represent visibly the "absence of the stories that belong to the Gitxsan," Abel's *The Place of Scraps* transforms Barbeau's writings into visual poetry that invokes landscapes, maps, and shorelines, and that carves the source texts into scattered words, letters, blank spaces, and brackets. Working also in performance and new media, Abel creates soundscapes and landscapes from Barbeau's recordings and photographs. Layering and remixing Barbeau's words, recordings, images of poles, and tattered archival documents through a variety of formats and media, Abel reverses the political implications of "salvage" anthropology in an act of repatriation.

In recent years, I have had the great fortune to engage in a variety of collaborative projects with Indigenous and non-Indigenous scholars, writers, and artists. Collaborative practice can become a way to talk about issues central to the task of decolonizing practices, including Indigenous and settler roles and responsibilities, as well as conflict as a site of creative and political productivity. Creating and sustaining collaborative relationships within and across differences is gratifying and demanding, in the best senses of those words. The field of Indigenous literary studies continues to need committed, inspired, and provocative contributors who are asking tough questions of the past . . . and looking to the future to imagine alternative directions.

WORKS CITED

Abel, Jordan. *The Place of Scraps.* Vancouver: Talon, 2013.

Aboriginal Healing Foundation. *From Truth to Reconciliation: Transforming the Legacy of Residential Schools.* Ottawa: Aboriginal Healing Foundation, 2008.

———. *Response, Responsibility, and Renewal: Canada's Truth and Reconciliation Journey* 2. Ottawa: Aboriginal Healing Foundation, 2009.

"About the Commission." Truth and Reconciliation Commission of Canada. *TRC.ca.* n.d. Web. 16 May 2014.

"About the LE,NONET Project." Office of Indigenous Affairs, University of Victoria. *UVIC.ca.* 1 March 2010. Web.

"About Us." Indian Residential School Survivor Society. *IRSSS.ca.* 10 November 2009. Web.

Absolon, Kathleen E., and Cam Willett. "Putting Ourselves Forward: Location in Aboriginal Research." *Research as Resistance: Critical, Indigenous and Anti-Oppressive Approaches.* Ed. Leslie Brown and Susan Strega. Toronto: Canadian Scholar's P, 2005. 97–126.

Acoose, Janice [Misko-Kìsikàwihkwè (Red Sky Woman)]. *Iskwewak—Kah' Ki Yaw Ni Wahkomakanak: Neither Indian Princess nor Easy Squaws.* Toronto: Women's P, 1995.

———. "The Problem of 'Searching' for April Raintree." *In Search of April Raintree: A Critical Edition.* Ed. Cheryl Suzack. Winnipeg: Portage and Main, 1999.

Adams, Howard. *A Tortured People: The Politics of Colonization.* Penticton: Theytus, 1995.

Adamson, Joni. *American Indian Literature, Environmental Justice, and Ethnocriticism: The Middle Place.* Tucson: U of Arizona P, 2001.

Akiwenzie-Damm, Kateri. "Erotica, Indigenous Style." *(Ad)dressing Our Words: Aboriginal Perspectives on Aboriginal Literatures.* Ed. Armand Garnet Ruffo. Penticton, BC: Theytus, 2001.

Alcoff, Linda. "The Problem of Speaking for Others." *Cultural Critique* 20 (Winter 1991–92): 5–32.

Alexander, M. Jacqui, and Chandra Talpade Mohanty, eds. *Feminist Genealogies, Colonial Legacies, Democratic Futures.* New York and London: Routledge, 1997.

Alexie, Robert Arthur. *Porcupines and China Dolls.* Toronto: Stoddart, 2002.

———. "Robert Arthur Alexie—An Author in Waiting." *Indian Country Today* 31 July 2002. Web. 30 April 2008.

Alexie, Sherman. *Flight.* New York: Grove Press, Black Cat, 2007.

———. *Indian Killer.* New York: Atlantic, 1996.

———. *Old Shirts and New Skins.* Los Angeles: American Indian Studies Center, 1993.

Alfred, Taiaiake. "Colonialism and State Dependency." *Journal of Aboriginal Health* 5.2 (2009): 42–60.

———. "Indigenous words for leadership." Email message to Jeff Corntassel. 28 September 2005.

———. "The People." *The Words That Come before All Else: Environmental Philosophies of the Haudenosaunee*. Ed. Haudenosaunee Environmental Task Force. Akwesasne, NY: Native North American Travelling College, 2007.

———. *Wasáse: Indigenous Pathways of Action and Freedom*. Ontario: Broadview P, 2005.

——— and Jeff Corntassel. "Being Indigenous: Resurgences Against Contemporary Colonialism." *Government and Opposition* 40.4 (2005): 597–614.

Allen, Paula Gunn. *The Sacred Hoop: Recovering the Feminine in American Indian Traditions*. Boston: Beacon, 1986.

Amnesty International Canada. *Stolen Sisters: A Human Rights Response to Discrimination and Violence Against Indigenous Women in Canada*. Ottawa: Amnesty International Canada, 2004. Web. 8 June 2010.

Anahareo. *Devil in Deerskins: My Life with Grey Owl*. Ed. Sophie McCall. Winnipeg: U of Manitoba P, 2014.

"analysis, n." *OED Online*. Oxford University Press, March 2015. Web. 19 March 2015.

Anderson, Kim. *A Recognition of Being: Reconstructing Native Womanhood*. Toronto: Second Story, 2000.

Anguksuar [Richard LaFortune]. "A Postcolonial Colonial Perspective on Western [Mis]Conceptions of the Cosmos and the Restoration of Indigenous Taxonomies." *Two-Spirit People: Native American Gender Identity, Sexuality, and Spirituality*. Ed. Sue-Ellen Jacobs, Wesley Thomas, and Sabine Lang. Urbana: U of Illinois P, 1997.

"The Anti-Sealing Campaign." *Canadian Arctic Resources Committee* 14.2 (1986). Web. 30 October 2014.

Apess, William. "Indian Nullification of the Unconstitutional Laws of Massachusetts Relative to the Mashpee Tribe: or The Pretended Riot Explained." *On Our Own Ground: The Complete Writings of William Apess, a Pequot*. Ed. Barry O'Connell. Amherst: U of Massachusetts P, 1997.

Aphrodite Recommends: Female Sexuality, n.d. Web. 24 October 2007.

Appleford, Rob. "A Response to Same McKegney's 'Strategies for Ethical Engagement: An Open Letter Concerning Non-Native Scholars of Native Literatures.'" *Studies in American Indian Literatures* 21.3 (2009): 58–64. Web. 7 February 2014.

Armstrong, Jeannette. "Land Speaking." *Speaking for the Generations: Native Writers on Writing*. Ed. Simon J. Ortiz. Tucson: U of Arizona P, 1998. 174–94.

———. "The Disempowerment of First North American Native Peoples and Empowerment Through Their Writing." *An Anthology of Canadian Native Literature in English*. Ed. Daniel David Moses and Terry Goldie. 1998. Toronto: Oxford UP, 2005.

———. *Looking at the Words of our People: First Nations Analysis of Literature*. Penticton, BC: Theytus, 1993.

——. *Slash*. Penticton, BC: Theytus, 1985.

——. "This Is a Story." *All My Relations: An Anthology of Contemporary Canadian Native Fiction*. Ed. Thomas King. Toronto: McClelland and Stewart, 1990.

——. *Whispering in Shadows*. Penticton, BC: Theytus, 2000.

——. "Writing from a Native Woman's Perspective." *In the feminine: women and words / Les femmes et les mots: Conference Proceedings 1983*. Ed. Ann Dybikowski et al. Edmonton: Longspoon, 1985.

Ashcroft, Bill, Gareth Griffiths, and Helen Tiffin, eds. *The Postcolonial Studies Reader*. London and New York: Routledge, 1995.

Atleo, Umeek E. Richard. *Tsawalk: A Nuu-chah-nulth Worldview*. Vancouver: UBC P, 2004.

Aupilaarjuk, Mariano, Emile Imaruittuq, Akisu Joamie, Lucassie Nutaraaluk, and Marie Tulimaaq. *Perspectives on Traditional Law*. Ed. Frédéric Laugrand, Jarich Oosten, and Wim Rasing. Interviewing Inuit Elders, vol. 2. Iqaluit: Nunavut Arctic College, 2000.

Austin, John. *Lectures of Jurisprudence*. London: John Murray, 1861–63.

Awiakta, Marilou. *Selu: Seeking the Corn-Mother's Wisdom*. Golden, CO: Fulcrum, 1993.

Bailey, Paul. *Wovoka: The Indian Messiah*. Los Angeles: Westernlore, 1957.

Baker, Madeline. *Spirit's Song*. Wayne, PA: Dorchester, 1999.

Baker, Marie Annharte. "An Old Indian Trick Is to Laugh." *Canadian Theatre Review* 68 (1991): 48–49.

——. *Coyote Columbus Café*. Winnipeg: Moonprint, 1994.

Bannerji, Himani. *Thinking Through: Essays on Feminism, Marxism, and Anti-Racism*. Toronto: Women's P, 1995.

Baraga, Frederic. *A Dictionary of the Otchipwe Language*. Montreal: Beauchemin Valois, 1880.

Barbeau, Marius. *The Downfall of Temlaham*. Toronto: Macmillan, 1928.

Bar On, Bat-Ami. "Marginality and Epistemic Privilege." *Feminist Epistemologies*. Ed. Linda Alcoff and Liz Potter. London and New York: Routledge, 1993.

Barker, Francis, Peter Hulme, and Margaret Iverson, eds. *Colonial Discourse/ Postcolonial Theory*. Manchester: Manchester UP, 1994.

Barlow, John Perry. "A Declaration of the Independence of Cyberspace." Electronic Frontier Foundation. *Projects.EFF.org*, 8 February 1996. Web.

Barnes, Trevor. "Worlding Geography: Geography as Situated Knowledge." *Reading Human Geography: The Poetics and Politics of Inquiry*. Ed. Trevor Barnes and Derek Gregory. London: Arnold, 1997.

Bartleman, James. *As Long as the Rivers Flow*. Toronto: Knopf, 2011.

Bass, Keith H. *Portraits of "The Whiteman": Linguistic Play and Cultural Symbols Among the Western Apache*. Cambridge: Cambridge UP, 1979.

Bastien, Betty. *Blackfoot Ways of Knowing—Indigenous Science*. Ph.D. diss., California Institute of Integral Studies (San Francisco), 1999.

Bataille, Georges. *Theory of Religion*. New York: Zone Books, 1989.

Battiste, Marie, and James (Sákéj) Youngblood Henderson. *Protecting Indigenous Knowledge: A Global Challenge.* Saskatoon: Purich Publishing, 2000.

Baudrillard, Jean. *Simulacra and Simulation.* Paris: Editions Galilee, 1981.

Beat Nation. www.beatnation.org.

Belleau, Lesley. *Sweat.* Sudbury, ON: Scrivener, 2013.

Benedict, Ruth. *Patterns of Culture.* Boston: Houghton Mifflin, 1934.

Benway, Elizabeth. "Indian Romance in Series." *Elizabeth's Book Collection and More.* 28 June 1999. Web. 24 October 2007.

Berkhofer, Robert F., Jr. *The White Man's Indian: Images of the American Indian from Columbus to the Present.* New York: Random House, 1978.

Bertrand, Karine. "The Wapikoni Mobile and the Birth of a New Indigenous Cinema in Quebec." *American Review of Canadian Studies* 43.2 (2013): 283–89.

Bevis, William. "Native American Novels: Homing In." *Recovering the Word: Essays on American Literature.* Eds. Brian Swann and Arnold Krupat. Berkeley: U of California P, 1987.

Bhabha, Homi K. *The Location of Culture.* London and New York: Routledge, 1994.

Bird, Gloria. "Breaking the Silence: Writing as Witness." *Speaking for the Generations: Native Writers on Writing.* Ed. Simon Ortiz. Tucson: U of Arizona P, 1998.

Bird, Louis. "Untitled Story [in which Weesakaytsak Becomes a Caribou]." Incompletely recalled, yet living in the memories of those who heard it at the University of Manitoba, 10 August 2010.

Bissoondath, Neil. "'I'm Just a Writer'—That's the Voice That Matters." *Globe and Mail,* 18 April 1991.

———. *Selling Illusions: The Cult of Multiculturalism in Canada.* Toronto: Penguin, 2002.

Blackburn, Carole. "Searching for Guarantees in the Midst of Uncertainty: Negotiating Aboriginal Rights and Title in British Columbia." *American Anthropologist* 107 (2005).

Blaeser, Kimberly. "Learning 'the Language the Presidents Speak': Images and Issues of Literacy in American Indian Literature." *World Literature Today* 66.2 (1992): 230–35.

———. "Native Literature: Seeking a Critical Centre." *Looking at the Words of Our People: First Nations Analysis of Literature.* Ed. Jeannette Armstrong. Penticton, BC: Theytus, 1993.

———. Unpublished manuscript in possession of the Native Critics Collective.

Blaisel, Xavier. "Trajet rituel : du harponnage a la naissance dans le mythe d'Arnaqta-aqtuq." *Études Inuit Studies* 17.1 (1993): 15–46.

Blanchot, Maurice. "The Absence of the Book." *The Infinite Conversation.* Trans. Susan Hanson. Minneapolis: U of Minnesota P, 1993.

Blaut, James M. *The Colonizer's Model of the World: Geographical Diffusionism and Eurocentric History.* New York: Guilford, 1993.

Blomley, Nicholas K. *Unsettling the City: Urban Land and the Politics of Property.* London and New York: Routledge, 2003.

Bloodland. Dir. Elle-Máijá Tailfeathers. 2011.

Boldt, Menno. "Residential School: Review of *Indian School Days* by Basil Johnston." *Canadian Literature* 124/125 (1990): 311–12.

Bolter, Jay David, and Richard Grusin. *Remediation: Understanding New Media.* Cambridge, MA: Massachusetts Institute of Technology P, 1999.

Borrows, John [Kegedonce]. "Constitutional Law from a First Nation Perspective: Self-Government and the Royal Proclamation." *UBC Law Review* 1 (1994): 1–47.

———. *Drawing Out Law: A Spirit's Guide.* Toronto: U of Toronto P, 2010.

———. "With or Without You: First Nations in Law (in Canada)." *McGill Law Journal* 41.3 (1996): 629–65.

Bose, Chris, and David McIntosh. *Vancouver, Crawling, Weeping, Betting.* Vancouver: Publication Studio, 2014.

Bourdieu, Pierre, and Loïc J. D. Wacquant. *An Invitation to Reflexive Sociology.* Chicago: U of Chicago P, 1992.

Bowerbank, Sylvia, and Dolores Nawagesic Wawia. "Wild Lessons: Native Ecological Wisdom in Ruby Slipperjack's Fiction." *Homemaking: Women Writers and the Politics and Poetics of Home.* Ed. Catherine Wiley and Fiona R. Barnes. New York and London: Garland, 1996.

Boyd, S. "What Knowledge Do You Privilege?" Conference Presentation. Graduate Student Conference for the University of Victoria, Studies in Policy and Practice, Victoria, BC, 18 November 2005.

Boyden, Joseph. *Three Day Road.* Toronto: Penguin, 2005.

Braidotti, Rosi. *Nomadic Subjects: Embodiment and Sexual Difference in Contemporary Feminist Theory.* New York: Columbia UP, 1994.

Brand, Dionne. "Jazz Ritual and Resistance: The Cultural Political of Drumming," Guelph Jazz Festival, Guelph, ON, 6 Sept. 1998.

Brant, Beth. "Coyote Learns a New Trick." *Mohawk Trail.* Ithaca, NY: Firebrand, 1985.

———. *Food and Spirits.* Vancouver: Press Gang, 1991.

———. *Writing as Witness: Essay and Talk.* Toronto: Women's P, 1994.

Brant, Beth, ed. *A Gathering of Spirit: A Collection by North American Indian Women.* Ithaca, NY: Firebrand, 1988.

Bredella, Lothar. "Toward a Pedagogy of Intercultural Understanding." *American Studies* 37.4 (1992): 565.

Brill de Ramirez, Susan Berry. *Contemporary American Indian Literatures and the Oral Tradition.* Tucson: U of Arizona P, 1999.

Brooks, Lisa. *The Common Pot: Indigenous Writing and the Reconstruction of Native Space in the Northeast.* Ph.D. diss., Cornell University, 2004.

———. *The Common Pot: The Recovery of Native Space in the Northeast.* Minneapolis: U of Minnesota P, 2008.

Brooks, Peter. "Kristeva's Separation of Spheres." *PMLA* 117.2 (2002): 296–99.

Brophy, Sarah. "Angels in Antigua: The Diasporic of Melancholy in Jamaica Kincaid's *My Brother.*" *PMLA* 117.2 (2002): 265–77.

Brown, Michael F. *Who Owns Native Culture?* Cambridge, MA: Harvard UP, 2003.

Bruchac, Joseph. *Roots of Survival: Native American Storytelling and the Sacred.* Golden, CO: Fulcrum, 1996.

Buendía, Edward. "Fashioning Research Stories: The Metaphoric and Narrative Structure of Writing Research about Race." *Interrogating Racism in Qualitative Research Methodology.* Ed. Gerardo R. López and Laurence Parker. New York: Peter Lang, 2003. 49–69.

Bulhan, Hussein Abdilahi. *Frantz Fanon and the Psychology of the Oppression.* New York: Plenum, 1985.

Burns, John F. "Canadian Prelate Quits In Clerics' Sex Scandal." *New York Times,* 20 July 1990. Web.

Buur, Lars. "Monumental Historical Memory: Managing Truth in Everyday Work of the South African Truth and Reconciliation Commission." *Commissioning the Past: Understanding South Africa's Truth and Reconciliation Commission.* Ed. Deborah Posel and Graeme Simpson. Johannesburg: Witwatersrand UP, 2002. 66–93.

Calloway, Colin G. *The Western Abenakis of Vermont, 1600–1800: War, Migration, and the Survival of an Indian People.* Norman: U of Oklahoma P, 1990.

Cameron, Anne. "The Operative Principle Is Trust." *Language in Her Eye: Writing and Gender.* Ed. Libby Scheier, Sarah Sheard, and Eleanor Wachtel. Toronto: Coach House, 1990.

Cameron, Anne. *Daughters of Copper Woman.* 1981. Madeira Park: Harbour, 2002.

Campbell, Maria. *Halfbreed.* Toronto: McClelland and Stewart, 1973.

——. *Stories of the Road Allowance People.* Penticton, BC: Theytus, 1995.

Canada. "Key Events." Indian Residential Schools Resolution Canada. Web. 23 August 2004.

Canada. "The Sophisticated Traveller." *New York Times Magazine,* part 2. May 17, 1992. Advertisement.

Canada. Canada Council for the Arts. *Recommendations of the Advisory Committee to the Canada Council for Racial Equality in the Arts and the Response of the Canada Council.* Ottawa: January 1992.

Canada. Royal Commission on Aboriginal Peoples. *Final Report of the Royal Commission on Aboriginal Peoples* 3.2. Ottawa: Aboriginal Affairs and Northern Development Canada, 1996. Web.

Canada. Royal Commission on the Donald Marshall Jr. Prosecution. *The Marshall Inquiry.* Halifax, 1989. Web.

Canada. "Statement of Reconciliation: Learning from the Past." Ottawa: Aboriginal Affairs and Northern Development Canada, 1998. Web. 17 March 2007.

Canada. Statistics Canada. *Aboriginal Peoples Highlight Tables, 2006 Census, All Census Metropolitan Areas (CMAs) and Census Agglomerations (CAs).* Web. 12 May 2008.

Canada. Truth and Reconciliation Commission of Canada. "Mandate of the Truth and Reconciliation Commission." *TRC.ca,* 11 November 2009. Web.

——. "Our Mandate." *TRC.ca,* n.d. Web. 16 May 2014.

Card, Claudia. *The Atrocity Paradigm: A Theory of Evil.* Oxford: Oxford UP, 2002.

Cardinal, Douglas, and Jeannette Armstrong. *The Native Creative Process*. Penticton, BC: Theytus, 1991.

Cardinal, Harold, and Walter Hildebrandt. *Treaty Elders of Saskatchewan: Our Dream Is That Our Peoples Will One Day Be Clearly Recognized as Nations*. Calgary: U of Calgary P, 2000.

Carr, A. A. *Eye Killers: A Novel*. Danvers, MA: U of Oklahoma P, 1996.

Carson, Ben. "The 'Cosmopolitan Consciousness' of Gerald Vizenor and Native American Literary Separatism." *English Studies Forum* 3.1 (Fall–Winter 2007). http://www.bsu.edu/web/esf/3.1/Carson.htm. Web.

Cassirer, Ernst. *The Philosophy of the Enlightenment*. Ed. James Pettegrove. Trans. Fritz Koelin. Boston: Beacon, 1955.

Cha-chin-sun-up. Interview with Chaw-win-is, 10 November 2009.

Chapman, Audrey R., and Hugo van der Merwe, eds. *Truth and Reconciliation in South Africa: Did It Deliver?* Philadelphia: U of Pennsylvania P, 2008.

Chrisjohn, Roland, Sherri Young, and Michael Maraun. *The Circle Game: Shadows and Substance in the Indian Residential School Experience in Canada*. Penticton, BC: Theytus, 1997.

Chrystos. *Fire Power*. Vancouver: Press Gang, 1995.

———. *In Her I Am*. Vancouver: Press Gang, 1993.

———. *Not Vanishing*. Vancouver: Press Gang, 1988.

Churchill, Ward. "Kizhiibaabinesik: A Bright Star, Burning Briefly." Preface. *In My Own Voice: Explorations in the Sociopolitical Context of Art and Cinema*. By Leah Renae Kelly. Winnipeg: Arbeiter Ring, 2001.

Clairmont, Don, and Jane McMillan. *Directions in Mi'kmaq Justice: An Evaluation of the Mi'kmaq Justice Institute and Its Aftermath*. Halifax: Tripartite Forum on Native Justice, 2001.

Clark, Kendall. "Defining 'White Privilege.'" *WhitePrivilege.com*, n.d. Web. 6 September 2005.

Clements, Marie. *The Unnatural and Accidental Women*. Vancouver: Talon, 2005.

Clements, Marie, and Rita Leistner. *The Edward Curtis Project: A Modern Picture Story*. Vancouver: Talon, 2010.

Clifford, James. *Routes: Travel and Translation in the Late 20th Century*. Cambridge, MA: Harvard UP, 1997.

Cobb, Amanda. Unpublished manuscript in possession of the Native Critics Collective.

Cole, Peter. "Aboriginalizing Methodology: Considering the Canoe." *Qualitative Studies in Education* 15.4 (2002): 447–59.

Coleman, Daniel. *White Civility: The Literary Project of English Canada*. Toronto: U of Toronto P, 2006.

Collins, Patricia Hill. *Black Feminist Thought: Knowledge, Consciousness, and the Politics of Empowerment*. New York: Routledge, 1991.

———. "Comment on Hekman's 'Truth and Method: Feminist Standpoint Theory Revisited': Where's the Power?" *Signs* 22.2 (Winter 1997): 375–81.

Colorado, Pam. "Bridging Native and Western Science." *Convergence* 21.2–3 (1988): 49–67.

Coltelli, Laura. *Winged Words: American Indian Writers Speak*. Lincoln: U of Nebraska Press, 1992.

"Compensation for Mount Cashel Victims Is Tangled Legal Web." *CBC News*, 10 November 2003. Web.

Conley, Robert J. *Cherokee Medicine Man: The Life and Work of a Modern-Day Healer*. Norman: U of Oklahoma P, 2005.

Connor, Ralph. *The Patrol of the Sun Dance Trail*. Toronto: Westminster, 1914.

Cook-Lynn, Elizabeth. "Who Gets to Tell the Stories?" *Wicazo Sa Review* 13.1 (1995): 46–51.

——. *Why I Can't Read Wallace Stegner and Other Essays*. Madison: U of Wisconsin P, 1996.

Coon Come, Matthew. "Is It Civilized to Push Indigenous Peoples in Canada to the Edge of Social, Political, and Cultural Extinction?" Unpublished written remarks. Dialogue and Declaration on Indigenous Civilisations: Towards Postcolonial Standards of Civilisation. Canadian Commission for UNESCO, Saskatoon, 22 November 2001.

Corntassel, Jeff, Chaw-win-is, and T'lakwadzi. "Indigenous Storytelling, Truth-Telling and Community Approaches to Reconciliation." *ESC* 35.1 (March 2009): 137–59.

Coulthard, Glen S. "Subjects of Empire: Indigenous Peoples and the 'Politics of Recognition' in Canada." *Contemporary Political Theory* 6.4 (2007): 437–60.

——. *Red Skin, White Masks*. Minneapolis: U of Minnesota P, 2014.

Coulthard, Glen S., and Leanne Simpson. "Leanne Simpson and Glen Coulthard on Dechinta Bush University, Indigenous land-based education and embodied resurgence." Interview with Eric Ritskes. *Decolonization: Indigeneity, Education & Society*, 26 November 2014. Web.

Cox, James. "Review of *Toward a Native American Critical Theory* by Elvira Pulitano." *American Indian Quarterly* 29.1–2 (2005): 316–21.

Cox, James H., and Daniel Heath Justice, eds. *Oxford Handbook of Indigenous American Literature*. New York: Oxford UP, 2014.

Cox, Wendy. "Government Paper Warns Risks of Apologizing for Residential School [Internal Report]." *Canadian Press News Wire*, 26 July 1998. Web. 17 March 2007.

Cruikshank, Julie. *The Social Life of Stories: Narrative and Knowledge in the Yukon Territory*. Lincoln: U of Nebraska P, 1998.

Culhane, Dara. *The Pleasure of the Crown: Anthropology, Law and First Nations*. Vancouver: Talonbooks, 1998.

Culleton, Beatrice. *April Raintree*. 1984. Winnipeg: Peguis, 1992.

Culleton (Mosionier), Beatrice. *In Search of April Raintree*. Winnipeg: Pemmican, 1983.

Dagle, Joan. "Linear Patterns and Ethnic Encounters in the Ford Western." *Ford Made Westerns*. Ed. Gaylyn Studlar and Matthew Bernstein. Indianapolis: Indiana UP, 2001.

Dances with Wolves. Dir. Kevin Costner. Tig Productions and Majestic Films International, 1990.

Darling, David, and Douglas Cole. "Totem Pole Restoration on the Skeena, 1925–30." *BC Studies* 47 (Autumn 1980): 29–48.

Dasenbrock, Reed Way. "Do We Write the Text We Read?" *Falling into Theory: Conflicting Views on Reading Literature.* Ed. David H. Richter. Boston: Bedford Books of St. Martin's, 1994.

Davies, Carole Boyce. *Black Women, Writing and Identity: Migrations of the Subject.* London and New York: Routledge, 1994.

Davis, David Brion. *The Problem of Slavery in Western Culture.* Ithaca: Cornell UP, 1966.

Davis, Kate. "Foreword." *Exposed: Aesthetics of Aboriginal Erotic Art.* Ed. Lee-Ann Martin. Regina: MacKenzie Art Gallery, 1999.

Day, Gordon M. *The Identity of the Saint Francis Indians.* Ottawa: National Museums of Canada, 1981.

de Certeau, Michel. *The Practice of Everyday Life.* Berkeley: U of California P, 2002.

de Vries, Maggie. *Missing Sarah: A Vancouver Woman Remembers Her Vanished Sister.* Toronto: Penguin, 2003.

Dean, Amber. *Remembering Vancouver's Disappeared Women: Settler Colonialism and the Difficulty of Inheritance.* Toronto: U of Toronto P, 2015.

Deep Inside Clint Star. Dir. Clint Alberta. National Film Board of Canada, 1999.

Delgamuukw v. Her Majesty the Queen. "Reasons for Judgment." 8 March 1991. 13.

Deloria, Philip J. *Playing Indian.* New Haven: Yale UP, 1998.

Deloria, Vine, Jr. "American Fantasy." *The Pretend Indians: Images of Native Americans in the Movies.* Ed. Gretchen M. Bataille and Charles L. P. Silet. Ames: Iowa State UP, 1980.

———. "Commentary: Research, Redskins, and Reality." *American Indian Quarterly* 15.4 (1991): 457–68.

———. *Custer Died for Your Sins: An Indian Manifesto.* London: Macmillan, 1969.

———. "Forward." *New and Old Voices of Wah'kon-tah: Contemporary Native American Poetry.* Ed. Robert K. Dodge and Joseph B. McCullough. New York: International Publishers, 1985.

———. *We Talk, You Listen.* Lincoln: U of Nebraska P, 1970.

Derrida, Jacques. *Specters of Marx: The State of the Debt, the Work of Mourning, and the New International.* Trans. Peggy Kamuf. London and New York: Routledge, 1994.

Diet of Souls. Dir. John Houston. Triad, 2004.

Dimock, Wai Chee. *Residues of Justice: Literature, Law, Philosophy.* Berkeley: U of California P, 1996.

Doxtator, Deborah. *Fluffs and Feathers: An Exhibit on the Symbols of Indianness.* Brantford, ON: Woodland Cultural Centre, 1988.

Dragland, Stan. *The Floating Voice: Duncan Campbell Scott and the Literature of Treaty 9.* Concord, ON: Anansi, 1994.

Driskill, Qwo-Li. "Call Me Brother: Two-Spiritedness, the Erotic, and Mixedblood Identity as Sites of Sovereignty and Resistance in Gregory Scofield's Poetry." *Speak *to Me Words: Essays on Contemporary American Indian Poetry.* Ed. Dean Rader and Janice Gould. Tucson: U of Arizona P, 2003. 223–34.

——. "Doubleweaving Two-Spirit Critiques: Building Alliances Between Native and Queer Studies." *GLQ: A Journal of Lesbian and Gay Studies* 16.1–2 (2010): 69–92.

——. "Stolen from Our Bodies: First Nations Two-Spirits/Queers and the Journey to a Sovereign Erotic." *Studies in American Indian Literatures* 16 (2004): 50–64.

Du Bois, W. E. B. *The Souls of Black Folk.* New York: New American Library, 1969.

Dubinsky, Karen. *Babies Without Borders: Adoption and Migration across the Americas.* Toronto: U of Toronto P, 2010.

Duchemin, Parker. "A 'Parcel of Whelps': Alexander Mackenzie among the Indians." *Native Writers & Canadian Writing.* Ed. W. H. New. Vancouver: UBC P, 1990.

duCille, Ann. "The Occult of True Black Womanhood: Critical Demeanor and Black Feminist Studies." *Signs* 19.3 (1994): 591–629.

——. "Postcolonialism and Afrocentricity: Discourse and Dat Course." *The Black Columbiad: Defining Moments in African American Literature and Culture.* Ed. Werner Sollors and Maria Diedrich. Cambridge, MA: Harvard UP, 1994.

Duggan, Lisa. *The Twilight of Equality? Neoliberalism, Cultural Politics, and the Attack on Democracy.* Boston: Beacon, 2003.

Dumont, Jim. "Anishinaabe Izhichigaywin." *Sacred Water: Water for Life.* Ed. Lee Foushee and Renee Gurneau. Lake Elmo, MN: North American Water Office, 2010.

——. Presentation. Elders Conference, Trent University, Peterborough, ON, 20 February 2010.

Dumont, Marilyn. "Circle the Wagons." *Native Poetry in Canada: A Contemporary Anthology.* Ed. Jeannette Armstrong and Lally Grauer. Peterborough, ON: Broadview P, 1985.

——. "Popular Images of Nativeness." *Looking at the Words of Our People: First Nations Analysis of Literature.* Ed. Jeannette Armstrong. Penticton, BC: Theytus, 1993.

Dunn, Marty. *Red on White: The Biography of Duke Redbird.* Toronto: New Press, 1971.

Duran, Eduardo, and Bonnie Duran. *Native American Postcolonial Psychology.* Albany: State U of New York P, 1995.

Duthu, N. Bruce. *American Indians and the Law.* New York: Penguin, 2008.

du Toit, Pierre. *South Africa's Brittle Peace: The Problem of Post-Settlement Violence.* New York: Palgrave, 2001.

Eco, Umberto. *Travels in Hyperreality.* Indianapolis: Mariner Books, 1990.

Eigenbrod, Renate. "Reading Indigeneity from a Migrant Perspective: Ruby Slipperjack's Novel *Silent Words*—'log book' or *Bildungsroman*?" *ESC* 26 (2000): 79–93.

——. *Travelling Knowledges: Positioning the Im/Migrant Reader of Aboriginal Literatures in Canada.* Winnipeg: U of Manitoba P, 2005.

Eigenbrod, Renate, and Jo-Ann Episkenew, eds. *Creating Community: A Roundtable on Canadian Aboriginal Literatures.* Penticton, BC, and Brandon, MB: Theytus and Bearpaw, 2002.

"Elders Statement on Truth and Reconciliation Commission." *TurtleIsland.org*, 14 November 2008. Web.

Emberley, Julia V. *Defamiliarizing the Aboriginal: Cultural Practices and Decolonization in Canada*. Toronto: U of Toronto P, 2007.

———. *Feminist Critique, Native Women's Writings, Postcolonial Theory*. Toronto: U of Toronto P, 1993.

En'owkin Centre Web Site. En'owkin Centre, n.d. Web. 2 January 2008.

Eng, David L., Judith Halberstam, and José Esteban Muñoz. "What's Queer about Queer Studies Now?" *Social Text* 84–85 (2005): 2.

Episkenew, Jo-Ann. "Socially Responsible Criticism: Aboriginal Literature, Ideology, and the Literary Canon." *Creating Community: A Roundtable on Canadian Aboriginal Literature*. Ed. Renate Eigenbrod and Jo-Ann Episkenew. Penticton, BC: Theytus, 2002. 51–68.

Episkenew, Jo-Ann, ed. *Taking Back Our Spirits: Indigenous Literature, Public Policy, and Healing*. Winnipeg: University of Manitoba P, 2009.

Episkenew, Jo-Ann, and Deanna Reder. "*Tâwaw cî?*: Aboriginal Students, Faculty and Content in the University English Department." *Academic Matters* (3 September 2008). Web.

Erdrich, Louise. *Love Medicine*. New York: Holt, Rinehart, and Winston, 1984.

Ermine, Willie. "Aboriginal Epistemology." *First Nations Education in Canada: The Circle Unfolds*. Ed. Marie Battiste and Jean Barman. Vancouver: UBC P, 1995.

Erno, Kim. "Political Realities: The Impact of Globalization on Indigenous Women." *Torn from Our Midst: Voices of Grief, Healing and Action from the Missing Indigenous Women Conference 2008*. Ed. A. Brenda Anderson, Wendee Kubik, and Mary Rucklos Hampton. Regina: U of Regina P, 2010. 57–68.

Essed, Philomena. *Understanding Everyday Racism: An Interdisciplinary Theory*. Newberry Park, CA: Sage, 1991.

Estrada, Jiménez V. M. "The Tree of Life as a Research Methodology." *Australian Journal of Indigenous Education* 34 (2005): 44–52.

Fagan, Kristina. "'What about You?': Approaching the Study of 'Native Literature.'" *Creating Community: A Roundtable on Canadian Aboriginal Literature*. Ed. Renate Eigenbrod and Jo-Ann Episkenew. Penticton, BC: Theytus, 2002. 235–54.

———. "Tewatatha:wi: Aboriginal Nationalism in Taiaiake Alfred's *Peace, Power, Righteousness: An Indigenous Manifesto*." *American Indian Quarterly* 28.1–2 (2004): 12–29.

———. "Weesageechak Meets the Weetigo: Storytelling, Humour, and Trauma in the Fiction of Richard Van Camp, Tomson Highway, and Eden Robinson." *Studies in Canadian Literature* 34.1 (2009): 204–26. Web. 7 February 2012.

Fanon, Frantz. *The Wretched of the Earth*. Trans. Constance Farrington. London: MacGibbon and Kee, 1965.

Fee, Margery. "Deploying Identity in the Face of Racism." *In Search of April Raintree: Critical Edition*. Ed. Cheryl Suzack. Winnipeg: Portage and Main, 1999.

———. "Romantic Nationalism and the Image of Native People in Contemporary English-Canadian Literature." *The Native in Literature: Canadian and Comparative Perspectives*. Ed. Thomas King, Cheryl Calver, and Helen Hoy. Downsview, ON: ECW, 1987.

———. "The Trickster Moment, Cultural Appropriation, and the Liberal Imagination in Canada." *Troubling Tricksters: Revisioning Critical Conversations*. Ed. Deanna Reder and Linda M. Morra. Waterloo, ON: Wilfrid Laurier UP, 2010. 59–76.

———. "Who Can Write as Other?" *The Post-Colonial Studies Reader*. Ed. Bill Ashcroft, Gareth Griffiths, and Helen Tiffin. London and New York: Routledge, 1995.

Ferguson, Adam. *An Essay on the History of Civil Society, 1767*. Edinburgh: Edinburgh UP, 1966.

Ferguson, Roderick A. *Aberrations in Black: Toward a Queer of Color Critique*. Minneapolis: U of Minnesota P, 2004.

Findlay, Isobel. "Working for Postcolonial Legal Studies: Working with Indigenous Humanities." *Law, Social Justice, and Global Development Journal* 7.1 (2003). https://www2.warwick.ac.uk/fac/soc/law/elj/lgd/2003_1/findlay/. Web.

Findlay, L. M. "The Future of the Subject." *English Studies in Canada* 18.2 (1992): 125–41.

Findley, Timothy. Letter. *Globe and Mail*, 28 March 1992.

———. "When You Write about This Country." *Canadian Forum* (September 1992): 8–14.

"A Forum for Native People." Editorial. *Edmonton Journal*, 25 April 1991.

Foster, Tol. "Of One Blood: An Argument for Relations and Regionality in Native American Literary Studies." *Reasoning Together: The Native Critics Collective*. Ed. Craig S. Womack, Daniel Heath Justice, and Christopher B. Teuton. Norman: U of Oklahoma P, 2008. 265–302.

Foucault, Michel. *The History of Sexuality*. Trans. Robert Hurley. New York: Pantheon Books, 1978.

———. "Nietzsche, Genealogy, History." *Language, Counter-Memory, Practice: Selected Essays and Interviews*. Ed. Donald Bouchard. Ithaca: Cornell UP, 1977.

———. *The Order of Things: An Archaeology of the Human Sciences*. London: Tavistock, 1970.

———. *Power/Knowledge: Selected Interviews and Other Writings, 1972–1977*. Ed. Colin Gordon. Trans. Colin Gordon et al. New York: Pantheon Books, 1980.

Fournier, Suzanne, and Ernie Crey. *Stolen from Our Embrace: The Abduction of First Nations Children and the Restoration of Aboriginal Communities*. Vancouver: Douglas and McIntyre, 1997.

Francis, Daniel. *The Imaginary Indian: The Image of the Indian in Canadian Culture*. Vancouver: Arsenal Pulp P, 1992.

Frank, Gloria Jean. "'That's My Dinner on Display': A First Nations Reflection on Museum Culture." *BC Studies: The British Columbian Quarterly* 125/6 (2000): 163–78.

Freeman, Michael. "Puritans and Pequots: The Question of Genocide." *New England Quarterly* 68.2 (1995): 278–93.

Freire, Paulo. *Education for Critical Consciousness*. London: Bloomsbury, 2005.

——. *Pedagogy of the Oppressed*. Trans. Myra Bergman Ramos. New York: Continuum, 1986.

Frideres, James S. *Aboriginal Peoples in Canada: Contemporary Conflicts*. 1974. Scarborough: Prentice Hall Allyn and Bacon Canada, 1988.

Friedman, Susan Stanford. "Beyond White and Other: Relationality and Narratives of Race in Feminist Discourse." *Signs* 21.1 (1995): 1–49.

Gagnon, Monika Kin, and Scott Toguri McFarlane. "The Capacity of Cultural Difference." *Canadian Heritage*. Department of Canadian Heritage, 23 April 2003. Web. 2 January 2008.

Gallagher, Susan Vanzanten. "'I Want to Say: / Forgive Me': South African Discourse and Forgiveness." *PMLA* 117.2 (2002): 303–6.

Garneau, David. "Imaginary Spaces of Conciliation and Reconciliation: *Art, Curation, and Healing*." *Arts of Engagement: Taking Aesthetic Action In and Beyond the Truth and Reconciliation Commission of Canada*. Ed. Dylan Robinson and Keavy Martin. Waterloo: Wilfrid Laurier UP, 2016. 21–41.

Gates, Henry Louis, Jr., ed. *"Race," Writing, and Difference*. Chicago: U of Chicago P, 1986.

Gay American Indians, and Will Roscoe, eds. *Living the Spirit: A Gay American Indian Anthology*. New York: St. Martin's, 1988.

Geniusz, Wendy Makoons. *Our Knowledge Is Not Primitive: Decolonizing Botanical Anishinaabe Teachings*. Syracuse, NY: Syracuse UP, 2009.

George, Chief Dan. *My Heart Soars*. Saanichton: Hancock House, 1974.

Gilley, Brian Joseph. *Becoming Two-Spirit: Gay Identity and Social Acceptance in Indian Country*. Lincoln: U of Nebraska P, 2006.

Godfrey, Stephen. "Minority Writers to Raise their Voices." *Globe and Mail*, 23 May 1992.

Gold, Joseph. *The Story Species: Our Life-Literature Connection*. Markham: Fitzhenry and Whiteside, 2002.

Goldie, Terry. *Fear and Temptation: The Image of the Indigene in Canadian, Australian, and New Zealand Literatures*. Montreal and Kingston: McGill-Queen's UP, 1989.

Goodfellow, John C. *The Totem Poles of Stanley Park*. Vancouver: Art, Historical and Scientific Association of Vancouver, n.d.

Gopinath, Gayatri. "Bollywood Spectacles: Queer Diasporic Critique in the Aftermath of 9/11." *Social Text* 84/85 ("What's Queer about Queer Studies Now?" special issue. Ed. David L. Eng, Judith Halberstam, and José Esteban Muñoz) (2005).

——. *Impossible Desires: Queer Diasporas and South Asian Public Cultures*. Durham: Duke UP, 2005.

Gottesman, D. H. *The Politics of Annihilation: A Psychohistorical Study of the Repression of the Ghost Dance on the Sioux Indian Reservations as an Event in the US Foreign Policy*. Ottawa: National Library of Canada, 1974. Master's thesis, McGill University, 1973.

Gould, Janice. "American Indian Women's Poetry: Strategies of Rage and Hope." *Signs* 20.4 (1995): 797–817.

———. "Disobedience (in Language) in Texts by Lesbian Native Americans." *ARIEL: A Review of International English Literature* 25 (1994): 32–44.

Grayson, G. W. *A Creek Warrior for the Confederacy: The Autobiography of Chief G. W. Grayson.* Ed. David W. Baird. Norman: U of Oklahoma P, 1988.

Groening, Laura Smyth. *Listening to Old Woman Speak: Natives and alterNatives in Canadian Literature.* Montreal and Kingston: McGill-Queen's UP, 2004.

Grossberg, Lawrence. "Wandering Audiences, Nomadic Critics." *Cultural Studies* 2.3 (1988): 377–91.

Grunebaum, Heidi. "Talking to Ourselves 'among the Innocent Dead': On Reconciliation, Forgiveness, and Mourning." *PMLA* 117.2 (2002): 306–10.

Guillory, John. *Cultural Capital: The Problem of Literary Canon Formation.* Chicago: U of Chicago P, 1993.

Gunew, Sneja. *Framing Marginality: Multicultural Literary Studies.* Melbourne: Melbourne UP, 1994.

Hadley, Margery Tanner. "Photography, Tourism and the CPR." *Essays on the Historical Geography of the Canadian West.* Ed. L. A. Rosenvall and S. M. Evans. Calgary: U of Calgary P, 1987.

Hames-Garcia, Michael. *Identity Complex: Making the Case for Multiplicity.* Minneapolis: U of Minnesota P, 2011.

Hall, Stuart. "Cultural Identity and Diaspora." *Identity: Community, Culture, Difference.* Ed. Jonathan Rutherford. London: Lawrence and Wishart, 1990.

———. "What Is This 'Black' in Black Popular Culture?" *Black Popular Culture.* A Project by Michele Wallace. Ed. Gina Dent. Seattle: Bay, 1972.

Hampton, E. "Memory Comes before Knowledge: Research May Improve if Researchers Remember their Motives." Conference Presentation. First Biannual Indigenous Scholars' Conference, University of Alberta, Edmonton, 1995.

Harding, Sandra. "Comment on Hekman's 'Truth and Method: Feminist Theory Revisited': Whose Standpoint Needs the Regimes of Truth and Reality?" *Signs* 22.2 (Winter 1997): 382–91.

Harjo, Joy. "In Love and War and Music: An Interview with Joy Harjo." Interview with Marilyn Kallet. *Kenyon Reviews* 15.3 (1993): 57–66.

———. "The Spectrum of Other Languages: Interview with Bill Aull, James McGowan, Bruce Morgan, Fay Rouseff-Baker, and Cai Fitzgerald." *The Spiral of Memory: Interviews.* Ed. Laura Coltelli. Ann Arbor: U of Michigan P, 1996.

———. *The Woman Who Fell from the Sky.* New York: W. W. Norton, 1996.

Harjo, Joy, and Gloria Bird, eds. *Reinventing the Enemy's Language: Contemporary Native Women's Writings of North America.* New York: Norton, 1997.

Harjo, Joy, and Poetic Justice. "A Postcolonial Tale." *Letter from the End of the Twentieth Century.* Silver Wave Records, 1997. CD.

Harlow, Barbara. *Resistance Literature.* New York: Methuen, 1987.

Harris, Marvin. *The Rise of Anthropological Theory*. New York: Crowell, 1968.

Hart, E. J. *The Selling of Canada*. Banff, AB: Altitude Publishing, 1983.

Hartsock, Nancy. "Rethinking Modernism: Minority vs. Majority Theories." *Cultural Critique* 7 (1987): 187–206.

Haviland, William A., and Marjory W. Power. *The Original Vermonters: Native Inhabitants, Past and Present*. Hanover, NH: UP of New England, 1994.

Hegel, G. W. F. *Phenomenology of Spirit*. Oxford: Clarendon Press, 1977.

Henderson, James (Sákéj) Youngblood. *First Nations Jurisprudence and Aboriginal Rights: Defining the Just Society*. Saskatoon: Native Law Centre, U of Saskatchewan, 2006.

——. "First Nations Legal Inheritance In Canada: The Mîkmaq Model." *Manitoba Law Journal* 23 (1995): 1–31.

——. "Postcolonial Ghost Dancing: Diagnosing European Colonialism." *Reclaiming Indigenous Voice and Vision*. Ed. Marie Battiste. Vancouver: UBC Press, 2000. 57–76.

Henzi, Sarah. "Bodies, Sovereignties and Desire: Aboriginal Women's Writing of Quebec." *Quebec Studies* 59 (2015): 85–106.

Highway, Tomson. *Kiss of the Fur Queen*. Toronto: Doubleday, 1998.

——. *The Rez Sisters*. Saskatoon: Fifth House, 1988.

Hill, Gord. *The 500 Years of Resistance Comic Book*. Vancouver: Arsenal Pulp P, 2010.

Hill, Sarah H. *Black Looks: Race and Representation*. Boston: South End P, 1992.

——. *Feminism Is for Everybody: Passionate Politics*. Cambridge, MA: South End P, 2000.

——. *Weaving New Worlds: Southeastern Cherokee Women and Their Basketry*. Chapel Hill: U of North Carolina P, 1997. 44.

——. *Yearning: Race, Gender, and Cultural Politics*. Boston: South End, 1990.

Hobson, Geary. "Barbara's Land Revisited—August 1978." *American Indian Chapbook*, The Beloit Poetry Journal. Eds. Gogisgi and Carroll Arnett. 30.2 (Winter 1979–80): 6–7.

hooks, bell. *Black Looks: Race and Representation*. Boston: South End, 1992.

——. *Yearning: Race, Gender, and Cultural Politics*. Boston: South End, 1990.

Horne, Dee. *Contemporary American Indian Writing: Unsettling Literature*. New York: Peter Lang, 1999.

Howe, LeAnne, Harvey Markowitz, and Denise K. Cummings. *Seeing Red—Hollywood's Pixeled Skins: American Indians and Film*. East Lansing: Michigan State UP, 2013.

Hoy, Helen. *How Should I Read These? Native Women Writers in Canada*. Toronto: U of Toronto P, 2001.

——. "'Nothing but the Truth': Discursive Transparency in Beatrice Culleton." *ARIEL: A Review of International English Literature* 25.1 (1994): 155–84.

Hulan, Renée. "Some Thoughts on 'Integrity and Intent' and Teaching Native Literature." *Essays on Canadian Writing* 63 (1998): 210–30.

Hulan, Renée, ed. *Native North America: Critical and Cultural Perspectives*. Toronto: ECW, 1999.

Hungry Wolf, Beverley. *The Ways of My Grandmothers*. New York: Morrow, 1980.

Hurst, Lynda. "Can(not!)lit." *Toronto Star*, 11 April 1992.

Hutchinson, Allan. "Giving Smaller Voices a Chance to Be Heard." *Globe and Mail*, 14 April 1992.

"Incorporating Truth and Reconciliation Commission Resources into Your Teaching and Learning." UBC Centre for Teaching and Learning Technology, *UBC.ca*, 5 September 2013. Web.

"Indian Residential Schools Settlement—Official Court Website." Indian Residential Schools Settlement. *ResidentialSchoolSettlement.ca*, 10 November 2009. Web.

Innis, Robert Alexander. *Elder Brother and the Law of the People: Contemporary Kinship and Cowessess First Nation*. Winnipeg: U of Manitoba P, 2013.

Ipellie, Alootook. *Arctic Dreams and Nightmares*. Penticton, BC: Theytus, 1993.

Irlbacher-Fox, Stephanie. *Finding Dahshaa: Self-Government, Social Suffering, and Aboriginal Policy in Canada*. Vancouver: UBC P, 2009.

Isernhagen, Hartwig. *Momaday, Vizenor, Armstrong: Conversations on American Indian Writing*. Norman: U of Oklahoma P, 1999.

Jackson, A. Y. *A Painter's Country*. Toronto: Clarke, Irwin, 1958.

Jacobs, Sue-Ellen, Wesley Thomas, and Sabine Lang, eds. *Two-Spirit People: Native American Gender Identity, Sexuality, and Spirituality*. Urbana: U of Illinois P, 1997.

Jaimez, Vicki. "Sexuality and the Invasion of America: 1492–1806." *Virtual School*, n.d. Web. 24 October 2007.

Jensen, Derrick. "Linda Hogan." *Listening to the Land: Conversations about Nature, Culture, and Eros*. San Francisco: Sierra Club Books, 1995.

Jiwani, Yasmin, and Mary Lynn Young. "Missing and Murdered Women: Reproducing Marginality in News Discourse." *Canadian Journal of Communication* 31.4 (2006): 895–917.

Joe, Rita. *Song of Eskasoni: More Poems of Rita Joe*. Charlottetown: Ragweed, 1988.

———. *Song of Rita Joe: Autobiography of a Mi'kmaq Poet*. Charlottetown: Ragweed, 1996.

Johnson, E. Pauline [Tekahionwake]. "A Strong Race Opinion: On the Indian Girl in Modern Fiction." *Collected Poems and Selected Prose*. Ed. Carole Gerson and Veronica Strong-Boag. Toronto: U of Toronto P, 2002.

Johnston, Basil H. *Anishinaubae Thesaurus*. East Lansing: Michigan State UP, 2007.

———. *Indian School Days*. Norman: U of Oklahoma P, 1988.

———. *Indian School Days*. Toronto: Key Porter Books, 1988.

———. *Moose Meat and Wild Rice*. Toronto: McClelland and Stewart, 1978.

———. "One Generation from Extinction." *An Anthology of Canadian Native Literature in English*. Ed. Daniel David Moses and Terry Goldie. Toronto: Oxford UP, 1998.

Jolly, Rosemary. "Desiring Good(s) in the Face of Marginalized Subjects: South Africa's Truth and Reconciliation Commission in a Global Context." *South Atlantic Quarterly* 100.3 (2001): 693–715.

Jordanova, Ludmilla. "Natural Facts: A Historical Perspective on Science and Sexuality." *Nature, Culture, and Gender*. Ed. Carol P. MacCormack and Marilyn Strathern. Cambridge: Cambridge UP, 1980.

Justice, Daniel Heath. "Beloved Woman Returns: The Doubleweaving of Homeland and Identity in the Poetry of Marilou Awiakta." *Speak to Me Words: Essays on Contemporary American Indian Poetry*. Ed. Dean Rader and Janice Gould. Tucson: U of Arizona P, 2003.

———. "Conjuring Marks: Furthering Indigenous Empowerment Through Literature." *American Indian Quarterly* 28.1–2 (2004): 2–11.

———. "Fear of a Changeling Moon: A Rather Queer Tale from a Cherokee Hillbilly." *Me Sexy: An Exploration of Native Sex and Sexuality*. Ed. Drew Hayden Taylor. Vancouver: Douglas and McIntyre, 2008. 87–108.

———. "'Go Away Water!' Kinship Criticism and the Decolonization Imperative." *Reasoning Together: The Native Critics Collective*. Ed. Craig S. Womack et al. Norman: U of Oklahoma P, 2008. 147-68.

———. *Our Fire Survives the Storm: A Cherokee Literary History*. Minneapolis: U of Minnesota P, 2006.

———. "Renewing the Fire: Notes toward the Liberation of English Studies." *English Studies in Canada* 29.1–2 (2003): 45–54.

Kane, Margo. "From the Centre of the Circle the Story Emerges." *Canadian Theatre Review* 68 (Fall 1991): 26–29.

———. "Moonlodge." *An Anthology of Canadian Native Literature in English*. Ed. Daniel David Moses and Terry Goldie. Toronto: Oxford UP, 1992.

Kearney, Richard. *The Wake of Imagination*. London and New York: Routledge, 1998.

Keeshig-Tobias, Lenore. "Lenore Keeshig-Tobias." Interview with Hartmut Lutz. *Contemporary Challenges: Conversations with Canadian Native Authors*. Ed. Hartmut Lutz. Saskatoon: Fifth House, 1991.

———. "The Magic of Others." *Language in Her Eye: Writing and Gender*. Ed. Libby Scheier, Sarah Sheard, and Eleanor Wachtel. Toronto: Coach House, 1990.

———. "Running on the West Wind." *An Anthology of Canadian Native Literature in English*. Ed. Daniel David Moses and Terry Goldie. Toronto and New York: Oxford UP, 1992.

———. "Stop Stealing Native Stories." *Globe and Mail*, 26 January 1990.

Keeshig-Tobias, Lenore, ed. *The Magazine to Re-Establish the Trickster: A Magazine of New Native Writing* 1.2 (1989).

Kehoe, Alice Beck. *The Ghost Dance: Ethnohistory and Revitalization*. New York: Holt, Rinehart and Winston, 1989.

Kelly, Jennifer. "Coming Out of the House: An Interview with Lee Maracle." *ARIEL: A Review of International English Literature* 25.1 (1994): 73–88.

Kennedy, David. "A New Stream of International Law Scholarship." *Wisconsin International Law Journal* 7.1 (1988–89): 1–50.

Kenny, Maurice. *Wounds Beneath the Flesh: Fifteen Native American Poets*. White Pine Press, 1995.

Kilpatrick, Alan. *The Night Has a Naked Soul: Witchcraft and Sorcery among the Western Cherokee*. Syracuse: Syracuse UP, 1997.

Kimpson, Sally A. "Stepping Off the Road: A Narrative (of) Inquiry." *Research as Resistance.* Ed. Leslie Brown and Susan Strega. Toronto: Canadian Scholars' P, 2005. 19–36.

King, Thomas. "Godzilla vs. Post-Colonial." *New Contexts of Canadian Criticism.* Ed. Ajay Heble, Donna Palmateer Pennee, and J. R. (Tim) Struthers. Peterborough: Broadview P, 1997.

———. "Godzilla vs. Post-Colonial." *World Literature Written in English* 30.2 (1990): 10–16.

———. *The Inconvenient Indian: A Curious Account of Native People in North America.* Toronto: Doubleday, 2012.

———. *The Truth about Stories: A Native Narrative.* Toronto: House of Anansi, 2003.

King, Thomas, ed. *All My Relations.* Toronto: McClelland and Stewart, 1990.

King, Thomas, Cheryl Calver, and Helen Hoy, eds. *The Native in Literature: Canadian and Comparative Perspectives.* Downsview, ON: ECW, 1987.

Kipling, Rudyard. "The White Man's Burden." *McClure's Magazine,* 12 February 1988. Web.

Kirby, Sandra, Lorraine Greaves, and Colleen Reid. *Experience, Research, Social Change—Methods beyond the Mainstream.* Peterborough, ON: Broadview P, 2006.

Knockwood, Isabelle, and Gillian Thomas. *Out of the Depths: The Experiences of Mi'kmaw Children at the Indian Residential School at Shubenacadie, Nova Scotia.* Lockeport: Roseway, 1992.

Konkle, Maureen. *Writing Indian Nations: Native Intellectuals and the Politics of Historiography, 1827–1863.* Chapel Hill: U of North Carolina P, 2004.

Kovach, Margaret. *Indigenous Methodologies: Characteristics, Conversations, and Contexts.* Toronto: U of Toronto P, 2009.

Krauss, Clifford. "Capone May Have Slept Here, Too, Canada Town Says." *New York Times,* 16 November 2004. Web.

Kristeva, Julia. "Forgiveness: An Interview." *PMLA* 117.2 (2002): 278–95.

Krupat, Arnold. *Ethnocriticism: Ethnography, History, Literature.* 1989. Berkeley: U of California P, 1992.

———. *For Those Who Came After: A Study of Native American Autobiography.* Berkeley: U of California P, 1985.

———. "Introduction." *New Voices in Native American Literary Criticism.* Washington: Smithsonian Institution P, 1993.

———. *Red Matters: Native American Studies.* Philadelphia: U of Pennsylvania P, 2002.

———. *The Turn to the Native: Studies in Criticism & Culture.* Lincoln: U of Nebraska P, 1996.

———. *The Voice in the Margin: Native American Literature and the Canon.* Berkeley: U of California P, 1989.

Kulchyski, Peter. "bush/writing: embodied deconstruction, traces of community, and writing against the state in indigenous acts of transcription." *Shifting the Ground of Canadian Literary Studies.* Ed. Smaro Kamboureli and Robert Zacharias. Waterloo: Wilfrid Laurier UP, 2012. 249–68.

————. "From Appropriation to Subversion: Aboriginal Cultural Production in the Age of Postmodernism." *American Indian Quarterly* 21.4 (1997): 605–20.

LaBarre, Weston. *The Ghost Dance: Origins of Religion.* London: Allen and Unwin, 1972.

Lachance, Lindsay. Unpublished letter (email). 12 January 2015.

Ladner, Kiera. "Women and Blackfoot Nationalism." *Journal of Canadian Studies* 35.2 (2000): 35–61.

LaDuke, Winona. *All Our Relations: Native Struggles for Land and Life.* Cambridge, MA: South End P, 1999.

————. *Recovering the Sacred: The Power of Naming and Claiming.* Toronto: Between the Lines, 2005.

LaRocque, Emma. "The Colonization of a Native Woman Scholar." *Women of the First Nations.* Ed. Christine Miller and Patricia Chuckryk. Winnipeg: U of Manitoba P, 1997.

————. "From the Land to the Classroom: Broadening Epistemology." *Pushing the Margins: Native and Northern Studies.* Ed. Jill E. Oakes et al. Winnipeg: U of Manitoba P, 2001.

————. "Métis and Feminist." *Making Space for Indigenous Feminism.* Ed. Joyce Green. Halifax: Fernwood Publishing, 2007.

————. "Native Identity and the Métis: Otehpayimsuak Peoples." *A Passion for Identity.* Ed. David Taras and Beverly Rasporich. Scarborough, ON: Nelson Thornes, 2001.

————. *Native Writers Resisting Colonizing Practices in Canadian Historiography and Literature.* Ph.D. diss., University of Manitoba, 1999.

————. "The Place of Native Writing in Canadian Intellectual Categories: Native Resistance Literature." Association of Canadian College and University Teachers of English, Université de Québec à Montréal, 29 May 1995.

————. "Preface, or Here Are Our Voices—Who Will Hear?" *Writing the Circle.* Ed. Jeanne Perreault and Sylvia Vance. Edmonton: NeWest Press, 1990.

————. "Teaching Aboriginal Literature: The Discourse of Margins and Mainstreams." *Creating Community: A Roundtable on Canadian Aboriginal Literature.* Ed. Renate Eigenbrod and Jo-Ann Episkenew. Penticton, BC: Theytus Books, 2002. 209–230.

Lawrence, Bonita. *"Real" Indians and Others: Mixed-Blood Urban Native Peoples and Indigenous Nationhood.* Lincoln: U of Nebraska P, 2004.

Leclair, Carole. "Métis Wisdom: Learning and Teaching across the Cultures." *Atlantis* 22.2 (1998): 123–26.

Lee, Sky. "Yelling It: Women and Anger across Cultures." *Telling It: Women and Anger across Cultures.* Telling It Book Collective. 177–85.

Lehto, Martti, Aki-Mauri Huhtinen, and Saara Jantunen. "The Open Definition of Cyber: Technology or a Social Construction?" *International Journal of Cyber Warfare and Terrorism* 1.2 (2011): 1–9. Web.

Leon-Portilla, Miguel. "Have We Really Translated the Meso-American Word?" *On the Translation of Native American Literatures.* Ed. Brian Swann. Washington: Smithsonian Institution P, 1992.

Leon-Portilla, Miguel, ed. "Introduction." *The Broken Spears: The Aztec Account of the Conquest of Mexico*. Boston: Beacon, 1992.

Lewis, David, Jr., and Ann T. Jordan. *Creek Indian Medicine Ways: The Enduring Power of Mvskoke Religion*. Albuquerque: U of New Mexico P, 2002.

Lewis, Meriwether, and William Clark. *The Journals of Lewis and Clark (Lewis & Clark Expedition)*. Ed. Bernard DeVoto. Indianapolis: Mariner Books, rev. ed., 1997.

Liamputtong, Pranee. *Researching the Vulnerable*. London: Sage, 2007.

Lionnet, Françoise. "'Logique metisses': Cultural Appropriation and Postcolonial Representations." *College Literature* 19/20.3/1 (October 1992–February 1993): 100–120.

Little Bear, Leroy. "Jagged Worldviews Colliding." *Reclaiming Indigenous Voice and Vision*. Ed. Marie Battiste. Vancouver: UBC P, 2000. 77–85.

Little Thunder, Beverly. "I Am a Lakota Womyn." *Two-Spirit People: Native American Gender Identity, Sexuality, and Spirituality*. Ed. Sue-Ellen Jacobs, Wesley Thomas, and Sabine Lang. Urbana: U of Illinois P, 1997.

Littlechild, George, et al. *In Honour of Our Grandmothers*. Penticton, BC: Theytus, 1994.

Littlefield, Daniel F. *Native American Writing in the Southeast: An Anthology, 1875–1935*. Jackson: UP of Mississippi, 1995.

Ljunggren, David. "Every G20 Nation Wants to Be Canada, Stephen Harper Insists." *Reuters*, 26 September 2009. Web.

Locke, John. "The Second Treatise of Government." *Two Treatises of Government*. Ed. Peter Laslett. Cambridge: Cambridge UP, 1970.

Lowenstein, Tom, trans. *Eskimo Poems from Canada and Greenland: From Material Originally Collected by Knud Rasmussen*. Pittsburgh: U of Pittsburgh P, 1973.

Lowman, John. "Violence and the Outlaw Status of Street Prostitution." *Violence Against Women* 6.9 (2000): 987–1011.

Lugones, Maria. "On the Logic of Pluralist Feminism." *Feminist Ethics*. Ed. Claudia Card. Lawrence: UP of Kansas, 1991. 35–44.

Lutz, Hartmut. *Approaches: Essays in Native North American Studies and Literatures*. Augsburg: Wissner, 2002.

———. "First Nations Literatures in Canada and the Voice of Survival." *London Journal of Canadian Studies* 11 (1996).

———. "'Is the Canadian Canon Colorblind?' On the Status of Authors of Color in Canadian Literature in English." *Zeitschrift für Anglistik und Amerikanistik* 44.1 (1996).

———. "Talking at the Kitchen Table: A Personal Homage to Rita Joe of Eskasoni Reserve, Cape Breton Island, Nova Scotia." *Down East—Critical Essays on Contemporary Maritime Canadian Literature*. Ed. Wolfgang Hochbruck and James O. Taylor. Trier: WVT, 1996.

Lutz, Hartmut, ed. *Contemporary Challenges: Conversations with Canadian Native Authors*. Saskatoon: Fifth House, 1991.

Lynch, D. *Wovoka and the Ghost Dance*. Lincoln: U of Nebraska P, 1997.

Lyons, Scott Richard. "Rhetorical Sovereignty: What Do American Indians Want from Writing?" *College Composition and Communication* 51 (2000): 449.

Mair, Charles. *Through the Mackenzie Basin*. Toronto: William Briggs, 1908.

Manalansan, Martin F., IV. *Global Divas: Filipino Gay Men in the* Diaspora. Durham: Duke UP, 2003.

Mannette, Joy, ed. *Elusive Justice: Beyond the Marshall Inquiry*. Halifax: Fernwood Publishing, 1992.

Maracle, Lee. "Coming Out of the House: A Conversation with Lee Maracle." Interview with Jennifer Kelly. *ARIEL: A Review of International English Literature* 25.1 (1994): 73–88.

———. "Goodbye Snauq." *Our Story: Aboriginal Voices on Canada's Past*. Toronto: Doubleday, 2004. 201–20.

———. *I Am Woman*. North Vancouver: Write-On, 1988.

———. "Native Myths: Trickster Alive and Crowing." *Language in Her Eye: Writing and Gender*. Ed. Libby Scheier, Sarah Sheard, and Eleanor Wachtel. Toronto: Coach House, 1990.

———. "Oratory: Coming to Theory." *By For and About: Feminist Cultural Politics*. Ed. Wendy Waring. Toronto: Women's P, 1994. 235–40.

———. "Oratory on Oratory." *Cerium*. Centre d'études et de recherches internationales, Université de Montréal. Web. 1 August 2014.

———. "The 'Post-Colonial' Imagination." *Fuse* 16.1 (1992) : 12–15.

———. *Ravensong*. Vancouver: Press Gang, 1993.

———. *Sojourner's Truth and Other Stories*. Vancouver: Press Gang, 1990.

Marken, Ron. "'There Is Nothing but White Between the Lines': Parallel Colonial Experiences of the Irish and Aboriginal Canadians." *Native North America: Critical and Cultural Perspectives*. Ed. Renée Hulan. Toronto: ECW, 1999.

Martin, Joel W. *Sacred Revolt*. Boston: Beacon Press, 1991.

Martin, Keavy. "Truth, Reconciliation, and Amnesia: *Porcupines and China Dolls* and the Canadian Conscience." *English Studies in Canada* 35.1 (March 2009): 47–65.

Martin, Lee-Ann, ed. "Reclaiming Desires." *Exposed: Aesthetics of Aboriginal Erotic Art*. Regina: MacKenzie Art Gallery, 1999.

Matas, Robert. "The Numbers Say." *Globe and Mail*, 19 June 2009. Web.

Maud, Ralph. *Transmission Difficulties: Franz Boas and Tsimshian Mythology*. Burnaby, BC: Talonbooks, 2000.

Mauss, Marcel. *The Gift: Forms and Functions of Exchange in Archaic Societies*. Trans. Ian Gunnison. New York: Norton, 1967.

McIntosh, Peggy. "White Privilege: Unpacking the Invisible Knapsack." *Independent School* (Winter 1990). Web.

McKay, Gail. "'Learning to Listen to a Quiet Way of Telling': A Study of Cree Counselling Discourse Patterns in Maria Campbell's *Halfbreed*." *Indigenous Poetics in Canada*. Ed. Neal McLeod. Waterloo, ON: Wilfrid Laurier UP, 2014.

McKegney, Sam. *Magic Weapons: Aboriginal Writers Remaking History after Residential School*. Winnipeg: U of Manitoba P, 2007.

———. "Strategies for Ethical Engagement: An Open Letter Concerning Non-Native Scholars of Native Literatures." *SAIL: Studies in American Indian Literatures* 20.4 (2008): 56–67.

———. "Writer–Reader Reciprocity and the Pursuit of Alliance Through Indigenous Poetry." *Indigenous Poetics in Canada.* Ed. Neal McLeod. Waterloo: Wilfrid Laurier UP, 2014. 43–60.

McKegney, Sam, ed. *Masculindians: Conversations about Indigenous Manhood.* Winnipeg: U of Manitoba P, 2014.

McKenzie, Stephanie M. "Canada's Day of Atonement: The Contemporary Native Literary Renaissance, the Native Cultural Renaissance, and Postcentenary Canadian Mythology." Ph.D. diss., University of Toronto, 2001.

McLeod, Neal. *Cree Narrative Memory: From Treaties to Contemporary Times.* Saskatoon: Purich, 2007.

McLeod, Neal, ed. *Indigenous Poetics in Canada.* Waterloo, ON: Wilfrid Laurier UP, 2014.

McLuhan, T. C. *Dream Tracks: The Railroad and the American Indian, 1890–1930.* New York: Harry N. Abrams, 1985.

McMaster, Gerald, and Lee-Ann Martin, eds. *Indigena: Contemporary Native Perspectives.* Vancouver and Toronto: Douglas and McIntyre, 1992.

Means, Russell. "I Am Not a Leader." *Mother Jones* (December 1980): n.p.

Medicine, Beatrice. *Learning to Be an Anthropologist and Remaining "Native": Selected Writings.* Urbana: U of Illinois P, 2001.

Memmi, Albert. "Attempt at a Definition." *Dominated Man: Notes toward a Portrait.* Boston: Beacon, 1969.

———. *The Colonizer and the Colonized.* Trans. Howard Greenfield. 1957. New York: Orion, 1965.

Mencken, H. L. *The American Language: An Inquiry into the Development of English in the United States.* New York: Knopf, 1921.

Mendoza, Durango. "Summer Water and Shirley." *American Indian Authors.* Ed. N. Scott Momaday. Boston: Houghton Mifflin, 1971.

Mendoza, Vincent. *Son of Two Bloods.* Lincoln: U of Nebraska P, 1996.

Mertens, Donna M. *Research and Evaluation in Education and Psychology: Integrating Diversity with Quantitative, Qualitative, and Mixed Methods.* Thousand Oaks, CA: Sage Publications, 2005.

Mesnak. Dir. Yves Sioui Durand. Kunakan Productions, Les Films de l'Isle, 2011.

Meyer, Manulani Aluli. *Ho'oulu: Our Time of Becoming.* Honolulu: Ai Pohaku, 2004.

Mihesuah, Devon. "Finding Empowerment Through Writing and Reading, or Why Am I Doing This? An Unpopular Writer's Comments about the State of American Indian Literary Criticism." *American Indian Quarterly*: 28.1/2 (2004): 97–102.

Miller, Bruce Granville. *Oral History on Trial: Recognizing Aboriginal Narratives in the Courts.* Toronto: UBC P, 2011.

Miller, D. H. *Ghost Dance.* New York: Duell, Sloan and Pearce, 1959.

Miller, J. R. *Shingwauk's Vision: A History of Native Residential Schools.* Toronto: U of Toronto P, 1996.

Mills, P. Dawn. *For Future Generations: Reconciling Gitxsan and Canadian Law.* Saskatoon: Purich, 2008.

Miranda, Deborah A. "Dildos, Hummingbirds, and Driving Her Crazy: Searching for American Indian Women's Love Poetry and Erotics." *Frontiers* 23 (2002): 135–49.

——. *The Zen of La Llorona.* Cambridge, MA: Salt, 2005.

Mitchell, Terry L., and Dawn T. Maracle. "Post-Traumatic Stress and the Health Status of Aboriginal Populations in Canada." *Journal of Aboriginal Health* 2.1 (2005): 14–25.

Mohanty, Chandra Talpade. "On Race and Voice: Challenges for Liberal Education for the 1990s." *Cultural Critique* 14 (Winter 1989–90): 179–208.

Mojica, Monique. "Postcolonial Traumatic Stress Syndrome: Ethno Stress." Address. Congress of Humanities of Social Sciences, University of Ottawa, May 1998.

Momaday, N. Scott. *House Made of Dawn.* New York: Harper Perennial Modern Classics, 2010.

——. "The Man Made of Words." *Indian Voices: The First Convocation of American Indian Scholars.* San Francisco: Indian Historian P, 1970.

——. "The Man Made of Words." *The Remembered Earth.* Ed. Geary Hobson. Albuquerque: U of New Mexico P, 1981.

——. *The Names.* Tucson, Arizona: U of Arizona P, 1976.

Monk, Katherine. *Weird Sex and Snowshoes: And Other Canadian Film Phenomena.* Vancouver: Raincoast, 2001.

Monkman, Leslie. *A Native Heritage: Images of the Indian in English-Canadian Literature.* Toronto: U of Toronto P, 1981.

Monture-Angus, Patricia. "Native America and the Literary Tradition." *Native North America: Critical and Cultural Perspectives.* Toronto: ECW, 1999.

——. *Thunder in My Soul: A Mohawk Woman Speaks.* Halifax: Fernwood Publishing, 1995.

Mooney, James. *The Ghost-Dance Religion and the Sioux Outbreak of 1890.* Chicago: U of Chicago P, 1965.

Moore, Christopher. "The Writers' Union of Canada, 1973–2007." *The Writers Union of Canada.* The Writers' Union of Canada, n.d. Web. 23 December 2007.

Moore, Thomas E. *Sour Sofke.* Muskogee: Hoffman Printing, n.d.

Morales, Aurora Levins. *Medicine Stories: History, Culture and the Politics of Integrity.* Cambridge, MA: South End P, 1998.

Moray, Gerta. "Emily Carr and the Traffic in Native Images." *Antimodernism and Artistic Experience: Policing the Boundaries of Modernity.* Ed. Lynda Jessup. Toronto: U of Toronto P, 2001. 71–93.

Morgan, Sally. *My Place.* 1987. Fremantle, Australia: Fremantle, 2008.

Morgensen, Scott. *Welcome Home: Settler Sexuality and the Politics of Indigeneity.* Minneapolis: U of Minnesota P, n.d.

Morningside (CBC Radio). "The Public Face of the Cultural Appropriation Debate: Who Speaks for Whom?" Radio transcript. *Textual Studies in Canada* 2 (1992).

Morris, Meaghan. "At Henry's Park Motel." *Cultural Studies* 2.1 (1998): 43.

Morrison, Toni. *Playing in the Dark: Whiteness and the Literary Imagination.* Cambridge, MA: Harvard UP, 1992.

Morrisseau, Norval. *Legends of My People, The Great Ojibway.* Ed. Selwyn Dewdney. Toronto: McGraw-Hill Ryerson, 1965.

Morse, Bradford. "Indigenous Peoples of Canada and Their Efforts to Achieve True Reparations." *Reparations for Indigenous Peoples: International and Comparative Perspectives.* Ed. Federico Lenzerini. Oxford: Oxford UP, 2008.

Morse, Garry Thomas. *Discovery Passages.* Vancouver: Talon, 2011.

Moses, Daniel David. *Coyote City.* Stratford, ON: Williams-Wallace, 1990.

———. "The Trickster's Laugh: My Meeting with Tomson and Lenore." *American Indian Quarterly* 28.1/2 (2004): 107–11.

———. "Whose Voice Is It, Anyway?: A Symposium on Who Should be Speaking for Whom." *Books in Canada* (January–February 1991): 15.

Moses, Daniel David, and Terry Goldie, eds. *An Anthology of Canadian Native Literature in English.* 1992. Toronto and New York: Oxford UP, 2005.

Mosse, George L. *Toward the Final Solution: A History of European Racism.* London: Dent, 1978.

Moustakas, Clark. *Heuristic Research: Design, Methodology, and Applications.* Newbury Park, CA: Sage Publications, 1990.

Mukherjee, Arun. "First World Readers, Third World Texts: Some Thoughts about Theory and Pedagogy." *Postkoloniale Literaturen.* Ed. Liselotte Glage and Martina Michel. Hamburg: Argument Verlag, 1993.

———. *Oppositional Aesthetics: Readings from a Hyphenated Space.* Toronto: TSAR, 1994.

Muñoz, José Esteban. *Disidentifications: Queers of Color and the Performance of Politics.* Minneapolis: U of Minnesota P, 1999.

Nurse, Andrew. "Marius Barbeau and the Methodology of Salvage Ethnography in Canada, 1911–51." *Historicizing Canadian Anthropology.* Ed. Julia Harrison and Regna Darnell. Vancouver: UBC P, 2006. 52–64.

Nadasdy, Paul. "The Antithesis of Restitution? A Note on the Dynamics of Land Negotiations in the Yukon, Canada." *The Rights and Wrongs of Land Restitution.* Ed. Derick Fay and Deborah James. London and New York: Routledge-Cavendish, 2009.

Nandy, Ashis. *The Intimate Enemy: Loss and Recovery of Self under Colonization.* Delhi: Oxford UP, 1983.

Narayan, Uma. "Working across Differences." *Hypatia* 3.2 (1988): 31–47.

Nason, James D. "Native American Intellectual Property Rights: Issues in the Control of Esoteric Knowledge." *Borrowed Power: Essays on Cultural Appropriation.* Ed. Bruce Ziff and Pratima V. Rao. New Brunswick, NJ: Rutgers UP, 1997.

Nehamas, Alexander. "What Should We Expect from Reading? (These Are Only Aesthetic Values)." Lecture, University of Wisconsin-Milwaukee, 1993.

Nielsen, Aldon Lynn. *Reading Race in American Poetry: "An Area of Act."* Urbana: U of Illinois P, 2000.

Nelson, Hilde Lindemann. *Damaged Identities: Narrative Repair.* Ithaca and London: Cornell UP, 2001.

Nelson, Melissa K., ed. *Original Instructions: Indigenous Teachings for a Sustainable Future.* Rochester, VT: Bear, 2008.

Neu, Dean, and Richard Therrien. *Accounting for Genocide: Canada's Bureaucratic Assault on Aboriginal People.* Black Point: Fernwood Publishing, 2003.

New, William H., ed. *Native Writers and Canadian Writing.* Vancouver: UBC P, 1990.

Newhouse, David. "Review of *Song of Rita Joe: Autobiography of a Mi'kmaq Poet* by Rita Joe." *Quill & Quire* (July 1996): 51.

Niedzwiecki, Thaba. "Print Politics: Conflict and Community Building at Toronto Women's Press." Master's thesis, University of Guelph, 1997.

Nietzsche, Friedrich. *Untimely Meditations.* Ed. Daniel Breazeale. Trans. R. J. Hollingdale. Cambridge: Cambridge UP, 1997.

Niezen, Ronald. *Truth and Indignation: Canada's Truth and Reconciliation Commission on Indian Residential Schools.* Toronto: U of Toronto P, 2013.

Noël, Lise. *Intolerance: A General Survey.* Trans. A. Bennett. Montreal and Kingston: McGill-Queen's UP, 1994.

O'Chiese, Peter. Interview. Trans. Harold Cardinal. Office of Specific Claims, Hinton, AL, 1 March 1976. Web.

Orenstein, Susan. "Television and Tradition in Sherman Alexie's *Flight.*" *American Popular Culture Magazine* (July 2007). Web. 15 December 2014.

Ortiz, Simon J. *The People Shall Continue.* San Francisco: Children's Book P, 1988.

———. *Speaking for the Generations: Native Writers on Writing.* Tucson: U of Arizona P, 1998.

———. "Towards a National Indian Literature: Cultural Authenticity in Nationalism." *MELUS Journal* 8.2 (1981): 7–12.

Osennontion [Marlyn Kane] and Skonaganleh:rá [Sylvia Maracle]. "Our World." *Canadian Woman Studies/Les cahiers de la femme* 10.2/3 (1989): 6–19.

"Our Truth." University of British Columbia, *UBC.ca*, 2013. Web. 5 Sep. 2013.

Owens, Louis. *Mixedblood Messages: Literature, Film, Family, Place.* Norman: U of Oklahoma P, 1998.

———. *Other Destinies: Understanding the American Indian Novel.* Norman: U of Oklahoma P, 1992.

———. *The Sharpest Sight.* Norman: U of Oklahoma P, 1992.

Pakes, Fraser J. "Seeing with the Stereotypic Eye: The Visual Image of the Plains Indian." *Native Studies Review* 1.2 (1985): 1–31.

Panetta, Alex. "Governor General Has a Heart—Raw Seal That Is." *Toronto Star,* 26 May 2009. Web. 30 October 2014.

Paris, Erna. "Letter to the Thought Police." *Globe and Mail,* 31 March 1992.

Parker, Pat. *Movement in Black: The Collected Poetry of Pat Parker, 1961–1978.* 1978. Ithaca, NY: Firebrand, 1989.

Parkhill, Thomas. *Weaving Ourselves into the Land*. Albany: State U of New York P, 1997.

Pelletier, Wilfried, and Ted Poole. *No Foreign Land*. Toronto: McClelland and Stewart, 1973.

Pels, Peter. "The Trickster's Dilemma: Ethics and the Technologies of the Anthropological Self." *Audit Cultures: Anthropological Studies in Accountability, Ethics, and the Academy*. Ed. Marilyn Strathern. London and New York: Routledge, 2000.

Peltier, Leonard. *Prison Writings: My Life Is My Sun Dance*. New York: St. Martin's, 1999.

Pennebaker, James W. *Opening Up: The Healing Power of Confiding in Others*. 2nd ed. New York: Guilford, 1997.

Pevar, Stephen L. *The Rights of Indians and Tribes*. New York: Oxford UP, 1983.

Pérez, Emma. *The Decolonial Imaginary: Writing Chicanas into History*. Bloomington: Indiana UP, 1999.

Peter, Aaju. "The European Parliament Shuts Down Seal-Product Imports—Again." *Above and Beyond* (May/June 2010). Web. 30 October 2014.

Petrone, Penny. *First People, First Voices*. Toronto: U of Toronto P, 1983.

——. "Indian Literature." *Oxford Companion to Canadian Literature*. Toronto: Oxford UP, 1983.

——. *Native Literature in Canada*. Toronto: Oxford UP, 1990.

Phelps, Teresa Godwin. *Shattered Voices: Language, Violence, and the Work of Truth Commissions*. Philadelphia: U of Pennsylvania P, 2004.

Philip, M. NourbeSe. *Frontiers: Essays and Writings on Racism and Culture*. Stratford, ON: Mercury, 1992.

"Pod Plays." Ed. Natalie Meisner. *Podplays.ca*, n.d. Web.

"Podplays." *NeworldTheatre.com*, n.d. Web.

Poliakov, Léon. *The Aryan Myth: A History of Racist and Nationalist Ideas in Europe*. London and Heinemann: Chatto and Windus and Sussex UP, 1974.

Potter, Mitch. "Jean's Seal Meal Sparks Feeding Frenzy." *Toronto Star*, 27 May 2009. Web. 30 Oct 2014.

Potts, Karen, and Leslie Brown. "Becoming an Anti-Oppressive Researcher." *Research as Resistance*. Ed. Leslie Brown and Susan Strega. Toronto: Canadian Scholars' P, 2005. 255–86.

Powell, Malea D. "Blood and Scholarship: One Mixed-Blood's Story." *Race, Rhetoric, and Composition*. Ed. Keith Gilyard. Portsmouth, NH: Boynton/Cook, 1999.

——. "Down by the River, or How Susan La Flesche Picotte Can Teach Us about Alliance as a Practice of Survivance." *College English* 67 (2004): 38–60.

——. "Dreaming Charles Eastman: Cultural Memory, Autobiography, and Geography in Indigenous Rhetorical Histories." *Beyond the Archive: Research as a Lived Process*. Ed. Gesa E. Kirsch and Liz Rohan. Carbondale: Southern Illinois UP, 2008.

——. "Listening to Ghosts: An Alternative (Non)Argument." *AltDis: Alternative Discourses and the Academy*. Ed. Christopher Schroeder, Helen Fox, and Patricia Bizzell. Portsmouth, NH: Heinemann, 2002.

———. "Rhetorics of Survivance: How American Indians Use Writing." *College Composition and Communication.* 53.3 (February 2002): 396–434.

Pratt, Mary Louise. *Imperial Eyes: Travel Writing and Transculturation.* London and New York: Routledge, 1992.

Preston, Jennifer. "Weesageechak Begins to Dance: Native Earth Performing Arts Inc." *The Drama Review: A Journal of Performance Studies* 36.1 (1992): 135–59.

Pulitano, Elvira. *Toward a Native American Critical Theory.* Lincoln: U of Nebraska P, 2003.

Qapirangajuq: Inuit Knowledge and Climate Change. Dir. Zacharias Kunuk and Ian Mauro. Igloolik Isuma Productions, 2010.

Qwul'sih'yah'maht [Robina Thomas]. "Honouring the Oral Traditions of My Ancestors Through Storytelling." *Research as Resistance: Critical, Indigenous, and Anti-Oppressive Approaches.* Ed. Leslie Brown and Susan Strega. Toronto: Canadian Scholars' P, 2005.

Rabinow, Paul. "Representations Are Social Facts: Modernity and Post-Modernity in Anthropology." *Writing Culture: The Poetics and Politics of Ethnography.* Ed. James Clifford and George E. Marcus. Berkeley: U of California P, 1986.

Rader, Dean. "Review of *Toward a Native American Critical Theory* by Elvira Pulitano." *American Indian Quarterly* 29.1/1–2 (2005): 330–34.

Radin, Paul. *The Trickster: A Study in American Indian Mythology.* With commentaries by Karl Kerényi and C. G. Jung. London and New York: Routledge and Kegan Paul, 1956.

Rasmussen, Knud. *Intellectual Culture of the Iglulik Eskimos.* Trans. William Worster and W. E. Calvert. Vol. VII, no. 1 of *Report of the Fifth Thule Expedition 1921–24.* Copenhagen: Gyldendal, 1929.

Razack, Sherene H. *Looking White People in the Eye: Gender, Race, and Culture in Courtrooms and Classrooms.* Toronto: U of Toronto P, 1998.

Red Shirt, Delphine. "These Are Not Indians." *American Indian Quarterly* 26. 4 (2002): 643–44.

Reder, Deanna. "Writing Autobiographically: A Neglected Indigenous Intellectual Tradition." *Across Borders/Across Cultures: Canadian Aboriginal and Native American Cultures.* Ed. Emma LaRocque, Paul DePasquale, and Renate Eigenbrod. Peterborough: Broadview, 2009. 153–69.

Reder, Deanna, and Linda M. Morra, eds. *Troubling Tricksters: Revisioning Critical Conversations.* Waterloo, ON: Wilfrid Laurier UP, 2010.

Regan, Paulette. *Unsettling the Settler Within: Indian Residential Schools, Truth Telling, and Reconciliation in Canada.* Vancouver: UBC P, 2011.

"Regulation (EC) No 1007/2009 of the European Parliament and of the Council of 16 September 2009 on trade in seal products." EUR-Lex: Access to European Union Law, 31 Oct 2009. Web. 30 Oct 2014.

Reid, Dennis. *Edwin Holgate.* Ottawa: National Gallery of Canada, 1976.

Rentelin, Alison Dudes. *International Human Rights: Universalism versus Relativism.* Newbury Park, CA: Sage Publications, 1990.

"Residential School Cash Has Deadly Fallout." *Calgary Herald*, 26 January 2009. Web.

"Residential School Finally Offers Some Closure." *ciquut: Tseshaht First Nation's Newsletter* 5.2 (2009).

Restall, Matthew, Lisa Sousa, and Kevin Terraciano, eds. *Mesoamerican Voices: Native-Language Writings from Colonial Mexico, Oaxaca, Yucatan, and Guatemala.* New York: Cambridge UP, 2005.

Rhymes for Young Ghouls. Dir. Jeff Barnaby. Digital Productions, 2013.

Rice, Alison. "Introduction: Interview with Julia Kristeva." *PMLA* 117.2 (2002): 278–95.

Richardson, John. *Wacousta.* Philadelphia: Kay and Biddle, 1832.

Richler, Noah. *This Is My Country, What's Yours? A Literary Atlas of Canada.* Toronto: McClelland and Stewart, 2006.

Ridington, Robin. "Cultures in Conflict: Problems in Discourse." *Native Writers and Canadian Writing.* Ed. W. H. New. Vancouver: UBC P, 1990.

Rifkin, Mark. *The Erotics of Sovereignty: Queer Native Writing in the Era of Self-Determination.* Minneapolis: U of Minnesota P, 2012.

————. *When Did Indians Become Straight? Kinship, the History of Sexuality, and Native Sovereignty.* Oxford: Oxford UP, 2011.

Rigby, Andrew. *Justice and Reconciliation: After the Violence.* Boulder, CO: Lynne Rienner Publishers, 2001.

Robinson, Dylan. "The Arts of Public Engagement: Moving Beyond Reconciliation in Canada." Banting Postdoctoral Research Project.

Robinson, Eden. *Monkey Beach.* Toronto: Knopf Canada, 2000.

————. *The Sasquatch at Home: Traditional Protocols & Modern Storytelling.* Edmonton: U of Alberta P, 2011.

————. *Traplines.* Toronto: Knopf, 1996.

Robinson, Frances M. P. Introduction. *Visitors Who Never Left: The Origin of the People of Damelahamid.* Ed. Chief Kenneth Harris and Frances M. P. Robinson. Vancouver: UBC P, 1974. xi–xxi.

Rooke, Constance. "Interview with Thomas King." *World Literature Written in English* 30.2 (1990): 62–76.

Roper, Edward. *By Track and Trail: A Journey Through Canada.* London: W. H. Allen, 1981.

Rorty, Amélie Oksenberg, ed. *Essays on Aristotle's Poetics.* Princeton, NJ: Princeton UP, 1992.

Rosaldo, Renato. *Culture and Truth: The Remaking of Social Analysis.* Boston: Beacon, 1989.

Roscoe, Will. *Changing Ones: Third and Fourth Genders in Native North America.* New York: Palgrave Macmillan, 2000.

————. *The Zuni Man-Woman.* Albuquerque: U of New Mexico P, 1992.

Ross, Rupert. *Dancing with a Ghost: Exploring Indian Reality.* Markham, ON: Reed Books, 1992.

Rotenstreich, Nathan. "Volksgeist." *Dictionary of the History of Ideas.* Ed. Philip P. Wiener. New York City: Charles Scribner's Sons, 1973.

Roth, Christopher F. *Becoming Tsimshian: The Social Life of Names.* Seattle: Washington UP, 2008.

Rousseau, Jean-Jacques. *The Social Contract and Discourses.* London: Dent, 1986.

Ruffo, Armand Garnet, ed. *(Ad)dressing Our Words: Aboriginal Perspectives on Aboriginal Literatures.* Penticton, BC: Theytus, 2001.

——. "Why Native Literature?" *American Indian Quarterly* 21.4 (1997): 663–73.

Rushdie, Salman. *Imaginary Homelands.* New York: Penguin, 1991.

Ryan, Allan J. *The Trickster Shift: Humour and Irony in Contemporary Native Art.* Vancouver and Toronto: UBC P, 1999.

Rymhs, Deena. "Appropriating Guilt: Reconciliation in an Aboriginal Canadian Context." *English Studies in Canada* 32.1 (2006): 105–23.

Said, Edward W. *Culture and Imperialism.* Cambridge, MA: Harvard UP, 1992.

——. *Orientalism.* New York: Pantheon Books, 1978.

——. *Reflections on Exile and Other Essays.* Cambridge, MA: Harvard UP, 2000.

——. *Representations of the Intellectual.* New York: Vintage, 1996.

Samson Occom Papers. *Mohegan Tribal Records.* Collection 1 (Box 1, Folder 16). Hartford, CT: Connecticut Historical Society, 1766.

Sands, Kathleen Mullen, and Theodore Rios. *Telling a Good One: The Process of a Native American Collaborative Biography.* Lincoln: U of Nebraska P, 2000.

Sangari, Kumkum. "The Politics of the Possible." *Cultural Critique* 7 (Fall 1987): 157–86.

Sarris, Greg. *Keeping Slug Woman Alive: A Holistic Approach to American Indian Texts.* Berkeley: U of California P, 1993.

Sartre, Jean-Paul. "Colonialisme et néocolonialisme." *Situation V.* Paris: Gallimard, 1964.

——. "Materialism and Revolution." *Literary and Philosophical Essays.* Trans. Annette Michelson. London: Hutchinson, 1968.

Sawatsky, Wendy. "J. J. Harper: 15 Years Later." *CBC Manitoba,* 7 March 2003. Web.

Sayer, John William. *Ghost Dancing and the Law: The Wounded Knee Trials.* Cambridge, MA: Harvard UP, 1997.

Scofield, Gregory. *kipocihkân: Poems New & Selected.* Gibsons: Nightwood, 2009.

——. *Love Medicine and One Song: Sâkihtowinmaskihkiy êkwa Pêyak-nikamowin.* Custer, WA: Polestar, 1997.

——. "You Can Always Count on an Anthropologist (To Set You Straight, Crooked or Somewhere In-Between)." *Me Sexy: An Exploration of Native Sex and Sexuality.* Ed. Drew Hayden Talyor. Vancouver: Douglas and McIntyre, 2008. 160–68.

Scott, Jamie S. "Colonial, Neo-Colonial, Post-Colonial: Images of Christian Missions in Hiram A. Cody's *The Frontiersman,* Rudy Wiebe's *First and Vital Candle,* and Basil Johnston's *Indian School Days." Journal of Canadian Studies* 32.3 (1997): 140–61.

The Searchers. Dir. John Ford. American Technicolor VistaVision, 1956.

Seelye, John. "Introduction." *The Adventures of Tom Sawyer*. By Mark Twain. New York: Penguin Classics, 1986.

Sequoya, Jana. "How (!) Is an Indian? A Contest of Stories." *New Voices in Native American Literary Criticism*. Ed. Arnold Krupat. Washington: Smithsonian Institute P, 1993.

Shakespeare, William. *The Tempest*. London: Dover, 1998.

Sherman, Jason. "Making a Bid to Reclaim the Native Voice in Literature." *Toronto Star*, 25 March 1989.

Shilling, Arthur. *The Ojibway Dream*. Montreal: Tundra, 1986.

Silko, Leslie Marmon. *Almanac of the Dead*. New York: Penguin, 1991.

———. *Ceremony*. New York: Penguin: 1977.

———. *Gardens in the Dunes*. New York: Simon and Schuster, 1999.

Simon, Lorne. "Freedom of Expression? Are Native Voices Being Silenced in the Name of Artistic Freedom?" *Canadian Forum* (July–August 1993).

Simpson, Leanne. *The Construction of Traditional Ecological Knowledge: Issues, Implications, and Insights*. Ph.D. diss., University of Manitoba, 1999.

———. *Dancing on Our Turtle's Back: Stories of Nishnaabeg Re-creation, Resurgence and a New Emergence*. Winnipeg: Arbeiter Ring, 2011.

———. "Politics Based on Justice, Diplomacy Based on Love." *Briarpatch* 42.3 (2013). Web. 21 August 2014.

Sinclair, Murray. "Aboriginal Peoples and Euro-Canadians: Two World Views." Ed. John H. Hylton. *Aboriginal Self-Government in Canada: Current Trends and Issues*. Saskatoon: Purich Publishing, 1994.

Sinclair, Niigaanwewidam James. "Responsible and Ethical Criticisms of Indigenous Literatures." Excerpt from "Trickster Reflections: Part I." *Troubling Tricksters: Revisioning Critical Conversations*. Ed. Deanna Reder and Linda M. Morra. Waterloo, ON: Wilfrid Laurier UP, 2010.

Sinclair, Raven. "Identity Lost and Found: Lessons from the Sixties Scoop." *First Peoples Child and Family Review* 3.1 (2007): 65–82.

Skins Workshops on Aboriginal Storytelling in Digital Media. skins.abtec.org. Web.

Sladen, Douglas. *On the Cars and Off*. London: Ward, Lock and Bowden, 1895.

Slapin, Beverly. *The Basic Skills Caucasian Americans Workbook*. Illus. Annie Esposito. Foreword Doris Seale. Berkeley: Oyate: 1994.

Slemon, Stephen. "The Scramble for Post-Colonialism." *The Post-Colonial Studies Reader*. Ed. Bill Ashcroft, Gareth Griffiths, and Helen Tiffin. London and New York: Routledge, 1995.

———. "Unsettling the Empire: Resistance Theory for the Second World." *New Contexts of Canadian Criticism*. Ed. Ajay Heble, Donna Palmateer Pennee, and J. R. (Tim) Struthers. Peterborough, ON: Broadview P, 1997.

Slipperjack, Ruby. *Honour the Sun*. Winnipeg: Pemmican, 1987.

Smith, Andrea. "American Studies without America: Native Feminisms and the Nation-State." *American Quarterly* 60.2 (2008): 309–15.

——. *Conquest: Sexual Violence and American Indian Genocide*. Cambridge, MA: South End P, 2005.

——. *Native Americans and the Christian Right*. Durham, NC: Duke UP, 2008.

——. "Queer Theory and Native Studies: The Heteronormativity of Settler Colonialism." *Queer Indigenous Studies: Critical Interventions in Theory, Politics, and Literature*. Ed. Driskill, Qwo-Li, Chris Finley, Brian Joseph Gilley, and Scott Lauria Morgensen. Tucson: U of Arizona P, 2011. 43–65.

——. "Unsettling the Privilege of Self-Reflexivity." *Geographies of Privilege*. Ed. France Winddance Twine and Bradley Gardener. London and New York: Routledge, 2013.

Smith, Donald B. *Long Lance: The True Story of an Imposter*. Toronto: Macmillan, 1982.

Smith, G. H. "The Problematic of 'Indigenous Theorizing': A Critical Reflection." Conference Presentation. AERA Annual Conference, Montreal, 11–15 April 2005.

Smith, Janet. "Michelle Olson Turns to Her Roots at Dancing on the Edge." *Georgia Straight*, 6 July 2011. Web.

Smith, Linda Tuhiwai. *Decolonizing Methodologies: Research and Indigenous Peoples*. New York: Zed Books, 1999.

Soldier Blue. Dir. Ralph Nelson. Avco Embassy Pictures, 1970.

Somerville, Siobhan B. *Queering the Color Line: Race and the Invention of Homosexuality in American Culture*. Durham: Duke UP, 2000.

Sontag, Susan. "Against Interpretation." *Against Interpretation and Other Essays*. New York: Picador, 2001. 3–14.

South Africa. *Truth and Reconciliation Commission of South Africa Report*. Vol. 1–5. 29 October 1998. Cape Town: The Commission, 21 March 2003. Web.

Sparrow, Quelemia. *Ashes on the Water*. Vancouver: Raven Spirit Dance and Neworld Theatre, 2011.

Spears, Heather. *Poems Selected and New*. Toronto: Wolsak, 1998.

Spelman, Elizabeth. *Fruits of Sorrow: Framing Our Attention to Suffering*. Boston: Beacon, 1997.

——. *Inessential Woman: Problems of Exclusion in Feminist Thought*. Boston: Beacon, 1988.

Spier, Leslie. *The Ghost Dance of 1870 among the Klamath of Oregon*. Seattle: U of Washington P, 1927.

——. *The Prophet Dance of the Northwest and Its Derivatives*. Menasha, WI: G. Banta, 1935.

Spivak, Gayatri Chakravorty. "Can the Subaltern Speak?" *Marxism and the Interpretation of Culture*. Ed. Cary Nelson and Laurence Grossberg. Urbana: U of Illinois P, 1988.

——. "How to Read a 'Culturally Different' Book." *Colonial Discourse/Postcolonial Theory*. Ed. Francis Barker, Peter Hulme, and Margaret Iverson. Manchester UP, 1994.

——. "The Post-Colonial Critic." *The Post-Colonial Critic: Interviews, Strategies, Dialogues*. Ed. Sarah Harasym. New York and London: Routledge, 1990.

————. "Three Women's Texts and a Critique of Imperialism." *"Race," Writing, and Difference.* Ed. Henry Louis Gates Jr. Chicago: U of Chicago P, 1986. 262–80.

Standing Bear, Luther. *My People the Sioux.* Lincoln: U of Nebraska P, 1928.

State of Vermont v. Harold St. Francis, et al., Vermont Supreme Court. 1989.

State of Vermont v. Raleigh Elliot, et al., Vermont Supreme Court. 1992.

Stegner, Wallace. *Where the Bluebird Sings to the Lemonade Springs: Living and Writing in the West.* New York: Modern Library Classics, 2002.

Steinhauer, Evelyn. "Thoughts on an Indigenous Research Methodology." *Canadian Journal of Native Education* 26.2 (2001): 69–81.

Stevenson, W. L. *Decolonizing Tribal Histories.* Ph.D. diss., University of California, Berkeley, 2000.

Steward, Julian H. *Theory of Cultural Change: The Methodology of Multilinear Evolution.* Urbana: U of Illinois P, 1955.

Stewart, Hilary. *Totem Poles.* Vancouver: Douglas and McIntyre, 1990.

Struthers, Roxanne. "Conducting Sacred Research: An Indigenous Experience." *Wicazo Sa Review* 16.1 (2001): 125–33.

Stump, Sarain. *There Is My People Sleeping.* Sydney, BC: Gray's Publishing, 1970.

Sturm, Circe. *Blood Politics: Race, Culture, and Identity in the Cherokee Nation of Oklahoma.* Berkeley: U of California P, 2002.

Sugars, Cynthia. "Settler Fantasies, Postcolonial Guilt: The Compromised Postcolonialism of Jane Urquhart's *Away.*" *Australian Canadian Studies* 19.2 (2001): 101–18.

Suleri, Sara. *Meatless Days.* Chicago: U of Chicago P, 1989.

————. "Woman Skin Deep: Feminism and the Postcolonial Condition." *Critical Inquiry* 18.4 (1992): 756–69.

Suttles, Wayne. "Linguistic Evidence for the Burrard Inlet as Former Halkomelem." *Working Papers for the 31st International Conference on Salish and Neighbouring Languages.* Vancouver: ICSNL, 1996. 283–96. Web.

"Swedish Erotica: Custer's Revenge." *MobyGames.com,* 24 October 2007. Web.

"Tanya Tagaq on the Polaris Prize, the Seal Hunt and the 'Sealfie.'" YouTube. 26 September 2014. Web. 30 March 2015.

Tator, Carol, and Frances Henry. "The Role and Practice of Racialized Discourse in Culture and Cultural Production." *Journal of Canadian Studies* 35.3 (2000). Web. 2 January 2008.

Taylor, Diana. *The Archive and the Repertoire: Performing Cultural Memory in the Americas.* Chapel Hill: Duke UP, 2003.

Taylor, Drew Hayden. *Funny, You Don't Look Like One: Observations from a Blue-Eyed Ojibway.* Penticton, BC: Theytus, 1996.

————. *Me Sexy: An Exploration of Native Sex and Sexuality.* Madeira Park, BC: Douglas and McIntyre, 2008.

Tedlock, Dennis. "The Spoken Word and the Work of Interpretation in American Indian Religion." *Traditional American Indian Literatures.* Ed. Karl Kroeber. Lincoln: U of Nebraska P, 1981.

Teuton, Christopher B. "Review of *Toward a Native American Critical Theory* by Elvira Pulitano." *American Indian Quarterly* 29.1/2 (2005): 334–37.

Thobani, Sunera, Glen Coulthard, and Dory Nason. "Teach In." Public remarks. University of British Columbia, Vancouver, BC, 13 September 2013.

Thornton, Russell. *We Shall Live Again: The 1870 and 1890 Ghost Dance Movements as Demographic Revitalization*. Cambridge: Cambridge UP, 1986.

Thrasher, Anthony Apakark. *Thrasher: Skid Row Eskimo*. Toronto: Griffin, 1976.

Tinsley, Sean A., and Rachel A. Qitsualik. *Ajjiit: Dark Dreams of the Ancient Arctic*. Toronto: Inhabit Media, 2011.

Todd, Loretta. "Aboriginal Narratives in Cyberspace." *Immersed in Technology: Art and Virtual Environments*. Cambridge, MA: Massachusetts Institute of Technology P, 1996. 179–94.

Todorov, Tzvetan. *The Conquest of America: The Question of the Other*. Trans. Richard Howard. New York: Harper and Row, 1984.

Tompkins, Jane. *West of Everything*. New York: Oxford UP, 1992.

Torsen, Molly, and Jane Anderson. *Intellectual Property and the Safeguarding of Traditional Cultures: Legal Issues and Practical Options for Museums, Libraries and Archives*. Geneva: World Intellectual Property Organization, 2010.

Trask, Haunani-Kay. "Ulu." *Light in the Crevice Never Seen*. Corvallis, OR: Calyx, 1994.

Travis, Molly. "*Beloved* and *Middle Passage*: Race, Narrative and the Critic's Essentialism." *Narrative* 2.3 (Oct. 1994): 179–200.

Trinh, Minh-ha T. *Woman, Native, Other: Writing Postcoloniality and Feminism*. Bloomington: Indiana UP, 1989.

Tungijuq. Dir. Félix Lajeunesse and Paul Raphaël. Perf. Tanya Tagaq and Zacharias Kunuk. Igloolik Isuma Productions, 2009.

Tyman, James. *Inside Out: An Autobiography by a Native Canadian*. Saskatoon: Fifth House, 1989.

Unger, Roberto Mangabeira. *Knowledge and Politics*. New York: Free Press, 1975.

———. *Law in Modern Society: Toward a Criticism of Social Theory*. New York: Free Press, 1976.

Van Manen, Max. *Researching Lived Experience*. London, ON: Althouse P, U of Western Ontario, 2001.

Vander, Judith. *Shoshone Ghost Dance Religion: Poetry Songs and Great Basin Context*. Urbana: U of Illinois P, 1997.

Verwoerd, Wilhelm. "Toward a Response to Criticisms of the South Africa Truth and Reconciliation Commission." *Dilemmas of Reconciliation: Cases and Concepts*. Ed. Carol A. L. Prager and Trudy Govier. Waterloo, ON: Wilfrid Laurier UP, 2003.

Vizenor, Gerald. *Bearheart: The Heirship Chronicles*. Minneapolis: U of Minnesota P, 1990.

———. *Dead Voices: Natural Agonies in the New World*. Norman: U of Oklahoma P, 1992.

———. *Fugitive Poses: Native American Indian Scenes of Absence and Presence*. Lincoln: U of Nebraska P, 1998.

———. *Manifest Manners: Postindian Warriors of Survivance.* Hanover and London: Wesleyan UP, 1994.

———. *Manifest Manners: Narratives of Postindian Survivance.* Lincoln: U of Nebraska P, 1999.

———. "Native American Indian Identities: Autoinscriptions and the Cultures of Names." *Native American Perspectives on Literature and History.* Ed. Alan R. Velie. Norman: U of Oklahoma P, 1994. 117–126.

———. "Native American Indian Literatures: Narratives of Survivance." *Native North America: Critical and Cultural Perspectives.* Ed. Renee Hulan. Toronto: ECW, 1999.

Vizenor, Gerald, ed. *Narrative Chance: Postmodern Discourse on Native American Indian Literatures.* Albuquerque: U of New Mexico P, 1989.

Vizenor, Gerald, and Robert Lee. *Postindian Conversations.* Lincoln: U of Nebraska P, 1999.

Wagamese, Richard. *Keeper'n Me.* Toronto: Doubleday Canada, 1994.

Wall, Bob. "Analyzing the Marshall Commission: Why It Was Established and How It Functioned." *Elusive Justice: Beyond the Marshall Inquiry.* Ed. Joy Mannette. Halifax: Fernwood Publishing, 1992. 13–33.

Walters, Anna Lee. *Talking Indian: Reflections on Survival and Writing.* Ithaca, NY: Firebrand Books, 1992.

Warrior, Robert Allen. "Native Critics in the World: Edward Said and Nationalism." *American Indian Literary Nationalism.* Ed. Jace Weaver, Craig S. Womack, and Robert A. Warrior. Albuquerque: U of New Mexico P, 2006.

———. *People and the Word: Reading Native Nonfiction.* Minneapolis: U of Minnesota P, 2005.

———. *Red on Red: Native American Literary Separatism.* Minneapolis: U of Minnesota P, 1999.

———. *Tribal Secrets: Recovering American Indian Intellectual Traditions.* Minneapolis: U of Minnesota P, 1995.

Waziyatawin [Angela Cavender Wilson]. *What Does Justice Look Like? The Struggle for Liberation in Dakota Homeland.* St. Paul: Living Justice, 2008.

Weaver, Jace. "Splitting the Earth: First Utterances and Plural Separatism." *American Indian Literary Nationalism.* Ed. Jace Weaver, Craig S. Womack, and Robert A. Warrior. Albuquerque: U of New Mexico P, 2006. 1–89.

———. *That the People Might Live: Native American Literatures and Native American Community.* New York: Oxford UP, 1997.

Weaver, Jace, Craig S. Womack, and Robert A. Warrior, eds. *American Indian Literary Nationalism.* Albuquerque: U of New Mexico P, 2006.

Weber, Max. *The Protestant Ethic and the Spirit of Capitalism.* New York: Scribner's, 1958.

Weigel, Sigrid. "Secularization and Sacralization, Normalization and Rupture: Kristeva and Arendt on Forgiveness." Trans. Mark Kyburz. *PMLA* 117.2 (2002).

Welch, James. *Winter in the Blood.* New York: Penguin, 1974.

Welsh, Christine. "Women in the Shadows: Reclaiming a Métis Heritage." *New Contexts of Canadian Criticism.* Ed. Ajay Heble, Donna Palmateer Pennee, and J. R. (Tim) Struthers. Peterborough: Broadview P, 1997.

Wenzel, George. *Animal Rights, Human Rights: Ecology, Economy, and Ideology in the Canadian Arctic.* Toronto: U of Toronto P, 1991.

Wickman, Patricia Riles. *The Tree That Bends: Discourse, Power, and the Survival of the Maskókî People.* Tuscaloosa: U of Arizona P, 1999.

William, Gerry. *The Woman in the Trees.* Vancouver: New Star, 2004.

Williams, Barney, Jr. Interview with Chaw-win-is. 10 November 2009.

Williams, Eric. *Capitalism and Slavery.* Chapel Hill: U of North Carolina P, 1944.

Williams, Kenneth. "Cultural Appropriation and Aboriginal Literature." *Windspeaker* Classroom Edition 3. The Aboriginal Multi-Media Society. Web. 19 May 2008.

Williams, R. A. "The Algebra of Federal Indian Law: The Hard Trail of Decolonizing and Americanizing the White Man's Indian Jurisprudence." *Wisconsin Law Review* (1986): 219–99.

Williams, Shirley Ida. *Gdi-nweninaa: Our Sound, Our Voice.* Peterborough, ON: Neganigwane Company, 2002.

Williams, Walter L. *The Spirit and the Flesh: Sexual Diversity in American Indian Culture.* Boston: Beacon, 1992.

Wilson, Waziyatawin Angela, and Michael Yellow Bird. "Beginning Decolonization." *For Indigenous Eyes Only: A Decolonization Handbook.* Ed. Waziyatawin Angela Wilson and Michael Yellow Bird. Santa Fe: School of American Research, 2005.

Winks, Quintin. "Port Alberni Residential School Destroyed in Ceremony." *Times Colonist,* 11 February 2009. Web. 10 November 2009.

Wiseman, Frederick Matthew. *The Voice of the Dawn: An Autohistory of the Abenaki Nation.* Hanover, NH: UP of New England, 2001.

Wolfe, Patrick. *Settler Colonialism and the Transformation of Anthropology: The Politics and Poetics of an Ethnographic Event.* London: Caswell, 1999.

Womack, Craig S. *Art as Performance, Story as Criticism: Reflections on Native Literary Aesthetics.* Norman: U of Oklahoma P, 2009.

———. *Red on Red: Native American Literary Separatism.* Minneapolis: U of Minnesota P, 1999.

Womack, Craig S., Daniel Heath Justice, and Christopher B. Teuton, eds. *Reasoning Together: The Native Critics Collective.* Norman: U of Oklahoma P, 2008.

Wong, Hertha. *Sending My Heart Back across the Years: Tradition and Innovation in Native American Autobiography.* New York: Oxford UP, 1992.

Woolford, Andrew. *Between Justice and Certainty: Treaty Making in British Columbia.* Vancouver: UBC P, 2005.

Wright, Ronald. *A Short History of Progress.* Toronto: House of Anansi, 2004.

Writing the Land. Dir. Kevin Lee Burton. National Film Board, 2007.

Yahgulanaas, Michael Nicoll. *Red: A Haida Manga.* Madeira Park, BC: Douglas and McIntyre, 2009.

York, Geoffrey. *The Dispossessed: Life and Death in Native Canada.* Toronto: Lester and Orpen, 1989.

Young, Iris Marion. *Justice and the Politics of Difference.* Princeton: Princeton UP, 1990.

Zebolsky, Kirk H. "Recent Works of Louis, Harjo and Silko: Emphasizing Land Rights, Subsuming Native Culture." Unpublished paper. Omaha: University of Nebraska at Omaha, n.d.

Ziff, Larzer. *Writing in the New Nation: Prose, Print and Politics in the Early United States.* New Haven, CT: Yale UP, 1991.

ABOUT THE CONTRIBUTORS

Janice Acoose is an Anishinaabekwe-Métis-Nehiowé educator whose roots stem from the Sakimay (Saulteaux) First Nation and her mother's Ninankawe Marival Métis Community. She wrote one of the first books on Indigenous literatures in Canada, *Iskwewak—Kah' Yaw Ni Wahkomakanak: Neither Indian Princesses nor Easy Squaws* (Women's P, 1995). She completed her Ph.D. at the University of Saskatchewan in 2011.

Robert Appleford is Associate Professor in the English and Film Studies Department at the University of Alberta. He has published many articles on Aboriginal literatures and theatre, and edited the anthology *Critical Perspectives on Canadian Theatre in English, Volume One: Aboriginal Drama and Theatre* (Playwrights Canada P, 2005).

Jeannette C. Armstrong is Syilx Okanagan, a fluent speaker of nsyilxcen, and an author and activist whose published works include literary titles and academic writing on a wide variety of Indigenous issues. The focus of her Ph.D. is on Syilx oraliture (oral story literature) and tmixwcentrism (syilx environmental ethics). She currently holds the Canada Research Chair in Okanagan Indigenous Knowledge and Philosophy at UBC Okanagan, and is Program Coordinator of and teaches in Indigenous Studies in Unit 1: Community, Culture, and Global Studies.

Kateri Akiwenzie-Damm is an Anishinaabe writer from the Chippewas of Nawash First Nation, and in 1993 founded Kegedonce Press, one of very few literary publishing houses in Canada devoted to Indigenous writers. She has edited two anthologies: *Skins: Contemporary Indigenous Writing* (with Josie Douglas, IAD P, 2000) and *Without Reservation: Indigenous Erotica* (Kegedonce P, 2003).

Kristina Fagan Bidwell is the first Associate Dean of Aboriginal Affairs in the University of Saskatchewan's College of Arts and Science. In this position, she is responsible for building Aboriginal student success and encouraging the College to engage meaningfully with Aboriginal communities and Aboriginal knowledge. As a researcher and teacher, she specializes in Aboriginal writing and storytelling in Canada. She is the co-editor of *Call Me Hank: A Sto:lo Man's Reflections on Logging, Living and Growing Old* (U of Toronto P, 2006) and *Orality and Literacy: Reflections across Disciplines* (U of Toronto P, 2011). Her current research is on autobiography and storytelling among her people, the people of NunatuKavut.

Kimberly Blaeser (Anishinaabe) is a widely published creative writer, photographer, and scholar. A professor at the University of Wisconsin–Milwaukee, she teaches Native American Literatures and Creative Writing. Blaeser has authored three collections of poetry, most recently *Apprenticed to Justice*, and is Wisconsin's Poet Laureate for 2015–16. Among her edited volumes is *Traces in Blood, Bone, and Stone: Contemporary Ojibwe Poetry*. Her current work brings her poetry and photography together in a new form she calls "picto-poems."

Lisa Brooks (Abenaki) is Associate Professor of English and American Studies at Amherst College. Her first book, *The Common Pot: The Recovery of Native Space in the Northeast* (U of Minnesota P, 2008) reframes the historical and literary landscape of the American Northeast.

Warren Cariou was born in Meadow Lake, Saskatchewan, into a family of mixed Métis and European heritage. Though he has lived away from Meadow Lake for many years, his art and academic work maintain a focus on the cultural and environmental questions that have preoccupied the people of his homeland. His books, films, photography, and scholarly research explore themes of community, environment, orality, and belonging in the Canadian West, with particular focus on the relationships between Indigenous and non-Native peoples. Cariou holds a Canada Research Chair in Narrative, Community and Indigenous Cultures at the University of Manitoba, where he also teaches in the Department of English, Film and Theatre and directs the Centre for Creative Writing and Oral Culture.

Jeff Corntassel is Tsalagi (Cherokee Nation) and is Associate Professor and Director of Indigenous Governance at the University of Victoria. His next book is an edited volume in collaboration with Kanaka Maoli professors in Indigenous Politics at the University of Hawai'i, Manoa, and is entitled *Everyday Acts of Resurgence: People, Places, Practices*.

Michelle Coupal is Assistant Professor of English at Laurentian University and a member of the Bonnechere Algonquin First Nation. Coupal specializes in both Indigenous literatures in Canada and Canadian literature. She is working on a book—*Teaching Trauma and Indian Residential School Literatures in Canada*—that provides a theory and practice of teaching Indian residential school texts from an Indigenous framework of understanding trauma.

Amber Dean is Assistant Professor in the Gender Studies and Feminist Research Program and the Department of English and Cultural Studies at McMaster University. She is the author of *Remembering Vancouver's Disappeared Women: Settler Colonialism and the Difficulty of Inheritance* (U of Toronto P, 2015).

Qwo-Li Driskill is a Cherokee Two-Spirit and Queer writer, activist, and performer, also of African, Irish, Lenape, Lumbee, and Osage ascent. S/he is author of *Walking with Ghosts: Poems* (Salt Publishing, 2005) and co-editor of *Sovereign Erotics: A Collection of Two-Spirit Literature* (U of Arizona P, 2011) and *Queer Indigenous Studies: Critical Interventions in Theory, Politics, and Literature* (U of Arizona P, 2011). Driskill is Assistant Professor of Queer Studies in the Women, Gender, and Sexuality Studies Program at Oregon State University.

Renate Eigenbrod served as head of Native Studies at the University of Manitoba until her unexpected passing in May 2014. She was also a member of the Manitoba Aboriginal Justice and Equality Coalition, a dedicated teacher and mentor, and an avid supporter of Indigenous writers in Canada. Her research interests revolved around theories of decolonization in relation to Aboriginal literatures in Canada and Indigenous literatures globally. The author of several books and articles, her final work, published posthumously, was the republication of a bilingual edition, in both English and Anishinaabemowin, of George Kenny's *Indians Don't Cry: Gaawin Mawisiiwag Anishinaabeg* (U of Manitoba P, 2014), accompanied by an afterword on the significance of the text.

Jo-Ann Episkenew was the Director of the Indigenous Peoples' Health Research Centre at the University of Regina, until her passing in February 2016 following a sudden illness. Previously she had worked as Professor of English at the First Nations University of Canada. An active researcher, her interests included Aboriginal youth health, applied literatures, and trauma studies. Episkenew authored *Taking Back Our Spirits: Indigenous Literatures, Public Policy, and Healing* (U of Manitoba P, 2009) and was the winner of two Saskatchewan Book Awards. In 2015, the YWCA Regina recognized her contributions by awarding her the Women of Distinction Lifetime Achievement Award. In 2016, she was awarded the Indspire Award for Education.

Margery Fee holds the David and Brenda McLean Chair in Canadian Studies at the University of British Columbia. Her most recent publications are *Literary Land Claims: The "Indian Land Question" from Pontiac's War to Attawapiskat* (Wilfrid Laurier UP, 2015) and *Tekahionwake: E. Pauline Johnson's Writings on Native North America* (Broadview P, 2015), co-edited with Dory Nason.

Marc André Fortin is Assistant Professor of English and Comparative Canadian Literature at l'Université de Sherbrooke. His research focuses on science and literature, early ethnography in Canada, modernism, and Indigenous representations in colonial archives. Fortin is the co-editor of the digital journal *Mémoires du livre/Studies in Book Culture*.

Daniel Francis is the author of two dozen books, principally about Canadian history. Born in Vancouver in 1947, he currently resides in North Vancouver. His books, which have won several awards, cover a diverse range of subjects, from prostitution in his native city to the global history of whaling.

David Gaertner is a settler scholar of German descent and an assistant professor in the First Nations and Indigenous Studies Program at the University of British Columbia. His research and teaching investigate new media and digital storytelling within a decolonial framework. He has also written and published articles on reconciliation, Indigenous literature, podcasting, and typeface. He blogs at novelalliances.com.

Allison Hargreaves is Assistant Professor and non-Indigenous teacher of Indigenous literatures at the Department of Critical Studies at UBC Okanagan in unceded Syilx territory. Her research investigates literary and policy interventions into gendered colonial violence in Canada, looking to Indigenous women's writing as an intellectual contribution to contemporary anti-violence debate.

James (Sákéj) Youngblood Henderson is Chickasaw, born to the Bear Clan of the Chickasaw Nation and Cheyenne Tribe in Oklahoma. Henderson is currently a member of the College of Law, University of Saskatchewan, and the Senior Administrator and Research Director of the Native Law Centre at the University of Saskatchewan. In 2005, the Indigenous Bar Association awarded him the honorary title of Indigenous People's Counsel in recognition of his significant and outstanding achievements and excellence in law in the service of the Indigenous community and the Creator, with honour and dignity.

Sarah Henzi recently completed an FRQSC-funded Postdoctoral Fellowship in the First Nations and Indigenous Studies Program at the University of British Columbia. Currently she is a Visiting Scholar at McGill University's Institute for the Study of Canada. She is also a Co-Organizer of and Lecturer at the International Graduate Summer School on Indigenous Literature and Film, held annually in July at the Centre d'études et de recherches internationales, Université de Montréal.

Helen Hoy is Professor Emerita, English, at the University of Guelph. She has published *Modern English-Canadian Prose* (Gale, 1983), *The Native in Literature* (co-edited, ECW, 1987), *How Should I Read These? Native Women Writers in Canada* (U of Toronto P, 2001), and numerous articles on Canadian fiction. She has taught at the universities of Toronto, Manitoba, Lethbridge, Minnesota, and Guelph.

Katsisorokwas Curran Jacobs is a young Mohawk woman from Kahnawake, Quebec. She is an educator in all facets of her life and a firm believer that it is possible to walk confidently in both the Indigenous and Western worlds. She is working diligently to ensure that other Aboriginal youth can find their own, similar paths.

Daniel Morley Johnson earned a Ph.D. in Comparative Literature in 2014 from the University of Alberta. He has taught numerous courses on Indigenous studies, Canadian literature, and community engagement. In addition to teaching, researching, and writing, he is active as a community advocate in Edmonton's inner city. He is a settler on Treaty Six land, where he works full-time at the Women's Emergency Accommodation Centre.

E. Pauline Johnson (also known as Tekahionwake) was a Mohawk writer and performer popular in the late nineteenth century. She was notable for her poems and performances, which were informed by and celebrated her Indigenous heritage. Her publications include *The White Wampum* (1895), *Flint and Feather* (1912), *Legends of Vancouver* (1913), and *Moccasin Maker* (1913).

Daniel Heath Justice (Cherokee Nation) is Canada Research Chair in Indigenous Literature and Expressive Culture in First Nations and Indigenous Studies at the University of British Columbia, on the unceded territories of the Musqueam people. Widely published in the field of Indigenous literary studies, his critical and creative work engages issues of Indigenous being, belonging, and other-than-human kinship in literature and the expressive arts.

Natalie Knight (Yurok/Diné) is a writer and poet born in northern California and currently living in Vancouver. She is a Ph.D. student at Simon Fraser University.

Margaret Kovach (Sakowew pîsim iskwew) is of Plains Cree and Saulteaux ancestry from southern Saskatchewan. She is Associate Professor at the College of Education, University of Saskatchewan. Her research and teaching interests include Indigenous methodologies, Indigenous lifelong learning, and decolonizing approaches to post-secondary education.

Emma LaRocque (Plains Cree Métis) is a scholar, author, poet, and Professor in the Department of Native Studies, University of Manitoba. Her prolific career includes numerous publications in Canadian historiography, misrepresentation, racism, colonization, violence against women, and First Nation and Métis literatures and identities. In 2005, she received the National Aboriginal Achievement Award. She is author of *When the Other Is Me: Native Resistance Discourse 1850–1990* (U of Manitoba P, 2010), which won the Alexander Kennedy Isbister Award for Non-Fiction, and *Defeathering the Indian* (Book Society of Canada, 1975).

Keavy Martin is a settler scholar of Indigenous literatures in Treaty 6 and Métis territory at the University of Alberta. Her book *Stories in a New Skin: Approaches to Inuit Literature* (U of Manitoba P, 2012) won the 2012 Gabrielle Roy Prize. She is also the co-editor of a new edition of Mini Aodla Freeman's autobiography, *Life among the Qallunaat* (U of Manitoba P, 2015).

Sophie McCall is a settler scholar and Associate Professor in the English Department at Simon Fraser University. She has published scholarly work in the areas of Indigenous literatures, reconciliation, and decolonization. With Métis artist Gabrielle L'Hirondelle Hill, she recently co-edited *The Land We Are: Artists and Writers Unsettle the Politics of Reconciliation* (Arbeiter Ring, 2015), a collection of essays, poems, artwork, and interviews.

Sam McKegney is a settler scholar of Indigenous literatures and Associate Professor at Queen's University. He is author of *Magic Weapons: Aboriginal Writers Remaking Community after Residential School* (U of Manitoba P, 2007) and editor of *Masculindians: Conversations about Indigenous Manhood* (U of Manitoba P, 2014).

Linda M. Morra is a settler scholar of Italian origin and a Full Professor at Bishop's University, where she teaches Canadian, Indigenous, and American literatures. She is the 2016–17 Craig Dobbin Chair of Canadian Studies at University College Dublin. Her book *Unarrested Archives* (U of Toronto P, 2014) was a finalist for the Gabrielle Roy Prize. She also co-edited *Troubling Tricksters* (Wilfrid Laurier UP, 2010) with Dr. Deanna Reder.

Laura Moss is a settler scholar and an associate professor of Canadian and African Literatures at the University of British Columbia. She is the editor of the journal *Canadian Literature* and co-editor (with Cynthia Sugars) of the two-volume *Canadian Literature in English: Texts and Contexts* (Penguin, 2008). Her current work concerns the intersections of public policy and the history of arts and culture in Canada.

Elviro Pulitano's research and teaching interests include Indigenous and Africana Studies, Caribbean Studies, Literatures of the African Diaspora, and theories of race and ethnicity, migration, diaspora, and human rights discourse. A Fulbright Scholar from Italy, she holds a Ph.D. in English from the University of New Mexico, where she specialized in Native American literatures and postcolonial studies. She edited *Indigenous Rights in the Age of the UN Declaration* (Cambridge, 2012) and *Transatlantic Voices: Interpretations of Native North American Literatures* (U of Nebraska P, 2007).

Deanna Reder (Cree-Metis) is Associate Professor in the Departments of English and First Nations Studies at Simon Fraser University. She is co-editor, with Dr. Linda Morra, of *Troubling Tricksters* (Wilfrid Laurier UP, 2010). She is the Series Editor of the Indigenous Studies Series at Wilfrid Laurier UP. For more information, see deannareder.com and thepeopleandthetext.ca.

Deena Rymhs is Associate Professor of English at University of British Columbia. She is author of *From the Iron House: Imprisonment in First Nations Literature* (Wilfrid Laurier UP, 2008), and is currently working on a second book, *Directing Traffic: Roads, Mobility, and Violence in Indigenous Literature and Art*.

Leanne Simpson is of Michi Saagiig Nishnaabeg ancestry and a member of Alderville First Nation. She holds a Ph.D. from the University of Manitoba and is the author of three books: *Dancing on Our Turtle's Back* (Arbeiter Ring, 2011), *The Gift Is in the Making* (HighWater P, 2013) and *Islands of Decolonial Love* (Arbeiter Ring, 2013).

Niigaanwewidam James Sinclair is Anishinaabe (St. Peter's/Little Peguis) and an Associate Professor in Native Studies at the University of Manitoba. He is co-editor of the award-winning *Manitowapow: Aboriginal Writings from the Land of Water* (HighWater P, 2011) and *Centering Anishinaabeg Studies: Understanding the World Through Stories* (Michigan State UP, 2013).

Drew Hayden Taylor is originally from the Curve Lake First Nation in central Ontario, but over the last two decades has been travelling the world and writing about it from an Aboriginal perspective. An award-winning playwright, author, columnist, filmmaker, and lecturer, he has managed to bridge the gap between cultures by tickling the funny bone.

Gerald Vizenor is Professor Emeritus of American Studies at the University of California, Berkeley. He has published more than thirty books, including *Blue Ravens* (Wesleyan UP, 2014), a historical novel about Native Americans in the First World War. He was the Principal Writer of the Constitution of the White Earth Nation in Minnesota.

Renae Watchman (Diné–Bitter Water), Ph.D., hails from Shiprock, New Mexico, and is Associate Professor of English and Indigenous Studies at Mount Royal University in Calgary, where she specializes in North American Indigenous literatures. Dr. Watchman's favourite pastimes are eating, hiking, hanging out in coffee shops, watching movies, and travelling.

Craig S. Womack, of both Creek and Cherokee heritage, is author of *Red on Red: Indigenous Literary Separatism* (U of Minnesota P, 1999) and *Art as Performance, Story as Criticism* (U of Oklahoma P, 2009). He teaches in the English Department at Emory University.

INDEX

Books in the INDIGENOUS Studies Series
Published by Wilfrid Laurier University Press

Blockades and Resistance: Studies in Actions of Peace and the Temagami Blockades of 1988–89 | Bruce W. Hodgins, Ute Lischke, and David T. McNab, editors | 2003 | xi + 276 pp. | illus. | ISBN 0-88920-381-4

Indian Country: Essays on Contemporary Native Culture | Gail Guthrie Valaskakis | 2005 | x + 293 pp. | illus. | ISBN 0-88920-479-9

Walking a Tightrope: Aboriginal People and Their Representations | Ute Lischke and David T. McNab, editors | 2005 | xix + 377 pp. | illus. | ISBN 978-0-88920-484-3

The Long Journey of a Forgotten People: Métis Identities and Family Histories | Ute Lischke and David T. McNab, editors | 2007 | viii + 386 pp. | illus. | ISBN 978-0-88920-523-9

Words of the Huron | John L. Steckley | 2007 | xvii + 259 pp. | ISBN 978-0-88920-516-1

Essential Song: Three Decades of Northern Cree Music | Lynn Whidden | 2007 | xvi + 176 pp. | illus., musical examples, audio CD | ISBN 978-0-88920-459-1

From the Iron House: Imprisonment in First Nations Writing | Deena Rymhs | 2008 | ix + 147 pp. | ISBN 978-1-55458-021-7

Lines Drawn upon the Water: First Nations and the Great Lakes Borders and Borderlands | *Karl S. Hele, editor* | 2008 | xxiii + 351 pp. | illus. | ISBN 978-1-55458-004-0

Troubling Tricksters: Revisioning Critical Conversations | Linda M. Morra and Deanna Reder, editors | 2009 | xii + 336 pp. | illus. | ISBN 978-1-55458-181-8

Aboriginal Peoples in Canadian Cities: Transformations and Continuities | Heather A. Howard and Craig Proulx, editors | 2011 | viii + 256 pp. | illus. | ISBN 978-1-055458-260-0

Bridging Two Peoples: Chief Peter E. Jones, 1843–1909 | Allan Sherwin | 2012 | xxiv + 246 pp. | illus. | ISBN 978-1-55458-633-2

The Nature of Empires and the Empires of Nature: Indigenous Peoples and the Great Lakes Environment | Karl S. Hele, editor | 2013 | xxii + 350 pp. | illus. | ISBN 978-1-55458-328-7

The Eighteenth-Century Wyandot: A Clan-Based Study | John L. Steckley | 2014 | x + 306 pp. | ISBN 978-1-55458-956-2

Indigenous Poetics in Canada | Neal McLeod, editor | 2014 | xii + 404 pp. | ISBN 978-1-55458-982-1

Literary Land Claims: The "Indian Land Question" from Pontiac's War to Attawapiskat | Margery Fee | 2015 | x + 318 pp. | illus. | ISBN 978-1-77112-119-4

Arts of Engagement: Taking Aesthetic Action In and Beyond Canada's Truth and Reconciliation Commission | Dylan Robinson and Keavy Martin, editors | 2016 | viii + 376 pp. | illus. | ISBN 978-1-77112-169-9

Learn, Teach, Challenge: Approaching Indigenous Literatures | Deanna Reder and Linda M. Morra, editors | 2016 | xii + 578 | illus. | ISBN 978-1-77112-185-9